ALSO BY MARTIN GILBERT

The Day the War Ended

May 8, 1945—Victory in Europe

Martin Gilbert

Henry Holt and Company
New York

Henry Holt and Company, Inc.
Publishers since 1866
115 West 18th Street
New York, New York 10011

Henry Holt® is a registered trademark of
Henry Holt and Company, Inc.

First published in the United States in 1995 by
Henry Holt and Company, Inc.
Originally published in the United Kingdom in 1995 by
HarperCollins Publishers Ltd.

Library of Congress Cataloging-in-Publication Data
Gilbert, Martin.
The day the war ended: May 8, 1945—victory in
Europe / Martin Gilbert. — 1st American ed.
p.   cm.
Originally published: United Kingdom: HarperCollins, 1995.
1. World War, 1939-1945—Campaigns—Western.
2. V-E Day, 1945. I. Title
D755.7.G55   1995   94-45809
940.54'21—dc20   CIP

ISBN 0-8050-3926-0

Henry Holt books are available for special promotions
and premiums. For details contact: Director, Special Markets.

First American Edition—1995

Printed in the United States of America
All first editions are printed on acid-free paper.∞

1 3 5 7 9 10 8 6 4 2

CONTENTS

LIST OF ILLUSTRATIONS

The Day the War Ended

LIST OF MAPS

PHOTOGRAPHIC SOURCES

ABC Press Service, Amsterdam, 13.
American Official Photograph: Hulton-Deutsch, 34.
Bernard Barnett, 37, 38.
Black Star Pictures, 8.
Bundesarchivs, 53.
Geiger/Planet Photo, 16.
Imperial War Museum, 2, 7, 11, 12, 21, 48, 49, 50, 51 and 54.
Keystone Press Agency: Hulton-Deutsch, 1, 14, 15, 17, 18, 23, 25, 26,
    29, 31, 36, 39, 40, 41, 45, 52, 56, 58, 59 and 61.
Leah Silverstein, 42.
Novosti Press Agency, 19.
Official Netherlands Photo, 57.
Official Photo, United States Army Air Force, 35.
Public Information Division, Department of the Army, Washington,
    44.
Photo Actuelle, Sarrebruck, 55.
Stern, 60.

United States Army Photograph, 3, 4, 5, 6 and 9.
Vestry House Museum, 28.
William Beatty, 30.

The Robert Hunt Picture Library provided the prints of 8, 13, 16, 19, 53, 55, 57 and 60. The John Frost Historical Newspaper Service provided the original newspapers and magazines for illustrations 22, 24, 32, 33, 43, 46, 47 and 62.

ACKNOWLEDGEMENTS

I am extremely grateful to all those who sent me accounts of their personal experiences on the day the war ended, or who let me see their wartime diaries and letters. I have acknowledged each individual contribution in the text itself, but would here like to thank, warmly and collectively:

Hermann Arndt (in Florence on VE-Day, a British soldier)
Christian B. Arriëns (Leyden, Holland, just liberated)
Joan Astley (London, War Cabinet Office)
Alex Auswaks (Shanghai, civilian internee)

Clare Baines (London, working at the Admiralty)
John Barham (England, schoolboy)
Bernard Barnett (Czechoslovakia: American soldier)
William E. Beatty (Paris, American soldier)
Edith Beer (Germany, in hiding)
Ernest Beiser (Barce, Cyrenaica, British soldier)
Moshe Bejski (Brünnlitz, Sudetenland, in Schindler's factory)
George Bendori (Britain, a schoolboy, refugee from Germany)
Edward Benedek (Urals, a prisoner in the gulag)
Valentin Berezhkov (Moscow, Stalin's former interpreter, in disgrace)
Tova Blitz (Toronto, giving birth)
Georges Bonnin (Toulouse, released prisoner of Gestapo)
Edwin Bramall (Hamburg, a British soldier)
Betty Broit (Grodno, an eight-year-old, leaving Europe with parents)
Jack Brauns (Dachau, survivor of the Kovno Ghetto)
Mania Breuer (New York State, refugee from Europe)
Aron Bunyanovitch (Caucasus, wounded Soviet soldier)

Milton M. Cahn (Linz, Austria, American officer)
Gordon Campbell (Germany–England, British officer)
Alan Campbell-Johnson (Ceylon, British officer)
Susan Cernyak-Spatz (Germany, liberated concentration camp prisoner)
Henry Crooks (England, army radiographer)

Reuven Dafni (Sea of Galilee, Palestinian parachutist)
Harry Dayan (Venice, Allied soldier)
Felicija Dobroszycki (Urals, nine-year-old girl)
Lucjan Dobroszycki (Sudetenland, a prisoner on the march)
Louis Dorsky (Bavarian Alps, American soldier)
Hirsch Dorbian (Neustadt, near Lübeck, released prisoner)

Alfred Doulton (Burma, British officer)
Alfred Drukker (Theresienstadt, from Holland, aged twelve)
Natalia Dumova (Moscow, schoolgirl)
Michael Dunnill (England, schoolboy)
Ruth Dyson (London, musician)

Martin Eisemann (England, schoolboy)
Joel Elkes (Birmingham, England, student)
Sara Elkes (London, nurse)
Walter Eytan (Bletchley, Signals Intelligence)

Peter Fane (Thailand, prisoner-of-war of the Japanese)
Charles Feinstein (Germany: United States First Army)
Shoshanah Feldschuh (London, doing refugee work)
Benjamin B. Ferencz (Germany, American officer, war crimes enquiry)
Charles V. Ferree (Frankfurt, US Air Forces)
Alice Fink (London, maternity nurse)
John Fink (Belsen, recently liberated German teenager)
Philip I. Freedman (Philippines, American soldier)
Dr Reinhard Y. Freiberg (Berlin, a child emerging from hiding)
Paul Fussell (France, wounded American soldier)

Benjamin Gale (Scott Field, Illinois, American airman)
Arye Gertner (Italy, with the British forces)
Ben Giladi (Theresienstadt, from Poland)
Eva Goddard (London, refugee from Germany)
Walter Goddard (Sweden, refugee from Denmark)
Mikhail Goldberg (Austria, Russian artilleryman)
Jack Goldfarb (Miami, United States Army Air Force base)
Arthur Goodfriend (Paris, editor of *Stars and Stripes*)
Frank Green (Lüneberg Heath, British officer)
Hana Greenfield (Belsen, liberated)
Ruth Gruber (Washington, civil servant, Department of the Interior)
Hugo Gryn (Gunskirchen, awaiting liberation)
Peter M. Gunnar (Nebraska, American airman)
Pinchas Gutter (Theresienstadt, awaiting liberation)

Grace Hamblin (Moscow, secretary with British Red Cross mission)
Ansel Harris (Winnipeg, British air force cadet)
Sylvia Harris (London, the last day of her honeymoon)
Robert Hastings (Palawan Island, Pacific, American officer)
Hyman H. Haves (Philippines, American airman)
Norman J. Hazell (England, schoolboy)
Cameron Hazlehurst (Liverpool, child)
Ben Helfgott (Theresienstadt, awaiting liberation)
Susana Herrmann (Theresienstadt, from Czechoslovakia)
Margit Herrmannova (Theresienstadt, from Czechoslovakia)
Irene Hertz (Jerusalem, housewife)
Chaim Herzog (Germany, British officer)

Acknowledgements

Peter Hewlett (London, seven-year-old child)
William Higgins (Britain, railwayman)
Roger Highfield (Italy, British soldier)
Wolfgang Homburger (Britain, schoolteacher)
Henry C. Huglin (Pacific Ocean, American officer)
David Hunt (Izmir, Turkey, British officer)
Norman Hurst (England, schoolboy)

June Jacobs (London, schoolgirl)
Marjorie Jaffa (New York City, clerk)
Hans Jakobson (Sweden, brought by Red Cross from Germany)
Henia Jakobson (Sweden, brought by Red Cross from Germany)

Michael Katz (Cracow, Poland, a refugee from Lvov)
Ruben Katz (Lublin, Poland, thirteen-year-old survivor)
Edward Kanter (London, schoolboy)
Robert Kee (Germany, released British prisoner-of-war)
Charles H. Kessler (Wörgl, Austria, American soldier)
Grigory Kleiner (Perm, Urals, schoolboy)
Sholem Koperszmidt (Soviet Central Asia, working in a slaughterhouse)
Ruth Krammer (Chicago, schoolgirl, born in Germany)
Daniel M. Krauskopf (Germany, American soldier)
Robert Krell (The Hague, hidden child)

John Laffin (Australia, soldier)
Kenneth Larson (mid-Atlantic, returning American POW)
Isabella Leitner (reaching the USA that day, from Auschwitz)
Zdenko Levental (Sarajevo, Yugoslav partisan)
Leonard Levine (Pacific Ocean, American radio operator)
Dr G. Lewin (South Africa, refugee from Germany)
Marion Loveland (London, a 'Wren')
Mirko Lowenthal (Zagreb, British soldier with the Yugoslav partisans)
Lore Lilien (Jerusalem, working for Royal Air Force)
Hugh Lunghi (Moscow, British interpreter)

Ronald McCormick (Manchester: naval trainee)
Canon Frederick A. McDonald (Germany, American padre)
Noel Major (Britain, schoolboy)
Yakov Malkin (Lebanon, a prisoner)
Noel Mander (Rome, British soldier)
David Manevitz (Okinawa, American sailor)
Edmund Marsden (Shillong, Assam, British officer)
Robin Maxwell-Hyslop (London, schoolboy)
Vladka Meed (Lodz, Poland, survivor of the Warsaw Ghetto)
Benjamin Meirtchak (River Elbe, Polish soldier with the Russian Army)
Ernest W. Michel (Germany, working on a farm)
Benjamin Mirkin (Manchuria, civilian internee)
Herbert Mitgang (New York, *Stars and Stripes* reporter)
Seymour Moses (England, American army hospital laboratory technician)

Alex Moussafir (Cape Town, student)
Henry J. Muller (Philippines, American soldier)
Jakob Murkes (Urals, engineer)

Harry Osborne (British soldier, Greece)

Alan Palmer (England, naval cadet)
Veronica Palmer (England, schoolgirl)
Abraham Pasternak (Theresienstadt, from Poland)
Alfred Peacock (Britain, schoolboy)
Roger Peacock (Britain, returned prisoner-of-war)
Xavier Piat-ka (East Prussia, already liberated)
Gabriela C. Pollack (Oxfordshire, at RAF Fighter Headquarters)
Miriam Porat (Sudetenland, awaiting liberation)
Iris Portal (London, husband serving with the forces)

Arthur Radley (Italy, British soldier)
Natasha Raphael (Brazzaville, Congo, French radio operator)
Arthur Rappoport (United States, hospital pathologist)
Alan Raven (Thailand, prisoner-of-war of the Japanese)
Morton A. Reichek (near Calcutta, American soldier)
Leib Reizer (Russian Poland, seeking a way out of Europe)
Dov Riegler (Toronto, student)
Frank Roberts (Moscow, British diplomat)
Stephanie Robertson (Amsterdam, emerging from hiding)
Silvia Rodgers (London, schoolgirl)
Edmund Rogers Jr (Austria, American officer)
Meir Ronnen (Australia, about to be a soldier)
Irving Rosen (Germany, American army)
Alexander Rotenberg (Switzerland, refugee)
Edmund de Rothschild (Italy, British army)
Hilary Rubinstein (Torquay, Royal Air Force cadet)
Peter Ruston (London, airman)

Mania Salinger (Belsen, being tended by British doctors)
Leon Sawicki (Bohemia, Polish army doctor)
Julian Schragenheim (Italy, with South African army)
Robert Schreiber (United States, schoolboy)
Herbert Scott (Scotland, British pilot)
Yehuda Sela (Luxembourg, American airman)
Zvi Shalit (London, merchant seaman)
David Shwachman (Pacific Ocean, American radio operator)
Abe Shenitzer (Germany, interpreter with the British forces)
Ruth Shykoff (Toronto, university student)
Leah Silverstein (Warsaw, former resistance fighter)
Joe Simons (Perth, Australia, British naval rating)
Henry Slamovich (Poland, after liberation)
Birdie Smith (Macedonia, British army officer)
James Spooner (London, schoolboy)

Acknowledgements

Dyne Steel (Germany, helping in a Displaced Persons camp)
Lucien Steinberg (Tel Aviv, student)
Robert K. Straus (Copenhagen, American officer)
Alan Stripp (Delhi, British Signals Intelligence)

Cornelia T. (Haarlem, Holland, hidden child)
Morton Teicher (Burma, American army medical corps)
Edward Thomas (Scapa Flow, British naval officer)
Lloyd Thomas (Zadar, Yugoslavia, British soldier)
Paul D. Thompson (Egypt, RAF)
George Topas (Germany, ex-camp inmate, with American army)
Harry Torem (Toronto, schoolboy)
Noemi Török (Budapest, schoolgirl)
Jack Trembath (British soldier, Greece)
Vladimir Trukhanovsky (San Francisco, Soviet diplomat)
Francis Tucker (England, air gunner)
Ilana Turner (Theresienstadt, awaiting liberation)
Dr Milo Tyndel (Germany,with Russian army)
Yaakov Tzur (Germany, released concentration camp prisoner)
Lois Tzur (Kentucky, schoolgirl)

Jack Unikoski (Buchenwald, released prisoner)
Irving Uttal (mid-Atlantic, American airman returning home)

Peter Vernon (London, first day of honeymoon)
Elliott Viney (Germany, returning prisoner-of-war)
Nigel Viney (Somalia, British colonial official)
Kurt Vonnegut (Germany, American prisoner-of-war)
Rudolf Vrba (Slovakia, partisan)

Keith Wakefield (Washington DC, Australian soldier)
Dorothy Wallbridge (England, Channel Island schoolgirl)
Bartlett Watt (Germany, Canadian soldier)
Vic West (Britain, returned prisoner-of-war)
Phillip Whitfield (Belsen, British doctor)
Tess Wise (Lodz, Poland)
Leonard Wolfson (London, schoolboy)
Cyril B. Woolf (Cape Town, South African Air Force)
Geoffrey Wigoder (London, student)
Herman Wouk (Pacific, on board ship)
Ursula Wright (Germany–Sweden, being repatriated)
Woodrow Wyatt (New Delhi, British officer)

Yaere Yadede (Jerusalem, delivering bread)

Maurice Zinkin (England: Indian civil servant on leave)
Taya Zinkin (England: a refugee from France, on her honeymoon)

and the anonymous witness of 8 May 1945 (Breslau, schoolgirl)

I have also drawn on the published diaries, memoirs and recollections of Ruth Andreas-Friedrich, Lord Attlee, David Ben Gurion, Tony Benn, Valentin M. Berezhkov, Lena Berg, Guy Blackburn, Lord Boothby, Mary Borden, Jan Brod, General Alan Brooke, Hugh L. Carey, R.D. Catterall, Peter Collister, Noel Coward, Anthony Crosland, Hugh Dalton, Milovan Djilas, Lieutenant G. Dlynnich, Alan Dulles, E.E. Dunlop, General Eisenhower, Michael Etkind, Sholto Forman, Saul Friedländer, Ben Giladi, Germaine Greer, Israel Gutman, Alfons Heck, Renate Hoffmann, Lali Horstmann, James Howie, Anna Hummel, Heinrich Jaenecke, Alfred Kantor, Robert Kee, Dr Lincoln Kirstein, Helmut Kohl, Nathanial Kutcher, Admiral William D. Leahy, Robert Bruce Lockhart, Kurt Meyer-Grell, Ernest W. Michel, Herbert Mittelstädt, Sir Harold Nicolson, Chaim Nussbaum, Dr Miklos Nyiszli, Pat O'Leary, Sir Richard Pim, Peter Quennell, Pat Reid, Leib Reizer, Frank Richardson, Andrei Sakharov, Christopher Seton-Watson, Field-Marshal Sir William Slim, Dyne Steel, Robert K. Straus, W.H. Thompson, Trumbull Warren, General Wedemeyer, Leo Welt, Alexander Werth, Lord Whitelaw and Marshal Zhukov.

I have also used material from the following public archives: Public Record Office, Kew (Admiralty papers, Cabinet papers, Colonial Office papers, Foreign office papers, Premier papers, Ultra papers and War Office papers), the Central Zionist Archives, Jerusalem; the Eisenhower papers, Abilene, Kansas; the National Maritime Museum, Greenwich, the Truman papers, Independence, Missouri; and the United States Holocaust Memorial Museum, Washington DC. I have drawn on contemporary letters and diaries in the private archives of William E. Beatty, Lord Camrose, Alfred Doulton, Paul Kavon, Charles Kessler, Benjamin Ferencz, John Frost, Benjamin Gale, Irene Hertz, Jakob Murkes, Elizabeth Nel, Templeton Peck, Sir Richard Pim, Aumie Shapiro, Marian Spicer-Walker, Elliott Viney and Geoffrey Wigoder. Anita Lasker gave me access to her unpublished memories, Eli Kavon sent me copies of the wartime letters of his father (Sergeant Paul Kavon), and Francine M. Goldberg-Schwartz made available the unpublished memoir of her father, Mikhail Goldberg.

I have quoted from the following wartime newspapers and magazines: *Auckland Star*, *L'Aurore* (Paris), *La Voce* (Naples), *The Bulletin* (11th Armoured Division news sheet), *Cape Times*, *Chicago Daily News*, *Chicago Daily Tribune*, *Cosmopolitan* (New York), *Daily Express*, *Daily Herald*, *Daily Mail*, *Daily Mirror*, *Daily Sketch*, *Daily Telegraph*, *Evening Despatch*, *Evening News*, *Evening Standard*, *Evening Star*, *L'Express* (Neuchâtel, Switzerland), *Le Figaro*, *Guernsey Times*, *Guernsey Weekly Press*, *Het Parool* (Amsterdam), *L'Humanité*, *Jersey Evening Post*, *Libres* (Paris), *Life*, *Lübecker Zeitung*, *News Chronicle*, *New York Herald Tribune*, *New York Journal-American*, *New York Times*, *Palestine Post*, *Pravda*, *Rand Daily Mail*, *Résistance*, *Stars and Stripes*, *The Times*, *Union Jack*, *Wakefield Express* and *Yank*.

I have drawn with gratitude upon wartime newspaper articles by Homer Bigart, Noel Coward, Ilya Ehrenburg, Michael Foot, De Witt Gilpin, Evelyn Irons, John F. Kennedy, Charles F. Kiley, Harold King, Ernie Leiser, Carl Levin, Norman Lourie, George McCarthy, Lachie McDonald, Ralph G. Martin, Ronald Matthews, François Mauriac, Herbert Mitgang, Mack Morris, Alan Nash, Sidney Olson, Cornelius Ryan, Louis Sobol, Peter Stursberg, Ronald Walker, Maurice Western and Don Williams.

Joseph Kleiner spoke to several former Soviet citizens on my behalf. Major Colin Crawford of the charity Combat Stress gave me the guidance of his expertise. Larry

Acknowledgements

Arnn, William Beatty, Alice Brikach, Professor Philip Hanson, David Sinclair and Enid Wurtman each sent me copies of various wartime newspapers. John Frost put at my disposal the resources of his Historical Newspaper Service. On points of detail I was helped by Dr Christopher Dowling and James Taylor (Imperial War Museum), Deborah Hall (Royal Geographic Society), David Irwin (Wiener Library), Susie Harries, Arthur Peck Jnr and Dr Harry Shukman. Robin Dennison pointed me in the direction of an important source.

For further help I am also grateful to Philippe Abplanalp, Director of Researches, International Committee of the Red Cross, Geneva; Dr Vojtech Blodig, Terezin Memorial, Czech Republic; Dr Christopher Dowling, Imperial War Museum, London; David Manning, Foreign and Commonwealth Office, London; Daniela Moravcikova, Attaché, Embassy of the Czech Republic, London; Jean Morton, Canadian High Commission, London; Barbara Pestritto, the Claremont Institute, Claremont, California; and Captain Arne Söderlund, Naval and Army Adviser, South African High Commission.

Translations were undertaken by The Language Factory (Victoria Solsona) and Fax Translations (Pat Argent), and by Ruth Partington and Irina Brook. I am also grateful to Arabella Quin, of HarperCollins, who made many extremely valuable suggestions of form and content, and Biddy Martin who read the book in page proof. I was helped in the archival research by Rachelle Gryn, and in preparing the index and proof-reading by Naomi Gryn. The text was scrutinised in typescript by Arthur Neuhauser and Kay Thomson, who also lessened the considerable task of correspondence involved in the book's completion. My wife Susie was, as always, an exceptionally wise guide.

INTRODUCTION

In May 1945 the war against Germany, which had begun five and a half years earlier with Hitler's invasion of Poland, came to an end. Victory-in-Europe Day, universally known as VE-Day, saw a great explosion of excitement and celebration, which was captured on film and in photographs in a dozen European capitals, and is vividly remembered by those who witnessed it. Allied soldiers celebrated in towns and fields where, only a few days earlier, the last battles of the war had been fought. Civilians rejoiced in cities that had been under occupation for as long as five years. Allied prisoners-of-war were on their way home, or had already reached home. Almost all the surviving inmates of the concentration camps were free, though still devastated by their ordeal. One camp, Theresienstadt, was liberated on VE-Day itself. Millions of families rejoiced that they were to be reunited. Millions more had suffered losses, the agony of which could not be assuaged.

For the Western Allies, the Second World War ended in Europe on May 8. For the Soviet Union it ended a day later. For those soldiers, sailors and air crews in the Far East and the Pacific, the war was still being fought. For them VE-Day was a brief moment in a continuing and bloody battle, with the prospect of many months desperate fighting ahead of them.

In Europe, many scores were settled by VE-Day; some still remained to be settled. The hunt for Nazi war criminals had only just begun. Many new problems were created at the very moment when the old ones were dissolving. World leaders looked with new hope and new fear at the world confronting them. In San Francisco, even as the war in Europe was ending, the recently established United Nations was seeking a mechanism of debate and action designed to prevent, and when necessary to combat, future aggression. Refugees were everywhere on the move. Hunger and deprivation continued to beset those who had been defeated, and whose cities were in ruins. Revenge and magnanimity jostled in the minds of the victors.

This book examines the events and moods of VE-Day from the perspective of all the war zones: through the letters, diaries and recollections of soldiers and civilians, of the young and the old, of the liberators and the liberated, of those whose battles were over and those whose battles were continuing.

The material on which I have drawn comes from four main sources: archival material, much of it letters and documents originating on VE-Day itself; the newspapers of the time, including eye-witness reports of war correspondents; published diaries, memoirs and histories; and the recollections of more than two hundred individuals who wrote to me while I was working on this book. The range of sources reflects the range of witnesses to that memorable day and the days around it. Most people, even those who were quite young at the time, can remember where they were on VE-Day. My own recollections are vivid: at the age of eight and a half, just outside Oxford, I listened to the King's victory broadcast and then hurried up the hill to watch the burning in effigy of Hitler and Mussolini. On the following day my friends and I solemnly stuffed our model aeroplanes with cotton wool, lit the wool with matches, and threw the planes up into the air to their destruction.

Personal recollections reached me from five continents: from Africa, Asia, Australasia, the Americas and Europe. Some letters came from those who were in the very centre of Germany that day, where the guns had just fallen silent. Others were from those in the Far East and the Pacific, where war still raged. Some came from civilians who were watching from afar the final actions of the war in Europe. Many came from people whose concerns centred around the continuing war against Japan. These letters revealed many different perspectives and attitudes on the part of those who had fought, or had been incarcerated, or had followed the course of the war through the newspapers. The nature of experiences and reactions was as varied as the settings in which people found themselves on that day of jubilation, sadness and reflection.

Several people sent me the diary entries they had written on VE-Day. Others sent the letters they had written that day to parents, wives and friends, describing the celebrations in the Allied capitals, or written from the former battlefronts. These letters encapsulated moods ranging from exhilaration that the war was over to horror at what was being found in the ruins of the Reich. The impact of the liberation of the concentration camps was felt by thousands of Allied soldiers who entered them as the German guards fled, and by the doctors and nurses who tried, often in vain, to bring the victims back to health. The survivors, among them the remnant of six million murdered Jews, have vivid, sometimes painful, but also joyous memories of the days of liberation, and of VE-Day, itself. The showing in the Allied capitals and towns of newsreel film of what had been discovered in the liberated concentration camps caused shock, anger and controversy.

For many people in Europe, the war ended before VE-Day, on some earlier day on which their city, camp or prison was liberated. For as long as the war was still being fought, however, some sense of danger or anxiety remained, especially for those who had family or friends still in action, or among the vast legions of those who had disappeared, most of them for ever.

When I first appealed for recollections, I imagined that these would provide an interesting, if essentially minor element to the book: a sideline to history. But the quality of so many of the letters I received, their clarity, their directness and the variety of experience they reflected, led me to make them an integral and substantial part of the narrative.

I have also drawn on the recollections of the young. Some were at that moment among the starving, emaciated flotsam and jetsam of Germany's battered cities and liberated concentration camps. Others were at school in lands which had known neither occupation nor deprivation; for them, the day the war ended in Europe was one of excitement.

Every story is different and every individual's fate is, in a certain sense, unique. In the span of a single volume only a small part of the historical tapestry can be presented, even when the focus is on such a short period in time. It is my hope, however, that these pages give at least a glimpse into experiences, aspirations and emotions of half a century ago.

Martin Gilbert
Merton College, Oxford
3 February 1995

I

Anticipations

1940–1944

Victory-in-Europe Day was proclaimed and celebrated in Britain, the United States and Western Europe on 8 May 1945. In the Soviet Union the celebrations were held on the following day. Newspaper photographs of VE-Day show dancing in the streets, fireworks, illuminations and scenes of jubilation. These moments of exhilaration remain fixed in the minds of all who took part in them, a high point of relief and rejoicing after the hardships, sorrows and privations of war.

VE-Day was the focal point of celebration and memory, but for many people, both soldiers and civilians, the war had ended earlier, for some much earlier. For the millions of military and civilian victims of combat, oppression and genocide, the war ended on the day of their death. Not a single day passed without the deaths of hundreds, in battle, in reprisal actions and in concentration camps. On average, more than twenty thousand people, soldiers and civilians, were killed each day of the Second World War; the same number that were killed on the first day of the Battle of the Somme in 1916. For those who survived battle, aerial bombardment, execution and incarceration, the war ended with their liberation or repatriation from captivity. There were also more than a million Russians, including hundreds of thousands of former prisoners-of-war, who were repatriated, not to freedom, but to the Soviet gulag.

Liberation had come to northern France in June and July 1944, within weeks of the Normandy landings. The citizens of Paris had celebrated their freedom in August 1944, those of Warsaw in January 1945. In the same month the Soviet army reached Auschwitz, liberating the few thousand survivors still incarcerated there. Most of the prisoners at Auschwitz had, however, been moved to concentration camps within Germany before Auschwitz fell; those who had survived these 'death marches' were freed in April 1945. Also liberated in April were many of the prisoner-of-war camps in which hundreds of thousands of Allied soldiers, sailors and airmen had been held captive, some for more than five years.

I

The series of Allied victories, which began in North Africa in 1942 and in Russia in 1943, and which eventually brought the war to an end, had been won at an extraordinarily high cost in human life. Britain had been at war, and Poland had been under German occupation, for more than five and a half years. France, Belgium, Holland and Norway had suffered nearly five years of occupation. Greece, Yugoslavia and western Russia had been occupied for nearly four years. At sea, in the air, and from the air, the war had taken a daily and relentless toll.

For some of those who participated in the early battles, the war had ended swiftly. Fifty-five years later one British airman, Sergeant Roger Peacock, shot down during a bombing raid over Germany in July 1940, recalled the abrupt conclusion to his war, and the events that led up to it: 'On September 3rd, 1939 I was already engaged on flying duties as the third, and least, member of the crew of a light bomber of 2 Group Bomber Command. It was not long before it became quite clear to the realists among us – most of us that is – that we were not likely to survive. By the time the French campaign began, on May 10th, 1940 (a day known irreverently to us as Woompit Day, a reference to the noise made by the copious light flak with which the enemy supported his advancing troops) a man fresh from Operational Training Unit and posted to a fighting squadron might expect to live rather less than three weeks. Some men – men at eighteen or so? – lasted a mere day. In July 1940 No 40 Squadron had three commanding officers; the second flew in at teatime one day, to replace his predecessor lost only hours earlier. He showed willing by putting his name on the Dawn Battle Order, took off next day at 3.30 am and failed to return. He had not even unpacked, which meant that tidying up his affairs was relatively simple.'

Each morning when Peacock awoke he inevitably wondered, like all his fellow-airmen, 'whether that day would be my last. I had prayed, of course, not for survival (which would have been cheating) but that I might be spared long enough to see the spring in my beloved England. My prayer was granted; it was in the closing days of July 1940 that Lachesis and Atropos caught up with me.[1] In the course of an attack on the Luftwaffe airfield at Jever, a few miles west of Wilhelmshaven, our kite was disabled. There was a comical failure of communication: the two men in front baled out at some 8,000 feet or so, but I sat calmly in the back while the aircraft descended in sweeping spirals, waiting to be told when to go. By the time I found that I was alone and knelt beside my

[1] Lachesis was one of the three Fates. Her task was to cut asunder the thread of life. Her sister Atropos directed the thread, which a third sister, Clotho, spun.

hatch, the kite was down to some four hundred feet and I wondered dispassionately, but briefly, whether it was worth while trying to use my parachute or whether an instant and painless death was preferable.'

Peacock jumped. 'There was just time to pull the D-ring before I found myself spreadeagled on my back in a potato field. Some determined twitching of my various extremities convinced me that once I had got my breath back I would be well. My pilot landed only a few yards away and together we turned our backs on the blazing wreck of our poor Blenheim. In vain: within a few yards I was accosted by a nervous gentleman in an unfamiliar uniform, holding a quavering pistol within inches of my chest, and demanding, *"Hände hoch: Sie sind mein Gefangener"*.[1] It was ironic that only recently – perhaps the previous day – I had committed to memory that very phrase, offered to its readers by the *Daily Express* as a guide to "How to Receive a German Paratrooper who lands in your Back Garden" (an invasion was expected daily). The next thing he said, having assured himself that I was unarmed was, "For you the war is over." Perhaps he had learned that from *his* paper?'[2]

Roger Peacock remained a prisoner-of-war for nearly five years. Ten million soldiers like him were to reach the end of their fighting war in a prisoner-of-war cage or prison barrack. More than three million Russian soldiers captured by the Germans on the Eastern Front died of deliberate exposure and starvation, their lives ending amid great cruelty and ignominy.

From the first serious reversal of the tide of war in Russia in the summer of 1943, hundreds of towns and villages in the East were freed from the Nazi oppressor. In southern Italy, liberation from fascism came in the autumn of 1943. While the outcome of the war was still uncertain, gravely injured Allied prisoners-of-war were repatriated from Germany, though not from Japan or, as far as German prisoners-of-war were concerned, from the Soviet Union. Civilian internees from Western countries were also returned home.

One such civilian internee, the British-born Ursula Wright, who had been held in various camps in Vichy France, including Vittel, since the end of 1940, later recalled the day in October 1943 when her war ended: 'I was repatriated through an exchange of prisoners, along with a number of other internees. We travelled by train through Germany, with many stops in railway sidings, and finally arrived at the port of Rostock. Here

---

[1] 'Hands up: you are my prisoner.'
[2] Roger Peacock, letter to the author, 26 August 1994.

we met Count Bernadotte who was negotiating our transfer through Sweden. We sailed to Trelleborg and went from there to Göteborg under the care of the Swedish Red Cross. I remember the lovely porridge, with thick cream, served on the train, so different from our camp fare.'

At Göteborg, those being repatriated were put on board the British ocean liner *Empress of Russia*, 'painted white to show she was a hospital ship, and there we met many British soldiers, mostly wounded, and their protected personnel aides. We were given a marvellous send-off, with a band on the quay-side, and I believe the King and Queen of Sweden were there. I know Princess Louise, the Crown Princess as she was then, was at our departure, talking to some of the wounded soldiers. She was, of course, English (of the Mountbatten family). After an interesting journey through the Skagerrak we sailed across the North Sea to Scotland, where we were welcomed by a flotilla of little ships and then I, and some soldiers from that area, were transported to Hull. There I was given, which I felt I didn't deserve, a sort of hero's welcome, as the people there had suffered much more from the war than I had.'[1]

During 1944 the pace of liberation grew. With it, in the East, came the imposition of Communist rule over large areas of inter-war Poland. In Yugoslavia, Tito's partisans were wresting much of the country from German control. In Italy, Allied forces entered Rome on 4 June 1944, having established an Italian anti-fascist administration in the south. From the first hours of the Normandy landings on 6 June 1944, French villages, and then towns, and finally Paris itself, were freed. For millions of French citizens the war ended that summer and early autumn. Georges Bonnin, who had been arrested early in July for refusing to work in Germany, recalled vividly the day that the war ended for him. It was 20 August 1944. 'I was then in a Gestapo prison in Toulouse. The wardens, ordinary soldiers of the Wehrmacht, asked our small staff to stand in a line, shook hands with us and with a hearty: "*Auf Wiedersehen! Alles gute!*" ("Good-bye, Godspeed") as if we were old friends, left in a small ambulance. They did not go very far, for they were caught in the Rhône Valley near Avignon. We were so lucky to escape with our lives. A few days earlier four of us had been taken away by the Gestapists and never returned. I learned later that, with two dozen from other prisons, they had been burned alive. It was a symbolic execution; the Wehrmacht general commanding in Toulouse had left giving the instruction to the Gestapo: "Liquidate the prisons."'

[1] Ursula Wright, letter to the author, 17 October 1994.

4

Bonnin also recalled what he described as 'a little twist' in the story. 'Among those wishing well to the departing wardens there was Frau P, who had been arrested by the French in 1939 as German, and re-arrested as Jewish in 1941 by the Germans when they occupied the South zone. She was a remarkable typist: During the interrogations of Jews, she was typing their confessions – she had to – translating directly into German if necessary. Incidentally they were beaten up and their screams could be heard through the open windows. When I arrived at the Nuremberg Trial, whom should I see? Frau P wearing a dark green United States uniform. "Where did I see you?" she asked, slightly alarmed. In the course of the conversation it appeared that she was in fact in touch with the wardens, still prisoners in Avignon. She was making sure that they would get their rations of cigarettes and chocolate. This is all part of the rich pattern of life.'[1]

During the first three months of 1945 the German forces, which had stood triumphant within sight of Moscow, and on the Atlantic coast of France, were driven back by their adversaries deep into Germany. Still they resisted the onward march of the Allies. Seeking to stave off defeat, and to hide the consequences of the Nazi system, they moved hundreds of thousands of slave labourers and concentration camp prisoners deeper and deeper into Germany, trying to keep them away from the advancing soldiers, fearful of what might be the Allied reaction to so many starved, emaciated and desperately sick prisoners and slave labourers. As the Allied armies advanced, enormous numbers of German soldiers laid down their arms. On the Loire, an American officer, Lieutenant Colonel J.K. French, from Virginia, co-ordinated the surrender of 19,000 German troops.[2]

As the Russian forces moved westward during the early spring of 1945, the war ended for the much-bombed, and latterly much-shelled inhabitants of a hundred towns in the regions that were overrun. But the torments of peace could be harsh. In Königsberg, once the capital of East Prussia, there was little to celebrate on the day the war ended, or in the days that followed. The occupation forces did little to feed the inhabitants, many of whom died of starvation. In the words of two historians, 'Rape, looting and pillage defined life'. A German woman in the city later recalled how, after she and her friends had been raped, 'we often asked the soldiers to shoot us, but they always answered: "Russian soldiers do not shoot women, only German soldiers do that."'[3]

[1] Georges Bonnin, letter to the author, 21 October 1994.
[2] See photograph number 1.
[3] Dennis L. Bark and David R. Gress, *A History of West Germany: From Shadow to Substance, 1945-1963*, Blackwell, Oxford, 1989, p. 33.

Nearly six million Germans left their homes and fled westward in front of the advancing Russians. An estimated one million died as they fled, from exhaustion and starvation, from bomb and machine-gun attack from the air, or accidentally caught up in the battle that continued to scar the eastern extremity of the Third Reich. As the German civilians fled, they often came in sight of other columns of men and women: of British and French prisoners-of-war being marched westward to avoid liberation by the Red Army, and of emaciated, terrified Jews, the men and women being marched separately, who were being taken from the slave labour camps of the East to new camps in the West.

By the end of March 1945, Allied armies were on the borders of Germany in both the East and West. France and Belgium had been freed. Fighting was continuing in northern Italy, in Yugoslavia and in Hungary. Holland, Denmark and Norway remained under German occupation. The threat of Hitler's secret weapons had ended: the terrors of the rocket bombs and the prospect of a renewed German submarine offensive were over. Yet the tenacity of the German army on all fronts meant that there would be no sudden collapse, as in 1918. The struggle to end the Second World War would bring the ferocity of aerial and artillery bombardment to almost every corner of the Third Reich. The siege of Breslau, where for eighty-two days the city defenders refused to surrender, and tens of thousands of civilians were blown to pieces in their homes and shelters, indicated that the struggle would have to continue until Germany was completely crushed.

When the First World War had broken out in 1914 there were those in every land who were confident that it would end by that Christmas. When 1945 opened there was equal confidence that the war in Europe would end by the summer, if not sooner. Looming over the prospect of imminent victory, however, was the spectre of the continuing war against Japan, in which American, British, Australian and Dutch troops were bearing the brunt of an implacable enemy. As Germany faced defeat, Japan was still holding on to part of Burma, was occupying Malaya, the Dutch East Indies, Indo-China and large areas of China, and was fighting a stubborn retreat across the Pacific Ocean island by island, determined to resist any landing on the Japanese mainland with all the considerable resources at its military and autocratic command.

II

The Beginning of the End

1–24 April 1945

At the beginning of April, fighting on German soil continued on all fronts. The American Ninth and Third Armies had been trying for several weeks to encircle the Ruhr and, on April 1st, in a pincer movement which electrified all Allied observers, they met at Lippstadt. 'The German industrial heartland was now severed from Germany,' wrote an American soldier, Charles Feinstein, who was serving in the 3rd Armoured Division. 'Germany could not now win the war (although plenty of fighting was left).'[1] The commander of Feinstein's division, Major General Maurice Rose, was killed a few days later in a small arms battle at an SS training camp in Paderborn. In the Ruhr pocket some 100,000 German soldiers had surrendered by the third week of April. It was the first mass surrender on German soil.

On April 4, American troops advancing deep into Germany reached a camp different from anything they had seen before. More than three thousand emaciated corpses lay in and around the barracks. It was a slave labour camp, Ohrdruf. There were no living prisoners there when the Americans arrived: the German guards had marched the survivors away to avoid their being liberated, or even seen, by the Americans. The Supreme Allied Commander, General Dwight D. Eisenhower, was alerted. He sent photographs of what had been found in the camp to both London and Washington. Members of Parliament and Congressmen were despatched to Germany to see the evidence at first hand. By the time they arrived, more camps, and with them thousands of emaciated prisoners and slave labourers, had been discovered.

On April 6, American troops reached the town of Merkers in central Germany. There, in a deep mine, they discovered a cache of paintings that had been looted by the Nazis from the art galleries of Europe, as well as paintings from the art galleries of Berlin, that had been brought

[1] Charles Feinstein, letter to the author, 21 September 1994.

to Merkers for safety a month earlier. The most recent assignment had arrived as late as March 30. As well as the works of art were a hundred tons of gold bars. Some of these bars had been made from the gold fillings and gold teeth taken from the mouths of murdered Jews at Auschwitz and a dozen other camps. As the Americans had approached the mine, the Germans made an effort to move the hidden treasures further south, but work on this transfer came to a halt when German railway workers insisted on observing Easter Sunday. 'One could tear one's hair,' Dr Josef Goebbels wrote in his diary, 'when one thinks that the Reichsbahn is having an Easter holiday while the enemy is looting our stores of gold.'[1]

Eisenhower, coming devastated from his visit to the camp at Ohrdruf, examined the haul. It included four hundred paintings from the National Gallery in Berlin, a million and a half books from the Berlin State Theatre and Opera, as well as thousands of opera costumes, and the gold: all were despatched by the Americans to Frankfurt ten days later, escorted by machine-gun troops, anti-aircraft units and continual air cover.

On the Eastern Front, in Slovakia, Russian forces had reached the area in which Slovak partisans had been fighting the Germans since the Slovak uprising eight months earlier. One of those partisans, Rudolf Vrba, had escaped from Auschwitz in April 1944 and, with a fellow-escapee, had brought out the first news of the nature and scale of the extermination process there. After Vrba's account had been passed on by courier and telegram to London and Washington, he joined the partisans. 'In the morning at four o'clock on April 7', he recalled, I had been wakened by fire from a German infantry unit retreating through the same forest and accidentally colliding with our partisan group. After a short fight in pitch dark (with four dead on each side) a small group of six men had been sent to make contact with the approaching units of the Red Army. As I was fluent in Russian, I was included in this contact group. We met the first Red Army unit at 11.00 a.m. on April 7. So I celebrated my first anniversary of freedom from Auschwitz by this meeting.

'The Red Army unit we had met was commanded by a twenty-one-year-old captain (a university student from Moscow). The men in his unit were mostly grey-haired uncles (I was twenty-one-years-old at that time) and all of them (about two hundred soldiers) kissed me after we had met. I learnt that they had been searching for us since they had found the remains of the German artillery unit (including the bodies of the

---

[1] Quoted in Lynn H. Nicholas, *The Rape of Europa, The Fate of Europe's Treasures in the Third Reich and the Second World War*, Macmillan, London, 1994. p. 312.

killed Germans) we had attacked on the day before. The Russian captain explained to me how lucky it was for us, otherwise he would have cleared his route of advance by heavy artillery and our partisan group would have been inevitably hit by that fire.

'On that day together with the Red Army units we were assigned the task of liberating the nearby town of Březova nad Bradlom. We attacked the Germans at 2200 hours after an artillery barrage of their positions. We were amazed at the efficiency of the Red Army's artillery – as partisans we never dreamt of being supported with such terrifying weapons. The Russians enjoyed our amazement with benevolent laughter. After we took the town, I heard a Russian colonel say about us: "Good soldiers, but they need to get accustomed to the artillery."

'This, as it turned out, was not necessary, as our partisan group was directed to the military hospital in the nearby spa of Piešťany for recuperation. We had spent more than two hundred days (and nights) in the forests, constantly in close contact with the enemy, without as much as one single bath.'[1]

On April 11, American troops were battling with the German Army in the vicinity of the concentration camp at Nordhausen. The Mittlebau-Dora factory at Nordhausen had been a vast slave labour camp, a central plank of Germany's plan to accelerate the mass production of the V–2 rockets which had been designed to reverse the tide of war even at the eleventh hour, and bring large-scale destruction to London.

The SS guards had left Nordhausen a few days earlier, after a heavy American bombing raid on the town which had killed hundreds of prisoners. One of the survivors of the bombing raid, Ben Giladi, a Jewish boy from the Polish town of Piotrków, later recalled: 'Utterly exhausted and hardly able to move, I joined forces with a Polish boy. We gathered some food from the burning SS canteen into a blanket and limped out of the smouldering camp. We settled in a large bomb crater in a nearby field.' While in his hole, Ben Giladi heard explosions 'from afar; also a heavy cannonade. Still we couldn't believe that freedom was near.' On the morning of April 11, he had left his hole 'answering a call of nature' when he saw a group of armed Germans not far away. 'This was the Landsturm, very young boys and old men, all armed with rifles, inspecting the area. They saw me but continued walking. I was wearing a dark, civilian suit over my striped prison garb in order to keep warm, so I looked just like any other victim of the bombing. Suddenly one of them, a young boy, stopped and pointed at me. My trousers were still down

---

[1] Rudolf Vrba, letter to the author, 2 December 1994.

and the prison uniform beneath was clearly visible. *"Das ist doch ein Häftling"* ("That is a prisoner over there") he screamed to the others. They all stopped abruptly. The boy slowly raised his rifle, aiming at my heart. An old German tenderly moved the barrel of the rifle aside. *"Lass Ihm doch zu Frieden,"* ("Let him have his freedom") he muttered. *"Das is doch schon die Ende"* ("It really is the end now"). They left without another word. I was shaking all over, suddenly realizing that I was reborn again at that very moment.'[1]

That same day, April 11, American troops reached Nordhausen. 'The day was ending and already the shadows of twilight cast a red tint on the naked, battered brick walls of the ruins,' Ben Giladi recalled. 'We crawled out from our hole and were standing with a few of the inmates from other bunkers near the main entrance of the camp. And then, all of a sudden, a convoy of jeeps, command cars and Red Cross ambulances appeared in the dark. This was the first image of our liberation! The olive-drab shadows with spotted capes and helmets embellished with leaves and branches, moving cautiously from the vehicles, submachine guns in one hand, grenades in the other. They appeared stalwart, unafraid.

'The GIs[2] became aware of our presence. They saw the multitude of skeletons, a gigantic scene of death. One of them, apparently the commanding officer, gave orders rapidly to all the others. The language sounded heavenly. There was a distinctive timbre of voice full of authority but also full of concern and compassion. A voice that could never be forgotten.

'The army interpreter briefed us. In a matter of hours, all the survivors were carried by stretcher to an American field hospital and tended gently, with magnificent devotion in order to bring us back to life.'[3]

Charles Feinstein was one of the American soldiers who entered Nordhausen on April 11. 'We smashed down the wooden gates with our tanks,' he later recalled, 'and behold (somewhat to our chagrin) the British were already in there, having smashed their way in from another direction. I remember seeing the mounds of dead bodies, naked and piled so high. I remember the stench. We all vomited.'[4]

Another of the American liberators of Nordhausen, Hugh L. Carey, recalled thirty years later how, 'as an officer in the US Army, I stood with other American soldiers before the gates of Nordhausen and wit-

---

[1] Ben Giladi, letter to the author, 20 August 1994.
[2] American servicemen: the term was coined in 1936, and derived from their General Issue (or possibly Government Issue) clothing and equipment.
[3] Ben Giladi (editor), *A Tale of One City*, Shengold, New York, 1976, p. 299.
[4] Charles Feinstein, letter to the author, 2 October 1994.

nessed the nightmarish horror of the slave labour camps and crematoriums. I inhaled the stench of death, and the barbaric, calculated cruelty. I made a vow as I stood there at Nordhausen, face to face with the survivors of death, that as long as I live, I will fight for peace, for the rights of mankind and against any form of hate, bias and prejudice.'[1] When he wrote these words in 1986, Carey was Governor of New York State.

Also liberated on April 11 was the concentration camp of Buchenwald. As with Nordhausen, reports, and later photographs, appeared in all the main newspapers in Britain and the United States. 'We are now reading,' wrote Captain Frank Foley, who before the war had been British Passport Control Officer in Berlin, 'about those places the names of which were so well known to us in the years before the war. Now the people here really and finally believe that the stories of 1938–9 were not exaggerated.'[2]

A sense of the war's imminent ending affected the Allied soldiers on all fronts. Julian Schragenheim was serving that April with the 6th South African Armoured Division in Italy. He had been born in Berlin and had emigrated to South Africa shortly after Hitler came to power. His aunt Else, known to the family by the nickname Hänschen (little Johnny), had committed suicide in Berlin in 1942, knowing that deportation was imminent. In her last message to her nephew, which reached him after the war, she had sent him his sports club song book, with the inscription 'For Julian, Deuteronomy, ch. xxv, 17–19.'[3]

While he was fighting in Italy that April, Julian Schragenheim recalled 'a feeling of sombre satisfaction when I took a short walk in one of our target-areas of a few hours earlier, near a place called Finale Emilia, and found, next to a burning German half-track, a German boot, with the foot still in it. What happened to the rest of the guy, I never found out. But his personal mail was scattered all over the ground next to the burning vehicle, and knowing German well enough, I read, *inter alia*, a letter from his mother from the Rhineland. While she was writing, they were under American artillery-fire. She also wrote that she was sending him a cake.

[1] Hugh L. Carey, 'Remembrance of Things Past', Ben Giladi (editor), *A Tale of One City*, Shengold, New York, 1976, p. 296.
[2] Captain Foley to Werner Senator, 19 April 1945: Central Zionist Archives, Jerusalem, 57/915.
[3] 'Remember what Amalek did unto thee by the way.... How he met thee by the way, and smote the hindmost of thee, even all that were feeble behind thee, when thou wast faint and weary; and he feared not God. Therefore it shall be, when the Lord thy God hath given thee rest from all thine enemies round about, in the land which the Lord thy God giveth thee for an inheritance to possess it, that thou shalt blot out the remembrance of Amalek from under heaven; thou shalt not forget it.'

Not many days later, I watched the Herrenvolk, emerging from the Italian roadside ditches, with their hands up. An entire infantry-section, complete with First-Aid man, not one of them appearing to be older than seventeen, walked into our control-post, to surrender.'[1]

In early April 1945, British and American leaders had learnt, from their most secret Intelligence source, the Germans' own coded radio signals, that the Soviet army was preparing to take political advantage of its advance along the Baltic by occupying Denmark. This knowledge altered Allied strategy and was to bring the British troops to the Baltic as the occupying, and for some the liberating, power. A top secret diplomatic despatch from the Japanese Ambassador in Sweden to the Foreign Ministry in Tokyo, which had been intercepted on April 7, showed that the Russian move and Britain's response had been noted. The despatch began: 'From the Russian declaration that Denmark will shortly be liberated it is plain that Russia intends to bring Denmark into her sphere of influence and thus secure an outlet from the Baltic into the North Sea. Moreover the Russians have recently been making covert inquiries about what the Danish people who have taken refuge in Sweden have been doing. These are probably intended to provide material for their designs on Denmark. It is a fact also that the free Danish minister here recently left for Moscow in company with Kollontay, the Russian Minister here.' The Japanese Ambassador went on to point out that while not a word had been said in public in Britain about Soviet intentions, 'the British have since changed the direction of the drive on the Western Front by Montgomery's armies and turned it towards Hamburg. Moreover the recent heavy bombing of Kiel seems not so much to have been directed against the Germans as intended to prevent the Russians from being able to use it.'

Viewing Anglo-Soviet disputes in the most optimistic light, from a Japanese perspective, the Japanese Ambassador told his Government: 'The problems of the future of Denmark, the Near and Middle East, the Aegean Sea and China are very likely to provide the motives for a third world war.'[2]

In Silesia, German forces were holding out for their fourth month in the besieged city of Breslau. In the suburbs of Berlin, they were fighting against the Russians street by street. Still there were those in Germany who hoped that the war might not be lost. Their hopes were momentarily

---

[1] Julian Schragenheim, letter to the author, 25 September 1994.

[2] 'British-Soviet relations', Top Secret Ultra, telegram sent at 12.30 p.m., 7 April 1945; circulated to the Prime Minister and others, London, 11 April 1945. Reference HW1/3683, Public Record Office, Kew.

stimulated on April 12 by the death of President Franklin D. Roosevelt. Recalling how he reacted to the news, Alfons Heck, a young German schoolboy whose home town, Wittlich, had already been overrun by the Americans, testified that he saw Roosevelt's death as 'a ray of hope' amid the humiliation of occupation. 'I shared Josef Goebbels' short-lived illusion that his demise might persuade his successor, Harry Truman, to settle for an armistice or even to join us against the Soviets.'[1]

In an Allied prisoner-of-war camp at Eichstätt, in Franconia, Major Elliott Viney wrote in his diary on April 13: 'On evening parade we had two minutes silence for Roosevelt.' American prisoners who had been brought into the camp that day had actually met an American army jeep in Nuremberg. The driver had said to them, as he drove off, 'Back for you in an hour', but they had been moved by the Germans before their would-be liberator could return with some extra vehicles to take them back to the American lines.[2]

On April 14 American tanks from General George S. Patton's Third Army advanced along the autobahn from Weimar to Chemnitz. They had been informed that there was a prisoner-of-war hospital at Hohenstein-Ernstthal, a small village just south of the autobahn. A small force of one tank and two jeeps was sent to investigate. R.D. Catterall, a British prisoner-of-war at Hohenstein, later wrote of the liberating unit: 'Unfortunately it ran into a group of German SS troopers and there was a sharp exchange of machine-gun fire. A German was seriously wounded and two Australian medical orderlies from our hospital volunteered to take out our antiquated ambulance and bring him in. They were caught in the crossfire between the two groups and the ambulance was hit several times. Titch Foster, a corporal captured in Tobruk in 1941, was killed instantly and his companion was badly wounded in the leg. A few minutes later the main American force swept up the autobahn and there was no further fighting.

'Later that morning, at 8.50 a.m. to be exact, a small group of us was standing by the main gate, which was unguarded for the first time. Two American tanks drove up and in the first was a battle-stained Texan who fixed me with compassionate eyes and said, "Say boy, how long you been

---

[1] Alfons Heck, *A Child of Hitler: Germany in the Days when God wore a Swastika*, Renaissance House, Frederick, Colorado, 1985, p. 198.

[2] Elliott Viney, diary, 13 April 1945. Private archive. Major Viney had been in action for less than three weeks when he was captured in 1940. His commanding officer having collapsed after a few days, and the second-in-command having been killed, he was commanding the battalion, at the age of twenty-six, when it was overrun. The camp in which he was held was Oflag VII B.

a prisoner?" "Four years," I replied hesitantly. "Gee," he said, "and you still alive." "I think so," I ventured, at which he disappeared into the inside of his tank and re-emerged holding a full bottle of Johnnie Walker whisky, which he placed firmly into my hands. It was obvious that the dose would be homeopathic for the large numbers now gathering round the tank, so I gave it to the Scottish padre to distribute. He solved the problem by taking a huge swig himself and then passing the bottle round, saying repeatedly, "Don't forget the others". The bottle passed his way more than once before it was finally emptied.'[1]

At Colditz, more than a thousand British, French, Polish, Czech, American and other Allied prisoners-of-war, all of them officers who had earlier escaped from other camps and been caught before reaching freedom, were confined within a formidable fortress. One of these prisoners, a British officer, Captain Pat Reid, recalled in his history of the castle prison the reaction of a fellow prisoner, Captain Dick Howe, at the sudden entrance into the prison courtyard on April 15 of a single American soldier, 'His belt and straps festooned with ammunition clips and grenades', sub-machine gun in hand. 'A brainstorm momentarily paralyzed the normal currents of his mind. His memory played tricks upon him, and switched, suddenly, to a scene which floated past his inward eye. He saw himself standing on a dusty road outside Calais in 1940 unarmed and a prisoner. A German soldier was passing and he shouted, *"Für Sie ist der Kreig zu Ende. Wir fahren gegen England. Sie gehen nach Deutschland."* ("For you the war is over. We are marching against England. You are going to Germany.") Now the irony of the words struck him. "For you the war is over." That was five years ago. And the German? He was probably dead years ago.'

An Allied officer standing near the gate advanced with outstretched hand and shook the hand extended by the American, who grinned at him and said, cheerfully, 'Any doughboys here?' The spell was broken.

'Suddenly, a mob was rushing towards him, shouting and cheering and struggling madly to reach him, to make sure that he was alive, to touch him, and from the touch to know again the miracle of living, to be men in their own right, freed from bondage, outcast no more, liberated by their Allies and their friends, their faith in God's mercy justified, their patience rewarded, the nobility of mankind vindicated, justice at last accomplished and tyranny once more overcome.

'Men wept, unable to restrain themselves. It was not enough that the

---

[1] R.D. Catterall, 'Strictly personal': *As You Were, VE-Day: a medical retrospect*, British Medical Association, London, 1984, pp. 41-2.

14

body was free once more to roam the earth. Feelings, pent up and dammed behind the mounting walls of five successive torturing, introverted years, had to erupt.

'They welled up like gushing springs, they overflowed, they burst their banks, they tumbled unhindered and uncontrolled. Frenchmen with tears streaming down their faces kissed each other on both cheeks – the salute of brothers. They kissed the GI, they kissed everyone within range. The storm of emotion burst. The merciful rain descended. The grey clouds drifted from the horizon of the mind, borne on fresh salt- and moisture-laden breezes across the unchained oceans of memory from the far-off shores of love. Home and country beckoned, loved ones were waiting. Wives and sweethearts, mothers, fathers, and children never seen, were calling across the gulf of the absent years.

'Man was at his finest amidst the grandeur of this moment of liberation. A noble symphony arranged by the Great Composer had reached its thunderous finale and, as the last triumphal chord swelled into the Hymn of Nations, man looked into the face of his Creator turned towards him, a vision of tenderness, mirrored for an instant by the purity of his own unrepressed torrent of joy and thankfulness. At such a moment, mountains move at the behest of man, he has such power in the sight of God.'[1]

Although millions of Americans had wept to hear of their President's death, and many American soldiers were distraught at the loss of their Commander-in-Chief, there was no weakening of resolve to see the battle through. Roosevelt's demand of unconditional surrender, which Winston Churchill and Joseph Stalin had endorsed, remained the Allied aim. The debates then, as later, about whether this was wise or not, made no impact on the fighting men. Indeed, three days after Roosevelt's death, an event took place which only stiffened the Allied resolve. On April 15, British tanks stumbled across the first of the large concentration camps, Belsen. To this camp, from the beginning of 1945, tens of thousands of Jews had been brought from the slave labour camps of Silesia and eastern Europe. The Germans did not want them to fall into the hands of the Russians; but at Belsen they had no work for them to do, unlike at the vast slave labour camp a hundred miles further south, at Nordhausen. Once at Belsen, prisoners who had already survived three, four, or even five years of the rigours of camp life elsewhere, were left, with almost no food or medical help, to starve and to rot.

A British officer, Gordon Campbell, recalled: 'On April 15, our

[1] P.R. Reid, *The Latter Days at Colditz*, Hodder and Stoughton, London, 1952, pp. 226–7.

Division and the accompanying armoured units discovered Belsen. The concentration camp happened to be on our line of advance. Many of our officers and men had witnessed horrors and carnage in the previous ten months but they felt a sense of outrage at what they found. There had been rumours that such camps existed, but this was the first to be discovered in the West. Here was the awful proof. The press arrived as we were moving on towards the Elbe, and in the following days newspapers were full of accounts and photographs. Belsen had no gas chambers, but its victims were left to expire miserably from starvation and disease. We were too late for Anne Frank.'[1]

One of those liberated in Belsen that day was Hana Lustig, a Jewish girl from the Czech town of Kolin, who recalled: 'How many times did we dream about this day? In how many different ways did we imagine it? It was the hope of living to this day that sustained us. Death was everywhere. It stared at us from everyone's eyes. The pitiful "Musselmen", the walking dead bodies, no longer knew where they were walking to or why. Everyone was searching for non-existent food. Our tongues were swollen for lack of water. The little water that was available was contaminated with typhoid. Some drank from it, no longer caring.'

Hana Lustig was amongst a group of five hundred Czech women sent to Belsen who had earlier been in Auschwitz. Liberation had been awaited from day to day. 'At night, we heard the guns of the advancing armies from Bremen. How much longer can it take before they reach us? How much strength will it take to stay alive until then? And then it happened. The first British tank rolled inside the camp, opened the gates of this indescribable hell, and a bull horn sounded the sweet words we had waited for, for so long: "YOU ARE FREE.... YOU ARE FREE.... YOU ARE FREE...." Those of us who were still alive became free, while thousands lay dead, no longer having had the strength or will to live.'[2]

For those who were behind the barbed wire as the British tanks entered Belsen it was a moment to be engraved on their memories all their remaining lives. 'These fragments have retained for me the precision and sharpness of a Goya painting,' the twenty-four year old, Warsaw-born, Abe Shenitzer wrote. 'I am looking up at the man in the lead British tank and asking him questions about the military situation. I feel quiet but intense contentment, a delightful absence of the chronic background fear that was the one constant of camp life. I am not hungry. I am wearing

[1] Gordon Campbell (Lord Campbell of Croy), letter to the author, 4 October 1994. Anne Frank, a Jewish girl from Frankfurt who had been in hiding in Amsterdam (before being deported to Auschwitz) died in Belsen in March 1945, three weeks before the arrival of the British forces.
[2] Hana Greenfield, letter to the author, 22 September 1994.

my striped outfit with the little yellow mark on the right of my Häftling number – 120548 – but outfit and number are now irrelevant and slightly absurd. A soldier in the first jeep behind the tank hands me a few packs of cigarettes and tells me to distribute the cigarettes among the prisoners. They stand some distance away from the soldiers and me, a huge and silent crowd.

'Another fragment. I recall the sound track that tells us in a number of languages that we have been liberated by the Allied army. To me it means that I can now spit out the undigested lump of my prisoner past. I remember a choking sensation. I am on the verge of tears. Never before have platitudes about freedom and liberation sounded so real to me.

'It is late in the evening and there are four of us in the room, three sergeants and I. I answer questions for hours. And all this time I savour the miraculous transformation. I am human again. There is no longer any need to pretend to myself that I am Häftling number – 120548 – and that I properly and rightly belong behind barbed wire. Hours pass. My interlocutors are worn out but I am not. We say goodnight. Two of the sergeants are gone. The third one hands me a bottle and says somewhat timidly that his girlfriend gave him a bottle of vitamins but I need them more than he does. I thank him, put the bottle in my pocket, and when he is out of sight I throw away the bottle. I don't need vitamins now. Nothing bad can happen from now on. I have a whole regiment of protectors. If I could survive years of forced labour and weeks of marching (from Bunzlau to Nordhausen) then there surely is no longer need to give any thought to survival.'[1]

The liberation of Belsen was a moment that transformed the Allied perception of the war. The war had certainly been fought to destroy tyranny, and yet the full nature of that tyranny had not been grasped. Individual photographs of atrocities had circulated, but they had been relatively few and overshadowed by the general war news. The British entry into Belsen produced a mass of film that within days appeared on the cinema screens, and photographic images that were reproduced in every newspaper. Ten thousand unburied bodies were seen stacked in piles in the camp, and scattered between the huts. There was a wave of outrage. The photographs and films of emaciated corpses, and of living

[1] Abe Shenitzer, letter to the author, 13 November 1994. Shenitzer added: 'When I talked to an immigration official in New York many years ago and asked him whether or not "Abe" was an acceptable short form of "Abraham", he looked at me for a while without uttering a word and finally said: "Young man, what was good enough for Lincoln is good enough for you."'

men and women scarcely different from the dead, brought indignation and revulsion against the perpetrators in the wake of horror.

The entry into Belsen also produced eye-witnesses. Allied soldiers, doctors and nurses, already hardened to the horrors of soldiering by all they had seen in the previous months, were quite unprepared for the evils of a concentration camp: a camp in which the inmates, for their last days, had been left to fend for themselves, without food or water, without any form of medical attention.

Another of those who was liberated from Belsen that day was the twenty-one-year-old Mania Tenenbaum, who had been born in the Polish town of Radom. 'I was up that morning as usual and looking up, saw the watch tower empty,' she recalled. 'Puzzled, I ventured outside a few steps further and noticed the next tower empty also. The surroundings were very still, no one in sight. I saw the first daylight of the morning. Scared but bewildered I walked further and then suddenly, amazed, I saw a white flag on a distant building. I ran back to my barrack screaming "We are free, we are free, the Germans are gone!"'

Mania Tenenbaum continued: 'It would take a much more talented writer then me with my simplicity to describe the scenes that followed. Hundreds and then thousands of skeleton-like figures were running to the front gates screaming hysterically. I was up front and saw the first English tank enter the camp. We almost tore these poor soldiers apart. Other tanks followed. Through the loudspeaker and with tear-filled voices they repeated over and over again in several languages: "You are free, we are with the English Army. Be calm, be calm. Food and medical help is on the way." Amidst all the chaos, somehow they set up stands with food, medical tents, etc. I think that the soldiers which first entered our camp were so shocked and so horrified that it took much longer to organise this terrible chaos than I remember. The soldiers opened the nearby men's camp which we didn't even know existed.

'How can I describe fathers finding daughters, wives finding husbands, sisters finding brothers? How can I describe those unbelievable hours? I found no one. No family, not even close friends. The clean up and body burning began. I saw my infected arm swelling and felt a temperature. An English army doctor made an incision and left it open for the pus to drain. There was a lot of it. I remember it splattered on the doctor's coat. The swelling continued upward over my elbow. I ran a high temperature and I was frantic! I can't die now! I am free, I saw it happen!'

The British troops moved the surviving camp inmates to new barracks which had previously been occupied by the German army. They then burned down the stinking, loathsome huts. 'I went to see the English doctor again the next day,' Mania Tenenbaum wrote. 'My arm had a red stripe along it (sign of infection) and the swelling continued. The decision was to amputate my right arm the next day to save my life. There was a nurse working in the clinic who knew me and she begged the doctor to give me a penicillin shot. She told him that I was her relative. With much reluctance because they had so little of it, he authorized to give me one shot of penicillin. . . .

'I was sent to a hospital and they cut my arm open again for drainage. I continued to run a high temperature. There were so many sick people that I received no care at all at that hospital. I was worried that I would just rot and die there. My determination and intense will to live prevailed again. I just got dressed and walked out of the hospital to a nearby dormitory, where I knew some of my friends were housed, and collapsed at their doorstep. They took me in, cared for me and nursed me back to health.'[1]

The first British doctor to enter Belsen was Phillip Whitfield. He had been serving since the previous summer as an MO[2] in Normandy, and was anxious to be nearer to the front. 'I had been provided with a jeep to cover my duties in Normandy and towards the end of March I found myself driving alone from one transit post to another along the line of the Allies' advance. I didn't know that the Allies had crossed the Rhine until I found myself driving across it in the dark on what I suppose was some kind of improvised bridge. I think my destination was Celle but at some point I must have been diverted to Bergen-Belsen where I was told to report to the Royal Artillery Regiment which had been given responsibility for garrisoning the area around the concentration camp, and which had no attached MO.'

Dr Whitfield was responsible for medical services not only in Belsen but in the surrounding countryside. 'Many of the prisoners who were able to walk short distances had "escaped" from the camp as soon as they could. Although a certain amount of medical care was being set up inside the camp – I believe a Casualty Clearing Station had already arrived – it would have been an impossible (and heartless) task to try to persuade the ex-prisoners back inside, unless they were actually *in extremis*. There were already little bands of walking skeletons in their striped-pyjama uniforms, sometimes in groups of the same nationality, unrealistically making for home – probably hundreds of miles away. I was provided with some Army

[1] Mania Salinger (née Tenenbaum), manuscript memoirs, United States Holocaust Memorial Museum, Washington DC.
[2] Medical Officer.

transport, a fifteen-hundredweight truck and later an ambulance, and a Jeep I think, and some stretcher bearers. Also a German nurse who turned up miraculously and worked with me all the time I was at Bergen-Belsen. She knew the area and could communicate with me in simple French. She could explain my requirements to the various German officials to whom I applied for assistance, mainly accommodation, beds, blankets and food suitable for the starving. I think the mayor of Celle and similar people were very willing to help, not surprisingly perhaps. This nurse was always meticulously correct and turned up each morning in spotless uniform. She gave a cachet to our little group which it would not otherwise have had.

'For several days we kept discovering groups of ex-prisoners. I remember for instance a derelict house which had been taken over by *die Zigeuner*, Gypsies, of whom there were many in Belsen, all prostrate with typhus. I think they all survived. The ex-prisoners who temporarily became my responsibility were the fitter ones, although many were mute and unable to help themselves at all. It was astonishing how quickly some responded to a little simple care and nourishment. There were some Jewish doctors among the ex-prisoners who gradually became able, and very willing, to help in the various residential places we had secured, former small hotels and boarding houses, residential schools, etc. Other prisoners identified themselves as nurses: some Lithuanians, I remember.

'During this time I was billeted (for sleeping only) in the house of a former official at the camp. It seemed a very comfortable house, with a spacious music room. We were not supposed to fraternise but I was very surprised to find that the official's wife was English by birth. My relationship with her was awkward. I felt she wanted to make excuses for Germany but knew it wasn't possible. She had a young daughter. I never asked anything about the husband or his whereabouts. Looking back on it, it is possible the husband was no more than a senior officer at the Panzer training school at Bergen-Belsen.'[1]

Those who had been brought to Belsen from the concentration and slave labour camps in the East in the first four months of 1945, and who had survived the deliberate starvation there, were never to forget the re-awakening of their lives which came with liberation. Even before Belsen, their war had been one of almost inconceivable hardship. The Czech-born Margit Schönfeld had been at Auschwitz. She had survived that torment, the death marches to the West, and several other camps, and had finally reached Belsen. The day the war ended for her was the

---

[1] Phillip Whitfield, letter to the author, 2 October 1994.

day on which the British troops had arrived. Her war was over, she later recalled, 'when a Scottish regiment, "The Ladies from Hell", liberated the camp. Pictures were taken, films were made. The German population was led to cinemas to look at what their masters had done to people. Not long after the liberation, a British soldier took me to the cinema to see an American film and I accepted gladly, having not seen a film since 1939 (Jews were not admitted to the cinema in Czechoslovakia under German rule). It was a comedy with the Marx brothers. There was a band playing, and one of the musicians was very incompetent. A row started, the whole band gave the impossible player a thorough beating up, and all the instruments were in shambles. The whole cinema roared with laughter. I sat there stupified and near to tears. "How can people laugh over cruelties?" I realised how deep the gap was between us and normal people, even soldiers who themselves had gone through hardships threatened by death.

'Not long after my visit to the cinema I fell ill. It took me a long time to recover. Let me assure you that I never longed for revenge. I was only tired, drained out and afraid to cope with a new life. It was no "happy end!"'[1]

News of the liberation of Nordhausen, Buchenwald and Belsen was published throughout the Allied lands, hardening attitudes towards the Germans at the very moment when their abilities in battle were ceasing to be formidable. Ansel Harris, a nineteen-year-old Royal Air Force cadet who was completing his flying training in the Canadian city of Winnipeg, later recalled: 'For a young, sensitive, isolated Jew, the only one in his unit, cut off from his family and friends, the news was unbearable. I applied to my Commander for release from my (expensive) training for a posting to Europe. This was turned down in no uncertain terms.'[2]

On April 16, the day after the liberation of Belsen, Allied troops reached one of the dozens of prisoner-of-war camps in the same area. Among those liberated that day was Gunner A.A. Winter, an Englishman, and in civilian life a senior clerk in an insurance company, who wrote in his diary: 'April 16th – LIBERATION! Well, it came all of a sudden today. I happened to be outside at 9 o'clock and heard a bit of a shout down by the main gate and rushed up as fast as I could, just in time to see the first British tank go past the camp followed by many more. It's what I've been waiting for for four years and it really brought a lump in my throat. The German sentries were disarmed and our boys took control. The whole camp turned out. Within an hour lads were smoking

---

[1] Margit Schönfeld (later Herrmannova), letter to the author, 12 September 1994.
[2] Ansel Harris, letter to the author, 12 October 1994.

English cigarettes and tasting a bit of real white bread and tins of biscuits and meat. Another great treat is to see English newspapers and the feeling to be behind the English lines is marvellous in itself.'[1]

On April 16 the prisoners-of-war at Eichstätt were evacuated by the Germans, in an attempt to prevent them from being liberated by the advancing United States forces. As they moved out on foot, their belongings on various improvised carts, they were caught in an Allied air attack. Although the Allied Air Forces were aware of the presence of the prisoners-of-war in Eichstätt, they mistook the column for part of a Hungarian military unit known to be in the vicinity, whose uniform was not the German field grey, but khaki, similar to the British. Elliott Viney described the attack in his diary on the following day: 'We were still opposite the gate of the married quarters and the column stretched for two miles or so ahead. A reconnaissance plane (a Mustang) circled round and very soon a group of Thunderbolts; they started by bombing (two each) the railway and road on the far side of the valley. Then they turned on us, diving across the column and machine-gunning. It felt just like that village in Belgium in May 1940. Most of them seemed to be half a mile up the column but we were hit two or three times and owing to the steep hillside and the fence opposite could not scatter. We were mostly in the ditch. One burst did a lot of damage and I smelt the smoke and one flicked my heel. Soon some got across the road and down to the married quarters where there was a cellar. Gradually we got the wounded down there and the gates to the camp opened, when we could begin getting them treatment.

'The Goons[2] in the married quarters (soldiers, women and children) were good, but the Kommandant emerged from his cellar and tried to shut the gates into the camp and make us march on. He was howled down and sat on by Raum who was in charge of the column. For the next hour we gradually poured back to the Lagerstrasse and we began to hear about casualties. I had helped carry Ben Jickling down, shot through the left shoulder so that, when we were carrying him down the slope, his arm fell and a great stream of blood came over me. He was already dead then. Humphrey Marriott was shot through the spine, Donald Price through the heart. Dick Troughton was hit in the hand. Douglas MacLennan, Ally Sim and Roger Stewart were all hit. In the hospital I

---

[1] J.W.J. Levien (editor), *Atlas at War*, Atlas Assurance Company, London, 1946, pp. 210–11.
[2] British prisoner-of-war slang for their German guards.

saw Johnny Cousens with his leg shot almost off: the .5 bullets made ghastly wounds. We all got to cover on the Lagerstrasse. I found myself among the bad potatoes and Paddy Brennen in the cellar. By twelve we were cleaning out our old blocks and the roofs were all painted "POW". Another recce plane came over at one and everyone was jittery. We got on to cleaning up the place and had a meal and sleep.

'I had seen most of my friends intact, but the full tally was eight dead including Ben, Donald, Pat Heenan and Michael Hart. This evening Humphrey died in hospital, Johnny and Ian Fraser lost a leg, Eric Arden an arm. Forty-two seriously wounded. Just before parade at four, I unpacked my rucksack and found a large bullet lodged in a gym shoe.'[1]

Inside Germany, the Third Reich still had sufficient initiative to try to counteract the outrage which the liberation of Belsen had created among its near-triumphant enemies. As further concentration camps were about to be overrun, the SS drove the surviving inmates on to the road again, or sent them by rail, to the few remaining camps still under German rule: to Mauthausen and its sub-camps in Austria, and to Theresienstadt in what had once been Czechoslovakia. From western and central Germany, thirty thousand Jews were sent to Theresienstadt. On one of these forced marches, which had started more than a week earlier from Berga, a sub-camp of Buchenwald, three young men had managed to escape. One of them, Ernest Michel, recalled: 'On April 18, the day I now celebrate as my real birthday, the three of us escaped by running into the woods. We were hiding in the daytime, walking at night. Direction West. Towards the American armies. We lived on grass, bark from young trees, drank water we found in a small brook. We even found a rotten potato and shared it but we were getting very weak. None of us weighed more than ninety pounds. We still wore the same clothing we had worn in the camp.'

Four days after Ernest Michel and his companions had escaped, 'desperate from hunger and thirst, we came across an isolated farmhouse early in the morning. The three of us discussed whether it was worth taking a chance, asking for food. What would happen if the farmer became suspicious, seeing our prisoner clothing and called the police or the Gestapo. But we could not go on much longer. We had to try. We knocked on the door. Dirty, unshaven for days, our shorn hair was just beginning to grow back. We must have been some sight. A middle-aged woman, probably the farmer's wife, answered and, taking a quick look at us,

[1] Elliott Viney, diary, 15 April 1945. Private archive.

23

wanted to shut the door. Since I spoke better German than my friends, I asked her quickly if we could at least get some food, explaining that we were foreign labourers, that our group was attacked by allied planes and that we had been separated from the rest. "Just something to eat and drink, please. We haven't eaten for days."

The farmer's wife took another look at the three apparitions and, without saying a word, turned around and closed the door. 'We just stood, didn't know what to do. Just as we were ready to leave she came back with some bread, sausage, and a pitcher of milk. Sausage! Milk! We had not tasted this in I don't remember how long. I decided to take a chance. "Can you use some farmhands?" I asked her, "We are willing to work just for food". That is how Honzo, Felix and I landed on three isolated farms in a small hamlet in one of the few parts of Germany that were never occupied, neither by the Russians nor the western Allies. We never revealed to the farmers who we were. Neither did they ask any questions. I guess they were glad to have some extra hands. Never once during the three weeks between April 22 and May 7 did we see a soldier or any SS men. It seemed that the world around us never existed. We had no idea what was happening in the world. The radio was inside the farmer's house, and they did not tell us anything.'[1]

On April 21, the Germans evacuated the concentration camp at Sachsenhausen, eighteen miles north of Berlin, marching the inmates towards the Elbe. One of the marchers, the Czech-born Kurt Cierer, then aged nineteen, recalled: 'We could tell the end of the war was coming; all along the way we saw signs that the German army was crumbling. I remember especially one notice from the Wehrmachtbericht (German Army Command) dated April 28, saying: "Our troops on the Elbe have turned their rear towards the Americans in order to lend outside support to the defenders of Berlin". What this really meant was that in the West the war was over.'[2]

At the very moment when Sachsenhausen was being evacuated on April 21, less than twenty-five miles to the south of the city Soviet forces reached and overran the headquarters of the German High Command at Zossen. That day the head of the SS, Heinrich Himmler, who was also commander of the Rhine and Vistula Armies (although both rivers had already been overrun by the Allies) met the deputy head of the Swedish Red Cross, Count Folke Bernadotte, at Lübeck. Himmler had a startling proposition to put to the neutral emissary. He would surrender

[1] Ernest W. Michel, letter to the author, 17 October 1994.
[2] Yaakov Tzur (formerly Kurt Cierer), letter to the author, 17 October 1994.

all the forces under his command to the Western Allies, but would continue to fight the Russians until British and French forces could themselves reach the Eastern Front, and, in conjunction with those German forces still under arms, continue to wage war against Stalin's forces.

Churchill, to whom Himmler's offer was transmitted as a matter of urgency, sent it on at once to Stalin, with the assurance that no such deal would be struck. The attack by the Western Allies on the German forces, Churchill wrote, 'on all sides and in all theatres where resistance continues, will be prosecuted with the utmost vigour.'[1]

Hitler still hoped to set up a defensive line south of Berlin, running through Jüterbog to the Elbe. But on April 22, the day of Himmler's failed attempt to persuade Britain and the United States to join forces with the Germans against the advancing Russians, Soviet soldiers captured the town of Treuenbrietzen, west of the proposed defensive line, almost encircling Berlin from the south. Hitler now told those who were with him in the bunker that the war was lost. There would be no attempt, as he had once proposed, to hold off the Allies in an Alpine redoubt south of Munich. He would remain in Berlin, and shoot himself, so he told them, when the end came.

For those being held captive by the Germans, the end of the war came suddenly and dramatically. As the Russian forces encircled Berlin from the south, they came across several thousand Allied prisoners-of-war being held at Luckenwalde. One of the British soldiers liberated there, Robert Kee, who had been shot down over the Frisian Islands in 1942 while minelaying, recalled: 'The end of the war for me was when our camp was liberated by the Red Army. A jeep with an officer appeared rather mildly down the camp road first, to be followed a little later by a column of tanks – rather frightening – but simply driving down the road. They weren't particularly interested in us as they were still fighting a sizeable number of German divisions whom they were in the process of encircling on their retreat westwards to the Elbe. When the political people moved in on us a few days later they made clear that we would be repatriated correctly, in accordance with the terms affecting prisoners-of-war in the Yalta agreement – i.e. via Odessa! – even though we were only about fifteen miles from the Elbe, which the Americans had reached some time before, but where they had stopped by previous agreement with the Russians.'

There ensued 'a rather frustrating time in the camp, during which a

[1] Prime Minister's Personal Telegram, number 629 of 1945, 25 April 1945. Premier papers III, Public Record Office, Kew.

number of people made their own way, at some danger to themselves, to the Elbe. I waited, hoping the Americans would come when the Russians reached the Elbe. They did eventually.'[1]

Among those liberated by the Russians on April 22 was Major-General Otto Ruge, the former Commander-in-Chief of the Norwegian Army, who had been captured five years earlier as he sought to slow down the advance of superior German forces into the heart of Norway.

On April 23, another group of British prisoners-of-war experienced the long hoped for freedom. One of their number, Vic West, had been captured in Greece in 1941 during the desperate British attempt to help the Greeks withstand the German onslaught. He had spent four years in different prisoner-of-war camps, in one of which he had been shown, by a German guard anxious to find a piece of barter with which to acquire a few Red Cross cigarettes, some horrendous snapshots of mass murder. Having been liberated by the Americans, West recalled how he and his fellow soldiers were not allowed to move for two days 'to avoid clogging the roads while "logistical" supplies were being brought up' for the advancing armies. There then followed 'a couple of days in a United States' tented hospital waiting for better flying weather, and days, simply days and days, in a British Reception Camp back in Britain.'[2]

Several prisoner-of-war camps in southern Germany were also liberated by the Allies, among them Hammelburg. An American sergeant who had witnessed the events there was Charles Kessler, who had fought with his tank-destroyer crew in Africa, Italy, France and Germany, and who had last been in action in January in the tank battles south of Strasbourg. Fifty years later he recalled: 'My most striking memory of the war: thousands of POWs, mostly Serbian and Polish, greeted us joyfully. Even today, fifty years later, I can visualize the freed POWs, dressed in their striped clothing, half-starved, wandering dazed along roads outside of the prison camp.'[3] What Sergeant Kessler did not know then was that his brother Robert, who had been captured in the Ardennes during the Battle of the Bulge, had died on April 9, while being held captive further east. With other American prisoners-of-war who were Jewish, he had been forced to leave the camp at Berga, where they had been systematically ill-treated, and to march eastward. He had died on the march. He was nineteen years old.

*   *   *

[1] Robert Kee, letters to the author, 11 and 31 October 1994.
[2] Vic West, letter to the author, 26 August 1994.
[3] Charles H. Kessler, letter to the author, 5 September 1994.

On the road on April 25 was one of Hitler's Field Marshals, Ewald von Kleist, whose Panzer Group had been the first to reach the Channel coast in 1940. Von Kleist had led the attack on Belgrade from the South in April 1941 and had fought in the Soviet Union from the first hours of the German invasion that June. Despite the Field Marshal's military successes, Hitler had not trusted him, saying that he was neither intelligent nor a National Socialist; at their last meeting, in March 1944, von Kleist had recommended that the Führer make peace with Stalin. Following his capture by an American infantry patrol, he was to be held in twenty-seven different camps. In 1946 the Americans handed him to the Yugoslavs. He was tried as a war criminal and sentenced to fifteen years in prison. Two years later the Yugoslavs handed him to the Soviet Union, where he was also brought to trial, remaining in Soviet captivity until his death nine years after the war.[1]

The roads of every liberated region of Germany were cluttered in the last week of April, with many different peoples: Allied soldiers who had been held as prisoners-of-war, Jews who had survived concentration camps and death marches, civilians who had been deported for forced labour from conquered lands throughout Europe, German soldiers, from Field Marshal to Private, who had laid down their arms and were trying to get home; and Nazis on the run, seeking a safe haven through anonymity, even in the prisoner-of-war cages in which the Allies had confined them. As the battles still raged on the diminishing fronts, the war's human victims, as well as some of those who had perpetrated the worst atrocities, were on the move.

[1] Samuel W. Mitcham Jr., *Hitler's Field Marshals and their Battles*, Leo Cooper, London, 1988, p. 103.

III

The Last Week of April

On the evening of April 25, the increasing army of radio listeners in every Allied land heard one of the most dramatic announcements of the war. American and Russian forces had linked up in the middle of Germany, cutting the Third Reich in two. Shortly after midday, an American Army officer, Lieutenant Albert Kotzebue, moving forward near the village of Leckwitz, on the western bank of the River Elbe, had come across a solitary Russian soldier. Crossing the river, Kotzebue met several more Russian soldiers encamped near the village of Stehla. Four hours later, ten miles north-west of Stehla, another American patrol, led by Lieutenant William D. Robinson, came upon yet more Russian soldiers at the village of Torgau.

The Allies rejoiced to have linked forces. Newspapers showed how, on the map, Germany was now in two pieces. In Moscow, 324 guns fired a twenty-four salvo in celebration of the Torgau meeting. In New York crowds danced and sang in Times Square. The meeting at Torgau signalled for Europe the imminent end to a war that had lasted even longer than the First World War.

Elsewhere on the globe, however, no end to fighting was in prospect. In the Pacific, the Japanese continued to resist, island by island, the advance of the American and Allied forces with whom they had been in violent conflict since December 1941. On April 25, the same day on which Germany was cut in half, the struggle for the island of Okinawa was still harsh and unresolved. In the skies above the Pacific, American bombers intensified their attacks on the Japanese islands, hoping to create the disruption needed for a successful invasion of the Japanese mainland, planned for that November, still seven months away. But in the highest realms of secrecy, even the continuing war against Japan had a glimmer of an end. For on that same April 25, the United States Secretary of War, Henry L. Stimson, went to see President Truman with the news which could conceivably alter the whole timetable of the final assault on Japan. 'Within four months', Stimson told Truman, 'we shall in all probability have completed the most terrible weapon ever known in human history, one bomb of which could destroy a whole city.'[1]

Three days after his dramatic bunker statement that all was lost, Hitler ordered the Berlin Defence Perimeter to be held at all cost. But within twenty-four hours of the waist of Germany being cut by the Allies, the Berlin Defence Perimeter was pierced by Soviet forces from the north, the east and the south-east. The suburbs of Moabit and Neukölln were both in Russian hands by nightfall on April 26. That same day, British Intelligence decrypted a top-secret message, sent to the SS leader Heinrich Himmler by his chief advisers, warning him that food for the civilian population still under German control would not last beyond May 10.

From April 26 to May 10 was a mere two weeks. In 1918 the starvation of Germany by Allied blockade had led to hundreds of thousands of deaths, food riots, and a demand to end the war backed by revolutionary socialist upheaval. That prospect now loomed again, but with the added pressure of actual military occupation of much of German soil. On the day of this message, so ominous for the survival of the Third Reich, Soviet forces, entering the Imperial German city of Potsdam, completed the encirclement of Berlin. German forces in the capital, from which Hitler had proclaimed his triumph in 1933, were now restricted to an area less than ten miles long from west to east, and only one to three miles wide. That day, unaware that Hitler had decided not to leave Berlin, units of the Red Army seized his last avenue of escape, the airfield of Tempelhof.

The future of Germany had been much discussed by the Allies. Less than a year earlier, in Washington, the Morgenthau Plan had envisaged the total destruction of German industry, aimed at the creation of a weak, agricultural state that would never bear sophisticated arms again. Other plans, some of which had been discussed three months earlier by Churchill, Roosevelt and Stalin at Yalta, envisaged breaking Germany up into several states, to create a much weakened, pre-Bismarckian entity. On April 26, a further plan was produced. It was set out in a top secret directive of the United States Joint Chiefs of Staff. Addressed to General Eisenhower, it was one of the first directives to be signed by Truman, exactly two weeks after he had become President. 'Germany will not be occupied for the purpose of liberation but as a defeated enemy nation,' it read. 'The principal Allied objective is to prevent Germany from ever again becoming a threat to the peace of the world.' The element of

---

[1] Stimson memorandum: Richard Rhodes, *The Making of the Atomic Bomb*, Simon and Schuster, New York, 1988, page 624.

retribution was spelt out clearly. 'It should be brought home to the Germans that Germany's ruthless warfare and the fanatical Nazi resistance have destroyed the German economy and made chaos and suffering inevitable and that the Germans cannot escape responsibility for what they have brought upon themselves.'[1]

In 1919 the Allies had justified the imposition of punitive economic reparations on Germany because of Germany's alleged responsibility for causing the war. In 1945 they were putting the blame on the German people for the massive Allied destruction of Germany's cities. The phrase 'fanatical Nazi resistance' did not refer to camps and atrocities, but to the fact that a nation so obviously broken in battle had continued to fight, throwing old men and boys into the front line, refusing to accept that the war should be brought to an end.

Another camp, which was reached by American forces on April 27, was at Flossenbürg, on the German-Czech border. It had been set up in 1938, shortly after Germany had annexed the Sudetenland. An American officer, Benjamin Ferencz, whose task was to find Nazi war criminals and assemble sufficient evidence to bring them to justice, was among the first Americans to reach the camp. A call having reached his office that a German concentration camp had been overrun four miles from the Czech border, he set off with a lieutenant and a driver. 'As we rode along the roads leading to the front,' he wrote to his fiancée in New York two days later, 'we were impressed by the steady flow of trucks bearing disgruntled German prisoners-of-war. We must have passed at least 10,000 such men, jammed fifty to a truck, and guarded by a small handful of soldiers who followed each prisoner convoy in a jeep. We realized we were approaching our objective as we came upon small groups of wandering prisoners. These men had been imprisoned by the Nazis because they had not echoed Hitler's battle cry, or because they happened to be Jews.' They were Poles, Czechs, Hungarians, Roumanians, Russians, Dutchmen, Frenchmen, Luxembourgers, Belgians, Norwegians 'or nationals of any other nation. Their only crime being that they were not liked by the Third Reich. Their striped uniform, long blue and white stripes on trousers and jacket, the numbers over the pocket, immediately indicated that these men had been in prison. But the thing that gave them away more than anything else was the weary bewildered look with which they greeted

---

[1] United States Joint Chiefs of Staff paper, JCS 1067, quoted in Dennis L. Bark and David R. Gress, *A History of West Germany: From Shadow to Substance, 1945–1963*, Blackwell, Oxford, 1989, pp. 28–29.

each American vehicle. They were too tired to smile, but a sad ray of appreciation managed to appear on each face and no more had to be said.'

These former Flossenbürg prisoners were many miles away from their camp. 'When the Nazis realised that the Americans were approaching Flossenbürg they started to "evacuate" their prisoners. There were about 20,000 of them when the "programme" began. In groups of between three and five thousand men the Nazis herded the victims to their doom. The stated destination was Dachau, another concentration camp about two hundred miles to the south. About a hundred SS men accompanied each group of prisoners, as they marched towards their new home. There was no food. Most of the prisoners were already suffering from malnutrition and many were on the verge of starvation. Thousands were ill from a multiplicity of diseases. Typhus and the deadly lice that caused the disease accompanied the pilgrimage. The SS men surrounded the herd of victims, and a special group followed behind to take care of those who faltered. As soon as a man fell out of line the SS were at his side. Another prisoner dug the hole, and the victim or victims were thrown in before they received a Nazi death bullet behind the ear.'

After three days without food the men were still being marched eighteen miles each day. 'Nor did they march along the highways. They moved only at night, and through the woods where the Nazis could conceal their crimes. Through the cold and wet nights these miserables dragged their weary bodies, and as they fell they found their graves. But the Nazis were not content to wait for men to fall. We came to one small village where a French soldier halted us. He told us that he had been a prisoner-of-war in that town for two years, and that he saw the approaching column of unfortunates. His entire commando of about fifteen French prisoners-of-war was called out by the SS and ordered to dig a big hole deep in the nearby forest. The men had no choice and they obeyed. When the hole was dug they hastily departed, for they knew very well what was in store and they dreaded to remain in the vicinity. They saw, as they fled across the fields, a small group of weary men, about forty or fifty of them, being hurried along towards the hole.'

Ferencz asked the French soldier to show them where the hole had been dug, 'and he very willingly got into our car and showed us the spot. Half of the hole had been covered over, and a few branches were thrown over the freshly tilled sod. "Here is the place", he said, "and there they lie." We could see only freshly turned soil, and so a shovel was removed from our car. I handed it to the Frenchman and told him to start digging where he thought the bodies might be. It took only a few strokes of his shovel and he uncovered the head of one of the victims. The glaring dead eye was all I had to see. "Cover him again," I told him. These dead had suffered enough.'

The two Americans, Ferencz and the lieutenant, went to a nearby farmhouse to get further evidence of this massacre. 'The farmhouse was full of "good German people" who were very eager to help. Yes, the hausfrau had seen the column approaching, and suspected what was going to happen so she did not venture forth. Once the band had disappeared in the woods she heard shortly thereafter a series of shots, at about one or two minute intervals, as each body received its mortal blow. There was apparently no resistance from the victims. The weary souls had lost all strength to struggle. Many probably welcomed the end. The Germans had not bothered to bury their former prisoners. They had left the uncovered dead lying in the hole, and it was the farmer and his son who had gone forth and finally thrown some dirt over the corpses to prevent the spread of disease.'

Ferencz took sworn statements from the farmers. 'Then they dared to start complaining that some of the Russians, who had been members of the column and who had been liberated when the American troops overtook them, had stolen some clothing from the farm and had taken away their food. The farmer's wife started crying, but I was in no mood for tears. I told her, in my best broken German, that she could only thank Hitler for anything that happened to her, and that she should be thankful that she wasn't in the place of those poor political prisoners.'

Ferencz, the lieutenant and their driver continued towards Flossenbürg. 'At regular intervals along the way were small mounds, under which lay two or three bodies. There must be between two and three thousand murdered people lying along this road. Some have not been buried, and the emaciated sprawling blue bodies had me crying furiously without tears.'[1] Reaching Flossenbürg, Ferencz found that there were still about 1,400 inmates in the camp. Despite the resourcefulness of the American medics, at least thirty were still dying every day.

The two dictators who had dominated fourteen wretched years, and brought havoc to Europe, were nearing their end. The first of the Axis partners to fall was Benito Mussolini. He had come to power in 1922, had been bound to Hitler since 1934 by the Pact of Steel, and for more than a year had been held as Hitler's effective prisoner in northern Italy. There, on April 28, his rule came to an ignominious end near the lakeside

---

[1] Benjamin B. Ferencz, letter dated 29 April 1945. Private archive.

village of Dongo, when he was caught and shot dead by Italian partisans. Also shot, in reprisal for the killing of fifteen Italian partisans in Milan nine months earlier, were fifteen of those who had been captured with him, including Alessandro Pavolini, the Secretary of the Fascist Party, and four Cabinet Ministers. His mistress, Clara Petacci, was also shot.

The partisans took the bodies of Mussolini and his mistress to Milan. There they were hanged, upside down. That afternoon representatives of General von Vietinghoff signed, at Caserta near Naples, the unconditional surrender of all German troops in Italy. In Moscow, a British officer, Hugh Lunghi, who was serving with the British Military Mission to Russia, went with some of his colleagues, with the news of the surrender of the German Army in Italy, to the Soviet Ministry of Defence. 'We were greeted with a surly, couldn't-care-less, acknowledgement: this attitude was reflected in the Soviet press where the news later rated a paragraph or two on the back pages, if that. The Soviet media, for ever in the past clamouring for a "Second Front" in France, had always treated the Allied campaign in Italy as a sideshow.'[1]

The news of Italy's defeat percolated throughout the regions Mussolini had once aspired to rule. In Somalia, a member of the British Colonial Development Survey, Nigel Viney, was in a remote area 'having breakfast with my little gang of helpers,' he recalled, 'when an old man came walking along through the bush. I gave him a cup of tea. Before he left he said to me, "By the way, Mussolini is dead." When I got back to my base, about sixty miles away, they said to me, "Oh yes, it was on the nine o'clock news last night." '[2]

In the areas of Germany that remained under German control, Nazi resistance was collapsing. On April 28 there was excitement in the Allied armies when Munich Radio announced that the 'Bavarian Freedom Movement' had taken over from the Nazis in the city. The radio even gave out vital intelligence for the Allies with regard to the location of Field Marshal Albert von Kesselring's headquarters at Pullach, six miles from Munich. It was, however, a false dawn. Later that day the Gauleiter of Munich, Paul Giesler, came on the same radio frequency to announce that 'the activities of the traitors have been stopped'.[3] For Munich, the war would go on for another forty-eight hours.

Among those liberated by the British on April 28 were several thousand Allied prisoners-of-war in Stalag 11-B, near Fallingbostel. One of them

---

[1] Hugh Lunghi, letter to the author, 22 September 1994.
[2] Nigel Viney, in conversation with the author, 27 October 1994.
[3] Geoffrey Dennis (editor), *The War of 1939*, Caxton, London, 1946, p. 261.

was a nineteen-year-old American soldier, Kenneth Larson, who had been born in North Dakota, and had spent his childhood in Washington State, on the Pacific. He recalled the first moments of liberation: 'I saw a tank charging through the hills and German guards running across the fields tearing off their uniforms. We were fed food given out from a British Army truck. Another American soldier and I had the bright(?) idea of visiting the nearby village near the prison camp. We saw a military training facility with slogans on the walls and also entered what seemed to be a large storage warehouse. Inside, we found all sorts of department-store items. I took some gold-coloured silverware but left it on my bunk when we were told to depart from the camp and take trucks to a nearby airfield. Our visit to the nearby village was not a very good idea – because the other soldier and I could have been shot by Germans or by guards or by civilians or police, etc. We were dressed in old military clothing, rubber boots, etc. We were lucky.'

Fifty years after his liberation, Larson retained vivid memories of captivity. 'We were not mistreated or hit with rifle butts but all suffered from lack of needed food. We slept with one blanket on hard wooden slats on bunks, ate out of tin pans, drank cold water, had some Red Cross parcels from Sweden or Switzerland, were kept distant from Russian soldiers who later escaped through the barbed wire to loot a large German warehouse and who came walking back near our encampment with large bags of wheat slung across their soldiers. Also, American officers were kept in separate compounds. I was an ordinary American Infantry soldier with the 106th "Golden Lion" Infantry Division that was hit first by the Germans in the Battle of the Bulge, December 16th, 1944, near Belgium and Luxembourg.

'We were strafed by Allied airplanes while in German trucks headed for the prison camp in the small German village (but we weren't hit when we jumped out of the trucks and headed for the ditches). I saw German V–1 rockets at night and in the daytime and heard them as they headed for France and England. I saw Allied-German dogfights in the air, bombers shot down, experienced a close bombing at night of a nearby German canal (the building shook and the sky was lit up).

'If the European war had continued, would we have starved? I don't know. We all lost weight badly, and there was little real food. In some cases, men went out in work projects to nearby cities and under guard to work at jobs – and they had better food. But I never did this. It might have been better if I could have stayed at the hospital in the small German town – but one never knew just what to do because everything was changing and life was so unexpected.'

Larson had been severely wounded during the Battle of the Bulge, by what is now called 'friendly fire'. As he was walking back in the dark to his slit trench and his sergeant 'a tree branch hit my metal helmet and knocked it off. Startled, I called out or said something. Just at this moment, an American soldier heard me. Without calling out or saying anything, he raised up his rifle and shot me in the dark. His rifle bullet (M–1) hit me in the right side and almost sliced the spinal cord. I saw a red flash like electricity, and I felt weak and then fell down on the ground.'

The sequel to his wounding was something Larson could never forget: 'Some American soldiers picked me up and carried me to the nearby command post of our company,' he recalled. 'One can imagine what the effect of the solitary rifle shot had on the troops in the slit trenches up ahead on the side of the hill. I lay on the floor, the soldier apologized for hitting me, and I was carried on a stretcher down the hill. I was taken to a kind of wooden hut and left there with other wounded. I don't know where the others came from, and I heard later in the camp that the next day our company had been shelled by German artillery while walking along a road and men had scattered. Sergeant Henry had been killed and the company executive officer had his leg blown off. The next day the German soldiers came in, and we were taken prisoner.'

One episode while Larson was a prisoner-of-war had brought him a moment of good cheer. 'On one chilly and damp morning around February, 1945, I happened to take a walk up to the main gate of the large international camp made up of American, British, Russian, French, and other nationalities. My spirits were very low, and I was cold and hungry. Just at that moment, a loudspeaker perched up on top of the main gate burst out into song, and I heard the marvellous voice of Bing Crosby singing Irving Berlin's song called "Blue Skies". When I heard the words and music, my morale went up and I knew then that I could hold on and make it through to the end of the war.

'Losing weight and getting more and more touchy and irritable, and even trying to cook grass on simple handmade stoves, and toasting bread near the stone fireplace within each prison hut, we heard over the radio the news that President Roosevelt had passed away in early April, 1945. We watched as massive fleets of Allied bombers passed over in the blue skies on their way to central Germany. At night, we heard what were probably lone German military scout planes pass overhead.'

Larson was held captive for four and a half months. As for so many prisoners-of-war, it was a painful experience, making liberation a moment of miracle. 'I felt then that the Lord had protected me and that somehow I had been lucky enough to get through and back to America. Many others didn't – as witness the many crosses in Europe on military burial fields.'[1]

Among those still under German control on April 28, and being marched westward, were several thousand women who had been held in Ravensbrück concentration camp north of Berlin. 'It seemed at that time,' one of their number, the Vienna-born Susan Eckstein, recalled, 'as if all of Germany was running westward. During a rest stop on a roadside some young German air force soldiers started talking to us, and when we asked them where they were going in such a hurry, they answered, "To our liberators, the Americans." They were obviously petrified of falling into Russian hands.'[2]

Freedom came on April 29 for more than ten thousand Allied prisoners-of-war, including those from Eichstätt who for the past two weeks had been on the road. They had been brought together at a vast camp near Moosburg. All ten thousand had been marched away since mid-April from the advancing Americans, and some from the Russians further east. Eichstätt had been overrun by the Americans only two days after the prisoners had been taken out. Major Elliott Viney recorded the events of the liberation of Moosburg in his diary: 'It is difficult to write much, things happen so quickly and are out of date in ten minutes. Last night we took over the camp and the Germans are standing by to surrender. An SS division are said to be (a) gone in the night (b) digging in outside. It poured all yesterday and I read Boswell all day. The wire is coming down in places so I walked through a hole. The chaos at HQ is indescribable. At five this morning the South African provost company went on duty and the camp is full of white armbands and patrols and our men are in the perimeter sentry boxes. I got up for my shave at 6.30 and cleaned my boots to the sound of gunfire.

'After breakfast the fun started. There are planes all overhead and two P–51 Mustangs came very low and rolled; we all cheered like mad in the open. Now there is a mass of machine-gun and rifle fire – certainly it is flying over the camp and cleared the Lagerstrasse pretty effectively just now. There are big bumps very close now. 12.00 AMERICANS HERE.'

As Major Viney was writing up his diary it was announced that on the previous night the camp commandant had sent for the Senior Allied Officer among the prisoners-of-war and taken him to an SS general who proposed a 'neutral area' around the camp, and then went on with a Swiss intermediary for about three miles, where they met the commanding

---

[1] Kenneth Lloyd Larson, letter to the author, 19 September 1994.
[2] Susan E. Cernyak-Spatz (formerly Susan Eckstein), letter to the author, 28 October 1994.

officer of the United States forces nearest them. He doubted that a 'neutral area' was acceptable, so the delegation went on another six or seven miles to see an American general. It was then four in the morning. The American refused the SS offer but, Viney noted, 'said he would accept surrender of all local Goons, and would postpone his attack, which apparently he did.' Viney's diary continued: '12.40. We have just seen the Stars and Stripes hoisted in the town, amidst stupendous cheering. 13.30. The guards have been marched off; a sort of 'Oranges and Lemons', chaps shouting whether each was "good" or not and getting a root up the arse.

'Three jeeps in the camp and all national flags hoisted. The boys brought in cigars, matches, lettuce and flour. The scenes have been almost indescribable. Wireless blaring everywhere, wire coming down, sentry boxes packed, other ranks wearing Goon bayonets and caps. The SS put a *panzerfaust* through the guard company's barracks when they refused to fight.'[1]

At ten that evening the freed prisoners were told that Allied troops had reached Munich, and that their own liberation had been announced on the BBC. 'A bash lunch and a potato-less dinner. So ends four years, eleven months and one day.'[2]

The British entry into Belsen on April 15 had shocked the Western world, which after five years of war had thought itself beyond further shock. On April 29, the war ended for the prisoners of another vast concentration camp, in the village of Dachau, ten miles north-west of Munich. Among the prisoners in the camp was Albert Guérisse, a Belgian doctor who had been a British secret agent, with the false identity of a Royal naval officer, Lieutenant-Commander Pat O'Leary. Guérisse later recalled how, as the first American officer, a major, descended from his tank, 'the young Teutonic lieutenant, Heinrich Skodzensky', emerged from the guard post and came to attention before the American officer. 'The German is blond, handsome, perfumed, his boots glistening, his uniform well-tailored. He reports, as if he were on the military parade grounds near Unter den Linden during an exercise, then very properly raised his arm he salutes with a very respectful "*Heil Hitler!*" and clicks his heels. "I hereby turn over to you the concentration camp of Dachau,

---

[1] The *panzerfaust* was a hand-held anti-tank rocket which could knock out a tank at sixty metres. At a labour camp at Schlieben, Jewish prisoners had been among those forced to make them: they were so much in demand by the German troops as the Allies advanced into Germany that trucks took them straight from the factory to the front.
[2] Elliott Viney, diary, 29 April 1945. Private archive.

30,000 residents, 2,340 sick, 27,000 on the outside, 560 garrison troops".'

The American major did not return the German lieutenant's salute. 'He hesitates for a moment', Albert Guérisse recalled, 'as if he were trying to make sure that he is remembering the adequate words. Then, he spits into the face of the German, "*Du Schweinhund!*" And then, "Sit down here!" – pointing to the rear seat of one of the jeeps which in the meantime have driven in. The major turns to me and hands me an automatic rifle. "Come with me". But I no longer had the strength to move. "No, I stay here –" The major gave an order, the jeep with the young German officer in it went outside the camp again. A few minutes went by, my comrades had not yet dared to come out of their barracks, for at that distance they could not tell the outcome of the negotiations between the American officer and the SS men. Then I heard several shots'.[1]

Lieutenant Skodzensky was dead. Within an hour, all five hundred of his garrison troops were to be killed, some by the inmates themselves, but more than three hundred of them by American soldiers who had been literally sickened by what they saw of rotting corpses and desperate, starving inmates. In one incident, an American lieutenant machine-gunned 346 of the SS guards after they had surrendered, and were lined up against a wall. The lieutenant, who had entered Dachau a few moments earlier, had just seen the corpses of the inmates piled up around the camp crematorium, and at the railway station.

More than 30,000 were liberated in Dachau that day, of whom 2,466 were to die in the following month and a half. Their war had ended, but neither medical care, food nor concern could save their lives. They had gone beyond the point of physical recovery.

In Berlin, on the evening of April 29, General Helmuth Weidling, the city commandant, reported to Hitler that the Russians had reached the Potsdam railway station, not far from the bunker. In addition, Weidling warned, there were no longer any anti-tank guns available for the defence of the Chancellery area. What, he asked, were his men to do once they had run out of ammunition? 'I cannot permit the surrender of Berlin,' Hitler replied. 'Your men will have to break out in small groups.'

That afternoon, the Citadel Commandant of Hitler's bunker, SS Major-General Mohnke, who had been the senior officer involved in the massacre of British prisoners-of-war at Paradis, near Dunkirk, in 1940, made the last two presentations of the once highly-prized award for valour, the Knight's Cross. One went to a French SS volunteer, Eugène

---

[1] Andrew Mollo, 'Dachau', *After the Battle*, No. 27, 1980.

Vaulot, for destroying six Russian tanks on the previous day. The other went to the German commander of the tank troops defending the Chancellery, Major Herzig.

At eleven o'clock that night, Hitler, in search of reinforcements to come back into Berlin and break the siege, telegraphed from the bunker: 'Where are Wenck's spearheads? When will they advance? Where is the Ninth Army?' British cryptographers, working around the clock at Bletchley, read these last desperate questions, and knew that the end must be very near. At one o'clock on the morning of April 30, Field Marshal Wilhelm Keitel informed Hitler that General Wenck's forces were 'stuck fast' south of the distant Schwiechlow Lake, and had no way of moving towards the capital, while the Ninth Army was completely encircled. This fact, too, the British eavesdroppers read, noted, and passed on to the Allied Commanders-in-Chief in the field.

As the Allied troops advanced through Germany, they came upon dozens of long columns of prisoners-of-war, their own soldiers who had been taken into captivity, some as early as 1939, others as recently as the Battle of the Bulge at the end of 1944. For these men the fighting war had ended when they had been taken prisoner. What remained had been the life of camps throughout the Reich, and, in the last phase, painful, seemingly purposeless, often quite directionless marches across Europe. One of these marchers, the British airman Roger Peacock, later recalled 'almost five years passed in various prison camps, taking me from Germany to Silesia to Memelland (or Lithuania: the territory had changed hands on several occasions) to Poland and to West Germany. Like my colleagues, I knew misery, desolation, fierce hunger, loneliness, occasional hope, the solace (occasionally) of prose and poetry and music, the fierce satisfaction of enjoying news of the wounds inflicted on the enemy described both in their own newspapers – I read three every day and the weekly *Das Reich* every Tuesday – and brought to us by our own most illicit radio. Through all that time we hoped, intellectually, for eventual release; emotionally, we could hardly accept it as a future reality.

'When the 21st Army Group crossed the Rhine at the end of March 1945 the German authorities split us, in Stalag 357, into parties of three hundred or so and sent us out to march north-eastward towards the Baltic somewhere near Lübeck. Their motives were obscure: to use us as bargaining counters? spite? to delay release as long as possible? At any rate, our party was on the move for almost a month: sleeping where we could – a barn if we were lucky, a ditch if we were not.

'We stole a sufficiency of food from the farms we passed: grain, eggs, potatoes, smaller livestock such as rabbits and chickens. Once, I remember clearly, we carved up a dead horse – very dead – we found lying beside the road. Despite this month of high living, when I was weighed on my return to England I weighed a mere six-and-a-half stones.[1] Half-way through that last month the neighbouring column, a few hundred yards away, was attacked by RAF Typhoons; there were some sixty or so casualties – deaths, disablements, lesser wounds – and thenceforth we were very conscious of that potential danger.

'Then one day at the end of April, I stood on top of a low hill beside a Mecklenburg lake and saw our own tanks moving past – and the impossible was suddenly reality. We raced down to the road and stood, waving and shouting, immensely moved – moved beyond any words – as later columns came past. That was the day when, for me, the war ended, even if I did not realise it at the time. Days later, by means of a stolen or confiscated or "liberated" car followed by a stretch in a DC3, I arrived back in England by Lancaster from Brussels.'[2]

Rumours abounded of an imminent end to the war, and on April 29 they appeared to move from speculation to certainty, when, from San Francisco, an Associated Press news flash declared: 'Germany has surrendered to the Allied Governments unconditionally'. The source for this spectacular turn of events was given as 'a high American official'. The story was as false as a similar one, issued by the United Press from New York on November 7, 1918, had been. On that occasion, Enrico Caruso had appeared on the balcony of his New York hotel and sung 'The Star-Spangled Banner', while in Washington excited crowds had converged on the White House. On April 29th, 1945, there was, as *Stars and Stripes* recalled, 'a wild hour of jubilation until President Truman and SHAEF denied the report.'[3]

On the morning of April 30, American troops entered Munich, the scene of Hitler's earliest political rallies, and of his greatest domestic triumphs. In Italy, American troops entered Turin. That same day, General Eisenhower informed the Soviet Deputy Chief of Staff, General Antonov, that American troops would not advance further into Austria than the 'general area of Linz' and the River Enns. In Istria, British and American forces, with no such self-denying ordinances, hurried to reach

---

[1] Ninety-one pounds.
[2] Roger Peacock, letter to the author, 26 August 1994.
[3] *Stars and Stripes*, 8 May 1945. SHAEF was the Supreme Headquarters Allied Expeditionary Force.

Fiume, Pola and Trieste before the Yugoslav partisan leader, Marshal Tito, could beat them to it.

Winston Churchill was angered by Eisenhower's promise to Antonov, and, fearful of the westward march of communism and its imposition of one-party rule on the former democratic state of Czechoslovakia, telegraphed to President Truman on April 30: 'There can be little doubt that the liberation of Prague and as much as possible of the territory of Western Czechoslovakia by your forces might make the whole difference to the post-war situation in Czechoslovakia, and might well influence that in nearby countries. On the other hand, if the Western Allies play no significant part in Czechoslovakian liberation that country will go the way of Yugoslavia.'[1]

To Churchill's disappointment Truman replied that he would leave the tactical deployment of troops to the military. In passing on the British request that United States forces liberate Prague, the American Chief of Staff, General George C. Marshall, told Eisenhower: 'Personally and aside from all logistic, tactical or strategical implications, I would be loath to hazard American lives for purely political purposes.'[2]

The same day, April 30, in Berlin, one of Russia's leading war photographers, Viktor Temin, persuaded Marshal Georgi Zhukov to let him photograph the Reichstag from the air. As he flew towards the roof of the building he saw, and photographed, a Red Army soldier placing the Red Banner on top of one of the ornamental balustrades. He then flew on, without permission, to Moscow, where his picture was published in *Pravda* on the following morning. Temin then flew back to Berlin, bringing with him 'an armful of copies of *Pravda*'.[3]

Less than a mile away from the flag being placed on top of the Reichstag, Hitler was still in his bunker deep underground. He had abandoned all hope of a counter-attack by Wenck, or by any other general. At half-past three that afternoon, having eaten his lunch, Hitler sent those who were with him in the bunker, Dr Goebbels, Martin Bormann, and his personal staff, into the passage. As they stood there waiting, they heard a single shot. Hitler had shot himself in the mouth. A few moments later Goebbels, Bormann and the others entered Hitler's room. The Führer was dead. So too was Eva Braun; she had swallowed poison.

With a single pistol shot, the Thousand Year Reich, proclaimed as such by Hitler with confidence and bravado in 1933, was to all intents

[1] Eisenhower papers, Abilene, Kansas.

[2] Truman papers, Independence, Missouri.

[3] Georgii Drozdov and Evgenii Rybako, *Russia at War, 1941–45*, Stanley Paul, London, 1978, p. 244.

and purposes at an end. It had been twelve years of tyranny, bloodshed, war and evil on a scale which, even in the retrospect of fifty years, defies the imagination of those who did not witness it, and defies the understanding of those who did. As Soviet shells still fell around the Chancellery, Hitler's body and that of Eva Braun were taken up from the bunker to the courtyard above, doused in petrol, and set on fire.

That same day, Russian troops entered the women's concentration camp at Ravensbrück, north of Berlin. There they were welcomed by 23,000 women: the survivors of more than 115,000 Jews and non-Jews, most of them women and children, who had been murdered in the previous two years in that one camp alone. As the Russian troops then advanced westward, they found on the roads several thousand women who had been driven out of the camp by their German guards in an attempt to get them beyond the reach of discovery. Five thousand had been killed on the march by the guards, or had died of privation, but several thousand were still alive. It would be many months before they returned to even a semblance of health, but their war had ended.

IV

The First Four Days of May

The death of Hitler and the fighting in the centre of Berlin marked two dramatic steps in bringing the war in Europe to an end. With them, the pace of the collapse of the Third Reich intensified. On Tuesday May 1, 1945, the German garrison in Rhodes surrendered. In Berlin that day, negotiations began between the Chief of the German General Staff, General Hans Krebs, and the commander of the Soviet forces, General Vasili Chuikov. Krebs asked for a truce. Chuikov telephoned Marshal Zhukov, who himself telephoned Stalin, who insisted upon unconditional surrender. Krebs returned to the bunker, where Hitler's body still lay three-quarters burned in the open air. In the bunker, Krebs found Martin Bormann, the head of the Nazi Party Chancellery, and Josef Goebbels, the Nazi propaganda chief, both of whom were determined not to give in.

The news that Hitler was dead was broadcast over Hamburg Radio at 10.30 p.m. on the night of May 1st. 'We realised it was all over when what was left of German radio announced the death of Hitler in the bunker,' a British Intelligence officer in northern Germany, Vivian Herzog, later recalled.[1] His feelings were widely shared. That anyone could inspire the German army to continue the fight for much longer was clearly impossible. The country was fragmented, its capital a battleground, its leaders either dead or in disarray.

The news of Hitler's death spread to the furthest regions that had been within his sphere. The seventeen-year-old Yakov Malkin was in prison in the Lebanon at the end of April. He and twenty other young Palestinian Jews had embarked two weeks earlier on a lark which turned sour: they had decided to cross illegally from Palestine to Lebanon in order 'to visit the snow' on the mountain slopes so tantalisingly visible across the border. A shepherd boy had proved amenable to their bribe and taken them across the border unseen either by the British or Lebanese frontier guards: 'We enjoyed ourselves enormously.' Unfortunately for

---

[1] Captain Vivian (later Chaim) Herzog, letter to the author, 6 November 1994. Herzog was later President of the State of Israel (1983–1993).

them, the shepherd boy found that the Lebanese police were willing to pay a second sum for their capture. Taken to a Druze village, they were held in a prison that had once been stables, and sentenced to a month's detention. 'One evening we heard terrible shooting, the noise of hundreds of guns. We climbed up to the barred window and saw that the whole area was illuminated by the flashes of gunfire. There was shooting from all the roofs. The Druze were shooting in all directions. It was a terrible hour of anxiety. We banged and shouted. A guard came in. "Hitler is dead," he told us. "The war is finished. This is how we Druze celebrate, we shoot." The shooting went on throughout the night. In the morning the commander of the prison came in and told us: "Now you are free." '[1]

Hitler's death was the main newspaper headline throughout the world on Wednesday, May 2. It seemed clear to every newspaper reader that the war must soon be over. Yet the fighting continued. Like a headless chicken, the German army still battled against its foes. German soldiers still drove their tanks, fired their guns, manned their ditches, and fought. Thousands, and tens of thousands, also surrendered, but the war in Europe still had five days to run.

In the newly liberated Flossenbürg concentration camp, Benjamin Ferencz had spent the night in the commandant's bed. 'While the thousands of prisoners under his charge lived in miserable, contaminated shacks, stuffed in like sardines in a can,' Ferencz wrote home, 'the prime Nazi of the neighbourhood lived in a luxurious home a stone's throw away.' The prisoners had designated May 1st as their official liberation day 'and decided to have a celebration. The Russians are the majority in the camp, and it is not merely a coincidence that they picked May Day for the event. A huge platform was built in the centre of the prison yard. Flags of the United States, Great Britain, and Russia decorated the front, and before them were painted pictures of Stalin, Churchill, and most prominent, the late President Roosevelt. All the inmates, dressed in clothing which had already been collected from the surrounding villages, paraded around the square. Each national group formed a separate unit, and the leader carried their national flag. Since most of the former prisoners were too weak to participate, only a few hundred could take part in the celebration. At the top of the platform was a neat sign:

---

[1] Yakov Malkin, in conversation with the author, 30 December 1994.

44

THANKS TO OUR LIBERATORS

(Yesterday they had asked me how to spell it) and representatives from each group made long winded speeches thanking the Allies, and condemning the capitalistic system. There were cheers and hurrahs at appropriate intervals, and the whole affair was very well conducted. For the prisoners it was quite a difference from conditions a week ago.'[1]

In the Austrian province of the Vorarlberg, a member of a German anti-aircraft unit, eighteen-year-old Herbert Mittelstädt, recalled his last day as a soldier. 'On May 1st, 1945, our lieutenant approached the twenty-five of us, and gravely announced, "I no longer believe that there is any way possible for us to win this war. I am going to discharge you, and whoever wants to, can continue to fight with me as a Werewolf." Only one guy raised his hand. His family was in East Prussia, and the possibility of his ever returning was extremely slim anyway. Since the lieutenant only had a single ally, he said, "The whole thing is not worth it. I'm going to discharge myself as well!"'[2]

During May 2, the news of Hitler's death spread to every corner of the diminished and ever-diminishing Reich. Susan Eckstein was on the westward march from Ravensbrück when, as she later recalled, she and her fellow-marchers were 'plied with drinks from a joyous population upon hearing the news of Hitler's death, regardless of the fact that we were concentration camp prisoners under SS guard'.[3] Two hundred miles to the south-east, in besieged Breslau, where the distraught women of the city had long urged the authorities to bring the appalling siege conditions to an end, the headline in the Nazi Party newspaper on the morning of May 2 was mendacious and uncompromising:

HEROIC DEATH OF THE FÜHRER[4]

Further south, at a small farm in the Sudetenland, a column of Jews who were being marched away from a labour camp at Sonnenberg were ordered to spend the night in a barn. One of their number, Michael Etkind, who had earlier been in the Lodz ghetto, later recalled: 'Again, there was no food. We crowded in and lay down on the straw. The

---

[1] Benjamin B. Ferencz, Czech-German border, letter dated 29 April 1945. Private archive.
[2] Herbert Mittelstädt, in Johannes Steinhoff, Peter Pechel and Dennis Showalter (editors), *Voices from the Third Reich, an Oral History*, Regnery Gateway, Washington DC, 1989, p. 490.
[3] Dr Susan E. Cernyak-Spatz (née Eckstein), letter to the author, 28 October 1994.
[4] 'Heldentod des Führers,' *Schlesische Tageszeitung*, 2 May 1945, p. 1.

guards, posted at the open doorway, sat on stools with their guns resting on their knees. They were talking quietly in their alien, Germanic tongue when someone close by overheard the words: "Hitler is dead". Those three words were like a match thrown into the barn: in seconds the fire had spread from mouth to ear, from ear to mouth. And then there was a moment of silence. Suddenly, the "Joker" – the man who'd kept the rest of us going with his humour and jokes – the man from my hut in Sonnenberg, jumped up. Like a man possessed, like a lunatic, he began to dance about waving his arms in the air; his high-pitched voice chanted with frenzy:

> I have outlived the fiend,
> my life-long wish fulfilled,
> what more need I achieve –
> my heart is full of joy.

The 'Joker' sang in 'a transport of ecstasy. We watched him in horror, speechless. His lanky frame was swirling round until it reached the open door. No one could move. He'd run into the field outside. One of the German guards lifted his gun, took aim. We saw the "Joker" lift his arms again, stand up, turn around, surprised (didn't they understand, hadn't they heard, that the Monster was dead?) and, like a puppet when its strings are cut, collapse into a heap.'[1]

German newspapers appeared on May 2 with black borders. One of these newspapers, soon to fall into the hands of the advancing British, bore the three-word headline: 'Unser Führer gefallen'.[2] By implication, 'our Leader' had fallen in battle, presumably during the Russian onslaught on Berlin. Hitler's successor as Chancellor, Grand Admiral Karl Dönitz, declared: 'It is my first task to save the German people from destruction by the Bolsheviks. It is only to achieve this that the fight continues. As long as the British and Americans hamper us from reaching this end, we shall fight and defend ourselves against them as well.' What the German people had suffered, Dönitz added, 'is unique in history'.[3]

As well as his speech, Dönitz issued an order of the day to the German Army. It read: 'My comrades, the Führer has fallen. True to his great idea to save the peoples of Europe from Bolshevism, he has risked his life and met with a hero's death. In deep veneration and mourning, we

[1] Michael Etkind, ' "Youth" Remembered', *Journal of the '45 Aid Society*, number 12, London, March 1985, page 7.

[2] *Lübecker Zeitung*, 2 May 1945.

[3] 'Text of Doenitz's Speech', *Stars and Stripes*, 2 May 1945, page 4, columns 2 to 3.

dip our colours before him. The Führer has appointed me his successor as head of the State and Supreme Commander of the Wehrmacht. I am assuming command of all branches of all services of the German armed forces with the will to pursue the struggle against the Bolsheviks so long as our fighting army and hundreds of thousands of German families are safe from slavery and destruction. Against the British and the Americans I shall have to pursue the fight so far and so long as they hamper my struggle against the Bolsheviks.'

The situation, Dönitz declared, 'demands further unconditional exertions from you who have already accomplished such momentous historical deeds and who are now wishing for the end of the war. I demand discipline and obedience. Only by executing my orders without reservation can chaos and annihilation be avoided. German soldiers, do your duty. The very lives of our people are at stake.'[1]

As news of Hitler's death spread, the Dönitz declaration that the war could still go on caused momentary distress. 'His statement spiked peace rumours which had been prevalent for more than a week in all the world capitals,' *Stars and Stripes* reported[2] on May 2, under the two-word headline

HITLER DEAD

A young German naval trainee then on the run with a group of fellow cadets, Heinrich Jaenecke, was unimpressed by the new Leader's call. 'We wanted to let the Grand Admiral conduct his war to the end alone,' he later wrote. 'We came through villages in which deserters hung from trees.'[3] The eleven-year-old Leo Welt, who was then living in Berlin, recalled: 'The SS shot a lot of German soldiers because they were not interested in fighting any more. They killed not only young boys who were crying they wanted to go home, but many soldiers because they had lost their will to fight. They were even hanged from the lampposts as traitors. And I remember quite clearly when my brother and his friends went into the basement of a house that had been bombed: there were five German soldiers sitting there, all shot.'[4]

In Berlin, as German artillery and tank fire pulverised the centre of

---

[1] 'Doenitz's Order of Day', *Stars and Stripes*, 2 May 1945, page 4, column 3.
[2] 'Doenitz at Helm, Vows War Will Continue,' *Stars and Stripes*, 2 May 1945, p. 1.
[3] Heinrich Jaenecke, article in *Stern*, 9 January 1981, quoted in Peter Padfield, *Dönitz, The Last Führer*, Victor Gollancz, London 1984, pp. 22–3.
[4] Leo Welt, in Johannes Steinhoff, Peter Pechel and Dennis Showalter (editors), *Voices from the Third Reich, an Oral History*, Regnery Gateway, Washington DC, 1989, p. 437.

the city, General Helmuth Weidling, whose earlier warnings to those remaining in Hitler's bunker had been ignored, decided there was no option but to surrender. Under flag of truce he made his way to a Soviet command post where, in the presence of Generals Chuikov and Sokolov-skii, he wrote out an order to the troops under his command: 'On 30 April 1945 the Führer took his own life and thus it is that we who remain – having sworn him an oath of loyalty – are left alone. According to the Führer's order, you, German soldiers, were to fight on for Berlin, in spite of the fact that ammunition has run out and in spite of the general situation, which makes further resistance on our part senseless. My orders are: to cease resistance forthwith.' This order was signed: 'Weidling, General of Artillery, former Commandant of the Berlin defence zone.'[1] Except for deleting the word 'former' from Weidling's description of himself, Chuikov and Sokolovskii were content to let the order stand. The battle for Berlin was over.

It was a quarter to seven on the morning of May 2. The cease-fire was to come into effect at three o'clock that afternoon. At the appointed time, the Soviet guns ceased to fire. 'A great enveloping silence fell,' the historian John Erickson has written. 'Soviet troops cheered and shouted, breaking out the food and drink. Along what had once been Hitler's parade route, columns of Soviet tanks were drawn up as for inspection, the crews jumping from their machines to embrace all and sundry at this new-found cease-fire. Something like the great clean-up had already begun in several sectors with the establishment of a *komendatura*, a town-major's office under a Soviet officer, and the installation where possible of local German administrators and officials. Every item of value was to be catalogued, every file faithfully scrutinized and hoarded – except, ironically, a giant card-index compilation of the Nazi government's suspects, flung about in gay abandon by gleeful Soviet soldiers.'[2]

The statistics of the month-long battle for the German capital were astounding. More than 300,000 Russian soldiers had been killed during the battle. During the siege as many as 30,000 Berliners had died. On the day of the city's surrender there were 40,000 wounded Germans in hospitals and casualty stations. Forty-five per cent of the city's houses had been destroyed. Twenty per cent were badly damaged. The siege was the final blow: over the previous four years, during an estimated 360 Allied air raids on the city, at least 50,000 Berliners had been killed. Of

---

[1] Text in John Erickson, *Stalin's War with Germany, The Road to Berlin*, Weidenfeld and Nicolson, London 1983, p. 827.

[2] John Erickson, *Stalin's War with Germany, The Road to Berlin*, Weidenfeld and Nicolson, London, 1983, p. 828.

the city's pre-war Jewish population of 160,000, constituting a major centre of Jewish scientific, commercial, literary and medical achievement, 90,000 had managed to find refuge before the war in other lands, but 55,000 had been deported to concentration camps and murdered, and as many as 7,000 had committed suicide. Just over a thousand had survived in hiding. As many as 4,700 had survived as 'privileged persons': Jewish men married to non-Jewish wives.[1] Elsewhere under German rule no such status could save anyone from deportation. In Berlin, as a result of a courageous collective protest by the wives in 1943, a permanent reprieve from deportation had been granted, and honoured.[2]

Russian soldiers, exploring the shell-scarred monuments of Berlin, scratched their marks of conquest on them. On the burned-out shell of the Reichstag, on the battered Brandenburg Gate, on the Victory Column, on the Bismarck Monument, and on the smashed equestrian statue of the Emperor William I, the Russian graffiti gave a terse summary of four years of battle. Some of their phrases were noted down by Alexander Werth, a British war correspondent with the Russian forces who entered the city soon after its surrender:

'Sidorov from Tambov',
'Ivanov, all the way from Stalingrad',
'Mihkailov who fought the Fritzes in the Battle of Kursk',
'Petrov, Leningrad to Berlin'.[3]

One Russian soldier scrawled three words on the wall of the Reichstag: 'Baranowicze-Sobibor-Berlin', and gave his name: Semyon Rozenfeld. A Jew from the eastern Polish town of Baranowicze, he had fought in the uprising of the prisoners in Sobibor concentration camp in 1943, when he was badly wounded. Hiding behind German lines for seven months, he was liberated by the Red Army which he then joined, was wounded again in the fighting near Lodz, but managed to return to his unit for the Battle of Berlin. He was a survivor of both genocide and war. At the age of twenty-three, his hair had turned silver-white.[4]

Marshal Zhukov and the Soviet Commandant of Berlin, General Berzarin, also wrote their names on the wall. 'Having thus learned who

---

[1] Anthony Read and David Fisher, *Berlin, The Biography of a City*, Pimlico, London, 1994, p. 241.
[2] Anthony Read and David Fisher, *Berlin, The Biography of a City*, Pimlico, London, 1994, p. 233.
[3] Alexander Werth, *Russia at War, 1941–45*, Barrie and Rockliff, London, 1964, p. 989.
[4] Rozenfeld's story was told by Misha Lev, 'Almost a Legend', *Sovetish Geimland*, Moscow, January–February 1964, pp. 78–93.

49

we were,' Zhukov later wrote, 'the soldiers surrounded us. We had to stay with them for an hour, talking heart to heart. The soldiers asked us many questions. They asked when it would be possible to go home. . . .'[1]

During the fighting in and around Berlin on May 2nd, the Red Army captured 134,000 German soldiers. That same day, in Hamburg, the mayor began negotiations for the unconditional surrender of his city. That evening, Churchill told the House of Commons that more than a million German troops had laid down their arms in northern Italy and southern Austria. But there were still areas under German control where the victims of Nazism struggled to survive. At a camp south of Schwerin, Neustadt-Glewe, Jewish women who had been brought from the Breslau area and from Ravensbrück had been made to dig trenches and anti-tank ditches: a cruel and futile German gesture of continuing defiance as the Allied armies prepared for their last assault. 'Everything was now a matter of physical endurance,' one of the inmates, Lena Berg, later recalled. 'The food was wretched; we slept on the floor; and we were tormented by lice. Only by gritting our teeth could we go on.'

An 'unusually warm spring', Lena Berg recalled, 'helped us to hold out'. It helped those women who, like her, had survived so many separate torments: the Warsaw Ghetto, Majdanek, Auschwitz, Stutthof and the death marches. To their surprise, on May 2nd the SS guards failed to appear at roll-call. The women were free. 'We walked out along the highway,' Lena Berg recalled. 'From the right a tank draped with an American flag was coming our way and behind it tall, slender boys in American uniform. They were terribly embarrassed when unappetising creatures who bore only a remote resemblance to women suddenly threw themselves at them, kissing and hugging them.' Back in the camp, she found wild enthusiasm. 'But I, who had unflinchingly believed that the moment would come, now for the first time felt bewildered and lost.'[2]

Susan Eckstein was among those Ravensbrück deportees who had been marched westward as the Red Army had approached Berlin. She later wrote of how, after two days and nights of walking, 'we came to an American checkpoint. The GIs manning the checkpoint did not quite know what to do with us, since we claimed not to be Germans, but nevertheless did not look too much different from the other refugees clogging that road. We had removed the numbers from our clothing when leaving Ravensbrück and chosen civilian clothing without paint

---

[1] Marshal of the Soviet Union G. Zhukov, *Reminiscences and Reflections*, Progress Publishers, Moscow, 1985, volume 2, p. 396.

[2] Lena Berg's recollections, in Alexander Donat, *The Holocaust Kingdom, A Memoir*, Secker and Warburg, London, 1965, p. 316.

stripes on the back, from the stores we were administering. We even had hair, though it was very short. Fortunately a prisoner from the Malchow satellite men's camp was with the GIs at the checkpoint and when we showed our tattoos he confirmed that we were from Auschwitz-Birkenau.

'The GIs who had never seen anything like it, did not know what to do with us, so they sent us to the village (Malchow), where they had set up temporary headquarters in the village inn. We walked the short stretch from the checkpoint to the village and I remember a distinct feeling of perhaps agoraphobia. For three years or more we all had been continuously under guard, never made a decision or took a step without being watched. The sudden feeling of no one watching, no one guarding was almost scary.

'We were fed and given bunk beds that had served for some German Air Force posts that had been located in that inn. As I was the only one who spoke English to some degree, I was urged by the soldiers and officers to tell them about where we had come from. The listeners were absolutely speechless during my narration, for they had never had an inkling of these conditions in Germany.

'We stayed with that outfit, which I believe belonged to the 82nd Airborne. Unfortunately I have lost the address book, with the names of the soldiers and officers. Two come to mind, Dr. George I. Mills, a captain, a dentist, who lives in Springfield, Missouri, and a young soldier, I believe from Nevada, whose name was Paul Harambasic.'[1]

At the concentration camp of Theresienstadt, to which more than 30,000 Jews had been sent in the previous ten days from camps throughout central Germany, May 2 saw the arrival of a senior Red Cross official, Paul Dunant, a representative of the Geneva-based International Committee of the Red Cross. One of those in the camp at the time, a twelve-year-old Dutch Jew, Alfred Drukker, later recalled 'the general atmosphere in the camp during the early part of May, when the war drew to its (unknown) end. We knew that Paul Dunant had come for his yearly inspection on behalf of the International Red Cross and had stayed to oversee the future developments. This, I remember very vividly, we interpreted as a good sign meaning "that the end was in sight". Spring was in the air, but also different feelings, probably best described as a mixture of tension and upheaval.'[2]

Dunant was offered by the German camp authorities the post of supervisor. Three days later he was able to replace the Germans as the effective

---

[1] Dr Susan E. Cernyak-Spatz (née Eckstein), letter to the author, 28 October 1994.
[2] Professor Alfred Drukker, letter to the author, 11 October 1994.

administrator of that vast prison. In Berlin, two other members of the International Committee of the Red Cross, Dr Otto Lehner and Albert de Cocatrix, were seeking to bring what practical help they could to the Berliners, in whose midst they had arrived while it was still under German control. There was little that they could do, either when the German army and SS had been in command, or during the first days of the Russian occupation. One historian of the Red Cross efforts, Drago Arsenijevic, has written: 'A young girl came to Albert de Cocatrix and begged him to take her and fifty of her companions under the protection of the Red Cross. They had been prisoners-of-war of the Yugoslav partisan army of Marshal Tito. "Even though we are wearing the Red Star very visibly," one of the young girls said, "the Russians push into the camp every night and act as if they were in a conquered country. Most of my comrades have been raped." All that de Cocatrix had been able to do was to give them some food parcels.'[1] After six weeks of trying to distribute such food and medical help as they could, de Cocatrix and Lehrer, together with their secretary and driver, were arrested by the Soviet authorities and deported to the Urals. It was not until late in October, after more than a hundred days in different Soviet camps, that they were allowed to return to Switzerland.

In Italy, the last 40,000 Germans under arms surrendered at 9.15 on the morning of May 2. Their surrender was conveyed in a radio message to the American 34th Division, and two American and one British officer went to the Alpine town of Biella, to await at the Albergo Italia the actual document of unconditional surrender. It was brought by Colonel Mallhauer, Chief of Staff to the German LXXV Armoured Corps, who arrived at the hostelry in a civilian Italian car flying a white flag. The Colonel promised to have all his troops assembled near Biella by noon on the following day.

In north-eastern Italy, one of Field Marshal Sir Harold Alexander's special formations, an Infantry Brigade Group made up entirely of Jewish volunteers, was at the end of a gruelling period of action. The commander of one of its artillery batteries, Major Edmund de Rothschild, recalled: 'We had just finished our own particular battle which was mainly against the Croats and certain Russian forces who were fighting alongside the Germans; both groups had behaved atrociously to the Italian civil population and the Free Italians who at one stage we supported in the liberation of Bologna. We were at Udine or in its vicinity. I remember just

---

[1] Drago Arsenijevic, *Voluntary Hostages of the SS*, France Empire, Paris, 1978, p. 274.

before the unconditional cease-fire took place that a hostile aircraft flew around and was just about to drop a bomb which I thought was going to come right in the middle of where we were gathered. I thought, "This is the end of the war and I'm going to be killed". It was the only time I ever took cover. It wouldn't have helped me in the least.

'All my men were so moved at the termination of hostilities but were terribly concerned with the fate of their relatives, so we were in a rather sombre mood. I therefore arranged for a service of thanksgiving to be held for all who were present. Thus the feeling of elation was not total. There were so many armed Serbian guerrillas who claimed they were fighting as partisans milling around our area, that we had to be extremely vigilant and the war was not completely over for our particular group.'[1]

It was mid-afternoon in New York when news reached the city that the war was over in Italy. In pouring rain, the denizens of Mulberry, Mott, Hester, Grand and Elizabeth Streets, the heart of New York's Little Italy, spread the news by word of mouth. On the following morning Milton Lehman, a staff writer for *Stars and Stripes*, cabled from New York to his Naples office: 'Some in "Little Italy" prepared special feasts last night, but many decided to wait for the real celebration when their sons, nephews and brothers returned from the fighting fronts.'[2]

Although the war in Italy was over, news of the German surrender had not reached the American 88th Division in the Alps, and they continued to fight. In what the American war correspondent Stan Swinton called 'a final tragedy of the Italian campaign', five men were killed and five more wounded. It was to be several more hours before the division tuned into a BBC broadcast and learned of the surrender. A few minutes later, official word of the surrender arrived from Corps headquarters. Swinton commented: 'By special order no firearms were discharged to celebrate the end of the fighting here. Life has gone on much as usual – outposts hold their places and vehicles drive with black-out lights. It is less a period of rejoicing than of thanks and personal contemplation.'[3]

On May 2, at Oberammergau, in southern Germany, American troops were approached by three German civilians, who gave themselves up. The first to reach them, and to explain who he was, was Dr Herbert

---

[1] Edmund de Rothschild, letter to the author, 20 October 1994.
[2] 'Italian People in US Hail Liberation of Native Country', *Stars and Stripes*, 5 May 1945, p. 5, cols. 1 and 2.
[3] 'GIs Die As Peace News Arrives Late', *Stars and Stripes*, 6 May 1945, p. 1, col. 1; p. 2, col. 5.

Wagner, one of Germany's leading guided missile designers. With him were two senior members of the Peenemünde rocket research staff, Wernher von Braun and General Walter Dornberger. These were the men whose technical expertise had created the rocket bombs that had recently fallen on London and Antwerp, killing thousands of civilians. The three men were hurried to Paris, and then to the United States. 'We were interested in continuing our work', von Braun later wrote, 'not just being squeezed like a lemon and then discarded.'[1] They may have been squeezed, but they were not discarded. A direct line of cause, effect and personnel was to run between that encounter at Oberammergau and the American Apollo 11 project which landed the first human beings on the moon twenty-four years later.

Also liberated that day were almost two hundred so-called 'prominent' people who had been held hostage at various concentration camps throughout the Reich. As the Allied armies moved across Germany, the prisoners had been taken southward under SS guard across the Austrian Alps to the village of Niederdorf, near Dobbiaco in the South Tyrol. The SS had orders to execute the entire group rather than let them fall into Allied hands, but a Wehrmacht officer, Captain von Alvensleben, reaching the village with a unit of fifteen men, intervened. The SS were defiant, but Alvensleben managed to call up reinforcements, and the SS were outnumbered.

Among those saved by Alvensleben, and then liberated by the Americans, was the former Prime Minister of France, Léon Blum, whose brother René had been deported in 1942 to Auschwitz and killed. Also liberated at Niederdorf were the former Chancellor of Austria, Kurt von Schuschnigg and his wife. It was Schuschnigg's challenge to Hitler in March 1938 which had exposed the strength of democracy in Austria and led Hitler to move in his troops. Another of those liberated was Pastor Martin Niemöller, the former leader of the Confessional Church in Germany. Niemöller, who in the First World War had been a U-boat commander, and was later a leading public opponent of Nazis, had been held, first in Sachsenhausen concentration camp, then in Dachau, and finally at Flossenbürg, for more than seven years.

Several generals suspected by Hitler of having been in the July 1944 plot against him were also found at Niederdorf, as were the widow, children, brother and nephew of Count von Stauffenberg, who had taken the briefcase with the bomb to Hitler's East Prussian headquarters and left it under the table. One unexpected prisoner liberated that day was

---

[1] Tom Bower, *The Paperclip Conspiracy, The Battle for the Spoils and Secrets of Nazi Germany*, Michael Joseph, London, 1987, p. 109.

Lieutenant Kokorin, the nephew of Vyacheslav Molotov, the Soviet Foreign Minister.[1]

During May 2, a Junkers 88, still with its Nazi markings, flew from Germany across France and on to Spain, landing at Barcelona. On board was Pierre Laval, former Prime Minister of Vichy France, whose relief at escaping 'from the ghastly turmoil of Germany's collapse' was tempered by his fear of landing in France and being arrested.[2] Franco's Spain was unwilling to give him asylum, however, not wishing to anger the Allies, and within three months he was flown in the same aircraft, its Nazi markings this time painted out, to the American zone of Austria, where he was taken into custody and then handed over to France for trial.[3]

Late on May 2, British troops of the 6th Airborne Division were on the Baltic coast at Wismar. Other British troops, of the 11th Armoured Division, reached Lübeck. As a result of this advance, the German forces in Schleswig-Holstein and in Denmark, as well as the seat of Admiral Dönitz's Government at Flensburg, were cut off from the rest of Germany. The way was also barred for the Russian army to continue along the Baltic coast, occupy Denmark, dominate the Baltic and gain an outlet on the North Sea. In Moscow, Hugh Lunghi recalled the moment when an urgent signal arrived from London that Montgomery's Northern Army group had reached the Baltic and cut off the German forces in Denmark. 'It had been suspected for some time that Soviet forces were planning to make a dash for that country. As I remember, we did not pass the news about Montgomery's capture of Lübeck to the Soviet Ministry of Defence.'[4]

On the following day, May 3, Russian forces linked up with the British at Wismar, east of Lübeck. A British war correspondent who was present watched as the Russians set up 'a little wooden barrier across the road. There was much hand-shaking and back-slapping and photography at the little barrier.' This meeting, he added, was 'the end, the dead end, of Hitler's Reich'.[5]

A British officer, Major William Whitelaw, later wrote: 'I always imagined that the ultimate surrender of the enemy would be an exhilarating

---

[1] Alan Dulles, *The Secret Surrender*, Harper and Row, New York, 1966, pp. 243–4.
[2] Antony Beevor and Artemis Cooper, *Paris after the Liberation, 1944–1949*, Hamish Hamilton, London, 1994, p. 191.
[3] Laval's trial began on 5 October 1945. He was sentenced to death four days later, and shot.
[4] Hugh Lunghi, letter to the author, 22 September 1994.
[5] Geoffrey Dennis (editor), *The War of 1939*, Caxton, London, 1946, p. 262.

occasion. For me, in fact, it was not.' He had been ordered to take the surrender of Lütjenburg, a small town near the Baltic, twenty-miles east of Kiel; a town that, like so many in that region, was 'overflowing with refugees'. Later he recalled the moment when he had taken the town's surrender. 'We were met by some smart German officers, beautifully turned out in field boots and breeches, putting to shame our rather dilapidated battle dress. The senior officer saluted and in perfect English declared, "I surrender Lütjenburg to you and with it all responsibilities." In typically British fashion, I thanked him rather lamely, not realizing until afterwards what he meant by "responsibilities". I had to find accommodation for our soldiers and this could only be done by forcibly evicting on to the streets huge numbers of desperate people. I knew a little German but, alas, *"Heraus"*[1] was the only word necessary, and the reaction was not easy to bear. Yet one had to remember that we had won and our troops had to come first. At that moment there was little pleasure in victory.'[2]

Emphatic at his pleasure when British troops reached the meadow in which he was hiding was Heinrich Jaenecke, the German naval cadet who had deserted and was on the run with a group of fellow-cadets. 'A deep feeling of liberation, of freedom arose,' he later wrote. 'In a second, everything, the whole dreadful edifice of fear and destruction in which we had lived, collapsed. It was ended. We lay in this meadow in Holstein and looked at one another. The tears ran down our cheeks, then we laughed until we were hoarse. It was the happiest moment of my youth.'[3]

'I really think the German war is drawing to a close,' Field Marshal Montgomery wrote to his son David on Thursday, May 3rd from his new headquarters on Lüneburg Heath, above the village of Wendisch Evern, and less than thirty-five miles from Belsen. 'We have taken one million prisoners in April, and the total since D-Day is now three million. Now that Hitler is dead I think we can expect large-scale surrenders on all sides.'[4] This sense of an imminent Allied victory was highlighted that morning by the Paris edition of *Stars and Stripes*, which listed in numerical order, under the headline:

[1] 'Out!'
[2] William Whitelaw, *The Whitelaw Memoirs*, Aurum Press, London, 1989, pp. 17–18.
[3] Heinrich Jaenecke, article in *Stern*, 9 January 1981, quoted in Peter Padfield, *Dönitz, The Last Führer*, Victor Gollancz, London 1984, p. 466.
[4] Letter of 3 May 1945: quoted in Alistair Horne (with David Montgomery), *Monty 1944–1945*, Macmillan, London, 1994, p. 335.

Nazis Crack Up

the six most recent developments:[1]

1. Foe Yields in Italy.
2. Reds Capture Berlin.
3. Goebbels a Suicide.
4. Confirm Hitler's Death.
5. Rundstedt Is Seized.
6. Peace Bid Admitted.

Confirmation that Hitler was dead had been made by Truman in Washington on the previous day, when he told journalists that he had learned it 'on the best authority possible at this time'. Although rumours were to persist for days, and even months, that Hitler might still be alive, Truman was right. As for Goebbels, a Russian communiqué issued on the night of May 2 had quoted the German Deputy Propaganda Minister, Dr Hans Fritsche, as disclosing that Goebbels had committed suicide in Berlin. This was true: he had also poisoned all six of his children before shooting his wife and himself. As to Field Marshal Gerd von Rundstedt, who on the eve of the Normandy landings had been given command of the anti-invasion forces, he had been captured on the night of May 1st by American troops south of Munich. He had been dining with his wife and son when apprehended by an American tank crew.

The three words 'Peace Bid Admitted' referred to the offer made by Himmler eight days earlier, in a meeting with the Swedish intermediary, Count Folke Bernadotte. The meeting had been held on German soil, at Lübeck, to arrange, as Himmler hoped, a German surrender on the Western Front but not against Russia. This the Allies had rejected. Everywhere Himmler's concentration camps were being revealed, to the anger and disgust of those who were uncovering them, and to the last-minute salvation of those who were being liberated.

As the Russian army had pressed in upon the few remaining German military enclaves in Latvia, Lithuania and East Prussia, several thousand Jews being held in concentration camps along the Baltic had been put into barges and sent by sea to what was left of German-controlled territory near Kiel and Lübeck. One of these deportees, the Latvian-born Hirsch Dorbian, from Libau, recalled these events from the perspective

---

[1] 'Nazis Crack Up', *Stars and Stripes*, 3 May 1945, page 1.

of a fourteen year old. 'We landed on the outskirts of Neustadt Holstein,' he wrote, 'where the guards abandoned us, leaving us stranded about three miles from shore. Fortunately for us, we had Norwegian and Danish prisoners with seafaring experience aboard. They were able to rig us some sort of sail which enabled us to get within walking distance to shore. With their help, the sick and weak were first to disembark. I was one who disembarked early. I remember being put down by a tree, where I was able to witness the other people getting off the boat. Then suddenly, out of nowhere, the guards reappeared, yelling and screaming that no one gave orders to disembark. They started shooting at people still on deck, waiting to go down the makeshift gang plank. Hundreds were killed like that – only a few hours before liberation. When the shooting stopped, those who survived were let off the barge, gathered up and marched to the town of Neustadt Holstein. There we were brought to a large naval base, which had formerly been used as a submarine base. Then we were taken and left on a soccer field. A few hours later, the Germans rounded us up again. By this time, the British tanks were already on the next road. But the Germans still tried to march us on.' It was on May 3 that British troops entered this vast camp at Neustadt where thousands of emaciated human beings had expected nothing but last minute execution. 'I was taken by British medical personnel to the Schleswig Holstein hospital,' Hirsch Dorbian recalled. 'Suffering from all sorts of ailments, I was scrubbed clean and my filthy clothes taken off my body and scrubbed with DDT[1] from head to toe.'[2]

In Bavaria, the tens of thousands of Allied prisoners-of-war who had been liberated by the Americans at Moosburg three days earlier were making their way westward in American lorries, forty to a lorry. Major Elliott Viney wrote in his diary that day: 'Most of the Isar bridges were effectively blown and there are miles of cable and a few guns. But as a drive it was pleasantly uneventful till we approached Landshut. Here bombing has made a detour necessary; the marshalling yards were obliterated and the fields looked like Flanders in the old days. The town itself is battered in places; it was only captured two days ago. We waited some time, then the occupants of some flats were given half an hour to clear out and we billeted ourselves here 28a Regensburgerstrasse, Flat 1. In my command there are six flats and an attic. There are three rooms in

---

[1] Dichlorodiphenyl-trichloroethane: a synthetic insecticide, highly toxic towards a wide variety of insects. Its insecticidal qualities had been discovered by a Swiss chemist in 1939. It was used against lice, fleas and mosquitoes (the carriers respectively of typhus, plague, and malaria and yellow fever) and could be applied as a dust or in liquid form.

[2] Hirsch Dorbian, letter to the author, 8 October 1994.

each. I am in the kitchen with the lads and Joe is baking cakes. The woman whose house it is was in all the rackets. A thousand Yanks went off today. We certainly ought to go alright tomorrow. The Yanks hate the Goons and treat them very rough; we of course fraternize, though the Indians shook them a bit. Two Indians were shot last night by two Hitlerjugend.'[1]

The Americans, Viney wrote the next day, 'are certainly the right people to deal with these bastards; we are far too sentimental. There were two more shot last night; they just turned two Shermans on to the block and filled it with phosphorus shells – just too bad a lot of others went up with it.' Before the Americans had arrived in Landshut, Viney wrote, 'the SS hung scores who ran up white flags here'. One cause of the American anger was an account which had reached them of how, north of Moosburg, the SS had taken over from the Wehrmacht an enormous camp full of tens of thousands of Russian, Polish and Serb prisoners and, Viney noted, 'killed (machine-gunned) 51,000. No wonder the Yanks don't accept their surrender.'[2]

In the former Czechoslovak town of Leitmeritz, on the Elbe, one of the industrial centres of the Sudetenland, a group of concentration camp survivors had arrived after a forced march from a slave labour camp at Rehmsdorf in Saxony. 'By this point,' one of their number, Lucjan Dobroszycki, recalled, 'many of the inmates were either terribly ill or starving to death, and only a handful of us managed to survive this last march. Even for those who did, there was little hope left. The camp was in chaos. There was no food or water. We all lay on the ground, awaiting the end. But the next morning, May 3, 1945, the head of the camp announced over the loudspeaker that not far from where we were, there was a Jewish ghetto – at Theresienstadt – that had been taken over by the International Red Cross. The Red Cross, he said, had expressed its willingness to accept us, and we should prepare to go there. He asked us to assemble at the camp square. No one believed him and, in any case, hardly anyone had the strength to get up and walk even the short distance to the square.

'Our minds changed, however, when after a while a nicely-dressed man appealed to us in Yiddish. He addressed us as *kinderlech* – an affectionate Yiddish word for children – and told us he was a representative of the Theresienstadt ghetto. He urged us to believe him and to get prepared for the trip, indicating that special carriages would be provided

---

[1] Elliott Viney, diary, 3 May 1945. Private papers.
[2] Elliott Viney, diary, 4 May 1945. Private papers.

to those unable to walk. His presence, his words, and the language with which he expressed them, gave us a glimmer of hope. After several hours, the remnants of inmates from the Rehmsdorf camp were at the gates of Theresienstadt. Our reception at Theresienstadt – a beautiful fortress town, filled with stylish brick buildings, canals and fancy bridges, built by Joseph II in honour of his mother, the Empress Maria Theresa before the Germans turned it into a concentration camp – exceeded all of our wildest expectations. First, representatives of the ghetto tried to give us food and drink. This was not easy to do, for instead of waiting in line, people rushed and grabbed, turning over tables covered with food and containers of tea.'[1] Although Theresienstadt was still behind German lines, it was no longer a scene of torment. The worst of Dobroszycki's war was over.

At 11.30 on the morning of Thursday, May 3, outside the village of Wendisch Evern, four German officers arrived from Flensburg at Montgomery's headquarters. They were led by Grand Admiral Hans Georg von Friedeburg, who had succeeded Dönitz as Chief of the Naval Staff, and General Hans Kinzel, Chief of Staff of the German North West Army Command. 'Who are you?', Montgomery asked them. 'I have never heard of you. What do they want?' When he came to the third emissary, Major Friedl, who was believed to be the Gestapo representative, he exploded. 'Major! How dare you bring a major into my headquarters!'[2]

The Grand Admiral, the General and the Major had come to surrender three German armies then facing the Russians. Montgomery rejected their offer. Surrender of the forces facing the Russians, he said, must be made to the Russians, and to the Russians alone. They could surrender to him only those armies facing the British; that is, all the German forces in Holland, north-west Germany and Denmark. Montgomery told them, as he reported to London: 'If they refused to agree as above, then I would go on fighting and a great many German soldiers and civilians would be killed.'[3] Major Trumbull Warren, a Canadian officer at Montgomery's headquarters, recalled: 'He told them to look at the maps that showed where we were and where they were. He told them that we had tremendous strength pouring into Germany on the ground and that we had sufficient aircraft for 10,000 bombers, day and night.'[4]

[1] Lucjan Dobroszycki, letter to the author, 12 November 1994.
[2] Quoted in Alistair Horne (with David Montgomery), *Monty 1944–1945*, Macmillan, London, 1994, p. 336.
[3] Telegram to Field Marshal Alan Brooke, quoted in Nigel Hamilton, *Monty, The Field-Marshal, 1944–1976*, Hamish Hamilton, London, 1986, p. 505.
[4] Trumbull Warren, 'The Surrender of the German Armed Forces', quoted in Nigel Hamilton, *Monty, The Field-Marshal, 1944–1976*, Hamish Hamilton, London, 1986, p. 506.

The German officers crossed back through the lines and returned to Flensburg, where they put Montgomery's conditions to Grand Admiral Dönitz and Field Marshal Keitel. At half past five on the afternoon of Friday May 4 the four German officers returned. An hour later they signed the instrument of surrender of all the forces facing Montgomery's. It would come into effect at 8 o'clock on the following morning. Listening at that moment to German radio traffic was Norman Cohen, a radio operator attached to Tactical Headquarters Staff, British 2nd Army. He heard, and translated on his note pad, a message from Admiral von Friedeburg to Admiral Dönitz: 'Have signed conditions, including shipping same zones. The cease-fire will take effect from 8 o'clock on May 5.'[1] Cohen kept the note pad as a souvenir.

All German forces in Holland, Denmark and northwest Germany would lay down their arms. German merchant shipping off the North Sea coast would likewise surrender. In Moscow that day, with the understandable pride of a British officer, Hugh Lunghi personally took the news of the German surrender to the Soviet Ministry of Defence. 'The Soviet media as good as ignored what for us was a momentous event: for months they had been reporting surrenders of many a German army to the advancing Soviet troops.'[2]

To the east of Berlin, the arrival of Soviet troops was causing consternation, leading to the westward flight of hundreds of thousands of German civilians. Renate Hoffmann, an officer's wife, had fled from a farm at Greifswald, near Peenemünde, as the front approached. 'We knew the Russians couldn't miss us,' she later recalled. 'We also knew that they had shot all of the owners of the neighbouring farms. They turned the houses upside down and behaved like madmen. We were told not to have the least bit of alcohol in the house. We also heard that the Russians attacked and raped women.' On May 4, after four days on the road with a group of refugees, she and a nurse who was with her found a secluded house in which they hoped to find food and shelter. 'Suddenly three Russian soldiers came around the corner. They pointed their guns at us and forced us into the house. We realized right away that we had walked into a trap. And we knew what they had in store for us. We were separated. They put their guns to our heads. Any attempt to defend ourselves meant certain death. The only thing you could do was to pretend you were a rock or dead. I don't want to talk about what happened next. . . .'[3]

---

[1] The text of the intercepted message was published by Alice Brickach in a letter to the *Narragansett Times*, 13 July 1994.

[2] Hugh Lunghi, letter to the author, 22 September 1994.

[3] Renate Hoffmann, in Johannes Steinhoff, Peter Pechel and Dennis Showalter (editors), *Voices from the Third Reich, an Oral History*, Regnery Gateway,Washington DC, 1989, p. 445.

For the 19th Canadian Army Field Regiment, Royal Canadian Artillery, then near Oldenburg, May 4 had dawned, in the words of its official history, 'cold and wet, without the slightest hint that the war was nearing an end'. Contact with the German forces facing the regiment had been re-established 'and resistance was stiffening'. Firing and manoeuvring for position took place all day. Then, at eight o'clock that evening, 'a BBC broadcast astounded officers and men with an announcement that the German armies in north-west Europe, the Frisian Islands and Denmark had surrendered to General Montgomery's 21st Army Group to take effect 0800 hours 5 May. While everyone was stunned and some more than a little sceptical, all waited tensely for confirmation to arrive from Headquarters 4th Division. At 2150 hours the order came through on the command wireless net: "Stop firing until further orders. Order to Cease Fire will be given at 0800 tomorrow."' As these words were coming over one wireless network, 'on the regimental set-up Major Hetherington was calling for fire to cover withdrawal of our own tanks which were pinned down by enemy shelling. Obviously the battle was still going on. However, news spread quickly and soon all was deathly quiet across the entire front.'[1]

In western and southern Germany, and in Austria, small teams organized by the United Nations Relief and Rehabilitation Agency were already visiting the many camps, more than a hundred in all, set up for displaced persons, known as DPs: non-Germans freed from German rule and captivity in the wake of the Allied advance. These DPs, mostly former civilian deportees, posed an enormous logistical and human problem for the Western Allies: how to feed them, how to restore and maintain their health, and how, above all, to enable them in due course to go home, or if 'home' was no longer a place they wished or were able to return to, how to gain them acceptance in other lands.

Dyne Steel, an Englishwoman who had herself been interned by the Germans in France during the war, was going from camp to camp with her boss, Hugh Nevins, compiling registers of the camp inmates. On May 4 they were in a camp in southern Germany comprising former Russian prisoners-of-war. Dyne Steel later recalled how, 'since it was quite impossible to communicate with them, we gave up trying to register their names and personal details.' The day was spent 'strolling around trying to look as if we found it perfectly normal to be surrounded by Kazakhs, Uzbeks, Turcomans and others of that ilk. We for our part,

[1] *19 Canadian Army Field Regiment, RCA, Regimental History, September 1941–July 1945*, Nederlandsche Diepdruk Inrichting, Deventer, Holland, 1945, pp. 103–4.

were evidently a huge attraction for the entire camp followed us every-where. From time to time we stopped, and Hugh made a short speech, perfectly aware that no one understood a single word, but which appeared to provide considerable entertainment for the audience. What neither they nor we knew was that at that very moment the Germans were surrendering at Lüneburg. It was the end of the war in Europe.'[1]

The war was ending all over Europe. In western Austria, the cities of Innsbruck and Salzburg surrendered that day to the Americans, who also entered Hitler's former mountain retreat at Berchtesgaden, in Bavaria, capturing two thousand German soldiers there. Also in Bavaria, one of Germany's most senior officers, Field Marshal Ewald von Kleist, was taken prisoner.

German armies were still fighting north of Berlin, and in Czecho-slovakia; Allied bombing raids against them continued. On May 4, in one such raid, a bomb killed Field Marshal Fedor von Bock, who had been the Commander of German Army Group Centre during the invasion of the Soviet Union in June 1941. Von Bock had been dismissed by Hitler early in 1942 when the offensive against Moscow was halted.

In Zagreb on May 4, the ruler of Croatia, Hitler's former ally Dr Ante Pavelic, made a final appearance in the streets of his capital. 'If we must die', he declared to his Ustachi militia, 'let us fall as true heroes, not as cowards crying for mercy.' Then, leaving most of his followers behind him, he hurried northward to the comparative safety of the Austrian border. He was eventually to make his way to Argentina, and to safety.

Also on the run that day, disguised as a German air force corporal, was Lieutenant-Colonel Adolf Eichmann, who from 1941 to 1944 had organized the deportation of Jews from all over Europe to their deaths. Captured by the Americans, he realized that his disguise was too flimsy. He, like all SS-men, was tattooed on the upper arm, and, changing his identity to that of an SS Lieutenant, bluffed his way through the interro-gations posing as a junior SS man of no significance. After a few months Eichmann made his escape. Like Pavelic, he made his way to Argentina, but in 1960 he was found there, taken to Israel, tried and hanged. Pavelic had died in his bed two years earlier.

A British war correspondent, Alan Moorehead, was a witness to the German plight during the final days of the Third Reich. His report, sent to the London *Daily Express* on May 4, was syndicated throughout the English-speaking world. 'The men are grey faced and dirty,' he wrote. 'Speak to them and they run to answer obsequiously. There is nothing

[1] Dyne Steel, *A 'One and Only' Looks Back*, Pentland Press, Edinburgh, 1992, p. 85.

whatever a German will not do at this moment, if ordered by us. How long all this will last I do not know. The basic sense – a sense of guilt – is lacking and you will never get any German to admit it. Instead he has an entire sense of defeat. He expects to be kicked around. The Germans' one hope is to get quickly into a British or American prison camp.'

Moorehead went on to describe the scenes that crowded into his mind that day, the things he had witnessed as the German will to fight collapsed. He had seen groups of German officers near Lüneburg 'flinging their pistols into a hedge, tearing off their uniforms and getting into tattered civilian clothes stolen from the nearest houses'. He had seen German looters in Osnabrück, the women 'shoving and tugging' at the men and crying out 'The men won't let us get any'. He had seen 'the carcasses of U-boats lying useless along the Hamburg docks'. He had heard the arms manufacturer 'in his green-walled study at Fallingbostel saying softly, "Yes, I know you will destroy my machines. It all happened before in 1918."' He had listened when a garage keeper told him, 'Yes, they took fifty Russian bodies off the train here and dumped them in a pit. I would not let my wife look. No, we did not dare to inquire what it was all about.' There was also, Moorehead wrote, 'the bare patch on the wall of every house showing where the picture of the Führer used to hang', and binding all these scenes together 'that monstrous, moving frieze of refugees along the road. They tramp and tramp for a thousand miles, half the nationalities of the world.'[1]

Among those in flight from east to west were tens of thousands of Russians seeking to escape the advance of the Red Army. Some were anti-Bolsheviks who had lived in Germany since fleeing the Soviet Union after the revolution of 1917. Others were Russian soldiers who had changed sides after being captured and made common cause with the Germans. Most were Russian soldiers who had survived the torments of German prisoner-of-war camps and who, under the Yalta Agreement signed in February, had to be handed back to the Soviet authorities for repatriation.

In demanding that the Yalta repatriation agreement be adhered to, the Soviet Repatriation Commissioner, Colonel-General S.I. Golikov, alleged in the first week of May that eight hundred Red Army officers who had been liberated by the advancing Americans had already been transferred to the United States, and that their whereabouts were being concealed from the Russian authorities. The British were also to be

---

[1] 'In Germany Today, Scenes From A Conquered Country', *Palestine Post*, 10 May 1945, p. 3, cols. 2 and 3.

accused of violating the Yalta Agreement by hindering the repatriation of Russians liberated by British troops, or captured while fighting with the Germans.

General Golikov was a former Chief of Soviet Military Intelligence, and a senior commander in the Moscow and Stalingrad battles of 1942. 'He could be, and usually was, most unpleasant', Hugh Lunghi, of the British Military Mission, recalled. 'There was not a shred of truth in his statement. But we were extremely concerned it would add to the existing obstacles to the repatriation from Russia of our own prisoners-of-war, including Commonwealth soldiers, who had been evacuated from the German camps to various parts of the Soviet Union. It had been a constant battle to extract from Golikov permission to visit them, many dying of undernourishment and disease.'[1]

On May 4, the State Department in Washington issued a formal statement declaring General Golikov's allegations unfounded. Golikov went on to claim that of the 150,000 Russian prisoners-of-war liberated so far, only 35,000 had returned to Russia. He did not know that the United States and Britain were about to issue the strictest rules for repatriation, rules that were to lead to great hardship and many suicides among those who feared to return to the Soviet Union.

In New York, preparations were being made to celebrate the defeat of Germany. 'Gotham's bustling Times Square was fencing itself in today against the excitement and celebration expected to follow VE-Day,' George Hakim reported to the American forces newspaper in Europe. 'Windows were being boarded and barricades erected, as Broadway's celebration-conscious shopkeepers took hurried steps to protect their shops from the huge crowds expected to blow off steam there when VE-Day comes.' In the State capital at Albany, however, Governor Thomas E. Dewey asked that VE-Day be observed, not in festivities but as a day of thanksgiving, work and prayer. 'Victory over Germany', he said, 'will be the occasion for prayers for our noble dead, prayers of gratitude and thanksgiving that the rest of our task may be consummated in the shortest possible time.'[2]

Governor Dewey could not know the extent of the euphoria that would surface with the news of Germany's defeat. It would be quite different to the subdued celebrations in New York's Little Italy two days earlier.

---

[1] Hugh Lunghi, letter to the author, 22 September 1994.
[2] 'New York City Prepared for VE-Day Celebration', *Stars and Stripes*, 5 May 1945, p. 5, cols. 4 and 5. (In both the headline and the article, as in several American publications and letters at this time, VE-Day was spelt V-E Day).

In northern Italy, high in the Alps, German troops who had intended to fight their way back into Austria were bewildered by the rapidity of the Allied advance, and of the collapse of German resistance elsewhere. At 7.35 the same evening, driving northward from Borgo, a group of American soldiers, led by the twenty-nine-year-old Colonel Beneker, found the commander of the 1st Paratroop Division, Major-General Schultz, who not only surrendered his division, but thanked the Americans for allowing his officers to retain their side arms. The Americans then drove on to Levico. A war correspondent who was with them, Norman Lourie, reported on how the streets of the town were 'lined only by German paratroopers waiting silently for things to happen. Peering through the windows were Italian faces just visible in the gathering dusk. Here and there, suppressed clapping greeted our jeeps as they raced through the town with full lights on.'

When the Americans reached the headquarters of the 1st Paratroop Division they found most of the officers still dining in their mess. The Germans stood up as the Americans entered. The senior German officers then went with the Americans into an adjoining room to discuss the details of the surrender. But the two German commanders, General Heidrich and General Trettner, were not there. They were at Corps headquarters at San Cristoforo, some miles away.

Shortly before 11 p.m. the Americans set off to San Cristoforo. Lourie, who was with them, described the scene in his report: 'Heidrich, short, heavily built, and almost bald, was very self assured and continually smoked cigars. There, in the General's bedroom, with a dachshund lying sleepily in a corner, arrangements were made for the formal surrender of 10,000 of Germany's best troops who now have no option. Various young paratroop officers went in and out. These young fanatics were very polite and subdued, continuously giving the Nazi salute. Then the Italian partisan chief of Trento turned up for consultation and, finally, near midnight, General Trettner himself joined the party which had grown considerably. An advance tank detachment had now arrived in the courtyard to relieve the German guards. Trettner is a mediocre looking man, however capable a military commander he may be.

'It was now well past midnight and everything was agreed for the procedure of surrender to take place that day (Saturday) of Germany's last pocket of resistance on the Italian Front. It was arranged that others should stay the night at Heidrich's headquarters. Breakfast was to be at 7.30 a.m. and 8 a.m. Lieutenant-General Geoffrey Keyes, II Corps Commander of the Fifth Army, and the American Divisional Commander, would arrive to bring the drama to a close and to supervise the descent into captivity of Nazi Germany's most notorious fighting men.'[1]

During May 4, British troops were ordered into Hamburg. 'This in itself was something never to be forgotten,' Lieutenant Edwin Bramall later recalled. 'The impact of Hamburg was, if anything, worse than that of Hiroshima, which I was to see eight months later. There was appalling devastation and destruction on all sides, with twisted and gutted buildings or shells of buildings, piles of rubble and with all the city's lake and waterways drained of water (as a protection against air attack). A few old people were pushing barrows with salvaged belongings on them, but in general, the centre of the place seemed dead and deserted. It reminded me exactly of H.G. Wells' *Shape of Things to Come*.'[2]

In the Pacific, off Okinawa, seven American ships were hit by Japanese suicide aircraft during May 4, and 446 sailors were killed.

In the British Lake District, far from the fighting, a high-ranking German prisoner-of-war, SS Major-General Kurt Meyer, heard the news of Germany's impending collapse while he was with several thousand fellow prisoners at Camp Windermere. He later recalled: 'We believed that somehow, after reflecting, the Europeans would prevent the Red Army from taking over Central and Eastern Germany. We were mistaken. Fate ran its course, leading the Asiatics to the Elbe and into the heart of Europe. The complete collapse of our homeland struck us in the marrow. Stories about the cruel events in the Russian zone nearly drove us insane. No one knew with certainty where his family was – or even if still alive. Was our fifth child all right? Had my wish for a son been granted or did I have another daughter? Day and night all of us worried about our homes. Despite these broodings there were no answers. Outside camp privileges were withdrawn gradually until our life shrank to confinement behind the barbed wire. Our walks were terminated. The civil law of the conqueror took over.'[3]

Victory in Europe was bringing with it a stern sense of punishment and retribution. There was little sympathy for the defeated Germany. Nazism, with its unredeemed catalogue of crimes, had cast a blight over a whole nation.

---

[1] Norman Lourie, 'How Nazi Paratroops Gave Up', *Palestine Post*, 9 May 1945, p. 3, cols. 1 to 4.

[2] Field Marshal Lord Bramall, letter to the author, 13 October 1994.

[3] Quoted in Tony Foster, *Meeting of Generals*, Methuen, London, 1986, pp. 439–40.

V

Further Surrenders

5–6 May 1945

On the morning of May 5 the German soldiers in north-western Germany finally laid down their arms. Edwin Bramall, who was still in Hamburg that day, recalled how, 'while engaged on the problems which were to occupy us for the next few days – the rounding up and appropriate disposal of German stragglers and displaced persons – the news of the beginning of the end came through. This was the announcement that the German forces opposing us in 21st Army Group had surrendered to Field Marshal Montgomery. The relief was enormous, after battling almost continuously from the Normandy beaches, and frequently wondering, at the back of one's mind when one turned in for the night, whether one would get through the next day all in one piece! The result was that *that* night was really VE-night for the battalion and most other British units in the area. I seem to remember that inquisitive members of the battalion had discovered a large wine cellar in the town and thus there was more than enough to drink for everyone. A very large quantity of ammunition was also discharged, mostly perfectly harmlessly into the air, but three rounds of mortar ammunition were somehow fired in the general direction of Brigade HQ, who were not impressed with the excuse that we were under attack by Werewolves! The next day was spent clearing up the mess, while hundreds of displaced persons milled around the town.'[1]

Frank Richardson, a senior medical officer with the 15th (Scottish) Division, was with his commanding officer when news of the German surrender arrived. 'Soon after the end of hostilities was announced,' he recalled, 'we members of the general's mess were sitting at breakfast in a small house in the hamlet of Hammoor, a few miles from Ahrensburg, where we eventually established our headquarters in the schloss. To our amazement a column of SS armoured vehicles drove slowly down the

---

[1] Field Marshal Lord Bramall, letter to the author, 13 October 1994.

main – well, the only – street. The soldiers appeared to be well disciplined; their weapons bristled a few feet from our table. Neither we nor, so far as I can remember, the divisional defence platoon did a damned thing about it. We later learned that this formation, refusing to accept their nation's surrender, had "holed up" in the Forest of Segeberg, through which I was soon to drive, on my way to sort out the medical problems in the great port of Kiel, occupied by our 46 Brigade. I was advised to drive through the forest as fast as I could without stopping, but, as usual, found it irresistible to get out and question the wandering tribes who swarmed everywhere in those troubled days – displaced persons of many lands, and parties of Germans, who had obviously been soldiers, all with one urgent impulse: to get as far away as they could from the Russians.'[1]

Captain Vivian Herzog was at Bremervörde when hostilities ceased in the Cuxhaven Peninsula at eight in the morning of May 5. Some 130,000 German troops were trapped in the peninsula that day, including the remnants of a number of crack paratroop divisions which had fought the advancing British at the crossing of the Rhine two months earlier. Herzog later recalled: 'The German Army Commander, General von Blumentritt and his Chief of Staff, attended by aides, came to surrender to General Horrocks at 14.30 hours on May 5. They came fully dressed with great-coats over their uniforms, and entered with much pomp and circumstance, not behaving exactly as if they represented the defeated army. I was in the room at the surrender ceremony. The General and his party sat in front of a plain table in the small building in which Corps Headquarters was set up, with his ADC standing behind him.

'At the appointed time, General Horrocks entered through the windows leading to the garden, dressed simply in battledress. All in the room stood up, including the generals, and General Horrocks sat down facing them, on the other side of the table. The proceedings were interpreted by Major Freddy Hindmarsh, who was absolutely fluent in German.

'After General Horrocks issued his orders for the surrender he finished with the words: "These orders must be obeyed scrupulously. I warn you we shall have no mercy if they are not. Having seen one of the horror camps my whole attitude towards Germany has changed." At this point, the Chief of Staff jumped to his feet and exclaimed in German, *"Nein, nein, es wahr nicht uns, es war die SS"* ("No, no, it was not us, it was the SS"), to which General Horrocks replied curtly, "Sit down, there were

---

[1] Frank Richardson, 'Scenes of action', in *As You Were, VE-Day: a medical retrospect*, British Medical Association, London, 1984, p. 132.

German soldiers on sentry duty outside and you cannot escape responsibility. The world will never forgive Germany for those camps." [1]

One of the first four western journalists to reach the heart of Berlin on May 5 was Ernie Leiser of *Stars and Stripes*. In a despatch to his paper that day he wrote: 'Berlin, the capital of defeat, today is a charred, stinking broken skeleton of a city. It is impossible to imagine what it looked like before. It is impossible to believe that the miles of disembowelled buildings, of cratered streets, of shattered masonry once could have been the capital of Greater Germany and the home of four million people. Only a handful of the four million still remain as the last clatter of machine-gun fire echoes through the hollow city. There are no factories left for them to work in, no shops, no theatres, no office buildings.

'But the handful were busy today. They are shovelling the rubble from the streets, sweeping the dead out of the way – working while the Russian conquerors still walk the streets with straggling columns of prisoners or wander around staring at the shells of once-great buildings of State. They are working, oblivious of the light, chill rain that is the only mourning for the death of their homes.

'The Russians are everywhere – their tanks rumble down the Charlottenburger Chaussee which slices through the great Tiergarten Park; a pert girl MP[2] smartly directs traffic at the west end of Unter den Linden; an infantry battalion forms up in front of the shrapnel-scarred statue of Wilhelm the Great; single armed soldiers wander in and out of cellars; cavalrymen wash their horses at the edge of the River Spree in shambles that was the city's centre. A Cossack rides down the Wilhelmstrasse raising a cloud of dust from the powdered stone and concrete that, despite the rain, coats everything. Horse and wagon convoys creak down Leipziger Strasse, past the bodies of two German soldiers, with mouths open, in a grin of death.

'Unter den Linden, which a 1929 guide book proudly calls the "most beautiful avenue in all the city", is grey with the universal powder, dead and broken as all the rest. We stopped to pick up a grim souvenir – a street sign with the enamel partly chipped off and a bullet hole through it. Beside the sign were a German man and woman, dead among the debris. Street fights are just coming to an end, and the smells of sewage and death are everywhere. It is one great tombstone.

'As you ride out of Berlin, on the single wall that remains in a whole block, near the city's southern limits, you see a sign, white-washed into

---

[1] Chaim (earlier Vivian) Herzog, letter to the author, 26 October 1994.
[2] Military Police.

the crumbling bricks. It says: *"Mit Unser Führer, Zum Sieg"*. Translated, that means: "With our Führer, to Victory".[1]

The rapid pace of Germany's collapse was inevitably the headline news among the victorious powers. But the clash of ideologies which had been set aside in June 1941 when Hitler invaded the Soviet Union could no longer be submerged. It had been surfacing steadily from the moment that the Soviet forces had brought with them into Poland at the end of 1944, a Polish civil adminstration that was both Moscow-trained and Moscow-controlled. The possibility of a Soviet occupation of Denmark had been another harbinger of conflict. At Yalta, the British and Americans had seen just how determined Stalin was to assert Soviet dominance over as much of Eastern Europe as possible, even to the Adriatic.

Another cloud appeared on the political horizon on May 5 which threatened to introduce a sour note in the imminent celebration. Radio Moscow announced that day that sixteen Polish emissaries who had gone under safe conduct to the Soviet military authorities outside Warsaw, had been taken to Moscow and, after disappearing for a while, were accused of 'diversionary activities'. These Poles were leaders of pre-war democratic parties. Under the Yalta Agreement, they were to have been given a place in Poland's post-war government. Churchill had worked particularly hard to ensure that they could participate, and, in an apparent concession at Yalta, Stalin had offered to welcome them into a coalition with the Soviet-sponsored Lublin Government, set up nine months earlier when the Red Army entered central Poland.

The accusations against the sixteen Poles had an immediate repercussion, when the British Foreign Minister, Anthony Eden, and the American Secretary of State, Edward R. Stettinius Jr., both of whom were in San Francisco for the founding conference of the United Nations, suspended all discussions on the Polish question, and demanded the release of the sixteen.

Canadian forces had been at the forefront of the final assault on the remaining German positions in northern Europe. Among these soldiers was an artilleryman, Lieutenant F. Bartlett Watt, 63rd Battery, 19th Army Field Regiment, Royal Canadian Artillery, 3rd Canadian Division. He had served with the division since the battles in Normandy the previous summer. On May 5 he and his battery were near Oldenburg. As he later

[1] Ernie Leiser, 'S & S Reporter Sees Ruined Berlin,' May 5 (Delayed), *Stars and Stripes*, 10 May 1945, p. 1, cols. 2–4 and p. 2, col. 5.

recalled: 'Our guns were firing up at 0740 hours on the morning of May 5. Cease Fire came down at 0800 hours. Six of the guns in my Battery were loaded at Cease Fire and had to be fired into a designated safety area. My feelings that morning were of relief – thankful to be alive and whole, and with a deep sense of loss that so many brave boys were not there to see the end. The Padre had a regimental Victory Thanksgiving which was really quite well attended but the feeling during the day for me was a let down, the war seemed to fizzle out in so many different ways and I think only the army routine brought us back to reality that day. There was that day, and for some time to come, the feeling that there might be some retaliation from the Germans, some landmines; we were not totally at ease.

'I am sure we all thought about the future and mine included my family, my fiancée and friends, it was somewhat daunting. There was also on the horizon the Army of Occupation, and as we were the life blood of the army there was some talk of our going to Burma. It was only after a few days that one really settled down to the fact that the war was over.'[1]

The American sergeant Charles Kessler, was in Austria on May 5. In a letter to his parents two days later he wrote: 'We pulled back from the front into a town for the night. Someone was driving a truck around like a wild man, blowing his horn and yelling that the war was over. Well, we had heard that one several times before so we didn't think too much of it. But all the GIs we asked seemed to confirm that statement, saying that they had just heard it on the radio. This was the first definite news we had that the war was finally over. I guess that I have never seen a happier bunch of men in my life. We opened up all the wine, schnapps, champagne, etc. that we had, which was plenty and had quite a celebration.'[2]

At Baldham, in southern Germany, a further unconditional surrender was signed at 2.30 p.m. on May 5. This time it covered all the German forces between the Bohemian mountains and the Upper Inn river. The German officer agreeing to the surrender was General Hermann Foertsch, to whom the American General, Jacob L. Devers, explained that this was not an armistice, but unconditional surrender. 'Do you understand that?' Devers asked Foertsch. 'I can assure you, Sir,' Foertsch replied, 'that no power is left at my disposal to prevent it.'[3]

That same afternoon, in Innsbruck, the German Nineteenth Army

[1] F. Bartlett Watt, letter to the author, 19 August 1994.
[2] Charles Kessler, letter to his parents, 7 May 1945. Private archive.
[3] Winston G. Ramsey, 'Germany Surrenders,' *After the Battle*, No. 48, 1985.

surrendered unconditionally. It had been driven by the Americans from the beachhead at St Raphael in the South of France across eastern France and southern Germany to the Austrian Alps. In the previous thirty-five days 100,000 of its men had been taken prisoner, forcing it to take into its fighting ranks many stragglers and rear echelon troops. Stan Swinton, a *Stars and Stripes* war correspondent, was a witness of the surrender scene: 'With a flick of his pen, scowling Lieutenant General Erich Brandenberger put into Allied hands forces holding much of the mountainous region where the Nazis once planned to make their final stand: the provinces of Vorarlberg, Tyrol and Allgäu and a portion of Salzburg province. The buffer of Germans remaining between the Fifth and Seventh Armies is thus erased and the front is cleared before the American VI Army Corps, veterans of Italy's grimmest battles, portions of the French 1st Army and XXI American Corps. The surrender took place this afternoon in a red-carpeted room of scenic Innsbruck's *Landrathaus*. Representatives of the US, France and Germany sat at a long conference table while, in the courtyard below, an infantry company and the 103rd Division band stood at attention. General Brandenberger, balding and wearing horn-rimmed glasses, signed first. Major General Edward H Brooks, 6th Corps Commander, followed. At 18.00 hours tonight all fighting was to cease.'[1]

Another German surrender signed that afternoon led to all German forces in Holland laying down their arms. It was signed at Wageningen shortly after 4 p.m., in the presence of a senior Canadian officer, Lieutenant-General Charles Foulkes. Also present, in his capacity as Commander-in-Chief of the Netherlands Forces of the Interior, was Prince Bernhard of the Netherlands, to whom the commander of the German forces in Holland, General Blaskowitz, showed unexpected deference. The Prince ignored him.

Among those who were liberated that day was Robert Krell, a four-year-old Jewish boy who had survived in hiding for three years. The last Christian family that had taken him in, saved him from deportation, and brought him up as if he were their own child, was the only family he could remember. On the day the war ended in Holland, they took him back to his mother. 'I was born on 5 August 1940,' he recalled, 'and the liberation of Holland was on 5 May 1945. So I was less than five years old. Yet two memories are crystal clear. One is that two of my hiders, Albert and Violette Munnik, took me to the roof of the apartment-style

---

[1] '19th's Nazi General Puts Pen To Paper, Climaxing 7th Army Push From Riviera', *Stars and Stripes*, 7 May 1945, p. 8, cols. 3, 4 and 5.

blocks where we lived at Loenenschestraat 147 in The Hague. We watched British planes drop food parcels from the sky and I heard people excitedly talking that they contained white bread.

'Also that day, we somehow or other went to the Rijswijkse Weg, the street in which my mother had hidden throughout the war. I do not know how we got there, nor do I remember her there, but by that time Mr and Mrs Munnik were to my mind, my *"moeder"* and *"vader"* and their sixteen-year-old daughter, my "sister" Nora. On this visit, I looked out of the front window. Trucks filled with German soldiers were rolling down the street and being actually chased by Canadian tanks. In retreat, the Germans were firing randomly into the street and I saw an elderly man shot, across from my vantage point. Someone dragged me from the window by my legs, way back under a table. It was still too dangerous to be outside. Some time that night I was put to bed about 7.30 p.m. back at Loenenschestraat.

'I was furious to be put to bed. I yelled and cried. I wanted to be out in the streets where I heard celebrations. It is only many years later that I realized that my anger was probably the first expression of normal childhood for me. I had never before protested against anything. I had been compliant, co-operative, and non-complaining, probably realizing that I was at the mercy of my hiders, and not to bother anyone or risk betrayal or discovery. The Munniks of course had nothing remotely evil in mind. But a neighbour in 1961 asked me on my first return to Holland after emigrating in 1951, why had I not thanked him for not betraying me.

'Liberation was not particularly liberating, for within a few days I was "liberated" from those I loved, (*"moeder"*, *"vader"* and Nora) to rejoin my father and mother who had each emerged from their respective hiding places. I cried in protest, and they had to prove I was theirs with photos taken when I was aged about one and a half. Of course, I was actually the luckiest of all children in having my parents survive. Try telling that to a five year old with no memory of them, after nearly three years with another family. My cousin, Nallie, was also hidden, but his parents had been deported and did not return.

'That was what my own parents faced on the day of liberation. They got back their son, but their parents had been murdered, as well as my father's two sisters and my mother's two brothers and sister. Of course they searched for a long time, but basically everyone knew that on that 5 May 1945 we were all that was left of our immediate family and we had lost an enormous extended family as well.'[1]

---

[1] Robert Krell, letter to the author, 22 September 1994.

1. German officers surrendering 19,000 troops on the Loire, September 1944. The American officer in the photograph (second from right) is Lieutenant Colonel J.K. French, of Fairfax County, Virginia. *See page 5.*

2. One of millions of Allied leaflets dropped behind the German lines, explaining to the German soldiers how to pronounce 'I surrender'. The message reads, 'This is the English and American pronunciation of the words "I surrender" Make use of it, if you have the opportunity.'

3. German prisoners-of-war are marched to the rear as American army vehicles go forward to the front, 29 March 1945.

4. French forced labourers, 175 in all, freed by an American reconnaissance unit, begin their journey home, 1 April 1945.

5. American troops advance through a ruined town in southern Germany, a photograph taken on 5 April 1945.

6. On 6 April 1945, at Merkers in southern Germany, American troops discover European art treasures stolen by the Germans – the first of several of such discoveries. The painting shown here is by Manet.

7. The concentration camp at Bergen-Belsen, liberated by the British on 15 April 1945. The photograph shows a soup kitchen operated by British soldiers. *See pages 15–21.*

8. A sign erected at Belsen.

9. American officers, part of a group of more than 7,000 former Allied prisoners-of-war, liberated by the Americans at Moosburg on 29 April 1945. *See page 36.*

10. German soldiers, some only young boys, surrender to the British in Bremen, 26 April 1945.

11. One of the young German soldiers surrendering to the British, 26 April 1945.

12. (*right*) As the concentration camps in central Germany were being liberated, 30,000 camp inmates were moved by the Germans to Theresienstadt in Czechoslovakia. This photograph shows a Jewish boy arriving in Theresienstadt in the last week of April 1945.

13. An American soldier stands guard at the gate of Dachau, which was liberated by the Americans on 29 April 1945. *See pages 37–8.*

14. Inmates of Dachau shortly after liberation.

15. German civilians fleeing westward across the River Elbe at Tangemünde. Determined to escape from the approaching Russians, they cross a destroyed railway bridge and reach the American lines, 1 May 1945. Six days later, the Russians began shelling the bridge with refugees still on it. *See pages 105–6.*

16. A Russian infantryman stands guard after the fall of Berlin on 2 May 1945. The British news agency caption read: 'Berlin Falls: Russia Breaks the Nazi Heart'.

17. Berlin, the courtyard of Hitler's Chancellery, after the fall of the city

18. Young German soldiers surrender to an American GI.

19. Field Marshal Montgomery reads the terms of surrender for all German forces in northern Europe to Admiral von Freideburg, Lüneberg Heath, 4 May 1945. *See page 61.*

Cornelia T had also survived the war in hiding in Holland. She was twenty-one years old in May 1940, when the Germans marched in. She had been sitting in the garden when she saw her first German soldier 'on a bike, rifle on the handlebars'. In 1943, while she was in hiding, her mother, brother and sister had been deported to Sobibor, the death camp situated on the River Bug where everyone was murdered on arrival, more than a quarter of a million people in all: there were no vast industrial enterprises, Krupp factories, coal mines, or armament manufacturers nearby clamouring, as at Auschwitz, for Jewish slave labour. Cornelia remained with different Dutch families, working as a 'Christian' nurse and studying for a medical diploma in Haarlem. 'Came the 5th of May 1945,' she later wrote, 'and at last the war was over – my reaction on that day, why were they (the public) singing and dancing in the street. Indeed the war was over, but I lost my entire family. I was devastated.'[1]

Across the Austrian border from southern Germany, tens of thousands of concentration camp inmates had been sent to Mauthausen and several camps nearer the mountains, in the hope of keeping them away from the advancing Allies. Among those at the camp at Ebensee that May 5, as the German guards prepared to flee, was Dr Miklos Nyiszli. He had been an eye-witness of the brutality of Dr Josef Mengele at Auschwitz. Like all the prisoners at Ebensee, he had survived several death marches, including one from central Germany to Mauthausen on which three thousand men set off and a thousand had been killed on the march. 'On May 5,' he recalled, 'a white flag flew from the Ebensee watch-tower. It was finished. They had laid down their arms. The sun was shining brightly when, at nine o'clock, an American light tank, with three soldiers on board, arrived and took possession of the camp. We were free.'[2]

An American officer, Nathanial Kutcher, who was among the forces to enter Mauthausen, wrote: 'General Patton ordered that all prisoners be evacuated by ambulances and taken to Linz, Austria, to hospitals which had been specially designated to receive them. Of course, this was *my* job. I ordered the men to pick up and place these victims in the ambulances to be transported for medical treatment. The stench made me sick, and caused my men to retch from the nausea. My First Sergeant came to me and said, "Captain, I'm having a problem with the men who have to do such a distasteful duty." I myself went to help pick up these poor victims who were more dead than alive. After picking up the first one, my officer's

[1] Letter to the author, 13 October 1994.
[2] Dr Miklos Nyiszli, *Auschwitz, A Doctor's Eye-Witness Account*, Panther, London, 1962.

uniform was spattered with fecal matter and urine, as these poor inmates were so weak that when they were picked up their body waste and urine oozed out of them uncontrollably. When my men saw what I was doing, their disgust evaporated and turned to compassion and pity. Everyone did his duty, willingly, without complaint.

'I am proud to say, that every single human being, both the living and the dead, were evacuated in this manner. The dead were transported to army mortuaries for decent burials. They numbered just under one thousand.'[1]

Once more the moment of freedom was one of deep shock for the liberators. When American troops reached Mauthausen, they found nearly ten thousand bodies in a huge communal grave. Of the 110,000 survivors, 28,000 were Jews. Confronted by so many starving skeletons, well-meaning American soldiers brought chocolate, jam and other rich foods which the camp survivors ate. Many could not digest them, and died. Some, too weak to stagger to the distribution centres to claim their share of these enticing foods, survived.

Here, repeated in every liberated camp, was another perversion of reality for thousands of Hitler's victims. Food, which had for so long been the life-giving substance, longed for with such desperation, proved to be the final blow. Because their bodies were beyond the point of repair when the Americans arrived, more than three thousand of the 110,000 survivors of Mauthausen and its sub-camps died after liberation. Among the dead was Andor Gelleri, the thirty-eight-year-old Hungarian novelist, who died of typhus two days after liberation.

It was at midday on May 5 that the war ended for several thousand Jewish prisoners at Gunskirchen, many of them survivors of Auschwitz, and in the previous four days, of a terrible death march from nearby Mauthausen. 'It was horrible, Gunskirchen', the then fourteen-year-old Hugo Gryn, from the Ruthenian town of Beregszasz recalled. 'People were literally dying by then. There was no food. Typhus was raging. Everybody was very ill, or dying – or dead. At the middle of the day we began to hear firing. We knew something was up when, suddenly, there were no guards. They were just not there. Most people were not in a shape to take it in. Then there were American tanks on the road, firing ahead of them, with troops crouching behind them, followed by troops in troop carriers. They saw what they saw: starvation on the face of people. They start to throw food, and then they moved on.'

[1] Colonel Nathanial Kutcher, *Mauthausen Remembered*, privately printed, Miami Beach, 5 March 1994.

The Americans were in hot pursuit of German military units making for the mountains. 'People take the food. Others go out of the camp, to nearby farms, and come back with chickens, with food. It was food that was the obsession. I was too weak and too ill to eat, which probably saved my life, and I was wanting to be with my father who was rapidly losing consciousness. He had a high fever, typhus. Then, in the afternoon, more troops arrived with trucks. They put us on these trucks and took us to Hörsching.' There, the barracks of a German air base (now the main airport of Linz) had been transformed into a makeshift hospital. 'German prisoners-of-war acted as medical orderlies. We had clean rooms, cleanish beds. Within two days, perhaps three, my father died. We were in the same bed. I went berserk. When the German orderlies came to collect him, I went for them like an animal. Then I passed out.'

For a few days Hugo Gryn was unconscious. 'When I came to, they told me my father had died. Nobody knew where they had taken him, and I never found out. One of the first pieces of news I got after that was that Roosevelt was dead. I cried.'

Hugo Gryn's father, Geza Gryn, was one of several thousand Jews who died after being liberated at Gunskirchen. His son gradually regained his strength. 'A few days later an SS man who had been at Mauthausen, Sergeant Kakadu, the vilest thing that lived, God knows how many people he killed just by hitting them, just for no reason, was brought to Hörsching. Suddenly word goes round, "Everybody go to the windows". Kakadu had been found. He was being strung up. The windows were thronged. The American soldiers stood around, there were not many of them. They didn't know what to do. It was the end of Kakadu.'[1]

The discovery of the concentration camps was to have an enormous impact in the West, as soon as the photographs taken in them were published, and the politicians who had been flown out to see them, from Britain and the United States, returned home. The first two photographs to appear in the American forces newspaper *Stars and Stripes* were published on May 5. Taken in Belsen two weeks earlier, but only just released for publication, they showed captured SS troops being made to load the bodies of victims into a truck for burial, and SS women placing the bodies in mass graves. The caption contained the instruction: 'Note the shrunken corpses. Starvation and disease killed hundreds of thousands imprisoned at the camp.' *Stars and Stripes* also reported that two United States Congressmen, Leonard W. Hall of New York and Gordon Canfield of New Jersey, who had just returned from visiting the camps at the invitation

---

[1] Hugo Gryn, in conversation with the author, 11 December 1994.

of General Eisenhower, stated on their arrival in New York 'that the American people should be permitted to see the pictures of German atrocities, especially those at the Buchenwald camp, despite their shocking effect.'

Although 'revolting in every respect', Congressman Hall told reporters, 'the pictures should be shown to Americans'. He added: 'Even the pictures cannot show the cruelty and depravity of a people who would treat human beings as the Germans treated those in detention camps.'[1]

One who had avoided the German concentration camps was Chaim Nussbaum, a Polish Jew born between the wars in a small town near Auschwitz, and taken by his parents to Holland as a child. When the Germans invaded Holland in 1940 he was serving as a chaplain with the Dutch forces in the Dutch East Indies, Singapore, and Java where, in 1942, he was captured by the Japanese. On May 5, 1945, Nussbaum was in a Japanese prisoner-of-war camp on the River Kwai. Through a clandestine radio, he and his fellow-prisoners learned that day that the war in Europe was all but over. 'What the news elicited in most of our minds,' he wrote in his diary, 'were the questions: how will the Japanese take it? Are they going to capitulate as well?' The answers came soon enough, when the Japanese guards responded with scorn: "Europeans no good. Italians, poor soldiers. Cowards. Germans cowards, afraid of dying, of being killed. Japanese number one. Number one soldiers. Never afraid. Japan have many peoples. Pacific Ocean big, very big. War going on long, very long time." Nussbaum commented despairingly, 'We realize that the war may drag on.'[2]

A few moments after midnight on May 5, the people of Prague rose up against their German occupiers. In doing so, they appealed for support from an unlikely ally, General Vlasov, the most senior Russian officer to have thrown in his lot with the Germans. For almost a year Vlasov, as head of the anti-Communist Committee for the Liberation of the Peoples of Russia (KONR), had commanded two divisions of former Soviet troops, mostly Ukrainians, on the Eastern Front, fighting as allies with the German army, resisting the Soviet westward advance, and retreating with the Germans. Having listened to a radio appeal by Czech patriots over Radio Prague early on the morning of May 6, Vlasov decided to turn against his German masters. This was very much the advice of the

[1] 'Ask Atrocity Photos Be Shown To Public', *Stars and Stripes*, 5 May 1945, p. 2, cols. 2–5.
[2] Diary entry, 5 May 1945, in Chaim Nussbaum, *Chaplain on the River Kwai, The Story of a Prisoner of War*, Shapolsky, New York, 1988, p. 253.

commander of his First Division, General Bunyachenko, whose forces were then less than twenty miles from Prague, having moved south from Germany to escape the advancing Soviet army. Anti-German feeling had been 'running high amongst both officers and men,' the historian Catherine Andreyev writes, and this, combined with the 'friendly reception afforded by the Czech population', was decisive. So too was 'the need felt by the Vlasovites to demonstrate to the Allies the fact that they were not Nazi hirelings and that they were opponents of Nazism.'[1]

In a radio broadcast on May 6, Vlasov promised the people of Prague that the Germans could be thrown out of their city with the help of his troops. The Czech patriots then issued an ultimatum over Radio Prague to all German forces in Bohemia and Moravia, telling them that the German administration had come to an end. The Germans agreed to a truce, but almost immediately tried to encircle the city with their tanks. 'It was then,' a British army broadsheet reported later that same day, 'that the Patriots launched urgent appeals from Prague radio to both US and Russian armies. Patton was asked to send tanks and planes to designated areas in and around the city; the Russians were besought to dispatch airborne forces in order that the enemy's last desperate throw might be thwarted. Then there was silence for a few hours, but at 6 a.m. this morning the Patriots broadcast the news that hostilities had ceased and that negotiations for surrender had been re-opened. As a sign of the times, Czech radio then went on to broadcast the BBC's Czech bulletin, eagerly listened in to in the past five years by virtually the whole nation despite German restrictions and severe punishments on those people unfortunate enough to be found out with their sets tuned to London.'[2]

The celebration and the enthusiasm were premature. The German forces in Prague had not given up. From their positions on Castle Hill they opened fire on the city, severely damaging several buildings in the centre. Three thousand patriots were killed as the fighting in Europe's last unliberated capital went on. The German troops included part of an SS Division. Against them were pitted one of Vlasov's two Russian divisions, men who had been the Germans' allies only a month earlier.

At six in the morning of May 6, the *Stars and Stripes* was being distributed in Paris and Naples, and in the German, Austrian and Italian war zones. Its main headline was a graphic summary of the previous day's events:

---

[1] Catherine Andreyev, *Vlasov and the Russian Liberation Movement*, Cambridge University Press, Cambridge, 1987, p. 74.
[2] 'Good King Wenceslas Looked Out', *The Bulletin*, 11th Armoured Division news sheet, issue No. 293, 6 May 1945.

79

KRAUTS SURRENDER IN NE GERMANY, HOLLAND, DENMARK

Its subheading was equally succinct: 'Million Nazis Quit; Homeland Crushed.'[1]

In Berlin, the rigours of the Soviet occupation did not abate. Writing in her diary on May 6, Ruth Andrea-Friedrich described a fearful scene: 'We visit Hannelore Thiele, a friend and classmate of Heike. Cowering, she squats on her couch. She barely looks up as we enter the room. "I should kill myself," she cries pitifully. "I cannot live like this." It's terrible to look at her swollen eyes, terrible to look at her distorted face. "Was it really so bad?" I ask. She looks at me pitifully. "Seven", she says and shakes with disgust. "Seven in a row. Like animals."'

The frontline Russian soldiers had, in the main, been disciplined fighters who maintained their discipline, and continued westward in pursuit of the German army. The soldiers who followed them into Berlin and occupied the city were for the most part undisciplined and brutal. 'The uncontrollable lust of our conquerors has fallen on the women of Berlin,' Ruth Andreas-Friedrich explained. After visiting Hannelore Thiele she had gone on to see another acquaintance in the suburbs. 'She is eighteen years old and knew nothing of love. Now she knows everything. Sixty times repeated. "How is one to defend oneself?" she says apathetically, almost dully, "when they hammer on the door and shoot mindlessly in all directions. New ones every night, different ones every night. When they took me the first time and forced my father to watch, I thought I was going to die."'

Two days before the surrender of Berlin, a school teacher had told the girls in her class: 'If a Russian soldier violates you, there remains nothing but death.' Ruth Andreas-Friedrich commented in her diary on May 6: 'More than half of the students draw the required inference and drown themselves in the nearest body of water. "Honour lost, everything lost." Poison or bullet, cord or knife? They kill themselves by the hundreds.' The phrase 'honour lost, everything lost' had been the words 'of a distraught father who presses a rope into the hand of his daughter who has been violated twelve times. Obediently she goes and hangs herself at the nearest window transom.'[2]

Suicide, the last resort for many of Hitler's victims, had become a way of escape for those whose world of normality he had destroyed.

* * *

[1] *Stars and Stripes*, 5 May 1945, p. 1.
[2] Ruth Andreas-Friedrich, *Shauplatz Berlin*, Suhrkamp, Frankfurt-am-Main, 1984, pp. 37–40.

At these very moments of horror, a senior British Intelligence officer, Colonel David Hunt, was on a tour of inspection of the Greek islands closest to the Turkish mainland. On May 6, he was on Chios. 'Also present on the island,' he later recalled, 'was a detachment of commandos and of the Special Boat Service, as piratical and Byronic a body of men as ever scuttled ship or cut a throat. Having heard that the Germans were about to sign an instrument of unconditional surrender the next day, the mood was celebratory. In the mess, established in a fine old merchant's house on the sea front, target practice against the ornamental plaster cornices produced plenty of dust and some startling ricochets as .45 rounds from our friends' revolvers hummed around the room. In the harbour outside, their motor launch sent tracer rounds into the night sky.'[1]

The three thousand German troops in the Channel Islands had been cut off from all contact with German-controlled Europe since June 1944. On May 5, a radio message had been sent to the German Commander-in-Chief of the islands, General Hüffmeier asking him to surrender. At 5.36 p.m. on May 6, the German radio station on the islands replied that the Commander-in-Chief 'receives' orders only from his own Government.[2]

Those who had committed themselves most fiercely to the Third Reich were on the run. On May 6, a top secret radio signal was sent from the German ruler of Norway, Reichskommissar Josef Terboven, who was then in Oslo, to Admiral Dönitz at Flensburg. This message, signed by Reischskommissar Terboven, was picked up by radio signal and decrypted by the British. It read: 'Walloon Führer S.S. Degrelle has just arrived in Oslo. He states that with your consent he is to be taken to Spain or Japan in a submarine. Please confirm whether a submarine is to be placed at his disposal. Heil Hitler.'[3]

Léon Degrelle, the leader of the Walloon fascist movement, as well as being a high-ranking SS officer, was trying to escape retribution.

From Tokyo came a formal public protest against the imminent German surrender. In a statement issued that Sunday, Shigenori Togo, the Japanese Foreign Minister, declared that any surrender would be a 'flagrant violation' of the Tripartite Pact of September 1940.[4]

---

[1] Sir David Hunt, letter to the author, 10 September 1994.

[2] War Office papers, 106/2997: quoted in Charles Cruickshank, *The German Occupation of the Channel Islands*, Oxford University Press, London, 1975, p. 295.

[3] Message dated 6 May 1945, 'Top Secret Ultra', CX/MSS/C532, HWI/3761, Public Record Office, Kew.

[4] 'Honourable Protest', *Palestine Post*, 7 May 1945, p. 1, col 8.

The last official acts of the European war were about to take place. At six o'clock on the evening of May 6, the commander of the German forces besieged in Breslau, General Nickhoff, accepted the Soviet terms for the surrender of his forces, 40,000 men in all, and of the city, after a siege lasting eighty-two days. Half an hour later, in the West, General Alfred Jodl flew from Flensburg to Reims, to sign the capitulation of all German forces still fighting or facing the Western Allies. At first, Jodl was determined to limit the surrender to the German forces facing westward. But, without prevarication or debate, General Eisenhower made it clear to him that the Germans agreed to a complete surrender of all their forces, East as well as West. Otherwise he would break off all negotiations and seal the Western Front, thereby preventing any more Germans transferring from East to West in order to give themselves up. General Jodl passed back this ultimatum by radio signal to Grand Admiral Dönitz at Flensburg. Shortly after midnight, Dönitz replied, authorizing Jodl to make a final and complete surrender of all German forces on all fronts.

In western Czechoslovakia, American forces, part of General George S. Patton Jr's 4th Armoured Division, had entered the city of Pilsen, less than fifty miles from Prague. Among those who were with them to witness their success was the war correspondent Cornelius Ryan. His report, which appeared under the headline 'A General's Death', told of the enthusiasm of the local Czechs, whose city had been occupied by the Germans more than six years earlier, in March 1939: 'Pilsen, the first Czech city to be captured by the United States Third Army, was the scene of the biggest demonstrations the American troops had seen since the liberation of Paris. The city was surrendered by Major-General George Majewiski, the garrison commander, who, after a brief ceremony, shot himself before his own staff and the American officer of the 16th Armoured Division, to whom he surrendered. When the General commanding the 16th Armoured Division appeared at an upper window of the town hall, the square in front was filled to overflowing with thousands of people who burst into song, repeating over and over again the National Anthem of Czechoslovakia. From every window and tower Czech flags were flying.'[1]

The American liberators of Pilsen were committed, under the agreement reached by Churchill, Stalin and Roosevelt at Yalta, to withdraw from western Czechoslovakia and a broad belt of land in central Germany as soon as the Soviet forces were ready to take it over. This agreement to

[1] Cornelius Ryan, 'A General's Death', *Daily Telegraph*, 8 May 1945.

withdraw was quickly honoured. In Denmark, where no Yalta agreement existed with regard to the zones of occupation, Soviet designs on Denmark had, however, been frustrated by the British dash forward to the Baltic. On May 6, the first British and American troops reached Copenhagen, by air. Robert Straus, an American then serving with Supreme Headquarters Allied Expeditionary Force, later recalled: 'We landed at Kastrup Airport, still the main airfield of Copenhagen, and on the field there must have been three or four hundred airplanes that the Germans had abandoned. We were told that all their arms were stacked inside the airport terminal building. I went looking for a few souvenir pistols, and they weren't difficult to find as one room was filled almost to the ceiling with the weapons. I picked up three P–38 pistols and one Luger and took them back with me to where my colleagues were waiting for the buses that were to take us into town. I distributed the P–38 pistols to various individuals who had asked for them, and kept the Luger for myself. The Luger stayed in my possession until 1949 when it disappeared during a move from East 91st Street to Gracie Square in New York. I presume one of the truckmen stole the only war souvenir that I had. I hated to lose it.

'Eventually a group of buses assembled in front of the terminal building to take us into Copenhagen. The welcoming Danes lined up on both sides of the road, cheered and waved English and American flags as we passed in celebration of the end of the war. This was the only victory parade that I personally participated in. It must have been about six miles to the Rathausplatz, the City Hall square, where Dagmarhaus was located. This building, which was to house our offices, had also been the head-quarters of the German High Commission that had ruled Denmark since 1940. Diagonally across the square was the Plaza Hotel, which we took over from the Germans as well, and where we lived during our stay in Copenhagen.

'The Danes gave us a wildly enthusiastic reception. They had been under occupation for five years, and it was not hard to understand the explosion of gaiety that occurred when they knew that the hated Germans were leaving.'[1]

In Prague, the Czech patriots and Vlasov's First Division had continued to push back the German forces sent to crush them. That afternoon one of Vlasov's commanders, Colonel Arkhipov, was summoned to a meeting of patriot leaders where, to his amazement, he found an American Army

[1] Robert K. Straus, *In My Anecdotage*, privately printed, Santa Barbara, California, 1989, pp. 279–81.

captain who had just reached the city at the head of an armoured scout column. The Americans wanted to know whether the population of Prague needed help. They were surprised to see Arkhipov, not because he was a Russian, but because he and his men wore German uniforms, as they had done during their year as Germany's fighting allies. The American captain explained that his armoured column 'was not the vanguard of approaching American forces, and they were not intending to enter Prague; he had been sent on ahead to see whether the insurgents could hold the city by themselves until it could be handed over to the ally of the USA, the Soviet Union. Arkhipov then realised that one of the chief reasons for taking part in the rising, to make contact with the American forces, was illusory.'[1]

Having offered Prague the possibility of Soviet rather than American help, the small American force withdrew. Within a few hours Vlasov's First Division decided to make its way southward to the American lines. On its journey, two of its most senior officers were captured and killed by Czech partisans and two others handed over to the Red Army. The change of sides, and their decision to fight alongside the Czechs, had come too late to save them.

Making their way through the front line to a schoolhouse at Reims, senior German emissaries, headed by Admiral von Friedeburg, began negotiations for unconditional surrender. The Allied officers who confronted them were in no mood for jest or delay. The private soldiers who had to accompany and look after them were also not amused by their high-ranking visitors. As the talks were in progress, an American war correspondent, DeWitt Gilpin, spoke to Private Fink of Detroit. 'Fink rode in the car that brought the Admiral to the German billets at 3 rue Carnot in Reims,' he wrote. 'Accompanying von Friedeburg in the car was an English major who, Fink recalls, brought the Admiral up-to-date on current events by telling him the lights had gone on again in London. Von Friedeburg just replied that he "hadn't had a good night's sleep in a month". He looked it, too, Fink says. Von Friedeburg also said he had been bombed out of his headquarters three times, and as the car rolled through the French countryside he remarked on the contrast with Germany, which he said must now be completely rebuilt.'

While he was in his billets, von Friedeburg 'smoked *beaucoup* cigars and drank *beaucoup* liquor without improving his disposition any. Once

[1] Catherine Andreyev, *Vlasov and the Russian Liberation Movement*, Cambridge University Press, Cambridge, 1987, p. 75.

during a discussion of US Army public relations he got angry and began pounding his fist on the table. What made him mad, according to what table waiter Private William Bittay said, was a copy of the *Stars and Stripes* with an atrocity picture from a German concentration camp.'

As the discussions among the admirals and generals continued, Private Frederick A. Stones told Gilpin: 'One of the things that the boys talked about, the enlisted men, I mean, was that our guys up front were still getting killed while this was going on. And somebody said that they ought to have settled this thing by talking five years ago.' Private Joyce Bennett of New York City, who had the job of managing the German officers' billet, disagreed. 'I hate the Germans as much as anybody else,' she said, 'but this is what's going to end the war.'

Commented Gilpin: 'Everybody agreed about the ending the war part, but there was a lot of bitching at some of the work details.' When Private Bennett asked two of the billet orderlies to straighten the beds of the German officers, they complained: 'We're usually assigned to Air Marshal Tedder, who straightens up his own bed, and these guys can too.'

'Agnes, who is from Tarentum, Pennsylvania, and who has a husband in a Third Army combat engineer unit, said, "I felt terribly uneasy serving them coffee. It was an awful feeling, and I can't get over it. And then some officer made a wisecrack about my serving coffee to Germans while my husband was still shooting them. He thought that was funny. I didn't. And that General Jodl, I'd like to have spilled hot coffee down his neck." Angela, a blonde from Kansas City, simply said "It's hard to keep remembering they are your enemies when they're sitting in a place like that all dressed up and acting like gentlemen. But I've only been over here six weeks." '[1]

American servicemen in Europe learned on May 6 that the coming of VE-Day, whenever it might be, would not necessarily be the end of their military service. In an article by a staff correspondent, Don Williams, published that day in *Stars and Stripes*, soldiers learned that 'no man or woman, no matter how long he or she has been in service, overseas or in combat, will be released from the Army if his or her services are required in the war against Japan'. Preference for demobilization would be based on a credits system, calculated according to length of service, time already spent overseas, combat decorations, and the number of dependent children at home. Soldiers under eighteen years old on VE-Day would also get credits. Those soldiers deemed essential for war duties, and those with insufficient credits, would either stay on as

[1] DeWitt Gilpin, 'The Surrender of Rheims', *Yank*, Victory Edition, 1945, pp. 2–3.

occupation troops in Germany, or be sent to the Pacific. 'In the mean-time,' Williams told his readers, 'don't write home and tell your mother or sweetheart that you'll be home next week or next month. For most of you, it just ain't so.'[1]

There were 8,300,000 Americans under arms as the war in Europe was drawing to a close. In Washington, following discussions with General Douglas MacArthur and Admiral Chester W. Nimitz, the Pacific Theatre commanders, the War Department announced that more than a million men would be released as a result of the ending of the war in Europe. 'Under an approved plan,' the War Department declared, 'we are now engaged in working toward an Army strength of 6,968,000 a year from now. That will give us all the strength we believe we can deploy effectively against Japan and also enable us to meet our occupation responsibilities in Europe and to maintain the necessary training and supply force in the United States.' The statement continued: 'Our best judgement is that we can defeat Japan quickly and completely with an army which a year from now will be 6,968,000.'[2]

'A year from now' would mean May 1946, a daunting prospect for those whose long service in Europe had only just finished, and who, that very day, learned from *Stars and Stripes* that it was General Patton himself, one of their toughest commanders, who had written the hitherto anony-mous lines about fear,

> I spare no class or cult or creed,
> my course is endless through the year.
> I bow all heads and break all hearts,
> All owe me homage – I am fear.[3]

---

[1] Don Williams, 'GIs In This Theatre Warned', *Stars and Stripes*, 6 May 1945, p. 4, cols. 4,5.
[2] 'WD Statement On Redeployment', *Stars and Stripes*, 7 May 1945, p. 1, col. 1, p. 4, cols. 4,5.
[3] *Cosmopolitan*, New York, May 1945 issue.

VI

False Dawn

7 May 1945

In Paris, Lieutenant-Colonel Arthur Goodfriend, editor-in-chief of *Stars and Stripes*, and those under him who were preparing the May 7 edition, were confident in the headline they chose for that day's front page:

VE-DAY IMMINENT

Their confidence was not misplaced. At 02.41 that morning, in a schoolhouse at Reims, General Alfred Jodl signed the unconditional surrender of all German land, sea and air forces, wherever they might be. General Walter Bedell Smith then signed for the Allied Expeditionary Force and General Ivan Susloparov for the Soviet High Command. Finally, General François Sevez signed as a witness for France. The surrender was to come into effect at fifty-nine minutes to midnight on 8 May.

After Jodl had signed, he asked the Allied generals for permission to speak. This was granted him. 'With this signature,' he said, 'the German people and armed forces are, for better or worse, delivered into the victors' hands. In this war, which has lasted more than five years, both have achieved and suffered more than perhaps any other people in the world. In this hour I can only express my hope that the victors will treat them with generosity.' He was heard in silence. What could any of the Allied soldiers present say with regard to Jodl's grotesque summary of Germany's war record, his continued self-delusion in the face of the cataclysm Germany had perpetrated.

Jodl was led into Eisenhower's office in an adjacent room. Eisenhower asked him if he 'thoroughly understood the provisions of the document he had signed'. He answered with one word: '*Ja*'. Eisenhower then told him: 'You will, officially and personally, be held responsible if the terms of this surrender are violated, including its provisions for German commanders to appear in Berlin at the moment set by the Russian high command to accomplish formal surrender to that government. That is all.'[1] General Jodl saluted and left the room.

Eisenhower, who had not been present at the actual signing, then went to the room where the signing had just taken place and told the assembled company: 'In January 1943, the late President Roosevelt and Prime Minister Churchill pronounced the formula of unconditional surrender for the Axis Powers. That formula has now been fulfilled.' Eisenhower went on to say that while the bulk of the forces that had carried out the Normandy landings eleven months earlier had been American and British, his command, which now contained five million men, contained 'elements from almost every oppressed country in Europe'. France had played a special part in the victory. 'I think that it is particularly fitting that this unconditional surrender should have been signed in the heart of France, a country which has suffered so much.'[2]

Before going to bed, Eisenhower telephoned the head of Churchill's Defence Office, General Sir Hastings Ismay, with news that the war was over. Ismay then telephoned John Martin, Churchill's Principal Private Secretary, with the news; but Martin, knowing that in 1940 Churchill had given instructions that he was only to be woken up if Britain were being invaded, decided not to wake his master. It was the officer in charge of Churchill's Map Room, Captain Richard Pim who, when Churchill awoke on the morning of May 7, took him the news. 'For five years,' Churchill told Pim, 'you've brought me bad news, sometimes worse than others. Now you've redeemed yourself.'[3]

For the public, the news that Germany had surrendered unconditionally and on all fronts did not emerge at once, or clearly. There was considerable confusion during much of May 7 as to what had actually happened at Reims. 'Millions of people waited tensely throughout yesterday for the official announcement of VE-Day', one British newspaper reported on the following day, and went on to explain: 'For many hours conflicting reports on Germany's surrender poured into Britain from various sources.'[4] The sense of waiting was graphically expressed by *Daily Mail* reporters in an article on the following day, when they wrote: 'Twelve elderly men stood yesterday for hours on end, with ropes in their hands and hope in their hearts, waiting to send the bells of St Paul's clanging in the paean of triumph. Outside the cathedral a couple of hundred people waited to celebrate with thanks to God the victory that

[1] Dwight D. Eisenhower, *Crusade in Europe*, William Heinemann, London, 1948, p. 465.
[2] Text (marked 'security delay') in *The Times*, 9 May 1945, p. 4, col. 6.
[3] Sir Richard Pim, memoirs (typescript). Private archive.
[4] 'All Britain stood by for the news', *Daily Mail*, 8 May 1945, p. 4, col. 1.

has been granted to the Allies. In the four hundred square miles of which St Paul's is the centre, physical and spiritual, 8,000,000 people waited breathless for the official news that never came.

'From early morning victory was in the air. Housewives queued for bread to last for the two days of official celebration; bakers worked all night shifts and then worked through the day to keep pace with the demand: bread for sandwiches – for who could trouble about meals on VE-Day? In suburb and fashionable quarter, in slum and great street, the shops were cleared of loaves and cakes and sweets. But the people were hungrier for news than for food.

'Food for the body, but flags for the spirit. Toyshops, decorators, department shops, and multiple stores brought out every red-white-and-blue piece of cloth to blaze in their windows. Those flags not bought up by the prudent on Saturday were sold for anything up to a pound. In the streets, hawkers were gaily a-flutter. A piece of bunting on a pole could fetch up to a £5 note, and there were more buyers than flags.

'Over the City came a trainer plane. His wings swooped and dipped, banking in the Victory roll. From the thronged streets, the crowded windows, a multitude of heads looked up as he zoomed upwards and dived again. Shading eyes against the sun-glare – 'Victory weather' after the dull week-end – people took the aerobatics for an announcement. A few began to cheer. But the airman flew away to the East – and the hundreds of thousands began to wonder again.'[1]

The news of the early morning unconditional surrender had been broadcast more than twelve hours after it had taken place. 'This news crackled through the town like summer lightning,' the London *News Chronicle* reported. 'But still the famous figures did not appear on the balconies.'[2]

The reason for the failure of the Allies to make May 7 the day of victory in Europe was unknown to the public. Eisenhower had wanted the announcement to be made at 6 p.m. London time that day, May 7, on the pragmatic grounds that the orders to the Germans to lay down their arms would be broadcast that day *en clair*[3] to the German troops, and could not then be kept secret. Churchill therefore proposed 6 p.m. on May 7, as the moment for the announcement, this being noon in Washington and 7 p.m. in Moscow.

Assuming that this timing would be accepted by Truman and Stalin,

---

[1] 'London: Monday, May 7, 1945', *Daily Mail*, 8 May 1945, p. 3, cols 1–3.
[2] 'London Put Out Its Flags And Waited', *News Chronicle*, 8 May 1945, p. 1, col. 5.
[3] Openly, not in code.

Churchill alerted the British Chiefs of Staff and War Cabinet to be ready to go together with him to Buckingham Palace at 6.30 that evening, when the announcement of victory would be made. By midday, however, it became clear that this plan was impossible. Stalin, as Admiral Sir Andrew Cunningham noted in his diary, was 'refusing to recognize the signatures at Eisenhower's headquarters, and wanting it done in Berlin and by Zhukov'.

Cunningham was one of the five guests invited to have lunch that day at Downing Street with Churchill. 'He is in great form,' Cunningham noted, 'but much annoyed with Russians.'[1] General Sir Alan Brooke, the Chief of the Imperial General Staff, who was also present, noted in his diary: 'It was a disturbed lunch. Winston was expecting a telephone call from the President which only came through after lunch. Meanwhile he received a telegram from Ike stating that it was likely he would have to fly to Berlin for the required Russian final negotiations. This necessitated a call being put through to Ike, which got through during the pudding period! In the intervals Winston discussed the pros and cons of elections in June. We stressed the cons from the military point of view, stating that it could lead only to dispersal of effort which would be better devoted to the war.'[2]

Stalin was insistent that the surrender of German forces on the Eastern Front must be made before VE-Day could be proclaimed. In a telegram to Churchill, he stated that German resistance 'is not slackening and, to judge from radio intercepts, an appreciable group of German forces is openly declaring its intention to continue resistance and not to obey Dönitz's order for surrender'. The Soviet High Command, Stalin added, would therefore like to hold up the announcement of the end of the war until such time as the instrument of surrender signed at Eisenhower's headquarters 'enters into force', a minute after midnight on May 8, that is, the first minute of May 9. Stalin therefore proposed delaying the official announcement that the war was over until 7 a.m. on May 9, Moscow time.[3] President Truman's first reaction was that he too would have to wait before making an official announcement 'unless Stalin approves an earlier release.'[4]

[1] Admiral Cunningham, diary, 7 May 1945. National Maritime Museum and Archive, Greenwich.
[2] General Brooke, diary, 7 May 1945, Arthur Bryant (editor), *Triumph in the West*, Collins, London, 1959, pp. 455–6.
[3] Stalin to Churchill, telegram, 7 May 1945: Foreign Office papers, 371/50581. Public Record Office, Kew.
[4] Truman to Churchill, telephone message, 7 May 1945: Foreign Office papers, 371/50581. Public Record Office, Kew.

At midday, as the disagreement over the timing of the announcement threatened to make a May 7 victory day impossible, although millions of German soldiers were then laying down their arms, Churchill telegraphed to Truman at the White House. In a 'personal and top secret' message, he pointed out to the President that Eisenhower thought it was 'hopeless' to try to keep the news of the German surrender secret until the following day. He would be grateful, Churchill ended, if Truman would telephone him 'on the open line as soon as you get this, asking for Colonel Warden, Whitehall 4433'. Churchill added 'I will address you as Admiral. We can then both tell UJ what we are going to do.'[1] By the time the telephone call took place four hours later, there had, however, been significant developments.

Although the Allied leaders had been unable during the morning of May 7 to agree on a public announcement that the war was over, a sense of comradeship was all-pervasive. At Wismar, on the Baltic, the Soviet Marshal Konstantin Rokossovsky and Field Marshal Montgomery, meeting for the first time, lunched together and toasted 'Churchill, Stalin, Truman and the memory of Roosevelt'. Then, at 2.27 that afternoon, the newly-appointed German Foreign Minister, Count Schwerin von Krosigk, broadcasting from Flensburg, the headquarters of the German Government, announced that Germany's fighting troops had surrendered and that the war was over. His words, although couched in the rhetoric of untarnished pride, were unambiguous. 'German men and women,' he said, 'the High Command of the German armed forces, on orders of Grand Admiral Dönitz, has today declared unconditional surrender of all German fighting troops. As the leading minister of the Reich Government, which the Admiral of the Fleet has appointed for dealing with war tasks, I turn at this tragic moment of our history to the German nation.

'After a heroic fight of almost six years of incomparable hardness, Germany has succumbed to the overwhelming power of her enemies. To continue the war would only mean senseless bloodshed and futile disintegration. The Government, which has a feeling of responsibility for the future of the nation, was compelled to act on the collapse of all physical and material forces and to demand of the enemy cessation of hostilities. It was the noblest task of the Admiral of the Fleet and of the Government supporting him, after the terrible sacrifices which the war

[1] Prime Minister to President, telegram number 36, 'Personal and Top Secret', 7 May 1945: Foreign Office papers, 371/50581. Public Record Office, Kew. Colonel Warden was one of Churchill's wartime aliases (he was Warden of the Cinque Ports). 'UJ' was Uncle Joe: Stalin.

demanded, to save in the last phase of the war the lives of a maximum number of our fellow countrymen. That the war was not ended simultaneously in the West and in the East is to be explained by this reason alone.'[1]

Reports of von Krosigk's speech were immediately relayed over the radio stations of the world. 'The evening papers hustled the news to the waiting streets,' the *News Chronicle* told its readers on the following day. 'The BBC proclaimed it. That was enough for London. Any minute now, said one to another in the buses, in the trams, in the pubs, and on the pavements, Churchill will pop up and say "It's V-Day".'[2] But Churchill did not and could not do so. The Russians were determined to fight for one more day, and to postpone the celebrations until May 9.

In the streets of London, and even in the newspaper offices, nothing was known of the complex diplomatic negotiations that were proceeding on two continents with regard to when the Reims surrender could be announced. But with Schwerin von Krosigk's broadcast, western listeners knew that the European war was over in the East as well as in the West. It was ironic that the news that had been hoped for so long, and waited for so impatiently in the last days, should come, not from an Allied spokesman, but from a German.

Behind the scenes, Britain, the United States and the Soviet Union were engaged in a frantic attempt to co-ordinate the victory announcement. Churchill, Truman and Stalin were each personally involved, with dozens of telegraph messages between London and Moscow, and London and Washington. Stalin did not want to announce that the war was over until the surrender already signed at Reims had been signed in Berlin, with the most prestigious Russian soldier, Marshal Zhukov, as the senior Allied witness.

The broadcast by von Krosigk had therefore to serve as the formal notice that the conflict in Europe was, to all intents and purposes, over. From Flensburg it was picked up by radio networks around the world, and re-broadcast in every land. Although it was not confirmed by either the British or American Governments, it became the catalyst for all that followed. News of the German surrender at Reims had been broadcast across the world. The message read: 'Flash. Reich Germany surrendered unconditionally to Western Allies and Russia at two forty-two a.m. today.' Commented the *Stars and Stripes*: 'Minutes later, in New York, Paris, London and other major cities of the world, extras hit the streets, radio

---

[1] English-language text in *Stars and Stripes*, 8 May 1945, p. 2, col. 5.
[2] 'London Put Out Its Flags And Waited', *News Chronicle*, 8 May 1945, p. 1, cols 4 and 5.

stations cut into programmes with special announcements, and the Allied peoples once more started to celebrate VE-Day.'[1]

It was 3.46 p.m., British, French and German time. The headline compositor for the early evening edition of the London *Evening News* was clear as to what had happened.

GERMANY SURRENDERS

was his two-word declaration of triumph. The *Stars and Stripes* writer Ernie Leiser was flying back from the Elbe that afternoon with a group of recently freed American prisoners-of-war. 'The C47 was heading from the Elbe River back to Paris,' he wrote. 'It had landed near Weimar when a GI walked up with the news "Have you heard?" he asked. "The war's over. It's on the radio." For a moment no one answered. Then a flyer, just liberated from a German prison camp and on his way home, said, "Hear that? The war's over? Hell, it ended for us when the first four American tanks came over the hill in sight of our stalag. This war's been over for us for two weeks".'

First Lieutenant Philip Burke, of Worcester, Massachusetts, who had been with the 45th Division from Africa to Austria, said, 'They may say the war's over. But, buddy, if there's a single pocket left over here and a single GI gets killed cleaning it out, this war's not over, and I don't care who says it is.' Sergeant Charles Harvey, the crew chief of the aircraft, who came from Steubenville, Ohio, commented, 'I've been waiting for this thing since the first day I got in the Army and now that it's here, I just don't have any real feeling about it. I just wonder where they'll send me next. If I have to go to the CBI[2] though, I'd like to go in the Troop Carrier Command."[3]

Arthur Goodfriend was on duty in the headquarters of *Stars and Stripes* in the rue de Berri in Paris. 'Normally the news operation was managed by staff,' he later recalled, 'but that day, alerted by the imminence of the German surrender, I manned the telephone when the call came through from Reims that the war in Europe was won. Our reporter in Reims shouted the details, but a bad connection, plus turmoil at both ends of the line, made it difficult to receive and record what he said, a problem accentuated by the nature of the news itself, so overwhelming

[1] 'News Service Jolts World Again With Premature Peace Report', *Stars and Stripes*, 8 May 1945, p. 8, cols 1 and 2.
[2] The China-Burma-India Theatre of Operations.
[3] Ernie Leiser, 'For a Liberated PW It Was Over Weeks Ago', *Stars and Stripes*, 8 May 1945, p. 8, col. 4.

in its impact as to numb a mind like mine, unused to coping with an event of such magnitude.'

The deskmen of the *Stars and Stripes* 'soon had the story under professional control and I, after composing an editorial commemorating the climax of the ETO[1] campaign, reeled into the streets of Paris where giddy girls and grandmothers clasped me to their breasts, drenched me with champagne, and danced me into oblivion, from which I awoke the next day with a hangover *sans pareil.*'[2]

All over the world the news of the unconditional surrender was sparking strong emotions. In the African city of Brazzaville, where General Charles de Gaulle had raised his standard of defiance in 1941, Natasha Kounin was working in the news department of the Free French radio station. 'My colleagues and myself awaited eagerly for the last seventy-two hours the imminent announcement of Germany's unconditional surrender,' she later wrote. 'I happened to be the responsible editor for the shift, and will never forget the overwhelming emotion which engulfed all of us when the long-awaited dispatch fell on my desk. It seemed as if six years of nightmare had come to a "happy end". . . . We wept, laughed, drank, and danced all the night.'[3]

It was still not clear throughout the afternoon of May 7, when VE-Day would be declared. In Washington, Jonathan Daniels, Presidential Press Secretary at the White House, told reporters eager to know the time and date of VE-Day: 'There is nothing official to announce here at this time. We do not know when there will be an announcement.'[4] One London newspaper told its readers on May 7: 'The *Evening News* will publish on whatever day is officially defined as VE-Day'.[5] It did not know what day that would be.

The telephone call for which Churchill had alerted Truman took place at 4.10 p.m. London time, less than two hours before Churchill wanted to make the historic announcement that the war was over. He spoke, not to Truman, but to Truman's Chief of Staff, Admiral William D. Leahy, whose secretary noted down the conversation:

LEAHY: 'Admiral Leahy speaking.'
CHURCHILL: 'It is me, the Prime Minister.'
LEAHY: 'Colonel Warden, yes, sir.'

---

[1] The European Theatre of Operations.
[2] Arthur Goodfriend, letter to the author, 19 October 1994.
[3] Natasha Raphael (née Kounin), letter to the author, 7 October 1994.
[4] Reported in the British Forces newspaper, *Union Jack*, on 8 May 1945, p. 8, col. 4.
[5] *Evening News*, 7 May 1945, p. 1, col. 2.

CHURCHILL: 'You've got my telegram?'

LEAHY: 'I have your telegram, sir. This is a message which the other Admiral asked me to convey to Colonel Warden'.

CHURCHILL: 'We are on the "Secret" now, so we can talk quite freely. A message that he asked you to convey to me was what?'

LEAHY: 'I convey the following message to you. In view of agreements already made, my Chief asks me to tell you that he cannot act without approval of Uncle Joe. Did you understand, sir?'

CHURCHILL: 'Will you let somebody with a younger ear listen to it? I am not quite sure I got it all down I have got my secretary here. My ears are a bit deaf, you know . . .'

The 'younger ear' was a member of Churchill's Private Office, John Peck, through whom Churchill asked for an announcement to be made that evening that the war was over. But Leahy said, on Truman's behalf, that the announcement must wait until May 9, as requested by Stalin. An hour later Churchill telephoned the White House again. 'Mr Churchill called me from London on the open telephone,' Leahy noted in his diary, 'telling me that crowds celebrating in the streets of London were beyond control and that he must make an announcement of the victory at noon.'[1]

Churchill made one last effort to persuade Stalin to accept that evening as the time when victory would be declared. In a telegram which was despatched to Moscow at 4.26 p.m. he set out for Stalin the text of Schwerin von Krosigk's broadcast, and went on: 'As the whole world has now been informed of the surrender I propose that I should make announcement at 6 p.m. our time this evening corresponding to noon Washington time and 7 p.m. Moscow time. Otherwise it will seem that it is only the Governments who do not know.'[2]

While awaiting Stalin's reply, Churchill continued to plan for an announcement of victory that evening. At 5.30 p.m. he summoned his secretary Elizabeth Layton and dictated three hundred words for a short broadcast. 'They were stirring and purposeful to a degree,' she wrote home that day. 'At 5.55 p.m. we finished, then suddenly a phone call came through and it was decided not to broadcast.'[3] 'It was an anti-climax to us,' Churchill's secretary Marian Holmes wrote in her diary, 'especially

---

[1] Fleet Admiral William D. Leahy, *I Was There*, Whittlesey House, New York, 1950, pp. 359–63.
[2] 'Most Immediate, Clear the Line,' Foreign Office telegram No. 2473 to Moscow, 4.26 pm, 7 May 1945: Foreign Office papers, 371/50581.
[3] Elizabeth Layton, letter to her parents, 7 May 1945. Private archive.

with the crowds thronging the streets and Whitehall and already celebrating Victory.'[1]

At 5.35 p.m., while Churchill was dictating his victory broadcast, there had been an announcement from Eisenhower's headquarters declaring that the Supreme Headquarters Allied Expeditionary Force 'had nowhere made any official statement for publication concerning the complete surrender of the German armed forces in Europe.'[2] This put a further public dampener on the idea of victory that day.

At the War Cabinet that evening, Churchill gave a full account of the day's exchanges between London, Washington and Moscow. 'In view of the numerous reports which were being broadcast throughout the world,' Churchill told his colleagues, 'he thought it unfortunate that the official announcement should be delayed, and he thought it a matter for special regret that the public in this country should be deprived of the opportunity for spontaneous celebration of the victory; but, on balance, he had thought it preferable to avoid the risk of a reproach from Marshal Stalin for having departed from the arrangements previously agreed between the three Powers.'

The War Cabinet endorsed Churchill's decision. At the same time, because the news of the Reims surrender had become 'so widely known on an unofficial basis, it was necessary to give some guidance to the public and, in particular, to let it be known whether workers should proceed to work on the following day'. The Minister of Information was asked to broadcast an announcement 'forthwith' that the following day, Tuesday 8 May, 'will be treated as Victory-in-Europe Day and will be regarded as a holiday'. The day following 'will also be a holiday'. The Ministry of Information would also state that on 8 May, at 3 p.m., Churchill would broadcast an 'official announcement' that the war was over. Churchill had hoped that the broadcast could be made at midday, but accepted that this would be too early for Truman to make a simultaneous announcement in the United States, where noon in Britain would only be six in the morning in Washington. Three o'clock it would be: the broadcast announcing VE-Day would come halfway through the day, and a day later than originally hoped.

There remained the problem of General de Gaulle, who was intending to broadcast news of the German surrender over French radio that Monday evening at 8 p.m. The War Cabinet agreed to ask him to postpone his announcement 'until a corresponding hour' on May 8. 'If, however,

[1] Marian Holmes, diary, 7 May 1945. Private archive.
[2] *Daily Express*, 8 May 1945, p. 1, col 5.

he were unwilling to accept this advice no further pressure could be brought to bear on him.'[1] De Gaulle agreed to give up his evening broadcast that May 7, and to speak instead on the newly declared VE-Day, but he chose to do so at the exact moment of Churchill's broadcast, a defiant assertion of his independence.

The War Cabinet having agreed that VE-Day would be May 8, Churchill telegraphed Stalin that he had decided 'with much regret', in view of the 'difficulty in concerting an earlier release', that he would postpone his broadcast announcement of victory from that evening, May 7, to the following day, May 8 at 3 p.m. British Double Summer Time, 4 p.m. Moscow time. A statement had already been issued to the Press, Churchill added, informing the British public that May 8 'will be treated as Victory in Europe Day and will be regarded as a holiday'.[2]

Churchill relayed this information in a telegram to Truman, explaining that the holiday was necessary, 'on account of the masses of work people who have to be considered. I have informed Marshal Stalin.'[3]

The public still had no idea of the postponement. Just before 6 p.m., 'as the news of the surrender was spreading rapidly,' *The Times* reported, 'three Lancasters flew low over London dropping red and green lights.'[4] Then, at 6 p.m. the BBC announced that VE-Day would be on the following day. In Parliament Street, Whitehall, a crowd had gathered during the afternoon in the expectation that the formal end to the war would be declared that evening. 'Some of the people who line the pavement had waited four hours in the hope of hearing a Churchill broadcast from the loudspeakers on the Ministry of Health building opposite,' one newspaper reported. 'They were disappointed.' Others had waited in Downing Street to catch a glimpse of Churchill on his way to make the broadcast. 'They were disappointed too. Mounted police moved them away.'[5]

At the very moment that the BBC was announcing that VE-Day would not be until the following day, an American radio broadcast did likewise, explaining that while Churchill and Truman were ready to announce the

---

[1] War Cabinet No. 59 of 1945, 6.30 pm, 7 May 1945: Cabinet papers, 65/50. Public Record Office, Kew.
[2] Prime Minister's Personal telegram number 815 of 1945, Foreign Office number 2483 to Moscow, 'Most immediate', 'Personal and Top Secret', sent at 9.10 p.m., 7 May 1945: Foreign Office papers, 371/50581. Public Record Office, Kew.
[3] Prime Minister to President, telegram number 37, 'Personal and Top Secret', 7 May 1945: Foreign Office papers, 371/50581. Public Record Office, Kew.
[4] 'Celebrating The Victory', *The Times*, 8 May 1945, p. 5, col. 1.
[5] 'They Waited Four Hours But The Loudspeakers Were Silent', *News Chronicle*, 8 May 1945, p. 4, cols 3–5.

capitulation, Stalin was not. The Soviet leader was insistent that Berlin, where his soldiers were in the ascendant, not Reims, be the scene of the final Allied triumph. At 6.14 p.m. a radio broadcast from Paris stated: 'Announcement of capitulation will probably be delayed until fighting elsewhere ceases': a reference to the fighting between Russian and German troops in Moravia. At 6.15 p.m. the *Daily Herald* reported that in London's Piccadilly, police officers gave the order, 'Move along; it's all off', whereupon, 'slowly, with disappointment on every face, the crowd edged away towards homes they had not expected to see until late at night. In fifteen minutes Piccadilly was almost deserted.'[1] There was to be no victory declaration that day in London, Paris or New York.

[1] 'Nothing Doing Ended Big Day', *Daily Herald*, 8 May 1945, p. 1, col. 5.

VII

Learning the News

7 May 1945

News of the German capitulation at Reims reached people in many different ways. For more than four years, Carmen Goldberg had worked at
Fighter Command Headquarters, Stanmore, as a Filter Plotter, helping
to track incoming German aircraft by plotting their course, speed and
height, co-ordinating the information coming in from different radar
stations. On May 7th she was at Wantage in Oxfordshire. 'I was walking
across a green lush meadow where cows were peacefully grazing on this
pleasant May morning,' she later recalled, 'when suddenly all the church
bells of Wantage, it seemed, started to ring, on and on and on. Of course
I knew what it should signify but literally I could not believe my ears. It
was true – the war was over! However my first reaction was a kind of
numbness followed by an immense sense of relief. No doubt the excitement, festivities and peace celebrations did take place but in fact I have
no remembrance of them. Suddenly my own future confronted me –
now!'[1]

Among those in London that day was the pianist Ruth Dyson, who
was rehearsing with her colleagues of the New English Trio. 'At noon
we dived underground into the Mainly Musicians' club for a hasty lunch.
The club was a cosy little refuge adjoining Oxford Circus tube station.
Run by the 'cellist May Mukle, it was always full of familiar faces and on
that occasion the conductor Vaughan Williams was there. In the middle
of lunch the receptionist, a modest lady whom most of us had only ever
seen seated behind her desk, walked into the restaurant and made a brief
and unemotional announcement: "Ladies and gentlemen, the War is
over".

'The place exploded. Vaughan Williams began by embracing all the
ladies who happened to be sitting near him, including myself and
my companion the violinist Gwynneth Trotter. A few minutes later he

---

[1] Gabriela Pollack (formerly Carmen Goldberg), letter to the author, 23 August 1994.

murmured to me; 'Who *was* that nice lady I've just kissed?' Later we all emerged up the dark little staircase into Argyll Street where it appeared to be snowing. Tons of ticker tape were showering down from office windows, whistles blew, sirens wailed the "All Clear", people danced – indeed the War was over.'[1]

In a quiet hotel in Bath, Maurice Zinkin, a member of the Indian Civil Service, on leave from India, was on his honeymoon. His wife Taya, whom he had not seen throughout their wartime courtship, which had been conducted by correspondence, had fled from Paris as the Germans entered the city in 1940. Reaching the safety of Spain, she had gone by sea to Cuba at a time when the Germans seemed about to march through Spain to Gibraltar. From Cuba she had been forced to flee to Santo Domingo. When the dictator, General Rafael Trujillo Molina, showed too keen an interest in her, she moved on to Haiti. In 1942 she was admitted to the United States, and before the war ended made her way by sea to Britain. The journey had been a frightening one, made 'by the last convoy to be chased by U-boats', she later recalled. 'The crossing had lasted three weeks. We had lost four ships with everyone aboard. The ocean ablaze with aviation fuel, a sheet of rippling gold dotted with dark specks of human debris was branded in my memory, fitting finale to the five years I had, with my brother and my parents, spent struggling to survive.'

On May 1, in London, Taya and her Maurice were married. Fifty years later she recalled how, in their honeymoon hotel: 'The radio finished announcing that Germany had surrendered. The Dowager Duchess of Somerset had to be helped to her feet for God Save the King. She was ninety-two. For a brief moment everybody was talking to everybody, so great was the relief on hearing that the war in Europe was over. We had been sipping a concoction misnamed "coffee" in the lounge of a hotel in Bath. Till then, as far as the other guests were concerned, we did not exist. Too young. I, twenty-six, Maurice a mere thirty. The next youngest person was well over sixty-five. For the past week we had listened, without having to eavesdrop since everybody was hard of hearing, to gossip about events going back to the end of the last century. Only yesterday Maurice had scanned *The Times* to discover what "young Claude" had done to deserve being mentioned. He had retired with the rank of Major General! When Maurice had booked us at the hotel for our honeymoon he did not know it had become a geriatric haven. "Be very quiet," the manageress had whispered when taking us to our room, "the lady next door is dying."

---

[1] Ruth Dyson, letter to the author, 30 August 1994.

It had taken the end of the war to propel us into fleeting existence as congratulations went round after the broadcast.

'The war in Europe was over at long last! My brother, an OSS counter-intelligence paratroop officer in the American Army, had been trained for sabotage in France. Predictably he had been sent to China, and was by now facing the Japanese somewhere in the Far East. The last news was from Kunming with a wedding present picked up in India on the way. When would the war end? Elation evaporated into concern as far as I was concerned. But in Europe at least there was going to be peace. No more bombs or U-boats.'[1]

Taya Zinkin's concern reflected that of many thousands of people in Britain that day, as well as in the United States, and also Australia, whose close relatives were in the Far East and Pacific war zones. Unknown to her on May 7, her brother had earlier been captured during his ninth parachute drop behind enemy lines, a clandestine mission to Japanese-occupied Indo-China, and was cruelly tortured. He survived the war, but, like so many who had been through the same tribulations, was unable to shake off the traumas left to him from his experiences in Japanese captivity. 'He had a dreadful war,' Taya Zinkin later reflected. 'He never completely recovered.'[2]

The *Evening Standard* published two statistics on May 7. Under the headline 'The Prisoner Haul' it stated that there were 'approximately five and a half million German prisoners in the hands of the British and American armies'. And in the stop press column it reprinted a press agency report: 'Twenty-two million people died in this war. They include soldiers of every nation, both Allied and enemy troops on every battlefield. They include civilians who died in southern England, Germans who died in the great Allied bombing onslaught. It was the worst war of all so far as casualties are concerned. Eight million soldiers died in the last war. But civilian casualties rose to nothing like the stupendous heights they did in this war.'[3]

The Soviet authorities, and above all Stalin, were determined not to recognize what had been signed at Reims, a predominantly American triumph, in which a little-known Russian general had been a mere witness.

[1] Taya Zinkin, letter to the author, 18 September 1994.

[2] Taya Zinkin, in conversation with the author, 11 October 1994. Her brother, Robert V. Ettinger, was the only American officer during the Second World War to receive the highest combat award of the French Foreign Legion.

[3] *Evening News*, 7 May 1945, p. 1, col. 8. The figure of twenty-two million was a considerable underestimate. If one includes the complete death tolls for Russia, China and Japan, and European Jews, the figure was nearly fifty million.

Hugh Lunghi, in Moscow with the British Military Mission, later recalled: 'On Monday May 7 we received the news that Eisenhower at his Reims headquarters had in the early hours of that morning accepted General Jodl's total capitulation of all German armed forces with a cease-fire at midnight on May 8. A General Susloparov had signed the surrender document on behalf of the Soviet Command. Again the Soviet media ignored the historic event.

'Instead of congratulations, we received a curt communication addressed to the then Head of our Military Mission, Admiral Archer, copied to the United States Head of Mission General Deane, from the Soviet Chief of Staff, General Antonov. He demanded that what he called the "temporary protocol" signed in Reims should be replaced by "an act of general unconditional surrender" which would be drawn up and signed in Marshal Zhukov's headquarters in Berlin on the following day, May 8.

'Stalin, it was obvious, intended that the only "real" surrender should be to a Soviet commander. Years later we learned from Soviet generals' memoirs that Stalin had been furious that a Soviet representative had added his signature to the Reims surrender: "Who the hell is Susloparov? He is to be punished severely for daring to sign such a document without the Soviet Government's permission." '[1]

At 7 p.m. Moscow time, the members of the British Military Mission gathered to hear the news of the Reims surrender, and to celebrate. Their guest of honour was Churchill's wife Clementine. A British journalist, Alaric Jacob, who reported that there was 'not the slightest end-of-the-war hysteria in Moscow tonight', described the highlight of the British celebration: 'Standing on a chair, Mrs Churchill made a speech, declaring that her tour of Russia had shown her how much the ordinary man and woman desired friendship with Britain.'[2]

There were several local German surrenders on May 7. At 2 p.m. Allied-controlled Danish radio announced that all German forces in Norway, 300,000 men, had laid down their arms. Their Commander-in-Chief, General Boehme, issued a final, defiant statement: 'The Foreign Minister, Count von Krosigk, has announced the unconditional surrender of all fighting forces. I know that this announcement will hit you hard. We are unbeaten. No enemy dared to attack us. Nevertheless, we shall have to submit to the enemy's conditions.'[3]

---

[1] Hugh Lunghi, letter to the author, 22 September 1994. A high-ranking member of Soviet Military Intelligence, General Susloparov was recalled to Moscow and demoted. In September 1945 he became Head of the Higher Intelligence Courses of the Soviet Army, and in 1950 Head of Intelligence Courses at the Military-Diplomatic Academy.
[2] 'No hysteria', *Daily Express*, 8 May 1945, p. 3, col. 1.
[3] 'No one dared attack us', *Daily Express*, 8 May 1945, p. 4, col. 1.

In the Adriatic, near Trieste, twenty-three German naval craft surrendered to Lieutenant-Commander T.J. Bligh of the Royal Naval Volunteer Reserve.

In the small north German town of Bad Zwischenahn, General Erich von Straube signed the unconditional surrender of the 30,000 German troops under his command in the Wilhelmshaven and Emden areas, and on the Frisian Islands. For several days he and his troops had been cut off from all access to the rest of the German forces. The signing took place after a two-hour discussion, the senior Allied negotiator being Lieutenant-General Guy Simmonds, Commander of II Canadian Corps. After the surrender had been signed, General von Straube was described as having been 'most co-operative'.[1]

In Wilhelmshaven, German civilian workers and naval ratings were at once put to work to clear the port of demolitions, under the vigilant eyes of the Polish Armoured Division, whose troops had been the first to enter the port.

Each Canadian brigade headquarters entering Holland on May 7th had orders to position itself near a German divisional headquarters. The Germans were to keep their weapons until they could be collected into assembly areas and disarmed. Major-General Harry Foster, commanding the Canadian 4th Armoured Division, went through German lines under German escort to meet the commander of the German XXX Corps, General Philipp Kleffel, to arrange the mechanics of the Corps' surrender. Foster later recalled: 'Much saluting and heel clicking all around. The old boy appeared genuinely co-operative and terribly worried about his family. He was a model train enthusiast and had the largest track layout I'd ever seen. He had placed most of the Gestapo behind bars already, saving us the trouble of rounding them up.'[2]

In Amsterdam, the arrival of the first British troops, the men of B Squadron, 49th (West Riding) Reconnaisance Regiment, 'produced the greatest liberation scenes I have known', John Redfern reported to his newspaper. The 'hated *Grunepolizei*', the German security police, was made to clear a way for them through the rejoicing crowds.[3]

In Denmark, it still seemed possible that German troops who had formally surrendered might go on fighting. As a British journalist, George

---

[1] 'A day of suspense', *Union Jack*, British Forces Daily, Eastern Italy edition, 8 May 1945, p. 8, col. 5.
[2] Quoted in Tony Foster, *Meeting of Generals*, Methuen, London, 1986, p. 444.
[3] 'Nazis clear way', *Daily Express*, 8 May 1945, p. 3, col. 1.

McCarthy, reported: 'Thousands of SS men in northern Germany and Denmark are threatening to fight on. I was for half an hour their prisoner on my way through Schleswig-Holstein to Copenhagen. This trip through the German lines, with thousands of armed German troops marching along the roads and patrolling the towns, was an almost incredible journey. There were no British fighting troops for miles around as our little party of four officers and twenty men, with five correspondents, raced forward to be the first to cross the thronged frontier of Denmark.

'On our way we settled disputes between Germans and the risen Danish Resistance troops, ordered a German general to provide hostages, and drove through the cheering towns and villages into the tumultuous welcome of beflagged Copenhagen. The SS refusal to surrender cannot last long, for already the 300,000 German troops in Denmark are delivering their arms to British soldiers. "It's a truce, not a surrender," was how the SS men put it.

'A German sentry announced that his orders were that if we passed his post on the main road the battle would begin. We stopped. It seemed that we were technically prisoners and that we might spend the next few days in a German cage. Finally a major of the Royal Corps of Signals prevailed on the German commander to telephone his general for fresh orders. They must have proved peremptory, for when a Royal Air Force convoy arrived we followed on behind and sailed past the sentry unmolested. At Schleswig we parted with the convoy and went on alone, and astonished German patrols gaped as our three jeeps and a staff car drove through. For us the relief was inexpressible. It was heartlifting to have emerged from sullen and beaten Germany into a land where once again we came as liberators and not as conquerors.

'There had been some shooting by SS troops so the German garrison commander was called in and told that we must be given hostages to ensure our safe journey to open Copenhagen. Then a new problem arose. The Danes insisted on arresting the Danish quislings[1] in the locality, but the German commandant protested that they were under his protection. To ease his conscience he was told that the local traitors would be held for a fair trial. So we drove on.'[2]

'In Copenhagen, the last vestiges of five years of German rule were being removed during May 7 when, it was reported in a British Forces

---

[1] Collaborators: named after Captain Vidkun Quisling, head of a puppet goverment in Norway from May 1942 to May 1945. He was arrested and tried as a traitor, and executed on 24 October 1945.

[2] 'SS, fighting on in Denmark, took me prisoner', *Daily Mirror*, 8 May 1945, p. 7, cols. 2,3,4.

newspaper, 'uniformed freedom fighters, acting under orders from the Government, marched more than four hundred arrested Danish Nazis past angry crowds lining the streets. Earlier in the day, Patriots seized a hundred Gestapo agents who had locked themselves in their headquarters since the liberation. Other traitors are being quickly rounded up.' Copenhagen, 'gay and sunlit', had gone on celebrating its liberation, 'but a sombre note was introduced when casualty figures were published on the fighting between Patriots and Danish quislings. Fifty-four Patriots were killed, and 255 wounded'. There had also been suicides among the German sailors still aboard ship in Copenhagen harbour. 'Some six sailors drowned themselves, apparently preferring death to defeat.'[1]

During the morning of May 7, a British journalist, James Wellard, witnessed what he called 'the last battle on the Western Front', at Tanger-münde on the Elbe. 'It was fought 200 yards from me between thousands of disorganised, hysterical, screaming Germans, and the implacable, ruthless Russian tanks and infantry. From the top of an American tank, which, if it had opened fire, could have slaughtered hundreds of Germans at point-blank range, I saw scenes so fantastic that they surpass anything I have seen in four years of war.

'Russian mortar shells burst in the midst of German soldiers and civilians waiting to cross the Tangermünde bridge to the American side of the Elbe, scores of women and children were killed or wounded. German soldiers pushed old women out of the boats in which they were trying to cross the river. German officers, stripped naked, paddled a rubber boat loaded with German soldiers and three women, with their baggage and bicycles. A German girl drowned in mid-stream after screaming for help. German soldiers swam the river in their vests, climbed up the west bank and were sent straight to the prisoners' cages, still in their vests. German soldiers panicked and rushed in waves towards the river as Russian tanks burst out from the woods.

'In the past five days 50,000 Germans have passed into our lines across a catwalk they built along the blown bridge which lies awash in the Elbe. Today about noon the Russian tanks arrived only 1,000 yards from the river bank. Some German rearguards were still trying to hold them. That is why the war continued in this place.

'I stood at the broken bridge and watched paratroopers, generals, high-ranking staff officers, nurses, tankmen and Luftwaffe men run across

---

[1] 'A day of suspense', *Union Jack*, British Forces Daily, Eastern Italy edition, 8 May 1945, p. 8, cols. 2, 3.

wild-eyed. From what I have seen today I accuse the German Army of being cowardly degenerates.'[1]

Fear of Soviet revenge for the atrocities committed on Russian soil against Russian civilians, more even than fear of the dark night of communism, drove the once-triumphant army to desperation. In 1939 it had crossed the Vistula, in 1941 it had reached the Moscow River, in 1942 it stood on the bank of the Volga. The humiliation of the precipitate retreat across the Elbe was nothing compared to the fear of capture.

During May 7, the British Army put into effect Operation Eclipse, the military occupation of Germany. It was the last British operation of the war. Previous highlights had been Operation Plunder, the crossing of the Rhine, and Operation Cricket, the capture of the port of Bremen. During May 7, the Reuter's correspondent with the British Second Army cabled his report: 'Operation Eclipse has now become the last Army code signal for hundreds of thousands of British fathers, husbands and sons before quitting Europe and getting back to Blighty.' One soldier told him 'Well, I'm certainly glad that the biggest part of Germany has been smashed. Now the sooner this so-called "master race" is exterminated the better. All I want is to get home to my girl and family and be allowed to live a peaceful life again.'

In the words of another private: 'I hope the remainder of the enemy surrender similarly and sensibly, and that peace is as successful as this campaign.' A corporal commented: 'At last. Let's hope we'll all benefit from this grim experience. The sooner we are back in civvy street the better.' In the entrance to Divisional Headquarters, the driver of Montgomery's headquarters caravan, who had been with the commander since the Battle of Alamein, added: 'The caravan has been all through the Desert, Sicily, and up the Normandy beaches, and I've driven it all the way. The news has come just right. I'm off home in three days.'[2]

At the Italian town of Alba, soldiers of the British Fifth Army took into custody one of Hitler's senior advisers, Hjalmar Schacht. Asked about Hitler's death, he said: 'I wouldn't believe it if he told me himself.' As to his own part in Hitler's regime: 'I was never a Nazi. Hitler never took my advice. He never understood money or the power of money.'[3] One by one, those who had been members of Hitler's inner circle, who had served him and sustained his regime, were distancing themselves from him, and from Nazism. Schacht was the first leading figure to do so.

*   *   *

[1] 'Last Curtain On The German Army', *Daily Express*, 8 May 1945, p. 3, col. 5.
[2] 'The Last Signals, Eclipse', *Star*, 7 May 1945, p. 4, col. 3.
[3] 'Hitler not dead, says Schacht', *Daily Express*, 8 May 1945, p. 1, col. 5.

More than a million Allied soldiers were on German soil on VE-Day. Many of them had been in action for more than five years. Some had fought all the way from the desert frontiers of Egypt and the scrublands of North Africa, through Italy, or across Europe. Others had marched from the outskirts of Moscow. The Roumanian-born Milo Tyndel had been recruited by the Soviets into the Second Polish Army in September 1944, after the Russians had reached his home town, Czernowitz.[1] He was thirty-four years old. The recruitment, 'was highly reminiscent of the eighteenth-century recruitment methods in Europe', he recalled. A centrally located "bribery centre" was set up for doctors who had the means to pay for the privilege of having their names removed from the list. Accepted values: gold and golden objects, furs and US dollars. The outcome was a list of thirty-eight doctors, myself among them, despite the acknowledged need of my services in Czernowitz. We were taken at a very slow pace across Poland to the Lublin region, through Warsaw, finally to Lower Saxony.'[2]

Tyndel served as a neuro-psychiatrist. He recalled how his war ended: 'I was stationed at Spremberg an der Spree (Niederlausitz, Germany, not far from Berlin), with nothing to do. Together with a few colleagues we spent the day basking in the sun on the bank of the River Spree, watching dead, bloated cows floating down the river. We had just heard the good news that the war had ended on that day. Suddenly there were gunshots ringing from a wooded hill nearby. Immediately we heard rumours to the effect that stragglers from the fleeing German Army were fighting their way out from encirclement. Fortunately the Russian *comendatura* was glad to inform us that it was their soldiers celebrating the end of the war by shooting into the air. We continued our sunbathing in good spirits.'[3]

From southern Germany, Benjamin Ferencz wrote to his fiancée that evening: 'About ten minutes ago, as I was passing by our new day-room on the way back from supper I stopped to join a group of fellows who were crowded around the day-room radio. An announcer from New York told us that the war was over. At one time I thought that I would go wild with joy if I heard that the war had come to an end. At other times I thought I'd cry. Actually I just listened silently and seriously, and it's still hard for me to believe. The other fellows seemed to feel the same way.

'There were no wild shouts, no hurrahs, and no tearing of papers and

---

[1] Since 1945, Chernovtsy, in the Ukraine

[2] Dr Milo Tyndel, letter to the author, 6 October 1994.

[3] Dr Milo Tyndel, letter to the author, 8 September 1994. Tyndel never returned to Czernowitz, but went to Vienna, where he practised and taught, emigrating to Canada in 1954.

confetti. Some said: "Guess we oughta celebrate", but to me it seemed as though celebrations would be had because it is considered the right thing to do. There is no added noise around here, and the end of the war is being greeted as just the end of another day.

'I wonder how it was with you, Dear. I'd guess that you were far more moved than the boys who are out here where the Germans are. Perhaps it is that soldiers are not people; they're just soldiers and that's something different. Perhaps an official announcement from Washington will bring a different reaction, but so far around here the signing of a surrender by Germany is just one step, and not the most important one in our lives. The big question which I'm sure is foremost in everyone's mind is: "When do we get home?"

'The Japanese war will now be regarded with more interest, for now it is a matter of CBI, or occupation. I know there is enough work in war crimes to keep a lot of people busy over here for quite some time, but I'm hoping that the army will turn the matter over to more competent hands. I'm pretty sure I'd select a trip to China for a thirty-day furlough at home. Anyway there's little sense speculating about it since the matter is completely out of my hands. I am the victim of circumstances and the draft. I just wait to see what will happen to me.

'This evening I received a little envelope from you, Dear saying, across the front, "Do not Bend". I knew it was a photo so I wasted little time in tearing it open. Sure enough, it was my pretty sweetheart! I thought it was beautiful, and now that you've told me it was the poorest one of all I can hardly wait to see the "good" ones. I didn't even notice "my mother's sweater" until you called my attention to it. It seems you are getting younger and prettier as time goes by. I have just posted your picture on the wall near my desk and marked it "Postwar Plan No.1." Now I've got something to fight for!'[1]

Others who had something to fight for that day were the survivors of the concentration camps. Most of them have vivid memories of the announcement that the war was over. In many of the camps that had been liberated in April, the former prisoners were still there on May 7, recovering from the desperate straits of privation. Ben Giladi was still at the Mittlebau-Dora slave labour camp which had been liberated almost a month earlier.'The scenic Dora was now bursting with all kinds of displaced people speaking so many tongues,' he recalled. On the afternoon of May 7, the loudspeakers emotionally announced the surrender of Germany. The war in Europe had come to an end. An imposing,

[1] Benjamin Ferencz, letter dated 7 May 1945. Private archive.

impromptu victory celebration was hastily arranged by the camp authorities. People were dancing and singing at the site of the old *Appellplatz*.[1] All kinds of performances took place. The orchestra played the popular songs of the era. The survivors enjoyed their new attained, precious freedom.'[2]

In Belsen, liberated nearly three weeks earlier, Margit Schönfeld remembered the day her war ended. 'I was in hospital with spotted typhus, very weak and confused with high fever. I heard from very far the sound of bells, somebody told me "the war is over" but I felt no joy. I knew that my whole family was wiped out. I felt miserable and thought I was dying. Probably I was really near death, unable to discern between reality and very vivid fever dreams.'[3] She recovered, and in due course made her way back to Czechoslovakia, rebuilding her life in the shadow of communism, emerging only in 1991 to the brighter light of freedom. But it was with her recovery at Belsen, after the bells had pealed out their triumphant news, that she regained her freedom.

With the guns having fallen silent, the Allied soldiers under Eisenhower's Supreme Command had time, on May 7, to write home, and to reflect. One of them, Sergeant Charles Kessler, who had witnessed the liberation of the prisoner-of-war camp at Hammelburg a month earlier, was particularly concerned about his brother Robert, who had been taken prisoner at the Battle of the Bulge, and whose fate he did not yet know: he had in fact been killed a month earlier, on April 9th, during a 'death march' from Berga prisoner-of-war camp. On May 7 Charles Kessler was near the Austrian village of Wörgl, typing a letter to his parents on a 'liberated' German typewriter which he had kept with him inside his tank during the last weeks of the war. 'It was only today,' he wrote, 'that I learned fighting was still going on in Czechoslovakia. A peace is expected there hourly and I expect that by the time this reaches you everything in the ETO[4] will be finished.'

Sergeant Kessler had more than a German typewriter with him in the tank that day, as he explained to his parents. 'It is strange that I have been looking for pistols for so long, and on the last day of the war, I have enough to set up a small store. We captured a supply dump containing hundreds of pistols, and naturally everyone helped themselves. I have, or had, about fifteen Walther automatics, all brand new. I believe that we are only allowed to bring one gun back to the States, so I am going

---

[1] The main square in every camp, and the scene of the daily roll-call.
[2] Ben Giladi, letter to the author, 20 August 1994.
[3] Margit Herrmannova (née Schönfeld), letter to the author, 12 September 1994.
[4] The European Theatre of Operations.

to get rid of them all. So far I have made a trade for a Luger. Sailors sometimes pay as much as a hundred dollars for a Luger, and if I get that offer I am going to sell. I have also set a price on my others of thirty-five dollars per gun, and expect to clean up. By the way, when I bring home a pistol it will be strictly for souvenir purposes. I am not taking any ammunition with me.

'It is hard to realize that we must not shoot all the German soldiers we see. There are thousands of them along the roads, all going home. Some of them have thrown away their uniforms. Most of them are walking, but occasionally we see bus loads, truck loads, wagon loads, etc., of enemy soldiers. Guns are lying everywhere, and burned and wrecked vehicles clutter all the roads. Throughout the Alps, the remnants of the once mighty Wehrmacht is everywhere. Cannons have been pushed over cliffs and out into lakes, and broken rifles are in every ditch. The German soldiers smile and wave at us, but I have never seen a GI return anything but scorn.

'I have just received a letter from the Red Cross saying that they could give me absolutely no help in obtaining information about Robert. Everything of that nature, they said, goes through the War Department. Very little mail has been coming through to me during the past month and it is possible that you have already written me the good word about Robert. Now that fighting is over I am quite sure that he is on his way home. It is probably a matter of time till you and myself hear from him. By the way the papers (*Stars and Stripes*) said that all released prisoners were eligible to a twenty-one day furlough in the States, but that they were also eligible for duty in the Pacific.

'Several times I have requested a watch, but now my time troubles are over. I have a wrist and pocket watch now, all obtained from German soldiers. I also have the prettiest camera you have ever seen. Film is scarce, but I have several rolls and am snapping photos as fast as I can find good objects. If you send me any more packages enclose several rolls of 120mm film.

'When I get back I am going to try to collect enough souvenirs to give one to everyone I know. There is so much stuff here that I hardly know where to start. Heavy objects like helmets I am going to leave here, but I will bring things back like caps, sweaters, belt buckles, insignias, flags, metals, etc.

'We have been kidding each other about going to the CBI for the past year. Now we are facing the question seriously. Quite a few men in my outfit, especially the newer replacements, will probably go directly to the Pacific. Guys like me with twenty-five months overseas expect to make the States shortly, but after that it is hard to say what will happen. Some I expect will get a furlough and then embark again. Others will get duty in the USA, while a few will be discharged. One thing I know, they'll have a hard time shipping me to the CBI, because I am going to have more things wrong with me than the doctor knew there were diseases. I will be satisfied with duty in the States, but I will say here and now that I am working for a discharge. I have seen all the fighting I care to see. I do not know exactly how many days of combat I have but it is more than the 36th Division, and they have 510. For the curiosity of it, I am going to try to figure that out later.

'Perhaps you noticed under my date line that I am now in Austria. It is Germany all over again as far as I am concerned. The people seem friendly enough, but . . .

'I should write lots more letters to everybody but right now I don't feel like doing anything but resting and taking things easy. I am perfectly content for the moment trying to fully appreciate the fact that I have made the war. What seems so unbelievable to me is that I have seen some of the worst fighting in the ETO and have come through without even a scratch, while lots of men I knew have been either killed or wounded several times. About half the men in my company have the Purple Heart award. So long, and keep well.'[1]

Under the terms of the Reims surrender, the war in Europe would continue until one minute to midnight on May 8. The leading article in the *Evening News* that afternoon, headlined

IT IS OVER

was premature.[2] The headline in the *Evening Star*, 'Tonight may be VE-night', was also wrong. Its political correspondent was right, however, when he forecast that: 'As soon as VE-Day is announced the public will, with few exceptions, stop work.' The *Evening Star* also told its readers that a thousand extra police had been chosen to take up positions at Buckingham Palace, Piccadilly, Trafalgar Square, Whitehall, Parliament Street, Oxford Street and Regent Street. 'Every man has been chosen for ability to handle good-tempered, happy crowds. Those selected are called the Dismounted "Courtesy Cops" because their job will not be to prevent people enjoying themselves, but to stop excesses.'[3]

[1] Charles Kessler, letter to his parents, Austria, 7 May 1945. Private archive.
[2] 'Victory', *Evening News*, 7 May 1945, p. 2, col. 2.
[3] 'London Puts Out The Flags Today', *Star*, 7 May 1945, p. 1.

Among those Londoners determined to celebrate without delay was Aumie Shapiro. A week later he wrote to a friend who was serving with the Royal Air Force in India: 'Rumours were running wild early Monday afternoon that VE-Day would be announced at any moment, and to ensure that flags, bunting and other decorative arrangements would be completed, the street organizing committees set to feverishly with the work. The Shapiro family hoisted the Jewish flag[1] side by side with the Union Jack. The Klein colony followed suit and at least in one area the Jewish nation was fully represented! The Botsman and neighbouring families were busy chopping down trees and stripping bombed houses of all wooden fittings so that sufficient material would be available for the street's bonfire.'[2]

The preparations for a Monday celebration were well under way, but premature. Despite the signing of unconditional surrender at Reims that morning, and the virtual cessation of hostilities on almost all fronts, the political leaders in London, Washington and New York had been unable to agree that May 7 should be VE-Day, but the men and women in the street had no reason to curb their celebratory zeal.

---

[1] A Star of David on a blue and white background.
[2] Aumie Shapiro, letter to a friend, London, 13 May 1945. Private archive.

VIII

War Recedes

7 May 1945

By late afternoon of May 7, the final problems of co-ordinating the British, American and Soviet declarations of VE-Day had been resolved, and a compromise reached, unsatisfactory to Britain and the United States, but unavoidable in the light of Stalin's attitude. The Soviet Union would wait for its official war ending until May 9. The Western Allies would celebrate on May 8. The British Ministry of Information issued its statement that 'in accordance with arrangements between the three Great Powers, an official announcement will be broadcast by the Prime Minister at 3 p.m. tomorrow afternoon, May 8. In view of this fact, tomorrow (Tuesday) will be treated as Victory-in-Europe Day and will be regarded as a holiday.'

From the German forces in Czechoslovakia came ominous news at 3.49 p.m., when Prague Radio broadcast a statement from the German commander-in-chief in Czechoslovakia, that Dönitz's capitulation applied only to the American and British. The statement went on to say that the announcement over Flensburg radio that Germany had surrendered unconditionally to the Soviet Union was 'enemy propaganda intent on breaking our troops' will to resist'. It was only against the Western powers that the Reich Government had ceased to fight. 'In our area the struggle will continue until the Germans in the East are saved and until our way back into the homeland is secured.'[1]

As the fighting continued in Czechoslovakia, Czech partisans in Prague seized the east bank of the Vltava River. During May 7, a Czech Spitfire squadron left Britain for an American-held airfield near Pilsen, intent on helping the Prague insurgents. Soon afterwards, as a London newspaper reported the next day: 'Large formations carrying Czechoslovak ground troops also took off for home, and the battle for the liberation of Prague. The commander, before leaving, said: "This is the greatest day of my

---

[1] English-language text in *Stars and Stripes*, 8 May 1945, p. 2, col. 4.

life." In a final burst of fiendishness, SS troops in Prague last night were firing the last shots of the war on helpless Czech civilians. SS men went through the streets driving people out of their homes as other SS troops waited to mow them down with machine-guns. The *Wehrmacht* commander announced that he did not recognize what he described as the "armistice". "German troops will continue to fight until they have secured a free passage out of the country", he added. Meanwhile Patton's famous 4th Armoured Division is speeding towards the capital. . . .'[1]

Two radio transmitters were broadcasting from Prague. One was in the hands of the Czechs, the other in the hands of the Germans. In its early evening edition, the London *Evening Star* reported a broadcast by the German-held radio station: 'All important military positions are in the hands of the German troops. The rebels have already been driven from a number of penetrations. German reinforcements are standing by at the fringe of the city.' A proclamation by the German Army commander in the city, in which he ordered a 10 p.m. to 5 a.m. curfew, warned: 'Civilians found in possession of arms will be summarily shot. Any excesses against the German civil population will be answered by reprisals against Czechs in German hands.'[2]

The last broadcast heard over the German transmission was at 5.30 p.m., in the strident style of the Nazi pronouncements; it made no reference to the fighting in Prague, but stated that strong flank attacks were being made against the Russian forces in Moravia, north of Olomouc, and also between Dresden and Chemnitz, where 'great battles' were in progress.[3]

Although the German broadcast had avoided any mention of the fighting in Prague, three hours later the Czech-held transmitter announced that the German position in Prague was precarious. In eight words the Czechs proclaimed: 'Help has come. Allied divisions are approaching Prague.'

General Patton's troops were only fifteen miles from the city. Inside the capital, the initiative no longer lay with the Germans. Hitherto, one of the largest homogeneous group of soldiers fighting alongside the Germans in Prague were the Russian forces under the command of General Vlasov. Strongly anti-Soviet, and loyal to the Germans for more than two years, they turned their backs on Germany and declared their loyalty to the Allies. This was made clear in a third broadcast from Prague that day, picked up by radio listeners in the West. 'General Vlasov's Army HQ

[1] 'Czech troops fly from Britain to save Prague – great day', *Daily Mirror*, 8 May 1945, p. 3, col. 2.
[2] 'Patton Fifteen Miles From Prague', *Star*, 7 May 1945, p. 1, col. 1.
[3] *Daily Sketch*, 8 May 1945, p. 8, col. 5.

appeals to all the German Armed Forces in Greater Prague to capitulate unconditionally,' the broadcast declared. 'Should these orders be disobeyed, all means will be used until complete extermination is achieved. Prague has been encircled by us. Signed, General Vlasov's HQ.'[1] With Vlasov's defection the Germans had lost any chance of maintaining effective power in Prague.[2]

While the struggle for control of the streets of Prague continued, three American Army vehicles reached the city. Shortly afterwards, so did the Russians. Within hours the Russians insisted, under an agreement reached some days earlier between Eisenhower and the Soviet High Command, that the Americans withdraw to Pilsen. The Americans complied. Under an agreement that had been made at Yalta they were committed to withdraw altogether from Czechoslovak soil.

In the areas which neither the Americans nor the Russians had yet reached, parts of Saxony, Bohemia and Moravia, Ernest Michel and his two friends were still in hiding, working for the German farmer and his wife who had saved them from starvation by giving them work and food. Ernest Michel recalled: 'On May 7, I was working in the field with a farmer, Hempel, who had given me a job on his farm in a little hamlet, Lindenau, in Saxony, Germany. We were repairing a fence and I was holding a two-by-four. At that moment Hempel's wife came to the field where we were working, bringing coffee and sandwiches. Almost as an afterthought, as if talking about the weather, she said in her heavy Saxonian accent: "*Der Krieg is vorbei: Ich hab's gerade am Radio gehört.*" ("The war is over. I just heard it on the radio.")

'Hempel didn't say anything. His wife turned around and went back to the farmhouse. I stood there, dumbfounded, not knowing what to do. I couldn't believe it. I had survived. It was all over and I was alive. My thoughts were interrupted by Hempel. "Don't just stand there! We got work to do." I handed him the two-by-four and we went back to fixing the fence. The three of us, Honzo, Felix and myself, had been together, inseparably, for over two years in Auschwitz, Buchenwald and finally in Berga. After five and a half years – 2,051 days – in slave labour, in concentration camps, all of a sudden we were free, and we didn't know what to do about it. Strangely enough, during all those years in the camps, we only thought about surviving, about the end of the war, without any idea what would happen afterwards. I had no education, having been

---

[1] 'Patton Fifteen Miles From Prague', *Star*, 7 May 1945, p. 1, col.1.
[2] As Russian forces entered Prague, Vlasov, knowing the Soviet hatred of his earlier change of sides, managed to reach the American lines. The Americans handed him over to the Soviet authorities, who tried and hanged him in 1946.

kicked out of school in Mannheim in the seventh grade. The only thing I knew was how to survive.

'Where were my parents? My sister? Were they alive? I doubted it. What happened to all the people I knew? Friends, family. We talked for a long time that evening. Honzo and Felix decided to leave the next day. Honzo wanted to go back to Prague. Felix decided to go with him. It was a strange farewell. Here we were, three young Jewish men, lucky enough to have survived what was later to become known as the Holocaust. We were as close to each other as human beings could be. Our lives had depended on one another. We could never have made it alone. So we stood there. We embraced, we hugged. Nobody said a word. There was nothing to say. We exchanged addresses, not knowing whether the places where we had lived still existed, but we wanted to stay in touch with each other. Then, after the final embrace, they turned around and left. I went back to Hempel's farm.'[1]

Ernest Michel's sister Lotte had survived, hidden by Catholic nuns. Only later did he learn that his parents, Otto and Frieda Michel, had been murdered in Auschwitz in 1942. Many of his close friends had also been murdered. At the Nuremberg Trials, where he worked as a journalist for the newly created Allied News Agency DANA, he looked down on the accused men day after day. 'Sometimes I wanted to jump from the press gallery to shake them by the shoulders and yell in their faces: "Why did you do this to us? Why did you kill my friend Walter? Why did you hang Leo, Janek and Nathan? Why? Why?"'[2]

In neutral Dublin, where an official visit of condolence had been made to the German Embassy after Hitler's death by President de Valera, Mass was celebrated on May 7 for Mussolini, at the Franciscan Catholic Church, at the request of members of the Italian community in the city.

Neutral Spain, whose leader General Francisco Franco, while maintaining his country's neutrality throughout the conflict, had sent Spanish troops to fight alongside Germany against Russia, acted on May 7 to dissociate himself from his earlier actions. 'Spain has severed diplomatic relations with Germany, it is officially announced in Madrid,' a press bulletin reported that day. This was published in one British newspaper under the laconic headline:

---

[1] Ernest W. Michel, letter to the author, 17 October 1994. Honzo (John Marek) met Michel again some ten years after the war: since then they have maintained a life-long friendship. Felix re-emerged only after the publication of Michel's memoirs in 1993: that same year, he, Honzo and Michel met for dinner on Thanksgiving Day.

[2] Ernest W. Michel, *Promises To Keep*, Barricade Books, New York, 1993, p. 116.

JUST IN TIME[1]

The Spanish decision to abandon neutrality beyond even the eleventh hour did not prevent the Spanish authorities from giving sanctuary to those who had served the now-enemy regime, and were on the run. On the same day that Spain severed relations with Germany, it was announced that the Belgian Fascist leader and Waffen SS General, Léon Degrelle, had found sanctuary in Spain, not escaping Norway by submarine as he had hoped, but by air. A pre-war leader of the Belgian Walloon nationalist Rexist Party, Degrelle had, during the war, commanded a detachment of Belgian soldiers on the Eastern Front, where he had been severely wounded several times. He had also been awarded the prestigious Knight's Cross for valour, and was personally decorated by Hitler.

Degrelle's ambition had been to rule a Nazi protectorate, Greater Burgundy, in emulation and imitation of the medieval Burgundian monarch, Charles the Bold.[2] But with the collapse of the Third Reich, having been condemned to death *in absentia* by a Belgian court, Degrelle flew across liberated Europe from Norway to Spain in a light aircraft. With his fuel tanks empty he crash-landed on a beach near the Spanish port of San Sebastian.

Many Belgian Waffen SS men were executed after their return to Belgium from Soviet prisoner-of-war camps. Degrelle remained in Spain, in hospital convalescing from the injuries he had sustained during the crash-landing. Having, at a late stage in the war, taken command of the scattered remnants of the Spanish Blue Division on the Eastern Front, he felt at home in Spain. Several appeals from the Belgian Government for his extradition were turned down. Then, in August 1946, he disappeared. Hidden for a decade by Spanish friends, when he reappeared the Belgians again sought his extradition, but he had managed to obtain Spanish nationality and could not be extradited. In 1983 the Belgian Government announced that if he did ever try to return to Belgium he would be expelled at the frontier as an *'étranger indésirable'*.[3] Forty-nine

---

[1] *Daily Mail*, 8 May 1945.

[2] During his ten-year reign (1467–77), Charles the Bold, Duke of Burgundy, united Flanders and Burgundy, and conquered Lorraine (in 1475). He also hoped to conquer Provence, Dauphiné and Switzerland. In 1476 he invaded Switzerland but was killed in battle the following year during the siege of Nancy.

[3] Martin Conway, *Collaboration in Belgium, Léon Degrelle and the Rexist Movement*, Yale University Press, New Haven and London, 1993, pp. 280–1.

years after his flight from Germany, Degrelle died in hospital in Malaga, on the Costa del Sol, at the age of eighty-seven.[1]

Throughout May 7, German forces continued to fight the Red Army north of the Czech town of Olomouc and in the town itself. On the long spit of land between Danzig and Königsberg, German troops continued to fight the Russians near the fishing village of Vogelsang. Just off the coast of Scotland, in the Firth of Forth, one mile south of the Isle of May, the German submarine U–2336, commanded by Captain Emil Klusmeier, sank two merchant ships, the Norwegian *Sneland I* and the British *Avondale Park*. On the *Sneland I* seven Norwegian merchant seamen were killed; two British seamen died on the *Avondale Park*. These nine merchant seamen were the last Allied naval deaths of the European war.

In five years and eight months of submarine war, 27,491 officers and men on German submarines had been killed. Of the 863 U-boats that had been sent on operational patrols, 754 had been sunk, or damaged beyond repair while in port. Their success had been considerable, however, with 2,800 Allied merchant ships and 148 Allied warships being sunk. Their own end was ignominious. Under Operation Rainbow, launched in that first week of May, 231 German submarines scuttled themselves rather than fall into Allied hands. Among those scuttled were many which had never put to sea, including, in Lübeck harbour, several submarines which were to have been powered by the new hydrogen-peroxide method. One of their inventors, Helmuth Walter, captured by the British on May 5, agreed on May 7 to give the Allies details of all new submarines and torpedoes then under construction at the nearby research stations at Eckernförde. One of the new type of submarines was shipped to America for trials, another to Britain.

The war at sea had been one of sudden dangers and terrifying forfeits. Ships that were sunk could be lost within a few minutes, and all on board drowned. The naval disasters of the war were to be counted, not in lost battles, but in lost lives. Those who served at sea had every reason to rejoice when, during the afternoon of May 7, the news reached them that hostilities were over. They did not need to wait for VE-Day to celebrate the ending of danger. A naval officer, Lieutenant-Commander Edward Thomas, who in 1944 had been awarded the Distinguished Service Cross for saving life at sea, recalled: 'I was on board the Home Fleet flagship at anchor in that glorious inland sea, Scapa Flow, one of the finest sights in the United Kingdom. It was filled with radiant northern sunlight in

[1] Obituary notice, *The Times*, 2 April 1994.

which the ships of the Home Fleet gleamed with an even greater beauty than they did ordinarily. This was the scene when signals arrived from Admiralty announcing the end of hostilities. For two years, as the Home Fleet's intelligence officer, my life had been bound up, to the exclusion of all else, with the Fleet's operations in northern waters, off the Norwegian coast, and on the Arctic convoy to North Russia.

'I had been intensely proud of having been in the thick of those operations, of my close association with the ships of the Home Fleet and its officers and men, and of the DSC which they had awarded me a year earlier. I loved the ships for their beauty and their embodiment of Britain's genius for engineering and the seamanship that had shaped Britain's history.

'But they were all essentially things of war; and with the Admiralty's sudden announcement the feeling equally suddenly came over me that all this glorious assemblage was now futile and without point. It was months before I could comfort myself with the reflection that there was a place in peace-time for all, or some, of it. But that reflection was poor recompense for all the sudden evaporation of that spiritual *élan* that had kept us all going through almost six years of war.

'The second feeling was of panic. The war had filled my life, and for hardly a moment had I thought of what might follow it. My lack of qualifications (except a poor BA) hadn't mattered during the war when insecurity and competition had been suspended. But I was now suddenly confronted with the collapse of that artificial stability. Ian Fleming at the Admiralty had undertaken to put forward my name for a job in Whitehall intelligence. But I hardly thought I had an earthly when pitted against the big, self-confident personalities I had met in wartime intelligence. Nor was I sure that that was what I wanted to do in life. A glory had gone out of things.'[1]

Edward Thomas's sad reflections at Scapa Flow were in contrast with the mounting excitement in London that evening. VE-Day might still be half a night away, but there were those who had no intention of waiting until the morrow. Among them was Aumie Shapiro, who wrote to his RAF friend a week later, describing how he and two friends spent the evening of May 7: 'On reaching Trafalgar Square we were rather disappointed, for few people were about. Both Sid and I remembered

---

[1] Edward Thomas, letter to the author, 30 August 1994. Thomas was later to be one of those responsible for the multi-volume history, *British Intelligence in the Second World War* (London, 1979–1992).

that the West End appeared less populated than at normal times, but reviewing the position in Hyde Park, we began to realize that the crowds were assembling. The spirit of fun and merriment was in the air and singing a rousing Hebrew song we made our way down Oxford Street to Regent Street. Then the fun really began! Sid decided that he was a poor down and out and began to sing beery renderings befitting the hard-working, hard-drinking good for nothing. We collected from the passers-by the noble sum of one half penny and an old boot! But the crowds were still on the quiet-cum-shy side and we wondered whether the celebrations would turn out to be nothing but a damp squib.

'As dusk fell, bonfires were being kindled throughout London. The sky soon resembled a London sky of 1940, only this time the reddened clouds were a sign of jubilation and not of wanton destruction. We were attracted by a bonfire off Regent Street and again we were rather disappointed at the tempo of the so-called festive spirit. We wanted action, bags of fun, madness. We wanted to see a crazy London! Perhaps five and a half years of war had made London forget how to be merry? After making a number of rude remarks to the local prostitutes we made our way into Piccadilly and here, at long last, the FUN had begun in real earnest!

'Simpsons, the famed hosiery store, was a blaze of light. Officially, floodlighting was not permissible until Tuesday night and the crowd, desiring to show their sympathy for Simpsons' "revolutionary" spirit, were cheering and yelling for all their worth. The road was impassable. A car attempted to force its way through the yelling mob and the crowd reacted by jumping upon the vehicle and refused to move off! The poor driver was kicking up a row about something or other, but no one took a bit of notice. Yanks, bless 'em, climbed on to the roof of the car and began to leap about. At any moment we expected the thing to collapse. We joined in the merriment with full blooded war-cries of *Ooskidavie, Ooskidavah!*, our Jewish youth club war cry, and shouted ourselves hoarse! It was mad, crazy: but so was war-torn London!'[1]

The atmosphere was very different in Cumberland. That night a train drew in to Windermere Station in the Lake District. On board were a number of German prisoners-of-war, bound for the prison camp at Grizedale Hall near Hawkshead. Three naval officers and two generals were among them. 'Five high-ranking Nazi prisoners', as one newspaper described them.[2]

---

[1] Aumie Shapiro, letter to a friend, London, 13 May 1945. Private archive.
[2] 'More Nazi generals arrive', *News Chronicle*, 8 May 1945, p. 4, col. 2.

For the victors, in Paris as in London and New York, it was impossible to prevent, even had anyone wished to do so, the outburst of patriotic zeal before the official day of victory. Among those who witnessed and participated in the Parisian explosion of joy was an American war correspondent, Ralph G. Martin, who had been with the soldiers throughout the war in Europe. He sent a report to his newspaper, *Yank*, the next day, with an account of how May 7 had begun, and how it evolved: 'It started out phoney. It started when a photographer staged a shot with some French babes kissing some slightly overhappy soldiers in front of Rainbow Corner. Watching the whole thing curiously, quietly, were several dozen soldiers sitting at the tables outside the Red Cross Club, sipping Cokes. "I keep telling everybody that the war is really over' said the Military Policeman at the door who was no longer checking passes, "but nobody believes me. I told one guy and he just said, "What . . . again . . . ?"'

'That was only part of the mood that afternoon. There was something else. There was this. Two paratroopers were just standing in front of the club when an excitable Frenchman ran up to them, waving a French newspaper, yelling "*La guerre est finie . . . La guerre est finie . . .*". After he raced by, spreading the news, one of the paratroopers simply said, "For him, not for us."'

'Then there was another soldier who listened to somebody tell him that the war was over and then said bitterly, "Which war, the war they're fighting in Paris?"'

'That was Monday afternoon, and then the mood changed. It changed slowly. You could feel it change; you could hear it. First the singing by small crowds, loud singing by people who had drunk lots of cognac and were walking down the Champs Élysées arm-in-arm until they had a small parade. Then the parades getting longer and the crowds getting bigger and the planes swooping down low dropping flares and dozens of people piling onto any jeep that slowed down.

'The Champs Élysées was the centre of it and every soldier had a girl or two girls or a dozen girls. And everybody was singing and everybody was everybody's buddy.

"Hiya Army . . . Hiya Navy . . .
"Hello beautiful . . .
"Goddammit, don't call me sir . . . today I'm a civilian.
 "Hiya civilian . . ."

'It spread fast. Some of it was forced. Some guys were getting drunk not just because they really wanted to, but just because they felt they had to.

But most of the soldiers on the Champs were just letting themselves go, catching the spirit of it.

> Show me the way to go home.
> Roll out the barrel, we'll have a barrel of fun.

' "We're forgetting about the CBI tonight. We're forgetting about every goddam thing," said Private First Class Nat Mangano of Company H. "We're just gonna have a helluva time, that's all. Why not?" There were very few lonely people. "I can't find anybody to celebrate with. I don't know anybody here. I'm just on a three-day pass. Every time I find me a girl she disappears. And I can't get a drink. All the bars are closed. But don't worry, I'll make contact before the night's over. I've gotta make contact. I'm going back to the outfit tomorrow." It looked like that about midnight at the Arc de Triomphe. It looked like it was going to last all night long and not stop for days and days.'[1]

An American serviceman in Paris, Staff Sergeant William E. Beatty, wrote to his mother and sister in Baltimore, Maryland, that evening: 'Paris is getting very excited tonight, for, as you on that side of the water no doubt know, from all indications the war is just about over. In fact it seems that VE-Day has poked its nose around the corner – or perhaps the people (we included) are poking our noses round the corner. All afternoon the bits of news we have been able to gather have been quite "hot". Morning papers of both Paris and London stated that it was only a few hours away. Later a news bulletin appeared on our bulletin board saying that the German Foreign Office had announced capitulation.[2] And finally the Paris evening papers burst out into full headlines with an AP[3] report of the actual signing of the armistice at Reims at 02.41 this morning. The hold-up seems to be the official announcement from Washington, London and Moscow, and naturally we were wondering if that will come in a matter of hours or days. But all indications seem that this really *is* IT.'[4]

Four days later, Sergeant Beatty sent his mother and sister an account of the rest of the events of May 7 in the French capital: 'Within about a half-hour after I came out from supper tonight crowds seemed to come from everywhere and gather on the Champs-Élysées. French policemen are as thick as flies, and the fences that have been piled up along the

---

[1] Sergeant Ralph G. Martin, 'The War Was Over', *Yank*, Victory Edition, 1945.
[2] This was the broadcast by Count Schwerin von Krosigk, made at 2.30 that afternoon.
[3] The Associated Press news agency.
[4] William E. Beatty, letter to his mother and sister, Paris, 7 May 1945. Private archive.

streets suddenly appeared along the curbs. Everybody was milling around, I suppose just waiting for the "last horn to blow". We know that the official time will be announced by sirens and church bells, and just as when we were expecting an air raid, whenever I heard a car start up or anything remotely resembling a whistle, it sort of made me jump. I suppose you'd call it "peace-jitters".

'I just heard the 8 o'clock news in French, and from what I could make out there is still fighting in Czechoslovakia where they refuse to accept the capitulation of the Wehrmacht. After the string of big news that came out in the papers for the past week or so, from the kicking of the bucket by Hitler and Musso, the big surrenders etc., the news of the Luftwaffe and submarines giving up took almost insignificant space in the papers. As it's now the middle of the afternoon where you are, I can't help wondering what's going on if the news is the same as it is here. I can imagine the papers are full of it and that they have been screaming extras for the past week, unless they've calmed down a bit after getting the country unduly excited a week ago.' [1]

The BBC broadcast that May 8 would be VE-Day was transmitted by national and local radios to every corner of the globe. Major Edmund Marsden was on leave in India. He later recalled: 'As my regiment was still fighting the Japanese in Burma, from which I had only just returned after a year which took me from Kohima to Mandalay, one looked forward to a rapid redeployment of forces and resources that would bring an early end to the Japanese war, certainly the liberation of Burma and Malaya and above all those held prisoner by the Japanese.'[2]

From Palestine, a British pilot, Flying Officer Anthony Wedgwood Benn, wrote home three weeks later of how, on the morning of May 7, he and two officer friends 'hired a rowing boat and rowed out into the Sea of Galilee, trying to pick out Capernaum on the side of the lake further up. Coming in, we entered a little Arab restaurant for refreshment and as we walked towards the place, a Jew hurried up with a smile and said "The war – finished!" We didn't know whether to believe it or not so we smiled back. It seemed to be confirmed by a special edition of the paper. So we solemnly celebrated with an orange squash and ice cream each – hardly believing it could be true, hardly thinking of it, it seemed so remote. Returning later to Shaar Hagolan, via another settlement, we found them preparing for a festival to celebrate peace. It was nearly ten o'clock and we understood that the King was to speak so we asked to

[1] William E. Beatty, letter to his mother and sister, Paris, 11 May 1945. Private archive.
[2] Edmund Marsden, letter to the author, 21 September 1994.

listen to the wireless. As you know, he didn't but in consequence we missed the gathering on the lawn when the leader of the settlement gave an address of welcome in Hebrew to "the three English officers". Think of the wonderful opportunity for replying with a speech – what we missed! I was disappointed.

'Outside on the grass an effigy of the swastika was burned and the settlement crowded into the eating hall, where a little wine and lots of biscuits and nuts were laid along tables. I asked for an orange squash and was given one, however, one old boy emptied half a cupful of wine into it, and I drank it up – it was practically communion wine – rather an appropriate beverage to celebrate peace. Then the national dances began, Germans, Czechs, Poles, Turks, Yugoslavs, all did their national dances. Then there was a pause and an announcement in Hebrew. Everyone looked at us and it was explained that the RAF officers would do an English national dance. Hurriedly deciding to do the boomps-a-daisy, two of us took the floor. It was an instantaneous success and everybody joined in.'[1]

Another of those by the Sea of Galilee when news that the war was over was broadcast by the BBC was the Yugoslav-born Reuven Dafni. A year earlier he had been parachuted behind German lines in Yugoslavia, a British agent living with the partisans, seeking as part of his dangerous mission to make contact with the surviving Jews of the region. Several of his parachutist colleagues and close friends had been captured by the Germans, tortured and killed. One of them, the Hungarian-born Hanna Szenes, had been executed in a Gestapo prison in Budapest. Dafni had flown out of Yugoslavia at the beginning of 1945 on an aircraft carrying wounded Yugoslav partisans to hospital in Italy. Listening on the radio to the news of the war's end, no longer a soldier but the captain of a small ferry-boat on the Sea of Galilee, he recalled: 'There was no joy in my heart, no feeling of victory, since I knew from my own experience what the Nazis (and their accomplices) did to our people. I was actually sad and at the same time relieved that the nightmare was over.'[2] Dafni's mother, his sister-in-law and her seven-year-old son had been killed by the Germans in Belgrade in November 1941. His grandmother, his two uncles and a cousin had been killed by the Ustashi is the concentration camp at Jasenovac.

*   *   *

[1] Letter of 20 May 1945, quoted in Ruth Winstone (editor), *Tony Benn, Years of Hope, Diaries, Letters and Papers 1940–1962*, Hutchinson, London, 1994, p. 90.
[2] Reuven Dafni, letter to the author, 11 September 1994.

Officially, the war was still not yet over. 'A great doubt as to whether today would be VE-Day,' Hugh Dalton wrote in his diary on the afternoon of May 7. 'Will it be announced tonight? It should have been, but the Americans and the Russians insisted on delaying it till tomorrow so as to get all the surrender business complete.'[1] In Washington, President Truman issued a statement to the Press that afternoon: 'I have agreed with the British and Soviet Governments that I will make no announcement with reference to the surrender of enemy forces in Europe or elsewhere until a simultaneous statement can be made by the three Governments. Until then there is nothing I can, or will, say to you.'[2]

Among those serving with the 6th Armoured Division in northern Italy was Captain Tony Crosland. In his diary on May 7 he described the scene as Italian workers who had been taken by the Germans for forced labour returned to their homeland: 'A sad never-ending procession, huge packs or cases on their backs, bent double beneath the weight. What they did for food, God knows, but if one gave them a cigarette they were so grateful it made one ashamed. They were amazingly cheerful, dogged, enduring, and could manage a smile though their hands were so tired they could hardly hold a cigarette from the trembling. Well, the slaves are free at last, thank God: but their release is costing them something near the limit of physical suffering.'[3]

Colonel Hunt, the British Intelligence officer who had been on the Greek island of Chios during May 6, decided, together with his friend Colonel Wheeler, to visit the Turkish city of Izmir. 'As we moved in to the jetty to tie up,' he recalled, 'a dignified figure in top hat and frock coat could be seen on shore. "It must be the harbour master", said Wheeler. It was indeed, and he showed the purpose of his visit by removing his hat with a graceful gesture and declaiming, in good and heavily emphasised English , "The war is over". It was three o'clock of the afternoon of May 7.

'I thought at once of a moment that matched. It was at Long Whittenham in Oxfordshire at midday on 1 September 1939. That time a colleague and I, who had come out from Magdalen for the first day of the shooting season, were stationary and watched someone approaching down a long straight road. It seemed a long time before he drew up to us and said, without introduction: "The war has started; they were bombing

---

[1] Ben Pimlott (editor), *The Second World War Diary of Hugh Dalton, 1940–45*, Jonathan Cape, London, 1986, p. 856.
[2] Full text in 'No Separate US Announcement', *Daily Telegraph*, 8 May 1945, p. 1, col. 3.
[3] Captain Anthony Crosland, diary, 7 May 1945: in Susan Crosland, *Tony Crosland*, Jonathan Cape, London, 1982, p. 37.

Poland this morning." In the six intervening years I had travelled a long way; but I never expected to end the war with a dinner at a Turkish fish restaurant at the next table to the lugubrious executive committee of the German-Turkish Chamber of Commerce.'[1]

Throughout May 7, British prisoners-of-war were returning to Britain, flown back from Germany as a priority. Among those who reached London that day was Viscount Lascelles, a nephew of King George VI, and his fellow prisoner-of-war the Master of Elphinstone, a nephew of the Queen. Both were 'welcomed home' that night at Buckingham Palace.[2]

While some Lancaster bombers brought former prisoners-of-war back to Britain, others were dropping more than a thousand tons of food over Holland, for the starving Dutch civilian population. An estimated six thousand Dutch civilians had reached the stage 'where the normal digestion of food is almost impossible.'[3] For them, two shipments of the protein preparation Amigen, had been flown from the United States to Britain, for despatch to Holland by the United States Eighth Air Force within forty-eight hours of leaving the Atlantic seaboard. Canadian army drivers were also taking food trucks deeper and deeper into Holland without incident, but the situation inside the country was still precarious. As many as 8,000 Dutch SS troops, many of whom had fought alongside the German army against Russia, were being arrested and disarmed by German troops committed to do so under the terms of their own surrender two days earlier. The 120,000 German troops who had surrendered on May 5 were also committed to build their own barbed wire enclosures, and had been moving throughout May 6 and May 7 to special areas set aside for them. Until reaching their destinations, they were allowed to keep their arms.

At nine o'clock on the morning of May 7, coming across the German border from the East, a British armoured car regiment was making for Utrecht, Hilversum and Amersfoort. It drove forward almost entirely unmolested. Only in the village of De Klomp were the armoured cars sniped at by Dutch SS troops. That day, General Blaskowitz assured General Foulkes that he had already arrested four hundred Dutch SS men.

A British newspaper correspondent, Peter Stursberg, in a despatch

---

[1] Sir David Hunt, letter to the author, 10 September 1994.
[2] *Daily Herald*, 8 May 1945.
[3] 'Food Raids Continue', *Palestine Post*, 8 May 1945, col. 7.

from Utrecht on May 7, wrote: 'The Dutch, whom we have always thought a stolid people, have outdone the Belgians and the French in their wild welcome to our troops during their victory march into Holland. The sound of cheering is still ringing in my ears as I write this in a hotel lobby here. I arrived in this ancient city with the first British armoured cars. All the way from our starting point on the Grebbe line we drove through lines of people, but it was not till we got to the outskirts of the city that we were almost mobbed.

'There had been some shooting in Utrecht between Nazis and Resistance men, and we stopped for a moment on a wide boulevard. A cheering, singing crowd descended on us and took over our vehicles. My coat was almost torn from my back, and I found that there was no room in the jeep for me except on the spare tyre. A girl had her arm round my neck, and a man was sitting on my knee. There were between forty and fifty persons on the jeep and trailer, and more got on as we entered Utrecht.

'This is the greatest liberation and the strangest, too. On our way up Germans drove past us in army cars and volkswagens, and for a time, as we slowly edged our way through the crowds, two Germans cycled beside us. They had machine pistols slung over their backs, and might have been our escorts. The Dutch just ignored them. The girl who had her arm round my neck stuffed golden tulips into my raincoat. Our jeep and trailer load – by now a full chorus of sixty voices – broke into "The Orange" as we passed a German headquarters.

'The effect of starvation is noticeable in the pinched faces of the people. Some are so weak from hunger that they can hardly wave to us. I talked with the leader of the Resistance Movement here, and he told me that there was so little food that people were going round from house to house begging for a potato.'[1]

Almost undamaged by war, Amsterdam had waited for liberation longer than any other large European city except Prague. On the morning of May 7, German forces were still present in large numbers. At vantage points in the city, members of the Dutch resistance movement had taken up guard. As news of the Reims surrender spread through the city, flags were hung out and people began to gather in the streets, in defiance of German orders. Some German soldiers opened fire, and the citizens hurried back into their houses. They did not have long to wait, as the first units of the Canadian Army, who had planned to enter the city only on the following day, accelerated their arrival. 'They are still dazed by the tumult which engulfed them as they drove in,' Ronald Walker, a

---

[1] Peter Stursberg, 'Dutch Beat All For Cheers', *Daily Herald*, 8 May 1945, p. 4, col. 1.

British war correspondent, wrote on the following day. 'We have been kissed, cried on, hugged, thumped, screamed at and shouted at until we are bruised and exhausted. The Dutch have ransacked their gardens so that the rain of flowers which falls on the Allied vehicles is endless.' Behind the joyous welcome was 'a stark background – food is terribly short'. There was no gas, electricity or coal. In one of their first acts as liberators, the Canadians imposed a curfew on the citizens from nine o'clock that evening, 'so that their former German masters can be transported by night without interference'.[1]

On the evening of May 7, in an ominous development for the Western Allies, Lublin radio, which was controlled by the Soviet-sponsored Polish Provisional Government, raised the issue of the arrest of General Okulicki, Commander-in-Chief of the Polish Home Army, and fifteen other Poles, mostly leading non-Communist politicians. The broadcast was uncompromising: 'Because the criminal activities of Okulicki and his accomplices were also directed against the reborn Polish State, it constitutes high treason. The Provisional Government reserves the right to demand that Okulicki and his accomplices be turned over to the Polish authorities to be indicted in the courts of the Republic.'

In response, Stanislaw Mikolaczyk, the Prime Minister of the London Poles, declared that the arrested Poles could not be accused of diversionary acts against the Red Army as they were 'sincere partisans of a Polish-Soviet understanding'. Mikolaczyk added that with the war coming to an end 'the problem of keeping the promises of a strong, free and independent Poland arose. The liberation of the democratic leaders and the honest execution of the Crimea resolutions were imperative.'[2]

Under the Crimean resolutions, signed less than three months earlier at the conclusion of the Yalta Conference, Stalin had assured Churchill and Roosevelt that free and democratic elections would be held in Poland at the earliest opportunity. Among the sixteen arrested Poles were several who would have played an important part in those elections, as Party leaders and respected wartime anti-Nazi leaders. Their arrest cast into jeopardy and turmoil the future of the Yalta Agreements, and the future of Poland.

Clearly the Soviet Union was going to lose no time to assert its rights and demands throughout the regions under its control, and even beyond

[1] Ronald Walker, 'Amsterdam rains flowers on Canadians', *News Chronicle*, 9 May 1945, p. 3, col. 8.
[2] 'Lublin Radio's Treason Charge', *Daily Telegraph*, 8 May 1945, p. 1, col. 6 (including the text of the Radio Lublin broadcast).

them. On the afternoon of May 7, New York radio reported that United States Ninth Army troops had already withdrawn from territory they had conquered east of the Elbe 'in accordance with the demarcation agreement with Russia.'[1] This item appeared immediately below the report of the 'treason' of the sixteen Polish emissaries. The newspaper also reported that Moscow radio's regular six o'clock news bulletin had made no reference to the German capitulation at Reims.

The Soviet capital was expected to hold a special gala at the Bolshoi Theatre on VE-Night. Before the Soviet decision to make May 9 the day of victory, invitations had been issued to all the foreign diplomatic representatives in the capital to a gala performance on the night of May 7. Among those who attended were the senior American and British representatives, George Kennan and Frank Roberts, who assumed that this was to be the moment when the victory would be announced. To their surprise, the gala was introduced, not as the celebration of the defeat of Germany, but as the fortieth anniversary of the birth of the alleged inventor of radio, A.S. Popov, for whom a commemorative postage stamp had been issued fifteen years earlier. Remembering this anti-climactic gala fifty years later, Frank Roberts recalled: 'At half time George Kennan and I went to Vishinsky and said, "We've nothing against your Mr Marconi, but we've got something else to celebrate" – and off we went.'[2]

The British radio announcement at six o'clock that evening, stating that VE-Day was not to be until the following day, was no deterrent to an immediate outburst of enthusiasm in London. A phrase was coined, 'VE-Eve', and beyond the phrase was the reality of unrestrained celebration. 'This is IT – and we are all going nuts', an exuberant newspaper reporter declared from the midst of the celebrations. 'There are thousands of us in Piccadilly Circus,' he wrote. 'The police say more than 10,000 – and that's a conservative estimate. We are dancing the conga and the jig and "Knees up, Mother Brown" and we are singing and whistling, and blowing paper trumpets. The idea is to make a noise. We are. Even above the roar of the motors of low-flying bombers "shooting up" the city.

'We are dancing around Eros in the black-out, but there is a glow from a bonfire up Shaftesbury Avenue and a newsreel cinema has lit its canopy lights for the first time in getting on for six years. A huge "V" sign glares down over Leicester Square. And gangs of girls and soldiers of all the Allied nations are waving rattles and shouting and climbing

[1] 'Elbe Withdrawal', *Daily Telegraph*, 8 May 1945, p. 1, col. 6.
[2] Sir Frank Roberts, conversation with the author, 1 November 1994.

lamp-posts and swarming over cars that have become bogged down in this struggling, swirling mass of celebrating Londoners.

'We have been waiting from two o'clock to celebrate. We went home at six when it seemed that the news of VE-Day would never come, but we are back now. And on a glorious night we are making the most of it. A paper-hatted throng is trying to pull me out of this telephone box now. I hold the door tight, but the din from Piccadilly Circus is drowning my voice. It is past midnight. We are still singing. A group of men liberated from German prison camps are yelling "Roll out the Barrel". They told me, "We sang it when we went to France in 1939 and we sang it as we tried to get out in 1940. Now we sing it for victory."

'Amid terrific cheers a New Zealand sailor climbed on the bonnet of a bus and from there to the roof. He stood there swaying above the crowds as the American Army swarmed up after him, but the police fought through the crowd and pulled them down. Traffic tried to push through the crowds, got lost to sight and came out with civilians, soldiers, airmen and sailors and their girls clinging to the running boards. Down in the East End, too, celebrations are terrific. When fireworks ran out they used slates which "popped" alarmingly as they hit the ground.

'But the biggest fun is in Piccadilly Circus. There is a brass band here now. They are banging out all the songs that saw this war through, and they are even trying amid the mocking cheers of the crowd, the song that did not see Germany to victory "Deutschland Awake"! And the noise goes on.'[1]

As the noise went on, it was heard loud and clear in the corridors and rabbit-warren rooms of the War Office building in Whitehall. Among those working there that day was one of Churchill's pre-war literary assistants, Maurice Ashley. His task, and that of those in the rooms near him, precluded celebration. Room 109 was the operational co-ordinating centre for South-East Asia Command. A newspaper reporter had been invited in to see that the war in the Far East was still very much in progress. 'As the news broke throughout London, and shouts of joy came up,' he wrote, 'a major in charge of SEAC Co-ordination was analysing cipher telegrams that told of troop movements, campaign plans, battle through swamp. Throughout the night, as gladness thrilled through London, and workers all over the nation stopped after five and a half years in thanksgiving and joy, the little pins moved slowly forward on the secret map in Room 109. There was still war in Room 109. I watched,

---

[1] 'London had joy night', *Daily Mirror*, 8 May 1945, p. 1, cols. 2–5 and back page, cols. 1 and 2.

fascinated, as the Major swiftly organised the constant flow of secret intelligence. . . .

'I followed the Major into a little annexe. He switched on a little light and drew back two heavy curtains. A wall was covered by a quarter-inch scale map of the whole of SEAC – Arakan, Burma, India, the whole vast war area. There were hundreds of coloured pin-heads showing troop dispositions and the whole picture of the battle. He moved a pin in Burma. Less than an hour before, while London laughed, some British troops had moved in the jungle – forward.

'Back in Room 109 three other staff officers, all experts in close touch with Chiefs of Staff, went on with the work that would carry them through VE-Night. For Room 109 the paper hats are yet to come.'[1]

At 10.40 p.m. the Foreign Office activated its long-prepared plan to inform all British embassies and overseas missions that Germany had surrendered. A single codeword had been chosen, ESCAPE, and this one word was now telegraphed across the world.[2] Twenty hours after the German surrender had been signed at Reims, British officials on five continents were to receive the news that Europe had escaped from the greatest bloodletting of the twentieth century.

At the theatre that evening, many performances ended with an announcement during the curtain call that VE-Day was to be on the following day. 'It was very emotional,' recalled Sylvia Harris, who was then working for the National Fire Service, and on the last day of her honeymoon. On May 1st she had married an American medical officer, Jack Harris, who was stationed at the 137th General Hospital in Shropshire. 'We were due to return back to Shropshire on May 8th. After we had checked out of the hotel we saw a copy of *Stars and Stripes* and discovered all leave was extended forty-eight hours. It was impossible to get our room back at the hotel or any other hotel, everything was booked. We even had to take a bus to Euston as all the taxis were on holiday! So while we were wending our way home crowds were pouring into London.'[3]

That midnight, Wolfgang Homburger, a nineteen-year-old school teacher who had come as a refugee from Karlsruhe just before the outbreak of war, and was teaching mathematics, Latin and scouting at a school which had been evacuated during the war from Essex to Wales, was waiting on Crewe Station, on the London, Midland and Scottish

---

[1] 'The war that is still to be won', *Daily Mirror*, 8 May 1945, p. 2, col. 1.

[2] 'Most Immediate', 10.40 p.m., 7 May 1945: Foreign Office papers, 371/50581. Public Record Office, Kew.

[3] Sylvia Harris, letter to the author, 25 October 1994.

railway, for the night train to London. 'A group of us gathered in the small restaurant on the up platform,' he later recalled, 'and joyously toasted peace with LMS tea, the only beverage available.'[1] In London, as the bells of midnight struck, there was a sense of euphoria. Veronica Cordell was a fifteen-year-old schoolgirl at the Ursuline Convent School in Forest Gate, where her father was vicar in what had been a much bombed, aerial-mined, and V–2-rocketed parish. She remembered joining other youngsters in a crowd outside East Ham Town Hall 'with one of the lads banging a drum as the Town Hall clock tolled midnight'.[2]

Aumie Shapiro wrote to a friend of London's continuing late night revels on May 7. 'Piccadilly Circus itself was a mass of slap-happy people. If one wanted to enter the famed area you had to form a rugger scrum and shove! Somehow or other we reached Eros and lustily singing we heightened the din by a number of points. Sid, in the Haymarket, suddenly decided that he was an Irish Communist and standing upon a street lantern was yelling to crowds about "we the masses of the working class etc. etc". A crowd soon gathered and led by Nat and myself we began to cheer Sid like mad! We then decided to carry him shoulder high through the Haymarket yelling "The Messiah – he comes!" Poor Sid had let himself in for more than he bargained.

'Rattles rattled, whistles whistled (Sid had one, and he insisted on blowing the damn thing on every possible occasion). People yelled, rockets exploded and fireworks banged; it was hell on earth! People were everywhere. They even climbed to the top of the street lanterns and any other available upright. The police joined in the fun and one poor copper was sozzled. Oh! What a beautiful sight! Strangers kissed each other, backs were slapped by all, everyone was the best pal of the guy next door. Piccadilly was just one big happy family! But mortals have to breathe, and to perform this function we penetrated through the crowds to Shaftesbury Avenue hoping to partake of some air.

'Moving into Coventry Street, close to the Lyons' Corner House, we linked up with a group of young Zionists by reason of our singing one of our songs to the tune of John Brown's Body, and we decided to dance a Hora there and then, but a bonfire, which had just been lit in Coventry Street itself, distracted us from our intention and we lost our Zionist friends.

'Whilst watching the bonfire in Coventry Street we learnt that the hour was past midnight. Joyfully but wearily we set our course for home

[1] Wolfgang S. Homburger, letter to the author, 17 October 1994.
[2] Veronica Palmer (née Cordell), letter to the author, 26 September 1994.

via Strand, St Paul's to Aldgate. On reaching Aldgate East Station a thunderstorm broke out and it seemed as if the very elements themselves had decided to "have a go!" The lightning was really beautiful. The clock showed 2.30 a.m. when I crawled into bed.'[1]

On the German shore of Lake Constance, French troops, lacking any fireworks, were celebrating with a massive display of fire power that lit up the lakeside. 'Stars are quenched by brilliant flares streaming red into the sky,' Evelyn Irons reported. 'there is a constant crack of rifles and revolvers and machine guns, and bullets rip up in the mad joy of victory.' It was not only the French troops who were rejoicing. In a lakeside hotel, French men and women who had been held as hostages in the Tyrol, at Itter Castle, were welcomed back to freedom by the French conqueror of southern Germany, General Jean Lattre de Tassigny. Among those reaching Lake Constance were two former French Prime Ministers, Edouard Daladier and Paul Reynaud, and two former wartime Chiefs of Staff, Generals Maurice Gamelin and Maxime Weygand. General de Gaulle's sister, Madame Cailliau, was among those released, as was the French tennis champion Jean Borotra, with whom Daladier had played deck tennis in order to keep fit during captivity.

'France will continue to fight alongside the Allies in the Pacific War,' was Reynaud's comment to Evelyn Irons.[2]

The Canadians were not be be outdone in their pre-VE-Day celebrations. In an eastern seaboard port that had been one of the main starting points for the transatlantic convoys, the exuberance of victory proved overwhelming. 'Mobs of civilians, servicemen and sailors staging V-Day celebrations in Halifax, Nova Scotia,' reported a British newspaper on the following day, 'became riotous, breaking into the two largest liquor stores and helping themselves to their contents. They burned a police patrol; wagon and a tramcar, and wrecked twenty others, causing damage estimated at thousands of dollars.'[3]

There were also riots in Dublin on the night of May 7, after students at Trinity College sang 'God Save the King' and 'Rule Britannia' and hoisted the Union Jack, the Stars and Stripes, the Tricoleur, and the Hammer and Sickle. A large crowd of neutral-minded Dubliners, resentful of this show of pro-Allied feeling in their midst, broke into the college and could only be dislodged by baton-wielding Civic Guards. A restaurant

---

[1] Aumie Shapiro, letter to a friend, London, 13 May 1945. Private archive.
[2] Evelyn Irons, 'German Lake Was Afire', *Evening Standard*, 8 May 1945, p. 5, cols. 5 and 6.
[3] 'V-Day rioters break into liquor stores', *Evening Despatch*, 8 May 1945, p. 1, col. 5.

in which the victory was being celebrated had its windows smashed. A hotel in which victory celebrations were also taking place was attacked to cries of 'Give us the West Britons and put out the traitors,' but the attackers retreated 'under the blows of the page-boys and hall-porters'.[1]

New York, like London, anticipated the long-awaited delights of VE-Day itself with spontaneous celebrations on May 7. 'Cheering thousands packed Times Square soon after 10 a.m.', reported a British journalist, John Sampson. 'Streams of paper floated from skyscrapers and the harbour was loud with whistles.' While people in Washington waited for confirmation that the war was over, 'in New York the news set off a contagious outburst of rejoicing unequalled since Armistice Day, 1918. Paper streamed down into the streets in one continuous shower with radio announcers frantically appealing to people, "Don't throw away paper; it's necessary to the war." Reminders that the country was still at war with Japan fell on deaf ears. People collected so quickly in Times Square that many vehicles had to be abandoned by their drivers and left in the midst of the milling mass.'[2]

A correspondent for *Stars and Stripes*, Herbert Mitgang was in New York on May 7, having earlier reported on action in North Africa, Sicily, Italy and Greece, where he accompanied the British parachutists sent to liberate Athens. After two and a half years overseas, he was within a week of his wedding. In a piece he sent that day to his paper for their Mediterranean edition he wrote: 'There was ticker tape in the streets and newspapers sailing down from buildings. There were school kids wondering if it would mean a day off. There were old World War One men waving small American flags bought from street hawkers. There were young girls kissing soldiers with overseas bars, and saying, "You'll never go back now."'[3]

Mitgang also wrote of 'the mothers ... One grey-haired woman, whose son is a captain in the Medical Corps in Germany, cried because she felt her little boy was safe now. In the back of her mind, she said, she was thinking of the next step: Would he have to go to the Pacific? A shoe store near Lexington Avenue had a picture in the window showing the famous flag-raising over Mount Suribachi, blown up to 4 feet, and a sign below: "We licked the Nazis, now let's finish the Nips."'[4]

[1] 'Baton Charges in Dublin', *Evening News*, 8 May 1945, p. 1, col. 4.
[2] 'New York went wild', *Daily Mirror*, 8 May 1945, p. 8, cols. 4,5.
[3] Herbert Mitgang, 'VE-Day called "Gift to Mothers"', 7 May 1945 (delayed), *Stars and Stripes*, 9 May 1945.
[4] Herbert Mitgang, 'VE-Day called "Gift to Mothers"', 7 May 1945 (delayed), *Stars and Stripes*, 9 May 1945.

This awareness of the war that still had to be won was the front-page story by Frank S. Adams in the *New York Times* on the following day, when, under the headline

WILD CROWDS GREET NEWS IN CITY WHILE OTHERS PRAY

he reported on how New Yorkers had reacted in two 'sharply contrasting ways' to the news of the unconditional surrender of the German armies. 'A large and noisy minority greeted it with the turbulent enthusiasm of New Year's Eve and Election Night rolled into one. However, the great bulk of the city's population responded with quiet thanksgiving that the war in Europe was won, tempered by the realization that a grim and bitter struggle was still ahead in the Pacific and the fact that the nation is still in mourning for its fallen President and Commander-in-Chief.

'Times Square, the financial section and the garment district were thronged from mid-morning on with wildly jubilant celebrators who tooted horns, staged impromptu parades and filled the canyons between the skyscrapers with fluttering scraps of paper. Elsewhere in the metropolitan area, however, war plants continued to hum, schools, offices and factories carried on their normal activities, and residential areas were calmly joyful. One factor that helped to dampen the celebration was the bewilderment of large segments of the population at the absence of an official proclamation to back up the news contained in flaring headlines and radio bulletins. With the premature rumour of ten days ago fresh in everyone's mind, and millions still mindful of the false armistice of 1918, there was widespread skepticism over the authenticity of the news.

'By mid-afternoon, loudspeakers were blaring into the ears of the exulting thousands in the amusement district, the news that President Truman's proclamation was being held up by the necessity of co-ordinating it with the announcements from London and Moscow, and that the formal celebration of the long-awaited VE-Day would be delayed until today.'[1]

Among those working in Manhattan that day was Marjorie Jaffa. 'It was mid-afternoon at work,' she recollected, 'when we all became aware of a tremendous roar coming from the street six floors below. Being a new employee my desk was an inner one, not by the window. Someone yelled, "The war is over!" and the office went wild, especially the Dutch national who was my supervisor. All of the windows were forced open.

---

[1] 'Wild Crowds Greet News In City While Others Pray', *New York Times*, 8 May 1945, p. 1, cols. 3,4,5,6.

No small feat since they were huge. It took about three secretaries to open each, as there were almost no men in this office.

'Then the paper storm began. The contents of the wastepaper baskets were torn to shreds and tossed below, followed by candy wrappers, newspapers, and anything of paper that could be torn to shreds. Then followed the toilet paper from all the bathrooms. Finally, the old insurance rate books and telephone books were being torn to shreds. The merriment was at its highest when the noise finally reached the inner sanctum and the head of the firm emerged shrieking for us to close and lock the windows. He then ordered the supervisors to go down to the street and search for anything with the company name on it. We were then ordered to restore the office to normal. When the supervisors returned, saying no documents or company records were on the street below, we were finally told: "Since I see I can get no more work done today, you might as well go home."

'It was a very emotional time for all, tears as well as laughter. It meant husbands returning home, no more lives to lose and a return to normalcy. For me, it meant that my husband Harry could finish graduate school, and that my brother and friends would be returning home safely.

'As I came out of the front entrance of our building I was astonished to find the paper scraps almost ankle deep, like snow on the ground. The sidewalks were crowded, but everyone was in a jocular mood. New Yorkers were actually talking with one another! Bringing up the rear of the parade was New York City's finest, the Mounted Police Patrol, and what a beautiful sight they were. Watching them in action was an event in itself. Believe me, they are effective in controlling crowds, one doesn't argue with a 1,000-lb horse with sharp iron shoes! Watching the Mounted Police in action was something I shall always remember.

'Since the parade disrupted the bus service, I started walking home. The paper drifts were varied, deeper in front of those high-rise office buildings and the ground almost bare in other places ... just like a snowstorm on the prairie. Halfway down Fifth Avenue I discovered the Sanitary Department workers already at work on that enormous task of clearing New York City of its paper storm.'[1]

In Australia, *HMS Pioneer*, an aircraft repair ship, was being fitted out in Perth harbour on May 7, for service in the Pacific. Its complement included Joe Simons, a radio mechanic with the Fleet Air Arm. Taking a bus from the town to the port, he recalled, 'I overheard local Australians quietly discussing the news and one said "Of course, it will not make

---

[1] Marjorie B. Jaffa, letter to the author, 13 November 1994.

much difference over here". Knowing the situation from
had heard on board ship, I inferred that the war in Europe
this was confirmed when we boarded ship.' The next day
given 'make and mend': a half-day holiday. 'Of course aft‿ ‿
to get on with our war against the Japanese.'[1]

In the New Zealand city of Auckland, where the flags and bunting had
already been unfurled in anticipation of VE-Day, Europe's false afternoon
news that the war was over came in the early hours of the morning,
before dawn. 'Some there were who had been sitting by their loudspeakers
through a night of waiting,' the *Auckland Star* reported on the following
day. 'To them, early, came the news. Germany had surrendered. It filtered
into bakehouses, into telegraph operating rooms, into engine sheds, and
was seized upon with avidity by early morning workers. Telephones
buzzed in awakening clamour in hundreds of homes as the news was
passed on. It sounded like VE-Day. And then came the announcement.'
VE-Day would be on the following day. 'The sun shone, though the
morning was cold with an early winter chill. It felt like a day for glad
tidings and celebrations. But the official voice said "No." '[2]

One city that did celebrate liberation on May 7 was Orléans. For five
years the Germans had forbidden any public manifestation of their historic day, on which Joan of Arc had driven the British from the city 526
years earlier. The British Ambassador, Alfred Duff Cooper, and the Papal
Nuncio, Angelo Roncalli (later Pope John XXIII), were both present
during the ceremonies.

Amid all the newspaper reporting on May 7, one source was strangely
silent: the journalist pool at Supreme Headquarters Allied Expeditionary
Force. The censorship rules there had still to be obeyed. Bitterly, a British
journalist, David Walker, cabled to his editor: 'This must be the greatest
single Press fiasco of all time. While the peace news has been broadcast
all over the world, British and American newspapermen's copy still lies
here pending the permission of officialdom. Even in their defeat, the
Germans can laugh at us for our confusion, and for those who have been
abroad on war stories since 1938 and 1939, this is the final humiliation.
It is a pity that SHAEF lacks the courage of Lord Nelson, who put his
telescope to a blind eye; the only advantage they seem to have over
Nelson is that they are more at sea.'[3]

*   *   *

[1] Joe Simons, letter to the author, 10 October 1994.
[2] 'This VE-Eve, Uncertain City. Poised For Peace', *Auckland Star*, 8 May 1945, p. 3,
col. 3.
[3] 'I can't tell you it's over', *Daily Mirror*, 8 May 1945, p. 8, col. 6.

Manya Breuer had been born in Berlin before the war. She was one of a thousand Jewish refugees who had been brought to the United States from Naples in August 1944, and given asylum for the duration of the war in a military camp, Fort Ontario, at Oswego in upper New York State. She recalled the cry going up from all over the camp: 'The war is over, the war is over!' It came from every direction. 'Could it really be true? Was it for real? Germany was defeated, Germany surrendered, or was I only dreaming of all this? People were running all over the place, in the barracks, outside, all the voices combined sounded like a swarming beehive. Oh God! I had to make sure and find out for myself. I picked up my little baby, Diane, from her crib and clutched her to my heart and, like a bird, flew down the stairs, out of the house, into the fresh, free air blowing at me from the clear blue waters of Lake Ontario that had cradled and safeguarded me from harm in the last few months. People laughing and crying while I was looking for my husband Ernest. I ran into Lisl, my sister and my friends Edith Semjen and Mrs. Munz. "Manja, Manja, the war is over! The nightmare is gone." We all hugged and kissed each other while tears were running freely from our eyes. Our emotions overpowering. My lips were softly forming prayers of thanks. Blessed be Thou, Oh Lord of Israel, King of the Universe, who has saved my life! Please let me find my Mama and Papa, Sigi and Willi and please let me find them safe back again.'[1]

Manya was anxious to speak to the woman who had been instrumental in bringing the thousand refugees to the United States. 'I had to find Ruth Gruber and share this with her. I am free and I am alive. No more running from the Nazis, no more concentration camps, no more separation from loved ones, no more bombs, hate and hunger! I have made it, and come out of this horror with the most grateful heart for the Allies, who so gallantly made this possible.'[2]

Ruth Gruber, a special assistant to the Secretary of the Interior, Harold L. Ickes, was working at her desk in Washington when Manya telephoned, 'Ruthie, the war's over. We're free. Maybe my father's alive. My mother. My brothers. Dear God, keep them alive!

'The camp's crazy,' Manya Breuer went on breathlessly. 'We're running from one barracks to another hugging, screaming, laughing, crying.'

---

[1] Manya Breuer's brother Willi survived the war in an Italian orphanage, disguised as a young Fascist. Her mother survived internment in Gurs, in southern France. Her brother Sigi survived Auschwitz. Her father survived in hiding in Italy, protected by an Italian priest in his church. 'My father found me due to a newsreel he had watched about the liberation of Rome which showed me kissing an American soldier.' Manya Breuer, letter to the author, 29 November 1994.

[2] Manya Breuer, letter to the author, 17 November 1994.

Then her voice dropped. 'But what's going to happen to us now? Will they let us out of the camp? Will we be allowed to stay in America?'

The decision to allow these thousand refugees into the United States had been made, at President Roosevelt's urging, after a long internal discussion among the officials concerned, and with one condition. Before boarding ship in Italy, the refugees had been asked to sign a paper promising to return to Europe when the war was over. 'For me,' Ruth Gruber later recalled, 'the day the war ended was a bittersweet victory. The joy that no more soldiers would be dying, no more Jews murdered, my brother would come home alive,[1] was darkened by the knowledge that the government had plans to return the thousand refugees to their countries of origin. "What's going to happen to us now?" Manya asked me, anxiously, while outside my office windows, bells were pealing, horns were honking, people were singing songs and celebrating.

Amid the peals of victory, Ruth Gruber had to help plan a strategy to persuade the policy makers to allow the refugees to stay permanently in the United States. 'The heads of the State, Justice and Treasury Departments insisted that they must keep their pledge to the dead President and send the people back to Europe,' she recalled. 'Ickes, in Interior, with the help of private agencies, fought to keep them in America. "How can a country like ours", he asked, "with only 137 million people, send back a thousand?" In the end, Ickes prevailed. Christmastime 1945, President Truman allowed the refugees in the camp to apply for citizenship.'[2] Only then, for Ruth Gruber, was the war truly over.

In the Far East, fighting had continued on all fronts throughout May 7. In both Britain and the United States, there was recognition that this struggle would be hard and prolonged. A communiqué from South East Asia Command that day reported the capture of Japanese guns and equipment at Yenanma in Burma, by General Slim's Fourteenth Army, but other troops were being hampered by the heavy monsoon rains. In Sydney, a spokesman at the headquarters of the British Pacific Fleet announced that eighteen Japanese planes had been destroyed in a com-

---

[1] In the Bavarian town of Bad Lippspringe, Ruth Gruber's brother, Dr Irving Gruber, a captain with the Ninth Army, had taken over, with a single enlisted soldier, a small hospital run until then by German nuns. Their patients were Russian slave labourers rescued from the nearby salt mines. 'Irving had enlarged the hospital to two hundred beds,' Ruth Gruber later wrote, 'and was running it the day the war ended.' Ruth Gruber, letter to the author, 30 September 1994.

[2] Ruth Gruber, letter to the author, 21 September 1994. Ruth Gruber has told the story of the Oswego refugees in *Haven: The Unknown Story of 1,000 World War Two Refugees*, Putnam, New York, 1983.

bined sea and air bombardment of airfields on the island of Miyaka, 550 miles south-west of Japan.

From the Washington bureau of the *Chicago Daily News*, Paul R. Leach told his readers: 'Germany has reportedly surrendered after five years and eight months of Hitler's attempt to rule the world, but for the United States the war is only half finished. Another would-be master race, Japan, remains to be taught a lesson for all time. For that reason the fighting Government, from President Truman down, is seeking greater public support than ever for a smashing finish – and peace for all our time.'[1]

In San Francisco, General Jan Christian Smuts submitted his suggested preamble to what was intended to be a new World Charter which would underpin the future work of the United Nations. This was the Declaration of Human Rights, which was to become a beacon of hope for political prisoners throughout the world, including those in the Soviet Union, one of its signatories.

On May 7, Truman took up official residence in the White House for the first time. Since becoming President on April 16 he had been living at nearby Blair House, while Eleanor Roosevelt remained at the White House. Her departure on April 30 had been followed by the arrival of painters, carpenters and renovators. Truman's daughter Margaret had brought in her piano, but, the *New York Herald Tribune* reported, 'No plans for entertaining of any kind are scheduled until the end of the thirty-day mourning period for the late President Roosevelt.'[2] Truman himself was to celebrate his sixty-first birthday on 8 May, his first full day at the White House.

During the night of May 7, and as May 8 dawned, there was a sense of elation throughout the liberated and Allied lands that an era had come to an end, and that justice had been done. In a London hospital, a maternity nurse, Alice Redlisch, who had come to Britain as a refugee from Berlin in 1938, recalled how, at that moment of triumph for the Allies, 'the babies born were called Victoria, Victor and such.'[3] They were to be witnesses of the exuberance of that moment for the rest of their lives.

A fifteen-year-old German boy had, like many hundreds of thousands of those of his age, been called up to serve in the last months of the war. For some months he had been assisting an anti-aircraft battery. On May

---

[1] 'US Job Half Done – Jap Next', *Chicago Daily News*, 7 May 1945, p. 1, col. 2.
[2] 'Truman's Move to White House On Eve of Victory and Birthday', *Herald Tribune*, 8 May 1945, p. 1, cols. 6 and 7.
[3] Alice Fink (née Redlisch), letter to the author, 1 November 1994.

7, he was walking home. 'We walked on the railroad tracks, because the roads were full of Americans. We had our Hitler Youth winter uniforms on, since we had no civilian clothes. We spent the night on straw in a signal box. The next morning we heard the news that the war was over.'[1] The boy was Helmut Kohl.

[1] Johannes Steinhoff, Peter Pechel and Dennis Showalter (editors), *Voices From The Third Reich, An Oral History*, Regnery Gateway, Washington DC, 1989, p. 488. Helmut Kohl later became Chancellor of the Federal Republic of Germany (1982–)

IX

VE-Day Dawns

8 May 1945

At one minute past midnight on Tuesday, May 8, VE-Day, so long awaited, began. In London, at his wartime headquarters in Storey's Gate, facing St. James's Park, the Prime Minister asked one of his secretaries, Elizabeth Layton, to come into his room for the nightly dictation. A mass of documents awaited his scrutiny: diplomatic telegrams, intelligence summaries, reports from the now-silent war zones, and reports from the British forces fighting in Burma. As his secretary entered the room he looked up from his desk with the words: 'Hello, Miss Layton. Well, the war's over, you've played your part.' She had been with him for more than three years, including his wartime journeys to Ottawa, Moscow and, five months earlier, to Athens amid civil war.

In a letter to her parents written when the dictation was over that night, Miss Layton described how, as she entered the room, 'an enormous thunderstorm broke – claps, bangs and crashes. He kept saying, "What was that? Oh, thunder", because it sounded like rockets, not because he thought it might be! Then he'd say "Might as well have another war. What was that? Oh, thunder."'[1]

VE-Day had begun with an explosion of nature. There had been a similarly violent thunderstorm on the night of September 2, 1939, when Neville Chamberlain was still hesitating to declare war on Germany, and a group of his Cabinet Ministers, angered by what they saw as a demoralising and possibly even sinister delay, hastened to Downing Street to insist that Britain carry out its treaty obligations to Poland at once.

Among the telegrams requiring Churchill's attention in the early hours of May 8 were several which gave more information about the recent arrest by the Soviet authorities, near Warsaw, of General Okulicki and the fifteen other Poles who were meant to be travelling to Moscow under safe conduct. The same Poland whose fate had led Britain and France to

---

[1] Elizabeth Layton, letter to her parents, London, 8 May 1945. Private archive.

declare war on Germany in 1939, was still not be be allowed to decide its own political future. From the British perspective, the villain in both cases was the Soviet Union, which in 1939 had signed a pact with Germany effectively sealing Poland's fate, and in 1945 was seeking to impose on Poland a Moscow-backed communist regime.

It was not until 3.45 a.m. that Churchill finished his work and went to bed. By then the newspapers were on the streets. In *The Times* there was a stark reminder of the cost of the war. The daily list of 'fallen officers' still had its place on the Court page. 'We have received news of the death of the following officers . . .' the column began.[1] The front-page headline of *Stars and Stripes* carried an implicit reminder that the war was still being fought against Japan. The headline read:

IT'S OVER, OVER HERE

An inside page declaimed:

SIX DOWN, TWO AXIS PARTNERS REMAIN TO BE PUT OUT OF WAR[2]

and an article on what remained to be done stated bluntly, 'Germany has been crossed off the list of Allied war enemies; the blasting of Japan lies ahead.'[3]

In the Far East the fighting was continuing without respite. Every VE-Day newspaper reported on the battles still being fought against Japan. On Tarakan Island, off the coast of Borneo, Australian and Dutch troops had taken full possession of the airfield, using tanks, flame-throwers and demolitions 'to reduce the maze of pill-boxes and inter-communicating tunnels'. In New Guinea, Australian troops, in a four-mile advance, had occupied Cape Wom, within three miles of the Japanese-held town of Wewak, and had captured 'quantities of equipment and supplies'. Other Australian forces had penetrated inland, seizing the village of Ranimboa. Heavy bombers had attacked the Japanese naval yards, arsenal and fuel depot at Saigon, in French Indo-China. 'Storage

---

[1] 'Fallen Officers', *The Times*, 8 May 1945, p. 8, col. 5. The officers were Commander R.I. Money, Royal Navy, Lieutenant W.H.J. Hogg (Irish Guards), Captain D. MacFadden (Parachute Regiment), Lieutenant H.R.H. Marriott (Buffs), Lieutenant T. Reeves (Grenadier Guards), Lieutenant R. Tudsbery (Royal Horse Guards), and three Air Force officers, Squadron-Leader R.P. Bacon, Flying Officer C.R. Fairbairn and Flight-Lieutenant D.G. Rochford.

[2] *Stars and Stripes*, 8 May 1945, p. 3, cols. 3 and 4. The six defeated powers were Germany, Italy, Bulgaria, Finland, Hungary and Roumania. The powers still at war were Thailand and Japan.

[3] 'The Final Battle Lies Ahead In Japan', *Stars and Stripes*, 8 May 1945, p. 7, cols. 1 to 4.

tanks were directly hit, and large fires and explosions were seen through-out the area, with smoke billowing 15,000 feet.'[1]

American soldiers in Europe, reading their *Stars and Stripes* on the morning of May 8, rejoiced in the one-word headline

VICTORY

and in a front page full of zeal and congratulations. On turning to page two, however, they found a column which gave details of the fighting against Japan. From American Field Headquarters in South China came a report of Chinese ground forces and American air forces 'fighting a full-dress battle against the Japanese in the interior of the country'. The newspaper added that for the first time in eight years of war in China, Americans were 'performing such activities as strategic planning, directing air cover, assisting in artillery attack and directing communi-cations'.

There was also a report of the latest casualty figures issued by General MacArthur in the Philippines. In the week ending May 5, a total of 11,028 Japanese soldiers had been killed and 462 taken prisoner. American losses that week were 391 dead and 1,323 wounded. Fighting was continuing on Mindanao Island, where Japanese hill positions had been attacked west of Davao City. In the seas nearest to Japan, American bombers had sunk or damaged twenty-four Japanese ships. The British Pacific Fleet, in its first major bombardment while operating with the United States Fifth Fleet, had shelled the southern Ryukyu Islands. Fifty American bombers, based on the Marianas, had attacked airfields on Kyushu, the southernmost island of Japan. On Okinawa, where three thousand Japan-ese soldiers had been killed during the previous week, American troops had 'resumed their general offensive.'[2]

The reaction of those troops to the news that the war in Europe had ended was described by a *Life* correspondent. 'Americans on Okinawa passed a heartbreaking few minutes when they heard the news about Germany,' he wrote. 'A war had ended for the people of Europe and for many Americans, yet for them the danger of death was still imminent. Reports of a conference trying to prevent future wars had a hollow ring to men still in battle in southern Okinawa, where the Japanese held

[1] 'Flame-throwers Drive Japs From Centre Of Tarakan', *Rand Daily Mail*, Johannesburg, 8 May 1945, p. 1, cols. 4, 5.
[2] *Stars and Stripes*, 8 May 1945. Editions of *Stars and Stripes* were being printed in London, Paris, Nice, Naples and Pfungstadt (Germany).

tenaciously to their line in the hills. At sea around the island Japanese planes kept up strong attacks against U.S. ships.

'Reports of German atrocities did not shock Americans in the Pacific. From the inner councils of MacArthur to the plainest private they had known they were fighting an enemy adept in cruelty. They were reminded by pictures of Japanese executions of captured fliers which were passed from hand to hand. The Pacific war was still grim and the Americans fought to advance it to a point where new forces from Europe could help them begin final offensives.'[1] To emphasize this point, *Life* printed on the facing page a full-page photograph showing a Japanese officer bringing down his sword on the neck of a bound and blindfolded Allied airman.

Through the pages of *Stars and Stripes*, the news of continued fighting against Japan reached the American troops who were celebrating the end of the war in Britain, France and Germany. For many of them it was a sobering, and even a fearful thought, that they might have to move, and move quickly, from Europe to Asia, and to another war. On VE-Day itself they had the dubious pleasure of reading an article by David A. Gordon, a staff writer with *Stars and Stripes*: 'Now that European shooting is over, and countless gallons of questionable cognac, half-passable wine and anaemic beer have been swallowed in celebration of the event, soldiers in the ETO[2] are asking "What now?" The first idea which soldiers might well throttle in their noggins is a return, *tout de suite*, to their homes. The transfer of ETO troops to the Pacific has been in progress for some time now, although on a small scale. Army officials have declared that there would be a rapid transfer of greater numbers immediately following VE-Day.' The decisive factor would be one of transport alone. 'The amount of shipping available,' Gordon explained, 'will determine the speed with which units are transferred to the Pacific or returned to the United States.'[3]

There was a detailed report of the fighting on Okinawa in the *New York Herald Tribune* on May 8. One of its correspondents, Homer Bigart, was with the XXIV Army Corps. In a wireless message printed on page one he reported that after seventeen days of 'bitter fighting' troops commanded by Major General John R. Hodge 'have entirely secured an abrupt coral escarpment (Hill 196) north of Shuri'. Bigart added: 'Nagging slowness and brutal exhaustion mark this struggle.'[4]

---

[1] 'Pacific War, Savage Battles Continue As Europe's Peace Comes', *Life*, Overseas Service Edition, 14 May 1945, p. 48.
[2] The European Theatre of Operations.
[3] *Stars and Stripes*, 8 May 1945.
[4] Homer Bigart, 'Hill 196 Taken In Bitter 17-Day Okinawa Fight', *Herald Tribune*, 8 May 1945, p. 1, col. 2.

In Burma, the reaction of the British troops to the news of victory in Europe was summed up by *The Times* special correspondent as: 'The war is over. Let us get on with the war.' Not all the troops in Burma had heard the news by May 8, but among those who had there was 'deep thankfulness and rejoicing'. Even for the men who were engaged in fighting the Japanese, the news of VE-Day held out certain avenues of hope. 'The thought uppermost in the minds of the British soldier is repatriation,' *The Times* explained. 'At last, he hopes, it will be possible to reduce the term of overseas service.' The senior commanders had another perspective on the news from Europe. For them, it was the prospect of an upsurge in landing-craft, flame-throwers, aircraft, trucks and shipping that loomed. 'At last we shall get the equipment we want. We have fought and won the Burma campaign on a shoestring, but the days of shoestring campaigning will soon be over.'[1]

On May 8, *Union Jack*, the British Forces newspaper in Italy published a full page headed,

THE EYES OF THE WORLD NOW TURN TO THE PACIFIC

Its large map of the Far East bore the caption: 'Before the fighting citizens of the Empire can pack up and go home there's one more score to be settled.' The article began: 'The other half of the war has still to be won. Perhaps it has had less attention than it deserves amid all the excitement of recent weeks over events nearer home. But there has never been any real excuse for forgetting that this is part of the same war.' In a war of attrition Japan 'might be able to hold out for a long time'. Her manpower situation was not yet critical. Her Fleet remained in being. Her hold over the Chinese land mass was considerable. There was no sign of 'her people's fanaticism' being broken. 'She will no doubt try to play the waiting, wearing game, seeking to drive the Allies into disunity or disillusionment. The answer will be to carry the war to the enemy with ever-increasing vigour until the job is finished.'[2]

An indication of how that job was going appeared in the stop press section of the newspapers which Londoners bought on May 8, in a British United Press report from Manila, in the Philippines, earlier that day. Under the headline 'Tarakan Nearly Cut In Two' the report as published in the *Daily Mail* stated: 'Allies cleared ground east of the main oilfield

---

[1] 'Our Special Correspondent', Rangoon, 8 May 1945, *The Times*, 9 May 1945, p. 3, col. 4.
[2] 'The Eyes Of The World Now Turn To The Pacific', *Union Jack*, British Forces Daily, Eastern Italy edition, 8 May 1945, p. 7, cols. 1–5.

of Tarakan, off Borneo, and advanced across the island to within a mile and a half of the east shore. Fighting continues for Tarakan town.'[1] This good news contrasted with an article in the same paper that same VE-Day, sent from Manila by Lachie McDonald, in which he described how American naval observers just back from Tarakan were 'shaking their heads dubiously' over the lack of adequate engineering equipment among the Australian troops who were bearing the main brunt of the fighting on the island.

In his report, which was not the most uplifting that day, McDonald wrote of the American naval officers: 'While full of praise for the ingenuity and energy of the Australian troops, they are openly fearful that lives will be sacrificed needlessly unless the Allied units doing these jobs in future have the right equipment in sufficient quantity. One of the Americans, Vice-Admiral Daniel E. Berbey, Commander of the United States Seventh Amphibious Force, had said on the previous day: "At Tarakan I saw lines of motor vehicles brought to a standstill all morning and part of the afternoon because the pontoons were not long enough. At least one pier was not repaired at the end of the second day, when great piles of supplies mounted up at the seaward end. This was not the fault of the Australian engineers and soldiers, who sweated all day and night. They laboured like mules because they had to use their hands and backs instead of machines. I saw engineers tackling with handsaws great piles that had to be cleared from a shattered section of the pier. They took three days to do a job which Americans on the spot told me could have been done in twelve hours with the right equipment. The Australians also heaved huge logs from the beach manually, when a machine could have done the job in a fraction of the time." '[2]

Surprisingly, this report was passed by the censor. More encouraging, though given far less space, was a report in the *Birmingham Evening Despatch*. 'More telling blows against the Japanese are reported from the Far East today – air blows on the Japanese mainland and China Coast, and important new gains by Allied forces on the four Pacific island battle-fronts of Okinawa, Mindanao, Luzon and Borneo. Shanghai was bombed for the second time within a week, its waterfront and shipping being one of the targets – in a series of air blows along the Chinese coast by nearly a hundred American planes of all types.'[3]

In its main leader-page article on VE-Day, *The Times* focused on the

---

[1] 'Tarakan Nearly Cut In Two', *Daily Mail*, 8 May 1945, p. 1, col. 8.
[2] Lachie McDonald, 'Allies Equipment In East Is Poor', *Daily Mail*, 8 May 1945, p. 4, col. 7.
[3] 'Important New Gains In Pacific', *Evening Despatch*, 8 May 1945, p. 1, col. 3.

work of the Royal Australian Air Force in the Far East. This was a sympathetic account by the newspaper's Australia correspondent of the dangers facing the Australian airmen. 'In Europe,' he wrote, 'you are over populated areas; if you bale out you are within reasonable distance of medical aid and food. Flying over the jungle and ocean of the south-west Pacific, your chances even of reaching the ground safely are remote, and you are dependent on yourself for survival. Possibly you are hundreds of miles from any habitation except perhaps a native village whose people may not be friendly.' Although the main Australian air base being used against Japan was at Leyte in the Philippines, nearly two thousand miles from Australia, 'the airmen look forward to further targets. They want a share in the attack on the Japanese homeland.'[1]

It was not only the war against Japan that intruded on to the pages of the celebrating newspapers on the morning of May 8, and dented their readers sense of joy and relief. From Radio Moscow that morning came the most 'stupendous' of all the details of wartime civilian deaths. Four months earlier Russian troops advancing through southern Poland had reached the site of Auschwitz. A Soviet commission of inquiry was immediately set up, and on May 7 its findings were published in *Pravda*. 'Over four million people were exterminated there,' *Pravda* reported. 'Three to five railway carriages packed with people arrived daily at the camp, and 10,000 to 12,000 persons were killed daily in death chambers and their bodies burned. This camp, set up directly by the German Government, was organized by Himmler, who personally inspected it and acquainted himself with the methods of mass extermination and himself gave instructions. On his orders the camp was extended and provided with new methods of extermination. Correspondence between the camp administration and German industrial enterprises on the construction of incinerators, gas chambers, and other equipment fell into the hands of the Soviet State Commission of Inquiry. On the direct initiative of the German Government a system of offering rewards for the killing of prisoners was introduced. It was suggested that a good way of collecting the cash was to kill the inmates during an alleged escape. None of these criminals from the organizer and chief hangman, Himmler, down to the rank and file will ever escape just punishment. They will be discovered in any of the hospitable neutral countries and on every uninhabited island.'[2]

This was the first report on Auschwitz to appear in print since the

---

[1] 'Over Jungle And Ocean', *The Times*, 8 May 1945, p. 7, cols. 6 and 7.
[2] 'Himmler Ruled Camp Horrors', *Star*, 7 May 1945, p. 4, col. 2.

revelations published the previous November by five escapees from the camp. The Soviet details, awaited since the camp was liberated in January, created a further chill of recognition of the scale of Nazi tyranny.[1]

The report was picked up and published in the British and American newspapers on VE-Day, mostly on their front pages.

REDS SAY NAZIS SLEW FOUR MILLION IN POLISH CAMP

was the headline in the *New York Herald Tribune*. The Russian report told of mass murder, described mounds of children's clothes and adults' gold teeth taken from the victims, and listed the systematic cruelties perpetrated against the camp's inmates.

Three features in particular of the published report are immediately striking. Nowhere in it was the name Auschwitz mentioned, only Oswiecim, the Polish name for the town. Nowhere did the name Birkenau appear, yet this was the adjacent camp in which by far the largest number of the killings had taken place. And nowhere in the published summary did the word 'Jew' appear, although more than eighty per cent of those killed in Auschwitz were Jews. *The Times* report referred to 'citizens of the Soviet Union, Poland, France, Belgium, Holland, Czechoslovakia, Yugoslavia, Hungary, Italy and Greece'. Yet with the exception of the Soviet Union, tens of thousands of whose prisoners-of-war were murdered there, the nationals of the other countries mentioned had been almost entirely Jewish. *The Times* also pointed out, from the Soviet report: 'Seven tons of women's hair was found, ready for despatch to Germany'.[2] It made no mention of the fact that the women from whom this hair had been shorn, shortly before they were murdered, were Jewish.

Another report issued on May 7, and published in the British newspapers on VE-Day, was the official British Government enquiry into the Bengal famine of 1943 and 1944, and the epidemics that followed it, during which a million and a half Indian men, women and children had died. The report was issued from Delhi. Although one reason adduced for the famine was the loss of Burmese rice as a result of the Japanese occupation of Burma, the Commission concluded that the famine could have been prevented 'by resolute action at the right time to ensure an

---

[1] The figure of four million was exaggerated, though the numbers murdered at Auschwitz, principally Jews, but also Poles, Russian prisoners-of-war and Gypsies, exceeded one million, The 10,000 to 12,000 a day figure related to the period between May and July 1944, when more than 400,000 Hungarian Jews were deported to the camp and killed there.

[2] '4,000,000 deaths at Oswiecim Camp', *The Times*, 8 May 1945, p. 5, col. 3.

equitable distribution of the available supplies', and found the Government of India 'culpable' of not setting up sooner than it did a system of planned movement of food and grains, including rice, between the surplus and deficit provinces.[1]

There were other items of news presented to British readers on May 8, which made for sombre reading. One was an official announcement of the British wartime civilian death toll. It was more than sixty thousand. In the *Daily Mail* this appeared as a small item on page three. In precise figures as published that morning, 26,920 of those killed were men, 25,392 were women and 7,736 were children. A further 537 of those killed were 'unclassified'.Those injured totalled 86,175, of whom more than seven thousand were children under sixteen.[2] In the First World War, the civilian death toll from German Zeppelin and bombing raids had been just over a thousand.

Another distressing item related to the showing of the British newsreel films of the liberation of Belsen. This had already become a subject of public controversy. In its VE-Day issue, the *Daily Sketch* published two letters which took opposing points of view. The first was from V. du Bedat Smythe in Bournemouth, who wrote: 'I feel that I should be lacking in a sense of duty and moral courage if I failed to voice a strong protest against the public showing of a film illustrative of the German Horror Camps. If it is intended to foster a spirit of hatred against persons of that nationality, were not many of the victims themselves German?'[3]

Underneath Smythe's letter the newspaper published one from Mrs Beryl Statham of Weston-super-Mare, who wrote, describing herself as a mother of three children: 'I suggest that the films showing the German atrocities be shown regularly every three or four years all over the country, so that our children, now too young to be allowed to see such horrors, shall see with their own eyes when they are old enough with what they will have to contend in the building of the peace. Real peace can only be obtained through education, and to see these films should be a part of every adolescent's education. These atrocities will mean nothing until they see them with their own eyes, and in their full belief in them lies the only hope for peace in their time.'[4]

The outrage felt at the films of Belsen had not diminished. In the

---

[1] 'Bengal Famine', *The Times*, 8 May 1945, p. 5, col. 5.

[2] 'Civilian Toll – 146,760', *Daily Mail*, 8 May 1945, p. 3, col. 6.

[3] In fact, at Belsen, as at Dachau, almost all the victims in each camp when it was liberated were Jews, mostly of Polish, Lithuanian and Hungarian origin, though this was not immediately clear at the time.

[4] 'Horror Camp Films', *Daily Sketch*, 8 May 1945, p. 2, cols 4, 5.

House of Commons on VE-Day, the War Minister announced that films of the concentration camps would be shown to all German prisoners-of-war in captivity in Britain.

On the morning of May 8, Stalin made one last effort to postpone the announcement of the Allied victory until May 9, on the grounds, Admiral Cunningham noted in his diary, 'that there was still fighting going on on the Russian Front'. 'This,' Cunningham added, 'will be resisted.'[1] In a telegram which reached Churchill just after midday, Stalin told him that the Soviet Supreme Command was not convinced that the German High Command order regarding unconditional surrender, although broadcast by Schwerin von Krosigk on the previous day, would be carried out by German troops on the Eastern Front. 'It must be borne in mind,' Stalin wrote, 'that the resistance of German troops on the Eastern Front is not slackening and, to judge from radio intercepts, an appreciable group of German forces is openly declaring its intention to continue resistance and not to obey Dönitz's order for surrender.'

The Soviet High Command would therefore prefer, said Stalin, to wait until the time when the German surrender actually entered into force, at one minute past midnight on May 8, 'and accordingly to postpone the Government announcement on German surrender until May 9 at 7 a.m. Moscow time.'[2] Churchill could do no more. As had become clear on the previous day, Moscow would celebrate the end of the war on May 9. London and Washington would stick to May 8, the second consecutive day on which crowds had gathered in the streets to celebrate. The Chiefs of Staff were as determined as Churchill to allow no further postponement. 'It will not be possible for me,' Churchill replied to Stalin, 'to put off my announcement for twenty-four hours as you suggest. Moreover, Parliament will require to be informed of the signature at Reims yesterday and the formal ratification arranged to take place in Berlin today. I have spoken with General Eisenhower on the telephone and he assures me of his intention to co-operate to the full, with all forces, against any fanatical groups of the enemy who may disobey the orders they have received from their own Government and High Command. This would of course apply to all British troops under General Eisenhower's command. I shall make it clear in my announcement that there is still resistance in some places. This is not surprising considering the

---

[1] Admiral Cunningham, diary, 8 May 1945. National Maritime Museum, Greenwich.

[2] 'Immediate, Secret and Personal, Marshal Stalin to Prime Minister', telegram of 7 May 1945, received 8 May 1945: Foreign Office papers, 371/50581.

immense length of the Front and the disorganized condition of the German Government.'[1]

Churchill now worked on the final text of his victory statement to be broadcast in two hours' time.

The Germans had surrendered, VE-Day had come, and yet Flensburg radio, still controlled by Admiral Dönitz and his Government near the Danish border, was reported on May 8 to be broadcasting 'anti-Soviet propaganda'. One sentence which monitors in Britain picked up, and which caused particular offence, was published in the evening papers on VE-Day. The German announcer had declared: 'In the last few hours of the war our troops were fighting hard to save Germany from Bolshevism.'[2] Scarcely a week earlier, in announcing Hitler's death, Hamburg radio had stressed that he had 'fallen in the fight against Bolshevism'. In the name of that fight, ten million Russian civilians had been killed, and several million Russian soldiers murdered in captivity.

When Dönitz himself broadcast from Flensburg on May 8, his reference to the Soviet occupation of the eastern half of Germany was oblique. The German people should walk in defeat 'dignified and courageous', he said, 'in the hope that our children may one day have a free, secure existence'. He was able to announce one change that the Allies considered essential in any future Germany. All connection between the German State and the Nazi Party had been severed. 'The Nazi party has left the scene of its activity,' he said.[3] A few hours later Flensburg radio announced that the Nazi salute, '*Heil Hitler!*', was abolished. That same day the German Navy, which the new ruler of Germany had commanded at the height of its powers, suffered its final humiliation, as all German submarines, the U-boats which had caused such enormous losses to Allied and neutral shipping and to the lives of sailors and merchant seamen, were ordered to surface and to report for instructions to the nearest Allied commanders. 'So is ended one of the most formidable of Hitler's threats to the United Nations,' commented the *News Chronicle*.[4]

On VE-Day morning the Channel Islands were still under German control. On Guernsey, 23,000 islanders had submitted to the swastika since June 1940. German troops were still in occupation of the island

[1] Prime Minister's Personal telegram, number 823 of 1945, 'Most Immediate, Clear the Line, Personal and Top Secret', 8 May 1945: Foreign Office papers, 371/50581. Public Record Office, Kew.

[2] 'German radio is still anti-Russian', *Evening Standard*, 8 May 1945, p. 1, col. 6.

[3] 'Dönitz Proclaims End Of Nazi Party In Reich', *Stars and Stripes*, 9 May 1945, p. 1, cols. 4 and 5.

[4] 'Sea Power', *News Chronicle*, 9 May 1945, p. 2, col 2.

when, at 10 a.m. on May 8, the two senior German officers on the island, Corvette-Captain Reich and Baron von Aufsess, called on the Bailiff and informed him that the war was over 'in Guernsey as well as elsewhere'. The two Germans then assured the Bailiff 'that until such time as the Allies arrive in the Island, they will on their side do all that is necessary to ensure that the discipline of their troops will be maintained and that they will govern themselves in an orderly manner *vis-à-vis* the civilian population.' At noon the Bailiff reported this to the Island's council, and announced: 'At 3 p.m. this afternoon all flags can be hoisted throughout the Island.'[1]

With the occupation forces still in place, and before a single British soldier had arrived, Guernsey's war was over, and with it all the restraints of occupation. For the first time it was possible to print the news that a Guernsey man, Major Wallace Le Patourel, had been awarded the Victoria Cross for his bravery in action in North Africa in 1942.

In Holland, May 8 witnessed the arrival of the second wave of Allied troops. At seven that morning the Canadian 1st Division crossed the frontier, driving along the autobahn through Amersfoort and Utrecht to Rotterdam. A senior Canadian officer who followed that route, Major-General Harry Foster, recalled: 'My first problem was with the Dutch underground. They were armed and wanted to shoot every German, Dutch quisling and collaborator they could lay their hands on. In several towns German soldiers and collaborators were executed before I could put a stop to it. It was hard to blame the Dutch. They had been through hell. God, how they hated the Boche! There was an immediate urgency to get the Germans out of Holland.'[2]

Over Britain, in line with the weather forecast, the day began bright and clear. For nearly six years the British people had been denied the traditional daily weather forecast in an attempt to prevent the Germans from gaining any useful information with regard to their own bombing and naval plans. On May 7 it had been announced that these restrictions were at an end, and so it was possible to publish the weather forecast on the morning of VE-Day. The forecast read: 'Wind freshening; warm and sunny at first but rain can be expected later. Last night the glass was falling a little: indicating that the sudden warm snap of yesterday will not continue.'[3]

---

[1] 'Fly Your Flag At Three This Afternoon!', *Guernsey Weekly Press*, 15 May 1945, p. 1, cols. 1 to 9.
[2] Quoted in Tony Foster, *Meeting of Generals*, Methuen, London, 1986, pp. 444–5.
[3] 'Weather – as before', *Daily Mirror*, 8 May 1945, p. 3, col. 2.

The forecast was wrong. After a thunderstorm in the night, when more than half an inch of rain fell in half an hour, the day had dawned bright and clear. By afternoon London was basking in what was known as 'King's weather', with a temperature of 75° Fahrenheit, fourteen degrees higher than the average for early May.

London was celebrating on May 8, with crowds larger than any since Armistice Day, 1918. 'A wonderful day from every point of view,' Noel Coward wrote in his diary. 'Went wandering through the crowds in the hot sunshine. Everyone was good-humoured and cheerful.'[1] June Caller, a fifteen-year-old London schoolgirl, was taken by her father to Whitehall. 'I remember being extremely frightened walking up Villiers Street and crowds came down. Of course they were happy crowds, but they were very scary.'[2]

George Bendori, who had been brought to Britain from the German Baltic port of Stettin in 1939 as an eleven-year-old refugee, later wrote: 'I was only sixteen, the day the war ended, but vividly remember for days sitting in front of the wireless, eagerly awaiting Jerry's collapse. When it came on the 8th, people thronged the streets, embraced one another, shed tears of joy and danced on the pavements. No doubt everyone was happy that the boys were going to come home, forgot having spent endless nights in the "Anderson Shelter" – a dug out in the back yard – or countless nights in the underground stations. The frightful "Blitz" was finished with and so was the horror of the "Doodlebugs", never knowing where they were going to land after their engine cut out.'[3]

More than three thousand Londoners had been killed between June and December 1944 by Hitler's last two secret weapons, the pilotless aircraft bomb the V–1, and the rocket bomb, the V–2, known as 'doodlebugs'. That menace, which had also killed hundreds of civilians in Antwerp, had been hateful and fearful to those who experienced it. Relief, as much as elation, was a predominant emotion on May 8, as Shoshanah Feldschuh, a true cockney born within the sound of Bow Bells, recalled: 'I thought it was good that my father could finish with his Home Guard duties and my mother was very busy as an unofficial social worker travelling most of the time from West Finchley, where we lived, to East Finchley, Highgate and other places to help families whose fathers were in the

---

[1] Graham Payn and Sheridan Morley, *The Noel Coward Diaries*, Weidenfeld and Nicolson, London 1982, p. 92.

[2] June Jacobs (neé Caller), in conversation with the author, 4 September 1994.

[3] George Bendori (formerly Rechelmann), letter to the author, 25 August 1994. 'My whole family, it was surmised after the war, were gassed in a German concentration camp' (letter to the author, 6 October 1994).

army. I was relieved that my brother could finish with his work setting up radar on ships at ports on the South Coast. Also as I travelled every day from West Finchley to Tottenham Court Road on the tube I must have thought it was wonderful that families no longer had to sleep on the platforms of the Underground and, the best of all, not to have to go everywhere with a gas mask!

'None of us really knew what horrible things had been happening in Europe,' Shoshanah Feldschuh added. Like so many others with families who lived in Europe, and had been trapped there when war broke out, it was not until after the war that the details of their fate became known. 'My mother lost her three brothers and their families in Warsaw, and I dread to think what happened to them.'[1]

Among the thousands of schoolboys taking advantage of a day off school on VE-Day was the seventeen-year-old Leonard Wolfson, who went by train from Worcester to London, hoping to see the King and Queen on the balcony at Buckingham Palace. On reaching Paddington he made his way to the Mall, but the crowds were already so thick that he could make no headway and walked instead across Horse Guards Parade and towards Birdcage Walk, hoping to get to the Palace from there. There were fewer people about, and Birdcage Walk, when he reached it, was closed off to the public. At that moment Churchill emerged from his wartime headquarters at Storey's Gate. Pushing through the small crowd, the excited schoolboy tried to touch him. A policeman pushed him back. Churchill, who saw what had happened, called out: 'Leave the boy alone' and gave a V-sign. 'What a moment that was for a schoolboy,' Wolfson recalled fifty years later.[2]

Churchill got into his car and was driven to the Palace for lunch with the King. It was a little after one o'clock. 'We congratulated each other on the end of the European War,' the King wrote in his diary. 'The day we have been longing for has arrived at last and we can look back with thankfulness to God that our tribulation is over.'[3]

For many of those whose war was over, there were still long and difficult journeys to be made. During May 8, two hundred Lancaster bombers brought back more than 13,000 former British prisoners-of-war to Britain. At the air base at Westcott the loudspeaker announced: 'We have now completed the landing of our 30,000th ex-prisoner-of-war at this

[1] Shoshanah Feldschuh (formerly Rose Crafchik), letter to the author, 29 September 1994.
[2] Lord Wolfson of St Marylebone, in conversation with the author, 14 October 1994.
[3] Quoted in John W. Wheeler-Bennett, *King George VI*, Macmillan, London, 1958, page 625.

station. Well done, boys and girls! Let 'em all come.'[1] Yet the homecoming of the prisoners-of-war was often hard, and their exposure to freedom difficult. A few found a hero's welcome, including the legless Wing-Commander Douglas Bader, who visited the House of Commons on VE-Day 'looking very fit after his years in a German prison camp'.[2]

The newspapers on VE-Day had good news for millions of serving soldiers, sailors and airmen in Europe and Britain: demobilization would begin in six weeks. But those between the ages of eighteen and twenty-seven who were working in factories no longer needed for war production would be called up for military service. Women in industry, whether married or single, would be allowed to leave their jobs, provided they had 'household responsibilities' or wished to join their husbands on release from the forces.[3]

When the House of Commons met at 2.15 p.m., one of the first questions related to returning prisoners-of-war, and their liability to be posted overseas after six months. In his reply, the Secretary for War, Sir James Grigg, while stating that this question was one of many 'to be reconsidered in view of the events of the last twenty-four hours', pointed out that he had come across cases where men who had been repatriated earlier on medical grounds from German prisoner-of-war camps 'had pressed and pressed to be allowed to fight against the Japanese'.

The question was then raised about the education of German prisoners-of-war in Britain. It was pointed out that Vera Brittain's book *Testament of Youth* 'had been forbidden circulation among English-speaking prisoners-of-war in this country'. This was indeed so, the Minister confirmed. The reason, he explained, was 'that one of the main theses of the book was that the Allies in the last war committed a great offence against the Germans because the Treaty of Versailles was too severe, and he certainly did not think that that was suitable for circulation among the German prisoners.' There were cheers at this answer.

A question was also asked that touched on one of the most sensitive final British acts of the war, the drive to the Baltic in order to prevent Russian troops entering Denmark. An Independent Member of Parliament, W.J. Brown, asked whether 'the dropping of airborne Russian troops on Denmark was part of the Allied strategical plan; or whether this action was taken by the Russian Government alone'. The implications of the question were avoided when the Chancellor of the Exchequer, Sir

---

[1] David Rolf, *Prisoners of the Reich, Germany's Captives, 1939–1945*, Leo Cooper, London, 1988, p. 186.
[2] 'Bader, Legless Ace, is Back', *Evening News*, 8 May 1945, p. 1, col. 3.
[3] 'Demobilisation May Start In 6 Weeks', *Daily Sketch*, 8 May 1945, p. 3, cols. 4, 5.

John Anderson, replied: 'It was no part of any inter-Allied strategic plan that Russian troops should land in Denmark from the air, and, so far as His Majesty's Government is aware, no Russian airborne troops have in fact been so landed.' There was laughter.[1]

As May 8 progressed, scattered German military garrisons and units were still surrendering. At 2 p.m. the German garrison at St Nazaire, on the Atlantic coast, surrendered to the Americans. An hour later the Dame of the small Channel Island of Sark raised both the British Union Jack and the United States Stars and Stripes over her tower. There were still 175 Germans on the island, and not a single Allied soldier. The British Army, three officers and twenty men, arrived two days later.

In the Austrian village of Strobl, eight miles east of Salzburg, SS troops had been guarding one of Hitler's most important hostages, King Leopold of the Belgians, whose armies had been overwhelmed in the first westward dash of German armour in May 1940. Local civilians had told the American troops in the area where the King and those with him were being held. A rescue mission was carried out at once, and on May 8 an Associated Press message from the United States Seventh Army announced that soldiers of the American 106th Cavalry had overpowered the SS and released the King, his mother, four children, and eighteen members of the royal staff. 'All were in good health.'[2]

Eire, which under the leadership of Eamon de Valera had preserved its neutrality throughout the war despite British pressure to join the Allies, was the last country in the world to have diplomatic relations with Germany. On VE-Day, the senior German diplomat in Dublin, Dr Hempel, called on de Valera, and handed over his legation to Eire's care. He and his staff would return to Germany. Unlike the German diplomats in Spain, Portugal, Sweden and Switzerland, who had been ordered by their host governments to leave their posts and return home, those in Dublin did so voluntarily.

On VE-Day two white-painted flying boats reached Stockholm. In one of them was a senior British officer, Brigadier-General R. Hilton, of Scottish Command, who was authorised to accept the capitulation of all German forces in Norway. Travelling with him was Crown Prince Olav, the Norwegian Commander-in-Chief, returning to his native land after five years in exile. Once the surrender was signed, all German forces had to make their way to the Swedish frontier and to internment in Sweden.

---

[1] *Hansard*, 8 May 1945.
[2] 'King Leopold of Belgium and Queen Freed by Yanks', *Chicago Daily Tribune*, 8 May 1945, page 1, column 4.

Norway, whose resistance forces had been active throughout the war, was free. Members of the Norwegian Government prepared to leave London for Oslo, followed by King Haakon.

In April 1940, in one of its most humiliating setbacks, the British Navy had failed to capture the principal Norwegian ports before the Germans arrived and Norway was overrun. Among the lost battles was that for Trondheim. VE-Day saw the reversal of that defeat when, with the German surrender, a British naval squadron entered the port. A further forty-eight British ships had entered Oslo Fiord. That same day, a British newspaper reported: 'Prison gates opened all over Norway yesterday to release the victims of five years of Gestapo terror – and the Norwegians are busy filling the prisons up again with quislings.'[1]

The Norwegian fascist leader Vidkun Quisling had tried to make his way to Sweden, but was turned back at the frontier that day by the Swedish authorities. Arrested by the new Norwegian authorities, he was put on trial, found guilty of treason, and sentenced to be executed by firing squad.[2]

In Sweden, ten thousand refugees from Nazi persecution had awaited the news of Germany's defeat with eager anticipation. 'When the news was announced on May 8,' Walter Goetz, then living in the town of Borås, recalled, 'everybody poured on to the streets. The cessation of hostilities, the fall of Nazi tyranny, was cheered no less enthusiastically in neutral Sweden than it was in liberated Denmark.'[3] Goetz had been one of nearly six thousand Danish Jews who in 1943 had been ferried to safety in a single night by the determination of the Danish people not to allow them to be rounded up and deported to Germany.

Switzerland, like Sweden, had managed to preserve her neutrality in both world wars, although, from the moment Italy joined the war in June 1940 and France capitulated, she had been surrounded by Axis or Axis-controlled powers. Her borders, although fortified and defended, were exposed to any German desire to crush her neutrality and acquire her wealth. The landlocked country's precarious position did not prevent those fleeing from Nazi tyranny from seeking refuge there. Indeed the only two effective avenues of safety from German-dominated Europe were across the Pyrenees into Spain, or into Switzerland. One of those who took the Swiss mountain route was Alexander Rotenberg, a Belgian-born Jew who, while a refugee in the South of France in 1941, before

---

[1] 'Our Warships In Norway – Quisling Tries To Bolt,' *Daily Mirror*, 9 May 1945, p 7, col 3.

[2] The death sentence on Quisling was carried out on 24 October 1945.

[3] Walter Goddard (formerly Goetz), letter to the author, 26 October 1994.

the German occupation of the Vichy zone, had helped a wounded British soldier, Sergeant Arnold Howarth, to escape from Europe and rejoin his regiment for the battle in Sicily. In September 1942, after a fourteen-hour trek across the high mountains east of Chamonix, Rotenberg reached Switzerland. 'The pro-Allied Swiss were subdued,' he later recalled. Hitler was still the master of western Russia and North Africa, and Rotenberg was held, with hundreds of other refugees, in an internment camp at Girenbad. 'We slept on a concrete floor on half an inch of straw.' After the Allied victories at Stalingrad and Alamein, the Swiss attitude changed, and, as the war came to an end, Rotenberg, then aged twenty-three, was studying philosophy at the University of Basle. 'I was doing my homework in my room,' he later recalled, 'when all of a sudden I heard screaming and newspaper vendors calling out, "The war is over". I was in tears. The owner of the apartment, a French Swiss, provided drinks, kirsch for everybody. "We're not going to let you cry", he said.'[1]

Most of Rotenberg's family had been deported by the Germans from Belgium and killed. His tears were those of a survivor, who in the moment so long awaited, knew that grim news could be expected. There were more than 100,000 refugees in Switzerland on VE-Day. That day, as a gesture of new-found independence, the Swiss Government dissolved the Swiss branch of the German Nazi Party, and expelled its leader, Wilhelm Stengler. It had already announced, on the previous day, that 'individuals who have committed acts in violation of the laws of war will not be granted asylum' and that every arrangement 'to prevent the entry of undesirable aliens, either by forged passports, by aeroplane, or by other means, has been made'.[2]

One individual who arrived in Switzerland that day, by air from Germany, was Haj Amin el-Husseini, the Mufti of Jerusalem, who had thrown in his lot with the Axis in 1941, supporting the pro-German Rashid Ali revolt in Iraq, and visiting Hitler in the hope of preventing the emigration of Bulgarian Jewish children to Palestine. In Bosnia, the Mufti had raised a pro-German military force. Described in the Swiss newspapers as a 'sworn enemy of Britain', the Mufti was escorted to the French frontier by Swiss police.[3] In the Middle East, the British Cabinet was later told, 'the fate and whereabouts of the Mufti have been the subject of frequent

---

[1] Alexander Rotenberg, in conversation with the author, 18 October 1994. In 1987 Rotenberg published *Emissaries, A memoir of the Riviera, Haute-Savoie, Switzerland and World War II*, Citadel Press, Secaucus, New Jersey.
[2] 'War Criminals', *Palestine Post*, 8 May 1945, p. 3, col. 5.
[3] *L'Express*, Neuchâtel, Switzerland, 9 May 1945.

rumours and widespread interest. He is still accepted as symbolical of Arab nationalism.'[1]

The Mufti managed to evade capture in France, making his way by various stages first to Cairo, and then to the Lebanon, where he died in 1974, at the age of seventy-seven.

Spain had also remained neutral throughout the war, even resisting Hitler's pressure after the fall of France in 1940 to allow German troops to march through the peninsula on their way to Gibraltar. British agents in Spain had succeeded in acquiring the stocks of cork needed for refrigeration of transatlantic food supplies. The British Government had promised Spain that in the event of a German invasion, Britain would undertake the training of anti-German guerrilla forces. Publicly, however, the allegiance of Franco's Spain seemed, overtly, to be very much on the side of Germany, which before 1939 had contributed arms and air power to the overthrow of the Republicans in the Spanish Civil War, and for whom Spain had provided troops to fight against the Soviet Union. Six years after the end of the Civil War, Spain remained a divided country. In Barcelona, memories of German air raids on the republican city were still vivid. It was hardly surprising, therefore, as P.H. Dorchy, Press Attaché at the British Consulate-General in Barcelona, reported to London three days after VE-Day, that news of the Allied victory in Europe 'was welcomed by probably ninety-five per cent of the population of Barcelona in their heart, but on the other hand, there was little sign of any external demonstration as a White Terror had been instituted by the Party thugs over ten days ago, most of which had been armed by the Spanish authorities'.

The Barcelona newspapers, Dorchy added, had received special instructions from Madrid 'to play down the Allied victory and play up Franco's part in keeping out of the war'. But the 'true feelings' of the people could be gauged by 'the avalanche of callers and the number of cards and letters received by the Consulate-General, apart from the innumerable verbal congratulations lavished on one wherever one went'. Any more open manifestation of delight was frowned upon. Those flying Spanish flags in celebration were ordered to take them down 'as it was not a Spanish feast day'. As many as thirty people had been arrested daily since the beginning of May for 'commenting favourably on the Allied victory'. Throughout May 8 and May 9, in contrast to the reported

[1] Cabinet Paper number 47 of 1945, 'Report for the Month of May 1945 for the Dominions, India, Burma and the Colonies and Mandated Territories, Report by the Secretary of State for the Colonies', 25 June 1945: Colonial Office papers, 323/1871/13. Public Record Office, Kew.

celebrations elsewhere in Europe, 'Barcelona presented a perfectly normal appearance, nobody daring to exteriorize their feelings in the fear of immediate repression from the Party patrols. One unfortunate wretch who did was seized by them and hung up for three hours by his wrists to a high railing.' He was finally taken down, 'but can get no redress.'[1]

In the last weeks of the war, under the courageous auspices of the Swedish Red Cross, thousands of concentration camp prisoners had been brought out of Germany to Sweden. Although Heinrich Himmler's attempt to gain some Allied support for his idea of a united Western Front against the Russians had failed, the efforts of the Swedish mediator, Count Folke Bernadotte, had resulted in the agreed transfer of human beings from imminent danger of death in eastern Germany to safety. Groups of prisoners were taken from Ravensbrück concentration camp north of Berlin, and from the harbour in Kiel, to which thousands had been brought by the Germans, from Stutthof and other concentration camps, across the Baltic.

Some of those who were brought to Sweden were too weak to survive, despite all the efforts of the Swedish Red Cross to nurse them back to health. One who did survive was Hans Jakobson, originally from the Latvian capital of Riga, almost all of whose family had been murdered there by the Nazis. In February 1945, as Russian forces approached the labour camp at Lenta, where Jakobson was working, he had been taken from there by sea in the hold of a cargo ship, first to a prison in Hamburg and then to a labour camp at Kiel. He had been one of the fortunate ones to be taken to Sweden on the last day of April, under Red Cross protection. He recalled: 'I experienced the May 8, 1945 in Malmö, Sweden. On this day I was in quarantine, with many other Jewish and non-Jewish fellow sufferers, in a school in Malmö, where we slept on mattresses placed on the floor in the classrooms. Everything brought by us from Kiel, such as clothes, shoes, etc., was taken from us and burned. We were given a shower, de-loused and disinfected. This was followed by a thorough medical, to see whether anyone had a contagious disease (typhus, dysentery, tuberculosis, etc.), which was the reason for this fourteen-days quarantine in Malmö. Many of our companions died in Malmö.

'On May 8 I was still alive and was saved, but at this time we were not sure if we wanted to live! I was physically emaciated, with a shell wound in my leg. My thoughts at that time were of my loneliness, with no relatives. All had died. This I knew, without being able to understand

---

[1] P.H. Dorchy, report: Foreign Office papers, 371/49588. Public Record Office, Kew.

the language of the country, without having graduated, without any money at all. Various thoughts went through my mind, as to what would happen to me. I was in a foreign country which had a different way of life, different customs and usages. Of course the people who were in charge of me were kind to me.

'I tried to be optimistic and enjoy life, and I had faith in the future. The medical rehabilitation proceeded, and on or about May 8 I was told that I was not suffering from any contagious disease and that I would soon be released from quarantine. In fact, I was released about a week later on. My mental condition was not the best at this time! The future was so uncertain.

'On May 8, 1945 I began to remember everything that I had been through, what I had lost, and what tortures and mortal fears that I had to undergo. During my long four camp years I had neither the time nor the inclination to think about things in a true perspective. At that time I was too concerned with the job of surviving. Now that I am free, I am asking myself how it was possible to go through all that and survive. Just surviving had been a miracle. On May 8, my thoughts were about all of the terrible things I had gone through, the times I had stared death in the face, yet in spite of everything had managed to survive! I was glad to learn that Germany had surrendered, and that I could spend the last week of the war in Sweden and not in that dreadful labour camp in Kiel-Hassee. The impossible had happened, I had been saved from this camp, from the criminal regime that had physically debased my life, away from those terrible SS people, who had humbled me so much.'[1]

A few days after VE-Day, an official from the Soviet Embassy in Stockholm suggested to Jakobson that he might consider returning to Latvia, which had been annexed to the Soviet Union. Jakobson declined. Instead, he would stay in Sweden. He did so, marrying Genia Dvorkin, another of those who had been brought to Sweden by Count Bernadotte in the first days of May, and starting a new life. Today, at the age of seventy-two, he can recall every episode of his wartime torment, and unexpected salvation. Genia Dvorkin recalled her first days of freedom, as a seventeen-year-old Polish girl, in quarantine in a camp in southern Sweden. 'After four years in camps', she wrote, 'and after suffering hard labour during this time I was in a poor state of health, my body weight was very low, and my lungs had been affected. It was here in this camp that I realized that I was alone in the world; all my family was dead. I nurtured a certain, if tiny hope, that someone might have survived. How-

---

[1] Hans Hirson Jakobson, letter to the author, 27 September 1994.

ever, it later turned out that I had been hoping in vain. I was totally alone. Despite the beautiful time of the year and the warm spring and despite the good care I received from the friendly people around me, I was like a fish out of water – in a country with a strange language, and with no anchor in my life.' On arriving in Sweden at the beginning of May, 'we were deloused, and we all had to hand in our clothes; our old clothes and shoes were burned because of the risk of contamination. At the time, we were told that if we had anything of value, we could keep it. I kept my concentration camp uniform with my prisoner number 6762 as a valuable (!) possession.'[1]

In Egypt, which had been threatened first by Italian and then by German armies four years earlier, a mass of military and air forces formed the main reserve of the Allied strength in North Africa, as well as the focus of intelligence activity throughout the eastern Mediterranean. Among those stationed near the Suez Canal was Leading Aircraftman Paul Thompson, from Denham in Buckinghamshire, who recalled: 'VE-Day on the 8th was what we'd all been waiting for! It took some time for such stupendous news to sink in. But, the Commander of our RAF base at Shandur, Great Bitter Lake, knew what to do! First, a day off, in which to celebrate. Next, open up the NAAFI, and every man for himself! Ever tried riding a donkey while inebriated?' Thompson added: 'My Service and Release book indicates that I was in the Middle East for forty-seven months and sixteen days!'[2] After many months of virtual stagnation as the war came slowly to an end, and the servicemen in Egypt had less and less to do, life suddenly went on 'at a quickened pace, for "Roll on that Boat" was on everyone's mind.'[3] Leave, and returning home, had become the aspiration of the hour.

Two hundred miles west of Egypt, Major Ernest Beiser, Royal Army Medical Corps, was at Barce in Cyrenaica on VE-Day. Born in Vienna before the First World War, he had made his way to Palestine shortly before the outbreak of the Second World War, and had enlisted in the British Army the moment 'enemy nationals' were allowed to do so. At his army base in Cyrenaica were British, Sudanese and Nigerian troops. 'The end of the war, long expected and overdue, left me with two contrasting feelings. The first was happiness and relief that the slaughter had ended with the fall of Hitler and his cohorts, thankfulness and admiration

[1] Henia Jakobson (formerly Genia Dvorkin) letter to the author, 27 September 1994.
[2] Paul D. Thompson, letter to the author, 7 August 1994.
[3] Paul D. Thompson, letter to the author, 20 September 1994.

for Churchill's leadership, the stamina of the British people, the unbelievable fighting spirit of the Red Army and Roosevelt's getting the United States into the war, greatly helped by the trigger of Pearl Harbour. On the other side I had no illusions of Hitler's promise that the end of European Jewry was about to materialize. All my family, parents, uncles, cousins perished in the camps. Through GHQ I sent cables to the Jewish communities in Vienna and in Boskovice, Moravia, the home cities of my parents and grandparents. My fears came back in cables two months later: "Deported, no further news available." One of my uncles, Dr Simon Batisl of Vienna, a First-Lieutenant in the Austrian Hungarian army in World War One was together with another 317 Jewish officers kept in isolation in Vienna and then deported to Yugoslavia in April 1943. All these officers were murdered by Croatian Ustashis, sure and devoted allies of the Nazis.

'In camp at Barce, the Officers Mess was heavy with smoke and happy drinking. The lieutenants, captains and a few majors discussed hopefully some leave before being shipped out into the Pacific Theatre of War to fight against the Japs. My Commanding Officer with his Military Cross was busily discussing plans to shift the victorious armies against Russia and finish off communism. Nursing one drink carefully, I was able to bring a good number of my brother-officers back to their quarters, most were stoned. The Other Ranks celebrated noisily and happily.

'So there was really "triumph and tragedy" in my mind. I was not yet thirty-four years of age, had a young, beautiful wife back in Tel Aviv, a baby boy of eight months, believed this to be indeed the end of all wars.'[1]

Beiser could remember the end of the First World War. He was just seven years old when his father took him to their local station at Boskovice, on the Vienna-Prague railway line, just as a train was drawing in. 'When the elegant express stopped for water and coal, I enjoyed the spectacle. While the train was just moving off, in the direction of Prague, a group of some ten excited men came to the station running, took down the station flag of the Austro-Hungarian monarchy, and replaced it by a new flag, Red, Blue and White, the flag of Czechoslovakia. There was no violence, but my father, a good German-speaking Austrian Jew, shook his head and said to me: "Something extraordinary is happening. We will see about the outcome." The Habsburgs were our Kaisers for centuries!

'This all happened to my father and me on 28 October 1918. I continued to go to my one-room schoolhouse. . . .' In March 1938 Hitler annexed Austria, and in October 1938 Boskovice was incorporated into

---

[1] Ernest Beiser, letter to the author, 25 August 1994.

the Third Reich. Four months later, Beiser had left for Palestine. But the fate of those with whom he had spent the inter-war years was always in his mind, from the moment he left Europe to VE-Day. 'The tragedy I feared on May 8th, 1945 involved family, friends, acquaintances. All of them indeed were long gone. With them went a world of culture, the Vienna of music, literature, medicine, journalism, the friendship with Gentile boys and girls, the good feeling there had existed between my parents and their Catholic neighbours. I met later two survivors of Auschwitz, and I felt guilty for the freedom and dignity I had experienced while serving in the British Army.'[1]

At Barce, Beiser recalled, 'night had fallen, and the noise had petered out, when I got a call to come urgently to the railway station. A young soldier, drunk, had slept on the flat roof of the station building, and had fallen some ten metres to the ground. I found a boy of seventeen, South African Signals, bruised but in good shape, no bone injury, no bad trauma. He had landed in a flower bed, was terrified that I would tell his Commanding Officer that he had been drunk. That was his only concern. I took him home to his barrack.'[2]

In French North Africa, several hundred miles west of Barce, VE-Day had a very different aspect. While France celebrated victory over Germany, with her army poised to take up its position as one of the four occupying powers, rebel nationalists in Algeria, who had been crushed in a series of punitive expeditions before the war, renewed their struggle. On the day the war ended in Europe, twenty-seven Europeans were murdered when a violent struggle erupted in the streets of Algiers and Oran. The disturbance spread rapidly. The British Consul-General in Algiers, J.E.M. Carvell, reported to London on an anti-French demonstration at Sétif, held under the guise of a victory parade: 'A scuffle then took place and a policeman drew his revolver and shot a native. More shots were fired both by the police and by French civilians who were watching the procession from balconies overlooking the street. Pandemonium then ensued. Indiscriminate firing by French and natives took place; unarmed natives seized chairs and anything on which they could lay their hands, and persons were attacked regardless of race, colour or creed.'

In Sétif and its immediate surroundings forty-nine Europeans, including the Mayor and the Headmaster of a school, 'both very popular with Europeans and natives alike', were killed. The secretary of the local

---

[1] Ernest Beiser, letter to the author, 1 October 1994.
[2] Ernest Beiser, letter to the author, 25 August 1994.

branch of the Communist Party 'had both his hands cut off by an axe'. The news of these events 'quickly spread eastwards by "bush telegraph" and the whole of the area between the sea and a line running from Sétif to Souk-Ahras flared up in open revolt. Armed attacks were made on guards. Farms were burnt and their occupants murdered. Europeans encountered on the roads were attacked and killed ... There were instances of rape and mutilation of corpses. A priest was killed and his heart was cut out and strung round his neck in mockery of well-known religious pictures. Nearly all the European casualties took place in the areas around Sétif (49 killed), Perigotville (21 killed) and Guelma (27 killed).' More than a hundred Europeans were killed that day.

The French authorities took immediate and strong counter-measures. 'Troops, including a Senegalese battalion, and armoured cars were despatched from Algiers, Sidi Bel Abbès, Biskra, Bougie and Constantine,' Carvell reported. 'At the request of the French authorities a detachment of seventy-five men of the Foreign Legion were conveyed from Sidi Bel Abbès in four Royal Air Force transport planes to a landing ground near Constantine. A French cruiser and a sloop were despatched from Algiers to Bougie and bombarded concentrations of rebels in the Souk el Taine area. Considerable air activity took place, it being estimated that approximately three hundred sorties were made by B26s and P38s during the period 8-14 May. While it is said that 250lb bombs were used, it is thought that action was mostly confined to machine-gunning and the use of anti-personnel bombs. Reports from aerial observers indicate however that whole villages have been destroyed. By May 10 the situation was well in hand.'[1]

Such was VE-Day and its immediate sequel in French North Africa. The French action was certainly effective in the short term. A British Intelligence report commented: 'The French authorities are understood to have carried out punitive air bombing in the Guelma district and to be bringing reinforcements by air from France. There is no reason to doubt that they have the situation well in hand.'[2] In the British Foreign Office there was greater scepticism. 'The French dealt ruthlessly with the revolt, but it may flare up again if economic conditions become worse,' one official commented. 'I am sure much bloodshed might have been avoided if the French military had not been so eager to engage in wholesale slaughter,' wrote another, and he added: 'As Syria has

[1] J.E.M. Carvell, British Consulate General, Algiers, report No. 86, Algiers, 23 May 1945: Foreign Office papers, 371/49275. Public Record Office, Kew.
[2] 'France', Weekly Political Intelligence Summary No. 293, 16 May 1945: Foreign Office papers, 371/50421. Public Record Office, Kew.

shown even more forcibly, they do not know how to deal with native unrest.'[1]

While French Algerian troops had been fighting against the Germans in northern Europe, new Muslim leaders had emerged in French North Africa whose aim was independence from France, and whose inspiration was the Koran. Three leaders in particular, Ferhat Abbas, Sheikh Brahimi and Hadj Messali were preaching violent revolution. Many of the Europeans who died that day were hacked to death. The day of revolutionary victory had not yet dawned, however. Hardly had the Parisian celebrations ended than General Duval, the French military commander of the Constantine region, took immediate punitive action. Whole villages were burned to the ground, 'and it was said that German and Italian prisoners-of-war were armed by the French to put down the insurrection'.[2]

Even as the VE-day riots were erupting throughout Algeria, the United Nations delegates in San Francisco had in front of them a telegram from the exiled President of the Front for the Defence of North Africa, Sheikh Mohamed al Khidr Hussein, who was then living in Cairo. 'Your congress, endeavouring to establish universal peace and freedom eliminating by this act oppression imposed on subject small nations by aggressive big ones,' he telegraphed, 'should remember that in North Africa, Tunis, Algiers and Morocco, twenty-five million Arabs maladministered severely oppressed and shamelessly deteriorated by France. The Front for Defending the Interests of these Nations is impatiently waiting the Congress initiative, which is benevolently directed for the happiness of all nations, to submit this case hoping it shall obtain full justice and declare their rights in full freedom and independence as these nations are of the principal one of the globe and peace can never be maintained without being content with what the Congress shall arrive at on their behalf.'[3]

No notice was taken by the United Nations of this telegraphic appeal, though it was considered provocative enough by the British authorities in Cairo to forward a copy to the Foreign Office in London. It was to be almost two decades, dominated by the war of independence which broke out in 1954, before Algeria obtained its independence from France: an act made possible in 1962 by the decision of General de Gaulle, who

---

[1] 'Native uprising in the Department of Constantine', Foreign Office papers, 371/49275. Public Record Office, Kew.

[2] Charles Williams, *The Last Great Frenchman, A Life of General de Gaulle*, Little, Brown and Company, London 1993, p. 300.

[3] Night Letter Telegram, Cairo, 24 April 1945, intercepted by the British authorities in Egypt: Foreign Office papers, 371/49275. Public Record Office, Kew.

on 8 May 1945 had celebrated the European victory in Paris while the Algerian insurrection entered a new and violent phase.

The British war with Germany had stirred in the Jews of Mandate Palestine a deep desire to join the war effort and to contribute to the defeat of Hitler. Thirty thousand, out of a population of only half a million, had volunteered to join the Forces. Several thousand had fought with the British Army. Many had served in the Royal Air Force and the Royal Navy. A few had volunteered for one of the most dangerous tasks of all, to be parachuted behind German lines. At the same time, the British Government's restrictions on Jewish immigration had generated deep hostility, and the likelihood of post-war British opposition to Jewish statehood had generated a spate of violent activities, led by two main terrorist groups, Etzel and Lehi. The main Jewish self-defence group, the Haganah, opposed this terrorism, and denounced it to the British, but the tensions between ruler and ruled were considerable. 'The Jewish celebrations on VE-Day,' the British Cabinet were told, 'took the form of ebullitions of nationalist sentiment. In Tel Aviv few flags save the Zionist blue and white and occasional red banners were in evidence.'[1]

Living in Tel Aviv at that time, and in the city on VE-Day, was the eighteen-year-old Lucien Steinberg. In 1943 he had fled with his mother from the pogroms and forced labour camps of Roumania. Four members of his father's family had been murdered by Roumanian fascists during the pogrom in Jassy in 1941. His father had died of a heart attack in 1942. Lucien and his mother had left Roumania and reached Palestine, travelling by train through Bulgaria, Turkey, Syria and Lebanon, then by boat to Haifa. 'On that VE-Day, in Tel Aviv,' he later recalled, 'the speech of Winston Churchill[2] on the radio was listened to with both attention and deep emotion. In the evening people danced in the streets. I definitely cannot say how the other people felt and why they danced; of course, the feeling that it was over and one's life preserved played the main role. But at that time Tel Avivians were not heavy alcohol drinkers, in fact the drunkards were exceedingly few. Drunkenness was the "privilege" of the British and accessory of the Australian soldiers. There were no more Aussies in Tel Aviv at that time, but they had left strong, friendly memories.

'One knew, on VE-Day, about the concentration camps Majdanek,

---

[1] Cabinet Paper number 47 of 1945, 'Report for the Month of May 1945 for the Dominions, India, Burma and the Colonies and Mandated Territories, Report by the Secretary of State for the Colonies', 25 June 1945: Colonial Office papers, 323/1871/13. Public Record Office, Kew.
[2] For Churchill's speech, see chapter 10.

Auschwitz, Treblinka, but of course mainly about Buchenwald, Dachau, Belsen. But – one was *not dead* and one could and did rejoice. I myself had lost part of my family in the pogrom of Jassy, but why should I not frolic on VE-Day in Tel Aviv, on the sea-shore with a very nice girl, whose name – shame on me! I do not remember?

'But then came a disturbing incident, at least for me: on Allenby Road, just in front of Wittmann's ice cream parlour – a well-known landmark even then – an elderly gentleman (maybe he was only about forty-five, but to me he seemed elderly) did not participate in the general joy. He said, more or less (I cannot quote, of course), that the war that had just ended was not a victorious one as far as Jews and particularly Jews in Palestine were concerned. "Our war, your war, is still to come!" he said.

'Was his voice prophetic? Did it seem so to me only in retrospect? Quite frankly, I could not swear to it, one way or another. One more remarkable fact: the Etzel and Lehi were already active against the British "occupant". However, most of the people, including the youth, were following the directives of the Haganah. But just before VE-Day and on VE-Day itself, there was an unproclaimed truce. Due, probably, to the illusion that the British would henceforth adopt a more friendly line towards the Jewish positions. Such British military as were in Tel Aviv were all but mobbed by the Jewish revellers and joined the dance.'[1]

In Jerusalem that morning, outside the King David Hotel, the British High Commissioner for Palestine, Field Marshal Viscount Gort VC, surrounded by senior civilian and military personnel, saluted the hoisting of the Union Jack and the flags of the other Allied nations. As the flags rose to the top of their mastheads the band of the Palestine Police Force struck up 'God Save The King'. The High Commissioner then proceeded to the Collegiate Church of St George for a noonday service.

During the day, 'in token of the overwhelming victory won by His Majesty's Forces and the forces of our gallant Allies in their fight to liberate Europe from oppression', Lord Gort granted an amnesty for a number of political prisoners, Jews and Arabs. Then the citizens of Britain's most troubled Mandate celebrated the victory. 'Gaiety broke bounds late in the afternoon,' the *Palestine Post* reported. 'Hundreds of flags and pennants and bunting flying from most of the buildings in the centre of the town and decorating the squares sprang into life in the cooling breeze. Cars and buses and trucks, also beflagged, sounded their horns, and suddenly the empty streets were jammed with crowds.' On the steep slope of Ben Yehuda Street wine flowed freely where 'out of

---

[1] Lucien Steinberg, letter to the author, 4 September 1994.

three huge barrels, servicemen passing the Carmel Mizrahi shop were served free drinks. By 6.30, 8,000 glasses had been poured.'

The free wine was welcome, but although most British soldiers joined in the celebrations 'they could not help feeling their homesickness more keenly on the great day,' wrote the *Palestine Post*, 'and many of them were heard to say, "What a time I would be having if I were in Blighty now".'[1] By contrast, Otto Lilien, from Jerusalem, was in England that day, and had been for some years, serving with the Royal Air Force photographic intelligence. He had helped to prepare the photographs needed for the liberation of France and Holland. His wife Lore recalled: 'When I returned from my work at the RAF Headquarters Jerusalem, where I worked as civilian typist, my two daughters met me very excited and I was so determined to do something special with them. We walked along King David Road towards the centre of Jerusalem. I had to give them a special treat. I bought each some *ice cream*. That was the greatest treat I could give them at the time.'[2]

Another Jerusalemite who celebrated that day was Yaere Yadede, who at the age of seven had survived the Arab massacre of sixty-seven Jews in Hebron in 1929 by hiding with his family in a basement. In 1945 he was employed by a local bakery to deliver bread throughout the city. This he did by bicycle, starting every morning at four and making a circuit of the city's hills. 'On that day,' he later recalled, 'I never made it to Mount Scopus, which normally would be a hair-raising ascent, on my faithful friend, the bicycle (accustomed, one way or another, to defy any British curfews over the Jewish-inhabited areas). For the moment I reached that other mountainous road, Ben Yehuda Street, my eyes beheld the celebrating crowd, and celebration it was. Halfway up the street, there was a huge "Carmel Mizrahi" wine barrel, the like of which I had never seen before, and, what shall I say, not having been accustomed to the good stuff, my prospective bicycling trip up the mountain to the university was literally washed out – in wine, that is.'[3]

Unknown at that moment to Yadede, his German-born mother had just reached the safety of a DP camp in southern Germany, having spent the war successfully concealing the fact that she was Jewish, first by pretending to be a refugee from the Allied bombing of Berlin, then under false Aryan papers as a 'regular' resident of the town of Memmingen. 'The worst period for her was the time between her "coming clean"

---

[1] 'V-Day Gaiety In Jerusalem', *Palestine Post*, 9 May 1945, p. 1, cols. 3 to 5.
[2] Lore Lilien, letter to the author, 24 August 1994.
[3] Yaere Yadede, letter to the author, 12 August 1994.

26. Crowds cheer as the ministers of the wartime coalition, headed by Winston Churchill, appear on a balcony overlooking Whitehall.

27. Churchill on the roof of his car amid cheering crowds, 8 May 1945. *See page xxx*.

28. A crowd gathers in Wood Street, Walthamstow, to listen to Churchill's broadcast. Two loudspeakers have been placed above the shop at number 93.

29. The Mall, London, 8 May 1945.

30. The Champs-Elysées, Paris, 8 May 1945.

31. Celebratory chaos in the streets of London, 8 May 1945.

32. An open-air street party in London, 8 May 1945.

(after the liberation) and her being admitted to a DP camp, since, after all, the good citizens of that nice German small town (read: Nazis) were "shamelessly" deceived by such a "Jewish swine" as her, and while the rulers had changed, the people remained the same. It was, she told me later, the most frightening thing, at the very point in time when she might have thought the moment for a sigh of relief had come.'[1]

In Transjordan, VE-Day was celebrated, according to a British Cabinet report, 'with more genuine and spontaneous feelings of relief and grati-tude than were apparent in Palestine, and pro-British sentiments were well to the fore'. But there was a darker side, as far as the British were concerned, when the inhabitants of Amman and other towns in Trans-jordan closed their bazaars in sympathy with the Syrian and Lebanese demand for independence from France. 'This was the first political dem-onstration since the beginning of the war, and hence significant as the apparent end of the self-imposed truce on political activities observed in Transjordan during the past year.'[2]

In Beirut, where Arab nationalist feeling was resentful at the obvious intention of the French to remain in control, the celebration of the defeat of Germany took on a one-sided aspect. A British Intelligence summary described it thus: 'VE-Day and those following were marked in Beirut by a display of French flags (distributed by the French); French lorries, decorated with *tricoleurs*, parading the town; *tricoleurs* attached to para-chutes rocketed overhead by the French; and the shouting of such slogans as, "This is your country, O de Gaulle!" As a result, incidents have not been lacking, and clashes between the French and the local population have occurred not only in Beirut, but also in Damascus and Homs. All this has done nothing to lessen the excitement already prevailing, and the atmosphere thus created can hardly be propitious for the negotiations due to be opened.'[3]

In Cape Town, Cyril Woolf, who had served as an aircraft electrician with the South African Air Force in the Middle East and Italy, was among the thousands who thronged the streets. 'Cars could hardly crawl along,' he later recalled. There was 'much shouting and car hooting and revelry.'[4] In the words of Alex Moussafir, a university student in Cape Town that

[1] Yaere Yadede, letter to the author, 8 October 1994.

[2] Cabinet Paper number 47 of 1945, 'Report for the Month of May 1945 for the Dominions, India, Burma and the Colonies and Mandated Territories, Report by the Secretary of State for Colonies', 25 June 1945: Colonial Office papers, 323/1871/13. Public Record Office, Kew.

[3] 'The Middle East', Weekly Political Intelligence Summary No. 293, 16 May 1945: Foreign Office papers, 371/50421. Public Record Office, Kew.

[4] Cyril Woolf, letter to the author, 25 October 1994.

day, 'everybody was in the streets singing, dancing and generally making merry. It was a huge euphoria.'[1]

Amid these celebrations in the southern hemisphere, there was an unpleasant reminder of the influence of strongly pro-German, and even pro-Nazi groups in South Africa during the war. A secret report submitted six weeks later to the British Cabinet related that Dr van Rensburg, 'the leader of the "Ossewa Brandwag", has gone out of his way to praise Hitler as a hero. This has served to remind South Africans that the organization, with its declared Fascist policy, still exists. A further reminder that the Government emergency regulations cannot yet be revoked came on VE-Day when subversive elements raided the office of the Chief Controller at Pretoria after overpowering the Guard.'[2]

More than 340,000 South African soldiers, sailors and airmen had made their contribution to the European war. Twelve thousand had been killed in action. On the day after VE-Day the *Cape Times* tried to encapsulate the meaning of the conflict, and to look ahead at the future, with the Japanese war much in mind: 'Long expected, long deferred, the end has come. Partly because the final defeat of Germany has been certain for many months past and its surrender foreseen, the event itself does not find us, as in 1918, suddenly moved to an exuberant joy, but rather, as a people, in a sober mood of quiet satisfaction. We are restrained too by the thought that over vast spaces and against a savage and truculent enemy, war is still raging and may last yet for an incalculable time. But let us not dim today's happiness or mar its thanksgivings. We have been delivered from a great peril, and the deadly threat to everything we hold dear has been swept from our path. It is a time to rejoice. The slaughter in Europe has ceased and the worst of the suffering is over. Peace reigns. Liberty has returned. Justice is triumphant. The prisoners are being released. Men can move freely and speak what they list. The gnawing, ceaseless anxiety in many homes for loved ones in danger has vanished like an evil dream.'[3]

[1] Alex Moussafir, letter to the author, 21 October 1994.
[2] Cabinet Paper number 47 of 1945, 'Report for the Month of May 1945 for the Dominions, India, Burma and the Colonies and Mandated Territories', 25 June 1945: Colonial Office papers, 323/1871/13. Public Record Office, Kew.
[3] *Cape Times*, 9 May 1945, p. 4, col. 5.

X

'The German War is at an End'

At three o'clock in the afternoon of May 8, Churchill made the broadcast he had originally intended to deliver the previous evening. The speech was listened to throughout Europe and beyond, and to those millions of people for whom the events of the previous twenty-four hours had been a mixture of hope and rumour, he declared with finality: 'Yesterday morning, at 2.41 a.m., at General Eisenhower's Headquarters, General Jodl, the representative of the German High Command, and Grand Admiral Dönitz, the designated head of the German State, signed the act of unconditional surrender of all German land, sea and air forces in Europe to the Allied Expeditionary Force, and simultaneously to the Soviet High Command.'

This agreement would be ratified in Berlin 'today'. Hostilities would officially cease at one minute after midnight that night. In the interest of saving lives, the cease fire 'began yesterday to be sounded along all the Front, and our dear Channel Islands are to be freed today. Today, perhaps, we shall think mostly of ourselves. Tomorrow we shall pay a particular tribute to our Russian comrades, whose prowess in the field has been one of the grand contributions to the general victory.'

In a brief survey of more than five and a half years of struggle, Churchill told his listeners: 'The German war is therefore at an end. After years of intense preparation, Germany hurled herself on Poland at the beginning of September 1939; and, in pursuance of our guarantee to Poland and in agreement with the French Republic, Great Britain, the British Empire and Commonwealth of Nations, declared war upon this foul aggressor. After gallant France had been struck down we, from this Island and from our united Empire, maintained the struggle single-handed for a whole year until we were joined by the military might of Soviet Russia, and later by the overwhelming power and resources of the United States of America. Finally almost the whole world was combined against the evil-doers, who are now prostrate before us.'

At the phrase 'the evil-doers, who are now prostrate before us', Harold Nicolson, who was among the crowd listening to the speech being relayed through loudspeakers in Parliament Square, noted: 'The crowd gasped.'[1]

Churchill continued: 'We may allow ourselves a brief period of rejoicing; but let us not forget for a moment the toil and efforts that lie ahead. Japan, with all her treachery and greed, remains unsubdued. The injury she has inflicted on Great Britain, the United States, and other countries, and her detestable cruelties, call for justice and retribution. We must now devote all our strength and resources to the completion of our task, both at home and abroad. Advance, Britannia! Long live the cause of freedom! God save the King.'

'The PM's voice broke as he said "Advance, Britannia!"', noted his secretary Marian Holmes.[2] 'A magnificent speech,' Noel Coward wrote in his diary, 'simple and without boastfulness, but full of deep pride.'[3] Churchill's wife telegraphed to him from Moscow as soon as the broadcast was over: 'My darling, here we in the British Embassy have all been listening to your solemn words. God bless you. M. Herriot is here and sends you his devoted greetings. Alleluia! All my love. Clemmie.'[4]

Edouard Herriot, then aged seventy-two, was a former French Prime Minister (on one occasion for only two days) and several times President of the Chamber of Deputies. He had been interned by the Germans near Berlin since 1942, and was liberated by Soviet troops a few days before VE-Day. Listening in Moscow to Churchill's broadcast, he wept, then told Churchill's wife: 'I am afraid you may think it unmanly of me to weep, but I have just heard Mr Churchill's voice. The last time I heard his voice was on the day in Tours in 1940 when he implored the French Government to hold firm and continue the struggle. His noble words of leadership that day were unavailing. When we heard the French Government's answer, and knew that they meant to give up the fight, tears streamed down Mr Churchill's face. So you will understand if I weep today, I do not feel unmanned.'[5]

Another of those who heard Churchill speak was his son Randolph, who in 1944 had been parachuted into German-occupied Yugoslavia to serve as a liaison officer with Tito's partisans behind German lines. 'Was greatly moved by your splendid speech, which I heard 8,000 feet above

[1] Harold Nicolson, letter of 8 May 1945, Nigel Nicolson (editor), *Harold Nicolson, Diaries and Letters, 1939–45*, Collins, London, 1967, p. 456.

[2] Marian Holmes, diary entry, 8 May 1945. Private archive.

[3] Graham Payn and Sheridan Morley (editors), *The Noel Coward Diaries*, Weidenfeld and Nicolson, London, 1982, pp. 92–3.

[4] British Embassy, Moscow, telegram of 8 May 1945, sent at 4 p.m., received at 6.50 p.m.

[5] Clementine Spencer Churchill, *My Visit to Russia*, London, 1945, pp. 56–7. From 1947 to 1954 Herriot was President of the National Assembly.

Dinaric Alps *en route* from Belgrade to Caserta,' he telegraphed to his father.[1]

In Prague, where Czech patriots had seized the centre of the city, a British Intelligence summary later reported that a German air attack 'was staged to synchronize with the relay of Mr Churchill's victory broadcast'.[2]

Listeners to Churchill's words had many different perspectives; the seventeen-year-old Dorothy Wallbridge, then living in the village of Shamley Green in Surrey, had been away from her home in the Channel Islands since the German occupation five years earlier. 'We like many others had our wireless on for all the news broadcasts,' she later recalled. 'When Winston Churchill said "Our Dear Channel Islands" will be freed tomorrow, we had big lumps in our throats, and tears were in our eyes. Someone, my mother I think, blew their nose, and said "Thank God for that, let's have a cup of tea." Then we felt fearful in case the Germans would harm someone before they surrendered, as we did not know what was happening in the islands.'[3]

At a luncheon party in London for two senior American airmen, General Doolittle and General Anderson, Churchill's broadcast marked the culminating high point. A British guest, Robert Bruce Lockhart, Director-General of the Political Warfare Executive, described in his diary how, when the BBC played "God Save the King", 'all the Americans made a half turn left from the table and stood stiffly to attention. It was a most solemn moment and gave me the impression of the choir turning to the east for the Apostles' Creed. Rather awkward, too, for the PM said: "Today we shall think mostly of ourselves; tomorrow we shall think of our great ally Russia." There was no mention of the Americans whose leading Anglophiles were at that moment entertaining us.' Bruce Lockhart later noted that on the following day the *Daily Express* 'tried to explain in a leader that "ourselves" clearly meant the Anglo-Americans. But the omission was a little unfortunate.'[4]

One couple listening to Churchill's broadcast were particularly euphoric. Peter and Dora Vernon had been married the previous evening. VE-Day was the first day of their honeymoon. They had intended to get

[1] Telegram F/72752 from Caserta, received 11.35 p.m., 8 May 1945. Public Record Office, Kew.
[2] Weekly Political Intelligence Summary No. 293, 16 May 1945: Foreign Office papers, 371/50421. Public Record Office, Kew.
[3] Dorothy Wallbridge, letter to the author, 22 October 1994.
[4] Kenneth Young (editor), *The Diaries of Sir Robert Bruce Lockhart, Volume Two, 1939–1965*, Macmillan, London, 1980, p. 431. Churchill had mentioned the Americans earlier in his broadcast (referring to 'the overwhelming power and resources' of the United States of America) but not in his conclusion.

married in June 1944 but Vernon was among those landing in Normandy on D-Day, with the 51st Field Artillery Regiment, and continued eastward to Falaise, Brussels, Walcheren, the Dutch–German border, the Ardennes and the Rhine. In April 1945 he had been among the British troops entering Belsen, where his knowledge of German and Yiddish (he had come to Britain before the war as a refugee from Vienna) was of considerable help. Twenty-four hours later he was sent from Belsen to a nearby 'crisis point' to stop rioting between Polish DPs and German villagers. The opportunity of home leave in the first week of May made marriage possible at last. His bride was also a refugee from Vienna who had been brought to Britain shortly before the outbreak of war. 'Our party,' he later reflected, 'was one of the biggest ones ever. Together with a hundred thousand others we were dancing first in Trafalgar Square and then moving to the Mall and Buckingham Palace, and the speakers at "our wedding party" were no other than the King and Winston Churchill.'[1]

Another of those listening to Churchill's broadcast in London was a university student, Geoffrey Wigoder, who had gone to the West End at midday. 'When I arrived at Trafalgar Square', he wrote in his diary, 'it was a mass of people – cheerful and goodhumoured – very hot and sunny. At 3 p.m. loudspeakers relayed Churchill's broadcast announcing the end of the war. There were some cheers (the loudest was for the announcement of the liberation of the Channel Islands) but no colossal demonstration. Afterwards move along in a terrific crush along Whitehall and take a stand outside the Ministry of Health balcony. Here I stood for an hour and a half and, eventually, Churchill appeared (45 minutes late). There were enormous crowds – crowds in the windows and on the roofs throwing paper.

'Planes swooping dropping parachute flares, and flares were lit from a roof. Churchill was accompanied by Bevin, Anderson, Lyttelton, Woolton and Morrison.[2] He 'V-ed' and everyone V-ed back. He made a short, typically Churchillian speech, and he seemed very moved. Afterwards Bevin stepped forward and called "Three cheers for Victory. 'Ip 'Ip", and everyone round me roared back "'Ooray". The crowd cheered and dispersed.'[3]

---

[1] Peter John Vernon, letter to the author, 18 October 1994. Peter Vernon and his wife contributed a two-page section to Barry Turner, *I Came Alone*, pages 347–8. They had been brought to Britain on special *Kindertransport* (childrens' transport). Their parents, who had to remain in Vienna, perished.

[2] The Minister of Labour, the Chancellor of the Exchequer, the Minister of Production, the Minister of Reconstruction, and the Home Secretary (and Minister of Home Security) respectively.

[3] Geoffrey Wigoder, diary entry for 8 May 1945. Private papers.

Also in London listening to Churchill's broadcast was Zvi Shalit, a merchant seaman who had never been in the British capital before. He had travelled from Hull the night before to be present for the celebrations. 'On the 8th of May 1945 I was privileged to be in London,' he recalled, 'and watched with great excitement and admiration, feeling I was participating in history, the celebrations, the happy crowds, which no words can describe, the festive atmosphere and exaltation. I heard our great leader W. Churchill declare on that memorable day, in the voice of a stern prophet, "War against Japan!" The next day I rejoined my ship and sailed from an assembly point off Land's End in a convoy of two hundred ships, to the United States still escorted by the Royal Navy, as some German U-Boats disobeyed their Admiral, did not surrender, and attacked Allied shipping for a short period. The war really ended for my shipmates and me when we were anchored in Colombo Bay, Ceylon, waiting for a floating crane to unload the torpedo boats which we had transported on deck from the United States, and the atom bomb was dropped on Hiroshima. That was the last day of the war for us.'[1]

In every Allied army camp in Germany, Churchill's broadcast was a high point of the day. An American soldier, Irving Rosen, wrote: 'On May 8, 1945 (VE-Day and President Truman's birthday) I was a Sergeant in the Field Artillery, US Army. We were pulled out of the lines a week or so before and we were in a little town, I think that it was Braunschweig, Germany. It was close to Leipzig. The war for all practical purposes had been over for about two weeks. I remember that it was a clear sunny day and somebody hooped up a loud speaker connected to a radio tuned into the BBC in London. I remember the announcer saying in a crisp British accent, "This is the BBC London with a special broadcast", and then Winston Churchill came on to announce that Victory had been won and there were cheering crowds in London.'

As the American soldiers in Europe listened to London's celebrations, Irving Rosen was among those who 'also received our orders that we were being redeployed to the Pacific.'[2] In June he sailed from Le Havre for the United States. After home leave, he was being shipped out of Fort Dix, New Jersey, on his way to further training at Camp Bowie, Texas, on the day the atomic bomb was dropped on Hiroshima.

Sergeant Mack Morris, an American war correspondent, was at an American army camp near Magdeburg, on the Elbe, as the war came to an end. 'Peace came to the weary infantry on the Elbe on a soft spring

---

[1] Zvi Shalit, letter to the author, 25 August 1994.
[2] Irving Rosen, letter to the author, 23 September 1994.

day,' he wrote, 'and the infantry nodded its head and went about its business. There could be, of course, no sudden order to cease fire because firing for the Ninth Army ceased days ago; so the infantry heard Churchill and told each other, "It's over" with hardly more enthusiasm than they might have shown toward the news that chow's up.

'For the infantry was preoccupied. A lieutenant in charge of the prisoner-of-war enclosure was sweating with the food problem. "I go over to see about feeding 2,100 people and come back and find I've 10,000 more they just brought in."

'The music that followed Churchill's announcement was still playing, but the lieutenant wasn't listening. He was staring gloomily at the huge mass of Germans. A Nazi kid with a placid face that had never known a razor approached the lieutenant and said in high school English, "I'm coming from Brooklyn. At which time do I eat?" The lieutenant stared at the kid, almost said something and thought better of it. He walked off without a word. The stately music heralding the peace played on.

'In Magdeburg, the infantry, already saddled with guard duty, met the peace with magnificent indifference. One dough,[1] "a character" in his company, rushed out shouting, "*Deutsches Kaput*," but both his buddies and the Germans only regarded him as people do when they hear already-ancient news. For peace, real peace, was now nothing more to them than the blessed inaction which had been theirs for days.

'A man with a bottle invited a friend to stop with him in a doorway. It's bad taste to drink in view of the beaten and bitter Germans and even worse taste to drink where an officer might see. The invitation was followed by the explanation "It's VE-Day," but the bottle was there before Churchill spoke and if it hadn't been VE-Day the invitation would have been backed by some other excuse or no excuse at all. The infantry talked with the age-old understanding of the infantry's lot: "Now what?" And in the manner of all infantrymen shrugged its shoulders.'[2]

Another American war correspondent, Sergeant Ralph G. Martin was with the soldiers in Paris as Churchill's speech was about to be relayed. 'At one of the big cafés at the Rond Point,' he wrote, 'Private Robert Sullivan put his arm around the Lieutenant-Colonel. Both of them had all kinds of ribbons and all kinds of clusters. Both were smiling and looking at the empty champagne bottles. When they had drained their glasses, Sullivan pointed to the Lieutenant-Colonel and beamed. "This

---

[1] The word 'doughboy', abbreviated to 'dough', was commonly used in the First World War for American soldiers.

[2] Sergeant Mack Morris, 'Some Merely Shrugged', *Yank*, Victory Edition, 1945, p. 8.

wonderful sonofabitch," he said. "If he wanted my right arm, I'd cut off my right arm right now and give it to him."

'The Lieutenant-Colonel kept beaming and refilled the glasses. "He was a second lieutenant and I was a private in his squad, and he was the best second lieutenant in the business and now he's a lieutenant colonel and I'm still a private and if he wants my right arm, I'll cut it off right now and give it to him. Honest to God." They were both still beaming when they finished off another glass of champagne.

'In another café, some WACS[1] were singing, "Mister Monsoor from Armentières, parlez-vous . . .". On the Rue de Berri, in front of the WAC hotel, a soldier and a WAC were in a clinch and the soldier said something and the WAC's voice came out of the darkness, "Nope, not even on VE-Day . . ."

'In the dayroom of the 108th General Hospital, a few boys were playing checkers, not listening to the radio. The radio was announcing the official end of the war in Europe. There were two soldiers sitting right next to the radio, listening very intently, as if they wanted to make sure they got every word. After Winston Churchill had finished speaking, I asked one of the soldiers how he felt about it. He turned around to stare with wide-open eyes and then his words came out so slowly as if it was painful for him to talk, as if he had to drag out every word separately. He said, "I have no feeling at all."

'Then he pointed to his head. "I got hit on the head with a dud," he said. "I don't remember too much. I don't remember what battalion I was with. I don't even remember what my rank is. I think I'm a T/5 but I'm not sure. Isn't that funny?"

'The other soldier was Private Ernest Kuhn of Chicago. He had just been liberated after five months in a Nazi prisoner-of-war camp. He still had some shrapnel in his throat. "I listened to Churchill talk and I kept saying to myself that I was still alive. The war was over and I was still alive. And I thought of all the boys in my division's band who were with me in the Ardennes who are dead now. We used to be a pretty good band."

'The nurse told how all the patients crowded to the balconies the night before to watch the planes drop the flares and how some of the planes spotted the hospital's Red Cross and all the crowded balconies, and how they came back and buzzed the hospital again and again, wiggling their wings, dropping so many flares that it looked like daylight. Then somebody started singing "God Bless America" and everybody joined in and

[1] More usually, WAACs: members of the Women's Army Auxiliary Corps.

179

some of the soldiers looked like they were crying. In one of the wards, Private Junior H. Powell told how he felt: "It's a great thing all right," he said "but I kinda wish it'd all happened a month ago." Then he pointed to his missing leg."[1]

At the British Military Mission in Moscow, Hugh Lunghi was frustrated by the Soviet refusal to accept May 8 as VE-Day. 'On Tuesday afternoon the BBC reported vast crowds joyfully celebrating victory and rejoicing in London and throughout the UK: we heard Churchill, we heard Truman. Nothing on the BBC from Stalin. At about the same time as the BBC reports of the celebrations in the UK we tuned in to Moscow Radio: it was broadcasting a fairy story. Still nothing from Stalin. Urgent enquiries to the liaison office of the Ministry of Defence elicited the reply that Soviet forces were "still fighting to liberate Prague and elsewhere". We could only guess word had gone out from on high that "the real victors" would declare victory at a time of Stalin's choosing. It left a sour taste. Russian friends whom we had invited to have drinks were hesitant and we had a job to persuade them we had heard Churchill and Truman welcoming the end of the war in Europe.'[2]

Although May 9 was to be VE-day throughout the Soviet Union, the British citizens in Moscow were not to be cheated of their own celebrations. Clementine Churchill's secretary, Grace Hamblin recalled, 'There was an enormous amount to be done in these final days of our journey.'

'Goodbyes to be said and written. A Press conference with the Russian Red Cross. The preparation of Mrs Churchill's farewell speech. And the usual packing; and I think I was too occupied to feel the true impact until we were entertained at lunch at the British Embassy where we later listened to Churchill broadcasting the great news from London. It was not until then that I became aware of the great surge of joy and thankfulness that was affecting, not only those immediately near to us, but people all over the world.

'Hearing Churchill's voice once more, after so many weeks, and listening to what he had to say, was incredibly moving, and made one long more and more to be home. In my diary I wrote "Even the Skymaster is panting to be off". A small service of thanksgiving was later held in the British Mission building, where the Dean of Canterbury gave a wonderful address. And later we were entertained at a special performance of Swan Lake at the great Bolshoi theatre.

---

[1] Sergeant Ralph G. Martin, 'The War Was Over', *Yank*, Victory Edition, 1945, p. 3.
[2] Hugh Lunghi, letter to the author, 22 September 1994.

'Mixed with the deep excitement and emotions of that great day was the awareness that this was not the same for our hosts the Russians, and perhaps of saving oneself a little, in order to share with them the tremendous joy of the next day, when they themselves would celebrate victory. Not that they had spared themselves in order to share OUR day.'[1]

Churchill's broadcast was listened to in many places where, in the recent past, it would have meant death to have been caught listening. It was even heard in the Sudetenland, on the clandestine radio at the labour camp still under German rule on May 8, in which the German factory owner Oskar Schindler was employing and protecting more than a thousand Jews, and where an SS garrison maintained the last dwindling law and order of the Third Reich. One of the prisoners in the camp, Moshe Bejski wrote: 'In the last days, the prisoners in Brünnlitz harboured hopes of liberation after five and a half years of suffering and torture, but their fear and dread also mounted. They knew of the Russians' progress from radio bulletins that they picked up secretly once each day, and explosions from the battles had been drawing closer for the past twenty-four hours. However, they were increasingly anxious about the possibility that their captors would take them out on a death march, as had been done at most of the camps before the Allies could effect their liberation. It was true that the Kommandant, Leipold, had left the camp by this time, but the junior SS men who remained might carry out an order to evacuate the camp or kill the prisoners before the Russians could arrive.

'The prisoners gathered in groups on the factory floor and discussed the possibility of escape, although this did not seem viable because the Front was nearby and there was nowhere to hide on the outside, even for a few days. Members of a group of people from Budzyn formulated practical plans, for they, along with a few others, were in on the secret of the arms cache at Schindler's small warehouse, the keys to which had been held for several weeks by my brother Uri Bejski. This group included several Polish Army officers and others who had been trained in the use of these weapons.

'When a report on Churchill's speech and the surrender of Germany came in at midday, prisoners on the smaller production floor where the boilers were made burst into consultations. It was decided that the weapons from Schindler's warehouse, including the grenades, would be distributed among the group members at once, and that guards would be posted at every corner of the plant. If an attempt were made to kill the prisoners or take them on a march, the armed group members would

---

[1] Grace Hamblin, letter to the author, 22 September 1994.

pounce on the SS men; rebellion and panic would ensue, and the prisoners would flee for their lives.

'After their years of oppression, suffering, and confinement in camps, most of the prisoners had evidently lost the capacity for independent thought and action. They had developed a dependency of sorts on the camp routine, focusing all their energies on the struggle for daily existence, on terms set by others. In the meantime, there was still fear that SS men, retreating Wehrmacht troops, and Vlasov's Ukrainian forces were circulating in the field. Compounding these fears was concern about Schindler's own impending departure, leaving us at a loss what to do that evening and the next day.

'It was Schindler who provided a little encouragement and dispelled our apprehensions. At his request, all 1,200 prisoners gathered on the production floor, whereupon he gave us a paternalistic parting speech. Schindler's remarks were not recorded and are difficult to reconstruct. To the best of my recollection, he noted with satisfaction that he had succeeded in keeping his promise to help and protect us to the best of his ability, and expressed hope that each of us would be able to return to his place of residence and even find some of his relatives. He asked us to behave with restraint and refrain from vengeance, and repeated several times that, just as he had promised, he would stay with us until five minutes after midnight, until after the SS guards left the camp and endangered us no longer.

'The group members shouldered their rifles after Schindler's speech, and the SS men made no attempt to enter the factory premises.

'Schindler kept his word: he and his wife, along with eight prisoners who had volunteered to escort him on his way as a refugee, set out in a car and a truck with provisions after midnight, when the cease-fire of the surrender went into effect and after the SS guards had left.

'Throughout the day of May 8, German forces could be seen retreating on the distant road and the sounds of artillery explosions came closer. When the SS guards pulled out that night, it became the duty of the Jewish guards to make sure that none of the prisoners would consider, even by way of temptation, the possibility of stepping past the camp fence for a taste of freedom. Gunfire was audible all around; shells penetrated the camp confines and wounded several people. How unjust it was to be wounded or killed on the day the war ended.

'It was a "white night". None of the prisoners attempted to climb onto his bunk; everyone crowded onto the large production floor. In fact, it was the first time that men and women could mingle and converse freely. The time had not yet come to ask what now? In the heat of emotion, the day's bread and coffee ration had not been handed out: the prisoners were beset with hunger pangs.'

Schindler's storerooms contained a large trove of dark blue fabric intended for German naval uniforms, thousands of litres of spirits, and an abundant quantity of cigarettes. Before he left, Schindler gave instructions for everyone in the camp to be given three metres of fabric for a suit, one litre of vodka, and some cigarettes. 'These commodities were worth their weight in gold at this time,' Bejski recalled. 'With them, the inmates could afford to begin their tortuous path toward home and their search for relatives who had survived. The distribution began the very next day.'[1]

Churchill's speech was listened to all over the world. In Cape Town it had to compete with the celebratory firing of artillery. 'Each salvo,' wrote Alan Nash, 'though it drowned Mr Churchill's speech periodically, was hailed with applause. When he spoke of the "toils and efforts that lie ahead", Mr Churchill was undoubtedly plumbing the thoughts of many in the streets yesterday. That phrase came to me through a solemn knot of listeners crowded round a car radio. Its implications of battle yet to be done and hardships still to be faced were dispelled only by the sirens and bells. Their joyous pealing shattered reserves of silence and thought.'[2]

Also in Cape Town on May 8 was a pre-war refugee from Dresden, Dr G. Lewin, a member in Cape Town of the People's Club, one of the few multi-racial institutions in the city. 'We celebrated in our club', he recalled, 'although we knew that it was also the end of the rather liberal time in South African politics. Those who had hoped for a lessening of Apartheid were soon deceived. The blacks who had been hoping their war efforts would be rewarded were very much disappointed. Many of the coloured people had been hoping for a Japanese victory and the day of "reckoning" with the whites, not realizing what the Japanese would have done in that case. Anyhow, there was not too much relief among them and the blacks – and one could well understand that.'[3]

On the western rim of Asia, Irene Hertz was on Mount Carmel, above Haifa Bay. In a letter to her father-in-law in England she wrote: 'So peace has come at last, and we were moved when we heard the Prime Minister's speech this afternoon, together with the children. We are grateful that our children do not know what war is, except from

---

[1] Judge Moshe Bejski, letter to the author, 23 October 1994.
[2] Alan Nash, 'The World Goes By', *Cape Times*, 9 May 1945, p. 2, col. 7.
[3] Dr G. Lewin, letter to the author, 21 November 1994.

conversation. When the news came through, Jonathan asked my father: "Are you happy *now?*"[1]

The Hertz family could not be as happy as many people were that day: Irene's uncle had last heard from her aunt when she was trapped in Poland at the outbreak of war. They had no idea on VE-Day what had happened to her and her family. In fact she had survived, but her parents had been killed, as had her four-year-old younger daughter. 'They hoped to find their lost daughter,' Irene Hertz recalled, 'and for years scanned the list of survivors. In vain.'[2]

In the Far East on May 8, at IV Corps Headquarters at Pegu, in Burma, Major Alfred Doulton, who wrote in his diary: 'It is the end of one war. It was half past seven this evening when we gathered in the open with a background of grasshoppers and bullfrogs revelling in the steamy atmosphere to listen to the words of the leader. His voice rang out clear in the well-known tones, despite the distance that separates us from home. A brief, restrained utterance, starting with a plain statement of the facts, rising in emotion to an expression of thankfulness and a mood of quiet rejoicing that never approached exultation. Every word befitted the occasion. At the end we should have sung "God Save the King", but we were silent as the full orchestra played. It was not, I think, that we were too deeply stirred by the greatness of the occasion or that we were stunned, scarcely able to credit that the struggle was over. Others know that their task is over and can give themselves up to rejoicing, secure in the knowledge that their lives are their own once more. We have no share in such feelings. There is no holiday for us, no relief from a long day in an oppressive climate. And tomorrow more lives will be lost. The hazards of war are still our lot and we have to grit our teeth and face an uncertain future.'[3]

[1] Irene Hertz, letter, Jerusalem, 8 May 1945. Private archive.
[2] Irene Hertz, letter to the author, 28 October 1994.
[3] Alfred Doulton, diary, Pegu, 8 May 1945. Private archive.

XI

Britain Rejoices

In Britain, as noon turned to afternoon, and afternoon to evening, the mood of VE-Day grew from excitement to tumult. Eva Loewenstein, a twenty-year-old refugee from Frankfurt-on-Main who was then living in London, took her disabled mother to the cinema in the West End that day. 'The day was just like any normal day,' she recalled, 'or what was termed normal after four years of war. While we were watching the world changed – coming out of the cinema we were confronted by a crowd of thousands cheering and chanting, and waving the Union Jack, and roaming through the streets and squares; and there was not a taxi to be had to take us home.'[1]

The exuberance of VE-Day in London was echoed throughout Britain. For the young, there were few constraints. Dorothy Wallbridge recalled that evening's celebrations at Shamley in Surrey: 'The village hall was packed. The band, "The Four in Harmony", or as we called them "The Four in Agony", played. We danced and sang, no one seemed tired. I remember dancing with one of the dads, when there was a loud bang in the porch, there were a lot of startled yells and screams, when they realized someone had let off a firecracker they had pinched from the Home Guard. No one was angry at the prank; there was a roar of laughter, as we had all jumped a foot in the air, by then even the band had recovered and we carried on singing and dancing till about 1 a.m. We still had to turn up for work next morning.'

Dorothy Wallbridge's parents, and several of the older people in the village, did not join in the celebrations at the hall. They were worried 'over the islands not getting liberated till the next day'. It was 'relief' rather than any less constrained emotion that she sensed among the adults, 'as so many boys were still out in the Far East. My father's brother, his wife and one of his sons were still in Jersey. The other son was out in the Far East, serving with the Chindits.'[2]

---

[1] Eva R. Goddard (née Loewenstein), letter to the author, 26 October 1994.
[2] Dorothy Wallbridge, letter to the author, 22 October 1994. The Chindits were the British long-range penetration force created in 1942 to operate behind Japanese lines in Burma. The name is derived from the Burmese word for the winged stone lions which guard Buddhist temples.

At a Royal Air Force station in Scotland, the Far East was also remembered, amid the elation, as Herbert Scott recalled: 'When the official announcement was made you could have heard the cheers from Banff miles away. In the officers' mess there was hugging and hand shaking which transcended rank. This was followed by a Tannoy broadcast by the Station Commander. In it he praised all ranks for their steadfastness in war and wished them all great joy that now their loved ones were safe after such a protracted period of deadly conflict. He also made special mention of all the personnel from countries in occupied Europe, some on our own Station, in particular some from Norway. He reminded us that there was still a deadly conflict raging in the Far East and to remember the millions of Allied Troops still engaged there.'

The Station Commander ended with a caution, 'that in celebrating this momentous occasion we should not do anything which transcended normal good behaviour and respect for the good name of the Royal Air Force. A senior Norwegian officer had requested authority from London to fly immediately to Oslo to take command of Royal Norwegian Air Force Station. This was given, and a Mosquito pilot flew him into Norway so that the Germans would not have another day in command of a RNAF station.'

Herbert Scott gathered all ranks of his own Flight together 'and echoed the Station Commander's call for them to temper their celebrations with goodwill and relief, stood down all flying for two days, and wished them well. As Flight Commander of a detached Flight, I had petrol coupons and the use of my car which at the time was a small Lagonda sports car. Even after calls for restraint in celebrating, I was worried about what high spirits might call for and so I hurriedly found a local farmer who put my car safely away in his locked barn after giving me a dram of his best malt whisky.' Along the coast, at Gardenstown 'the local hostelry was hosted by an ex-Pipe Major and he has never played better to an audience more ripe to enjoy it to the full. And so ended a day to remember for as long as I live.'[1]

Dr Sholto Forman, a Scot who had seen action in Burma, was in London on VE-Day, in the midst of the crowds, hugging and being hugged by total strangers. 'For me, as for tens of thousands of others,' he later explained, 'the war started again at the end of leave. I was due to sail for Bombay in a month and could expect exile for three years (some said seven before repatriation); that is for those of us who survived. Tomorrow I was to meet the girl I knew I loved. But was it zany to think

---

[1] Squadron Leader Herbert C. Scott, letter to the author, 1 October 1994.

of marriage at this stage of the game? Anyway, how would we find each other? We had known each other for six months before I left, separated in different parts of England for three of them. Born a cautious Scot and analytical by training, the demand for instant decision on this far-reaching matter put all my concepts to the test. For it has always gone against my grain to be pushed into action before the instinctive time for decision arrives. I felt no affection for the Japanese that day. But if hopes had been dupes, fears turned out to be resounding liars. We were married at three days' notice in the kirk I had been christened in at Beattock in Dumfriesshire.'[1]

At Kinnerley in Shrophire, William Higgins remembered VE-Day as 'work as usual' on a military light railway linking a large ammunition store with the main line. 'My memories of this notable day, 8 May 1945, was one of relief after being a conscript in the British Army from 15 November 1939. During my army service, Cupid enabled me to find my dear wife Betty. On this day my thoughts were of her and of our firstborn. My thoughts also turned to the acute housing shortage which then faced Britain. That evening I broke new ground and spent a convivial hour or so in a nearby pub. Several of my comrades were present and we all sang heartily.'[2]

In Staffordshire, John Barham was at school, six weeks from his six-teenth birthday. 'On the morning of VE-Day,' he later recalled, 'I went down the steep hill from the school with friends and caught a train to Derby. We had managed to buy cigarettes and one memory of that day is of smoking on every possible occasion, although two years later when I went into the army I was a non-smoker and still am! We had lunch in a café or restaurant and then went to the cinema where, of course, we could smoke. An airman and his WAAF girl friend were sitting in the row behind us and a few minutes after the lights went out one of our group said the following exchange had taken place. The airman said to the WAAF that he wanted to ask her something to which she agreed. He asked her to marry him! She said she would, so they got up and left. I suppose even on that day he needed the darkness of the cinema to provide a cover for his shyness.'[3]

Noel Major was at a boarding school just outside Worcester. Rumours about 'a great street party' near the cathedral led him and about eight fellow boarders to slip out of school, through a window on the first floor

---

[1] Sholto Forman, 'Family celebration', in *As You Were, VE-Day: a medical retrospect*, British Medical Association, London, 1984, p. 71.
[2] William Higgins, letter to the author, 2 September 1994.
[3] John Barham, letter to the author, 13 September 1994.

and down a drainpipe, and make their way to the celebrations. But the centre of the town was, he recalled, 'disappointingly dark and silent. No crowds, no music – nothing. Standing in an uncertain group near the Cathedral, we not unnaturally attracted the attention of a policeman who quickly found out who were, and what we were doing. He advised us to return to the school as soon as possible.' At that moment a passing car hit the First World War memorial. The driver and passenger ran off. The policeman went to investigate and the boys returned to school as secretly as they had left. The next day the police, seeking information about the car incident, visited the school to speak to the boys who had witnessed it. They were swiftly brought before the headmaster and accused of truancy. The punishment was to be confined to the school grounds for the next six weeks. 'One result of this incarceration,' Major recalled, 'was that we applied ourselves to our studies.' The result was a very successful exam result. 'It could be said, at several removes, that Hitler had a greater influence on my education and subsequent career than he could ever have intended.'[1]

In Yorkshire, Norman Hazell had celebrated his thirteenth birthday three weeks before VE-Day. A grammar schoolboy living on a council estate, he was one of six brothers and sisters. 'It poured with rain in the morning,' he later recalled, 'but stopped so that we were able to enjoy the bonfire, on waste ground in the centre of Wakefield. Slum clearance had left many such "gaps", rows of little back-to-backs demolished, families moved out to the new Council estates, then the war came along to stop any city centre redevelopment. But I'm sure this was reflected right across the North of England.

'I can clearly remember the way in which everyone in the road in which I lived, all fairly new, semi-detached Council houses, ran about, knocking on doors. A large street party was arranged and I can still picture the long table (made up of many individual ones) with masses of happy children, while parents stood in groups on the grass verges. No traffic of course. I remember the big bonfire on the evening of VE-Day. Dad took we older children, while Mum stayed at home with the baby.'[2]

That night's bonfire in Wakefield was devised as a dramatic culmination of a day of enjoyment. At 11 p.m., as the local newspaper reported four days later, 'the "body" of Hitler was found. And it was here in Wakefield! To Wakefield had fallen the pleasure of seeing to it that

---

[1] Noel Major, letter to the author, 4 October 1994. His 'subsequent career' was forty-two years in the building and engineering industry, starting as an articled pupil in the office of a consulting civil engineer.

[2] Norman Hazell, letter to the author, 26 September 1994.

Hitler was well and truly disposed of. With fitting ceremonial, a hearse containing the coffin was drawn by upwards of fifty servicemen and women, from near the Town Hall, to the scene of the *auto-da-fé*.

'Accompanying the Mayor were the "doubles" of Mr Churchill, Mr Stalin, Mr Truman, General de Gaulle, General Smuts, and General Chiang-Kai-Shek, realistically impersonated by members of the Wakefield Operatic and Dramatic Society. The roll of drums and the funereal dirge played by the instrumentalists, was remarkably effective. Mr Stalin was the star hero of the ladies. Unfortunately, owing to their boundless enthusiasm, he disappeared in the crush of feminine admirers before he could be rescued! A search party failed to locate him in time to witness the final scene.

'Nearer and nearer drew the hearse, and brighter and brighter burned the flames as if they hungered for what was to be fed to them! Herr Hitler was unceremoniously bundled out of the hearse and on to the fire. But the Führer's intuition evidently had prepared a last kick, for he promptly rolled out of reach of the dancing flames. He was quickly hurled back and, to make doubly sure, the hearse was also thrown into the flames! Hitler having met his doom, the crowd returned to Wood Street, where dancing, interspersed with community singing, was continued until long after the "witching hour." '[1]

There were many for whom VE-Day was a catalyst to sombre thoughts. Henry Crooks was a radiographer, working in a military hospital in Shaftesbury. Much of his wartime work had been with the wounded and the dying. Recalling a walk just after dawn that day across the fields near the hospital, he later wrote: 'My early morning thoughts would have extended to being thankful (having had a few narrow shaves) for being spared, while many virile young men lost their lives, and I could have contemplated the fully laden Dakota crash nearby when all, except the pilot, were killed. The bodies were brought to us, many with missing limbs, and I, being the orderly sergeant major for the night, had to organize a team to deal with this sad emergency. I later X-rayed the delirious pilot in the presence of his mother.'

Another harrowing experience that Crooks could not shake out of his mind was dealing with the victims of the Imber Down tragedy two years earlier. 'Of the sixty or so high ranking officers brought to us at Shaftesbury Military Hospital many died or were dead on arrival. Doctors, Sisters, Nurses and VADs[2] and all other ranks worked flat out for several

---

[1] 'VE-Day Celebration', *Wakefield Express*, 12 May 1945.
[2] VADs: members of the Voluntary Aid Detachment, nurses who volunteered for hospital service in Britain and abroad.

days (and nights) tending to the wounded. The account given to me was that, during a military exercise on Imber Down, the enclosure containing the senior staff was accidentally strafed by the pilot of a Hurricane fighter aircraft.'

After his morning walk, and after breakfast in the sergeants' mess, Crooks continued with his radiographic duties. He would wait until the 'relative freedom of the weekend' for a celebratory lunch in a nearby pub.[1]

From the nearby village of Histon, Alfred Peacock and a friend had bicycled into Cambridge for the evening. Their destination was a jazz concert held on the bandstand at the Guildhall, given by Leslie 'Jiver' Henderson's West Indian band. 'When it was all over, just before mid-night', Peacock later recalled, 'my friend and I, having spoken to the musicians and collected their autographs, went to collect our bikes. My black, utility, lightweight, back pedaller had gone! We told a policeman who, I recall, looked very old and seemed singularly unconcerned. "Where do you live?" he asked. "Histon," I replied. "I can see the law's going to get broken tonight then," he said laconically. Well the law *was* broken. My friend gave me what in Yorkshire is known as a "croggy", but which we, less imaginative, more down to earth, called a "bar" – a ride on his handlebars.

'We went down Arbury Road to avoid the traffic and policemen, past Unicam and over the railway crossing, then down Mill Lane and into Orchard Road. To our amazement, at least three hours after my parents' bedtime, No. 8 was ablaze with light, and when we went in we saw that, in addition to my mother and father, the Ambroses from No 6 were there, and so, too, were the Watsons from No 4. "I've had me bike pinched", I announced, noticing that there were bottles of cheap sherry and port around. I do not know what response to this I expected, but the reply turned out to be a show stopper. "Never mind about your bike", my mother said, "the war's over". So it was, in Europe anyway.'[2]

Norman Hurst was a schoolboy in Surrey, in the middle of taking his school certificate. Like many of his friends he had been shocked in the last weeks of April by cinema newsreels showing 'the sickening sights' in Belsen and other concentration camps. 'Even though we had often been conned by the newsreels for propaganda purposes there was no doubting the authenticity of these scenes.' Newspaper reports at the end of April and beginning of May of large-scale German troop surrenders in North-

---

[1] Henry Crooks, letter to the author, 14 September 1994.
[2] A.J. Peacock, letter to the author, 1 October 1994.

ern Europe had also made a strong impact on him. 'It was apparent from maps in the newspapers it was only a question of time before it ended.' On the evening of VE-Day, he later recalled, 'a friend and I and a couple of girls walked up to Old Coulsdon, a commuter community centred on a 12th-century church, a village green, a pub and a parade of shops. Someone had built a large bonfire around which we stood and talked. Most of the evening was spent, in the Victorian sense, promenading. It was all very tame really – no excessive drinking or misbehaviour. Thinking back there did not seem to be many older people around, my parents did not say much or celebrate in any way.

'Life suddenly went flat. The end we had so longed for had arrived, no more bombing, no more danger, no more excitement, just life. Nearby was a small prisoner-of-war camp in the grounds of the Territorial Barracks. For some time it had been a liberal regime with either Germans or Italians free to come and go. There did not seem to be any animosity.

'I can't recall when the blackout restrictions were officially relaxed, but certainly people took steps on May 8 to bring out fairy lights and light up the exterior of their houses. We lived on rising ground to the east of the Brighton Road. The ground to the west is much steeper, and before the war it was referred to as looking like Fairy Land after dark. It did again on VE night, when we saw the lights in all the windows over a large area illuminated for the first time in nearly six years. But rations were so tight it was out of the question to have a celebratory meal.'

What, Norman Hurst later asked, were his principal lasting memories of the war, and he answered his own question: 'The sound of a Merlin engine; Churchill's voice, particularly when imparting unwelcome tidings; and the last seconds of the engine of a flying bomb as the note rises slightly prior to cutting out and the silence that follows until detonation. Whenever I hear the latter on the radio or in a film I still feel inclined to dive for cover!'[1]

Ronald McCormick was an eighteen-year-old naval cadet in training at Wetherby in Yorkshire. 'Against all warnings from the officers, I decided to hitch a lift from Leeds to Manchester. Lack of funds plus Naval Police "infesting" the railway stations made me take the alternative mode of transportation. I travelled on the back of a lorry from Leeds (over the Pennines!) to Ashton-under-Lyne. I then "risked" public transport to Sale, which lies five miles south of the city. My father had hung a huge Union Jack from the front bedroom window, the only sign of the "victory" in the whole of the road. Seeing me, he was very annoyed that

---

[1] Norman Hurst, letter to the author, 28 August 1994.

I had gone AWOL[1] – not really the case because the Royal Navy had given us the day off. Returning to Leeds entailed playing hide and seek on the Manchester Railway Station, my father and brother helping out. There were many other servicemen apart from myself running the gamut. When I reached Wetherby in the evening a bonfire had been lit and there was dancing in the streets.'[2]

Training for the Royal Air Force on VE-Day was Hilary Rubinstein, who recalled being billeted in Torquay in 'what would have been a pre-war three-star hotel; the grub was adequate, the officers civilized, and it didn't look as though we were likely to see active service even though we were due to be trained as pilots at the end of the course'. He and a friend decided to hitch-hike that day to Buckfast Abbey and then on to Dartington School, where they found everybody 'exceptionally hospitable to two young airmen in uniform'. Rubinstein's London house had been destroyed in the Blitz four years earlier. His brother had died while in the Middle East with the Royal Air Force. But, as he reflected later, 'I never really felt the emotions of the day. I enjoyed a day off. There may have been dancing and boozing in the streets of Torquay when we had hitch-hiked home. There may have been a church parade. I don't remember. It wasn't until a day or two later that the newsreels in the local cinema were showing scenes from Belsen. That has stuck in my memory all right.'[3]

Able Seaman Alan Palmer, a university graduate naval cadet, was among those training for the Royal Navy on VE-Day 'I was with other ex-University Naval Division cadets training at HMS *Raleigh*, a shore establishment at Torpoint. All training ceased for the day, but I was, technically, already detailed for "Duty Watch" that evening and therefore knew perfectly well that I ought to stay "aboard". The "duty watch" did, however, slip out to the local pub as dusk fell and we then had to take quick evasive action on the approach of our training lieutenant before scuttling back to base. Much more vivid in my memory is the sight, a few days later, of three or four U-boats moored just south of Brunel's Tamar Bridge.

'On VE-Day itself I do remember being totally convinced that the war with Japan would be over long before we finished our training (which it was). But I don't think this conviction rested on any logical argument, merely a feeling that the pace of events had accelerated over the last two

[1] Absent Without Leave.
[2] Ronald McCormick, letter to the author, 19 September 1994.
[3] Hilary Rubinstein, letter to the author, 11 October 1994.

months. After all, it was only six weeks before VE-Day that I saw rescue workers digging among the rubble of the Vallance Road flats at Bethnal Green which were struck by a V–2 on March 27, killing more than 130 people.[1]

The shadows cast on VE-Day were many: Dr James Howie, the deputy assistant director of pathology at the War Office, who was mingling with the crowds in London that day, recalled: 'On VE-Day the recollection of the death of one particular friend and colleague focused my feelings of grief for all the terrible losses and waste of good effort. My friend was Dr E. C. (Ted) Smith, a Dublin microbiologist, who was medical director of the Medical Research Laboratory outside Lagos. He served the medical war effort in Nigeria in countless unselfish ways. It was Smith who backed up and urged acceptance of the idea of a field test to discover, against the odds, if vaccine might be used to make the west African airfields into genuinely yellow fever free zones. He resisted all pressures to take home leave until the summer of 1943, by which time the victory in North Africa had greatly reduced the risk to convoys from submarine warfare. On the voyage to Freetown a lone raider dropped a bomb down the funnel of his ship, and Smith's cabin was exactly where the bomb exploded. For me personally the sadness of that particular waste of precious life was overwhelming.'[2]

In the War Cabinet offices in London, the men and women who had been at the centre of some of the most secret aspects of the war had been able for some days to relax their daily, and nightly, vigil. One of them, Joan Bright, later wrote: 'I seem to have spent VE-Day on the second floor of the War Cabinet offices, gossiping, talking, aimlessly, with equally gossiping, talking and aimless colleagues. There seemed no more for us to do.'[3] To the north of London, at Bletchley, those who had been monitoring the most secret German radio messages for nearly five years had likewise seen the intensity of their work diminish as VE-Day approached. The day itself, Walter Ettinghausen recalled, 'was nothing special. We knew it was coming.'

More closely than any other group in Britain, the codebreakers at Bletchley had followed the final disintegrating hours of the German war machine. They had decrypted, and passed on to those who could make effective use of them, the final orders sent out from Berlin for such

[1] Alan Palmer, letter to the author, 26 September 1994.
[2] James Howie, 'New thinking and actions', in *As You Were, VE-Day: a medical retrospect*, British Medical Association, London, 1984, p. 86.
[3] Joan Bright Astley, letter to the author, 22 October 1994.

remaining defensive action as the German air, sea and land forces were still capable. They had extracted from the air waves the very last messages of the German military, naval and air commanders as their positions became hopeless and they laid down their arms. Throughout May 6 and May 7 they had heard, as if it were an audible sound, the last fitful gasps of the Third Reich.

At Bletchley, as so often elsewhere, it was some small local touch that remained in the memory that day. May 8 happened to be the birthday of two of the women officers there: Jane Bennett of the ATS and Thelma Ziman, a 'Wren'. These birthday celebrations were as immediate as the victory. Then routine took over. 'We cleared up arrears, things that had been too complicated to resolve on the previous few days,' Ettinghausen recalled. 'There was a tremendous amount of knowledge of those last few days, and other backlog, to be filled in. And then I had to set down an account of what we had done since 1941. Meanwhile, the Japanese work went on.'

Ettinghausen also remembered how, as an eight-year-old British boy living with his mother in Switzerland on November 11, 1918, the maid had burst into the room and shouted the one word, *Armistice*. That single word meant that his father, who had been held as a civilian internee in Ruhleben camp near Berlin since 1914, would be a free man. The ending of the Second World War held less rejoicing for the son. Among the thousands of secret German messages that he, a Jew, had seen during his work at Bletchley was one from a German naval captain in the summer of 1944, reporting that his ship was carrying Jews as part of the 'final solution'. Ettinghausen was never to forget that ominous message. A colleague at Bletchley later told him that she had seen a similar message, also from a ship's captain, that there were Jews being transported on his ship, 'some giving birth, some dying', on their way from a Greek island to the mainland.[1] The deportees were then taken, though neither Ettinghausen nor his friend knew it at the time, across the Balkans, through central Europe and Poland, to the death camp at Treblinka.

In the village of Westerham, near to which Churchill had his country house, Chartwell, there were no public celebrations that night, and the village green, on which Churchill's statue now stands, was silent. 'The villagers had decided not to celebrate while the war in the Far East is still on,' one newspaper reported.[2]

---

[1] Walter Eytan (formerly Ettinghausen), in conversation with the author, 25 August 1994.
[2] 'Short Circuit Of The News', *Daily Mirror*, 9 May 1945, p. 7, col. 2.

Others could not celebrate because they still felt, and were never to cease feeling, a sense of personal loss. A schoolboy of those days, Michael Dunnill, who lived in Bristol, later wrote: 'Yes, indeed I do remember VE-Day but not, alas, as a day of great rejoicing in our household. My brother who was twelve years older than me had been killed the previous November and this cast a gloom over my father and mother which never really lifted for the rest of their lives. My father, who was a surveyor with a good job since 1938, had a bad time in the early 1930s during the recession and had been without work. As a consequence my brother had to leave school without going to university but had joined the Army and done well. He survived the disastrous Norwegian campaign in 1940 as a platoon commander . . . After arrival in Normandy on June 10, 1944 he became a company commander and on July 15, was involved in fighting near Vendes where he was wounded and was awarded the Military Cross. He was flown back to the Queen Elizabeth Hospital in Birmingham and had shrapnel removed from his legs. Shortly after this he rejoined the battalion and took part in the assault on Le Havre where he was again wounded but not severely. The battalion progressed through France and Belgium, and he had heard that he was soon to go to the Staff College when, on the 4 November, he was killed while the battalion was attacking Oude Stoof clearing the Germans out of the country up to the line of the Maas.

'At the time we were living in a gardener's cottage on a large estate in Sneyd Park, a suburb of Bristol, many of the houses in Clifton having been requisitioned. Not that this cottage overlooking the Avon gorge was all that safe. One night in 1941 no fewer than seven unexploded bombs dropped in the vicinity. I have never believed in telepathy, but I have the most vivid memory of returning from school one afternoon in November 1944 and as I made my way through the grounds to our house I had a premonition that something awful had occurred. On opening the front door I realized at once what it was. My father, who was an emotionally robust and jolly individual, was in the drawing room weeping, something I had never witnessed before and the memory of which upsets me even fifty years on. My distraught mother handed me the letter from my sister-in-law giving us the news that my brother had been killed in action. It is true to say that my parents never regained their old sparkle and gaiety which had seen them through so many adversities.

'On VE-Day we had a holiday which was spent quietly at home. I was working for my higher school certificate and a scholarship, which was necessary for me to go to medical school, and was glad of the time to study. Although living in Bristol we were surrounded by large grounds and I do not remember anything of local street parties and the like, but we did listen to the wireless and heard the crowds outside Buckingham Palace. Not a great saga I am afraid but that is how it was.'[1]

Joel Elkes, then living in Birmingham, had been educated in the Lithuanian city of Kovno. He had come to England for a year in 1931, and had stayed. His younger sister Sara joined him in 1937. His overriding thought as the war ended was the fate of his parents. His father, Dr Elchanan Elkes, was a distinguished physician who had been elected by the Kovno Jewish community to accept the leadership after the Germans had forced them to live in a sealed ghetto. For three years he had led his community with immense courage and dignity, loyal to their needs and disregarding his own safety. He had persistently refused Gestapo demands to participate in the selections for deportation, and, amid increasing hunger and privation, had done his utmost to maintain morale, work and hope in his trapped community.

On VE-Day the thirty-two-year-old Joel Elkes was working in his medical laboratory in Birmingham. 'The radio carries the news,' he recalled. 'I decide to call it a day in the lab, run to the bus, and am home in the late afternoon. On the way, cars are tooting, people are rattling dustbins in their courtyards in celebration, and there is much singing in the streets. The pubs are filling up, the smell of smoke and beer wafting as we pass. Home, in our small third floor flat at 220 Broad Street, Charmian, my wife, greets me. We pull back the rough curtains (made of dyed sackcloth) and throw the windows open. The warm breeze sweeps through the rooms. We have our supper, and watch the sun set, and wait through dusk into the night. We do not turn on the lights, but light candles and put them into our wrought iron candlesticks, our present to each other soon after we got married.

'We sit quietly, and watch the city lights flicker below. "It's over," we say, "it's over, it's over." We say it again and again, trying to grasp the full meaning of the day. Inside me, though, there is a large, dark, numb presence which I dare not look at. The last I heard of my parents was the rumour that they had escaped to Yakutsk, Siberia. I refuse to contemplate the alternatives.'[2]

Joel and Sara Elkes had frequently spoken about their parents, forced, as the war came to an end, 'to face the unfaceable and speak the unspeakable', as Joel Elkes expressed it.[3] In Britain, Sara's life had been hard,

[1] Michael Dunnill, letter to the author, 11 October 1994.
[2] Professor Joel Elkes, letter to the author, 4 November 1994.
[3] Professor Joel Elkes, in conversation with the author, 4 November 1994.

'scrubbing floors, lighting fires at five in the morning', she recalled. She had often gone hungry. During the war she became a nurse in London. She was twenty years old. As the Allied armies fought their way into Germany, and the terrible extent of the atrocities against Jews became clear, she realized that 'something dreadful' had happened to her father. Devastated at the thought that he must almost certainly have perished, she was taken ill, and her hands broke out into suppurating boils. She went to the Matron to ask for some time off. 'Nurse, you've got to pull yourself together and get on with it,' was Matron's reply. Literally running away from the hospital, Sara Elkes found lodgings elsewhere. On VE-Day she was lying in bed racked with pain, anxiety and foreboding. 'I was lying there with my septic hands, with the fireworks going off in the streets.'[1]

It was a long time before Sara Elkes recovered her equanimity. Later that summer she and her brother learned that their father had died in Dachau in October 1944, three months after having being deported there with four thousand of his fellow Jews, from Kovno, and less than a week before the Russian army liberated Kovno. Fifty years later Sara Elkes learned, from someone who had been with her father in Dachau, that he had refused a German demand to point out who were the weakest and sickest of those with him, and had gone on hunger strike to protest against these selections, which invariably led to the killing of those who were selected. Dr Elkes had died of starvation, on a matter of principle.

The death of a parent in such terrible circumstances not only clouded the days of victory, but the months and years that followed. Joel Elkes recalled, 'I was working in a laboratory, and a letter came from someone I had been at school with in Kovno, a British journalist who had visited Dachau immediately after liberation. It told of my father's death. My chief was in his Officers Training Corps uniform. I found myself sobbing helplessly against the khaki. I could not handle it. I couldn't speak about it. That dark numb state remained with me for the best part of twenty years.'[2]

In London, his broadcast over, Churchill had to get to the House of Commons. His detective, Walter Thompson, later recalled: 'The car was literally forced through the crowds. No engine power was necessary. Everyone seemed determined to shake him by the hand. In Parliament Square the cheering crowds closed right in. Mr Churchill came forward

[1] Sara Elkes, conversation with the author, 28 October 1994.
[2] Professor Joel Elkes, in conversation with the author, 4 November 1994.

to stand on the front seat of the open car with me while mounted police cleared the way.'[1] 'The vast crowds of cheering people in Parliament Square made it almost impossible for the car to get through, and Churchill did not reach the Chamber until almost 3.30 p.m. Harold Nicolson, who was among the six hundred Members of Parliament there to greet him, wrote that night of how 'a slight stir was observed behind the Speaker's chair, and Winston, looking coy and cheerful, came in. The House rose as a man, and yelled and yelled and waved their Order Papers. He responded, not with a bow exactly, but with an odd shy jerk of the head and with a wide grin. Then he started to read to us the statement that he had just made on the wireless.'

Nicolson noted that after Churchill had finished he put his manuscript aside and with 'wide gestures' thanked the House of Commons for its 'noble support' throughout the war years.[2] During his words of thanks, Churchill spoke of his deep gratitude to the House of Commons, which had proved itself, he said, 'the strongest foundation for waging war that has ever been seen in the whole of our long history.'

In the House of Commons twenty-six years earlier, Churchill had been present when Lloyd George had announced that Germany had accepted the armistice. 'I recollect well, at the end of the last war, more than a quarter of a century ago,' Churchill said, 'that the House, when it heard the long list of the surrender terms, the armistice terms, which had been imposed upon the Germans, did not feel inclined for debate or business, but desired to offer thanks to Almighty God, to the Great Power which seems to shape and design the fortunes of nations and the destiny of man: and I therefore beg, Sir, with your permission to move: "That this House do now attend at the Church of St Margaret, Westminster, to give humble and reverent thanks to Almighty God for our deliverance from the threat of German domination." This is the identical Motion which was moved in former times.'[3]

The House of Commons then adjourned, its members walking across Old Palace Yard to St Margaret's for a service of Thanksgiving. At the end of the service the Speaker read out the names of the twenty-one Members of Parliament who had been killed during the war.

Returning on foot to the House of Commons, Churchill moved 'That this House do now adjourn'. It was 4.31 p.m. When Churchill was passing through the Central Lobby, Nicolson wrote, 'the crowd there broke into

[1] W.H. Thompson, *I Was Churchill's Shadow*, Christopher Johnson, London, 1951, p. 157.
[2] Harold Nicolson, letter to his son, 8 May 1945, Nigel Nicolson (editor), *Harold Nicolson, Diaries and Letters 1939–1945*, Collins, London, 1967, p. 457.
[3] *Hansard*, 8 May 1945, cols. 1867–9.

loud clapping. He hesitated and then hurried on. A little boy dashed out: "Please, sir, may I have your autograph?" Winston took a long time getting out his glasses and wiping them. Then he ruffled the little boy's hair and gave him back his beastly little album. "That will remind you of a glorious day," he said, and the crowd clapped louder than before.'[1]

Churchill then left the Palace of Westminster for Buckingham Palace: the King had asked him to look over the text of the royal broadcast. 'On the way, Winston asked me for a cigar,' his detective later recalled, 'but in the excitement I had forgotten to bring his case. He laughed and said: "Drive to the Annexe and I will get one. I must put one on for them. They expect it." '[2]

At six o'clock that evening King George VI broadcast to his nation. For millions of listeners the broadcast was a high point of the evening. 'Much hard work awaits us,' he said, 'in the restoration of our own country after the ravages of war, and in helping to restore peace and sanity to a shattered world.' One newspaper reported: 'Women and men fainted at a rate of about ten a minute in the enormous crowd gathered at London's Victoria Station to listen to the King's broadcast. Police estimated that there must have been 100,000 people there. Ambulance men and police fought to clear a path for the victims of too much VE-Day, but had to resort to lifting them high over the shoulders of the close-packed crowds.'[3]

Everyone who could do so gathered around a wireless, as they had done in the bleak days of 1940. 'We listened to the King's broadcast,' Noel Coward wrote in his diary, 'then to Eisenhower, Monty and Alexander. Then I walked down the Mall and stood outside Buckingham Palace, which was floodlit. The crowd was stupendous.

'The King and Queen came out on the balcony, looking enchanting. We all roared ourselves hoarse. I suppose this is the greatest day in our history.'[4]

Thousands of mothers took their small children to see the King and Queen that day. The impressions made on the seven-year-old Peter Hewlett remained vivid for fifty years. One of ten children, he had been evacuated from London to the country. 'When we came back from the country our parents were amazed: we cleaned our teeth and washed our

---

[1] Harold Nicolson, letter to his son, 8 May 1945, Nigel Nicolson (editor), *Harold Nicolson, Diaries and Letters 1939–1945*, Collins, London, 1967, p. 458.

[2] W.H. Thompson, *Sixty Minutes with Winston Churchill*, Christopher Johnson, London, 1953, pp. 88–9.

[3] 'Londoners were there by the acre', *Daily Mirror*, 9 May 1945, p. 5, col. 2.

[4] Graham Payn and Sheridan Morley (editors), *The Noel Coward Diaries*, Weidenfeld and Nicolson, London 1982, p. 29.

faces.' Waiting in the vast crowd, the small boy remembered the long periods when nobody came on to the balcony, and how the crowd responded with a roar to every movement of a curtain or a window. At one moment he saw a bird settle on the flagpole and pointed up excitedly, calling to his mother. She looked and pointed, the people around looked and pointed, and a roar went up in the belief that someone had been seen in one of the Palace windows.[1]

Among the hundreds of thousands gazing at the royal balcony that night was Clare Boulter, whose work at the Admiralty was to examine top-secret captured German naval documents. As many as 50,000 files had been seized a few weeks earlier and flown to Britain. 'I was assigned to a group concerned with war crimes,' she later wrote. 'Where among these 50,000 files might there be evidence against the twenty-two shortly to be tried at Nuremberg? Here luck and doggedness were more to the point than expertise, and we found many things that proved useful, among them the evidence of collusion between Quisling and the Germans before the invasion of Norway.' This was something that the Norwegians were able to use at Quisling's trial, to great effect. 'Among our other successes was also the identification of the U-boat responsible for sinking the *Athenia* on the first day of the war.'[2]

Like millions of Londoners, Clare Boulter and her colleagues had set aside their work that day. She later recalled: 'The King and Queen did their balcony bit, we roared and cheered. I was intrigued by a spontaneous ceremonial on our fringe of the crowd: a very solemn group had made a bonfire and was feeding it with Green Park chairs, each one being passed from hand to hand with a bow, the last in line placing it on the flames with courtly deliberation.

'All this was not easy on the feet and as my party included one allergic to crowds and another inadvisedly wearing high heels, we departed the scene at 10.30 p.m. How I spent the rest of May 8, 1945, I can't now remember. Perhaps I couldn't even remember on May 9.'[3]

The radio reports told of how Churchill had joined the King and Queen, and the two Princesses, on the Palace balcony, after the King's speech. One of those in the crowd was Iris Portal, whose brother, R.A. Butler, was Minister of Education in Churchill's coalition government. 'I had never been in such a vast crowd before, but there was no need to

---

[1] Peter Hewlett, conversation with the author, 18 October 1994.
[2] Clare Baines, 'Special Duties in World War Two', p. 9. I am grateful to Edward Thomas for a copy of this typescript.
[3] Clare Baines (née Boulter), letter to the author, 9 September 1994.

feel nervous. The people were exuberant but disciplined. I remember no incident of disorder. It seemed as if the amazing comradeship and good will that one had experienced during the war in London, in the black-out as well as the day time, in public transport, in air raid shelters – everywhere – still existed. All the way through the darkest days from 1940 onwards "brother clasped the hand of brother, stepping fearless through the night". That atmosphere was very present in the huge crowd which awaited the appearance of the leaders of the Nation, who had stood by us from beginning to end.

'When the Royal family and the Prime Minister stepped out on to the balcony the crowd cheered and cheered with genuine warmth and affection. Some people were in tears. No one (or so it seemed) was there from curiosity. Princess Elizabeth wore WRAC uniform. Princess Margaret was still a schoolgirl. They had been based at Windsor most of the war, and the King and Queen in London, where they shared our dangers and were often with us at scenes of death and destruction. For Winston Churchill, I think that this was his finest hour. Only a few months later, when I was working in Islington at the time of the General Election of 1945, I heard him booed as he drove through the streets, standing up in a Land Rover. But on 8 May 1945 people remembered that without his leadership we might have had German troops before Buckingham Palace, and possibly Nazi leaders on the balcony.

'We stayed for an hour or more. The Royal Family appeared several times, the crowd waved little Union Jacks, sang songs, and cheered and cheered. Everyone was friendly and relaxed, though it seemed unbelievable that we could now be free of fear. I did not myself celebrate later . . . Like many others I was on my own. My husband was still on active service in the Middle East. I believe that in many parts of London there were street parties that night and festivities in hotels and restaurants. But I was in no mood for revelry. We still had a long way to go.'[1]

Among those celebrating in London that night was Corporal Seymour Moses, an America laboratory technician with 306 Station Hospital, just outside Reading. He was already in London that day on a three-day pass, and was automatically entitled to leave extension were he to be away from the hospital when war ended. He took the extension with alacrity, 'mixing in with the throng'. His hospital was treating German prisoners-of-war who had been brought over from Europe after D-Day. On his return there he continued his work as before. 'My reaction on being in the actual presence of German soldiers was quite mixed,' he recalled. 'On

---

[1] Iris Portal, letter to the author, 5 October 1994.

the one hand, what I saw before me seemed to be ordinary city or country boys caught up in a war who would rather have been home. And on the other hand, I had the knowledge of the atrocities being perpetrated by the Nazis. What made it most horrible to me was the fact that before me were "ordinary human beings".'

Most of the wounded Germans, Moses added, 'were quite docile but seemed to be well indoctrinated and believed that New York had been bombed. They had also failed to accept the fact that the Allies were advancing in Europe which I pointed out to them on a large map I had on the wall. I was quite wary of the officer POWs as well as the young German boys who were drafted toward the end of the war. They seemed to be rabid Nazis. We did have one elderly POW who bemoaned the fact that he was a prisoner-of-war in World War I and now, again, in World War II.'[1]

German prisoners-of-war in the West were far more fortunate than those who had been taken captive in the East. Their camps were well maintained, food was plentiful by war-time standards, and Red Cross parcels brought them cigarettes and chocolate. The Red Cross also ensured a regular exchange of letters from home. As a young schoolboy I remember much local bitterness that the prisoners-of-war on our hill just west of Oxford received from time to time fresh eggs for breakfast while locals had to subsist on powdered egg. Within a year of VE-Day most prisoners-of-war held in the West had returned home, including hundreds of thousands who had been shipped to Canada.

One London schoolboy with particularly vivid memories of VE-Day was Edward Kanter, who had earlier seen at close hand, having been blown across the street by the blast, the horrors of a V–2 rocket explosion. 'I looked up and there was a tree with a person's body hanging on it or part of a body. I ran towards the site where the rocket had fallen and started to tear away with others at the planks and bricks and the dust and the turmoil of this horrendous scene. There is no way that I can accurately record what I saw, it was too horrendous for a boy of my age to comprehend.'

Kanter was fourteen years old. On VE-Day, he later recalled, 'I was playing with my brother and some other kids at the bottom of Merchant Street, Bow, with an improvised cricket bat that I had made out of a banister from a bombed out house and a plank of wood. My brother hit the ball into a reservoir built by the Government, I think they were

---

[1] Seymour Moses, letter to the author, 28 October 1994.

labelled EWS (Emergency Water Supplies). Anyway what the officials had done was to brick up or fill in bomb sites with water so that the fire brigade would have access to it.

'I climbed over the wall to collect the ball that my brother had knocked into it and slipped, I remember well, going down and down, and then hitting bottom and then coming back up, and on my way back up facing the wall I passed a fireplace and hanging crookedly over it an old picture. It was as if the whole of that home had been captured and frozen in a solitary moment of time, locked and fixed in a death trap. I reached the surface and my brother was screaming and trying to pull me out but he was too frail and I went down again, coming up for the second time I felt a massive hand reach out, grab me by the shoulder and heave me over the side. It was Ginger Harry, a well-known character who was a fish porter in the market.

'Having coughed up as much of the muck as I could I then to my horror realised that I had ruined my clothes and that my poor mother would be distraught and so with my brother we tried to reach our home over bombed out buildings and crawled in so that I could change and wash my dirty clothes in the bath. Alas we were caught, but when my mother heard the story all was forgiven.'

All that happened on VE-Day. 'There was a massive street party organised. Every family in the street were asked to put two shillings into a bag, those who could not afford it, would be supported by the others. Trestle tables were hastily erected, bunting came from nowhere and the whole street was ablaze with colour and children laughing – none of them knowing why all this excitement was taking place. Then suddenly from the pub at the top of the road a publican who was known as "Hunch Back Harry" had managed to save a wooden barrel of beer, and how I can remember him pulling this out of his Public House – he was a little man – and shouting, "There you are, its all for you" and kicking the barrel down this road where it rolled and rolled until it was stopped by the men, broken open, and drunk.'[1]

One aspect of London's celebrations on VE-Day remained vivid in the mind of one schoolboy for fifty years. Robin Maxwell-Hyslop, was less than a month short of his fourteenth birthday, when he had made his way to London from his boarding school in the north by train. 'Every nook and cranny of London buzzed with excitement, which manifested itself in diverse ways,' he recalled. 'The rubber-shortage interdicted the production of celebratory toy balloons: but the most enterprising breed

---

[1] Edward Kanter, letter to the author, 23 October 1994.

of street-traders, then known as "spivs", were assisting patriotic celebrations by offering for sale two types of "French letters" tied to the top of thin canes; those known as "with teat", which had a little bulge at the end, sold for two-and-sixpence each, and the less sophisticated variety for a florin (two shillings). Both found a ready market, particularly among servicemen and women, who brandished them triumphantly thereafter. Long before night threw her very incomplete mantle over Green Park couples were joyously copulating all over the grass. So natural and appropriate an expression of universal relief at the end of the War in Europe did that seem, that not even the old ladies, who normally clicked their tongues as drakes from the lake accosted more than willing ducks, expressed anything but a benign sharing of the universal happiness. I had only five shillings to last me through the day, including lunch and transport back to Euston Station: so as evening fell, I resold my florin's worth of joy to a deprived sailor at cost price, which enabled me to get back to the station by bus.'[1]

Amongst the vast crowds that milled through the centre of London during the evening were many individuals who could not fully share the almost universal rejoicing. One of them, Silvia Szulman, had come to Britain in 1939 as an eleven-year-old refugee from Germany. She recalled: 'The mood at home that day was sombre but I spent the evening with a girl from school who lived above her family's fish and chip shop, whose clothes always smelt of rancid oil and whose father was in the last stages of syphilis. She was tallish, gawky with large feet and clumsy shoes. A nice girl but no one's friend in particular. All the other girls were celebrating with their families, at home or outside pubs, but this girl and I met at Acton Town Underground station after supper and took the tube into the West End. There we joined the crowds drifting towards Whitehall and watched as Winston Churchill and others waved from the balcony of a government building. The crowd cheered and sang. We joined in and I think the group on the balcony joined in, too. But then they went inside, the doors were shut and the crowd around us started to dance beginning with the Lambeth Walk and Hokey Cokey-like dances. After a few minutes we went home. Perhaps, we felt out of place because we looked young for our age, but that was not all.

'I don't know about my friend, but I wanted to join in. I wanted to dance, to be merry but I felt no elation. I was certainly relieved that I was now safe from Nazi persecution. As well as being Polish Jews, my parents had been active in the underground Communist Party in Berlin

---

[1] Sir Robin Maxwell-Hyslop, letter to the author, 25 October 1994.

where we had all lived in constant fear till March 1939. Then, just after my eleventh birthday, we were lucky enough to come to England but throughout the war, I dreaded that the Germans would catch up with us.

'And so on May 8, I might well have rushed through the streets of central London, or of Ealing where we lived, skipping, dancing, shouting Halleluya! and praising the Lord, even if I did not believe in him. What held me back and my parents too, was that we feared that the very worst had happened to our relatives in Poland and in Paris.

'Of course, we were glad the war had ended, but like the relief felt after surviving a hurricane or earthquake, our sense of deliverance was tempered by apprehension of how much devastation we would find. The liberation of Paris, with its absence of Jews, had been ominous enough. One of two of my mother's sisters, who lived in Paris, had been lucky enough to have been hidden in the countryside near Tours with her four-year-old son, and both returned to Paris. But the actual end of the war, I associate with a letter from her husband, Michel. He had returned from several concentration camps. One was Auschwitz/Birkenau, another, Mauthausen in Austria, and according to him, the most horrendous. "Forgive me," the letter began, "but I have to write and tell you about all the things that happened. Everything I saw in the camps. Everything that happened to me. It is so gruesome, so hideous, so painful I have to tell you about it. Perhaps writing it down will make it feel better for me. It is driving me mad and I cannot keep it to myself."

'My parents were merciless with me. I had to know the letter's monstrous contents. "It is your duty, it is good for you". I could not read the letter myself as it was written in Yiddish, and so they sat down with me and read it out, translating it into German whenever necessary. After only a few paragraphs of atrocities, unimaginable if one is not a crazed sadist, I begged them to stop. But they would not spare me. "You only have to listen! What about those who had to endure it!" I listened on. I listened as Michel wanders into a room with rows and rows of tables. On each table lies a body of a naked woman. The women have been used for medical experiments carried out without anaesthetic. He touches one body with a buttock cut out. "I touched her and she quivered. She was still warm."

'I ran out and locked myself into the bathroom and in between sobbing bathed my eyes to no effect. To make up for my cowardice, I watched the film of Belsen showing at the local Odeon. I sat in the back row and could hardly believe those people were my people and that what had happened to them, had been scheduled for me. I howled. When the usherette asked: "Are you all right?", I went home. The truth was that I did not want to know. It may have been my duty, it may have been "good for me" but I did not even want to think about it. I did not want to dwell on what might have happened to me, on the horrors meted out to people like me but who had not been lucky enough to catch a train and a boat to Harwich in 1939. Apart from the brutality, what upset me then and alarms me now, is the anonymity. The corpses, whether still alive or already dead, had been eroded of any vestige of identity and individuality. When they were tipped into the mass grave, it was like tipping a month's delivery of coal down a shute.

'I had already seen photographs of the death camps in newspapers in the days leading up to May 8. These had been quite enough to make anyone shudder and I had been told that all our relatives in Poland, and I had met many of them, had disappeared either in the Warsaw ghetto or in concentration camps. But what my parents, who had insisted that I knew all the details of Michel's letter, kept from me, was the fate of Regina, another sister who lived in Paris, and Helene her little girl whom I knew and loved. "We have no idea where Helene is", they told me. It was like "missing presumed killed", one of the cruellest and most futile sentences. From then on and till I heard the truth some years later – they died in the ovens at Auschwitz/Birkenau – I fantasized about finding Helene. But I must have guessed the truth.

'Newsreels and newspapers also showed the destroyed towns of Germany. My mother's communist heart was warmed by the link-up of American and Soviet soldiers, and the ruins of Berlin made me coldly glad. It served them right, I told myself. Not till I went to Berlin decades later and saw that every house that I had ever lived in had been destroyed, did I allow myself to weep at the loss. In May 1945 it was only the loss of close relatives, especially my little cousin, and just about all the children I ever went to school with in Berlin, that hurt.

'Our New Year's Eve parties at home in Berlin before 1938 – that's how I wished we could have marked the end of the war. Lots of friends, food and drink, champagne and streamers at midnight, boisterous singing and dancing, rejoicing and exuberance.'[1]

Past memories of happiness and present agonies were a frequent feature of VE-Day for those whose early days, families and friends had been bound up in another country, another era. For each individual there was some particular focus that made or marred the celebrations. One of those

[1] Silvia Rodgers, (née Szulman) letter to the author, 12 August 1994.

for whom they were special was the sixteen-year-old Martin Eisemann, then at school at Shefford, in Bedfordshire. In January 1939 he had come to Britain from Frankfurt with his parents and sister. 'The end of the war was of enormous emotional significance to me,' he recalled. 'Somehow I made my way from Shefford to London, some fifty miles, and found myself on this tremendous day outside Buckingham Palace with roughly a million other loyal subjects. I remember the entire royal family coming out to the nation and the joy, jubilation and relief defy any description. Then the crowd moved on to outside the Ministry of Health. Mr Churchill and the Cabinet came out to the balcony and the great man called down: "This is your victory!" The cheering was tumultuous! I have never in my life again witnessed and experienced so much joy and happiness on such an enormous scale.'

Martin Eisemann added, as an afterthought: 'A number of times I passed the Ministry of Health and wistfully looked up to that balcony where great moments of history were made. It was empty!'[1]

The East End had been the worst hit of all the London residential areas by bombs and rockets. On VE-Day the sight of the East End was one of devastation. Alan Palmer later noted, of the victory celebrations: 'People accepted that there was a war to win in the Far East, for many had sons or brothers serving in Burma, but the strain of battle was over and there was a widespread desire to live peacefully within a more equitable society'.[2]

Not only was the war in the Far East still to be won, but a political battle was about to begin that was to see an electioneering Churchill booed in the streets of East London, and was to bring in the first Labour Government for more than fourteen years. Other political battles found a focus in London on VE-Day. The Zionist leader, David Ben-Gurion was in the city, and wrote a single sentence that day in his usually voluminous diary: 'Victory day – sad, very sad.'[3] The knowledge that six million Jews had been murdered had caused Ben-Gurion to sink into a deep depression. So too had the British Government's clear reluctance to agree to Jewish statehood now that the war was over. If England did not alter its policy, he told a press conference a few weeks later, 'there is a possibility of resistance in Palestine.'[4]

---

[1] Martin Eisemann, letter to the author, 11 September 1994.
[2] Alan Palmer, *The East End, Four Centuries of London Life*, John Murray, London, 1989, pp. 148–9.
[3] Ben-Gurion, diary, 8 May 1945: quoted in Michael Bar-Zohar, *Ben-Gurion, A Biography*, Weidenfeld and Nicolson, London, 1978, p. 125.
[4] Quoted in Michael Bar-Zohar, *Ben-Gurion, A Biography*, Weidenfeld and Nicolson, London, 1978, p. 125.

Among those who reached Britain on VE-Day was Squadron Leader Peter Ruston. For the previous week he had been crossing the Atlantic on the ocean liner *Normandie*, then serving as a troopship, with 15,000 men on board: they had shared seven to a cabin, with two meals a day in rotation. On leaving the United States, Ruston later recalled, 'we had no idea that the end of the war was so close'. Landing at Liverpool they were greatly surprised to learn that it was over. 'I was on my way to my then wife's house at Newport, Monmouthshire but took a train via London where the celebrations were in full swing. VE-night in London was a mad throng of servicemen and women and civilians. I went to my normal wartime haunts; the Brass Ass (Brasserie Universal) in Piccadilly and the Shepherds Tavern in Shepherd Market and ended up at a private party which ended at near dawn when I caught a train to Newport.'

Within a month, Squadron Leader Ruston had flown out to India. 'VJ-night was spent at Madras; I had been flying during the day and got very drunk trying to catch up with my friends.'[1]

Another of those who reached Britain on VE-Day was the former prisoner-of-war, Roger Peacock, who had been made captive in 1940. His experiences as a prisoner also served to blunt his rejoicing. As he recalled: 'The reality was too much. I cannot speak for my friends, but for myself the capacity to react to events was overloaded. I could not feel. My emotions were in shock and remained so. Let heartsickness pass beyond a certain bitter point and the life of the heart is over – or that is how it seemed. I pretended affection and joy and happiness but it was all merely an act. I felt nothing. I arrived home in the afternoon of VE-Day but the acceptance was intellectual, merely.

'There were, of course, great rejoicings in the city centre; bands, dancing in the streets, excited crowds, free drinks and meals for men in uniform, and so on. I didn't bother. Effectively, VE was, a *dies non* – a non-day – as was its successor. I wasn't excited, I didn't drink (in those days); I was well fed, with double ration cards and ample offerings from sympathetic neighbours, to whom I offered (I hope) convincing gratitude. So I listened to the radio, tried to respond to my family, especially my mother, read whatever I could find of interest, and retired early to bed. The family, who had obviously been briefed by "Authority" on how to treat returned prisoners, forbore to harry me and complied with my obvious wish for the minimum of fuss.

'Only those who had shared captivity with me could have understood; only with them could I have been at ease – and they were dispersed all

---

[1] Air Commodore Peter Ruston, CBE, DFC, letter to the author, 17 October 1994.

over the world. I could only hope that they were happier than I was.'[1]

Another returning prisoner-of-war, Vic West, had reached home a few days earlier. 'By May 8, I was in Chiswick with a pile of ham sandwiches, and three bottles of hooch. I wasn't the least impressed by the Victory junketing going on in London or radio reports of Churchill on the Balcony at the Palace. *I'd made it.*'[2]

Later that evening, in his rooms overlooking St James's Park, Churchill was studying the most recent telegrams from Moscow. One of them, from the British Chargé d'Affaires Frank Roberts, concerned a complaint from the Soviets about the way the British Government was protesting about the sixteen Polish emissaries who had been seized outside Warsaw, and were being held in prison in Moscow. 'We are utterly indifferent,' Churchill telegraphed to Roberts in reply, 'to anything that the Soviets may say by way of propaganda. No one here believes a single word.' When it became 'worthwhile', Churchill added, 'devastating replies can be made in Parliament'. At present, however, the British Government was endeavouring 'to shield the Soviets'. The breach with the Soviet Union was almost complete. 'It is no longer desired by us,' Churchill informed Roberts, 'to maintain detailed arguments with the Soviet Government about their views and actions.'[3]

Shortly after 10 p.m. Churchill made his way through the vast block of Government offices to make his second appearance on the balcony of the Ministry of Health, overlooking Whitehall and Parliament Square. A friend, the newspaper proprietor Lord Camrose, wrote in his diary: 'I accompanied him on the long walk from the Annexe through the various Government buildings, and the roar of enthusiasm which came up from the crowd at the sight of him and his grandson, Julian Sandys, was deafening. I went on to one of the adjoining balconies. Not only was the space immediately in front of the building packed, but there was a sea of faces stretching far up Whitehall and right down to Parliament Square.'[4]

'The roaring and cheering,' wrote Churchill's secretary, Elizabeth Layton, who was also on the adjoining balcony, 'exceeded by double anything I can remember at the Coronation.'[5] During his speech, Churchill told the thousands of people assembled below him: 'My dear friends,

---

[1] Roger Peacock, letter to the author, 26 August 1994.
[2] Vic West, letter to the author, 26 August 1994.
[3] Foreign Office telegram No. 2505 to Moscow, 8 May 1945, despatched at 10.05 p.m: Foreign Office papers, 371/50581. Public Record Office, Kew.
[4] 'VE Night, 8th May 1945', notes written by Lord Camrose on 9 May 1945. Private archive.
[5] Elizabeth Layton, letter to her parents, 8 May 1945. Private archive.

this is your hour. This is not victory of a party or of any class. It's a victory of the great British nation as a whole. We were the first, in this ancient island, to draw the sword against tyranny. After a while we were left all alone against the most tremendous military power that has been seen. We were all alone for a whole year. There we stood, alone. Did anyone want to give in?'

'No,' came the reply.
'Were we downhearted?'
'No!'

As the roar subsided Churchill continued: 'The lights went out and the bombs came down . . .' At that point, Churchill's detective recalled, 'quite accidentally, the flood-lights that were upon him from the opposite side of the road went dim. The crowd roared with laughter, and when he realised what had happened, he joined in."[1]

Churchill then took up his speech again: 'The lights went out and the bombs came down. But every man, woman and child in the country had no thought of quitting the struggle. London can take it. So we came back after long months from the jaws of death, out of the mouth of hell, while all the world wondered. When shall the reputation and faith of this generation of English men and women fail? I say that in the long years to come not only will the people of this island but of the world, wherever the bird of freedom chirps in human hearts, look back to what we've done and they will say "do not despair, do not yield to violence and tyranny, march straight forward and die if need be – unconquered". Now we have emerged from one deadly struggle – a terrible foe has been cast on the ground and awaits our judgment and our mercy.'

Turning to the war in the Far East, Churchill told the crowd: 'But there is another foe who occupies large portions of the British Empire, a foe stained with cruelty and greed – the Japanese. I rejoice we can all take a night off today and another day tomorrow. Tomorrow our great Russian allies will also be celebrating victory and after that we must begin the task of rebuilding our hearth and homes, doing our utmost to make this country a land in which all have a chance, in which all have a duty, and we must turn ourselves to fulfil our duty to our own countrymen, and to our gallant allies of the United States who were so foully and treacherously attacked by Japan. We will go hand in hand with them.

[1] W. H. Thompson, *Sixty Minutes with Winston Churchill*, Christopher Johnson, London, 1953, p. 89.

Even if it is a hard struggle we will not be the ones who will fail.'

The crowd replied by singing 'Land of Hope and Glory' and 'For He's a Jolly Good Fellow'. Churchill's detective later recalled how his master 'joined with the people in singing "Land of Hope and Glory," and indeed conducted them as they did so.'[1] Churchill then returned to the Annexe, where he spent the rest of the evening. As he worked through his ever-bulging box of telegrams and official correspondence he told Lord Camrose, his only guest, that the Americans had advanced '120 miles farther than was expected and, in accordance with the arrangement made with Stalin, would have to come back that distance'. Stalin would have 'eight capitals in his control.'[2]

Churchill told Camrose that he 'was making sure' of Italy, the Istrian peninsula and Greece. He had 'agreed the European line' with Stalin, he said, and 'while it was not all he could wish, it gave some guarantee for the future.'[3]

At eleven o'clock the King, the Queen and the two princesses made their sixth appearance on the balcony of Buckingham Palace, waving for ten minutes to the cheering crowds below. The princesses, in an unprecedented and spontaneous breach of protocol, had earlier slipped out of the Palace to join the revellers, accompanied by two Guards officers. Half an hour after midnight the King and Queen appeared again on the balcony. The crowd was as large and as enthusiastic as before.

Among those who were celebrating in London was Geoffrey Wigoder, who wrote in his diary: 'It was an amazing evening. Everywhere were enormous masses of people, drinking, wandering, dancing, singing. In Piccadilly Circus up the front of the London Pavilion surged a few youths and swung Harold Lloyd-like from the top. Then they got buckets of water and doused the people below. Some of the people below got rockets and directed them up at the youths above. Everyone is happy and good-humoured. Not as much drunkenness as I might have expected. With dark the lights come on. Streets of flares. Admiralty Arch, Nelson's Pillar, Big Ben and Buckingham Palace all stand out in the floodlighting. We go to the Mall and stand with the crowds in front of the Palace but the royal family have gone in for the night.

[1] W. H. Thompson, *Sixty Minutes with Winston Churchill*, Christopher Johnson, London, 1953, p. 89.
[2] Warsaw, Prague, Budapest, Bucharest, Sofia, Belgrade, Berlin and Vienna.
[3] 'VE Night, 8th May 1945', notes written by Lord Camrose on 9 May 1945. Private archive. The 'agreed' line had been established by Churchill and Stalin in Moscow in October 1944, whereby the Soviet Union would have the predominant influence in Hungary, Roumania and Bulgaria. Yugoslavia would be 50–50, and Britain and the United States would be predominant in Greece and Italy.

'We talk to everyone and everyone talks to us. We listen and watch the singing and dancing multitudes. Fireworks go up from the top of Admiralty Arch. Bonfires are lit. Searchlights dance around the skies. It is now 1 a.m. People everywhere are singing, dancing, courting (especially on the lawns along the Mall) and doing *meshuggas*.'[1]

Wigoder was ready to go to bed, but on his way home, an incident occurred that was to give him, a Jew, a sleepless night. 'As the tubes are closed, I have to walk an hour and a half back to my digs in Maida Vale. A couple of American soldiers with girls approach me and ask if I know where they could get a hotel for the night. I hear one girl say to an American, "You Americans have no culture. I admit Hitler was wrong in a lot of things but he was right about culture." Only a few days ago I went to a news theatre in Piccadilly Circus to the first films of the liberation of Bergen-Belsen and as the horrors were being shown, three young men got up at the back and shouted "Lies! Frauds! Fakes!". As I get to bed I wonder if we are going to have to go through it all again.'[2]

Aumie Shapiro was a witness of the final hours of the VE-Day celebrations in London. A week later he wrote to his friend who was serving in India: 'Until late hours of the night and even into the early hours of the morning, we mingled with merry London crowds, crowds which, although jubilant and carefree, were nevertheless well-behaved. St Paul's clock showed the hour to be one of the morning, as we stood to behold the breathtaking scene of floodlit St Paul's. The very cold stones seemed to come to life and with the red-clouded sky serving as a background (reflecting the many bonfires east of London) the beautiful picture of a victorious and gallant city cathedral personified the hopes of a new humanity.

'Again we footed our way home but on this occasion the time was close on 3.30 a.m. when I laid myself to sleep.'[3]

That night, more than a thousand high-spirited celebrators, some carrying dustbin lids, others armed with signs which they had removed from shops and pubs, tried to storm the Savoy Hotel. The hotel's loyal commissionaires barricaded the doors. Whether the attack was a social protest or mere high spirits is not recorded.

One of those who could not be 'jubilant and carefree' that night was Gordon Campbell, one of the officers who had entered Belsen on April 15, and who, during the fighting in the very last days, had been severely

[1] Lunacies.
[2] Geoffrey Wigoder, diary, London, entry for 8 May 1945. Private archive.
[3] Aumie Shapiro, letter to a friend, London, 13 May 1945. Private archive.

wounded. 'On May 8, 1945, I was thankfully aware that the war in Europe had ended, but I was in no condition to celebrate. I was in hospital, having been wounded three days before the cease-fire; and I was to remain in hospital for more than a year. The war for me, a Major in a Scottish division, was ended by a bullet through the middle at close quarters, fighting on the other side of the Elbe, after the attack across the river's half-mile width, near Hamburg, in assault boats. This was the day before Hitler committed suicide.

'I had an immediate operation in a field hospital, was flown to Brussels and then, in a Dakota full of stretcher cases, to RAF Lyneham. For reasons of civilian morale, wounded were moved by night, so that at about 5 a.m. on May 4 I arrived at Friern Barnet, formerly a mental hospital and then being used as a first treatment and clearing unit. I found myself there, in what had been a padded cell, on VE-Day. I was not in a good state and I remember little. On the 4th a nurse had telephoned to my father, a General in the War Office, and this was the first that he or my mother heard about my being a casualty. They had much to bear at that time because my brother, a Spitfire pilot, had been missing for a year and a half (eventually his death was reported – he had been challenged and shot after a daring escape as a prisoner-of war).

'The Scottish division in which I had fought, through the strenuous and wearing weeks of the Normandy campaign and the battles in Belgium, Holland and Germany, had suffered crippling casualties. Many of my friends in other units and members of my personal forward teams and their replacements had lost their lives. Although my faculties were not functioning normally on VE-Day, I could be thankful that the war against Hitler had been won and that I was still alive, although the war against Japan was continuing. I did not know what my own future would be. It was indeed a long time before an assessment could be made of my injuries and their degrees of permanancy. On May 14, I was moved to Barts,[1] at that time evacuated to Hertfordshire, and their skilled surgery and treatment gave me the best chance of returning to normal life over a year later, although I was not yet able to walk.

'I was twenty-three when I was wounded and twenty-five when I emerged from hospital. I was twenty-one when promoted to Major and given command of my field battery in 1942. We were very young!'[2]

Two others who also found it hard to rejoice in Britain on VE-Day

---

[1] St Bartholomew's Hospital.
[2] Lord Campbell of Croy, letter to the author, 4 October 1994.

were Megan Spooner and her twelve-year-old son James, whose father, Vice-Admiral E.J. Spooner, had not been heard of since the start of the war with Japan three and a half years earlier. 'We were still in the dark,' James Spooner recalled, 'as to where my father was. We subsequently learned from his Flag Lieutenant that he died on the little island of Tjebia, where they had been marooned in 1942 after escaping after the fall of Singapore'.[1]

That night, in his 'Evening Editorial' broadcast from London for the 'Voice of America', Templeton Peck, a familiar voice over the airwaves of Europe for almost a year, told his listeners that the Americans who had died on the battlefields 'in fighting for their own freedom, ... died for yours too ... whoever you are. Think of these Americans as your dead too. The cause that brought them into battle was the simple proposition that your freedom is inseparable from their freedom, and that your enslavement held the threat of their ultimate enslavement. Now, you who were enslaved are free, and those men who belong to Kansas and Mississippi and New York must turn, not homeward, but eastward to the last battleground, in Asia. From the lands of Europe their fathers came to America, seeking freedom, and to Europe their sons returned, still seeking it. Now that they have helped secure it, now that the "ceasefire" has sounded, let us post sentries and never again dismiss the guard that watches over our indivisible freedom.'[2]

---

[1] Sir James Spooner, letter to the author, 6 October 1994.
[2] Templeton Peck, broadcast: text communicated by his brother, Austin Peck Jr, letter to the author, 6 November 1994.

XII

Liberated Lands

The excitement in Paris on VE-Day echoed that of the city when it had been liberated eight and a half months earlier, but now the danger was gone. No snipers wreaked last minute havoc from rooftops and windows, and the people of the capital could rejoice unhindered. One of the strange sights of Paris that day, a British newspaper correspondent reported, 'was the British Ambassador, Mr Duff Cooper, driving a coupé very sedately, as if he didn't know that sixteen girls and soldiers were also aboard. For the young people of Paris and particularly for the thousands of very pretty girls who emerged like mushrooms in the strong sunshine, the Order of the Day was twenty-four passengers, and "it's nice to be kissed by a soldier." '[1]

The recent battles in eastern France and southern Germany, in which French troops had fought alongside their Allies, crossing the Rhine and advancing deep into Germany, were a source of deep satisfaction. In an article in *Le Figaro*, François Mauriac wrote of the 'unimaginable dream which has now been fulfilled: the French flag flying in Stuttgart and Ulm, along with the glorious standards of our American and British brothers. Let their sacrifice, and that of the innumerable soldiers of the Red Army, be forever inscribed in the memories and hearts of the schoolchildren of France.'[2]

The newspaper *Résistance* recalled the French soldiers who had fallen in the battle for France in 1940. 'You fought with all your strength,' it declared, 'opposing the monstrous tanks of a too powerful enemy.' *Résistance* also addressed itself to those French men and women who were punished by the German occupation authorities by deportation. 'You, men and women of France deported to Germany because you had chosen danger as a companion, risk as a friend, heroism as a guide, you who over the years battled against the enemy, affirming yourselves as the best of the French, were exiled ignominiously for your active and doubly determined patriotism. You who suffered vile torture in Buchenwald,

[1] David Walker, *Daily Mirror*, 9 May 1945, p. 7, col. 3.
[2] François Mauriac, *Le Figaro*, 8 May 1945, p. 1, cols 1–3.

Belsen, Dachau or elsewhere, were submitted to horrific treatment, you who are returning exhausted but with the flame of hope in your eyes, and you, alas, who are dead there in those citadels of pain; no, you have not succumbed and you have not experienced the cruellest hours in vain because today victory is here!'

There were also the French soldiers, sailors and airmen captured by the Germans in battle. To them, *Résistance* wrote: 'And you, prisoners, some now returning after more than five years behind the sinister barbed wire; you who, despite adversity and isolation, suffered the terrible isolation of being lost in a crowd – who kept your heads up high and resisted the enemy who kept you in captivity; you who had no news of your loved ones for months, who had to toil in factories or fret in dismal barracks; and you, the others, waiting to return home where you hope for certain deliverance and very soon, no, you have not suffered in vain as the victory which you never doubted is here at last!'[1]

The French newspapers on May 8 were filled with news of liberation. *L'Humanité* reported that nine hundred lieutenants and officer cadets who had been held as prisoners-of-war at Fürstenberg, on the Oder, had been liberated by Soviet forces two weeks earlier and would soon be on their way home.[2]

Among the deportees who returned to France on VE-Day were ninety political hostages who had been held, some for more than a year, at a camp near Berlin. That afternoon they reached Le Bourget by air and were driven into Paris. Among them was Yvon Delbos, who had served as Foreign Minister from 1936 to 1938, as a senior member of the Popular Front coalition, determined to resist German pressure. Later he had voted against the Vichy Government and been deported to Germany. 'The former Minister,' reported *L'Aurore*, 'exhausted by many months of captivity, almost all of them spent in prison cells, seemed happy to come back to Paris on this day of victory.'[3]

Also reaching Paris on May 8 was the seventy-seven year old Francesco Nitti, Prime Minister of Italy for twelve months in 1919–20 and an implacable opponent of Mussolini. He had been liberated by French troops a few days earlier. Not so fortunate was the elderly Madame Pétain. Although the newspapers announced that day that she had chosen a defence lawyer for her husband, 'she remains interned at the fort at Montrouge, but in a separate apartment to that of her hus-

---

[1] 'The Voice of Paris', *Résistance*, 8 May 1945, p. 2, col. 1.
[2] *L'Humanité*, 8 May 1945, p. 1, col. 3.
[3] *L'Aurore*, 8 May 1945, p. 1, col. 7.

band.'[1] She was later released. Her husband, sentenced to death for treason, had his sentence commuted to life imprisonment on the Ile d'Yeu, where he died six years later, still a prisoner, at the age of ninety-five.

The bitterness of former members of the resistance and supporters of de Gaulle towards those who had worked for Vichy was intense. In his article in *Le Figaro* on May 8, François Mauriac highlighted this aspect, appealing to those who had gone so far as to want to declare war on Britain in 1940: 'Rejoice with us and with all the peoples delivered from the monstrous servitude. Shudder with joy as Europe had been reduced to slavery by the torturers and assassins and because it has again become the home of free men, and has not been abandoned, and our eyes have seen the manifestation of justice.'[2]

The cost of making Europe a 'home of free men' will never be calculated. A comprehensive listing of the dead and wounded, and of those scarred by war, absence or loss, appears in no registry or reference work. Among the American soldiers who had been wounded during the battles on French soil two months earlier was Paul Fussell. 'On May 8, 1945, I was still in a hospital in Épinal,' he later recalled, 'recovering from wounds to my back and thigh received in the Seventh Army attack of March 15. The one in my thigh became infected and without penicillin I would have lost my right leg. I left the hospital only in July. My men had been badly dealt with by a German tank, and many were killed and wounded. At one of the hospitals on my way back to Épinal, I was seized with an unstoppable fit of crying, motivated, I think, both by shock and by guilt. My platoon sergeant, an older man (I was twenty) was killed, and we had been very close. I was persuaded that if I'd been leading better as a young officer, he might have, like me, survived – not to mention the others killed and maimed on that occasion. To this day, I've not got over this "survivor's guilt," if that is what it is. There's shame mingled with it too.

'The telegram arriving at my parents' home in California told them that I had been seriously wounded, and the event profoundly affected their lives too. Their own little boy of whom they'd been so proud had been badly damaged, and they weren't certain that the war was worth the price. (I am, by the way, perfectly fine now: forty per cent disabled, but nothing shows outwardly.) The sorrow occasioned by all the losses I saw in France stays with me fifty years afterwards. It emerges often as

[1] *L'Aurore*, 8 May 1945, p. 1, col. 8.
[2] François Mauriac, *Le Figaro*, 8 May 1945, p. 1, cols. 1–3.

irony and satire, since I don't feel able to face it without twisting it into some apparently tough literary actions.'[1]

At three o'clock that afternoon, precisely when Churchill was addressing the British people, General de Gaulle, whom the British had hoped would wait until later in the day, broadcast to his fellow-Frenchmen. 'The war is won!', he declared. 'Victory is won!' His address was followed, Carl Levin reported for the *New York Herald Tribune*, 'by the shrieking sound of the last air raid All Clear signal France ever wants to hear.'[2] After his speech, de Gaulle went to the Arc de Triomphe to lay a wreath at the Tomb of the Unknown Soldier, one of the million and a half French dead from the First World War, the war in which de Gaulle himself had been taken prisoner. As he turned from the ceremony to leave, the vast crowd surged forward, trampling on the special guard of honour of crippled French First World War veterans.

A witness of the zeal and antics of the Parisians that day was the American serviceman, Staff Sergeant William E. Beatty, who wrote home to his mother and sister three days later with a full account of the day. 'The *Stars and Stripes* and *New York Herald* had huge three- or four- inch headlines

VICTORY

French papers had equivalent banners; the time was published: 3 p.m. Paris time would be officially VE–Day. So, we went to work, doing our best to get our papers "drafted" with several others to represent the Office of the General Purchasing Agent at an assembly in the Palais de Chaillot at 2 p.m., where we were to officially help celebrate the end of the war.

'The huge auditorium, a modern theatre comparing favourably to Radio City, was filled with representatives of the various units in Paris. It was timed so we would get the President's speech at 3 o'clock. To fill in time, the Glenn Miller Band (minus Glenn Miller, you know he was

---

[1] Paul Fussell, letter to the author, 7 November 1994. Paul Fussell was to write a series of books in which the realities of war were seen and explored through their later uses and abuses, and through their literature. In his essay 'My War', in *The Boy Scout Handbook and other Observations* (Oxford University Press, 1982), he considered his reactions and shame as a 'survivor'. He dedicated his book *The Great War and Modern Memory* (Oxford University Press, London 1975) 'To the Memory of Technical Sergeant Edward Keith Hudson, ASN 36548772, Co. F 410th Infantry, Killed beside me in France, March 15, 1945.'

[2] Carl Levin, 'De Gaulle Says "War Is Won" As Jubilation Sweeps Paris', *Herald Tribune*, 9 May 1945, p. 1, cols. 4 and 5.

lost *en route* to here from England) gave a short concert of mostly swing music. At 2.55 p.m. the program, or service, I haven't yet decided which it was, started. It was a mixture of religious and patriotic features. First we sang "Battle Hymn of the Republic". Then we heard President Truman proclaim the end of the war in Europe, direct from Washington. I could not help wishing, the same as the President stated, that he wished President Roosevelt had been able to see this great day, and I'm sure it would have given me a much greater thrill to hear him announce it.'[1]

Truman's radio broadcast, like Churchill's earlier, was transmitted throughout the world. The President declared: 'This is a solemn but glorious hour. My only wish is that Franklin D. Roosevelt had lived to witness this day.' American rejoicing, he said, was 'sober and subdued by the supreme consciousness of the terrible price we have paid to rid the world of Hitler and his evil band. Let us not forget, my fellow-Americans, the sorrow and heartbreak in the homes of so many of our neighbours – neighbours whose most priceless possession has been rendered as a sacrifice to redeem our liberty.'

The war against Hitler had cost 132,000 American lives, and more than half a million casualties in three years, four months and seven days of fighting in the Mediterranean and European theatres. Yet one task remained to be completed. 'We must work to finish the war,' Truman told his listeners in every land. Only when the last Japanese division had surrendered unconditionally 'will our fighting job be done'. Unconditional surrender did not mean, he said, 'the extermination or the enslavement of the Japanese people', but it would mean the end of the influence of those military leaders 'who have brought Japan to the present brink of disaster'. Truman then appealed to every American 'to stick to his post until the last battle is won. Until that day, let no man abandon his post or slacken his efforts.'[2]

After Truman had spoken 'we had prayers by the Catholic, Protestant and Jewish Chaplains,' William Beatty wrote home from Paris, 'interspersed by a selection by the combined Communication Zone and Seine Section Choirs, which had rehearsed only a few minutes before the programme. They sang "God of our Fathers". The feature, next to the President's speech, was a talk by Lieutenant-General John C. H. Lee, Commanding General of Communications Zone (Com Z) which as you know is our headquarters. Following his speech, we sang "America the Beautiful", then the orchestra played all four National Anthems: the

---

[1] William Beatty, letter to his mother and sister, Paris, 11 May 1945. Private archive.
[2] 'Mr Truman To America, Work The Watchword', *The Times*, 9 May 1945, p. 4, col. 6.

stirring "Marseillaise" of France, the new and martial "Madelon" of Russia,[1] the majestic "God Save the King" of Great Britain, and finally the grand and glorious "Star Spangled Banner".

'At the close of the National Anthems there seemed to be a pause in which nobody knew just what to do, so General Lee stepped out into the middle of the stage and said very informally: "Thanks to the Orchestra, Thanks to the Choir" – then making the V-sign, shouted "VE-Day!" Everyone clapped and cheered, and went outside to see how the rest of Paris was carrying on.

'As we came out of the theatre, people seemed to be everywhere. The fountains in front of the palace were turned on for the first time since the war. Airplanes were flying all around, mostly very low. A Mitchell Bomber flew *under* the Eiffel Tower. I had heard of a small plane in the last war flying through the Arc de Triomphe, but with my own eyes I saw that beaten. I spent the rest of the afternoon walking around, watching Paris celebrate Victory.

'I walked along the Avenue de Tokio and Cours la Reine to Place de la Concorde. Everyone seemed to be everywhere. Jeeps, trucks, both civilian and military were packed with people, both civilian and military. I don't think any jeep had less than twenty people on it and trucks as many as they could hold and more. Flags were flying from the vehicles; horns were blowing and everything sort of gave the impression of a huge informal Fireman's Parade. MPs[2] and French police tried their best to direct traffic, but I don't think they had much luck. People were all over the streets, but when a vehicle came along, they slowly made room and it would pass thru with no casualties.

'Place de la Concorde was packed with people; soon a Piper Cub plane came over, flying low, dropping streamers of papers, which were picked up as fast as, or before, they landed. From the top of the wall bordering the Tuileries Gardens I could see a solid mass of people reaching all the way up to the Arc de Triomphe. I barged my way up Rue Royale to Place de la Madeleine: the same thing was going on there, people everywhere. Finally, after about an hour or so walking through the crowds I had made a complete circle and was back to the mess hall, I should say restaurant, for supper.

'It was a terribly hot day. We've had hot weather all week, so surprising, as just a week before VE-Day we had an inch of snow – on May lst.'

---

[1] The original 'Madelon' was a French soldiers' song in the First World War. Written just before the outbreak of war, it was popularised by a professional singer who served with an artillery regiment.
[2] American Army Military Police.

William Beatty decided to go to the cinema with some fellow GIs. Then, 'we did a little more exploring, to see the people and town lit up. The town only, I mean, was lit up: there seemed to be surprisingly little drinking and wild celebrating, at least the part we saw. Of course if we had toured Montmartre we'd probably have found some wild parties going on in the cafés. We just walked – and walked, eventually ending back at the Trocadero. By this time it was just about dark, and the fountains were illuminated – again for the first time since the beginning of the war. It was really beautiful, comparing only to the New York World's Fair. Perhaps it wasn't nearly so colourful, there really weren't any colours, but what made them seem so pretty was what it meant – the first time Paris could really be called the "City of Light" in over five years. We were too tired of walking by then to do anything but sit down and take it easy again, so sat by the fountains getting a slight spray from them. People were wandering around between the jets of water, getting mildly soaked. It seemed very much like a park or seashore at home.

'From there we walked up Avenue Kléber, along the same street which was strewn with burned out tanks and trucks when we arrived here last September, but this time it was, just as every other main street, full of people: people going from anywhere to anywhere, glad to be able to walk around in peace time in a city full of lighted streets. Fireworks were being shot off from the ground and from airplanes. The streets were lighted as much as possible. There is of course no blackout, but the pre-war lighting hasn't yet been put back into operation. All lights aren't lit, and to save "juice" they aren't as strong as usual.

'There was a bottleneck in the human traffic at the Place de l'Étoile, where stands the Arc de Triomphe. Here it was packed and jammed. Still nothing exciting happening, just people, people, and more people, watching the rest of the people who were out too. Well, just to be out. After all, it was VE-Day, and the people in France consider this their day perhaps more than any other country.

'About midnight, we started out to fight our way through the crowds back to our billet. We supposed that there wouldn't be any bed-check that night. Certainly nobody would be around to see that all the good little GIs were tucked up into our comfortable little trundle beds at midnight on VE-Day! The streets were just as full of people as ever, perhaps more so. There was no Victory parade, just everything very informal with numerous groups, particularly of students, barging through the crowds singing and giving what I suppose were school cheers.

'About half way down the Champs-Élysées a group of about a dozen students who were proceeding down the street broadside practically surrounded us and yelled "American Army – Hip Hip Hurray!" – for an instant it made us feel as though we *were* the whole Army and personally responsible for winning the war! Finally we reached our destination, our happy GI home, and turned in for the evening, or rather the rest of the morning. It may sound like peculiar behaviour for VE-Day when all of Paris, the US Army included was out, but as far as I was concerned I'd seen enough crowds for one day, and not being one to tear around felt the best thing was to turn in, but the heat and the noise outside was not at all conducive to sleep.

'The city seemed to be alive all night, but evidently the crowds all went home *eventually*, for when we went to breakfast Wednesday morning everything seemed very calm, like a deserted village.'[1]

Nearly two hundred miles south of Paris, in the village of Montluçon, lived the thirteen-year-old Saul Friedländer. In 1942 he had been saved from deportation by his parents, who had given him to Catholic nuns, with whom he had been brought up as a Catholic. The loyalty of the nuns had been to Marshal Pétain and Vichy. Neither the triumph of the Free French, nor the exhilaration of VE-Day, could change those attitudes, as Friedländer recalled: 'The church bells pealed and the whole town celebrated. "It's not like in 1918," Madame Robert said to us regretfully. "And then there's our poor Marshal. Let us pray for him." We went for our walk despite all this, and as I remember, the general manifestation of popular joy seemed monstrous and indecent to us.' But even at Montluçon, 'crowds were jostling each other everywhere, and people were kissing each other, obliging us to lower our eyes – without, however, causing us to make an abrupt *volte-face* the way we had when one day, on one of our walks, we sighted the troops of female boarding students from Sainte-Jeanne. On the walls, crosses of Lorraine and the hammer and sickle had replaced the Allied snail pasted up by the Germans, and the whole was topped with posters showing the smug, stupid face of the imperturbable Fernandel.[2]

'There was no *Te Deum* to celebrate the German surrender at our school, as I remember, but instead a constant concern for the lot of the victor of Verdun. When, later on, Pétain's trial began, we faithfully read the speeches of his defence counsel, Maître Isorni, whereas the State Prosecutor, who was doubtless a Freemason, was unanimously held up

---

[1] William Beatty, letter to his mother and sister, Paris, 11 May 1945. Private archive.
[2] Fernandel, a popular French comedian born in Marseille in 1903, whose visual trademarks were comic facial contortions and a wide, toothy grin. In 1930 he made the first of more than a hundred films. He died in 1971.

to obloquy. The portraits of the Marshal remained on the walls for a long time, and when they were finally taken down, it was the end of an era at Saint-Béranger, too.

'The war was over; my parents had not come back. The Red Cross thought that it had been able to identify a couple at Theresienstadt whose names corresponded to those of my father and mother, but a typhus epidemic had put the camp in quarantine, and we had to wait. An unreal wait: the days went by without a sign, and during all this time I kept asking myself: How will I greet my parents? Will there be any way to express my happiness?'[1]

Saul Friedländer's parents did not come back. They had been murdered by the Nazis.

In Luxembourg, which Germany had overrun in the first hours of the western *Blitzkrieg* in May 1940, Yehuda Sela was with the United States Army Air Forces on May 8. For the citizens of the principality, victory was marked by a procession in the main streets. For Sela, however, who was a member of a small photographic reconnaissance unit, the celebratory aspect was overshadowed by the work he was doing. 'The period before and after that day,' he later recalled, 'I was busy printing copies by the hundreds of photos my boss (officer) had taken in Dachau. As soon as the area around Munich was freed, we had taken off for a visit to the company manufacturing the Rollei cameras, the Schneider works, I believe. We were the advance party of the outfit to demilitarise the German Air Force. Dachau was near there. We had no automation in those days. Every print was handled individually. I'll never forget those corpses, those skeletons and all the rest that's common knowledge these many years. I couldn't look the other way even if I wanted to.'[2]

The failure of the parachute landings at Arnhem in September 1944, and the subsequent flooding by the Germans of vast areas of southern Holland, had forced the Allies to by-pass the Dutch cities as they advanced into northern Germany. Even after British forces had reached the Baltic, most of Holland, three hundred miles to their rear, was still under German control, and many of its citizens on the verge of starvation. An early sign of the German occupation forces' failure to administer the country had been their appeal to the Allies for food to be dropped to the starving Dutch. It was not until May 8 that the Allied forces finally reached the

---

[1] Saul Friedländer, *When Memory Comes*, Farrar, Straus and Giroux, New York, 1979, pp. 127–8.
[2] Yehuda Sela, letter to the author, 6 November 1994.

principal Dutch cities, which by then had known five years of German rule. Among those in Amsterdam that day was Steffi Tikotin, who had come to Holland in 1938 as a refugee from Dresden at the age of fifteen, with her parents. 'I had been in hiding at two addresses in North Holland for about four years,' she later recalled. 'Our part of the country was liberated on the 5th of May. Of course that day is indelible in my memory.' Her parents had been arrested in the north of Holland in 1943, 'the day after I was taken by kind people to stay with an elderly nurse near Hoorn. They were taken to Westerbork, and sent east in October 1944. My father was sent to the gas chambers almost straight away, my mother survived "somewhere" until February 1945 according to the Red Cross. By the 8th of May I was still unaware of my parents' death. I had been re-united with an uncle, aunt and cousins, who had also been in hiding. The lists from the camps were only just coming in. They were pitifully short, which worried me. It was a time of terrible upheaval, and although extermination camps were mentioned, I did not want to believe the horror of it all.

'I had been in Amsterdam to see the Canadian forces enter, and that was a moment of great jubilation. I was free and had met up with my uncle. I was almost twenty-one years old and the idea of having survived and being free overwhelmed me. I felt I wanted to make up for all the things I'd missed and was very unsettled and bewildered. I had been very lucky to be given shelter at my second address, specially with people who were kind, and found myself surrounded by young people. Nevertheless, from the moment I went into hiding under a false name and lost contact with my former life, I felt isolated and lost my identity, and it took years to regain it.'[1]

Among those who had given Steffi Tikotin a place to hide was a district nurse, Sister Ewoud, with whom she stayed for two and a half years until the hiding place was betrayed, and Thames Commandeur, a widower with six daughters and a son. 'They treated me as one of the family,' she later wrote. 'It restored my faith in humanity.'[2]

In the Dutch city of Leyden, Krik Arriëns, an aspiring Dutch civil servant, had been living clandestinely for five years. At midday on May 8, he described in his diary how liberation arrived in the city 'in the shape of the long-awaited Canadians. So far not more than a few score cars and tanks. It was a pleasant sensation and I found myself laughing and waving at the attractive, sun-tanned men (many "lads" and many mous-

---

[1] Steffi Roberston (née Tikotin), letter to the author, 20 October 1994.
[2] Steffi Roberston (née Tikotin), letter to the author, 25 October 1994.

taches!). But it did not thrill me to the extent I had expected earlier. Granted, for us it has come about in a very gradual way. For me the great moment will remain Friday evening, May 4th, at nine minutes past ten.[1] Then I felt something stir within me, something of deliverance and deep joy.

'Now I am, perhaps, too tired to feel anything intensely; I mean also mentally tired. I do not bother to try and let the significance of this event penetrate me. But maybe that wouldn't be possible anyway; maybe it is something which cannot be forced. Above all: it isn't something simple and clear. The very first sensation of relief, yes, that is something else – and that we did experience. However, as is emphasised in every pamphlet, the state of war has been so violent, and the war has lasted so long, that it is still making itself felt heavily, even now. Hence, probably, we cannot yet tear ourselves away from its impact.

'Well, I don't seem to have a clear inner perception of my emotions, let alone that I should be able to put them into words adequately. Accordingly, I shall not go on trying, all the more so as they keep changing continually. At this moment I experience mainly a sense of quiet; a feeling, yes, of "peace". In the morning however, it was preponderantly something melancholy; then again restlessness and vague disappointment. Perhaps I should try to draw up a balance-sheet of these five war years for myself; but I'm afraid that for the time being I shall not have the push to do so.'

That evening Arriëns joined the crowds of his fellow-citizens in the streets of Leyden. In his diary he recorded the scenes around him. 'My present mood is very different from that of this afternoon. But, then, who could have imagined that we should yet have to digest such strong emotions! Before dinner I went out into the street because from the direction of the Korevaerstraat there came again shouts of jubilation, evidently marking the arrival of more Canadian troops. This group included a number of cars belonging to the Irene-brigade, Dutch Soldiers ... And then, right after this sensation, there came another, even bigger one, when one of those people (to be exact, the bread-delivery man whom I had continued to greet in the street) told me that Japan had capitulated. This was a piece of information which, firstly, I considered to be highly improbable, and which, secondly, I couldn't possibly digest in such a short time. So that eventually I couldn't be overly disappointed when it proved to be untrue. All the same it caused several hours of such extra

[1] When Radio Orange had broadcast the news of the surrender of the German forces in Northern Europe to Montgomery. Leyden was still occupied by the Germans.

suspense that I couldn't shake off my excitement. And no wonder, for wouldn't it have been the greatest, the ultimate thing which could have happened at this moment: the idea that my parents, my brother, and many more relatives and friends in the Indies also might be free! Alas, the rumour was false. So be it; but soon it will happen. I felt (and I still feel) that I would promptly enlist as a volunteer if at this moment a summons should have been issued.

'At 8.15 p.m. together with K to the intersection Breestraat/'t Gang-etje/Steenschuur in order to listen, in a dense crowd, to a broadcast of Radio Orange and to hear definitive reports regarding Japan. Right at the start there came this disappointment; Churchill's speech ended with his remark that Japan still had to be beaten. Radio Orange then broadcast the sounds of the crowd at Piccadilly Circus. Finally the tolling of the bells: Armistice Day. The short radio-broadcast had immediately rendered that notion much more vivid. It surely must be something immense for all those millions in England, in America, etc. Just as thrilling as after the First World War.'

The rest of the evening, Arriëns noted in his diary, 'still brought the emotions of the rounding up of several NSB-members[1] in our neighbour-hood, among others B and my former neighbour V. In the morning I had already accidentally witnessed the arrest of P and Van der W. Tonight the bawling and jeering multitudes which surrounded the captives and their escorts were even bigger. An unforgettable sight which, by the way, filled me with mixed feelings. Undoubtedly the victims deserve something like it, as a small part of their punishment. But the spectacle did not please me as a human being. And I was surprised to see the intense pleasure which M and J derived from it.

'We have concluded the evening with a frugal supper of the left-over macaroni; and for the smokers a Players cigarette. Due to the absence of electricity this took place by the light of a candle, but – with open curtains! At this very moment the bells are ringing twelve o'clock. After exactly one minute the armistice will officially become effective. Peace. In Europe. For how long?

'I went outside for a moment. A beautiful starry night, with here and there dark patches of clouds. The Summer-Triangle, with Altaïr[2] just above the horizon. Otherwise everything dark; only now and again a flash of light in the east, and one or two sparsely lit windows. In the distance

---

[1] The Dutch National Socialist Movement, the main Dutch fascist party. Its leader, Anton Mussert, was later captured, sentenced to death and executed by firing squad.

[2] The brightest star in the constellation Aquilla.

the drone of a motor car (or tank?) and just one sharp rifle-shot. Otherwise only the rustle of the wind in the trees and shrubs, the soft flapping of the flag from the church-steeple. And – abiding in the background – the peaceful and familiar croaking of frogs. Maybe I shall retain something of this ambience in my memory.'[1]

At Landshut in Bavaria, thousands of released Allied prisoners-of-war were awaiting repatriation. Some, like Major Elliott Viney, had been free for more than a week, and were impatient to get home. As he wrote in his diary on the following day: 'Tuesday 8 May, VE-Day and for me one of the greatest days ever, dawned fine with mist over the Isar. I got up at six and we were all ready to move at eight as we were alarmed about the Yank other rank battalion which had stayed on the air field, getting in first. The Colonel (Chadwick) did not arrive till nine and we moved off gently then. There was a cool breeze and we did not get so hot as on Monday. Everyone was cautious, but still hopeful. No food was thrown away! A plane came in when we were on the road; once we arrived they poured in. Quite early on, I counted sixteen on the ground and forty-three circling round waiting to land. Before we left there were over a hundred, a great sight.

'We were pushed to three different planes and actually got into a fourth, but the pilot refused to take us – would only take Yanks. However we got a good pilot; he asked me where we wanted to go! I said "straight home", but he wasn't allowed to, but said he would take us direct to Brussels if the petrol lasted. We took off at midday and landed at Nivelles, south-west of Brussels, two and a half hours later. It was a good trip, sunny with small cumulus clouds. We started at 2–3000 feet and later went up to 5–6000. It was quite warm. I picked out Ingolstadt alright and could see almost to Eichstätt; we followed the Danube till it curved south and headed across the Swabische Alps to cross the Neckar and then the Rhine at Karlsruhe, whose layout looked splendid from the air, but the bombing had been pretty extensive, as at the Saar towns further on. He went nearly to Metz (their base), but finding he had enough petrol took us straight on and very soon we were over the Ardennes, the Meuse and so down to Nivelles.

'We were the first plane to land on the strip. It was most dramatic, for we stepped straight on to a lorry which took us to the canteen, where, as we entered, Churchill began his victory speech; the national anthem

---

[1] C.B. Arriëns, letter to the author, 31 October 1994.

followed, the first time I had heard it since 12 May 1940 and I must admit I was almost in tears as I drank my tea.

'We then had a splendid twenty-five kilometre truck drive to Brussels. I sat in front. A terrific welcome from the *Belgiques* (how like 1940!), for it was a national holiday. In a way the biggest thrill of the day came now for I suddenly saw a signpost to "Ferme Hougemont" and sure enough there was the Waterloo monument; a minute or two later and we passed the big farm where I had my company position on 15 May 1940. We landed up at the Artillerie barracks, Boulevard Saint-Michel, where again we were first in, got deloused, checked and paid. After a quick wash I had some tea in the mess, then came back for a cold, but long bath. Four in a room with two-tiered beds; still with Douglas, Joe and Jimmy. I have a new flight, A 358, with a nucleus of our original set.

'The hour before dinner was ennobled for others by whisky and for me by a gin and lime. The meal was exceedingly hilarious and then everyone dispersed for the evening. We four set out, not having the vaguest idea where even the centre of the city was, but after one false start we got a lift from a Belgian in British battledress driving an expensive American staff car. He took us round the royal palace – the king had returned during the day – and then dumped us and we headed for the Plaza, which is a sort of officers' restaurant, run by the NAAFI.[1] It was jam-packed with a mob of women in mysterious uniforms. I gathered they were mostly Belgian. I had hardly entered before I was greeted by Kenneth Hunter, who is a REME[2] captain on maintenance here. We drank beer all evening and later had a meal downstairs. It was what I wanted as I didn't want to have a hangover today. Nor have I. We left at midnight having heard the King speak and a lot of singing. The streets were packed, there were confetti and streamers (in my American jacket I got a lot of confetti) and rockets and Verey lights going up everywhere. After two or three failures to find a truck we found an American one to take us to their November 11 leave club, from where we could walk, getting in at 1.30 a.m. in good form.

'On looking back I should have mentioned the wonderful collection of "scarlet majors at the base"; there was one 18-stoner, monocled, last war medals and wearing *a kilt*.'[3]

In Italy on the morning of May 8, the British forces daily newspaper *Union Jack* appeared with a three-word headline:

[1] The Navy, Army and Air Forces Institutes.
[2] The Royal Electrical and Mechanical Engineers.
[3] Elliott Viney, diary, 9 May 1945. Private archive.

GERMANY: THE END

It also had a cautionary word to the troops reading it. 'The eyes of the world now turn to the Pacific. Before the fighting citizens of the Empire can pack up and go home there is one more score to be settled.'[1]

It was not Japan, however, that was on the mind of Sergeant Major Harry Dutka that morning at his army base in Rovigo. In the early hours of VE-Day he had invited the men of his Royal Army Service Corps company to accompany him on a victory day excursion. 'We left on a pick-up at about 05.00,' he later recalled, 'and after passing completely destroyed sections of Padua arrived in Venice. It seemed we were the first soldiers and there were still gondolas in abundance waiting for clients. It was still quite cool and the water was smooth like a mirror. It seemed unbelievable to be able to admire the wonders of this fantasy town, untouched by war, just less than twenty-four hours after the war was over and to tread over ground which was yesterday still enemy territory. To say our feelings were uplifted would be an understatement.

'Arriving at St Mark's Square we found many outside sculptures and decorations of the buildings encased in timber, this in spite of Venice having been declared to be an open city.[2] The place was still quite empty, except for the pigeons. Our small group took another gondola to explore the canals around the centre of town and when we returned to the Piazza at about noon the place had started to get filled to quite an extent. Sailors, soldiers and airmen from quite a few armies, not to forget the ATS, had streamed into town, and when the centre became really crowded we were happy to leave again, being led by a local civilian happy to do us that favour. On returning to camp we were pleasantly surprised to learn that VE-Day was prolonged to include also the 9th of May.'[3]

Not every soldier on duty near Venice managed to get to the city on May 8. Major Arthur Radley later recalled: 'When I got to the airfield at Treviso, north of Venice, on the actual VE-Day, the Royal Air Force were totally in command and in no doubt whatsoever that a second celebration was in order. All who could had already swanned off to

---

[1] *Union Jack*, British Forces Daily, No. 437, 8 May 1945.

[2] A city which would not be bombed or attacked by any of the combatants, in view of its special historic and artistic treasures. This was a local arrangement between the German and Allied forces in northern Italy.

[3] Harry Dayan (Dutka), letter to the author, 18 September 1994. Born in Vienna in 1920, Dutka had reached Palestine as an illegal immigrant in 1938. In 1943 he volunteered for the British Army, with which he served in Egypt, Libya, Italy and Austria, until his discharge in 1946.

Venice, and except for those actually on duty, it was gin and tonic all round. I was there on duty too, but who was I to resist their hospitality? I explained that I was still a British Liaison Officer for Special Operations Executive (SOE) helping the Italian Partisans to "set Europe ablaze", as Churchill had directed, and I had to collect the food for their Victory Dinner which was to be flown in.

'The Nino Nanetti Division of the Italian partisans had been operating behind the lines in the mountains to the north, and had been supplied by SOE with parachute drops of weapons and sabotage material. They had fought courageously against Hitler's Germans and Mussolini's Fascists and had just accepted the surrender of 10,000 Germans themselves. The Nino Nanetti men had then moved down into the largest of the local towns, Vittorio Veneto, where another defeated army, the Austrians, had surrendered in 1918, and were looking forward to a double Victory celebration.

'But we of course had to find the eats, and arranged with our bosses in Siena, over our special radio link, for a worthy Victory Meal to be flown in. That is why I was there on Treviso airfield. Just me and my jeep. And in came this splendid Dakota from the south. It was American, and out came a Colonel who just handed me a piece of paper and made me sign for both the plane and its cargo. I had of course presumed that his crew would have helped me offload it, but not a bit of it. They were off to Venice faster than light, with visions of Harry's Bar and gondolas on the Grand Canal, and the Colonel was ever so sorry, but they had done their bit, and he couldn't help any further. And, as could be well imagined, neither could the RAF by now.

'So I had a look at the cargo to see what supreme delicacies were in store for the expectant and fastidious partisans, if I could only just get them out. Caviare from Joe Stalin? Saltimbocca alla Romana from Rome itself? Zabaglione frothing with all the eggs in Italy to cap it all? Not a bit of it. No such luck. Just tin after tin of corned beef, good old Bully. All that the victorious British Army could spare for the victorious volunteer Freedom fighters.

'This was our Victory Dinner: that is, if only I could get it out. The problem got more pressing every moment. And then I became aware, increasingly acutely, of an odd sound coming from all sides of the airfield on the perimeter. Could it be digging, and if so what? I had a look: it was just that, and moreover the diggers were none other than old friends of mine from Malta days, the Basuto Pioneer Corps from South Africa. They typified the co-operation of the whole British Empire of those days. In Malta they had done all the donkey work of digging it out from the

German/Italian air-raids: and here they were, almost in Germany, the source of a war which they certainly wouldn't have called their own in normal circumstances. And they were still digging, in this case slit trenches for air defence all round the perimeter.

'I recognized their Sergeant: we exchanged Victory greetings, and with some hefty Pioneer labour, the stuff was out in no time at all. I thanked him profusely, but couldn't resist just one question. "Do tell me, Sergeant George, why are your magnificent men still digging slit trenches for anti-aircraft defence? No-one's going to attack us any more now: the War's over, or so they say." "Well, Sir," he replied smartly. "*You* know it is, Sir. And *I* know it is. But the *men*, Sir: if I were to tell *them* there'd be no holding 'em. Sir."'[1]

The Basuto labourers went on digging, and the Italian partisans got their celebratory dinner of bully-beef.

In Rovigo, the men of a company of the Royal Army Service Corps heard over the radio at four o'clock that afternoon that Churchill would speak in an hour's time. 'All work was stopped,' Sergeant Major Harry Dutka later recalled, 'and the whole platoon assembled around the only wireless set we had. Punctually at five the historic announcement came through. At the end of his address Churchill declared the 8th of May to be Victory Day. It was so sudden that at the beginning we could not grasp the actual meaning. It seemed so unbelievable, that the expressions of joy were somewhat subdued. I now remembered that in fact, during the last few days, no gunfire had been heard, and it later transpired that a cease-fire had been in force since May 2.'[2]

Also in Italy that day was Julian Schragenheim, a signaller with the South African forces, who later recalled how 'we suddenly and on the authority of no less a person than Churchill, himself, found ourselves without a war, on the shores of Lake Como. The operational tension had, in our case, already terminated a few days earlier, near Treviso, north of Venice. There I had met an Italian with a red scarf and a Schmeisser, who first looked very suspiciously at one of my companions, who had a rather square head, but, then, said, "Io Partigiano", and gave me a glass of grappa, which almost blew the scalp off my skull. But then it transpired that some German troops, in the Milan area, needed some encouragement to surrender. So the whole of the 6th Armoured Division was brought right across Italy, from east to west, and the German general, whoever it was, saw reason pretty quickly.'[3]

[1] Arthur Farrand Radley, letter to the author, 26 August 1994.
[2] Harry Dayan (formerly Dutka), letter to the author, 18 September 1994.
[3] Julian Schragenheim, letter to the author, 25 September 1994.

Christopher Seton-Watson had seen active service as an artillery officer since May 1940, when he had been evacuated from Dunkirk. He had fought in Greece in 1941, in North Africa from 1941 to 1943, and in Italy throughout 1944. On May 8 he was stationed near Bologna, writing in a letter home: 'Never did I think the end would come so suddenly, like a dam bursting and sweeping away all that was left of Hitler's proud empire in the space of a few days. And now today is VE-Day (horrible phrase), and the future has taken on the shape of one huge question mark of glorious possibilities. One always used to say that in wartime one never knew where one would be twenty-four hours later, and that the future was quite unpredictable. But now that the war is over, the future is a hundred times more uncertain than it ever was. No one has a ghost of an idea as to what happens next. So the only thing to do is to be patient and wait till the very important persons make up their minds.

'We have been listening to accounts of rejoicings in London and all over the world, as described on the wireless, and have had to make our own celebrations here, in the depths of the green Italian plains. We live in a backwater of country peace, far from great crowds and flags and speeches. Which I think is just as well. This afternoon we lined up our eight guns, sat round the wireless to hear Churchill's speech, then fired a salute of twenty-one rounds. Tonight we will listen to the King, then I shall ceremonially light our Victory bonfire, and we will all stand round it drinking hot rum punch and singing at the tops of our voices. About eleven the officers and sergeants will probably slink away to celebrate more privately, and leave the rest of the battery to their revels, which will last well into the small hours. And tomorrow the Peace in Europe begins.'[1]

Hermann Arndt was in Florence on May 8. For him, as for many of those with him, the end of the war had been anticipated with a wager. 'As the front line from East and West drew closer, with the dramatic meeting of the Russians and the Western Armies near the River Elbe,' he later recalled, 'we all knew the war was coming to an end. In effect we placed our bets on the day of the final, unconditional German surrender. In the event I won the bet as I had gambled on my wife's birthday, the 8th of May. I will never forget that mild spring day in Florence when suddenly, in the late afternoon, all of the mighty church bells started their deafening chorus in unison announcing the end of the war. People looked at each other, there was no need to speak. Every one knew: almost

---

[1] Christopher Seton-Watson, diary, 8 May 1945: *Dunkirk-Alamein-Bologna, Letters and Diaries of an Artilleryman 1939–1945*, Buckland, London, 1993, pp. 227–8.

six years of bloodshed and unspeakable misery had come to an end. The mighty German war machine, which during the first two years of the war seemed to be invincible, had been crushed and totally defeated.'[1]

Arndt, who had been born in Frankfurt-on-Oder and emigrated to Palestine in 1938, was serving as a member of a small mobile unit attached to the British forces in Italy, specialising in the interrogation of German prisoners-of-war. 'We certainly carried on interrogating Germans after the 8th of May,' he recalled. 'All kinds of war criminals, spies and collaborators. I do not remember many details but I definitely remember that amongst others we interrogated the wife of Reichsführer-SS Himmler, who had been a witness to her husband's suicide.'[2]

Near the north Italian town of Udine, Sandor Gärtner, who had been born in the Transylvanian city of Cluj, was a corporal in the British Army, in a vehicle workshop company with which he had served throughout the North African and Italian campaigns. To his amazement, on VE-Day he received a card from the Red Cross informing him that his parents, whom he had not seen for more than six years, had not only survived the last year in German-occupied Hungary but had arrived in Switzerland, having been sent from Belsen by train as part of a negotiated rescue in which more than a thousand Jews were brought out. Looking at the map, Corporal Gärtner saw how near he must be to his parents, Herman and Rosa. 'I immediately sought to reach the Swiss–Italian border in order to meet them,' he later recalled. 'At first I was denied permission since the Alto Adige area in that region was still in the hands of the Germans and travel would be dangerous despite the cease fire. Just then, I met a fellow soldier who had lived in the area. He offered to accompany me in reaching the Swiss–Italian border. Together we were able to convince my Sergeant-Major to allow us to go and even provide us with a vehicle. We crossed the Brenner Pass diagonally enabling us to reach the Swiss border at Munstair. I was now faced with the challenge of entering Switzerland. My efforts were in vain. However, the Swiss guards did offer to phone my parents to arrange a meeting at the border. The first available transport, a postal bus, would arrive only the next morning so we had to find overnight accommodation. The commander of the Italian Bersaglieri Alpine unit at the border allowed us to spend the night with them. As may be imagined, this was the longest night of my life.

'The next morning, my mother and father came. I saw them from a distance. As they approached, I first noticed their hair. It was as white as

---

[1] Hermann Arndt, letter to the author, 14 September 1994.
[2] Hermann Arndt, letter to the author, 30 September 1994.

the snow covered mountain peaks around us. When we separated years ago, their hair was jet black! Our meeting was beyond description. We fell on each other, embracing, crying and kissing. It was a long time before we could express our feelings in words.

'The Swiss authorities who were so strict the day before, now permitted my parents to cross into Italy. The Alpine commander accommodated them for the day. Our excitement must have been infectious. Before their return to Switzerland in the late afternoon with the last postal bus, the commander and his men joined us in celebrating this memorable day by putting on a display of fire-works, a local custom reserved for special events.'[1]

At Argenta, south of the river Po, Roger Highfield was a member of the Survey party of the 97th Field Regiment, Royal Artillery. 'Two points I chiefly remember. It fell to me to help organise a celebratory dinner. This meant buying chickens by barter from the local population and seeing that they were properly cooked in the communal oven of the nearest village. I had to book space in the oven, which was gladly given, and arrange for the chickens to be thrust into it on a wooden implement with a very long handle. Then, when the signore announced that the chickens were ready, to put them on a hand cart and to have them run along the lanes and footpaths to the camp where their arrival was eagerly awaited. My second memory is of the surprise which I felt when one of the Indian Other Ranks asked me "Jani, why can't we fight Russia?" '[2]

A British soldier, Noel Mander, who had been in action in Tunisia and southern Italy, was stationed on the outskirts of Rome on VE-Day. Having been taken ill from exposure during the battle for the Gothic Line, he had been medically downgraded, and relegated, to his great annoyance, to the Army Pay Corps headquarters at Centocelli. VE-Day had come only a few days after he had arrived. 'We were given the day off,' he later recalled, and transport was laid on for those who wished to go to Rome. 'The city was throbbing with excitement and jubilation, drinks were pressed on everyone, bands playing. Towards the evening celebrations became rowdy, Americans became particularly aggressive. Many girls were on the streets offering their favours. I, and some others, felt that it was time to get back to Headquarters, even there celebrations were in full swing and quite a few ladies were seen around.

'There was one sad element that not many gave thought to at that

[1] Arye Gertner (formerly Sandor Gärtner), letter to the author, 3 November 1994.
[2] Dr Roger Highfield, letter to the author, 30 September 1994. 'Jani' was Indian soldiers' slang for 'Johnny'.

time. A week or so before pictures of the concentration camps had been released in the press and on the cinema screens. While everyone was horrified, those of the base-wallahs were much more muted than those of us who had been at the front. "Wish that I had been there", was what many of us felt, we could have got a few more." [1]

As the Allied troops in Italy celebrated VE-Day, the Supreme Allied Commander in the Mediterranean, Field Marshal Alexander, who had been one of the last soldiers to leave Dunkirk in 1940, and had been evacuated from Burma in 1942 in the face of the Japanese onslaught, broadcast to his men. 'Some of you will be going home,' he said. 'Others will go to defeat the last remaining aggressor, the Japanese, who are already in a sorry way, and know what is coming to them. We and our Allies, by means of the same united strength which has at last brought us victory in Europe, shall now proceed to clean up the Japanese once and for all.' Alexander's Deputy, General Joseph T. McNarney, also broadcast that day. He too spoke of the war in the Far East. 'By crushing Germany,' he said, 'we are free at last to unleash our full might against Japan – to strike quickly and hard – to bring this long war to an end.' For those who would never see their homes or families again, 'we must fight on. For them we must achieve a world victory so total and complete that what has happened to them and to us can never happen again.' [2]

A Czech doctor serving with the British army, Jan Brod, was at a hospital between Pompeii and Salerno on May 8. 'The whole staff of the hospital,' he recalled, 'together with the patients, celebrated VE-Day by a thanksgiving Mass under the open sky and by a dance with the nurses. On May 13 many of us went to nearby Salerno to see at the local theatre Verdi's *Masked Ball* with Benjamino Gigli as Ricardo – unfortunately, too fat at that late period of his life and with only short spells reminiscent of his fabulous voice.' [3]

In Naples, *La Voce* published on May 8 a leading article headed 'Forward towards a new world!' Writing of the tricolour flag of Italy the article praised 'our brave soldiers, airmen and sailors, and our glorious partisans, who on September 8 picked it up from the mud where fascism and the fascist monarch had thrown it and held it firmly in their grasp again. From the tragic abyss, from the dark and fearful void of Hitler's Germany, which has surrendered only under the crushing weight of the

---

[1] Noel Mander, letter to the author, 28 August 1994.

[2] 'Texts of Alexander, McNarney VE-Day Talks', *Stars and Stripes*, 9 May 1945, p. 3, cols. 2 to 5.

[3] Jan Brod, 'Italian scenes': *As You Were, VE-Day: a medical retrospect*, British Medical Association, London, 1984, p. 37.

biggest coalition of peoples which ever went into battle to defend civiliz-
ation, comes a solemn warning: "We shall not forget! We shall destroy
fascism for ever!" Only thus will the world be reborn from the ruins and
go forward towards a future of peace, progress, justice and freedom.'[1]

The Italians were fortunate. Despite the creation and excesses of the
German–Italian Axis, the overthrow of Mussolini in 1943 had brought
Italians into the war on the Allied side, and in the fighting that followed,
Italian partisans had been one of the extra arms of the Allied war effort. At
the same time, despite the large communist element both in the partisan
movement and in Italian public life, Italy remained in the Western democratic orbit. Just over a year after VE-Day a republic was declared, in
1947 a peace treaty was signed with the Allies, and in 1949 Italy entered
the western defence system.[2] Only nine years earlier, Italy's military and
air attack on France, at the very moment when the German armies were
sweeping towards Paris, had brought down upon her the censure of the
western democracies.

Since the liberation of Greece from German occupation at the end of
1944, British troops had been involved in disarming and controlling the
Greek communist forces whose leaders had, with great reluctance,
accepted the regency of Archbishop Damaskinos. A British artilleryman,
Sergeant Harry Osborne, was in the Greek town of Agrinion when, as
he recalled later, 'we heard on our wireless that the war was finished and
we informed Captain Atkinson, our commanding officer immediately.
He then informed the Lord Mayor and in no time at all the word got
round and the local populace gathered in the small square. The Mayor
and the Captain made quite good impromptu speeches to rousing cheers.
Quite a lot of shots were fired in the air and several Bren guns arched
streams of tracer in crimson arcs. Meantime, quite unawed by the proceedings, some of us including myself "liberated" a large demi-john of
retsina and if I remember rightly toasted VE-Day, VE-Day Plus 1, VE-
Day Plus 2 etc .' Being in an isolated area, constantly on guard against
Greek communist guerrillas, Osborne and those with him 'did not have
much of a chance of celebrating apart from the release of tensions by
loosing off a few rounds from Brens, etc.'[3]

Stationed in Athens that day was another artilleryman, Sergeant Jack
Trembath. 'It became obvious as we followed the war news from Europe

---

[1] *La Voce*, Naples, 8 May 1945, p. 1, col. 1.
[2] In 1951 an Italian admiral was appointed to the NATO naval command in the Mediterranean.
[3] Harry Osborne, letter to the author, 16 November 1994.

that the end was approaching, so when it finally came to our backwater I for one accepted it with considerable relief and gratitude. But I cannot recall there was any great jubiliation or exuberant celebrations. In fact the houses where we were billeted were very quiet. My main reaction, rather naïvely perhaps, was to speculate on the possibility of the regiment being sent, in the not too distant future, to the Far East to participate in the fight against Japan. Perhaps our lack of enthusiasm to display any great emotion was the fact that we were not in at the death and had been out of action for some months leading a rather complacent existence.'[1]

Another British soldier, Captain Birdie Smith, who was then stationed in Macedonia with the 4th Indian Division, later recalled how, on VE-Day, 'we were patrolling the area, keeping the peace and searching for arms. But, at the same time, we had been told, unofficially, that once the war in Europe was over, then our Division would return to India, prior to fighting the Japanese. So, in all honesty, VE-Day did not mean as much to us as it obviously did to citizens elsewhere. The prospect of fighting the Japanese, after our year in Italy, definitely cast a shadow over our lives – and desire to celebrate prematurely.'[2]

In the event, British troops in Greece were not transferred to Japan, so that Birdie Smith spent VJ-Day as he had VE-Day, in Macedonia, 'drinking a bottle of sherry with another young officer – celebrating the fact that we would *not* have to fight the Japanese!'[3]

---

[1] Jack Trembath, letter to the author, 11 November 1994.
[2] Brigadier E.D. Smith, letter to the author, 29 September 1994.
[3] Brigadier E.D. Smith, letter to the author, 21 October 1994. Brigadier Smith published his memoirs, *Wars Bring Scars*, R.J. Leach, Arlesford, Kent, in 1993.

XIII

Poland

Poland had been liberated only four months before VE-Day. In five years of occupation, the Nazis had murdered six million of her thirty million citizens. Half of the murdered Poles were Jews, all but a few thousand of Poland's pre-war Jewish population. When the time came to celebrate the victory, there was no Polish family that had not suffered terrible losses. Polish Jewry had been destroyed. The capital, Warsaw, had witnessed some of the cruellest expressions of occupation known to history. Thousands of Poles had been shot dead in the streets in individual executions, for acts of resistance, or as reprisals. Hundreds of thousands had been deported to slave labour camps. Almost all the half million Jews of the capital had been starved in the ghetto or deported to Treblinka and murdered. Thousands more Jews had been murdered in April 1943 after the ghetto revolt. Tens of thousands of Poles had been killed during the Warsaw uprising in August 1944 and in the savage reprisals after it.

Not until January 1945 had Soviet forces crossed the Vistula and driven the Germans from the city. The new rulers were Polish politicians who had been trained in the Soviet Union and whose loyalty was to the Soviet perception of the post-war order. Even as the new communist regime was being imposed, the city faced formidable problems of reconstruction. Almost all the buildings in the central part of Warsaw had been completely destroyed or gutted. The principal Jewish section, once the home of nearly half a million people, had been deliberately levelled to the ground after the ghetto uprising had been crushed two years earlier. Amid the ruins of a once-vibrant metropolis, the slow process of rebuilding had begun. It was to take more than a decade to complete.

Yet even in Warsaw, with its terrible past, the excitement of May 8 was palpable. Leah Hamersztejn, a twenty-year-old Jewish woman who had survived the vicissitudes of Nazi rule in hiding, continually moving from town to town, later recalled that day in Warsaw as 'a memorable day, a day of victory. I remember it quite distinctly. I lived then in a *kibbutz* (a commune) together with other remnants of the Jewish Fighting Organisation. This place on 38 Poznanska Street became a gathering point for Jews who survived the war. It became a temporary home for all those who finally came out of their hiding places, for those returning from concentration camps, for partisans coming out of the woods, and for repatriates from the Soviet Union. Many of them were haggard, destitute and insecure. Officially the communist government treated Jews benevolently, but unofficially the Polish masses were hostile. The bulk of survivors was looking for a way to get out of Poland, hoping to arrive in Palestine.

'So, on that morning of May 8 I got up early. I was going, with a couple of friends, to Praga, the suburb on the right bank of the Vistula. We were going to the Committee of Polish Jews which was established prior to the liberation of Warsaw on 17 January 1945. Survivors were going there to register and to search for surviving members of their families and friends. I was excited because Praga is my birthplace and I love the place dearly.

'Imbibing the delightful morning sun we walked briskly along the streets of Warsaw. They still bore the signs of war destruction: after-bombs, craters, burned out and bombed out houses, debris along the sidewalks. We came to the Vistula. The view from the bridge was heartwarming. It brought back childhood memories, the murmur of the water beneath was the same as always. It was so good to be alive again! We were young, exuberant and could hardly believe that life could be fun again. A sense of incredulity was mixed with a new born hope for a free world.'

One of the friends with whom Leah Hamersztejn walked that day was a Jewish soldier who had served in the 1st Polish Infantry Division, a division which had been formed in the Soviet Union during the war and had fought under Soviet overall command on the Eastern Front. Another was a Jewish girl, Sara Sokoler, who was in a concentration camp at the end of the war, and was raped by Soviet soldiers when they liberated the camp.

'During the five terrible war years,' Leah Hamersztejn reflected, 'we could not indulge in simple pleasures that life offers to normal people. All our efforts were directed towards fighting the enemy and surviving. Now, for the first time since 1 September 1939 we could unwind and be normal again: to walk the streets without the fear of hearing the hated *"Halt!"*, without the fear of being rounded up by Germans and pushed into military trucks. No more *"Achtung, Achtung!"* coming down from the street loud-speakers. No more ghettos, no more starvation, typhus, gas chambers, *Einsatzgruppen* (killing squads).

'The intense fear and persecution were over. What the Nazis left behind were millions of brutally murdered people, ancient towns turned into piles of rubble, art treasures destroyed or stolen. For me it was hard to believe that the worst is over, that I really survived. I, an insignificant young woman survived, while so many important, learned, wise people perished. It seemed to me like an extraordinary privilege to be among those who lived to see the collapse of the Third Reich. How many did not live to see that day!

'On our way back home we had an argument with the taxi driver because he asked an exorbitant amount of money for the ride. But it didn't really matter. In the evening we went to a restaurant. Again this exhilarating feeling that we could eat and drink to satiation. The dishes on the menu had exotic names and we did not know what they contained. So we laughed and chose a dish with the most mysterious name. When the waiter brought the food to the table it turned out to be pork knuckles and green peas! This was the finale of that memorable day.'[1]

In Lodz, Vladka Meed lived with terrible memories of the destruction of the Warsaw ghetto and of her time in hiding in a Polish village, masquerading as a Christian, fearful of betrayal or capture. Her war had ended with the arrival of the Russian army in January 1945, but her sorrows remained. None of her family seemed to have survived, no one brought her news of them, the only near-certainty was that they had been deported from Warsaw to Treblinka and murdered there. Three-quarters of a million Jews had been deported to Treblinka from throughout Poland. Less than three hundred had survived the war. The camp had existed only for the purpose of murder. It had no vast labour camp component as at Auschwitz, only gas chambers and a tiny labour force. It was known as a 'death camp'. Vladka Meed knew this, and trembled. 'The war was coming to an end,' she later wrote, 'but I did not feel any joy, any happiness. Although life around me started to normalise, I did not feel part of it. I felt like an outsider, still waiting, waiting for something. Maybe one of mine will show up after all.'

On the walls of the Jewish Community Centre survivors pinned up messages, appealing to anyone who might know the whereabouts of their nearest and dearest. 'I read every day the written messages on the walls. I even put up my own note. Maybe, after all, my sister, my brother, they were so young, maybe they were sent somewhere else – to a work camp – and maybe they survived.' But there was nothing. 'And so came May 8, the end of the war, welcomed but without rejoicing. The day was like any other day. The official news of Germany's surrender had been expected for days. We greeted it without excitement: I, with a little bit

---

[1] Leah Silverstein (née Hamersztejn), letter to the author, 20 September 1994.

of new hope; maybe I will learn more about my closest ones; but futile were my hopes of mine returned.'[1]

In Cracow, more than three months had passed since the Red Army had driven the Germans from the city. Miraculously, the fiercest fighting had been some distance away, and scarcely any damage had been done to the ancient centre of the town. For the Poles of Cracow, the ending of the war in Europe was a moment to rejoice again that the Nazi tyrant, whose Gestapo had brought such suffering to the city, had been defeated. Before the war, the city's Jewish population had been a large and flourishing one. Deportation to the death camp at Belzec, in eastern Poland, had destroyed it. With the end of German occupation, the few surviving Jews from throughout the Galician region had come to the city, their own towns and villages holding no more life for them, only terrifying memories. Among the Jews in Cracow that day was Michael Katz. His city, Lvov, had been taken from Poland a few months earlier and incorporated into the Soviet Union, together with all of East Galicia, of which it was the principal town. Hundreds of thousands of Poles had begun to leave this eastern region to escape from Russian rule.

For Michael Katz there was the double loneliness of being dispossessed, like the Poles, and of being part of the tiny remnant of Lvov's once substantial Jewish community. 'On the 8th of May,' he later wrote, 'the end was more an absence of pain and a relief than – as one might have anticipated – an exuberant pleasure. There was a rally on the Market Square in Cracow that evening and, for the first time in years, the city lights went on. In that brief moment I felt excited.

'I met a girl at the rally, who was also a Jewish survivor. She too had no family left and, like me, felt no elation. We went for a long walk, hardly speaking to each other, but feeling an enormous kinship, and we wondered whether there were many other Jews who had survived. We began looking for them as we walked through the streets. And so my new world began with a whimper. I was seventeen, I was all alone, and my prospects for the future seemed dim. It was only afterwards that I became very angry and this saved me from depression.'[2]

The seventeen-year-old boy's family was no more. 'My relationship with my stepfather was exceptionally good,' he later recalled, 'and he was,

---

[1] Vladka Meed, letter to the author, 13 October 1994.

[2] Michael Katz, letter to the author, 9 August 1994. Of the girl who shared his VE-Day, he writes: 'We saw each other twice more and on one of these occasions went to hear a lecture in Yiddish on Flaubert at the newly opened Jewish cultural centre. We listened with awe, even as neither of us – classical assimilated Jews – knew Yiddish, but simply because Yiddish was spoken again.'

in a way, an auxiliary father to me. He perished first. One evening in January of 1942 there were some shots exchanged in the street where we lived. Shortly afterwards the Germans arrested all men they could round up in the immediate neighbourhood. My stepfather, an uncle and a family friend were all included. Only my grandfather, a younger cousin, and I were left behind with the women. It is almost certain that the men were all shot several days later in a mass execution at the top of Lyczakowska Street. My mother, her parents, and her sister began working in the municipal workshops. In the major "action" of August 1942, they were all (including my cousin, who was with his mother) taken, whereas I, working elsewhere in an army auto repair facility on Janowska Street (near the camp) was spared. I have no knowledge of their specific fate, but I imagine that they were taken to Belzec and killed there. All my post-war efforts at finding them failed, but a lingering, albeit minimal, doubt has persisted in my mind.

'My father and his wife had made their way from Lodz to Warsaw earlier, and at the end of 1942 were taken away from the ghetto in one of the transports. I know nothing more about it, but presume that it went to Treblinka.'

It was not until three or four months after VE-Day that it began to be clear to Michael Katz that his entire family had perished. Until then, he searched for them in vain. Then, as it became 'more and more obvious that we in Poland would end in the Soviet clutches', he made his way through Austria and Germany to the United States. 'A dozen years later, during my military service in the US Navy, I saw an old American newsreel of the troops returning home from Europe in 1945, and the crowds that greeted them as they disembarked. There were families waiting for them with hugs and kisses and laughter. I was an adult then, a physician, and an officer in uniform, and I began to cry.'[1]

---

[1] Michael Katz, letter to the author, 26 September 1994. Katz added: 'Some pain is never assuaged. This is why my four-year-old son gets so many hugs that he may think he is shackled.'

XIV

Germany Prostrated

A report in the London *Evening News* summed up the situation in Germany on VE-Day: 'More than sixty million Germans cooped in compounds, waiting in bread queues, wandering about and living aimlessly, have to be controlled.'[1] The newspaper's diplomatic correspondent, C.F. Melville, noted that day: 'This is the first time in history that a Great Power has emerged from a war in such a state of utter disintegration; but it is a condition of affairs inherent in the situation which the Germans themselves have created.'[2] *The Times*, in its VE-Day editorial, was even more emphatic: 'In a score of great cities of Germany scarcely a building stands intact; the Russian armies have swept like an avenging hurricane over the shattered avenues and palaces of Berlin. In the factories where, through the length and breadth of the Reich, all the resources of a rich and populous nation were harnessed, even in times of peace, to the making of engines of destruction, the wheels of industry have stopped. The fields are left untilled by the liberation of the foreign slaves upon whose labour German agriculture had come to depend. Famine and pestilence lower over Germany; only by the efforts of her conquerors can she hope to escape or moderate their ravages. More terrible in the perspective of the human story even than the material ruin is the universal execration that the years of domination have earned for the German name. The Third Reich goes down to destruction unmourned, even by those nations which in the time of its prosperity were content to appear its friends.'[3]

On the day that so many nations celebrated the defeat of Germany, the German people learned of the fall of Breslau, the capital of Silesia, to the Russians. For eighty-two days the city had been under siege. The suffering of the inhabitants had been acute. One of them, then a young schoolgirl, recalled: 'My father was German, and his family had managed to keep me and my mother in Breslau all through the war. When the Russians were approaching, in the winter of 1944, we couldn't get out

---

[1] *Evening News*, 8 May 1945, p. 1, col. 1.
[2] 'The German State is no more', *Evening News*, 8 May 1945, p. 2, cols 6 and 7.
[3] 'Victory', *The Times*, 8 May 1945, p. 7, col. 2.

of the city. For three months we were under siege, with continuous shellings, and we took shelter in the cellar. Food was scarce. All the women were in favour of surrendering, but women didn't count. On May 2, a local newspaper announced that Hitler was dead, so the demand for surrender increased. The women turned for support to the priests, who promised to speak to the officers. On the morning of May 7, there was complete silence all around. We realized that the fighting was over, and the Russians would be coming soon.

'The Russian soldiers reached our cellar the next morning, May 8. Women of all ages were raped openly, in sight of everyone, including their own small children. A drunken soldier pushed me to the floor and raped me, but he was only the first. The next day the women didn't ask one another, "Were you raped?", they just asked: "How many times?" '[1]

Also in Breslau that day was Kurt Meyer-Grell, a German Air Force pilot. 'We were all beset by a sense of doom,' he reflected, 'because we were afraid of being put at the mercy of the Russians. Even in 1945, many of us believed the Russians didn't take prisoners. And I remember very clearly that when we were marched out and loaded into a truck, many of us expected to be taken into the nearest ditch and shot.

'I recall how my men and I sang the national anthem from the bottom of our hearts in front of Breslau city hall on the evening of May 6. The next day we surrendered in good order, wearing our decorations and our sidearms. Officers were permitted to retain their weapons, but I'd thrown my service pistol into the river the day before. So we marched into Russian imprisonment singing.'[2]

That singing did not last very long: the period in Russian captivity was to be harsh and prolonged. Only a few thousand German soldiers were sent back to Germany each year until, a decade after the war, the bleak and remote prisoner-of-war camps were finally emptied. Even then there was additional hardship for those who could not return to their pre-war homes – in Pomerania, Silesia or East Prussia – regions which had been transferred to Poland in 1945. Others went from communist-controlled captivity to communist-ruled East Germany. Kurt Meyer-Grell was fortunate: returning from Russia, he became a civil servant in the German Federal Republic.

Anna Hummel, once a fervent Nazi, later remembered her sense of

---

[1] Letter to the author, 17 October 1994. For understandable reasons, the letter writer wishes to remain anonymous.

[2] Kurt Meyer-Grell, in Johannes Steinhoff, Peter Pechel and Dennis Showalter (editors), *Voices from the Third Reich, an Oral History*, Regnery Gateway, Washington DC, 1989, pp. 511–12.

relief that the war was finally over. 'There won't be any more dying, any more raids. It's over. But then the fear set in of what would happen afterwards. We were spiritually and emotionally drained. Hitler's doctrines were discredited. And then the desperation set in of realising that it had all been for nothing, and that was a terrible feeling. Surviving, finding something to eat and drink, was less difficult for me than the psychological emptiness. It was incomprehensible that all this was supposed to be over, and that it had all been for nothing.'[1]

At an American military hospital at Erfurt, R.D. Catterall, one of the many former British prisoners-of-war, was recovering from the physical effects of his incarceration. He recalled: 'I was still waiting to go home. I was also experiencing the charms and joys of feminine company, of which I had been deprived for over four years. When I first met the nurses of the American field hospital situated near Weimar I felt clumsy and ill at ease. I rapidly fell in love with a dazzling lieutenant from Boston, who became the object of my dreams and the most beautiful girl in the world. She understood the difficulties of adjusting to normal living and gradually brought me back to a feeling of comfort and assurance in female company.

'In the evening there was a huge turkey and cranberry sauce dinner and dance to which I was invited; but a form of agoraphobia took hold of me and I was reluctant to go to it. Instead, my Lieutenant organised a quiet dinner for two, my first bottle of champagne for five years, and her undivided attention for me alone. My VE-Day was very private, full of tenderness, and very therapeutic.'[2]

On Lüneburg Heath, the guns had fallen silent at the time of the German surrender in northern Europe on May 5. The anticipation of possible fighting further east, however, as German forces still battled against the Russians, had kept the men alert. One of them, Lieutenant Frank Green, an Intelligence Officer with the Royal Engineers, recalled: 'In April 1945 I was one of the first to liberate the Arbeit Macht Frei camp[3] at Celle and shortly after that visited Bergen-Belsen. On the morning of 8th May I was somewhere near Lüneburg in flat heath country, sharing a caravan with my CRE (Commander Royal Engineers), studying aerial recce pictures to determine our advance eastward from a Sappers

---

[1] Quoted in Johannes Steinhoff, Peter Pechel and Dennis Showalter, *Voices From The Third Reich, An Oral History*, Regnery Gateway, Washington DC, 1989, p. 527.
[2] R.D. Catterall, 'Strictly personal', British Medical Association, *As You Were, VE-Day: a medical retrospect*, British Medical Association, London, 1984, pp. 43-4.
[3] At the entrance to all concentration camps was a gate with the motto 'Arbeit Macht Frei': 'Work liberates.'

point of view (we were to finish up eventually as far east as Schwerin only to give it up to the Russians). There was an unusual quietness broken only by bird song and the hum of mayflies. My batman brought my monthly bottle of whisky. The field telephone rang, the colonel answered. "It's all over," he said. "They've surrendered."

'I went outside and stood with a few of my friends looking up the road from where we could at first hear, and then see, the beginning of a column of grey men in grey uniforms. The sound of their boots and the beaten look on their faces told the whole story. The column continued past us for hours, thousands of them. We could not hate them, although I, who had seen Bergen-Belsen had good enough reason, although I, who had been wounded and had wasted precious years, might have done. There was no hate, there was a feeling of relief and gratitude that we had survived. Feelings of elation were limited and short lived. By the evening I had finished my bottle of whisky, I was in a melancholy mood and was probably spouting poetry which was my habit when drunk.'[1]

Daniel Krauskopf, an American corporal with the 294th Field Artillery Observation Battalion, had been attached to the British Second Army. On VE-Day his battalion was at Hagenow, near Schwerin. 'Our mess truck driver, a heavy drinker from the hills of Kentucky, found a mirror image, a heavy short, squat hard-drinking Ukrainian soldier, who offered us huge unlimited amounts of vodka and accordion music for breakfast. More serious things were happening. We joined the mass burial of dead slave labourers on the lawn of the mayor's mansion. I remember a heavy, sweating German, something out of George Grosz, who was helped by his daughter to dig a grave for a thin dried-up body.'[2]

At Lübeck, on the Baltic, British troops had taken up position between the Danish border and the Russians to the south-east. John Frost, a private serving with the 11th Armoured Division, wrote home to his mother that evening: 'It's VE-Day, fighting has ceased. It finds Stan and me safe and well. We have much to be thankful for. Our celebration will come when we walk up the garden path. I think it will come before Christmas for both of us. This afternoon we all listened to Churchill broadcast over the radio. It put the official touch to things that it was all over. It's now eight o'clock, at nine we shall be hearing a speech from the King.

'Along this road today have passed thousands more German soldiers

---

[1] Frank Green, letter to the author, 7 October 1994.
[2] Daniel M. Krauskopf, letter to the author, 28 October 1994. George Grosz was a German painter who portrayed the savage, ugly side of German society, post-1918.

and airmen. They drive their own vehicles, they look battle-worn and completely tired. They prefer to give themselves up to us than to the Russians. Also on the roads making their own way away from the Russians are hundreds of German civilians. Those that have horses and carts have household belongings piled up on the carts. Many are walking, women and children too. VE-Day is very different in Germany.

'There is not too much Victory to be seen here in the Army. Today we have been holding the usual parades and working as usual. We still carry our rifles loaded everywhere we go. You can't trust every German to surrender quietly.

'This is our third week without bread. It's biscuits and bully beef, not forgetting good old tinned sardines, pilchards and powdered potatoes. There is no beer for the boys. So VE-Day is just another day out here. Some people I'm thinking have as much idea of how British forward troops live as the man in the moon. The last time I saw an English girl was when I got the boat at –¹ coming back from leave. Since then I've enjoyed one shower and haven't changed my underwear yet.

'In a few moments the King will speak. The hut here is crowded. There are several German beds in here for it was formerly a German soldiers' billet. The radio is German too. The reception is excellent. Some of the boys are in bed writing letters, others are sitting up and all ears are open. The anthem has just played. The Major is present. The speech is over. The King has certainly improved in his manner of speaking. The news is now on. I'm sure you too are listening, Mum. And so Mum I come to a close. What the picture will be, not many people know but let's pray that this is the last war in Europe.'²

Prayers were being offered up that day in every Allied headquarters and in every army camp. At Bad Wildungen, General Omar N. Bradley's headquarters, plans were made to broadcast the service to the United States over the National Broadcasting Company. It was to be conducted by the Reverend Frederick A. McDonald, who later recalled his jeep ride 'through a bucolic part of Hesse still resembling 19th-century prints: timbered houses lining cobbled village streets, streams arched by stone bridges, farms with fat cattle feeding on rich green grass. My own ease was disturbed when I reached Bad Wildungen and learned that not a three-minute prayer but that a full service, only fifteen minutes in length

---

¹ An experienced soldier, Frost left the name of the port blank, a habit acquired from several years of knowing that his letters would go through the military censorship.
² Letter from Private E.J. Frost, 6462216, 11th Armoured Division, dated by Frost: 'May 8th, '45, Tuesday . . . **VE Day** – ' (his dot, dot, dot, dash being the morse code for V). Private archive.

because of radio time requirements, involving a hymn, lesson, prayers and address was expected.

'The service was set for 3 p.m. and was to be attended by General Bradley and his Staff. Censorship required that every word spoken had to be written and approved before use, so I sat down and sweated in finding a suitable scripture lesson, and a terse appreciation of the moment from myself. I felt deeply conscious of the historicity of the moment and wondered was there a chaplain when Grant had finished his meeting with Lee at Appomattox? General Bradley and his Staff had masterminded the strategy with the strongest forces central to victory on the Western Front. The very weight of this moment of vast change – to have the destruction and militarily-continued killings end with healing, healing to spring from the wounds of a ruined social order and multitudes of injured souls, frightened me and I entered the service with knees trembling.'

In his address, McDonald said: 'Many centuries ago, a prophet in Israel charged men with the duty of "Proclaiming liberty, every man to his neighbour". No text can be more appropriate to this Victory in Europe Day. In the ages that lie between the sounding of Jeremiah's message and this day, the human family has suffered many wars and oppressions. Too frequently, the close of the wars have themselves established the oppressions. It is not difficult for us to imagine how incredibly frightful would be this day had our enemies won this war, had they established their own "diktat" peace, with its consequent Dachaus, Buchenwalds, and Nordhausen concentration camps in Connecticut, Kentucky, and California. Thank God, the conflict ends with victory for the United Nations!

'With what joy we can "Proclaim" this Victory Day. Certainly we have every right to hope that liberties for all people will grow from the multitude of sacrifices that have been made. May this new era be a period of realisation of the Prophet's dream, when every man would proclaim liberty to his neighbour.

'Reflective minds must watch with concern the course chosen by the delegates to the United Nations' Conference in San Francisco. Here is the first step toward building Victory into durable peace. Will we find in the world of tomorrow an international outlook with the breadth of vision and freedom that has characterised our country's growth? If not, we may find a world bearing more resemblance to Alcatraz, the prison-rock in San Francisco harbour. Yet the thoughtful mind remembers that that is a choice with which we are always faced, if we are free to choose. Victory has brought us freedom of choice, and given the people of the Earth real hope. Truly that is cause for celebration.

'Days of war are hard times and breed many griefs. They are, too, times of testing and development of character. The reward that remains, however, is the peace. Surely today we may exchange for the spirit of heaviness the garment of joyful praise!'[1]

A seven-year-old German boy, Reinhard Freiberg, later recalled VE-Day near Berlin. 'I had lived in hiding for the last two years of the war at a place called Stolzenhagen (near Wandlitzersee), about thirty kilometres from Berlin, in a wooden shack behind a country house of friends, where they kept their gardening equipment. There were no friends, no contacts, almost no light since I broke, by accident, the only window glass. I never ventured outside for over two years (and still have a kind of claustrophobia whenever in an elevator or closed room). I felt in a cage, not knowing or discerning the exact reasons why. We were "Germans", weren't we? I didn't understand what it meant to be "Jewish", or, as my parents taught me, of "Jewish extraction". I was a child, curious, frightened by the unknown, the isolation, the loneliness, the carpet-bombing over nearby Berlin. I was hungry, cold and joyless.'

The young boy later recalled how, when the Russians reached his hiding place, 'I experienced freedom – and more hunger, since the 1945– 46 winter (I was eight) was truly terrible for everybody, victims included. I still can't throw away any food. On May 8, 1945 I was a happy child, understanding that the war was over, the fear was over (I never "feared" the Russian soldiers who were always kind to children). Little did they know that among the "German" children were a few "Jewish" children, a miracle! And as I experienced them, they would not have cared – we were all children, innocent victims of events beyond our comprehension. I started to make "friends" among the mostly young Russians, begging for food, spending even nights at their encampments to be fed. I can't remember how we ever communicated so intensely and in what language. I only knew German and a bit of French (my mother came from a French background), no Russian whatever. Shortly after May 8, 1945 we were given a temporary home in one of Berlin's suburbs (Frohnau), which later became the French sector of Berlin (to our greatest delight). My memories are totally overshadowed by the cold, hunger and homelessness, surrounded by so many others in equally terrible conditions. I was too young to "judge", to "understand" why we were all (Germans and the few surviving Jews) in such a horrible situation. When I learned that my father had died in Buchenwald, I started prematurely to ask questions, "Why" this, "why" that, "why" us – and quickly my comprehension of

---

[1] The Reverend Canon Frederick A. McDonald, letter to the author, 16 September 1994.

the world around me became a second nightmare, the realization of events and their meaning. On May 8, 1945, among the rubble of the city I was born in (in 1937) and which "under normal circumstances" would have been my home, a cosmopolitan centre of Europe (as my mother who survived continued to impress upon me with her nostalgia for the intensively lived "Golden Twenties" in the Weimar Republic Berlin) – that Berlin of 1945 continued to haunt me.'[1]

Yoav Freiberg reached his eighth birthday on June 27, 1945.

Susan Eckstein and the women with her on the march from Ravensbrück had been liberated by the Americans five days before VE-Day. 'On May 8,' she later recalled, 'all of us, and the soldiers of the outfit, had a gigantic party with lots of liquor, and frankly I don't know what it was, but the next morning we all had gigantic hangovers. Freedom with all its ramifications was something one had to get used to slowly, and I guess on May 8 we wanted to taste it all, and overdid it slightly.'[2]

The experiences of Susan Eckstein mirror a vast vale of tears on that day of victory and rejoicing. Born in Vienna, a refugee in Prague from 1938, deported to Theresienstadt after the German occupation of Prague and from there to Auschwitz, she was still only twenty-two when her war ended. Her mother, who was also at Theresienstadt, had been deported to Sobibor and murdered. Her father, an officer in the Austro-Hungarian army in the First World War, had been fortunate to find a sympathetic German commandant in Brussels, army and not SS, and had survived. Her own survival at Auschwitz – 'I was a very low number . . . Auschwitz-Birkenau 34042' – she ascribes to the hierarchy that was created in that camp through survival itself. 'The longer you survived,' she later recalled, 'the more you belonged to the élite.'[3] Reaching the United States, she built a life as a university teacher. Fifty years after the end of the war, she remains, through her public lectures, a witness to the worst enormities of her time, lecturing most recently in Germany, the land from which her torments sprang.

The German officer's wife Renate Hoffmann,[4] and the German refugees who were with her from Greifswald, had continued to shelter in the house in which she and the nurse had been raped on May 4. 'Every

---

[1] Dr Reinhard Yoav Freiberg, letter to the author, 25 October 1994. Dr Freiberg served from 1963 with the United Nations Children's Emergency Fund (UNICEF)

[2] Dr Susan E. Cernyak-Spatz (née Eckstein), letter to the author, 28 October 1994.

[3] Dr Susan E. Cernyak-Spatz (née Eckstein), in conversation with the author, 8 November 1994.

[4] For her earlier story, see page 61.

morning we all spread out to pick grass for our injured horse. He ate and appeared to get better. Then one day we heard a commotion and shouts of joy coming from the road. We couldn't understand the Russian words, but we assured each other, "That can only mean that the war is over and they have won!" We all had the same thought: "My God, the war is over and we're still alive!" The sun was shining, it was a beautiful day. We were about to resurface after the flood. We got back out on the road and headed for Greifswald, where we went directly to a friend's house. He was a professor at the university there. He didn't recognize us. After all, we hadn't washed in a week, and we had wrapped our heads in awful scarves to look as bad as possible. It took a while, but our friend finally said, "It's you! Of course you all can stay here. We have three rooms upstairs we don't use." We asked if he was sure that the Russians couldn't climb up the wall and into the windows at night. Our friend laughed at us and said, "But here in the city everything is over with! You have nothing to be afraid of!" But we were all still so frightened that we – the old man, the women, and the seven children – camped out together in one room that first night. We had discovered that human beings are like animals, and feel much more secure in a pack.

'The next morning, the Professor asked the obvious question, "Did anything happen to you women?" We immediately knew what he was referring to and said "Yes." Then he told us we had to go to the clinic with him right away: "In the university clinic we only have enough medication left for a few days. Right now we are treating about 500 women."' These included Renate Hoffmann's mother and aunt, both of whom were over fifty, and had been raped 'by young Russian soldiers'. Later she went to Munich where she found her husband in hospital: a night-fighter pilot, he had been badly burned. 'We fell into one another's arms. We talked and I immediately realized it was the same voice, nothing had changed. My husband got out of bed and put on his robe – the same motions, the same movements, the same figure. But it had still been a shock, because the face was no longer there – it was gone.'[1]

As the war came to an end, Lali Horstmann was in a village fifteen miles east of Berlin, not far from the bombed-out country house where she and her husband had lived and entertained before the war. Among those living with them was a young East Prussian woman, a refugee, like so many in the village, from the earlier fighting. 'We were woken up by

---

[1] Renate Hoffmann, in Johannes Steinhoff, Peter Pechel and Dennis Showalter (editors), *Voices from the Third Reich, an Oral History*, Regnery Gateway, Washington DC, 1989, pp. 441–9.

an unusual stir in the streets,' Lali Horstmann later wrote, 'motor horns were hooting and truck-loads of soldiers were singing in high spirits. This activity went on all day, even when a thunderstorm broke and darkened the sky with pelting rain. We avoided going out and tried in vain to interpret the mysterious signs from our windows, but they were like a book written in an unfamiliar language; we could not guess their meaning.

'After the storm, the day was transparently clear until far into the evening. We were lying on our beds looking at the outline of a fir tree black against the liquid turquoise sky, in which gleamed a solitary star. There was a knock and the young East Prussian woman looked in. "My French friend has just told us that an armistice was signed at six o'clock last night," she said in a casual tone and then closed the door. It was in this matter-of-fact manner, as trivial gossip, that we heard of the end of the war, the end of death and hatred. We had waited so long and had often pictured it as a spectacular event, marked by a snowstorm of leaflets and a festive chime of bells.'[1]

There were no festive chimes in Germany that day. Even the euphoria that had engulfed the Allies elsewhere was not widespread, even among the victors on German soil. Too much blood had been spilled in battle, and too many horrific scenes had been encountered on the last stage of the road to victory, to allow for rejoicing. On VE-Day Charles Feinstein was in the centre of Germany. He had been fighting with the American forces since the Normandy landings eleven months earlier. 'I landed on Omaha Beach in June 1944 with the first wave of the invasion. I was in the 3rd Armoured Division which was part of Bradley's First US Army. A lifetime later we met the Russians at the Elbe and it was over in Europe. I rode an armoured artillery vehicle called an M7, which was really a tank with no turret, in order to accommodate the 105-millimetre cannon it carried.'

While in Belgium, Feinstein had been for a short while out of the vehicle 'on watch'. Two German shells landed inside the tank and, as he wrote, 'all three, repeat all three, of my comrades were instantly killed and cremated as it was compounded by our own ammunition exploding. The shells meant the German gun was large and a great distance away. It didn't even shift an inch as it fired (which would have resulted in the second shell landing many yards away). Mazzano, Hale and Jimmie were the three dead. I had both eardrums shattered and remained in action for days so that continuing explosions from our guns inflicted great dam-

---

[1] Lali Horstmann, *Nothing for Tears*, Weidenfeld and Nicolson, London, 1953, p. 122.

age. At age twenty-nine I was now a deaf "old man". But I am still here and my friends are killed and blown up, so I guess I was the "lucky one".'

'We won the war with an army in semi-shock,' Feinstein later wrote, 'but we were so well trained we were able to function and perform all (quite complicated at times) military orders. When we landed on Omaha Beach some of the biggest guys, and high ranking officers lay down and broke into uncontrollable crying and kicking their feet and screaming, "I want my Mama", but most of us kept going. We kept going because we were somewhat insane from what we were facing. Looking back I realise the hysterics were the only sane ones. *They* were the only ones who knew what was happening!

'How did I feel on May 8th?' Feinstein asked rhetorically fifty years later, and he answered his own question: 'Dazed, still in semi-shock and angry as a person can get – in an inner rage! Because I knew that nobody really gave a shit about us, and by some miracle those of us who survived were now being prepared to land on the Japanese beaches and we knew, they missed us on Omaha Beach, but they couldn't miss us twice – and nobody cared! Nobody except my mother and Harry Truman. I was so goddam mad on May 8, I was ready to kill someone, anyone, because having survived the war in Europe nobody gave a good goddam that they were now going to send us to the Japanese beaches and they knew we couldn't have survived it twice.' Charles Feinstein had a further reason for his anger. 'We overran Nordhausen. I saw all the live bodies and the dead bodies. That's when I became a Jew.'[1]

The impact on every soldier who entered the concentration camps was dramatic. On VE-Day, Benjamin Ferencz was just inside Austria. By rank a sergeant, he had with him a letter from General Patton requesting that he be given, by anyone from whom he needed it, all assistance for the work of his war crimes unit. 'May 8 was just another business day,' he recalled. 'There was a job to be done and it couldn't stop for celebrations. I managed to escape from my office assignment and get back into the field to help in the investigation of the Mauthausen camp. On May 8, I may have been on the road or may have reached Mauthausen where dysentery and typhus were rampant, so I spent nights in a commandeered apartment in nearby Linz. From Mauthausen I went to Ebensee and more trails of dead bodies and mass graves. I didn't give a damn what day it was – that made no difference! It was all Hell and horror!'[2]

In Belsen, the largest of the concentration camps to have been liberated

---

[1] Charles Feinstein, letter to the author, 20 September 1994.
[2] Benjamin B. Ferencz, letter to the author, 21 August 1994.

by the British, Dr Phillip Whitfield was, by VE-Day, in the third week of trying to save the lives of the camp inmates. During the week following liberation, three hundred former prisoners had died each day from typhus and starvation. For the next two weeks, even under the determined care of Dr Whitfield and his helpers, the death rate had still been as high as sixty a day. Between liberation and VE-Day, three thousand of the liberated inmates had died. Their war had ended, but they had been far too weak to survive. Whitfield was too absorbed in trying to save life to remember VE-Day itself. 'If there were any celebrations,' he later recalled, 'they must have been quite subdued: not like pictures of celebrations in London! Perhaps we had an extra drink in the Mess but I remember nothing of the kind.'

Like hundreds of thousands of other soldiers, Whitfield also knew that his tour of duty might soon continue in Burma or Malaya. 'I realised that the war was far from over for me. I had only done three years in the Royal Army Medical Corps, and I knew that Japan would be my next destination – and further long periods of separation from my wife. We had married in June 1943.' After his tour of duty in northern Germany, Whitfield was promoted company commander of a Field Ambulance and sent to the Egyptian desert, he later wrote, '*en route* to Canada and Japan. (This was in spite of Hiroshima and Nagasaki)'. Not until January 1946 was he back in England. His war, which had culminated in the nightmare of Belsen, was finally over. After almost a year since the liberation of the camp, his life returned to normal. 'On April 1st I had my first day as a civilian in general practice.'[1]

Among those liberated by the British in Belsen was Hans Finke. Born in Berlin, he had witnessed as an eighteen-year-old the Nazi destruction of synagogues in the city in November 1938; *Kristallnacht*, or the 'Night of Broken Glass'. That night, and in the frightening days that followed, ninety-one German Jews were killed and 60,000 sent to concentration camps at Dachau, Sachsenhausen and Buchenwald, where several hundred were killed. Hundreds more committed suicide because of the harsh brutality of the guards. This sudden increase in physical persecution, and the widespread destruction of Jewish property that November, led to a dramatic rise in the stream of emigrants seeking safety abroad. War came less than a year later, however, making further emigration impossible. After September 1939 almost no Jews were allowed out of the expanding borders of the Third Reich: and by the end of 1941 the deportation of German Jews to the East had begun.

Hans Finke was deported to Auschwitz in 1943. He was made to work

[1] Phillip Whitfield, letter to the author, 2 October 1994.

in the adjacent Buna synthetic rubber factory. Thousand of those with him were sent to the nearby gas chambers when ill-health or physical weakness overcame them. Two of his fellow prisoners at Buna, Primo Levi and Eli Wiesel, later became well known authors and wrote of their experiences there. When the Russian army drew near to Auschwitz in January 1945, Hans Finke was among nine thousand prisoners sent westward, first on foot and then in railway cattle trucks. Those who became sick were shot by the Gestapo on the railway stations 'in full view of the civilian population'. Eventually the deportees reached Berlin, Finke's birthplace, where he recognised the city's radio tower. The convoy was taken first to Sachsenhausen, then to Flossenbürg, and finally to Belsen. 'Liberated by the British forces,' Finke later wrote, 'weighing eighty pounds, hardly alive, we tradesmen who worked before for the SS, were asked by the British engineers to help them restore power for the camp. To get out of the barracks where death and sickness was rampant, we moved into the electricians' workshop. Here only the bed-bugs were after us. We lost the food we were given, everybody was sick. We had a radio assembled and we heard "Big Ben" and Chopin on the BBC news on the 8th of May, and that the Germans were finished. But as sick persons, we were more afraid of death and the victory did not sink in as fast as it should have done.'[1]

So shocked were the British at what they found at Belsen that they made the inhabitants of all the nearby towns of Bergen and Celle visit the army cinema and watch the film that they had taken of the mass burial of the corpses.

The British troops had taken former inmates to act as interpreters for them. One of these, twenty-year-old Abe Sienicer, who had been born in Warsaw, had been liberated by men of the 113 Light Anti-Aircraft Regiment. 'I worked for the regiment as an interpreter practically from day one,' he later recalled. His liberation day, April 15, made an indelible impression, 'but May 8 left just a ripple on my memory.'[2]

Among the thousands of prisoners liberated by the British five days earlier in the camp at Neustadt was Hirsch Dorbian, whom British doctors and nurses had been tending since then, slowly bringing him back to life. Dorbian recalled VE-Day thus: 'The 8th of May was spent by me in a clean and white bed for the first time in three years and I was all of fourteen and a half years of age.'[3]

*   *   *

[1] John Fink (Hans Finke), letter to the author, 25 October 1994.
[2] Abe Shenitzer (Sienicer), letter to the author, 16 October 1994.
[3] Hirsch Dorbian, letter to the author, 8 October 1994.

At the German North Sea port of Bremervörde the officers and men of the British XXX Corps were co-ordinating the surrender and disarmament of the German forces facing them when VE-Day was declared. 'Apart from the festive consumption of much alcohol,' Captain Vivian Herzog later wrote, 'I do not recall anything special.'[1] The work of disarming the vanquished went on as before. Lieutenant Edwin Bramall's battalion, which had, like Captain Herzog's, celebrated its end of the war on May 5, was still in Hamburg on VE-Day. Bramall recalled how 'on VE-Day itself the battalion moved to a town called Pinneberg, north of Hamburg, where it set about the serious business of clearing up the area and liaising with and controlling the local German Corps HQ, who had the task of organising the German stragglers. The whole area was in chaos, with everyone on the move and the SS and other potential war criminals trying to avoid capture. It was therefore greatly to our relief when two or three days later the battalion was given orders to move into Denmark to supervise the surrender of the German forces there. So, battling against this mass of humanity, the battalion soon crossed the German frontier at Flensburg, where Dönitz had set up Germany's final Supreme Headquarters, and entered a different world full of cheering and welcoming crowds and with a countryside free from the ravages of war and where food and female company were plentiful.'[2]

Bramall knew that the next stage of the war for him would be the Far East. That summer he was posted to Central India, where he trained with I Airborne Corps for the invasion of Malaya. He was still training when Japan surrendered. It was as a captain with the British Commonwealth Occupation Force of Japan that he landed on the Japanese mainland in January 1946.

In the Bavarian Alps, Major Edward French and Sergeant Louis Dorsky, his radio operator, were scouting in a jeep and a half-track for a suitable house or castle to use as their headquarters now that hostilities had ceased. After driving for about an hour they came to a small town. 'The place looked empty,' Dorsky later recalled. 'I didn't see any people anywhere.' It was Saalfelden. 'My driver stopped our half-track under a tree so that he might nap. I, being a restless person, started to walk round to look the place over and take some photos. A short distance away I saw a bend in the road. I walked to the bend to see what was around the corner. What I saw frightened me. There were hundreds of German soldiers sitting and lounging there with their military equipment (wagons,

---

[1] Chaim (formerly Vivian) Herzog, letter to the author, 6 November 1994.
[2] Field Marshal Lord Bramall, letter to the author, 13 October 1994.

trucks, guns) nearby. I turned around and left as soon as I could, thinking that I should wake my driver so that we might decide what to do. I also knew that if we left, Major French wouldn't know what had happened to us. Before I got to the half-track, I saw a tall German officer wearing a beautiful, clean uniform with a sword hanging at his side. He came toward me and gave me a snappy salute; I was wearing a pair of rumpled fatigues. He told me that the German High Command wanted to surrender.'

Field Marshal Kesselring and his staff were awaiting the arrival of the Americans, the German officer told the American sergeant. 'I told him that my officer was not here at the moment,' Dorsky recalled, 'but would be back shortly, and that he should go and return with the Marshal. He saluted me and left. I didn't know what else to do. I woke my driver, told him what had happened and told him to make ready in case we had to leave. About ten minutes later I saw the Major's jeep racing down the road from the corner. Without stopping he passed us and signalled for us to follow him. The half-track being much slower than a jeep, we could barely keep up with him. We tried to signal for him to stop, but he kept going. The road was too narrow and difficult to manoeuvre. We didn't stop until we got back to our Headquarters. The Major must have seen the same group of soldiers that I had seen; he got scared and took off. When he finally exited his jeep I went over to him and said, "Major, you just lost the war." '[1]

The 101st Cavalry was quick, however, to rectify the situation, and by nightfall Kesselring, 60 staff officers and 250 men were safely under American control, as was Hitler's personal railway train, the bizarrely named *Amerika*, which Kesselring had been using as his headquarters at Saalfelden station. Further south, at Zell am See, three thousand wounded German soldiers were found in the town's three hospitals. The final count of prisoners taken by the 101st Cavalry, its official history recorded, 'was over fifteen times our total strength, and then we thought we had paid our way back home.'[2]

During VE-Day, an Allied journalist was exploring Hitler's mountain home at Berchtesgaden overlooking Salzburg. A syndicated Reuter message published on the following day held fascination for millions of people

---

[1] Louis Dorsky, letter to the author, 5 October 1994. 'Shortly after, we were sent back to the States to be re-equipped and sent to Japan. Luckily, before we were sent, the war came to an end. Four and a half years in the 101st Cavalry and I'm still around.' (Louis Dorsky, letter to the author, 17 October 1994).

[2] Major Mercer W. Sweeney (editor), *Wingfoot, Rhineland and Central Europe Campaigns, 101st Cavalry Group (Mechanized)*, Weinheim, Germany, August 1945, p. 99.

who sought some glimpse of how Hitler had lived. The house contained 'priceless treasures of art and literature looted from the nations of Europe', Reuter reported. 'The innumerable rooms of the great underground labyrinth cut into the living rock also hold thousands of tins of food of all sorts, and a vast stock of the best wines of Europe.

'The whole place, captured without a fight, is one huge air-raid shelter and fortress, which looked as if it could have resisted siege for years. One of the most interesting features is Hitler's library of gramophone records which, as well as the finest musical works played by the world's greatest orchestras, also contains records of all Hitler's speeches, though judging by the rubble underfoot, it is not likely that much of the collection is left. Here, too, lying in dust and mud, are many thousands of yards of cinema film, showing Hitler in conference or at the executions of opponents. The hundreds of passages in this great honeycomb, with their kitchens, pantries, store rooms, bedrooms, and living rooms, stretch for miles. The whole is air-conditioned, lit by electricity, and inter-connected by telephone. There is enough food, blankets, clothes, and medical supplies to solve the feeding problem for thousands of slave labourers.

'Above ground all semblance of order disappears with the ruins of the once beautiful Berghof still smoking from the last RAF visit. The famous view room with its great window looking towards the Austrian Alps across the valley has gone. The Eagle's Nest is now occupied by parachute troops who fought their way up 12,000 feet of the peak, but are now unable to get back to the road as the SS men have blown up the bridges. The journey to the "nest" takes an hour by jeep as well as a four-hour climb on foot through deep snow.'[1]

These mountain-top ruins had already become a souvenir-searching ground for soldiers. In many an American and French home, some dusty photograph album, faded snapshots or deckle-edged postcards are a reminder of the scattered relics of what had been Hitler's most exotic residence.

As the Reuter's correspondent reported, there was at Berchtesgaden an incredible array of art treasures, looted by Goering from all over Europe, and brought at the last moment to his villa near Hitler's home by train, in the hope of being protected from any final Allied assault. Even as the Third Reich had been losing its borders and its chance of survival as a political entity, its leaders had looked for corners in which they, their families, and their spoils of conquest, might be safe. Among

---

[1] Reuter report, Berchtesgaden, 8 May 1945, published as: 'In Hitler's Home', *The Times*, 9 May 1945, p. 3, col. 2.

the treasures discovered, in disarray, at Berchtesgaden, were a Rubens that had once belonged to Richelieu, several Rembrandts, and a fifteenth century sculpture, *La Belle Allemande*, which had been taken from the Louvre. There were paintings which Goering had taken from some of the leading Jewish art dealers and collectors, as well as his much-vaunted Vermeer, *Christ with the Woman Taken in Adultery*. This, when examined some weeks later by the chief curator of the National Gallery of Art, turned out to be a fake 'which must have been painted four years ago for him.'[1]

The return of the forged Vermeer to Holland led to one of the stranger post-war trials, that of the forger, Hans van Meergeren, who was arrested not for fraud but for 'economic collaboration' with the Germans. Acquitted, he became something of a folk hero, but was retried for forgery in 1947. He died soon after the trial.

Much of the genuine art looted by the Germans was never recovered. Some of the paintings captured by the Americans in 1945 had a chequered history. In June 1941, within a few days of the German invasion of the Soviet Union, Hitler himself had taken the magnificent Dürer drawings, twenty-seven in all, from the Lvov museum. These had been donated to the Lvov museum by the Lubomirski family in the 1840s. In 1947 Prince Georg Lubomirski, then living in Switzerland, claimed the drawings and was given them by the Americans. He promptly sold them. Following the Ukrainian declaration of independence in 1991, the Lvov museum considered making an international claim for their return.[2]

In the Pomeranian town of Laueneburg, which was already being transferred to Polish rule, the twenty-five-year-old Izrael Jutan was also celebrating. He was among the few survivors of the once-vibrant Vilna Jewish community. 'It was a bright May day,' he later recalled. 'The sun was warming our thin bodies and our small group of Vilna men and women survivors were sitting outside a house we occupied in the outskirts of Lenbork (Lauenburg) not far from the Baltic Sea. We had been liberated early in March by units of the Red Army, advancing on Berlin. I was then sick with typhoid and not yet fully recovered, my still-to-be wife was also recovering slowly from the same illness.

---

[1] John Walker, diary, National Gallery of Art archive, Washington DC, quoted in Lynn H. Nicholas, *The Rape of Europa, The Fate of Europe's Treasures in the Third Reich and the Second World War*, Macmillan, London, 1994, pp. 344–5.

[2] Lvov (as Lemberg) was in the Austro-Hungarian Empire until 1919, was Polish (as Lwów) from 1919 to 1939, under Russian occupation from 1939 to 1941, part of the Soviet Union from 1945 to 1991, and of the Ukraine since 1991.

'A Jewish Russian officer used to help our group with some food and most importantly with protection from rape-intending, Asian-looking Red Army soldiers. The Polish-language newspaper *Wolna Polska* (Liberated Poland) announced the Victory Day and a parade in town, but we were not yet in good enough shape to attend. So we talked about the event, although for us the war ended two months ago. Will the defeated Germany be punished now for all the atrocities it committed against the Jews and other nations? What will the peace bring to our lives?

'Some of us wanted to go back to Vilna. Even though we were not communists, we still longed to see "home". Perhaps someone in our families is alive. Others with the full knowledge of the tragic fate which occurred to their nearest, hoped to start a new life in Palestine or in the countries where they remembered some of their relatives were living.

'I knew already that my father, a doctor, had died in the Panemünde camp, near Königsberg, I was the only child and my divorced mother lived in Paris. I had a postcard from her early in 1941, while I was still in Vilna. I thought of her a lot and hoped to contact her as soon as possible. I tried to remember the names and locations of my relatives in England and the United States. On that day, I thought of Allied victory over Nazism with a hope that my girlfriend's health, as well as my own, would improve soon, and we would begin a new life not marred by hatred against Jews. I wanted to believe that everyone would try to help us to forget our terrible experiences of past years.

'Our Russian officer, now our friend, came with a parcel of food and drinks. "Let's celebrate – *Na Zdarovye!*", his smiling face radiating good news. He was going back to Minsk, to his wife and family. We wished him well. Most of us knew, for sure, that we did not have a home to return to. Our nearest, our families, were gone and would soon begin to drift in various directions, mostly to the west. We drank the sweet lemonade, and his Crimean wine (he did not allow us to drink vodka, as our stomachs were still not in a healthy state), and enjoyed the lunch-boxed food, specially prepared for the V-Day, as he said.

'Drunken soldiers were marching past our house, carbine shots of celebration were heard, and shouts *"Za pabyedu"*: "For Victory". The realisation dawned on us that a new era of rebirth would now commence. Chayela, who was the singer in the Vilna ghetto theatre, started to sing *"Ich veel noch einmol zain mein heim"* – "I want to see my home again", and we cried. The Russian Jewish officer cried with us.

'In the evening we were joined by some Hungarian girls, who came to say goodbye. They were returning to Budapest with help from the Russians. We were expecting news from the Jewish Refugee Committee in Bydgoszcz about our status and travels. Long into the night we spoke about our plans, hopes and dreams. For each of us "tomorrow" was an uncertainty and the day the war ended was another day in our struggle on the way to recovery of our own selves."[1]

Izrael Jutan eventually made his way to South Africa, to a new life on another continent, far from the world in which he, his family and his people had suffered so much.

Like so many survivors of German persecution, Izrael Jutan changed his name, in his case to Xavier Piat-ka. The old names held no attraction to those for whom they were a perpetual memory of suffering, degradation and loss. Jutan, like the majority of survivors, was fortunate to reach the West. Other survivors were trapped in the East, becoming the citizens of communist countries that had little or no respect for individual and civil liberties. Only with the fall of communism in 1991 did their skies brighten.

During May 8, the German troops who had been cut off for many months in northern Latvia surrendered, as did those in the Dresden-Görlitz area. Only around the Moravian city of Olomouc did German troops fight on, but theirs was a brief and hopeless resistance. Olomouc fell during the day, as did the town of Sternbeck, further north, overrun by troops of Koniev's First Ukrainian Army.

Among those fighting against the Germans on the Russian Front was Lieutenant Benjamin Meirtchak, a Jewish soldier born in the Polish city of Wloclawek in 1917. All his superior officers having been killed in battle during the previous week, he found himself in charge of his tank battalion. A member of 1 Polish Panzer Corps, he later recalled the question that had haunted him and his men since they had crossed the River Neisse on April 16: 'How to survive the last days of the war?' In that short period two of his closest friends had been killed, and he himself had been wounded. 'The Germans, in spite of their hopeless situation, continued to fight hard.'

On May 8, Lieutenant Meirtchak's battalion had reached the River Elbe at Bad Schandau. There, he received an Order of the Day stating that the Germans had capitulated. 'Vodka was supplied for the units in unlimited quantities. Kisses and embraces, and salvoes from all arms, marked this great event.' Meirtchak had another reason to celebrate the end of the war. 'A few weeks earlier I had received official information that my sister Hannah had survived the war, was living in Lodz, and

---

[1] Xavier Piat-ka (formerly Izrael Jutan), letter to the author, 11 September 1994.

expecting my return. The battalion celebrated the good news with a special field dinner, with vodka, shouting "long live our lieutenant and his sister!" '

The Polish Panzer Corps had received orders not to disturb the demobilised and unarmed German soldiers and officers on their way home. 'Thousands of them passed our positions day and night on the eastern high bank road of the Elbe. They passed us in silence, still in good physical shape. The orders we had been given were frequently violated by our soldiers, specially against German officers, and SS women officers, who preferred for their safety to take off their epaulets. "*Za moju mat*" ("For my mother!"), "*Za mojego otca*" ("For my father!") was heard in Russian, followed by shots. We officers didn't react. The bodies were pushed, by the passing Germans, into the Elbe.

'It was "vengeance" for our mothers, fathers and families who had been killed. On our battle path west from the Russian tundra, passing cities and villages in the Ukraine and Poland; we saw the results of the terrible tragedy, the "Final Solution". No more Jews in Europe, no more Jewish families! Are we the last, and only survivors of European Jewry – we Jewish soldiers?

'Now my greatest wish was to meet Hannah, my sister, as soon as possible. And I remembered my last farewell telephone talk with my dear late father Moshe, from Warsaw to Wloclawek (my birthplace) on September 3, 1939, and my father's last words: "Beniek, be brave!" I was brave, my dear father. I fought the Germans. I took my "*nekume*", my "revenge." '[1]

On the afternoon of VE-Day, troops of the United States Ninth Army who had reached the Elbe were trying to convince the Germans that the war really was over. 'An armoured car with a loudspeaker was touring the sun-drenched streets of shattered Magdeburg this afternoon', a British war correspondent, Ronald Matthews, reported. ' "*Achtung*" it would announce, and go on to recount the German High Command's surrender and Dönitz's orders to isolated groups to offer no more resistance to us. Even at two o'clock the announcement was news to a good number of Germans, whose radios were smashed or were not working for lack of current. Sometimes the tidings were greeted with ragged cheers, some-times with a burst of clapping, but most often with silent stares.'

The question most in the minds of the citizens of Madgeburg, however,

---

[1] Benjamin Meirtchak, letter to the author, 22 September 1994. On 15 November 1994 Meirtchak was awarded the Officer's Cross of the Polish Republic.

which was causing them 'a great deal of anxiety', was: 'Are the Russian occupation troops coming here?'[1] They were. Under the Yalta Agreement on zones of occupation in Germany, the Americans would withdraw, leaving Madgeburg under Russian, and communist rule, for forty-six years.

East of Magdeburg, some of the British prisoners-of war who had been liberated by the Russians in the third week of April were still wandering in the area overrun by the Russians, hoping to find the American or British demarcation line. One of them, Robert Kee, later recalled: 'I quite enjoyed myself up to a point, as I had learnt enough basic Russian to be able to wander around the vicinity (during which incidentally I did meet a few demoralised retreating German soldiers trying to make their way west, who had little idea of what was happening, and I remember telling them that Hitler was dead and Mussolini strung up). Just after VE-Day the Americans came. They took us to Leipzig, then in the US temporary zone, and we were flown back about a day later. VE-Day and all it had meant to civilians was over by then, but in any case their celebrations seemed rather to belong to a different world from ours.'[2]

In a novel, which he wrote about his liberation after his return, Robert Kee described the first sight of the English countryside as seen from the train on his way to London; the first sight of England after more than three years in captivity in Germany and German-occupied Poland: 'Brown cows, small fields, hedges everywhere, watery green grass, fond motherly trees spreading against a sky where the clouds were white and inconsequential and the light blue had a temperamental charm, children standing at gates, girls holding bicycles at level crossings, families staring restfully from the fields, sedate stuffy hoardings – "Hall's Distemper" – and always the greenness soft and dear, the wandering hedges and the full spreading trees. The unfamiliar friendliness, like an old memory from childhood, of the English countryside. The train swayed and rattled south towards London. In the carriage was the same old English smell of cigarette ends and sooty plush, the same fading photographs of Aberystwyth and the golf course at Penzance.'[3]

In Dachau, several thousands of the prisoners who had been liberated nine days earlier were slowly recovering under American medical help. One of them, Jack Brauns, who had survived as a boy in the Kovno ghetto, was still in Dachau, and in quarantine, on VE-Day. He later

[1] Ronald Matthews, 'Germans Hadn't Heard It', *Daily Herald*, 9 May 1945, p. 1, col. 6.
[2] Robert Kee, letter to the author, 11 October 1994.
[3] Robert Kee, *The Impossible Shore*, McGraw-Hill, New York, 1950, p. 265.

recalled: 'With the sunrise, May 8 arrived and my ninth day of freedom started. The winds were sending rumours to all the corners of Dachau. The subjects of the rumours varied from some credible to some incredible situations. The rumours included what food would be served today; the different concentration camps that were liberated and the fate of the inmates; the fighting of the Allied forces and the surrender of the Wehrmacht in different locations of Europe.

'My father and I were walking between the barracks to the Appel Platz. People were walking, talking and some were congregating in small groups where the rumours were discussed, and comments were added to the rumours. The inmates were wearing the same clothes. They were still emaciated, but their faces had changed. From the look of despair, you could see an occasional gentle smile.

'My conversation with father centred on our concern about the fate of my mother and brother. We had last seen them one year ago at Stutthof. Rumours about the fate of the inmates were discouraging, but all the information obtained was based on rumour and speculation as well as wishful thinking. We tried to console ourselves and not consider the possibility that our family might be incomplete. I tried to imagine how my mother and brother looked after enduring one year of Stutthof. We were concerned with how we would manage to reunite with them and where we would live.

'But with all the turmoil that was consuming my brain, the ninth day of freedom was a special day. I received an orange from an American GI and shared it with my father. It was my first orange in four years. I will always remember May 8th, the ninth day of freedom, and the taste of that first orange.'[1]

That day, Jack Brauns did not know that his mother had survived but that his brother Harry was dead. Harry had been fourteen years old when the two had last seen each other in Stutthof. 'I never found out where Harry was killed. Perhaps it was Stutthof, perhaps it was Auschwitz. He was five years younger than me. On May 21, thirteen days after VE-Day, I was twenty-one. From a caged animal, who had survived day by day, I had to plan life, without plans. I had to readjust from a day-to-day challenge of survival to a planned future without plans.'[2]

Among those who had been liberated by the Americans in Buchenwald on April 11 was Izrael Unikoski. He was one of only a thousand Jewish boys between the ages of eleven and nineteen, most of them from Poland

[1] Jack Brauns, letter to the author, 27 October 1994.
[2] Jack Brauns, conversation with the author, 27 October 1994.

and Hungary, who had survived the final horrific months in the camp. He himself had been born in the Polish town of Kalisz. 'On the 8th May 1945, we boys were still "living" in Buchenwald,' he recalled, 'in the barracks deserted by the SS. We were assembled in one of the barracks, some of us still dressed in our striped uniforms, some of us in Hitler Youth uniforms. At the assembly we were told the great news, that Germany had signed an unconditional surrender and that the war was over. I said that, together with the joy I felt that Nazi Germany had lost the war and we had survived, I felt that for me the liberation had come too late and that I, too, had lost the war, having lost my whole family, my parents, brothers and sister (my older brother Isser died of hunger in the Lodz ghetto aged nineteen).'[1]

A German woman living in Brandenburg, west of Berlin recalled the ending of the war with particular emotion. 'A few days earlier the Russians had occupied the town and, in the course of the fighting, the home where I had been living for the last three years was burnt out. I had met a neighbour and we entered an empty flat, whose owners had run away. Both of us had a baby in a pram. Almost all the windows in the flat were broken, the door did not close, there was no gas, no electricity and no running water. We had to fetch every drop of water from a hydrant down the road and carry it up to the second floor. There was of course nothing to eat. But in all that misery I was happy, unspeakably happy, as the Nazi nightmare had disappeared and again I could be Jewish.'[2]

Since the deportation of Jews from Germany and Austria had begun at the end of 1941, Edith Beer had managed to hide her identity. Born in Vienna, she had been working at a forced labour camp when she was sent home to be deported. A Christian friend, Christine Denner, gave her the use of her personal documents, enabling her to create a new identity. With this she had left Vienna for Brandenburg, and had married. Her husband, after being drafted into the German army, was captured and deported as a prisoner-of-war to Siberia, from which he returned long after the war. Edith Beer continued to live as 'Christine Denner' and thus survived.[3]

At noon on May 8, the representatives of the Western Allies arrived in Berlin to witness the second and final unconditional surrender. Field Marshal Keitel, Chief of the Combined General Staff, was the senior

[1] Jack (Izrael) Unikoski, letter to the author, 12 October 1994.
[2] Edith Beer, letter to the author, 15 October 1994.
[3] Edith Beer, letter to the author, 29 October 1994.

German officer present. Since his first meeting with Hitler in 1933 he had idolised him, and was to do so until the day he died. Citing the Russian officers who were looking after the Germans during the surrender ceremony, Marshal Zhukov wrote: 'Keitel and the other members of the German delegation were very nervous. Turning to the people surrounding him, Keitel said: "When we were driving through the streets of Berlin, I was terrified by the extent of destruction." One of our officers replied: "Mr. Field Marshal, were you not terrified when on your orders, thousands of Soviet towns and villages were wiped off the face of the earth and millions of our people, including many thousands of children, were buried under their ruins?" Keitel grew pale and shrugged his shoulders nervously but said nothing.'[1]

An hour before midnight, the second and final negotiations began of the surrender already signed at Reims almost forty-eight hours earlier. The negotiations took place in the former German Army engineering college at Karlshorst, a suburb of Berlin. One of the German delegates, for the German High Command, Grand Admiral Hans von Friedeburg, was about to sign his third instrument of surrender in four days. The two other German negotiators were General Hans-Jürgen Strumpff, Goering's successor as Head of the German Air Force, and Field Marshal Keitel.

Four Allied witnesses were present to add their names to the surrender document: Marshal Zhukov for the Supreme High Command of the Red Army, Air Chief Marshal Sir Arthur Tedder for the Allied Expeditionary Force, General Jean de Lattre de Tassigny, General Commanding-in-Chief of the First French Army, and General Carl A. Spaatz, commanding the United States Army. An American eye-witness, Charles F. Kiley, wrote of the mood of the meeting: 'Keitel, tall and erect, was a model of Prussian arrogance to the end. After he had been called from the German delegates' table to the one occupied by the Allied officers, to sign, he returned to his seat and bitterly argued a point in the surrender.' His concern was that he had not been given enough time to inform all the German forces of when hostilities were to end. But no more time was to be granted. It was already more than twenty-four hours since the surrender at Reims. It was now two minutes to eleven at night, Berlin time. Kiley's account continued: 'The three principal German delegates took their seats at a table separate from the Allies.'

Air Marshal Tedder then addressed the Germans, 'I ask you: Have

---

[1] Marshal of the Soviet Union, G. Zhukov, *Reminiscences and Reflections*, volume two, Progress Publishers, Moscow, 1985, p. 398.

"*Here you are—don't lose it again*"

33. 'Here you are – don't lose it again': a cartoon by Philip Zec in the *Daily Mirror*,
8 May 1945.

34. President Truman reads the text of the announcement of unconditional surrender to news reporters, a few minutes before broadcasting it to the American people, Washington DC, 8 May 1945. Around Truman are several senior officers, members of his Cabinet, his wife and his daughter.

35. Sergeant Benjamin Gale, watched by senior officers, addresses 16,000 American troops at Scott Field, Illinois, on VE-Day. *See pages 299–300.*

36. VE-Day in New York: the crowd celebrates in Times Square beneath a replica Statue of Liberty. *See page 293.*

37. *(right)* An American victory plaque, Konstantinovy Lazne, Czechoslovakia , 8 May 1945.

38. American troops celebrate VE-Day inside Czechoslovakia.

39. The Prague uprising of 7 and 8 May 1945. One of the 1,600 barricades erected in the city.

40. The people of Prague celebrate their victory 9 May 1945.

41. Soviet troops enter Prague, 9 May 1945.

42. Four Poles in Warsaw on VE-Day. The soldier on the right was a Jew serving with the 1st Polish Infantry Division. Next to him is Leah Hamersztejn, who during the war had been a courier for the Jewish underground. *See pages 238–40.*

43. The American Army weekly, *Yank*, Victory Edition, 'The last full measure of devotion.'

44. The war against Japan: American heavy artillery on Okinawa, 26 May 1945.

45. The war against Japan: a British soldier, Lance Corporal T. Watson, from Carlisle, brings in a Japanese sniper captured by the 14th Army Pegu, Burma.

Amid the Laurels

An Enemy Yet to Conquer

ELATION over the brilliant victories achieved in Europe should cause no one to forget that conquest of the Fascists and the Nazis does not end the war for America.

However, the war with Japan calls for innumerable other types of materials, and the plants in which these are produced will have their continuing tasks.

Moreover. the Government will

46. 'An Enemy Yet to Conquer', a cartoon published in the *New York Journal American* on 9 May 1945.

you read this document on unconditional surrender? Are you prepared to sign it?' After Tedder's questions were translated, Keitel replied: 'I am prepared to sign.'

Zhukov then 'motioned Keitel to a seat on the side of the table occupied by the Allies, the Nazi Chief of Combined Staff removing a glove from his right hand and adjusting a monocle to his left eye. While Strumpff was signing and the documents were being passed to Zhukov, Tedder, Spaatz and de Lattre, Keitel first became annoyed by the score of Russian photographers darting around the room, then called the Russian interpreter to discuss the possibility of having the "end of hostilities" agreement changed.'

The meeting ended when Zhukov stood up and said: 'I now request the German delegation to leave the room.'[1] It was half an hour before midnight. The ceremony had taken thirty-three minutes. On behalf of the Soviet Supreme Command, Zhukov then congratulated all those present on the long-awaited victory. 'Incredible commotion broke out in the hall,' he later recalled. 'Everybody was congratulating one another and shaking hands. Many had tears of joy in their eyes.'[2]

The choice of Berlin for the final surrender was widely approved, the *News Chronicle* pointing out that the signature of the armistice in 1918 in Compiègne had been a mistake. The German army, and later Hitler, had been able to claim that Germany had never been defeated. Then, the armistice had been signed on French soil. The last battles had been fought inside France and Belgium. The war had ended without a single Allied fighting soldier on German soil. 'This time,' wrote the *News Chronicle*, 'the last act in the decline and fall of Hitler's monstrous dictatorship has been staged in the ruins of the Fuehrer's capital. His people have been given such an object lesson as no nation, lusting after power, has ever had before. If the Germans are not this time well and truly convinced of the folly of their ways, their minds are indeed impermeable.'[3]

---

[1] Charles F. Kiley, 'Terms Ratified in Berlin', *Stars and Stripes*, 10 May 1945, p. 1, col. 1 and p. 8, col. 2.
[2] Marshal of the Soviet Union, G. Zhukov, *Reminiscences and Reflections*, volume two, Progress Publishers, Moscow, 1985, p. 401.
[3] 'Full Circle', *News Chronicle*, 9 May 1945, p. 2, col. 2.

XV

Austria in Turmoil

The Allies had decided in 1943 that Austria would be treated as the first victim of German expansion, rather than as an enthusiastic participant in the expansion and conquests of the Third Reich. They came as conquerors, in as much as German (and Austrian) forces continued to fight on Austrian soil throughout the first week of May 1945, but they also came as liberators, especially to the concentration camp at Mauthausen and its sub-camps at Gunskirchen and Ebensee.

A British Army surgeon, Guy Blackburn, was among the British troops in Austria on VE-Day, at Klagenfurt. 'Final news of victory in Europe on May 8 produced a measure of euphoria, almost in disbelief,' he recalled. 'This inevitably was expressed in riotous celebration, accompanied by Austrian beer and wine in incredible quantities – I had seen nothing like it since the fall of Tunis, when wine actually ran down the gutters in the streets. The sequel to this extravaganza in 1945 varied from unit to unit, my own colleagues in the field surgical unit suddenly experiencing a desire to catch horses (there were so many free) and ride them, albeit without any previous riding experience. The subsequent crop of fractures of the pelvis in CMF,[1] with and without complications, produced surgical problems of a new variety.'

Blackburn's thoughts also encompassed 'an intense thankfulness among us that London and our cities in the British Isles were no longer the targets for "doodlebugs" and "buzz bombs", of which we had no personal experience. High explosive aerial bombing and landmines were familiar to us from the days before we left the UK but later variations of aerial attack – like pilotless planes and guided missiles – were largely an unknown quantity. It was then a marvellous relief to know that the banshee wailing of sirens would no longer harbinger attacks on civilian targets, indeed on our families and friends in civil life, whose lot we all knew had often been harder to bear than our own.'[2]

---

[1] The Central Mediterranean Force.
[2] Guy Blackburn, 'Lessons in surgery, geography, and much else', *As You Were, VE-Day: a medical retrospect*, British Medical Association, London, 1984, p. 29.

In the Austrian village of Aigen-Schlegel, near the Czech border, the Polish-born George Topas spent VE-Day with the American troops who had liberated him sixteen days earlier, and had made him one of their number. 'I recall awakening to a nice, sunny day,' he later wrote. 'For a moment I thought that I was dreaming. The war was finally over and my life had been spared. Scarcely sixteen days ago I was concentration camp prisoner 14993 on a death march from Flossenbürg concentration camp, on the verge of collapse from hunger and exhaustion, which meant certain death at the hands of the SS guards. And now, as a volunteer serving with the US Army, I had survived and lived to see the end of this terrible war.

'I was a witness to both the victorious German onslaught on Poland in 1939 and their ultimate defeat. Passing before my mind's eye was the incredible ending to my ordeal which had started five and a half years ago. For I had been allowed to join the 104th Regiment, 26th Yankee Division of the Third U.S. Army in the little Bavarian town of Neuburg, where only two days earlier 161 prisoners of our death march column had been killed by the SS.

'My personal rejoicing also was muted by the knowledge that I might be the only survivor of my immediate family. (Something which became known to me later as a fact.) Nevertheless, the mood of excitement was contagious and I could not help feeling uplifted by the general merriment around me. After all, I thought, I was not the only one bereaved of his family; there were many others. Also, the nations of the Allied forces had made great sacrifices to defeat this, the most vile tyranny known in the annals of mankind. A friendly GI from Texas named Savage tried to cheer me up. "George," he said, "put the past behind you, you will come to America and start a new life."

'Eugene Martin, another GI from Scranton, Pennsylvania, signed a photo for me, which showed him sitting on a white mount that I had liberated from a German officer a few days earlier and which we had taken turns riding around on.

'The only other individual who seemed not to let himself get caught up in the excitement of the moment was an Indian named Tuvinu, a big strapping fellow who carried a Browning automatic rifle and a friendly smile on his face. I also recall that Savage, who was fond of singing, played a western tune on his hand-held harmonica for the benefit of the handful of men around him.

'As time passed I sought solitude and began to think and wonder whether anyone in my family had survived. Had my friend Mark survived? I thought about Gina, the girl whose family befriended me during the early part of the war, and wondered whether she was alive. I began to feel a sense of anxiety that displaced the mood of hopeful expectation. I was not yet fully aware that the world I once knew existed no more. Only that I had no home, no country, and as yet no one to return to, except for my Grandmother Etta Topas who had come just before the outbreak of the war for a visit to the USA and presumably still lived there. This was my only personal pleasant prospect. Yes, I thought, I will go to my grandmother in America and will try to rebuild my life there.'[1]

Units of the American Army were in the Austrian city of Linz on May 8. Captain Milton Cahn, in charge of a medical company of five officers and 120 men, recalled how he had just been ordered 'to set up a command to evacuate the camps and hospitals from Innsbruck to Vienna. I had absolute control of the situation, and the first thing I did was to go into Linz, where there was a large contingent of Jews who had been about to be sent to Mauthausen. The US government in its infinite wisdom (stupidity) ordered that all the internees were to be sent back to their countries of origin, Poland, Lithuania, Russia, etc. (where they knew they were not wanted).' In fact, the concentration camp internees were not sent back to eastern Europe: they could go back if they wished, which some did, or they could stay where they were in their Displaced Persons camps, living on Red Cross rations, while officials of the United Nations Relief and Rehabilitation Agency, UNRRA, worked over several years to obtain permission for them to enter the countries of their choice, predominantly the United States.

Cahn and his men found several storerooms in Linz 'packed with Red Cross Parcels, never dispensed, and we broke open the lockers and distributed these to the survivors. We were also able to get equipment and materials to forge Italian passports, and, later, I ordered up a train and we sent these people to Italy, where an understanding colonel helped them get to Palestine (I was age twenty-seven at the time). It took me five months to clear up the mess – but I left feeling good!'[2]

The end of the war for Captain Cahn came, as for so many hundreds of thousands of Americans, after a long and often painfully slow forward march which had, in Cahn's case, started in Normandy two weeks after D-Day. Each stage of the journey was remembered, the evacuation of the wounded and the liberation of Europe, in a line on the map : 'Omaha Beach, Caen, St.Lô, Le Mans, Chartres, Reims, Bar le Duc, Épinal,

---

[1] George Topas, letter to the author, 10 October 1994. In 1990 Topas published *The Iron Furnace, A Holocaust Survivor's Story*, The University of Kentucky Press.

[2] Dr Milton M. Cahn, letter to the author, 6 September 1994.

Lunéville, Nancy, Metz, Ludwigshafen, Mannheim, Heidelberg, Stuttgart, Munich, Oberammergau, Garmisch Partenkirchen, Innsbruck, Salzburg, Linz.'[1] In Austria itself there was, Cahn reflected, 'no destruction, and very little effect of the war'. That was until he arrived in Vienna, after VE-Day, 'which was severely damaged and looted by the Russians'. Elsewhere it was near to normality: 'I remember that concerts started in Salzburg almost at once.'[2]

On the River Enns, a tributary of the Danube, American troops advancing rapidly eastward had been halted. One of their officers, Edmund Rogers, recalled: 'We – 261st Infantry, 65th Division, Third U.S. Army – had been halted at a bridge on the Enns River. The Russians were directly on the other side, fully armed and totally unco-operative. The previous few days had been spent accepting Jerry units in surrender. They had been caught between us and the "Russki" and were desperate not to be prisoners of the latter. A Swedish legation of twenty-five men and women had crossed furtively over to our lines at night. We hid them (even from our commanding officers). The Russians came to search for them. They returned empty-handed.

'An entire Panzer division – completely staffed and equipped – beat the Russians across that bridge by six hours and laid down their arms outside our HQ.'

Headquarters on May 8 was 'a huge German military complex called "The Kassern". It was château-like, two storeys, white stone, and sat on fifty acres. We were standing in front of a pair of glass French doors leading to a small garden, when the door behind us opened and the S-1 called, "The War is over. It's official".

'At that exact instant there was a ping and a crash of glass. We looked down and a sizeable piece of shrapnel lay on the ground at our feet. It had come through the bottom of the glass French door. It was completely spent. It could not have done more than accidentally scratch us. It was still hot. But it was a pseudo-dramatic touch to an historic moment; and I used to boast that the last shot of the Nazi war machine lay at my feet – exhausted.'[3]

In southern Austria, just across from the borders of Italy and Yugoslavia, an ominous drama was beginning to unfold. On May 8 a British War Office report gave details of the surrender that day, to a British Division,

---

[1] See map preceding the index.
[2] Dr Milton M. Cahn, letter to the author, 21 October 1994.
[3] Edmund Rogers Jr, letter to the author, 18 October 1994.

both of a 5,000-strong Caucasian Division and 2,500 women and children, and of a Cossack Division of 10,000 troops 'and many thousand women and children'.[1] The men of these two divisions had been fighting, most recently in Yugoslavia, as allies alongside the German army, under German command. The women and children had travelled with them for safety, fearful of the vengeance of the Soviet Union, from which they had fled. On the day of their surrender to the British, however, the Caucasians and Cossacks, some of whom had fought alongside the British against the Bolsheviks during the Allied intervention in 1919, believed that they had found a safe haven from Stalin and Soviet Russia. An almost unnoticed drama had begun.

The British watched the arrival of these exotically dressed newcomers without hostility. Nikolai Tolstoy, the historian of their fate, has written: 'When Brigadier Musson arrived at Kötschach on May 8 to accept the surrender of General Domanov's Cossacks, he came upon the rearguard of what appeared to be a whole people on the march rather than a military detachment. For fifteen to twenty miles ahead, over the pass into the next valley, straggled thousands of men, women and children, dragging their possessions on waggons and camping in groups where they stopped. Amongst them moved bodies of disciplined cavalry, but the majority were dispirited and suffering from the effects of the hazardous climb over the Plöcken Pass.'

Seventy-five miles to the east of Kötschach, near the village of Griffen, British troops watched while the men of XV Cossack Cavalry Corps paraded for the last time before their senior German officer. 'The commander, General Helmuth von Pannwitz, sat his horse at the head of a mounted escort. With drawn sabres glittering in the fresh spring air, his veterans gazed stiffly ahead. Many had fought in the army of the Tsar, and bore themselves as they had once when reviewed by their Orthodox Emperor. Then the Trumpeter-Corps of the 1st Cossack Cavalry Division mounted on white horses, raised their instruments and struck out into the stirring "Prinz Eugen March". At once the 1st Don Cavalry Regiment broke forward in perfect parade order, and passed at full gallop, squadron after squadron, before their General. They were followed by the 2nd Siberian Cavalry, dressed in white furred caps with rifles slung across their backs. Officers and men were armed with curved swords, all wore the traditional skirted *cherkess* borne by their ancestors in battle for centuries. The senior officers were almost exclusively Germans, drawn

---

[1] 'War Diary Narrative, 8th May 1945', War Office papers, 170/4183. Public Record Office, Kew.

from the noblest families of Germany and Austria. The whole scene, with its setting of snow-capped mountains and sunshine, seemed a last triumphant reminder of the pageantry of warfare before the advent of mechanisation. It was on this note that the last fighting units of national Russia had come to end their existence. To British officers watching, many of whom were themselves cavalrymen, the sight of so many splendid horsemen executing perfect drill was supremely stirring.'[1]

The magnificence of the scene could not hide the political reality. Von Pannwitz was a German general believed to have committed atrocities against Russian and Jewish civilians in the western Soviet Union during the autumn of 1941.[2] As to those serving under him, under the Yalta Agreements Britain and the United States were committed to the repatriation to Russia of all "Russian" prisoners-of-war and of all Soviet citizens who had fought with the Germans. The fact that some of these Cossacks had left Russia after the revolution, and that many of them had their families with them, did not make them an exception in the eyes of the senior Allied officials who would be responsible for carrying out the agreement, and doing so under considerable Russian pressure. It did not help the cause of these Cossacks that their German commanding officer was an alleged war criminal. His surrender to the British, and that of his men, was no guarantee that he, and they, would not be handed over to the Soviets. Within three weeks of VE-Day, they were being sent across the Russian lines. Like all those repatriated to the Soviet Union, a few were shot, some imprisoned, and more than half sentenced to five or even ten years in the labour camps of the gulag. Their fate was terrible: cut off from their families, employed in forced labour, surrounded by the brutality of guards and fellow inmates, cursed by hunger and cold, amid the remoteness and isolation of a hundred camps, they were, some for more than a decade, unable to re-enter the hard but normal life of Soviet citizens in the cities, towns and villages from which they had gone four years earlier to fight in the battlefield.

Fifty miles east of Berchtesgaden, where so many valuable stolen paintings and other art treasures had been discovered just before VE-Day, advance units of the American Third Army reached the Austrian mountain village of Altaussee on May 8. The first troops to reach the town, Major Ralph Pearson, two jeeps and a truck full of soldiers, was concerned lest the

---

[1] Nikolai Tolstoy, *Victims of Yalta*, Hodder and Stoughton, London, 1977, pp. 223–4.
[2] The British handed von Pannwitz over to the Russians. He was taken to Moscow, tried for war crimes, and executed.

Germans were about to carry out their threat of resisting to the last in the centre of the Alpine Redoubt. The Americans had been told that there was yet another large repository of paintings and other art objects hidden in the mine there. The armed guards at the mine offered no resistance. Inside was an Aladdin's cave of treasures. Two American experts were sent for: Captain Robert Posey, the Monuments Officer, and the art historian Dr Lincoln Kirstein, both of whom, in the wake of the army's advance, had already examined several large caches of stolen works of art and looted artefacts. The two men were held up on the road for several hours by fully armed German troops; soldiers who had accepted the surrender while in the mountains and were making their way back down the Alpine valleys, past Ribbentrop's former lakeside villa at Fuschl, to the prisoner-of-war cages in the plain near Salzburg.

Reaching the mine, the two experts found, among other stolen artefacts hidden deep in the mine, more than 6,000 paintings, 2,300 drawings, nearly 1,000 prints, 137 pieces of sculpture, 129 pieces of arms and armour, and 122 tapestries. Among the treasures were eight panels of the Ghent altarpiece, *The Adoration of the Lamb*. 'The miraculous jewels of the crowned virgin,' wrote Kirstein, 'seemed to attract the light from our flickering acetylene lamps.'[1]

On May 8 a broadcast from somewhere in southern Austria had given the names of the members of a 'Provisional Government of Carinthia'. That same day, a radio station broadcasting from Graz declared the formation of a 'Provisional Government of Styria'. Russian forces were even then crossing the southern Austrian border from Yugoslavia. As with the citizens of Warsaw in August 1944, some at least of the citizens of Graz hoped to establish their own authority over the town before the Russians arrived. Within twenty-four hours, however, a further broadcast set out the orders of a Russian officer, calling himself the Town Major, who said that 'complete powers were concentrated in his person as the representative of the High Command of the Red Army'. A British Intelligence summary commented: 'It would appear that two self-appointed and, perhaps, anti-Russian Provisional Governments have been suppressed by Russian action before the British arrived.'[2]

In Vienna, the city's leading churchman, Cardinal Innitzer, who in

---

[1] Dr Lincoln Kirstein, 'In Quest of the Golden Lamb,' *Town and Country*, September 1945, p. 183, quoted in Lynn H. Nicholas, *The Rape of Europa, The Fate of Europe's Treasures in the Third Reich and the Second World War*, Macmillan, London, 1994, pp. 346–7.

[2] 'Austria', Weekly Political Intelligence Summary No. 293, 16 May 1945: Foreign Office papers, 371/50421. Public Record Office, Kew.

March 1938 had publicly welcomed Hitler to the city when Austria was annexed by Germany, celebrated a Thanksgiving Mass for Germany's surrender. Austrian fears that their country would be trapped behind the Iron Curtain were eventually dispelled. Stalin adhered to the Allied agreement for a Four-Power regime in Austria, which was divided into four occupation zones. In May 1955, under the provisions of the London Treaty, France, Britain, the United States and the Soviet Union withdrew their troops from Austria, and Hitler's first territorial conquest became a neutral state, forbidden to unite with Germany or to build a large army, but freed from the incubus of defeat. In October 1955, the new Austria declared its permanent neutrality.

XVI

Germany's Vassals Lose Their Chains

Even as the Berlin surrender ceremony was in progress, the German forces under arms in western Czechoslovakia were still fighting. That day, two urgent radio messages from the region of Velke Mezirici had been picked up by the American Third Army. The first message read:

> GERMANS ARE SEARCHING EVERYTHING AND SHOOTING PEOPLE. SEND ARMS QUICKLY OR OTHER MILITARY HELP.

The second message was more detailed:

> VELKE MEZIRICI FREED 7TH MAY BY REVOLUTIONARY FORCES, BUT RETAKEN BY GERMAN PANZERS TODAY. IMMEDIATE NEED OF WEAPONS AS GERMANS ACTING AS DEVILS. GERMANS EXECUTING MEMBERS OF CZECH REVOLUTIONARY FORCES SHOOTING CIVILIAN INHABITANTS AND BURNING HOUSES WITH NATIONAL FLAGS. TODAY SEVENTY CZECH OFFICERS AND MEN IMPRISONED LAST NIGHT IN VELKE MEZIRICI WERE TORTURED AND EXPECTING EXECUTION.

The British response had been to try to send air sorties from bases in Italy, but the authorities in London reported 'great difficulty' in obtaining sanction for this from the Russian authorities.[1]

At eight o'clock that evening Marshal Ivan Koniev broadcast to the German forces still fighting that they must surrender. When, by 11 p.m., the Germans had made no reply, he ordered his artillery to launch a new barrage, and his troops to resume military operations. As the first day of peace came to an end, the full panoply of war was resurrected in Bohemia, to rapid and, for the German forces, devastating effect.

Millions of people were on the move on VE-Day as refugees. Others were in a state of shock as a result of their ill-treatment for so many years. Somewhere in the limbo world between Germany and the former

---

[1] Lieutenant-Colonel Peter Boughey, report of 8 May 1945, including the text of the two radio messages: Foreign Office papers, 371/47086. Public Record Office, Kew.

Czechoslovakia, among those marching, or being marched, away from the advancing Red Army, was a group of about a hundred American prisoners-of-war. They had been captured during the Battle of the Bulge five months earlier. This particular group had been employed by the Germans to dig in the rubble and ruins of Dresden, in search of the corpses of those who had been asphyxiated in their underground shelters during the Allied bombing raid of mid-February, the fire storm of which had sucked the air out of even the deepest shelter. One of those Americans, Kurt Vonnegut recalled: 'We marched south and into the country-side south of Dresden for a couple of days, reaching a vacant schoolhouse in a little village, Peterswald, on May 6th or so. Our guards, acting entirely on their own by then, told us to sleep there as best we could. When we awoke the next morning, they were gone.

'We began to wander, and soon found thousands of PWs[1] and slave labourers and concentration camp survivors and lunatics and convicts who had also been turned loose where they could do the least harm. There were also fragments of German military units still under arms. When they found out we were Americans, they tried to surrender to us.

'It was generally believed that Hitler, a suicide, was lying in state in a cathedral in Berlin. Not true, of course. Everybody was equally certain that Patton was in Prague, and we should head for there. Also not true, of course.

'We were strafed from time to time by Soviet Union fighter planes. We foraged, stripping farms of anything remotely edible. We took an abandoned Wehrmacht wagon and two horses, and headed for Prague. That might have been on May 8th. On May 10th or so, we were arrested at a USSR roadblock, and sent to Halle, where we were locked up in a conventional jail. On May 16th or so, we were taken to the Elbe, where we were traded to our own army, man-for-man, for USSR nationals in American hands, many of whom were subsequently executed or imprisoned.

'While we were still wandering, incidentally, we found one of our guards, severely wounded on the Eastern Front before being made a guard, and he said, "I have completely wasted the past ten years of my life." '[2]

To the east of the wandering Americans, on both banks of the Elbe, lay the town of Bodenbach-Podmokly. It too was in limbo on May 8, between its post-1938 German and pre-1938 Czechoslovak identities.

---

[1] A frequent American variant for POW.
[2] Kurt Vonnegut, letter to the author, 14 Otober 1994.

The German army had left but Russian troops had not yet arrived. One of those who had found refuge in the town, the Slovak-born Anna Klein, recalled having reached the town less than two weeks before 'on foot, together with my very ill comrade, a girl of eighteen. I was then twenty-three years old. We walked the distance of two hundred kilometres from Leipzig, first in a forced march column with the SS. After escaping from them, we wandered on the nearly empty roads of Germany. Ten days before the armistice we arrived in Podmokly and were employed by two families as domestic servants. My comrade, Agi, was too weak for such heavy work, and anyway her employers fled from their homes soon after she came to them, so she asked and was allowed to join me in the house of my employers. I served as maid in the spacious house of a retired chief gamekeeper of the neighbouring forests. My predecessor in this work was a Ukrainian young girl, who ran away to the surrounding hills with her comrades, to await the liberation by the Russian Army.'

The gamekeeper and his family were Sudeten Germans. 'In his house we found many signs of their being true Nazis in their past,' Anna Klein recalled. 'So, we were here, in a strange German town, far away from home, knowing that our parents and families were killed by the Nazis in Auschwitz. Here we heard the news on the radio: the German army has capitulated. Around us, on the rooftops of the houses appeared, one after another, white flags made of bedsheets and table cloths. White flags everywhere, but not a single one in the colours of the Allies. No moves of any army were seen, no army was there to leave the town, and on the first day no army had appeared yet to occupy the town. The weather was balmy, the town was silent and the streets deserted. This was finally the end of the cruel long war. Not the happy end we were dreaming about, but anyway it was the end.

'Immediately on hearing the news of the capitulation, I went to meet the gamekeeper. I told him that my original story of my being a Hungarian labourer, bombed out from my quarters in Dresden, with no papers left, was not true. The truth was that I am a Jewish girl of Hungarian origin, who escaped a death march and was formerly a prisoner in concentration camps in Auschwitz, Bergen-Belsen and Markkleeberg near Leipzig. I think that he suspected us, Agi and myself, of being Jews, but he did not mention it to us until the day of the armistice. He congratulated us on our survival and told his wife and daughter to prepare a meal for us.

'The table was laid for us in the dining room. After a whole year of dire suffering, we had a square meal beside a table laid with a clean tablecloth, china and silverware, with plenty of time for finishing it undisturbed. On this day we did not want to think of the many difficulties which awaited us, not of the future and not of the illness of Agi, which unfortunately killed her in a year. We only enjoyed the wonder of our survival and of being alive on this day of victory of the good over the evil.'[1]

Throughout the morning of May 8, radio monitors in London heard a series of appeals from Prague Radio for Allied help, 'telling the victory-celebrating world that its hospitals and civilians were being shelled by the Germans'.[2] Prague Radio also reported that the Germans were shooting captured Czech officers.

That afternoon, an agreement was signed in Prague between the commander of the Czech National Army and the German commander. All fighting would cease at 8 p.m. that evening. All German army units, SS troops and German State organizations would begin to leave Prague and its surroundings. The Czechs had liberated their capital. In the last substantial blood-letting of the war in Europe, eight thousand Czech civilians and patriot-soldiers of the Czech National Army had been killed fighting in the streets of their city. Entering Prague in the wake of its self-liberation, the First Ukrainian Army, commanded by Marshal Koniev, acquired the prize that Stalin had so desired.

American troops had entered western Czechoslovakia in force, including the 97th Infantry Division, which had established its headquarters not far from the city of Pilsen, 'waiting there', Sergeant Bernie Barnett recalled, 'for the word to enter the city'. The American tanks that had entered Pilsen in advance of the infantry, bringing Czechoslovakia into the European Theatre of Operations of the United States forces, were soon ordered back, as part of Eisenhower's agreement with the Soviet High Comand that western Czechoslovakia would be in the Russian sphere. 'I recall hearing from some of the tank crews,' Barnett wrote, 'about the jubilation of the locals, who showered them with flowers, wine etc.'[3]

Sergeant Paul Kavon, who was also serving in the 97th Infantry Division, had taken part during the first week of May in the fiercest American battle on Czech soil. 'I am enclosing a picture post card of Eger,' he wrote to his parents on May 8, 'the important city we captured after days of bitter fighting on the outskirts and finally from house to house. Many of our buddies were killed and wounded in this battle. Our own platoon

---

[1] Miriam A. Porat (formerly Anna Klein), letter to the author, 18 October 1994. In 1982 she published her memoirs in Hebrew (Eked publishing house, Tel Aviv) and in 1993 in German: *Nicht befreit, Erinnerungen aus der Zeit des Holocaust*, Der Kleine Verlag, Düsseldorf.
[2] 'Prague Huns give in – Barbarians to the last', *Daily Mirror*, 9 May 1945, p. 3, col. 3.
[3] Bernard Barnett, letter to the author, 9 October 1994.

lieutenant was killed and all of us that came through it alive have to thank the All–Mighty for protecting us every moment.'

That VE-Day morning, Kavon told his parents, 'we received the announcement that the German High Command has unconditionally surrendered to the Allies, that the war was over in the entire ETO with the exception of resistance still going on in parts of Czechoslovakia and Bohemia. That is the principal reason why we are still in this sector of operations cleaning out the remaining Nazis in this part of Europe. We've been taking countless numbers of prisoners all along and we have liberated many of the Russians, Poles and other nationalities that were confined in German concentration camps, some for more than five years.'

On the previous day, a group of Russians who had been imprisoned by the Nazis 'were freed by our outfit, and we caught their Nazi prison keepers and guards. We had the Russians guard them on the way back to the prisoner-of-war compound and you can just imagine how those Russians reacted with the tables finally turned. They made the Krauts run all of the five miles back to the PW camp and if any of them lagged behind the Russians hit them with their rifle butts and really made them keep on moving. When we came in contact with the liberated Russians, they cried for joy, cheered us, shook hands, saluted and tried to show us in every way possible how much they welcomed the sight of the American Army.'

Stressing the dark side of the coin of liberation, Sergeant Kavon continued: 'Folks, I have seen enough proof of the atrocities the Nazis committed all through the countries they overran. You can readily believe all the stories now slowly drifting back to the States. We saw many Russians with either their right or left arm cut off, something they told us the Krauts had done as punishment. We met five Jewish girls near here, the first Jews I have met since I arrived in the ETO. The Nazis had taken them from their homes in Hungary and put them in concentration camps. You can just imagine how these girls looked and they told us about the whole thing. Every time the Krauts would have to flee from a town, they would not leave the Jews behind, but instead made them keep up with their retreat. They told us that (one day) the Germans marched them twenty-five kilometres (about eighteen miles), many of them barefooted, and all the Germans fed them the whole day was *three* potatoes! One little boy saw some beets in a field and ran out to pick some because he was starving. He didn't get very far because the Germans shot him before he could get to the food. They related so many things to us that to tell you all of them would require that I write you a book about it. One finds it hard to believe that humans could possibly live through something like that, but a few managed to survive and were able to tell us these things.'

The five Jewish girls spoke 'a beautiful Yiddish and were surprised to find American soldiers who could also speak the language and who were brought up in a religious atmosphere. After seeing these girls, believe me, all that has been said about the German dogs is not propaganda, but true facts. Just to hear about these things is not enough. When you see it with your own eyes it makes a much greater impression on you. Oh yes, before I forget to mention it, we haven't met any Jewish men yet wherever we've been.'

Another incident in one of the towns through which the Americans had recently advanced was, Kavon wrote, 'typical of what has occurred throughout the lands conquered by the Nazis'. While standing guard outside the house they were quartered in, he had noticed a building 'with all the windows broken and roof torn down and generally in a deplorable state. I knew it couldn't have been from bombing because the surrounding homes where we were quartered were in good shape despite the war'. It proved to be a synagogue. 'My best friend in the company, Georgie Skolnik from New Haven, Connecticut, and myself went about investigating. The Germans told us it was a temple and when we inquired about the whereabouts of the Jews of the town, they said that only six remained and that they had all died of *old age*. The door of the temple was locked but we got the key, and upon opening the door a sight greeted our eyes that enraged us more than anything before. The Nazis had used it as the *City Dump*! The bastards had thrown every type of filth and decay in there, but more than that after a bit of rummaging about we came upon bones, carcasses we could not identify.'

The two Americans also found half burnt prayer books. 'Our anger was beyond words, and if it had been in our hand we would have riddled the town with our heavy machine guns. Instead, we went to the prisoner-of-war compound to try to get some Krauts to clean out the entire building, or what was left of it, but at the compound they told us that we would be moving out shortly and couldn't stay long enough to have them complete the job. We were determined to do something about it, and for a while we waited to see if we could capture a few Jerries ourselves and get them for the job. We gave up finally and went back to our headquarters to start moving out.'

Sergeant Kavon and his friend George Skolnik had been in the same section for more than two weeks and had become good friends. 'We usually have the job of chasing Germans out of homes that we need to garrison troops. We both walk in, rifles ready, and tell them to get out. We've had great satisfaction doing that and innumerable times we've scared hell out of them by telling them we are both Jews. They move and they move fast. Our turn has come to give the orders and give them we do as they look down the business end of a rifle or heavy machine gun!'[1]

Leon Schatzberg, a graduate of the Lvov Medical School, was a doctor serving with the 8th Infantry Division of the Polish Second Army in Czechoslovakia when the war ended. He recalled: 'During the offensive which started on the day President Roosevelt died, I became part of a mobile team composed of one "real" surgeon, three nurses – and myself. Our Commander-in-Chief was General Swierozewski. He was not the greatest military strategist, judging by the disarray caused by the onslaught of a crack SS-Division marching from Czechoslovakia towards Berlin. Somehow the Second Army, badly beaten, survived and was directed to turn south towards Prague. Somewhere north of Prague, and south of a town called Melnik, I found myself on the sunny day of the 8th or 9th of May 1945 in a wooded area. There I saw a German officer, with his girl secretary and his car, surrendering to some Polish officers. They took away all his cigarettes and whatever else. He said to his secretary *"C'est fini"* and how right he was! All German troops I saw at that time had in their pass books an annotation: "demobilized due to surrender".

'There was a night after that day. And what a night! Victory! All guns blazing towards the star-filled skies with all colours of the rainbow. Although not shrapnel, these "dummies" when falling towards the ground caused lots of casualties. For the immediate vicinity of where we were at the time, we treated more than thirty wounded. I have no idea if there were also some fatalities.'[2]

At Theresienstadt, a small Czech medical staff of five physicians, fifty nurses and six disinfection specialists, arrived in the camp on May 4 and were allowed to work in the ghetto and prison, under the protection of Paul Dunant of the Geneva-based International Committee of the Red Cross. On May 5, the SS guards made their escape. On May 7 the first food arrived from several nearby Czech towns, as well as from the Red Cross. That day, sixty-five people died of malnutrition and disease. Until the evening of May 8, retreating German and SS troops passed the ghetto continuously: it was located astride the main road from Prague to Dresden. The 30,000 prisoners could make no move. On the afternoon of

---

[1] Paul Kavon, letter to his parents, Czechoslovakia, 8 May 1945. Private archive.
[2] Leon Schatzberg (later Sawicki), letter to the author, 16 November 1994.

May 8 retreating SS troops fired several shots into the ghetto, but did not enter it. 'There were some injuries, some of them heavy,' the archivist of the ghetto museum writes. 'In the evening one gun shot, some people say it was a Russian shell fired by mistake, hit the house near the barracks of the Czech gendarmes. One person died and one was seriously injured.'[1]

Among those who had been brought to Theresienstadt in April, from a slave labour camp in Dresden, making munitions, was Halina Reingold, who later recalled: 'I was sixteen when I arrived in Theresienstadt, after a forced march from Dresden where I worked in a munitions factory. We received no food; many did not survive. I dragged my mother, who for the last three days of the march was unable to walk, and for most of the time was unconscious. A dear friend helped me. Mother was cared for at the Theresienstadt hospital, and survived. She lived to be eighty-eight. She was a fighter.' On reaching Theresienstadt, Halina weighed a mere twenty-two kilogrammes.[2] 'Along with other girls, I lied about my age in order to be accepted in a children's home. The social worker said, "You poor child, you are thirteen years old? I thought you were eleven (I was sixteen). This lie gave me a mattress and a pillow. I was rich!'

At nine o'clock that night the first Soviet tanks passed Theresienstadt on the main road. By midnight, the prisoners were free. 'I went to the hospital,' Halina Reingold later recalled, 'and found my mother crying. "Don't cry Mama" I said. "The war is over". She could hardly talk, but she whispered, "Today they gave us rolls for breakfast; do you remember what rolls are?" I kissed her and left. The streets were full of people. Some were too weak to walk. Some were crying, some were laughing. I felt like a bystander. Tears wouldn't come and laughter was a thing of the past.

'I returned to my room which I shared with three other girls. A kindly elderly man brought us a big pot full of milk and told us to boil it. After years of hunger, we were not quite sure when the boiling would be completed. The milk started to rise and I shouted "it is boiling over, what shall I do?" "Close the door so it doesn't run away", said the man. And that's what I did.

'I went to sleep, but sleep wouldn't come. I thought of all my close relatives and friends, wondering if I shall ever see them again. At last I slept.'[3]

Halina Reingold's family was unusual: both her parents survived the

---

[1] Dr Vojtech Blodig, Terezin (Theresienstadt) Memorial, letter to the author, 10 October 1994.

[2] Forty-eight pounds.

[3] Ilana Turner (formerly Halina Reingold), letter to the author, 29 August 1994.

war. She herself had been deported to Auschwitz from the Lodz ghetto, but after three days in that terrible camp she was deported, with several hundred women, to another camp, Stutthof, on the Baltic. There she had been kept for three months. 'Degradation, humiliation and tragedies of Stutthof', she later wrote, 'are another story.'[1]

It was the unknown fate of brothers, sisters, parents, closest relatives and friends that filled the minds of every prisoner liberated that day. Susanna Herrmann was one week short of her eighteenth birthday. 'I was a prisoner for three years, one month and ten days,' she later wrote. 'We knew that the Red Army was going on to Prague, and people who had a home there followed them. I stayed, and hoped to see again my fifty-two-year-old parents and twenty-three-year-old sister. They had been sent to the "East" in October 1944.' The "East" was Auschwitz, though neither she nor they knew it at the time. Later she learned that her parents had both been gassed on the day of their arrival at Auschwitz, and that her sister 'perished in Bergen-Belsen, one day before liberation.'[2]

Also in Theresienstadt that day was Abraham Pasternak, who had been born in Bethlen, Transylvania, twenty-one years earlier. Between the German occupation of Hungary in March 1944 and liberation in May 1945 he had been in a 'ghetto' established in an open field near the town of Dej, then at Auschwitz for ten days, then at Buchenwald, then at a slave labour camp at Zeitz, and finally at the slave labour camp at Schlieben, where he had worked on, and helped to sabotage, the German anti-tank rocket, the hand-held *panzerfaust*. 'We were told that if we poured sand with the sulphur into the missile, the missile would misfire. We did that whenever we could.'

At the end of April, Pasternak had left Schlieben in one of the last deportations by train to Theresienstadt. Later he recalled the impression the new camp made on him. They were very different from his previous scenes of torment: 'There were all kinds of people there. German officers were walking among us as we just sat on the ground. They were smiling at us and we were puzzled by all that smiling. Rumours were rampant that they were going to kill us, machine-gun us. While we were sitting, we were waiting to be assigned to the Caserna, the Dresden barrack, where I finally was housed. There I met my brother, from whom I had been separated since Zeitz. He told me that my other brother was in the infirmary.

'The mood: confused, dazed, weak and sick. We were fearful of the

---

[1] Ilana Turner, letter to the author, 4 October 1994.
[2] Tamar Susana Herrmann, letter to the author, 30 October 1994.

killing; but mixed with those rumours were those of the end of the war. We had no idea what was true or false. We were then told to report to the administration office where we were given clothes. I wound up with a lady's nightgown, some underwear, shirt, pants, a jacket, no shoes. There was very little food. I was able to steal three potatoes. When I found my brothers, we hugged, cried, and then separated. We talked briefly about our parents but nothing else.

'The day before liberation, we sat. Worried. I was with my brother until he was taken to a different barrack. We had no idea that liberation was coming. It happened suddenly, as those people rushed in. We sensed that something was going on, but we didn't know what. We expected the Americans, not the Russians. I remember no sounds of fighting nearby. There was confusion, pandemonium and rampant rumours. Many lice, lots and lots of lice; it was unbelievable how many lice there were. It was the filthiest place you can imagine.

'On the morning of May 9, those with more strength came into the barracks yelling the war was over. "The war is over! We're liberated. The Russians are here." I got dressed and went out. I saw a soldier with a red star on his cap. I had never seen a Russian soldier before. I said *"Drosviche tovarich"* ("Welcome comrade"). He asked why I hadn't gone underground, why didn't I go into the partisans. I left him as he marched off.

'Germans were coming from one direction, and as I walked with my friend, he said to a German officer: *"Nehmen sie die Stievel herunter"* ("Hand me over your boots"), and the officer did! I couldn't believe it! A group of Germans approached, one with combat boots on his shoulder and I asked for them. He gave them to me. They were American combat boots. Then a man in a Hungarian uniform came and held a pistol in front of me and demanded the boots. He spoke Hungarian and I gave them to him.

'As we walked I saw a lot of Deutschmarks on the ground, in one place in a rucksack. I left them.'[1]

Thirty thousand concentration camp inmates and slave labourers were liberated at Theresienstadt. Pinchas Gutter, whose parents and twin sister Sabina had been murdered by the Nazis in Poland, later recalled: 'I remember the day of liberation quite vividly because of the horses. The day started when the Czech gendarmes and the Germans who were guarding Theresienstadt disappeared and Russian front-line soldiers, mainly Tartar and Uzbeks, started coming through the gates. After a

---

[1] Abraham Pasternak, letter to the author, 4 October 1994.

while we all rushed out and found ourselves on the main highway where a multitude of German refugees were being expelled, or fleeing to Germany. Families with children, *peklach*,[1] with hand wheel-barrows, horse-drawn wagons, bicycles were making their way and were being assaulted mainly by Czechs, some Russian soldiers and very few survivors.

'I was with a band of children and I remember very clearly my own sentiments of pity and commiseration towards these people because they reminded me of my own suffering. I remember similar sentiments were expressed by my companions. After all these years I still find it intriguing that instead of an intense hatred which I should have felt for these people because they were Germans, all I felt was pity and commiseration.

'After a few hours we went to some farm houses to beg for food. While we were going through a field, I noticed a pair of horses hitched to a wagon grazing in the field with nobody around. My companions ran to forage for food but I was so fascinated by these two horses that I forgot everything, including my hunger, and just sat there watching them. After a while I plucked up my courage, I climbed on to the wagon, picked up the reins and shouted "*Voi!*" like I remembered from before the war. The horses responded and I drove them to Theresienstadt.'[2] There, Pinhas Gutter worked for the Russian and Czech administration in the camp, delivering food for the Russians, for German prisoners-of-war, and for SS men who were being held for trial as war criminals. As he had no food allocation for the horses to whom he had become so attached, 'I had to scavenge what I could like stale bread which I soaked in water, hay cut from the ditches and dried in the sun, and some groats from a sympathetic Russian field kitchen sergeant.'

The time came for Gutter to leave Theresienstadt, on a special scheme whereby more than seven hundred young survivors were taken first to hostels in Windermere and elsewhere in Britain, to be trained for a new life. 'I became so attached to these horses,' he later recalled, 'that I refused to leave them behind and wanted to take them with me to Windermere. It took a lot of effort on the part of some Czech official who was very kind, and many more tears on my part, before I agreed to be parted from those horses. I suppose they were my family and that is why parting was again so full of sorrows.'[3] Gutter flew to Britain, and later emigrated to Canada.

* * *

---

[1] packages.
[2] Pinchas Gutter, letter to the author, 12 September 1994.
[3] Pinchas Gutter, letter to the author, 24 October 1994.

Sarajevo, the city which had seen the fatal shot fired in June 1914 which had precipitated the First World War, had seen some of the most savage fighting of the Second World War. German rule had been harsh, with a bitter war waged against the occupation forces by Tito's partisans, supported from 1943 by British, American and Russian arms and supplies.

By the beginning of 1945 Sarajevo was firmly in partisan hands. Among the partisans in the city on May 8 was Lieutenant Zdenko Levental, a doctor responsible for the medical needs of the garrison of nearby Gorazde, which had recently seen internecine battles between Mikhailovic's Chetniks and Tito's partisans. These were now over, and Levental had walked over the mountains to Sarajevo, to find out the fate of his parents and his elder brother. 'Everywhere the Wehrmacht had been defeated and forced to retreat,' Levental later recalled. 'Nonetheless, we did not care to guess how long it might be before the war finally came to an end. It was hardly surprising that we sat by our radios for hours on end, for fear of missing any important news.

'Then, on 8th May, at about 11 o'clock in the morning, our attention was suddenly distracted by the sound of a crescendo of gunshots coming from the street outside my host's house. We cautiously opened a window to see what was happening below us. The entire street was full of people scurrying in all directions, some of them in uniform, firing shots from pistols and rifles. We were horrified, as our first reaction was that the town had once again been overrun by the enemy. During the period from 1941 to 1945, we had become so accustomed to the idea of being at war, with all its stark horror and insecurity, that we were resigned to yet another flare-up of hostilities.

'After the shooting had subsided a little, we suddenly heard bells chiming in a nearby church, which only made us even more uneasy. Then, quite suddenly, the astonishing truth dawned. On the radio that we had listened to for so long, the normal programme was interrupted by an announcement that the headquarters of the German military forces had signed an unconditional surrender. Shortly afterward, we could hear renewed shouts of joy from the street below: "The war is over!"'

'In the evening, as I finally began to calm down, I lay awake in my bed, wondering uneasily whether, as far as I was concerned, the war had finally come to an end. I suspected that there would continue to be repercussions, in public and political life as well as in my own private domain. Many years later, it transpired that my misgivings were fully justified. Shortly before I fell asleep, some of my dearest wishes drifted into my semi-consciousness, dreams that I had cherished for so long. These included a new Crombie overcoat and something more commonplace, that I hadn't tasted for years: a large plate piled high with pancakes, filled, naturally, with delicious apricot jam. Then I finally fell asleep. The next morning, I had to report back to my command in Gorazde.'[1]

Unknown to Levental at that time, his brother Mirko had survived the war as a partisan in Croatia, fighting against both the Germans and the Ustachi. Towards the end of the war he was serving as a wireless operator with a British unit operating behind German lines. Their parents and their eldest brother had also survived. They were another fortunate family. One and a half million Yugoslav civilians perished during the war, including 60,000 of the 72,000 Jews of pre-war Yugoslavia.

Budapest had been the scene of ferocious fighting in mid-February, before being overrun by the Russians. Among those who recalled VE-Day in the city was Noemi Török. Shortly after the arrival of the Russians, the house in which she and her mother were living was expropriated, together with their belongings. 'There were no flats available,' she recalled, 'because about eighty-five per cent of the houses were damaged or totally destroyed. Food was scarce in the capital, but peasants in the country had reserves. People who had some belongings made trips, sometimes on the top of wagons, to make the then-fashionable exchange of goods: a concert piano for an elderly goose, some precious jewels for some flour or eggs (of course the peasant had to go and fetch the piano). But a sparking cultural life emerged from the ruins.'[2]

Budapest suffered severely during the Russian siege, which had begun on December 24. Pest, on the east bank of the Danube, had fallen to the Russians on January 18. The German forces in Buda, the west bank, held out until February 18. More than 49,000 Germans were killed and 110,000 taken prisoner during the fighting, and large areas of the city were destroyed or badly damaged.

The cultural life that re-emerged was of a vivid Hungarian variety, and yet quickly overlaid by the less joyful hand of communist autocracy, against which, in 1956 the Hungarians rebelled courageously, but in vain. Only in the 1980s did Hungary's rulers turn to older values and seek new horizons.

A month before VE-Day, a British military unit, the 16th Base Workshops, Royal Electrical and Mechanical Engineers, hitherto based in the south Italian port of Bari, had been sent across the Adriatic by sea to the

---

[1] Zdenko Levental, letter to the author, 17 September 1994.
[2] Noemi Török, letter to the author, 10 November 1994.

former Italian port of Zara, which had been occupied by the Yugoslav partisans and incorporated into Yugoslavia. Among the British soldiers was Lloyd Thomas, who later recalled the VE-Day celebrations: 'Early in the evening I attended a concert given by a local choir performing Yugoslavian Folk Songs, and afterwards I took part in an impromptu dance held in the town square. One of the girls I "danced" with was a uniformed partisan fighter, complete with a revolver in her holster. Although neither understood a word the other spoke, I felt it advisable to tell her, with a glance at the revolver, that I was a gentleman and that she was safe in my arms!

'I "danced" wearing army boots, and my wife, who has suffered from my clumsiness on the dance floor, suggests that I have never been in graver danger, as partisan fighters are noted for being hot-tempered and unforgiving.

'Although the European war had been won, we were immediately re-issued with rifles as our usefulness to Yugoslavia had come to an end, and we were ordered to leave the country.'[1] Marshal Tito did not want British troops on the soil of his new patrimony. For Lloyd Thomas it was the end of a war that had begun with crossing the English Channel to Le Havre at the beginning of April 1940.

For the Yugoslavs, a new struggle had begun, between Tito and Stalin, culminating in Tito's defection from the communist bloc in 1948, and inside Yugoslavia, between communists and non-communists. The Croat Ustachi and Croat nationalists (Tito was himself a Croat) were an enemy to be kept from all power or influence. The unity of post-war Yugoslavia was to be the dictatorial unity of Tito-style communism. It survived his death in 1980, but broke up ten years later when, following democratic elections held in 1990, Slovenia and Croatia both declared their independence, followed by the secession of Bosnia-Herzegovina in 1992, and Macedonia in 1993.

In the former Czech province of the Sudetenland, small groups of Jews, under German guard, were still being shunted by rail away from central Germany on May 8. In groups of up to a thousand, they were being taken towards Theresienstadt, though, unknown to the guards, this camp too had been deserted by its former overseers by then, and by nightfall had been liberated by Soviet troops. A prisoner in one of the groups still being taken there by train, Alfred Kantor, later wrote of how, towards eleven o'clock that night, their guards suddenly fled. 'We can't believe

---

[1] Lloyd Thomas, letter to the author, 12 August 1994.

it's over!' he wrote. Of the thousand men who had begun that particular rail journey less then two weeks earlier, only 175 were still alive. Kantor noted that night: 'Red Cross trucks appear, but can't take 175 men. We spend the night on the road – but in a dream. It's over.'[1]

---

[1] *The Book of Alfred Kantor, An Artist's Journal of the Holocaust*, Piatkus, London, 1987, plate 120.

XVII

The New World

Among those who were on their way to the New World on VE-Day were several thousand American servicemen, returning home from Europe. One of them was a former prisoner-of-war, the nineteen year old Kenneth Larson who had been liberated by British troops on April 28. 'I was in the middle of the Atlantic Ocean aboard an American troopship that had sailed from Camp Lucky Strike near Le Havre, France,' he recalled. 'We were headed toward New York City and the Statue of Liberty. On May 8, 1945, the captain of the troopship announced over the ship's loudspeaker that the war in Europe had ended. We broke into cheers and looked forward to reaching New York City.'

The actual announcement, Larson remembered fifty years later, 'was not an overwhelming celebration. We heard the announcement, let out a cheer, and went back to our duties. We might have been hit by a torpedo from a German submarine when we approached New York, but we weren't. Our morale was higher, and the experience in the German prisoner-of-war camp forty miles north of Hanover was a thing of the past. We were returning to America and home.'[1]

Another American serviceman who was crossing the Atlantic on VE-Day was Irving Uttal, who later wrote: 'I was returning from the UK to the USA on the *Ile de France*, a former luxury liner. I had completed the last of thirty-five B–17 missions over Germany with the 390th BG of the Eighth Air Force on 11 April 1945. My tour consisted almost entirely of English winter flying – fog, icing, minimum daylight – which grounded operations in the previous years of the Eighth in England.

'I was delighted that my crew survived without a casualty when the Eighth's loss rate was 3.5% per mission. I hated and feared combat; yet air warfare had infused me with an opium-like addiction, which left me craving more and suffering withdrawal pains as I lay in my bunk on my ship.'[2]

Another ship, the *Brand Whitlock*, was also crossing the Atlantic as the

---

[1] Kenneth Lloyd Larson, letter to the author, 19 September 1994.
[2] Lieutenant-Colonel Irving L. Uttal, letter to the author, 12 December 1994.

war came to an end. On the afternoon of VE-Day itself, after five weeks at sea, it docked at Newport News, Virginia. On board were several hundred former American prisoners-of-war who had been repatriated by the Russians through the Black Sea port of Odessa. On the same ship were three sisters, Isabella, Regina and Berta Katz. Their mother had been killed in Auschwitz. An FBI security enquiry stated, after they had been questioned: 'Subjects possessed no identifying papers, but in panel interview they claimed to have been born in Kisvarda, Hungary, and to have been interned in German concentration camps at Auschwitz, Poland, and Birnbaumel, Silesia, from May 1944 to January 1945, because of their Jewish ancestry. They stated they escaped from internment in January 1945 and reached Russian occupied territory; Russian Army Official sent them to Odessa, where the United States Army Mission placed them aboard instant vessel to come to the United States to live with their father, Melchior Katz, Brooklyn, New York. Subjects detained aboard instant vessel by Immigration and Naturalization officials pending hearing in Baltimore, Maryland. Ship departed Hampton Roads for Baltimore, Maryland during evening of May 9, 1945.'[1]

These three girls were the first survivors of Auschwitz to land on American soil. 'In our battered being,' Isabella Katz recalled, 'we carried the innocent, charred souls of millions of children, women and men. And we thank this America, this best of all countries, for putting its healing arms around our weeping hearts.' Speaking of Hitler, Isabella Katz asked: 'Did I really outlive the monster by fifty years?' Her father having emigrated to the United States, she and her sisters now had somewhere to go. During the war his efforts to get them the necessary papers to leave Hungary had been in vain. 'He tried day and night to get papers for us. They weren't given to him in time. Then he tried to get Palestine certificates, and succeeded. But by the time they reached us Hitler had been in Hungary for some weeks. We used the certificates as toilet paper.' As to her other two sisters, her younger sister Helen died on a death march in January 1945, and her oldest sister, Jolan, in Belsen, a few days after liberation. 'Nobody died,' she later reflected, 'they were murdered.'[2]

During their interrogation by the FBI, the three surviving sisters spent almost a whole day testifying, through a Hungarian interpreter, against Irma Grese, one of the worst of the Nazi concentration camp women guards. Grese, who was only twenty-two when put in charge of 18,000

---

[1] Federal Bureau of Investigation, File No. 195–6539–3, declassified 27 June 1983.
[2] Isabella Leitner (née Katz), letter to the author, 22 October 1994.

women prisoners at Auschwitz, was captured by the Allies, brought to trial as a war criminal, and hanged.

Off the Newfoundland Banks on May 8 there was a thick fog, making navigation hazardous. Among the ships that had come to anchor was a British merchantman, the Cardiff-registered tramp steamer *Umberleigh*. One of her crew, F.T. Attenborough, later recalled: 'The master, Captain Jones, a teetotaller (no booze on the ship), and Welsh Methodist, called all hands to No.3 hatch, appeared from his cabin and said in his Welsh accent, "Well boys, the war is over", and he gave us a short prayer and said, "Let us give three cheers". That was my celebration of the ending of the war in Europe.' Attenborough and his fellow crewmen had to wait another ten days, until after docking in Hull, before they could make their way to the nearest pub and down a pint.[1]

The premature celebrations in New York on May 7 did not deter those who wished to mark the true VE-Day. The headlines in the *New York Times* on the morning of May 8 were four lines deep, the first line complete with exclamation mark, the last line reporting success in the Pacific:

THE WAR IN EUROPE IS ENDED!
SURRENDER IS UNCONDITIONAL
V-E WILL BE PROCLAIMED TODAY
OUR TROOPS ON OKINAWA GAIN.

The front-page photograph showed New Yorkers on the previous day 'massed under the symbol of liberty': a model of the Statue of Liberty that had been set up in Times Square. In his 'Letter to a Soldier' column in the *New York Journal-American*, Louis Sobol wrote to 'a pal overseas' about the VE-Day celebrations: 'Frankly, the excitement was greater around town than I had anticipated. Actually I thought the VE announcement would be anti-climactic, coming as it did upon the heels of the first false announcement, and then the daily reports of wholesale surrenders. But the people went hysterical. There were wild scenes, especially in Times Square, all through the day. There were shouts, and tears, and people kissing each other and banging each other on the back. And, of course, there were thousands who went to church or stayed indoors, remembering that VE-Day had come too late for a husband, a brother, a sweetheart, a son who wasn't coming back – who'd never come back.

---

[1] David A. Thomas, *The Atlantic Star 1939–45*, W.H. Allen, London, 1990, p. 263.

Came too late for some of the Joes in the hospitals who would never see again – or walk again.'

Sobol went on to comment on the German surrender. 'One thing is certain,' he wrote, 'the German general will no longer be able to boast of his superiority as a war strategist. The German soldier loses his place in history as a valiant, fearless, unbeatable foe. When they were beaten in World War I there were a dozen excuses advanced. This time we know them for what they are, whiners and crumble-uppers when the going gets tough. As for the Yanks, I leave it to you. When have they ever been licked.'[1]

The returning Americans were not without worries of their own. Herbert Mitgang, a writer for *Stars in Stripes* who was in New York on VE-Day, recalled: 'What did I hope to do after the day the war ended? Well, in the foxholes and offices overseas, one heard talk of getting a steady job after the war that paid "$100 a week for the rest of my life". This was a generation that came out of the Depression, and $100 was a great deal of money at that time. So the first consideration was getting a good job, perhaps leaving an old profession and finding a new one, sometimes in a different part of the country. Many soldiers had never been far from where they had been born and discovered other parts of the States. The second aim was to get married or if already married to rejoin your family. Then children. Then, perhaps, a third aim: to vote for leaders of the calibre of Franklin D Roosevelt. I was old enough to vote for him on a soldier ballot in November 1944 (the age was twenty-one then; I was twenty-three), my first vote. We believed in FDR and the New Deal. What we did not want was another war, not a cold or hot war, and for me, especially, the cold war was a tragedy after VE-Day.'[2]

On May 13, in Brooklyn, Herbert Mitgang was married, thus fulfilling his second aim a mere five days after VE-Day. He had spent two and a half years overseas, and reported on seven campaigns.[3]

It was at nine o'clock on the morning of May 8 that Truman broadcast to the American people. 'If I could give you a single watchword for the coming months,' he said, 'that word is – work, work, work. We must work to finish the war. Our victory is but half-won. The West is free, but the East is still in bondage to the treacherous Japanese. When the

[1] Louis Sobol, 'New York Cavalcade', *New York Journal-American*, 9 May 1945, p. 17, cols. 6 and 7.
[2] Herbert Mitgang, letter to the author, 7 September 1994.
[3] North Africa, Sicily, Corsica, three in Italy, and Greece.

last Japanese division has surrendered unconditionally, then only will our fighting be done.'

Among those in Washington on VE-Day was Major Keith Wakefield, a member of the Australian Military Mission, who drove into the city with a fellow Australian major. 'The crowd around the White House was huge and happy and both of us were relieved of our caps and our Australian mudguard flag. This was a forerunner of the manifestation of a universal desire of Washingtonians to strip us of our uniforms. Lasses of all shapes and sizes invaded our car and made interesting suggestions. We went home and became civilians and returned to the celebrations. The lawns around the Washington, Lincoln and Jefferson monuments were teeming with joyous people. At Union Station there was a pool with an active fountain and naked and partially naked men and women were cavorting in and out of it – nobody seemed to mind this pagan ritual. We got caught up in the ecstasy of the moment and joined a raucous motorcade through Rock Creek Park finishing up at the Wardman Park Hotel where we drank several toasts to fallen companions, past defeats – so many – and this night of final Victory in Europe. Early next morning I addressed my usual chore of moving the pins on the maps and rejoicing that there would be more warlike stories available successfully to prosecute the war in the Pacific.'[1]

An American schoolgirl, Ruth Krammer, had come to the United States before the war as a refugee from Nazism. She had been born in the city of Hildesheim. 'On May 8, 1945, I was a High School Senior in Chicago,' she recalled, 'swamped with the thoughts of final exams and graduation, along with the constant thoughts of my first great love, a soldier in the US Army, named Paul, who was serving with the 30th Infantry Division, somewhere in the midst of some of the most dangerous places on the Western Front. He had participated as a scout before the Normandy invasion, was wounded several times, always returning to his beloved division, causing those of us, left behind, to live from mail delivery to mail delivery, grasping at the little V-Mail airletters. Since we lived in the same building, his sister and I ran home from school each day, tearing open the mailboxes and sharing each other's precious letters, and always hoping that there wouldn't be another dreaded telegram or letter from some hospital. Like the rest of the world, we just wanted this to be over.

'Our next step was always to turn on the radio news broadcasts. And there it was – the wonderful news – VE-DAY had finally arrived. We

---

[1] Keith Wakefield, letter to the author, 31 October 1994.

were at home, two teenagers, at the home of his parents, sharing the news. We all cried, our reaction wasn't spectacular or different from anyone else – though we felt a big brick drop from our hearts. At the same time, another friend of mine, a young lieutenant named Tony, who was the brother of one of my schoolfriends, also in our building, and who had served in Europe until beginning May 1945, had been transferred to the Pacific, and he was killed immediately. This news was also received on VE-Day, casting a heavy shadow on all of us, and in the end obliterating our joy.'[1]

More than forty-five thousand Canadian troops had been killed in the war in Europe. Across the country, VE-Day became a spontaneous holiday. Harry Torem, a schoolboy in Toronto, later remembered someone coming into his classroom during the history lesson and announcing: 'The war is over', whereupon 'everyone stood up to leave. There was no one, teacher or staff, to say a few words. Suddenly, one student picked up a glass inkwell with blue-black ink inside and threw it against the blackboard, smashing it and showering the contents everywhere. We left the classroom for the balance of the day.'[2]

An eighteen-year-old university student, Ruth Shykoff, was writing her final exams that day. 'All 152 of us were assembled in the examination hall at 9 a.m.,' she later wrote. 'In addition to the examination anxiety we were all a-buzz with the knowledge that the war in Europe was done. Professor Bailey (always a favourite) walked to the desk at the front of the hall to tell us that the war was officially over. VE-Day was today. Our exam was postponed until tomorrow evening 8 p.m. to 10.30 p.m. The enthusiastic joy was dampened by tears – many of us had lost brothers and other family members in the European "theatre", and many still had loved ones in the Pacific. Most of us had been in High School since September 1939, when Canada first went to war, and although we were never in personal danger from the hostilities, every one of us was profoundly affected by the world news. We all joined the celebrating throngs singing and dancing and crying in downtown Toronto – then each of us joined family members in our homes – to rejoice and mourn.'[3]

There was a moment of whimsical amusement in one of the maternity wards in a Toronto hospital that day, when Tova Blitz gave birth to her son Andrew, whilst a son was born to a Mrs Berlin in the same ward.

---

[1] Ruth Krammer, letter to the author, 9 October 1994.
[2] Zvi (Harry) Torem, letter to the author, 14 October 1994.
[3] Ruth Shykoff, letter to the author, 9 November 1994.

'The nurses, doctors and patients were buzzing with the report of this coincidence,' Tova Blitz recalled.[1] Also in Toronto that day, David Riegler remembered sitting with a group of friends in a youth club building downtown, 'excitedly talking about the end of the war, when one of our members entered our room and told us that a huge crowd had gathered on North Younge Street and was marching south down to the centre of Toronto. He was bursting with laughter as he pointed out how completely conservative and law-abiding the Torontonians are because, as this huge excited crowd surged south, they came to an intersection where the traffic light was red and they stopped for it till it turned green!'

For the Riegler family of Toronto, the laughter amid the celebration of victory was mixed with sorrow when his grandmother, Bracha Selznick, was notified by the American Government 'that her son, Abe Selznick, had died on the death march on the island of Luzon in the Philippines, along with many more American servicemen who were held prisoner by the Japanese and brutally forced to die. He was the observer on an American plane which was shot down by the Japanese.'[2]

In schools across Canada and the United States, as news of the end of the war in Europe reached the classrooms, a holiday was declared for the rest of the day. Robert Schreiber, in Rockford, Illinois, recalled how he spent the afternoon 'listening to my short wave radio (which still sits in my basement) with a long wire strung out of my bedroom window and fastened to a nearby tree. The reception was awful – the signal faded in and out until evening when it became quite clear. At each piece of news, I would run down the stairs to inform my mother. When my father came home from work, he said something like "Thank G-d" and my mother cried because she felt that her brother would survive.[3] We were eager for news and the radio in our living room was switched from one station to another quickly to hear the same meagre news over and over again.

'My last clear memory is of huddling next to the radio late into the night to hear more news of which there was precious little. And then I did my homework for the next day.' For Americans 'in our corner of the country', Schreiber added, 'the war was not yet over.'[4]

For many in the United States, especially in middle America, and especially the young, the war in Europe had seemed very far away indeed. The

---

[1] Tova Blitz, letter to the author, 6 October 1994.
[2] Dov (David) Riegler, letter to the author, 28 August 1994.
[3] He did: he was then serving with the American forces in Europe.
[4] Robert J. Schreiber, letter to the author, 10 October 1994.

fourteen-year-old Lois Kleinman, living in Louisville, Kentucky, later wrote: 'For me, and I think for many Americans of my age, the Japanese were more terrifying, and war in the jungle was the stuff of nightmares.'[1] Peter Gunnar, who had taken part as a bombardier in the first American daylight air raid on Berlin on March 6, was at an air base in Nebraska on VE-Day, getting ready to fly his next combat tour against Japan. 'When in the evening of 8 May 1945 some of us from the Army Air Force Base arrived, the broad street in front of the Cornhusker Hotel in Lincoln, Nebraska, was filled with a joyous, cheering crowd. It had gathered spontaneously to celebrate "Victory in Europe", the end of our war across the Atlantic. Officially in that state capital, there was no celebration of victory, no bands, no parade, no speeches. President Truman had proclaimed, "Our victory is but half-won", and called for sober and subdued celebration with his watchword of "work, work, work"' for the final triumph. He set the next Sunday as a day for prayer and thanksgiving.

'Nebraska's governor and Lincoln's mayor followed Truman's lead. General Electric gave its workers the day off, but Goodyear, Elastic Stop-Nut, Lincoln Steel, and other war supplies manufacturers did not. Churches held noon or evening services. The Air Base paused in its regular activities for only thirty minutes. Its commander also ordered all bars on the base closed until further notice, which may have helped increase the evening crowd in the street. The Lincoln *Evening Journal Star* headlined:

GRIM QUIET MARKS CITY REACTION

But joy could not be gainsaid. For many in this town of 90,000 who had sons, fathers, brothers, at war in Europe, VE-Day meant the end of fighting, wounding, and dying. It signalled *finis* to silent fears during anxious days and troubled nights. It beckoned release in joy and celebration that could not be bottled up.

'"Celebration" hardly says it adequately for those thousands. Heartfelt cheers, ably amplified by university students and quite a few military, some inspired by base-banned bottled enthusiasm, roared forth wave after wave. After a grey cloudy day made unseasonably chilly by a north wind, that spring evening was, I remember, lovely and warm. The sun, not yet fully set, still glowed golden on sun-break clouds. As it slowly sank across

---

[1] Lois Tzur (née Kleinman), letter to the author, 17 October 1994. A Jewess, Lois Kleiman was later to marry, in Israel, a Holocaust survivor from Czechoslovkia, Kurt Cierer (Yaakov Tzur).

the rolling prairie of large farms and small towns into the western horizon, its soft light murmured almost audibly, "May Peace be with you."

'I was there in Lincoln that day because I had volunteered for a second tour of combat, this time to be in the Pacific. Unlike most in our crowd in Lincoln that evening, my thirty-two missions over Nazi Europe in B–24 Liberator bombers out of Old Buckenham in Norfolk kept bringing my mind back to bombed and blacked-out Britain. I knew and admired the war-weary Brits, saw the rubble the German bombers left, went through the V–1s and V–2s, and left there only eight months before. This VE-Day evening, I found myself wondering how long the screaming thousands in London, whom we had heard on radio, could keep it up, it now being past midnight there. And here in the heart of America, I ardently added my grateful cheers to those of the millions in Old Blighty.'

Gunnar did not, in the end, have to proceed to the Pacific. The holder of a Distinguished Flying Cross, and the Air Medal with four Oak Leaf Clusters, he had accumulated enough points under the American system to be separated from the service. 'With "my" almost six-year war in Europe over and with more than enough angry countrymen to finish the Pacific war, I decided to call my active service completed.' Throughout the war, his Australian-born mother had organised British War Relief in Chicago by day, and by night had distributed Red Cross coffee and doughnuts to airmen in transit through the city's airport. At six each evening she listened over the radio to reports that 'American bombers were out today, and fifteen – or thirty or forty – failed to return to base,' not knowing if her son was one of those lost. In 1946 she was awarded the King's Medal for Service to the Cause of Freedom. Three years later, aged fifty-five, she died, exhausted by her efforts, another war casualty.[1]

Technical Sergeant Benjamin Gale, a radio gunner on a B–25 Mitchell bomber, had seen action in North Africa, flown twenty-seven missions over Italy, and been hit by flak and crash-landed. A veteran of eighteen months' aerial combat, he had been decorated three times. On VE-Day he was in the United States, at Scott Field, Illinois. 'We celebrated with a victory parade. It was an especially moving experience for me because I was given the honour to deliver the VE-Day address in the presence of 16,000 troops.'[2]

Sergeant Gale told the assembled troops: 'This day of our victory over the Nazi barbarians is a day of rejoicing and thanksgiving. It is a day of rejoicing and thanksgiving for liberty-loving people all over the world.

[1] Peter M. Gunnar, letter to the author, 17 August 1994.
[2] Benjamin Gale, letter to the author, 1 September 1994.

We thank God with all our hearts. We have conquered a powerful and ruthless foe who threatened to enslave us all. Overseas, I have seen my buddies killed in the air over enemy targets and on the ground. There were several I knew who were former students of Scott Field. They have paid with their lives for this victory.

'Let's remember that we are still fighting a fanatic foe in the Pacific. Our shoulder must remain at the wheel until we destroy him. We must also win the peace to follow. Only then can we truthfully say that their supreme sacrifice has not been in vain. After December 7, 1941 our slogan ought to be something like this: "Remember to keep faith with those who gave their lives". In the words of Joshua, that great military leader of Biblical days, "Be strong and of good courage for our country and God." '[1]

At the 2,000-bed Fletcher General Hospital in Cambridge, Ohio, Lieutenant-Colonel Arthur Rappoport, the Chief of Laboratory (Pathology) Service in the hospital recalled on VE-Day, 'the sense of ecstatic joy which swept through the institution caring for ill and wounded military patients evacuated from Europe, including many still severely injured personnel from the invasion of June 6, 1944'. Rappoport had never been posted to Europe during the war, and still expected to be sent overseas. 'Shortly after VE-Day,' he wrote, 'I was transferred to another hospital to participate in the invasion of Japan.'[2] Like millions of American soldiers, sailors, and airmen, because of the atom bombs dropped on Hiroshima and Nagasaki, he never saw this distant war zone.

As the war came to an end Staff Sergeant Jack Goldfarb was at the vast Air Transport Command base at Miami, after having served for two years overseas with the United States Army Air Forces. There his task was to help prepare the configurations and loading of service personnel, freight and mail aboard dozens of aircraft leaving each day for the war zones and overseas bases. 'On May 8, 1945, I was at my desk at Miami Airport,' he later wrote, 'in the vast hangar where we prepared the configurations and loading of personnel, freight and mail aboard dozens of aircraft each day departing for the war zones and overseas bases. 'With slide rule and pen in hand,' he later recalled, 'I had one ear cocked to the radio on a co-worker's desk. The momentous news broke through that an unconditional surrender had ended the war in Europe. The announcement was followed immediately by the playing of "The Star-Spangled Banner". All the military personnel and civilian workers in the

---

[1] 'VE-Day Speech', Scott Field, Illinois, 8 May 1945. Private archive.
[2] Arthur E. Rappoport, letter to the author, 18 October 1994.

hangar stood rigidly at attention. Then the celebrations broke out – cheering, shouting, singing, as all work came to a halt. But somehow I didn't think that was the way to mark the end of a war. I was very moved, and felt the moment should be observed in private. I stepped outside onto an empty loading platform where I could be quiet and alone. Alone to murmur prayers of thanks to God. But I really wasn't alone. Out there I heard and felt the voices and hearts of countless millions around the world, each giving thanks in his and her own way.'[1]

In San Francisco on May 8, the Foreign Ministers of the victorious powers were in session, establishing the ground rules for the United Nations Organisation. Among the delegates was Clement Attlee, Britain's Deputy Prime Minister and leader of the Labour Party, who recalled: 'While we were at the Conference the news came through that the war against the Nazis had ended. We gathered to celebrate the event in a room at the top of a skyscraper. In San Francisco the Japanese War was nearer and of greater concern to the citizens than the European contest and we were sorry not to be at home for the celebrations.'[2]

One of the delegates at San Francisco, the South African Prime Minister Jan Christian Smuts, had taken a leading part in the founding of the League of Nations immediately after the First World War. It was he who drafted the preamble setting out the aims of the new world organisation. The United Nations was to be a forum in which every sovereign state, including in due course the defeated nations, would have a place and a voice, but the leading Allied powers insisted upon a veto, in any discussion about the use of force against a member State. The Prime Minister of New Zealand, Peter Fraser, was particularly opposed to the veto as a device, but Britain, the United States and the Soviet Union were insistent that a veto was needed, as the ultimate sanction against any proposed collective action with which they disagreed. The senior Soviet delegate, Vyacheslav Molotov, had in 1939 seen the League of Nations, as its last collective decision before its demise, condemn the Soviet Union for its invasion of Finland. He did not want the Soviet Union to be singled out for active censure again.

Vladimir Trukhanovsky, a member of the Soviet United Nations delegation, was in San Francisco that day. He recalled that his, and his Soviet colleagues' 'main feeling was the pride for their country and their people'. They felt also the 'great friendliness and gratitude of the common

---

[1] Jack Goldfarb, letter to the author, 16 October 1994.
[2] C.R. Attlee, *As It Happened*, William Heinemann, London, 1954, p. 134.

people of San Francisco.'[1] Whilst in San Francisco, however, Molotov dropped a bombshell. As a British Conservative politician, Robert Boothby, who was there as a journalist, later wrote: 'During the conference Stalin collected half Europe; but no one seemed to notice until, one evening, Molotov blandly told Stettinius and Eden in the corridor of our hotel that sixteen members of the Polish Government in Warsaw, who had gone to Moscow at the request of the American and British Governments to negotiate a treaty of peace, were all in prison. I was immediately behind them: and they were visibly shaken.'[2] In an anguished article published on VE-Day in the *Daily Herald*, a Labour journalist (and future leader of the Labour Party), Michael Foot, described the impact on the conference when Molotov had announced the arrest of the sixteen Poles. According to his contemporary report, the offending remark had come 'almost casually' towards the end of an otherwise cordial dinner. 'He could hardly have caused a greater sensation if he had upset the whole table and thrown the soup in Mr Stettinius's smiling face.'

Foot's concern, as a man of the Left, was the impact the arrests would have on American Right-wing opinion. 'The tragedy and the enigma,' he wrote, '(apart from the measureless agony of the Polish people) is that the Soviet Union, which certainly appeared eager to play its full part in the world organization, has handed a weapon more powerful than any they themselves could fashion to the most sinister American enemies of international collaboration.'

Foot was also concerned that both the United States and the Soviet Union would 'contract out and kill' the new United Nations Organisation if they felt that the international system being proposed 'appeared to threaten too strongly their own immediate national interests': hence their respective insistence on the veto. His suspicions of the 'formidable' American Right were intense, but even from his Left-wing perspective he could find no words of justification for the way that Russia had treated the Polish emissaries. 'Poland could not be excluded from the conference. She is here, mocking us with her strife, but still pleading with her wounds.'[3]

In the same VE-Day issue in which Michael Foot's telegram from San Francisco appeared, a news item reported Lublin Radio's broadcast 'last night' accusing the sixteen arrested Poles of high treason, and demanding that they be brought to trial.[4]

---

[1] Vladimir Trukhanovsky, letter to the author, 9 November 1994.
[2] Lord Boothby, *Recollections of a Rebel*, Hutchinson, London, 1978, pp. 203–4.
[3] Michael Foot, 'The Mystery of Molotov', *Daily Herald*, 8 May 1945, p. 2, cols. 1–4.
[4] 'Lublin May Try Arrested Poles', *Daily Herald*, 8 May 1945.

Another young journalist who sent a report from San Francisco on VE-Day was a veteran of combat in the Pacific War, John F. Kennedy. In a despatch to the *New York Journal-American*, entitled 'A Serviceman's Views', he wrote: 'San Francisco took VE-Day in stride. This city overlooks the Pacific and to the people here "the war" has always been the war against the Japanese. The servicemen who crowd the streets have taken it calmly too. The war in the Pacific is the only war that most of them have ever known – and when you have just come home from long months of fighting and are returning to the war zones in a few days, it is difficult to become excited about "the end of the war". V-Day for them is a long way off.'

The end of the war in Europe had, however, Kennedy reported, 'acted as a stimulant' to the United Nations conference. 'England and Canada will hold an election shortly and many of the delegates will be candidates. The French, Belgians and other Europeans want to return to their countries in order that they may participate in the gradual transition from military to civil control.'

The question of the Soviet Union had dominated the conference. 'Molotov's work was about done. He leaves the other delegates divided in their attitude toward him and the entire Russian policy. Some are extremely suspicious, while on the other hand there is another group which has great confidence that the Russians in their own strange and inexplicable way really want peace. The arguments of these delegates boils down to this: It starts with the assumption a nation can usually be depended upon to act in its own best interests. In this case, Russia needs peace more than anything else. To get this peace, she feels she needs security. No one must be able to invade her again. The Russians have a far greater fear of a German come-back than we do. They are therefore going to make their western defences secure. No governments hostile to Russia will be permitted in the countries along her borders. They feel they have earned this right to security. They mean to have it, come what may.'[1]

Kennedy's summary encapsulated Soviet intentions: the pre-war independent States of Poland, Roumania, Hungary, Czechoslovakia and Bulgaria would form a belt of subordinate and subservient client-states between Russia and the West, in which no hint would be allowed of

---

[1] *New York Journal-American*, 9 May 1945, p. 5, col. 1. In a biographical note the newspaper explained: 'John F. Kennedy, one-time Navy lieutenant in command of a P-T boat, decorated for bravery in action, is covering the San Francisco United Nations conference from a serviceman's viewpoint for the *N.Y. Journal-American*. He is the son of former Ambassador Joseph P Kennedy, and, before the war, author of the best seller *Why England Slept*.'

anything considered by Moscow to be hostile to Soviet interests. Robert Boothby, in his despatch home on the night that Molotov had announced the arrest of the sixteen Polish emissaries, warned that Britain had to decide where to stand. 'So far as Europe is concerned,' he wrote, 'the Western Democracies, including Scandinavia, constitute for us an essential minimum; and our continuing failure to form a regional group of those countries which fringe the Atlantic is greatly to be deplored.' The alternative to such a regional group, Boothby warned, was 'a dangerous and increasing sense of insecurity, and a return to the situation with which we are all horribly familiar.'[1] Five days after VE-Day Boothby wrote again to his paper, the *News of the World*: 'Meanwhile the development of American and Russian policies proceeds apace. The US have already signed the Act of Chapultepec, under which the American Republics agree to co-operate in the economic field, and jointly to take care of any threat to peace in this hemisphere. They also hope to establish a measure of economic domination over the rest of the world. The Russians are engaged in the construction of a regional bloc in Eastern Europe with a speed which is almost embarrassing.'[2]

The Soviet domination of Poland, which so shocked the Western delegates and journalists at San Francisco, led within four years to what Robert Boothby called the 'fringe' countries of the Atlantic coming together in the North Atlantic Treaty Organisation. This predominantly military organisation, with its emphasis on nuclear weapons, was to face and outlast the Communist threat.[3]

There were those on May 8 for whom neither the immediate celebrations of VE-Day, nor the wider worries about Soviet intentions, were to be the final memory. That day, at Fort Oglethorpe, Georgia, a few minutes after Colonel Howard Clark, the commanding officer, addressed his men to announce the end of the European war, he was handed a War Department telegram announcing that his youngest son, First Lieutenant William A. Clark, had been killed in action on Luzon three weeks earlier.[4] The war in the Pacific continued to cast its shadow.

---

[1] Lord Boothby, *Recollections of a Rebel*, Hutchinson, London, 1978, p. 204.
[2] Article of 13 May 1945, quoted in Robert Boothby, *I Fight To Live*, Victor Gollancz, London, 1947, p. 336.
[3] The twelve founding signatories of the North Atlantic Treaty in 1949 were Belgium, Canada, Denmark, France, Iceland, Italy, Luxembourg, the Netherlands, Norway, Portugal, the United Kingdom and the United States. Greece and Turkey joined in 1952; West Germany in 1955 and Spain in 1982.
[4] 'Colonel Hails Victory, Finds Japs Slew Son', *New York Journal-American*, 9 May 1945, p. 2, col. 6. Lieutenant Clark was killed on 18 April 1945.

XVIII

Fighting Against Japan as Europe Celebrates

War in China had begun almost two years before the outbreak of war in Europe, with the Japanese invasion of Tientsin and Peking in December 1937. By the start of the war in Europe, Japan was already in control of most of northern China. As the fighting continued over much of central China, as many as two and a half million Chinese were killed. It was therefore understandable that, at Chinese Nationalist headquarters in Chungking, the end of the war in Europe had an immediacy that belied its distance. The Chinese were also looking to the time when the military attentions of the Western Allies could be focused in their entirety on the East. On VE-Day General Chiang Kai-shek broadcast to the world: 'We Chinese share with our whole hearts the inexpressible satisfaction which this German surrender gives the civilized world. The whole stupendous weight of humanity now comes down on Japan'.[1]

The most recent Japanese offensive in Western Hunan had, however, been halted, a Chungking military spokesman reporting with enthusiasm that 'at one place 3,000 Japanese were killed', that Chinese forces had been brought to the region by air, and that these troops included 'battle-tested units who were equipped with modern American weapons'.[2]

Near Ledo, in Assam, close to the border between India and Burma, an American doctor from Philadelphia, Morton Teicher, had been working for two years in the 20th General Hospital, and was there on VE-Day. It was a thousand-bed hospital. Most of the patients were American soldiers who had been ravaged by some of the terrible diseases that were endemic in that area. Some were wounded soldiers and those suffering from 'combat fatigue'. Some were wounded Chinese soldiers and a few were wounded Japanese prisoners-of-war. 'My great personal recollection,' he later wrote, 'is that both patients and medical corps personnel

[1] Text in *Daily Express*, 9 May 1945, p. 4, col. 4.
[2] Spokesman's report of 5 May 1945: Weekly Political Intelligence Summary No. 292, 9 May 1945: Foreign Office papers, 371/50421. Public Record Office, Kew.

were exceedingly happy with the news. To celebrate, the commanding general of the hospital declared that all the medicinal liquor in the hospital stores was "unfit for human consumption" and we proceeded to have a wild and joyous cocktail party. It was quite a celebration!'[1]

In the Pacific, news of the defeat of the German armies in Europe was received by men who were still fighting a fierce daily battle. Robert Hastings was then stationed at an airstrip in Palawan, the southernmost island in the Philippines. That day, as Air Combat Intelligence Officer, he was absorbed in his Navy Bomber Squadron's current mission, to bomb strategic areas occupied by the Japanese in Borneo and the Celebes, Singapore and Indo–China. 'All our efforts were focused entirely on these objectives, which we had just undertaken. We were so absorbed in flying these missions that when the announcement of VE-Day came through, almost all of our aircraft and men were then on ten- and twelve-hour flights. There was no celebration at all. But I do have a very distinct recollection of being in the operations tent with one of our air crewmen, nervously awaiting the return of our planes, when a radio message came through from Admiral Nimitz's headquarters in Guam that the war had ended in Europe. This air crewman, and I, hoped and prayed silently to ourselves that this might bring an end to the war with Japan and that we would not be sent to Okinawa to prepare for the invasion of Japan itself. I remember the first words spoken by this man: "Hot dog – maybe I will be home sooner than I expected and get fucked."

'My own recollection was that my thoughts, which were unexpressed, were for my wife and daughter, and my father and mother, brother and sisters, and I prayed that the good Lord would continue to help me do my duty and eventually bring me back to them. I did not at that time know that my brother, a doctor in one of General Patton's tank battalions, had been shot in France saving three soldiers from the German enemy crossfire and was then hospitalized in France. (I am happy to say that my brother survived and was highly decorated for his bravery.)

'I reported this VE news to our Squadron Commander at the earliest opportunity, after he landed from one of the missions. He passed the good news along to all of our squadron mates as soon as possible. As I remember, there was general jubilation and prayers, followed on by the business at hand as if the more important thing for our squadron was to bomb the hell out of the Japanese in Borneo, the Celebes, Singapore and Indo–China.'[2]

[1] Morton I. Teicher, letter to the author, 17 October 1994.
[2] Robert Hastings, letter to the author, 21 September 1994.

The intensity of the American bombing raids was noted by a British War Office survey, which listed among the most successful activities that month the bombing of the Hiro naval aircraft plant at Kure, and the laying of sea mines off Tokyo and Nagoya and in the Straits of Shimonoseki, between the main Japanese islands of Kyushu and Honshu, and 'heavy incendiary attacks' on Tokyo and Nagoya, 'where the Mitsubishi aircraft assembly plant was set on fire.'[1]

At Admiral Nimitz's headquarters on Guam, the news of the German surrender had been accepted with 'quiet satisfaction', the *New York Herald Tribune* reported on May 8. 'Officers and men, while fully ready to continue killing Japanese to a bitter finish, discussed the possibility of enemy capitulation. This unofficial speculation was based on the assumption that Japan might seize the fall of her last Axis partner as a face-saving opportunity to accept unconditional surrender.'[2] General MacArthur, the American supremo, was less sanguine but still hopeful of the beneficial effects of Victory in Europe. 'I rejoice that this command will now be reinforced by those vast and powerful resources which were previously employed by the battlefields of Europe,' he declared in a special broadcast. 'The Japanese Empire will be more speedily vanquished, and with greater economy of life than would otherwise be possible.'[3]

On many of the islands captured from the Japanese, American troops were in training for what was clearly going to be an assault on the Japanese mainland of far greater magnitude and danger than the Normandy landings almost a year earlier. One of the soldiers, Philip Freedman, later recalled: 'On May 8, 1945, I was a teenage soldier, two weeks short of my nineteenth birthday, in an artillery battalion on the island of New Caledonia. We were engaged in manoeuvres to whip us into a battle-ready condition. Frightened by the prospect of invading Japan and facing the *kamikazes*, my only reaction was "Good. Now get the European troops over here *fast*. Don't waste time celebrating; move your asses!"' That, Freedman reflected, 'was pretty much the reaction of most of my fellow GIs'.[4]

Freedman's unit had been assigned to the assault on Japan's second largest and most southerly island, Kyushu. He was still on Leyte in the Philippines when the atom bombs were dropped.

*   *   *

---

[1] 'General Notes on Operations,' May 1945, War Office, London: War Office papers, 193/ 394. Public Record Office, Kew.

[2] 'Quiet Pleasure Is Mood At Guam Headquarters: Men Think Japan May Take Opportunity to Quit', *New York Herald Tribune*, 8 May 1945, p. 3, col. 8.

[3] Text in *Daily Telegraph*, 9 May 1945, p. 5, col. 4.

[4] Professor Emeritus Philip I. Freedman, letter to the author, 8 October 1994.

Throughout the Pacific the Americans fought on, as they had done since December 1941. They were no longer the almost-beaten victims of sudden attack, but the would-be victors. Yet, as victory came to their forces in Europe, they could not minimize the scale or ferocity of the battles that lay ahead against Japan. Some wished they were in Europe all along: Sergeant Leonard Levine, a radio operator with the 345th Bomb Group on the tiny island of Ie Shima, 'arranging air strikes in preparation for the terrible invasion of Japan proper', recalled that his three years in the Pacific 'were quite enough, especially since I was twenty-one, and years before had enlisted to fight the Germans.'[1]

Sergeant David J. Shwachman, a Jew like Sergeant Levine, and also a radio operator, had enlisted 'to help liberate Europe from the scourge that was devouring our people'. He had been sent instead to the Pacific, and on VE-Day was serving with 72nd Squadron, 5th Heavy Bomber Group. He recalled the way he saw his war ending: 'We now had a system of points, and those of us who had been overseas for a long time looked forward to being replaced by some new "eager beavers". We knew what lay ahead, our opponents being fanatic *kamikazes*.'[2]

'I was out in the Pacific, "steaming as before",' Herman Wouk later wrote.[3] He was executive officer on the destroyer-minesweeper *Southard*. Of the end of the war in Europe he reflected, 'The *Southard* was either already on patrol station off Okinawa, or on the way there. In any case, I haven't the faintest recollection of an announcement of the German surrender. That doesn't mean that we didn't hear of it, of course. We received regular navy news broadcasts, and unquestionably it rated a bulletin, and perhaps was the lead story. It just didn't matter much to us, I guess. "Our war" was happening in the Pacific, at the moment around Okinawa, and our best estimate at the time was that beating the Japanese might take another couple of years, granted their amazingly undaunted fighting spirit. Indeed, has any other nation ever produced an entire cadre of poorly trained air pilots ready and willing deliberately to immolate themselves on the motto, "Sure hit, sure death"?'[4]

The Commander-in-Chief of the Japanese Combined Fleet, Admiral Soemu Toyoda, had made it clear in his instructions to the Japanese Navy that 'the fate of the Japanese Empire depended on the issue of the Okinawa battle'. Hitherto, the newspaper *Domei* pointed out, *kamikaze*

[1] Leonard Levine, letter to the author, 10 September 1994.
[2] David J. Shwachman, letter to the author, 27 September 1994.
[3] Herman Wouk, letter to the author, 30 August 1994.
[4] Herman Wouk, letter to the author, 11 October 1994.

attacks had been a 'special means' of attack, but in the fighting for Okinawa 'this method had become a common practice and not only the Air Force, but some units of the Japanese Fleet were engaged in attacks from which they did not return. The object was to annihilate the American forces.'[1]

Another American serviceman on the Marianas on May 8 was Henry Huglin, the commander of the 9th Bombardment Group, with 2,200 men and 48 aircraft under his command. They were based on Tinian Island. Huglin later recalled: 'The announcement of VE-Day was but a "blip", though a happy one, on my consciousness. Exactly two months before VE-Day, General LeMay ordered us, and the rest of the Marianas-based B–29 outfits, to attack Tokyo at night from 5,000 to 7,000 feet altitude with incendiary bombs, a major change in tactics. Our three hundred B–29s burned fifteen square miles of that city on that one raid and that marked the beginning of the end for the Japanese. By VE-Day the B–29s were conducting almost continuous operations against Japan, with virtual impunity, with a mixture of daylight and night incendiary attacks on urban industrial areas, daylight precision attacks on factories and refineries, and laying Navy mines which were strangling Japan's shipping.'[2] Such, on VE-Day, as on the days before and after it, was the dominant focus of the United States bomber crews in the Pacific: the all-pervading need to reduce the military power of Japan to the lowest possible point before a landing on the mainland.

On the Philippine island of Luzon, Henry Muller was an officer with the 11th Airborne Division. His attitude to the news of the end of the war in Europe was, he later recalled, 'one of cautious relief, rather like the player whose team has successfully completed the first half of the big game'. On Luzon, the major Japanese army units had been defeated, the remnants withdrawing to remote, heavily-forested mountain tops. They would be left to moulder there. MacArthur's plan, Muller recalled, 'was to reconstitute the strength of the combat units and get them ready for the coming invasion of Japan. We knew we would be a part of the enormous operation (four full armies) against the Japanese mainland. The Navy was opening the sea routes and the Air Corps was pounding the war-making capacity of the Japanese. We understood, however, that the actual attack against the mainland would not begin until the end of the war in Europe, which would permit redeployment of troops for two more armies in the

---

[1] *Domei*, 6 May 1945, reported in Weekly Political Intelligence Summary No. 292, 9 May 1945: Foreign Office papers, 371/50421. Public Record Office, Kew.
[2] Brigadier-General Henry C. Huglin, letter to the author, 2 October 1994.

Pacific. For us then, this was a major consequence of the victory in Europe.'[1]

Hyman Haves was on the island of Mindoro in the Philippines as the war in Europe came to an end. 'I lost two bottles of whiskey in the celebration,' he recalled. 'The bottles were filled by my storing the whiskey shorts each of us received upon a return from a mission. With more than thirty missions under my belt, and not being a drinker, I always had whiskey on hand to share. My own reaction was a quiet one for reflection and private prayer. Hitler's suicide made me realize the war in Europe was over. As the Acting Jewish Chaplain at the base and at others on the island, at the Friday night service later that week, I commented on Hitler, Nazism and Germany and what its import would be on Jews around the world. But most of all, we prayed to be spared with life, as victory in Europe would now mean an increase in missions against Japan. Formosa was a major target for the 380th Bomb Group (B–24s, the 5th Air Force). I was lead navigator with the rank of 1st Lieutenant.'

Lieutenant Haves was near the end of his tour. He was to celebrate VJ-Day in New York. Looking back after fifty years, he reflected: 'The death of Franklin Delano Roosevelt hit me harder than all other losses. I sermonized that America must never again find itself in a position of weakness when dictators arise to challenge humanity.'[2]

David Manevitz was with the American forces on Okinawa when the war in Europe ended. 'To us in the Pacific, the war ending in Europe (VE-Day) was *news*, but not at all like that in the Pacific theatres,' he later wrote. 'In May 1945, alone, we were racing to general quarters some fifty times, due to attacks by *kamikaze* suicide planes. We "fought back" with fog and smoke generators. Anti-aircraft fire was useless. Many times we were *almost* hit; but Somebody was watching us.'[3]

On Tarakan Island, the 26th Australian Infantry Brigade prepared to attack the oilfields in the north of the island on VE-Day. They found them unoccupied, and continued their advance to the coast. The Japanese were 'still offering stubborn resistance in the mountainous country in the interior', but a War Office survey pointed out that as the oilfields, and the airfield already captured were the main object of the island campaign, 'the campaign is virtually complete.'[4]

* * *

[1] Brigadier-General Henry J. Muller, Jr, letter to the author, 11 October 1994.
[2] Hyman H. Haves, letter to the author, 18 November 1994
[3] David Manevitz, letter to the author, 26 August 1994.
[4] 'General Notes on Operations', May 1945, War Office, London: War Office papers, 193/394. Public Record Office, Kew.

In several of the many prisoner-of-war camps throughout Thailand, in which the tens of thousands of prisoners had been forced to build a railway linking Thailand with Burma, news of what was happening in Europe was picked up on a clandestine radio, and passed from mouth to mouth. Captain Peter Fane, who had been captured at Singapore at the beginning of 1942, later remembered the impact which the news of Germany's defeat had in the camp at Chungkai. 'It was absolutely wonderful. But we were terrified that the Japs would know from us what had happened if we went about being cheerful or singing. In fact, the Jap soldiers weren't told about it for another week. We just wondered how long it would be before the Jap war ended.'[1]

Another prisoner-of-war of the Japanese, Lieutenant Alan Raven, was at Kanchanaburi camp when news came through on their clandestine radio that the German war had ended. 'If the Japs knew one had a radio, they killed you,' he later recalled. 'Two fellows were beaten to death because they had a radio. On VE-Day we had a radio going in the officers camp at Kanchanaburi. It was very important that we hid our elation that this had happened. The Japs weren't keen on passing bad news even to their own people if they could help it. But it leaked out. The Korean guards – one or two of them came into our hut and said, "Germans finished" or words to that effect. Work proceeded as usual. I think I was pumping water at the time. In fact, I pumped it for a solid year for the Japs, for the camp and for ourselves, five men to a team.'[2]

While Britain celebrated VE-Day, hundreds of thousands of British troops were in the jungles of Burma, also facing the tenacious Japanese enemy. Detailed knowledge of Japanese military strength, tactical schemes and strategic plans, was being pieced together at the Wireless Experimental Centre in Delhi by the experts in Signals Intelligence, who patiently and anxiously decrypted the top secret Japanese radio signals. One of their number, Alan Stripp, later recalled: 'What we read in the press and heard on All-India Radio was reinforced by what we were constantly reading from our Japanese decrypts, emphasizing the scale of the Japanese defeat, yet reminding us of the massive task still ahead in Burma and Malaya, *en route* for Singapore. There was certainly plenty to celebrate in the wonderful news from Europe. Yet I cannot recall any whooping-up.' What was good news that day for the men in the Far East was 'that May 8 was the day that the port of Rangoon was cleared of mines and was beginning to be useful to us'.[3]

---

[1] Peter Fane, in conversation with the author, 20 October 1994.
[2] Alan Raven, in conversation with the author, 20 October 1994.
[3] Alan Stripp, letter to the author, 20 September 1994. Alan Stripp is the author of *Codebreaker in the Far East*, Frank Cass, London, 1989.

Unknown to the soldiers at the Front, May 8 marked the first day of a forward plan intended to drive the Japanese out of Malaya. 'Planning will proceed for an amphibious operation to secure a bridgehead in the Port Swettenham/Port Dickson area, and for the earliest possible advance south overland and by sea with the object of capturing Singapore,' the Supreme Allied Commander South East Asia, Admiral Lord Louis Mountbatten informed his air, sea and land Commanders-in-Chief that day. 'You will appoint force commanders forthwith and instruct them to prepare their Joint Plan for a D-Day in latter half of August.' The Joint Planning Staff would assemble in Delhi in two weeks time.[1]

For one British officer in Delhi on May 8, VE-Day had 'a singularly cheering aspect'. While on leave in England after the Normandy campaign, during which he had been mentioned in despatches, Major Wyatt had been adopted as the Labour candidate for the Aston division of Birmingham. Although, as he later wrote, he faced 'a hefty Tory majority' in the election, Army regulations required that he be given leave to return to England at once to fight in the election, 'which made a change from military campaigns.'[2]

Seventy-five miles north of Calcutta, Morton Reichek was a United States Army sergeant at a China–Burma–India Theatre air base on VE-Day. He was the chief clerk in a signal company supplying and maintaining electrical equipment to the troops in China and Burma. 'I learned about the German surrender from a newscast on the local Army radio station,' he recalled. 'My knowledge of what had been going on in Europe had been derived largely from the station's skimpy newscasts, out-of-date publications mailed to me from home, and from the English-language newspapers in Calcutta. My army buddies and I were obviously elated about the end of the war in Europe. To celebrate, someone smuggled several bottles of gin into our barracks in violation of regulations. For the only time in my life, I got smashed. One of my duties as company clerk was to prepare a morning report for higher headquarters, disclosing the status of the troops. I do not recall preparing one for May 9. But when I had sobered up the next day, I was astonished and delighted to find a meticulously prepared carbon copy of a report for the day that had been faithfully submitted.[3]

[1] 'Operations leading up to the capture of Singapore', 'Top Secret', 8 May 1945: War Office papers, 172/1762. Public Record Office, Kew.
[2] Lord Wyatt of Weeford, letter to the author, 12 October 1994. Wyatt won the election contest, left the army, and was a Member of Parliament from 1945 to 1955 and again from 1956 to 1970. In 1987 he was created a Life Peer.
[3] Morton A. Reichek, letter to the author, 29 October 1994.

In Calcutta itself, Peter Collister was one of a group of British officers whose regiment, the Glosters, had been badly mauled in Burma; of the thirteen officers with him who had first seen action in March 1942, five had been killed that month and three wounded. As VE-Day approached, Collister was awaiting home leave. 'During the campaign,' he later wrote, 'going round the trenches in the evenings, chatting to the sections as they sat, mess tins and mugs in hand in the cool period before standing-to, our two great topics of conversation were the rival merits of Gloucestershire and other counties, and how we would celebrate the end of the war. As it became increasingly apparent that the European war would be over whilst we were still in the East I had thrown out a general invitation for everyone to celebrate with me when the great day came, a sort of morale boosting throwaway remark which cost nothing whilst anticipating a particularly heavy bout of shelling; but one which came home to roost sooner than I had expected.'

When VE-Day came, Collister and two friends 'were lying sweating it out under the whirring fan, just thinking about getting up in the early evening after an afternoon's siesta (known as 'Egyptian PT' or 'staff college study') when we heard a steady tramp of heavy army boots in the passage and voices enquiring of the bearer where Collister *sahib* was to be found. A heavy knocking was followed by half the platoon, Corporal George Bate in the van. We trooped down to the dance floor area which was crammed with a mass of people intent on celebrating. The band thumped away, the little Eurasian girls were whirled around and we all sat in a large circle, order following order as we laughed our way through the brighter moments of the campaign. From somewhere or other we had picked up a very young officer reinforcement for the Glosters, a version of myself several centuries ago, shy and awkward with the men and awed by our talk. He was an early casualty. The band did not last very long either as the evening grew more troublesome and the dance floor area, littered with broken chairs and empty bottles, began to resemble a battlefield at dawn the next day. But it was good whilst it lasted, and I spent all my accumulated savings in one glorious night.'[1]

Among the many British officers in Ceylon on May 8 was Wing-Commander Alan Campbell-Johnson, whose diary entry that day was brief: 'VE-Day, Chungking Restaurant'. Campbell-Johnson later recalled the restaurant itself, 'a small open air establishment in Kandy not far from the Temple of the Tooth to which, with half a dozen of my HQ

---

[1] Peter Collister, *Then a Soldier*, Churchman Publishing, Worthing, 1985, p. 238–9.

SACSEA[1] staff friends and colleagues, I repaired for an informal celebratory dinner rather than adjourning to our otherwise entirely acceptable Officers' Mess. Nothing official had been laid on. The central event
for us was getting into Rangoon five days earlier on the 3rd May, in the
process just beating the monsoon, thus crowning the brilliant encircling
advance of General Slim's 14th Army and completing the re-occupation
of Burma. Specifically for us VE-Day meant the prospect of substantial
reinforcements which would enable Mountbatten to develop his long
awaited amphibious strategy involving plans to inch our way up the South
China Sea in support of an American ground assault on mainland Japan
by early 1947 at the latest. The imminence of the Atom Bomb was still
an unknown and unimaginable *coup de grace*.'

Campbell-Johnson also recalled the way in which 'reports of Hitler's
suicide in the Berlin bunker on 1st May made their delayed impact, and
I remember being impressed by and speculating upon the dramatic irony
arising from Roosevelt's passing on the 12th April, at the beginning of
his fourth term as President, and Hitler's *Götterdämmerung*[2] so closely
linked to each other. Hitler had preceded Roosevelt to power by just
thirty-two days in January 1933 and Hitler had outlasted Roosevelt by
just eighteen days in 1945 – for Hitler, eighteen days of freedom after
twelve years of being haunted by the man he chose in his paranoia to
describe as a degenerate cripple but whom deep down he must have
recognised as his most formidable and deadly adversary on the world
stage.'[3]

As Campbell-Johnson had been chosen as a Liberal candidate for
whenever the first post-war General Election would be, he was quickly
granted leave to return to Britain. He was defeated in the election, but
his war was over.

As VE-Day was being celebrated in Europe, British troops in Burma
were contemplating the next phase of the battle after the fall of Rangoon.
For the men of IV Corps (the 17th and 5th Indian Divisions, and 225th
Tank Brigade) the previous week had seen three violent days of battle
for the capture of Pegu, forty miles north of Rangoon. The Japanese had
put up a fierce resistance at Pegu. The 17th Indian Division, hoping to
join in the liberation of Rangoon, resumed its advance on May 1, but that
same afternoon, two weeks early, the monsoon burst. Within twenty-four

[1] Headquarters, Supreme Allied Command, South East Asia.
[2] Twilight of the gods.
[3] Alan Campbell-Johnson, letter to the author, 3 November 1994.

hours the countryside was flooded and further advance became impossible. Others had taken the palm when Rangoon fell on May 3 to a joint
land and sea assault.

Among those in Pegu on May 8, at the headquarters of IV Corps, was
Major Alfred Doulton, Deputy-Assistant Quarter-Master General, who
wrote in his diary that day: 'Our resources for making merry are scanty
enough at this time[1] and there was conspicuously little inclination on the
part of the gayer members of the mess to indulge in an outburst of
revelry. The clerks were similarly subdued. The end of our task is nearer
but not near enough to arouse us to unbounded rejoicing. Many at home
will not understand this mood which comes near to determined resig-
nation to continued toil and discomfort. Not for us the waving of flags,
the throng before the Palace and the exultant crowd in the Circus.'[2]

On the following day Doulton again wrote in his diary. 'The morning
opened with a record of the King's broadcast last night and the singing
of "God Save the King" by full choir and orchestra. That is how it should
be rendered for it is never mere routine played thus – thereafter we put
aside thoughts of the armistice and turned to our own war. Truth to tell
we are in a parlous plight. Having been splendidly sustained by the air
transports throughout the advance, we are now suffering strangely at
their hands. In part this has been due to the weather and the consequent
loss of lift when the whole Corps has to be maintained by drop. But the
airfields have dried out for the time being and the stores should be
pouring in. Not a bit of it! They shower down thousands of gallons of
petrol on an isolated company fifty miles away from where they should
be landing and they land a quantity totally inadequate to our needs. We
ought to be putting on a little fat after the stringent existence we've led.
Instead we are on half rations, having had to cut down the incoming
drink ration to a bottle of beer per head and have to eat this foul Army
biscuit instead of bread. It's the one item in the diet I abominate. Bully
I'll eat until the cows come home and enjoy it. But these biscuits, they
give me the creeps! That's the fare we have for celebrating V-Day. No
complaint, merely a statement of inescapable fact.'[3]

On the battlefield, the troops advancing from Prome to Rangoon had
covered nearly a hundred road miles by May 8. 'No considerable opposition was encountered,' the War Office was informed, 'and efforts to
make contact with the enemy reported in the hills west of the road have

[1] The troops at Pegu were then on half rations.
[2] Alfred Doulton, diary, Burma, 8 May 1945. Private archive.
[3] Alfred Doulton, diary, Burma, 8 May 1945. Private archive.

been unsuccessful.' Fifty sick and wounded Japanese infantrymen had been captured, and boats trying to take troops across the Irrawaddy had been sunk. On the Arakan coast 'mopping up operations continue.'[1] A report on Japanese air activity stressed that almost a year had passed since any 'serious attempt' had been made by the Japanese air force to challenge Allied air power in South East Asia: 'Their lack of spirit has brought them to their present sorry pass'.[2]

A report to the British Cabinet on the effect of the end of the war in Europe on the British and Indian troops in Burma was succinct. 'British troops have been optimistically speculating that VE-Day will considerably hasten release or repatriation,' it declared. 'Indian troops, on the other hand, must regard the release scheme as the end of attractive employment rather than the opportunity to return to civil life and a probably lower standard of living.'[3]

The war in Europe was half a globe away from Australia, whose soldiers, sailors and airmen were at the very moment of VE-Day in action against the Japanese. One of them, John Laffin, who had recently been in the thick of the fighting, recalled: 'On VE-Day 1945 I was in Sydney, having just returned from a campaign in Borneo. As a twenty-two-year-old veteran platoon commander, I had been posted back home as an instructor. With other officers and NCOs of much infantry experience I was to retrain experienced soldiers who had been traumatized by war and were returning to the Army after rest and treatment. As you can imagine, they would have resented being handled by anybody other than junior leaders who had themselves been through the fire of combat. In Sydney I joined my even younger wife who was hoping that this posting might mean the end of my active service career.

'Australians heard the news of the end of war in Europe without excitement. We had never been involved in that war on the ground. Many aircrew flew with the Royal Air Force and there were Royal Australian Air Force squadrons; the Royal Australian Navy had ships in the Mediterranean.' But Australian troops had left North Africa in 1942. 'Alamein,

---

[1] India Command, Weekly Intelligence Summary, number 184, 11 May 1945, 'Secret', 'South East Asia Command, Military': War Office papers, 208/813A. Public Record Office, Kew.

[2] 'Enemy Air Activity, 3–9 May, 1945': War Office papers, 203/5346. Public Record Office, Kew.

[3] Cabinet Paper number 47 of 1945, 'Report for the Month of May 1945 for the Dominions, India, Burma and the Colonies and Mandated Territories', including 'Report by the Secretary of State for India', 25 June 1945: Colonial Office papers, 323/1871/13. Public Record Office, Kew.

and service in Greece, Crete and Syria, were a long way behind us. When we heard about the jubilation in Britain and on the Continent, generally we were puzzled, even resentful. "How can the British be so cheerful?" Hazelle asked. "Don't they know about the 8th Division?" She was referring to the Australians still in Jap hands after the fall of Singapore. She knew, of course, that British and Indian troops were also among the Japs' POWs, but here focus of sympathy was on the Australian Imperial Forces' 8th Division; we all knew men in that division. I can remember Hazelle saying bitterly, "I suppose the Japs are allowing our boys to cheer today."

'For me, that day, the real war was still going on and I saw no prospect of its end. Only a few days before I had seen another close friend killed in action; none of my real mates survived the war. I suppose that had we seen immediate films about the celebrations in London we could have been infected by the peace hysteria. Newsreels took a couple of weeks to arrive.

'On VE-Day Australian newspapers were carrying columns of casualties in recent fighting in the south-west Pacific and Borneo. British papers still had reports of casualties in Burma. Those Australians who knew about the campaign there no doubt felt that celebrations in Britain about the end of the European war were premature.

'I have to admit to a certain amount of envy of the British that they were no longer at war in Europe, especially when I paraded my men in the training camp next day. Some of them were broken almost beyond repair and I (with others) had to restore their morale and motivation. We realized that it was going to be even more difficult now that one part of the war was over. Sooner or later the Japs would be beaten and none of my men wanted to be the last Australian killed in action.

'I do not know any Australian who celebrated VE-Day *in Australia* or in the Pacific. That would have seemed a betrayal of those servicemen still risking their lives.'[1]

Some celebrations did take place, however, of a lighthearted nature. In Melbourne they were led by a group of discharged war veterans at the Royal Melbourne Institute of Technology. These veterans were known for never smiling, and for wearing identical sportscoats. Meir Ronnen, who had not yet seen active service, later recalled: 'VE-Day was definitely an occasion to be marked in some way. The "sportscoats" confided to me they had a plan. A bombing was to take place. We repaired to the roof of the faculty, which was located almost in the centre of the city.

---

[1] John Laffin, letter to the author, 18 October 1994. Laffin later became a distinguished historian of Australian's contribution in both world wars.

One of the "sportscoats" produced a large packet of specially purchased French Letters, known in those days as Frenchies. They were filled with water, tied up, and dropped several storeys on to startled passers-by, most of them bursting on the pavement. I thought it was rather a stupid prank, but for the first time I saw that all the "sportscoats" were smiling. By the end of 1945, the "sportscoats" had vanished and shortly after I sailed to Japan with the occupation force. Luckily, I suppose, it was too late to earn a medal.'[1]

By the time of the Japanese surrender, the Australians had lost more than 40,000 soldiers, sailors and airmen killed in action.

In Japanese-occupied China, the end of the war in Europe was marked in an unusual way. In the Manchurian city of Harbin, which had been occupied by the Japanese for thirteen years, one of the many thousands of civilian internees, Benjamin Mirkin, recalled: We had to suppress our reactions and feelings for fear of reprisal after hearing of the defeat of Germany.'[2] Alex Auswaks, one of several thousand civilian internees in Tientsin, later recalled: 'The Japanese treated us very decently. My clearest memory of the day the war ended in Europe (I was just over eleven years old and a schoolboy) was huge signs put up by the Japanese authorities all over Tientsin, in Chinese, Japanese and *English*, that Germany had *betrayed* Japan by surrendering, whereas Japan would fight on to victory.'[3]

[1] Meir Ronnen, letter to the author, 24 October 1994.
[2] Benjamin Mirkin, letter to the author, 6 December 1994.
[3] Alex Auswaks, letter to the author, 29 August 1994.

XIX

VE-Day in Russia

9 May 1945

Under the terms of the unconditional surrender signed first at Reims and then in Berlin, the war against Germany ended officially at one minute before midnight on Tuesday, May 8. In the Slovak town of Piešťany, Rudolf Vrba, recuperating after a partisan battle a month earlier, recalled: 'I was woken up by fire from all available weapons at midnight of the 8th May. The Russian soldiers celebrated the outbreak of peace by spending all ammo they could lay hands on. It was very noisy.'[1]

At Karlshorst, where the final German surrender had been signed just before midnight, the early hours of May 9 were enlivened by a banquet at Marshal Zhukov's headquarters. Zhukov wrote in his memoirs: 'The banquet ended in the morning with singing and dancing. The Soviet generals were unrivalled as far as dancing went. Even I could not restrain myself and, remembering my youth, did the *Russkaya* dance. We left the banquet hall to the accompaniment of a cannonade from all types of weapons on the occasion of the victory. The shooting went on in all parts of Berlin and its suburbs. Although shots were fired into the air, fragments from mines and shells, and bullets fell on the ground and it was not quite safe to walk in the open on the morning of May 9. But how different it was from the danger to which we had grown accustomed during the long years of the war!'[2]

Because the Soviet Government had decided that May 9 would be Victory Day, Moscow radio had maintained a discreet silence throughout May 8 with regard to the festivities elsewhere. From the earliest hours of May 9, however, the restraints imposed by officialdom on the previous two days were swept away. The celebrations began at ten past one in the morning, nine minutes after the official end of the war, when Yuri

[1] Rudolf Vrba, letter to the author, 2 November 1994.
[2] Marshal of the Soviet Union G. Zhukov, *Reminiscences and Reflections*, vol. two, Progress Publishers, Moscow, 1985, pp. 401–2.

Levitan, the chief announcer of Radio Moscow, told the Russian people, and the world: 'Attention, this is Moscow. Germany has capitulated. This day, in honour of the victorious Great Patriotic War, is to be a national holiday, a festival of victory.'[1] Two historians of Moscow at war have described the sequel to Levitan's announcement: 'Suddenly the whole population of Moscow was on the streets, many still in their nightclothes or carrying children, dancing, praying, sobbing, laughing and shouting, "Victory! Victory!" By early morning, a mass of people was sweeping through the broad streets, below the western walls of the Kremlin, past the university and the Lenin Library to the Moscow River, lining the embankments, packing Red Square each side of St Basil's Church, towards the Theatre Square, and into the dark streets of Chinatown.'[2]

On May 9, inside the Kremlin, Lavrenti Beria, the head of the NKVD (later the KGB), brought Stalin a decree for his signature. It was a draconian document. All Soviet soldiers who had been taken prisoner by the Germans in battle, and all Soviet citizens liberated by the Allied forces on German territory and repatriated by the Allies, were to be placed in camps. Each camp would be designed to hold 10,000 people. 'Some camps may be set up on Polish territory'. In all, a hundred camps would be set up: sufficient for a million people. Stalin signed.[3]

Pravda that morning lauded the great achievements of the Soviet leader in prose and verse. The leading article, 'Triumph in the Capital' declared: 'The capitulation of Germany carried through the Moscow night like the wind. The people had waited four years for this great historical moment. The great Stalin foresaw it, he predicted it on that grim day of 3rd July 1941. And now the great moment has arrived. Moscow was sleeping. It was three o'clock in the morning. The windows of the houses shone brightly. The Kremlin warders light up the pre-dawn blue of the sky. The fires of victory emanate from the heights of the grey towers. It is as if they had never burned with such a bright light. A nationwide celebration began. On the streets were more and more people, more and more cars. There is a crowd of people at the Kremlin walls. People are embracing, kissing. Today there were no strangers.'

The Ukrainian poet Maksim Rylski contributed that day's poem, 'The Day of Victory':

[1] Georgii Drozdov and Evgenii Rybako, *Russia at War, 1941–45*, Stanley Paul, London, 1978, pp. 230–1.
[2] Cathy Porter and Mark Jones, *Moscow in World War II*, Chatto and Windus, London, 1987, p. 210.
[3] Decree submitted to Stalin on 9 May 1945, signed by Stalin at midnight 11 May 1945: Dmitri Volkogonov, *Stalin, Triumph and Tragedy*, Weidenfeld and Nicolson, London, 1991, p. 492.

Exalt, rejoice, for it is here, the day of victory!
We have waited for it, like the field awaits spring
We have thought of it, vanquishing all ills
Under the thunder of the Molotovs, under the thunders of war
We have lived for this day, loving and hating
In our dreams each night we have seen it
We have trodden a hard march, seeing in the distance beneath the
   ashes
Its dawning sacred triumph
And now it is with us: beautiful, carefree
It spreads its radiant wings
So here it is, this day, Stalin has gifted it to us
To our own Stalin – glory and praise!
To Marshal Stalin – glory and praise!
Marshal Stalin's – glorious deeds:
The hordes of fascists have been thrown to the ground
To Stalin – eternal glory!
He brings peace to all the peoples of the earth
The wild beast is vanquished, it dies in the dust.
Joy blazes in free hearts:
To Stalin – eternal glory!

An article in *Pravda* by Ilya Ehrenburg looked lyrically to the future. 'The last volleys have fallen silent, and after the long years Europe has found a great gift – tranquillity. Mothers can calmly caress their children – the shadow of death no longer lies over their cradles. The flowers blossom, the seeds grow, the cornfields rise, the caterpillar tanks do not crush them . . . A new era is beginning: of ploughmen and brick-layers, doctors and architects, gardeners and teachers, scribes and poets. Europe lies, washed with the tears of spring, covered with wounds. She has much need of labour, persistence, of daring souls and wills that she might heal the wounds.'[1]

Victory did not come without its shadow, however, to a land where the Party and secret police had ruled with ruthlessness for almost three decades. Even for someone as privileged as Valentin Berezhkov, who had interpreted at some of the wartime conferences, and had even been at Stalin's side, the reality of Soviet life cast a dampener on the celebrations. For six months he had been out of favour, deprived of his Kremlin pass, and relegated to the sidelines on the editorial board of the weekly foreign-language magazine *New Times*, a vehicle for Soviet propaganda

---

[1] Ilya Ehrenburg, 'The Morning of Peace', *Pravda*, 9 May 1945.

overseas. 'On Victory Day nobody came to see me or even called to share the joy,' he later wrote. 'To think that only recently they were jostling to have me as their guest. On May 9, 1945, only two men, my former servicemen in the Navy, stopped in at the office with a bottle of champagne, and we headed for Red Square, packed with jubilant crowds.'[1]

The people of Moscow had taken to the streets in unrestrained celebration. 'It is hard to describe the joy of thousands of people in Red Square and around the whole country,' Berezhkov later recalled. 'The pride that victory was finally won over a treacherous and foul enemy, the grief for the fallen (and we did not know then that nearly thirty millions were killed on the battlefields), hopes for a lasting peace and continued co-operation with our wartime allies – all this created a special feeling of relief and hope.'[2]

The mood in the Soviet Union, where the war losses had been so enormous, was summed up by Joseph Kleiner, who, though born after the war, spoke fifty years later to many of those who had fought in it, or who remembered May 9. Their recollections, he reported, were of 'immense joy and a great feeling as if something terribly hard had disappeared. If it was on the front line, a sea of vodka and shooting in the air. If it was in the depths of Russia, a sea of tears, and at the same time of joy and relief. Almost each and every family lost someone. The tears of ordinary people, it was something common to every one and to all of them.'[3]

Every Soviet soldier rejoiced on May 9 that the war was over. The Soviet Union had suffered the heaviest losses by far of any of the Allies. Not only had several million Soviet soldiers been killed in action, but several million more had been murdered after their capture, having been denied the most basic rights of a prisoner-of-war; food and shelter. These statistics defy the imagination, but every individual soldier understood them through his personal experiences. Mikhail Goldberg was serving in the 46th Heavy Artillery Brigade. 'We were given special helmets with ear covers because no human ear could take the sounds for long.' He had fought with his brigade in western Russia, Roumania, Transylvania, Hungary, Slovakia and Austria. 'We witnessed terrible massacres, with thousands of casualties on the field, horrible wounds, and cripples who were moved back to the east in special field ambulances. I reached the point where human suffering no longer affected me, and also understood what my friend Orlov had meant when he told me not to rush to war.'

---

[1] Valentin M. Berezhkov, *At Stalin's Side*, Birch Lane Press, New York, 1994, p. 353.
[2] Valentin M. Berezhkov, letter to the author, 4 November 1994.
[3] Joseph Kleiner, in conversation with the author, 9 November 1994. Kleiner was born in Kaliningrad after the Second World War. His parents live in Kirovograd, in the Ukraine.

Wounded in February, Mikhail Goldberg had spent six days in a coma. He then returned to the battlefield. In April, he and his brigade reached the German border in northern Austria. 'We could sense already the dying resistance of the German army. Finally arrived May 9, 1945, and the terrible war came to an end. I had lived to see the day of which I had dreamed for over four and a half years, and I thanked God that I had survived without a scratch.'[1]

Other Soviet soldiers were not so fortunate that day. Alexander Isayevich Solzhenitsyn was in the Lubyanka prison in Moscow. Having joined the Soviet Army in 1941, he had commanded an artillery battery 'continually and uninterruptedly in the front line' until February 1945, when he was with his battery in East Prussia.[2] Captain Solzhenitsyn had been awarded two decorations, the Order of the Fatherland War and the Order of the Red Star. But then, while still with his battery in East Prussia, he had been arrested and charged with 'conducting anti-Soviet propaganda among his friends and undertaken steps to establish an anti-Soviet organization.'[3] Two months after VE-Day he was sentenced to eight years in prison, after which he was forced to remain in exile until 1956. In the following year he was rehabilitated. But on VE-Day, like thousands of other Soviet citizens who had made some minor criticism, he was awaiting a trial, the outcome of which was never in doubt.

Throughout May 9, Moscow continued to replicate the sights and sounds of London, Paris and New York. Hugh Lunghi, still in Moscow, was amongst those who witnessed the events of the day. 'The morning was chilly,' he later wrote. 'With two other officers I set out to walk the mile or so to our Embassy via Red Square. The crowds, unusually colourful as the fitful sunshine picked out the many colours of their kerchiefs, were not yet as enormous as they were to be later in the day. As we approached the Square through History Museum Passage, exultant groups, noticing our uniforms, bore down on us, skipping, dancing, cheering, suddenly hugging and kissing: pushed and pulled into Red Square we were lifted onto shoulders then tossed in the air.

'Regaining our feet we looked across the neighbouring New Manezh

[1] Mihkail (Moshe, Michael) Goldberg, unpublished memoirs, p. 60. I am grateful to Francine M. Goldberg-Schwartz for sending me her father's memoir. One of her sisters, her grandfather (then aged fifty), two of her aunts and two of her uncles were murdered in her father's home town, Pinsk, when the Nazis destroyed the Jewish community there in October 1941.

[2] *Sovietskaya Rossiya*, 28 November 1962, quoted in Leopold Labetz (editor), *Solzhenitsyn, A Documentary Record*, Allen Lane, London 1970, p. 3.

[3] Decree of the Special Board of the NKVD of 7 July 1945, quoted, from the decree of rehabilitaion, in Leopold Labetz (editor), *Solzhenitsyn, A Documentary Record*, Allen Lane, London 1970, p. 2.

Square to the huge crowds gathering in front of the American Embassy, singing, embracing American servicemen, doing all they had done to us and more, cheering Roosevelt, though he had died a month ago. We made our way through the crowds across the river to the British Embassy on Sofiiskaya Embankment. Here, some distance on the opposite side of the river to the Kremlin and Red Square the crowds and cheers were lighter.

'There were drinks at the Embassy, including Soviet and French champagne. The ambassador, Sir Archibald Clark-Kerr, had left for the inaugural conference of the United Nations in San Francisco. The Chargé d'Affaires was the Minister, Frank Roberts. His guest of honour was Mrs Churchill. The crowds, now filling all the approach roads to Red Square, Gorky Street, Hunter's Row, Revolution Square, New Manezh Square and, further along, Comintern Street, blocked our return to the Mission and our living quarters. We struggled through, not without many judicious detours.'[1]

In Moscow, a salvo of a thousand guns marked the climax of the day's celebrations. Natalia Dumova was a girl of twelve, living in the city when the war ended. Later she wrote of how she remembered 'masses of people in the streets and common feeling of happiness and great hopes for a better future.'[2] At ten o'clock that evening Stalin broadcast to the Russian people. 'My dear fellow-countrymen and women, I am proud today to call you my comrades. Your courage has defeated the Nazis. The age-long struggle of the Slav nations for their existence and independence has ended in victory. The war is over. Now we shall build a Russia fit for heroes and heroines.'[3]

The Russian losses had been staggering. As well as the soldiers who had been killed on the battlefield or while prisoners-of-war, several million civilians, including more than a million Soviet Jews, had been murdered in mass killings and mass reprisals. A Russian historian gives the total Soviet war dead as between twenty-six and twenty-seven million.[4] But the hope of so many Russians that their suffering would lead to a change in the system was not to be fulfilled. The post-war Soviet Union was to maintain the pre-war tyranny and terror: one-party rule by the Commu-

---

[1] Hugh Lunghi, letter to the author, 22 September 1994.

[2] Natalia Dumova, letter to the author, 9 November 1994.

[3] Georgii Drozdov and Evgenii Rybako, *Russia at War, 1941–45*, Stanley Paul, London, 1978, p. 231

[4] Dmitri Volkogonov, *Stalin, Triumph and Tragedy*, Weidenfeld and Nicolson, London, 1991, p. 505.

nist Party, the control of movement and speech by a vast army of interior ministry troops, police and security personnel, and a harsh prison and labour camp system for those who dared to challenge any aspect of Party rule.

On the night of May 9, however, the stern realities of Soviet communism were briefly submerged in the enthusiasm of victory. 'That night we decided to see what was going on in Red Square again,' wrote Hugh Lunghi. 'We were assured by Russians there would be a tremendous firework display, outdoing all the by now almost too familiar "Victory Salutes" which in the final two years of the war had regularly greeted the Red Army's capture of towns and cities. We were not disappointed. They were the best fireworks to date and included a picture of Stalin.'

The acting head of the British Military Mission in Moscow, Colonel Brinckman, decided to celebrate that evening with Eddie Gilmore, the American Associated Press correspondent in Moscow. Hugh Lunghi and two other members of the mission thought they would try to follow them in Lunghi's staff car. 'We lost them before we reached the Square, then caught sight of them not far from Lenin's mausoleum. They had stopped. Brinckman had managed to get out of his car and was watching something going on just beyond the dark red and black marble block of a tomb. As we inched our way nearer we saw the scene clearly in the lights of the searchlights constantly sweeping the Square: at first, over the heads of the crowd, just a pink bald head circled with flowing white locks, sweeping the air, then a body in frock coat and gaiters. We got near enough to hear frightened squeals as the shape was tossed in the air. We had experienced the same treatment earlier in the day, but this body could probably give us a few decades.

'We soon recognized the figure: it was the Dean of Canterbury, Hewlett Johnson, the "Red Dean". He had arrived in Moscow only a few days previously. A picture flashed through my mind of the last time I had seen him. It was, I remembered, shortly before the outbreak of war, in the Randolph Hotel in Oxford. He had impressed me, so had his description of Stalin which I had read somewhere: "a man of kindly geniality . . . leading his people down new paths to democracy" or words to that effect. After nearly three years in Russia I had a very different picture of Stalin. But now our Colonel, we felt sure, was going to the Red Dean's rescue, regardless. Before he reached him we saw that the crowd had let him go, gently.

'Brinckman returned to the car. It looked as though some of the crowd were trying to lift it. We couldn't see who was driving: whoever it was inched the car firmly through the friendly revellers. Anxiously I followed until we emerged onto the bridge down the slope below St Basil's Cathedral.'[1]

Mrs Churchill's secretary, Grace Hamblin, who was also in Moscow that night, recalled 'going into Red Square with some of the officials who had travelled with us on our long journey, and watching a tremendous display of fireworks – and kissing them all good-bye!'[2]

The enthusiams of VE-Day in Moscow were echoed across the Soviet Union, but not always in the same spirit of unconfined joy . In the Soviet Central Asian city of Djambul, Sholem Koperszmidt was among many hundreds of Polish Jews who, having escaped from German-occupied Poland at the end of 1939, had been imprisoned for two years by the Soviets in the gulag, and then, after the Anders–Stalin agreement of 1943, had been allowed to leave prison for other parts of the Soviet Union. At Djambul, he worked in a slaughterhouse. 'It was on the night of 8 May 1945', he later wrote, 'our Russian neighbour knocked at the door where we lived, with a bang. Screaming to me and my wife, "Sasha" (it was my name in Russian) "and Genia, Get up, Get up! The war is over." We got dressed and went to their place, husband George and she Dusia hugged and kissed and cried together for joy, and all the neighbours on the streets thought about those who would never return, their sons, fathers, husbands perished on the fronts. My wife and I cried also for joy mixed with sadness now that the bloodshed had ended. We knew the Jewish community perished from the hands of the Germans and their collaborators. I worked then in a meat factory and when I went to work all workers and managers were assembled in the courtyard, and hugged and kissed each other, and some vodka, sausages, bread and sugar commodities hardly obtainable without ration card appeared. The director and Party executives on the podium started speeches and glorifying Stalin without stop for hours. In the meantime a message was received from Party headquarters. All workers, the whole population, were to come to the town square. We went arm in arm, with all the workers – red flags floating, singing and laughing with joy. All the population was present. The mayor and the Party secretary and soldiers were present. The speeches and glory for "Stalin" and the Communist Party were without end and again vodka, bread and sausages appeared without limits, the drinking and dancing did not stop till nearly midnight. It was such an event hardly to forget. This merriness lasted two to three

[1] Hugh Lunghi, letter to the author, 22 September 1994.
[2] Grace Hamblin, letter to the author, 22 September 1994.

days without stop. All of a sudden produce started to appear in the empty shops without any limits. The population was merry as never before. The newspapers with Stalin's portraits and glory for him were never-ending.'[1]

The Hungarian-born Edward Benedek was a member of a Jewish Labour Battalion who had escaped with seven other young men and ended up in Russian captivity. They had been arrested in the town of Beregszasz while trying to obtain documents confirming their former forced labour status. Put with five thousand Hungarians, the defeated enemy, they were unable to persuade the Russians that they were victims, not vanquished. 'There was no way to get out', Benedek recalled. They had been put in cattle trucks three weeks before the war ended and taken eastward 'like dead beasts on an endless lane to oblivion, shunting, stopping, jerking and stopping again. Locomotives changing in the middle of the night. Riots ignited by unbearable hunger and thirst. It seemed a miracle when the wagons were unsealed for a batch of *suharim* or a pail of water – and then shut again.' 'Suharim' were rock-hard pieces of bread which had been cut by machine to form the staple diet of the Russian soldier. 'Tasteless and dark,' Benedek remembered them. 'Russian soldiers were carrying it round in their back packs, with dry white salted fish, dry like a bone. Rats and mice ate it.'[2]

Reaching the Urals, Benedek recalled how, 'an earth shattering whistle signalled our arrival and the swirling steam vanished into the sulphurous air. We arrived at our destination, Krasnokamsk, in the bosom of the Ural mountains. From a crack in the car I could see a huge field. Fifty feet from the railroad tracks were clumps of prisoners with signs on wooden posts interspersed. They were dressed in ragged German uniforms with ancient Bolshevik pointed caps on their heads. On their bare feet they wore clumsy wooden shoes. Their hair was bleached from the fumes emanating from the smoke-belching chimneys. It was a horrifying scene from the Inferno. The doors to our cattle cars were opened and we descended on buckling knees to the Workers Paradise. We began unloading those who had not survived the long trip.

'We were addressed by Captain Ostrapez, telling us of our good fortune in being guests of the Soviet Union and being in this safe haven where we were under the protection of Stalin. He then explained to us what their expectations were of us and ended, almost with an aside, "On this very day, you should know that, by the glorious fighters of the Red

---

[1] Sholem Koperszmidt, letter to the author, 25 November 1994.
[2] Edward Benedek, in conversation with the author, 9 December 1994.

327

Army, the war in Europe has ended". No mention of his glorious Allies. It was May 9, 1945.'[1]

In the city of Molotov, formerly (and later) Perm, a fourteen-year-old schoolboy, Grigory Kleiner, had become familiar with the huge German prisoner-of-war camp near his home. 'On that day there was great rejoicing also among them,' he recalled. 'They cried out all the time, "*Hitler kaput*". They thought that now they would go home. They did go home – after five years.'[2]

In the Urals, there had been hints on May 8 that the war was over. 'The telephone operators had heard rumours,' the nine year old Felicija Herszkowicz later remembered of that day in a small settlement near Kamiensk-Uralsk. 'Immediately the news came on the radio on May 9 my mother dressed up and walked to a friend some way off who did not have a radio, whose husband was at the Front. She wanted her to know. She wanted to put her mind at rest.'[3] Thus the news spread throughout the distant nether regions of the combatants who had suffered most.

At the southern end of the Ural mountains, near Orsk, a former Polish prisoner in the gulag, Jakob Murkes, was working in a vast mining camp being managed by American engineers. Murkes was twenty-five years old. His life as a prisoner in the Soviet Union had begun in November 1939, when he fled from Poland to escape the perils of the German occupation. In an account which he wrote at Orsk a week after VE–Day, he recalled: 'On the morning of the 8th of May, one of our secretaries brought some drawings from the American office and told us that Mr Park had heard that night on the radio that the war was over. This news provoked a sense of joy somewhat stifled by the lack of confirmation on Russian radio. I met Wilner that afternoon and he confirmed this information. There's no doubt about it. There will be official confirmation in the next few hours, maybe even in the next few minutes. A gang of carpenters is already preparing a rostrum.'

On May 9, Murkes woke up at six in the morning. 'I slept badly that night, as I had so much to think about and got over-excited. The weather is beautiful, sunny. I get dressed quickly and run to my office. Almost everyone is already there. Poltinnikov declares that the official news was announced on the radio at 5 a.m. Germany had signed an act of uncon-

[1] Edward Benedek, letter to the author, 19 October 1994.
[2] Grigory Kleiner, communicated by Joseph Kleiner, in conversation with the author, 27 October 1994.
[3] Felicija Dobroszycki (née Herszkowicz), in conversation with the author, 1 November 1994.

ditional surrender! At last! The long-awaited, long-hoped-for moment had arrived! People congratulate each other, laugh, chat, drunk with happiness. A demonstration is announced for all the departments of the Trust. Poltinnikov promises us generous rations of vodka. People converge on all sides towards the square where the podium has been erected. Everywhere red flags, portraits of Stalin. Several speakers stand up. Unfortunately, all but one spoil the atmosphere of real joy by finishing their speeches with a well-worn phrase: "Comrades, now that the war is over we must work even more relentlessly to repair, as soon as possible, the vast damages caused by the Nazi barbarians!" Even this joyful, historical occasion serves as a pretext to urge people to work! Only one speaker dared omit this admonition and simply say: "The war is over – rejoice, comrades!". I think we were grateful to him.'

It was 'a crazy day,' Murkes wrote, 'a day where one was drunk with joy. A day that one can only live once in a lifetime. A day where everyone, literally everyone rejoiced. People danced in the streets, embraced each other. It was a real day of brotherhood. Bosses kissed their employees and drank together. The American delegates were the centre of attention: everyone shook their hands, as if to express joy and gratitude to the most powerful allies. Poltinnikov gave out ninety litres of vodka and invited all his staff to his place. His wife prepared hors-d'œuvres, there was endless singing and laughing. All this excitement and excess alcohol had given me a heavy head. In the afternoon, I went home for a little rest but as soon as I lay down, Liova came in with Sonia and suggested a more intimate party at home. I set off to find Zoya, which was not easy. Today everyone was in motion, twirling in a state of intoxication. That evening everyone was so stunned by the day's events that we danced and sang without even realizing it. Towards 11.00 p.m. I could take no more and went out to walk Zoya home.

'The air was warm, but fresh after a short spring shower. We went via the park which at this hour was completely deserted. The night sky was clear, sprinkled with stars. In the far distance one could hear laughter and music, but in no way did that disturb the peace and silence of the park. We sat down on a bench, huddled against each other, held by the spell, listening to distant voices, intoxicated by the atmosphere of this night which promised a new era for mankind, together and as individuals. A feeling of gratitude arose within me, gratitude for having this young girl next to me, for not finding myself abandoned, alone, this enchanted night. For never had I feared solitude as much as at this moment. All these last years I was mostly alone, except on very rare occasions, alone on the northern latitudes, alone on the southern latitudes, but I always retained the hope that one day

329

this solitude would end. But now, on this night of fulfilment, I was no longer sure. I had the vague feeling that at the end of this pilgrimage, the end which started tonight, solitude awaited me, a more cruel, more permanent solitude than up until now. At least at this moment I wasn't alone, I could feel my young companion quivering, my arm protective around her. We stayed sitting like that for a very long time, enveloped in a great nocturnal calm, unable to break the enchantment which paralyzed us.'[1]

In the north Caucasus city of Ordzhonikidze,[2] Aron Bunyanovitch, who had been severely wounded in the Battle of Kursk in August 1943, was still recuperating from his wounds. 'On the night of 8 to 9 May 1945', he later wrote, 'I was awakened by cries, gunshots and fireworks. Already that evening telegraphists knew that an important announcement was imminent. As battles were raging in Berlin, everyone knew that the end of the war was near. I dressed quickly and made my way to transport headquarters. My leg ached. I walked with the aid of a stick.

'On our street corner stood an Armenian, his face gleaming with joy. He held a little cask of wine, which he poured into a mug and offered to all passersby, congratulating them with Victory. I had a drink with him and it went to my head. At transport headquarters the lights suddenly went out. In the darkness I stumbled into some chap in the corridor. From his voice, I recognized Ivan Nikitich Hollandra, our telegraphist. He began to kiss me and to congratulate me with Victory.

'Nobody worked on May 9. Everyone went about starving, but endlessly happy. On everyone's mind and on their lips were the names of frontline troops, everyone hoped they would get in touch to say they were alive. But there were the tears of widows, mothers and orphans of those who, it was known, had died.

'I came home. Mother and I remembered Solomon Reissman, the husband of my aunt Anna Mineevna (on my father's side) who perished in 1942. I remembered many fallen comrades and those of my school mates who had perished.

'Crowds of people went daily to the railway station to meet the train from Moscow, in the hope that their relations were returning from the Front. Some were lucky, but not many.'[3]

*   *   *

[1] Jakob Murkes, diary, 15 May 1945. Private archive.
[2] Earlier (and later), Vladikavkaz.
[3] Aron Bunyanovitch, letter to the author, 31 October 1994. Bunyanovitch's father had disappeared during the purges in 1936 and his family were told that if they 'behaved' he would be allowed to return. It was only after Gorbachev came to power in 1985 that Bunyanovitch learnt that his father had been shot shortly after his arrest.

Throughout the Russian liberated and occupied areas of Eastern Europe, the Russians were making strenuous efforts to ensure the dominance of Moscow. When the Bulgarian Government asked that a British message should be sent to Sofia, praising Bulgarian efforts since September 1944 on the Allied side, the deputy head of the Foreign Office, Sir Orme Sargent, opposed this. 'I see no reason why we should boost either the Roumanian or Bulgarian achievements against the Germans,' he wrote. 'We have not the slightest idea what they have done, as the Russians have not allowed us to have anyone on their Fronts where the Roumanian and Bulgarian troops were supposed to be operating. Besides, if we recognize that these two enemy countries have rendered services in the war we shall find it increasingly difficult to resist the demand that they should be given Allied status, and this is certainly what the Soviet Government wants to obtain for Bulgaria.'[1]

The dominance of the Bulgarian Communist Party distressed the British Government, but when the possibility arose, at the very moment of victory, of protesting at disabilities being imposed on the Agrarian Party, it was decided that nothing could be done. 'Even if we felt inclined to back the Agrarians against the Communists,' one official noted on the telegram from the British Minister in Sofia on May 9, 'we have no power with which to see that our will prevails, and the only result of the intervention by us could be a further loss of face in the country.'[2]

Bulgaria, like Hungary and Roumania, had been placed firmly inside the Soviet sphere of control, confirmed on a single sheet of paper, put by Churchill to Stalin in Moscow in October 1944. Known as the 'percentages agreement', this piece of paper was recognition by Churchill of Stalin's predominance in three enemy countries where Soviet troops were already in occupation or on the eve of conquest: ninety percent in Roumania, seventy-five per cent each in Hungary and Bulgaria. Returning to Sofia from Moscow in 1945, the veteran Bulgarian communist, Georgi Dimitrov, became head of the communist-dominated Central Committee of the Fatherland Front and, after elections in October 1946 which formally established communist rule, Prime Minister. British and American influence plummeted from the twenty-five per cent allowed on Churchill's sheet of paper to nil; and for forty-five years Bulgaria lay firmly behind the Iron Curtain.

*   *   *

[1] 'Bulgarian Army operations against the Germans', Foreign Office papers, 371/48124. Public Record Office, Kew.
[2] Note by M.S. Williams, 14 May 1945: Foreign Office papers, 371/48125. Public Record Office, Kew.

331

In parts of Czechoslovakia the fighting continued even on May 9. At half past nine that morning a radio message from Prague was picked up in London. 'The situation in Prague is getting better,' it read. 'Our units are gradually gaining more ground. The units of the Wehrmacht are surrendering. There are cases that the surrendering units are being attacked by SS formations, because of their refusal to carry on the fighting. In spite of the agreement concluded with General Toussaint, SS units continue in shelling Prague. Amongst others, the following objectives are under fire: Pankrac, the electric power station in Holesovice, the Old Town Guild Hall at Staromestske namesti, Masaryk Railway station.' A briefer message transmitted over the radio at a quarter to ten stated: 'The firing is still going on.'

A third radio message was received at ten minutes to ten: 'The Germans are attacking by gunfire the Prague Castle. The withdrawing SS units are looting shops, especially food shops. There were cases that they have driven women and children out of blocks of flats and shot them.'[1]

These were the very last spasms of German military might. By the early afternoon of May 9 the German troops were gone. That evening the Russians arrived in the city to celebrate the victory. Fifty miles to the south-west, the men of General Vlasov's First Division, who had made their contribution to the liberation of Prague, were seeking safety from the Soviet forces against whom they had earlier fought. While still on Czech territory, near the town of Schlüsselburg, they made contact with tank detachments of the United States Third Army. Negotiations began, and they were disarmed. The area in which they had met the Americans was on the Soviet side of the imminent divide. When they asked the Americans to be allowed to continue southward to the American side, this was refused.

In Yugoslavia, the communist forces under Marshal Tito were still fighting against the Croat Ustashi forces. One of Tito's closest aides, Milovan Djilas, later wrote: 'On May 9, we leaders greeted the unconditional surrender of Germany, Victory Day, in bitter loneliness. It was as if that joy were not meant for us. No one invited us to the feast, even though, both as a movement and as a people, we had helped prepare it through the most terrible sufferings and losses. It is certain that 305,000 partisans lost their lives; that for the better part of the war this new Yugoslav army tied down on its territory over twenty German divisions; that according to official statistics, Yugoslavia lost between 1.7 and 1.8 million inhabi-

---

[1] Messages timed at 9.30, 9.45 and 9.50 a.m., 9 May 1945: Foreign Office papers, 371/47086. Public Record Office, Kew.

tants. This includes deaths in camps, massacres, and bombings, and both
those who died fighting against Communism and those whom we Communists executed. One always gives round figures, as if human beings
were not involved. It was not even possible to establish an exact figure:
hundreds of thousands were killed anonymously, uncounted. That
number may even be larger, though it seems to me, perhaps this is wishful
thinking, that the total is exaggerated, unless it also includes the German
national minority which fled or was expelled. But even without the min-
orities, the losses were horrible, particularly for a country of sixteen
million inhabitants. At that time these losses were felt wherever one went;
they were present in everything we touched or thought about.

'The world celebrated peace and victory, while we were still waging
war on a grand scale. Revolutions have their own peculiarities; they create
special situations and mental states. Not even the Germans dared surrender to us, to say nothing of the Chetniks, the Ustashi, and other bitter
mortal enemies. This may explain why I don't remember how and where
I spent Victory Day on May 9. It had an impact on my consciousness,
but not on my mood. Joylessness and bitterness overcame most of the
leading comrades.'[1]

May 9 was not only Victory Day in Poland. It was also a day on which
the Polish authorities loyal to Moscow were continuing to arrest those
Poles who had been in contact during the war with the government-in-
exile in London. This included Poles who had participated in the London
wing of the underground struggle against the German occupation.

Under the Yalta Agreement, and as a result of Russia's military victories
and predominance, Poland had lost one-third of its pre-war territory to
the Soviet Union, including the cities of Vilna and Lvov.[2] She had been
given as compensation a swathe of German land in the west, up to the
Rivers Oder and Neisse (Nissa) and the Baltic Sea, including the German
port of Stettin and the industrial heartland of Silesia. In Warsaw on
May 9, during the victory celebrations in Theatre Square, in view of the
monument of the Polish Unknown Soldier, a resolution was moved that
'the Polish frontiers on the Oder, the Nissa and the Baltic, which have
been gained by the heroism of our soldiers, cannot be changed.'[3] Fifty
years later these former German territories are Polish still.

The Polish city of Lublin had seen the setting up of the first

---

[1] Milovan Djilas, *Wartime*, Secker and Warburg, London, 1977, p. 443.
[2] In Polish, Lwów. In Lithuanian, Vilnius; in Ukrainian, Lviv; in German Lemberg.
[3] 'Poland', Weekly Political Intelligence Summary No. 293, 16 May 1945: Foreign Office
papers, 371/50421. Public Record Office, Kew. In German, the Nissa is the Neisse.

pro-communist and pro-Soviet government in Poland, while the war was still being fought, and while Warsaw was still under German rule. Before the war the city had been a centre of both Catholic and Jewish learning. During the war, under Nazi occupation, both these beacons of culture were extinguished, and tens of thousands of Polish citizens imprisoned or shot in the city's medieval fort. The large Jewish community was destroyed after being deported, some to the concentration camp at Majdanek, in the city's suburbs, others to more distant camps.

One of the few Jewish survivors who was still in Lublin when the Soviet forces arrived was a young boy, Ruben Katz. 'On 9 May 1945 I was thirteen years old,' he recalled, 'and lived in a Home for Jewish child survivors, in Lublin. I really had nothing much to celebrate about, since most of my family had been taken to camps deep in Germany and Austria, and I knew nothing of their fate at that time. I recall the Red Army triumphantly celebrating VE-Day, however most of the Polish population did not demonstrate the same enthusiasm. There was a Victory Parade in Lublin, in which I took part with a contingent of the older boys and girls from the Home. We were, then, full of admiration for our liberators and proudly marched in step, singing Russian and Partisan songs and swinging our arms high, from side-to-side, Red Army style. Bemedalled Red Army men and buxom Russian girl soldiers formed circles in the streets, performing Cossack dancing to music played on *harmoshkas*[1] and concertinas. A lot of *bimber*[2] and vodka was consumed and the celebrations went on until the early hours, and even spilled into the next day, as only the Russians knew how!'[3]

Ruben Katz had survived in hiding on the Christian side of Lublin, outside the ghetto. One of his four brothers had died in the ghetto. It was only some time later that he learned that his father, and another brother, had died at Gusen concentration camp in Austria only a few days before the end of the war. His mother survived Auschwitz and Ravensbrück. Two brothers survived Mauthausen and Gusen. His sister also survived, like himself, in hiding on the 'Aryan side' of the ghetto. 'Compared to other families,' he later reflected, 'I suppose one could say we were lucky.'[4]

---

[1] harmonicas.
[2] homemade spirit.
[3] Ruben Katz, letter to the author, 11 October 1994.
[4] Ruben Katz, letter to the author, 18 October 1994.

XX

VE-Day Plus One

It was not only east of the Oder that 9 May 1945 was a day of celebration. Those in the western European capitals who danced through the night of May 8 were still celebrating as May 9 came, and many went on celebrating throughout that second day. In Britain, May 9 had been declared a public holiday. It was known colloquially as VE–2. That day, at 7.14 a.m. Major General Heine, the German second-in-command on the Channel Islands, signed the instrument of surrender on board HMS *Bulldog*. His commander-in-chief, Admiral Friedrich Hüffmeier, was unable to be present because of unrest among his troops. Ordered by the instrument of surrender to ground his aircraft, Hüffmeier said he could not do so, since he had no serviceable aircraft left. Ordered to safeguard the documents of his administration, he replied that these had been destroyed 'day by day and systematically' during the last months of the occupation.

The signing having taken place, the small German craft were summoned alongside the *Bulldog*, their swastika flags hauled down, and the White Ensign run up in their place. An advance party of British troops then went ashore and hoisted the Union Jack.[1]

For the people of Guernsey, liberation brought news that had been withheld from them during almost five years of German occupation. It was from one of the first soldiers to come ashore that the parents of Leonard Zabiela learned that their son had been killed in action.[2]

On Jersey, another of the Channel Islands, the end of the war was celebrated on May 9, even though the British troops had not yet arrived. In a leading article headed

THANK GOD!

the island's evening newspaper declared: 'At last the day has come for which we have all so long and anxiously waited. We in Jersey are free. The troops of occupation are still on the island, and communication with

---

[1] War Office papers 106/2985 and 2986: quoted in Charles Cruickshank, *The German Occupation of the Channel Islands*, Oxford University Press, London 1975 pp. 296–7.
[2] 'Roll Of Honour', *Guernsey Times*, 15 May 1945, p. 4, col.1.

England is not fully restored, but all fighting on the Continent has ended – the War in the West is over – and these are the things that count; other details will be adjusted in the course of time. For some days it has been evident that, as one speaker graphically described it, "this war was fast drawing to its untidy end", and a wave of expectancy, growing in intensity, has swept the island. News of surrender after surrender began to come through, first in Italy and then in Germany, but whilst we naturally rejoiced, we waited with intense longing for the news of the liberation of the Channel Islands. For nearly five years we had been separated from loved ones and severed from associations which were very dear to us. Is it surprising that we yearned intensely for that freedom and Liberty to which we had so long been accustomed?"[1]

In the early hours of May 9, at 2 o'clock, the first edition of the *Daily Mail* was leaving Fleet Street for the news stands. A photograph on the front page, showing St Paul's Cathedral illuminated, bore the caption: 'Last night the gold cross of freedom shone out over London from the great dome of St Paul's – made illustrious by searchlights that once probed the skies for the Destroyer.'[2] A reflective article by Noel Coward used a moment in the past, when Britain stood alone, to look to the future. 'Let us try with all our concentrated will to maintain the spirit that upheld us in 1940. Let us remember – disregarding political tact and commercial expedience – that it was our inherited, stubborn integrity that gave the future of the civilized world a chance and a glimmer of hope.' Now, amid 'the rather deafening cacophony of trumpets, one or two gentle fanfares on British bugles should not strike too sharp a discord. We have seen one Victory Day, but there were greater Victory Days in 1940 for us and for the world, for then it was the beginning, and now it is still a long way from the end.'[3]

The leading article in the *Daily Mail* pointed a contrast in cities and morality: 'London, battle-scarred but triumphant, dons her gayest apparel for victory. Berlin, in ruins, sits in sackcloth and ashes. Justice has been done.'[4] That day, from Berlin itself, a Reuter correspondent, Harold King, sent a despatch that was syndicated around the world: 'Berlin is a city of the dead,' he wrote. 'As a metropolis it has simply ceased to exist. Every house within miles of the centre seems to have had its due. I toured the German capital from the east to centre and back to the south this

---

[1] 'Thank God!', *Evening Post*, p. 1, col. 1.
[2] 'The Cross of Freedom', *Daily Mail*, 2 a.m., 9 May 1945, p. 1, cols. 5,6.
[3] Noel Coward, 'This above all', *Daily Mail*, 2 a.m., 9 May 1945, p. 2, cols. 4, 5, and 6.
[4] 'Justice has been done', *Daily Mail*, 2 a.m., 9 May 1945, p. 2, col. 2.

morning with Air Chief Marshal Tedder and the Russian military Commander of Berlin, General Berzarin. Among hundreds of well-known
landmarks which have disappeared or been irreparably damaged are the
former Palace, the Opera House, the French, British, American and Japanese Embassies, Goering's Air Ministry, Goebbels' Propaganda Ministry, and the Bristol and Adlon hotels. Hitler's Chancellery is like some
vast abandoned ancient tomb of the dead. It had several direct hits and
it is impossible yet to tell who lies buried beneath the rubble – perhaps
Hitler himself.'[1]

The rumour that Hitler might not have been burned at the entrance
to his bunker was hard to dispel. The Russians had taken his body back
to Moscow, where they shrouded their subsequent investigations in the
strictest secrecy. Almost fifty years were to pass before they were to
publish the findings of their 1945 enquiry, and officially to confirm that
the body found shot and burned at the entrance to Hitler's bunker was
indeed that of Hitler. Various suggestions were made in the weeks following VE-Day that he might still be alive, stimulating a variety of fanciful
illusions. Hugh Trevor-Roper, an Oxford don who had served in the war
in British Intelligence, was commissioned to establish the historical
record. His conclusion was emphatic: Hitler had shot himself in the
bunker, and his body taken outside by his subordinates and burnt: 'the
Viking funeral.'[2]

During May 9 there were several further surrenders; the German garrisons on the Aegean islands of Milos, Leros, Kos, Piskopi and Simi; the
German garrison on the Baltic island of Bornholm, a part of Denmark;
and the German troops still holding out in East Prussia and around
Danzig. But the German forces in western and central Czechoslovakia
fought on against the Russians during much of the day, as did German
troops likewise still fighting in Silesia, where local memorials record the
death on May 9 of more than six hundred Soviet soldiers.

Also surrendering that day was the German garrison at Dunkirk, which
had been surrounded for more than six months, most recently by Czech
troops commanded by Major-General Alois Liska. To the surprise of the
Czech, British and French officers who accepted the surrender of
Dunkirk, the German fortress commander, Vice-Admiral Friedrich Fris-
ius, arrived at General Liska's headquarters with his own surrender document already signed.

Meanwhile, entering southern Austria that day with the 6th Armoured

[1] Harold King, 'Berlin Dead', *Palestine Post*, 10 May 1945, p. 1, col. 4.
[2] Hugh Trevor-Roper, *The Last Days of Hitler*, Macmillan, London, 1947, p. 219.

Division, Captain Tony Crosland was the witness of another strange sight, writing in his diary: 'Once over the frontier, we were presented with the astonishing spectacle of the German Army still free and in occupation. They had been ordered to stay put, and concentration had not yet begun: so they were lounging about the cafés, standing in the roadside, often armed, watching us curiously, in fact behaving quite normally. Austrian flags have appeared everywhere, thus giving the impression that we have liberated a friend rather than occupied a foe. Sitting on top of an AFV,[1] I got a good deal of satisfaction from watching their rather awed reaction (especially the soldiers) to our unending stream of tanks and trucks passing through. No doubt this pleasure would be even greater in Germany proper, but it won't do the Austrians any harm to have a good look at this display of force.'[2]

In Copenhagen harbour, on which the Germans had descended in April 1940, an armada of German warships was at anchor. On May 9 these vessels surrendered to a British naval flotilla. A British military report listed 'the powerful cruisers' *Prinz Eugen* and *Nürnberg*, two large destroyers, one small destroyer, two torpedo boats, ten minesweepers, thirteen flak ships, nineteen armed trawlers and two armed merchant ships. Captain H.W. Williams, commanding two British cruisers and four destroyers, had taken the surrender. 'Cheering crowds greeted the arrival of the British warships.'[3]

During May 9 the War Department in Washington announced the numbers of American army casualties (up to April 1). The figure was 139,498 dead and 72,374 missing, presumed dead. The number of wounded was 467,408. A further 52,990 soldiers, listed as prisoners-of-war, were already on their way home.[4]

Throughout Europe, former British prisoners-of-war were also being brought home. On May 9, when one of the aircraft crashed on its way across the Channel, twenty-five of the returning prisoners-of-war were killed.

In London that day, Churchill set off by car after lunch for the American, Soviet and French Embassies. 'At the Russian Embassy,' noted his Private Office, 'the Prime Minister made a short speech and toasts

---

[1] AFV: Armoured Fighting Vehicle.
[2] Captain Anthony Crosland, diary, 9 May 1945: Susan Crosland, *Tony Crosland*, Jonathan Cape, London, 1982, pp. 36–7.
[3] 'Northern Region Intelligence Review No. 89, Denmark, for week ending May 11th, 1945', Foreign Office papers, 371/47253. Public Record Office, Kew.
[4] 'ETO Casualties Top 750,000', *Stars and Stripes*, 10 May 1945, p. 1, col. 1.

were drunk.'[1] As he drove on to the French Embassy, Churchill's progress was witnessed by a large crowd, among whom was the writer Peter Quennell, who later wrote: 'Around him, their horses' hooves ringing over the tarmac, mounted policemen slowly cantered. Although his cherubic face shone, and he waved his hat and his cigar, he had a remote and visionary look, an air of magnificent self-absorption, as he rode in triumph high above the crowd.'[2]

The celebrations of victory in London, so enthusiastic on May 8, had carried on with almost no diminution, as Londoners continued to take to the streets in celebration. 'Wandered by myself in crowds and had a lovely time,' Noel Coward wrote in his diary that day. 'I sat on a stone balustrade in Trafalgar Square for over an hour and signed a few autographs and watched London rejoicing, and Nelson in his spotlight seemed to be watching too. Friendliness and kindness everywhere.'[3]

Clare Boulter, who was working at the Admiralty on captured German Navy documents, recalled the events on May 9 in a letter to her parents two days later: 'I was in the office all day on Wednesday and when I got back to Quarters for supper, there were only six other people in the mess, none of whom I really knew. I didn't want to stay in all by myself for the whole evening, so I decided to go out on my bicycle to see what was going on. I started off about nine and went first of all to Hyde Park. There, people were strolling around rather aimlessly, and but for their expressions, one would never guess that it was a day of public rejoicing; they were, however, obviously enjoying themselves in a quiet and satisfying way – that is, I suppose, an English attribute. There were a few speakers at Marble Arch, an arrant socialist, a Catholic, and several people singing hymns, apart from the usual folks who always start a crowd if they talk loud enough.

'From there, I went down Oxford Street and into the byways of Mayfair. Here, there was more sign of revelry (mostly due to the Americans), and the outskirts of the Piccadilly mob. I was advised by a policeman not to take my bicycle up to the Circus and I doubt if I could have got it up there because of the people. On a shelter in the Haymarket there was a man doing an impersonation of Hitler, and you can guess what sort of a reception he got from the crowd!

---

[1] Private Office diary, 9 May 1945, quoted in Martin Gilbert, *Winston S. Churchill*, vol. eight, Heinemann, London, 1988, p. 3.

[2] Peter Quennell, *The Wanton Chase, An Autobiography from 1939*, Collins, London, 1980, p. 57.

[3] Graham Payn and Sheridan Morley (editors), *The Noel Coward Diaries*, Weidenfeld and Nicolson, London 1982, pp. 29–30.

'Pall Mall was the first of the lighting I saw; there was a whole row of real outsize torches burning outside the clubs, which seemed to have livened up inside as well. Whole numbers of processions passed me here; they had a varied selection of instruments to bang, from inverted dustbins up. Leicester Square was also lit by the cinemas, all in coloured lights, but it wasn't time for the flood-lighting yet so I cycled down the Strand to fill up time. The first building I saw floodlit was the Guildhall. It wasn't quite dark then, but the effect of this brilliant frontage against a dusk and slightly cloudy sky was perhaps more lovely than the more dazzling effect gained later in the night. I had a talk with the keeper of the place, who told me that it only needed a new roof to be quite whole again. From there, I went to the Tower and on to the bridge. The Tower was not lit up but several windows had lights showing which made it look less like an historical monument and more like an inhabited house. London, by then, was just beginning to spring into light, and I watched them come on over the river.

'St. Paul's was a dream. Lots of people had come to see it in its glory, which pleased me because it meant that, although far from the other sights, it does mean something to Cockneys. Riding along Fleet Street one might have been anywhere, with that large number of people out to see what was going on, but somehow one *couldn't* have been anywhere but in London. There is something indefinable about the place and, on an occasion like that, one forgets the slabfacedness of its inhabitants (or they shuffle it off for a while) and there is something indefinable about them too.

'I went on to Waterloo Bridge (for the first time) too, to see Somerset House lit in a very soft colour with a silhouette of trees in front. Trafalgar Square, too, was a marvellous sight: Nelson had a searchlight on him, with the column in darkness: that was a thing they didn't do at the Coronation. When I got to Parliament Square, there was a large crowd assembled who were listening to a speech by the PM from the Air Ministry. I couldn't see him from there so I went down Cannon Row and just got into a position to see him and sing Rule Britannia with the rest in lusty tones. It was a moving experience.

'Certainly, everything had livened up by this time. I met some other Wrens from Quarters then and we trooped down Birdcage Walk to the Palace where there was less of a crowd than on the previous night. After a little put-on cheering and some "We want the King", to which we contributed not a little, the two of them appeared and there was a lot more cheering and waving done. There were also coloured flares and rockets let off. It was a marvellous sight.'

Clare Boulter's letter home ended with 'a little footnote, not seen by me but by one of the others: in a train coming to town from Earl's Court, at each successive crowded station it stopped at, there was this heard: "Now let them get off the train first, make way here!" from the people themselves waiting to get on. I don't think that has been heard under the circumstances since the beginning of the war.'[1]

The controversies which had been stirred by the war included the question of German atrocities. There was indignation in one British newspaper, the *Daily Mirror*, on May 9, because a woman from Oxford had written to the paper to say she did not believe ten per cent of the stories about the German concentration camps. 'Such people as "Oxford" should be taken to the camps and made to live there for a month,' was the comment by another woman, who signed herself 'War Widow'. The newspaper editor was emphatic as to where the problem lay: 'We have received more than a hundred letters in similar strain; and three saying that the writers also do not believe the reports. Well, now, we do not believe that the disbelievers are mad; we believe they are the remnants of the Mosley crowd and the Blackshirts still in our midst. Mark them folks!'[2]

The dispute between 'Oxford' and 'War Widow' was to have repercussions for the next fifty years, as 'revisionists' and 'Holocaust deniers' sought to cast a pall of doubt on the facts of mass murder. It was a theme given prominence in the *Daily Telegraph* that same day, through the lead letter in the correspondence column. It was written by George Campbell, a Londoner. 'One notes that MPs who visited Buchenwald are getting letters from people who do not believe in German atrocities,' he wrote. 'Perhaps we should not be surprised that there are still people who refuse to accept the evidence of countless better men's senses. There are always some people who will believe, and disbelieve, anything. Particularly when they want to. The sceptics in this case affect a charity, a judicial calm which comes easy to people who have suffered nothing. In reality, as any psychologist will tell them, their attitude springs from motives very different – the vanity of men who love to think they know better than others; sympathy, in some cases, with race hatreds and the aims of Fascism generally; and, above all, the instinct of self-defence.

'Secretly they suffer from a sense of shame and guilt; in the battle for humanity they have not done their share; and the only way they can bolster their egotism is by pretending that the cause was not worth fighting for. The motive is as old as man, but none the less despicable. In

---

[1] Clare Baines (née Boulter), letter to the author, 2 September 1994.
[2] 'Those Camps', *Daily Mirror*, 9 May 1945, p. 6, col. 6.

face of the horrors constantly being unveiled in Germany, in face of the thousands of skeletons and charnel-houses and trainloads of corpses, in face of the systematic extermination of millions, such complacency cannot be covered any longer with the cloak of scepticism and toleration. There comes a time when refusal to look at crime passes from cowardice to moral complicity.'[1]

In Paris, the French and Allied revellers of May 8 had mostly gone to sleep by dawn on May 9. Staff Sergeant William E. Beatty, having gone to bed earlier, was up the next day by mid-morning. As he wrote two days later to his mother and sister at home: 'It was possible by this time to walk up the Champs-Élysées on the *pavement* and not on the heads of the people! Paris had celebrated its first day of peace, and was collectively taking the day off. Not a shop was open, only the American Army seemed to be carrying on with "business as usual".

'The real significant thing is what is behind it all; and from my several months of living here, I naturally form my own impressions as to what may be behind the behaviour of a few of the millions of people who were celebrating in their own ways. It still gives me an indescribable thrill to see the flag-bedecked windows: flags of all the United Nations waving in the spring air from every window, house, and post; and to see the thousands of people going about their business in freedom once more, walking down the same streets that not many months ago echoed with the steps of the goose-stepping Nazis.

'All of these are a few things that continue to make impressions, equally hard to describe. And, it is almost as hard to believe at times that there actually is no more war in this part of the world. It seems a long time since we first heard on our radios the outbreak of war in Poland, listened to the broadcasts from around the world, hearing news from the world capitals, the descriptions of the children being evacuated from London, etc. Then we realize that at just this time last year we were looking for D-Day to come most any time. Perhaps when it did finally come we expected things to go faster than they did, and then at times things looked pretty black too. But the realization that peace has now come is the real keynote to all the celebration that went on here.

'Being one small part of Uncle Sam's Army, I quite well realize that it isn't all over yet . It's like a double-header with another game to be won before we can be sure that we'll be home for good. When the final

---

[1] 'There are None So Blind...', letter from George Campbell, London W.1, *Daily Telegraph*, 9 May 1945, p. 4 col. 7.

V-Day comes, whatever it's called, I'm sure I have no idea where I'll be. I might be here in the Army of Occupation, maybe on the other side of the world, maybe in the USA. Uncle Sam hasn't let me in on the secret yet. But, I'm prepared to continue to "sweat it out" wherever and in whatever way it may be necessary.'[1] In the event, Beatty was spared a spell of duty against Japan.

Among the Paris newspapers celebrating on May 9 was *Libres*, which had been founded during the German occupation by the French National Movement of prisoners-of-war and deportees.

VICTOIRE!

was its one-word headline that morning. On its front page it had an article by its publishing director, and senior member of its editorial board, François Mitterrand, who, in his confident role as a supporter of the French struggle against Germany, wrote: 'This people which clenched its fists during the ordeal and for four years accepted all the risks of interrupted war, obstinately refusing to be humiliated, this people, abandoned and enslaved, but nevertheless present at Bir-Hakeim, Cassino, Colmar and Ulm, today deserves to strike up the hymns of the victors. Ah, yes, hope was the truth.'

Expanding on his theme that 'hope was the truth', Mitterrand went on to write in emotional language about 'These young men, moved in herds to enemy camps, these young men, subjected to the rigours and most terrible threats of death, these young men, our brothers imprisoned and deported, also fought their fight. In darkness and sorrow they believed in the light and the joy of future triumphs. In slavery they patiently wanted liberty. Escaped prisoners from Rawa-Ruska, martyrs of Buchenwald and Dachau, these are the ones who can today in truth vindicate their hope.'[2]

France did not quickly or easily recover from the traumas of wartime collaboration. Mitterrand himself, later President of the Republic, had, in 1943 been flown to England from a landing strip near Angers, and returned two months later by motor gunboat to Beg-an-Fry, to begin active resistance contact with French deportees and prisoners-of-war. It was discovered fifty years after the war, however, that in 1942 he had served in the Vichy Government's Commissariat General for

---

[1] William Beatty, letter to his mother and sister, Paris, 11 May 1945. Private archive.
[2] '*Oui, l'espérance était la vérité!*', *Libres*, 9 May 1945, p. 1, cols. 1 and 2. Mitterrand was elected a Deputy in 1946, at the age of thirty. He was elected President in 1981, and was re-elected in 1988.

Prisoners-of-War and been decorated with the Pétainist medal, the Francisque Gallique, before he joined the Resistance.[1] But the efforts at reconciliation had begun. On May 9 General de Gaulle and members of the French Government attended a solemn *Te Deum* at the Cathedral of Nôtre Dame. That day a British Intelligence summary noted: 'The General was escorted to and from the West Door by the Cardinal Archbishop of Paris who was excluded from the *Te Deum* after the liberation of the capital, but may now be presumed to be officially rehabilitated.'[2]

On May 9 the Jews in Oskar Schindler's labour camp at Brünnlitz were without their patron and without their German guards, but Russian troops were still nowhere near the town. 'Apart from the 1,200 Jewish prisoners,' one of their number, Moshe Bejski, recalled, 'there was a German *kapo*[3] in Brünnlitz who had reached the confinement camp as a convicted habitual criminal. His treatment of the Jewish prisoners from Plaszow and Gross-Rosen concentration camps had been terrifyingly brutal, the suffering he inflicted surpassing that of the SS. As soon as the SS guards left the camp at midnight, the *capo* was arrested and placed under guard. The next morning, it was discovered that a group of activists (apparently including some of those who possessed arms) had decided that the *capo* should be executed by hanging, because he had killed not a few of their number with his bare hands.

'Several people (myself included) attempted to prevent this act of revenge, arguing that vengeance without a proper trial was inconceivable. As the correct alternative, they recommended that the *capo* be turned over to the Czech police along with prisoners' testimonies that would serve as a basis for his prosecution. This view was not heeded; some believed that summary execution was the *capo*'s just fate and that judgement should be exacted then and there. The *capo* was hanged. Some regretted that the first day of liberation began in this fashion; others believed that the *capo* had received his just deserts.'[4]

Vengeance had been taken, but still the Russian liberators had not arrived. The town of Brünnlitz and the factory camp remained in limbo, neither captive nor freed.

*   *   *

[1] John Laughland, 'Mitterrand's murky war', *The Times*, London, 18 October 1994.
[2] 'France', Weekly Political Intelligence Summary No. 293, 16 May 1945: Foreign Office papers, 371/50421. Public Record Office, Kew. In August 1942 Suhard had insisted on giving the absolution in the service of blessing for the Legion of French Volunteers about to leave for the Eastern Front to fight alongside the German Army.
[3] Concentration camp police (*Kontzentrationspolizei*).
[4] Judge Moshe Bejski, letter to the author, 23 October 1994.

In the western part of Czechoslovakia, which the Americans had liberated, Sergeant Paul Kavon wrote home to his parents for the second time in two days, heading his letter 'VE1'. The cease-fire order had been given to those in the Eger sector of operations. 'The weather is really getting nice over here in Czechoslovakia and you can feel the tinge of summer coming on. It's surprising how the climate changes from day to day over here. Just a few days ago it was actually snowing and it was really freezing weather. Right now we are catching up on a little rest, sorely needed and we have received a few hot meals. You can imagine what that means after being continually in combat and having to eat K and C rations all along.[1] There were days in combat when they could get no *chow* to us at all. During the battle for Eger there was a day and a half that we went without eating, but believe me folks, all of us were interested primarily in self-preservation and staying alive rather than eating or missing a few meals.'

Kavon hoped that now his unit had 'stopped racing through towns that we captured', mail would have a chance to reach him, and also a package with cigarettes, chewing gum, cake and candy. These 'are really luxuries, and when one of the guys gets a package from home, we all hit it like vultures who haven't eaten for days.'[2]

In Holland, the main task of the Allies on May 9, as General Blaskowitz's troops were making their way to assembly points to hand in their arms, was to continue to feed, by air drop and truck, the starving population. That morning the newspaper *Het Parool* published a letter, in English, from a Canadian journalist, Maurice Western, of the *Winnipeg Free Press*: 'We know that a dark nightmare has been lifted from your hearts and minds,' he wrote. 'While Germans in the end would have been driven from Holland regardless of any decisions which Blaskowitz could make, most of us feared that the country would be ravaged by the grimmest kind of war before freedom was secure again. Now as if by a miracle your dreads and ours are banished for ever and you have expressed your joy in rousing demonstrations that literally swept us off our feet and off our jeeps.'[3]

Blaskowitz surrendered with his men. He was on the list of Germans whom the Allies intended to bring to trial. In 1939 he had commanded

[1] American army rations; 'C' rations were issued to general combat troops and 'K' rations, which were lighter, to paratroopers. K rations came in three types: breakfast, lunch and supper, and included cigarettes, chewing gum, water purification tablets and toilet paper.
[2] Sergeant Paul Kavon, letter to his parents, Czechoslovkia, 9 May 1945. Private archive.
[3] Maurice Western, 'A Great Day', *Het Parool*, Amsterdam, 9 May 1945, p. 2, col. 3.

the German Eighth Army during the invasion of Poland, and had received the surrender of Warsaw. Unknown to the Allies as the war ended, in November 1939 and again in February 1940 he had protested, in a secret communication to Berlin, about SS atrocities against Jewish and Polish civilians. Hitler had dismissed this as a 'childish attitude'. On 5 February 1948 while awaiting trial, Blaskowitz was found dead in his prison cell at Nuremberg: fellow prisoners believed that he had been murdered by SS men.[1]

The 30,000 inmates at Theresienstadt had been awaiting liberation since May 5, when the SS guards and the camp commandant had disappeared. 'Throughout the last few days,' one of the prisoners there, the fifteen-and-a-half year old, Polish-born, Ben Helfgott recalled, 'there were rumours that we were going to be liberated, that the Allies were nearby. In the last few days we never went to sleep. We were awaiting the arrival of our liberators. On the night of the 8th I couldn't keep my eyes open because I had not slept the previous nights. A few hours later I was awakened by a big noise and somebody shouting: "Wake up! We are liberated". It was a kind of anti-climax. I suddenly realised that I was on my own. I was free, yet I had strange feelings, above all a feeling of loneliness.

'I got up and with many others went out of the camp. Outside were Russian soldiers, and Hungarians in German uniforms running around unarmed. The Hungarians had been taken prisoner, but they were running around. I had a pair of shoes with hardly any soles left, so I decided to get hold of a pair of boots from one of the Hungarians. I demanded his boots. He took out whatever he had in his pockets. I said, I don't want what is in your pockets, I want your boots. I picked up a piece of wood and threatened him with it. Russians soldiers were near. He sat down and gave me his boots. I gave him my virtually soleless shoes.

'I left the camp and went into the town of Theresienstadt, to walk into Leitmeritz. In Theresienstadt town there were pavements. I cried out, "I'm walking on a pavement." For the past three years we were always forced to walk in the road being escorted. I jumped for joy, being able to walk freely on a pavement. Theresienstadt was on the border of the Sudetenland. The Czechs were chasing the Sudeten Germans out of the nearby town of Leitmeritz. As I went towards Leitmeritz there were

[1] Robert Wistrich, *Who's Who in Nazi Germany*, Weidenfeld and Nicolson, London 1982, pp. 18–19.

German women and children walking on the road. They had been chased out of their homes. Two Hungarian Jewish survivors, young girls of seventeen or eighteen – older than I – were beating up a German woman who had two children with her, a baby in a pram, and a boy not much older than my own sister was when she was killed by the Germans, nine years old. The baby was crying. I told them to stop it. They said, "But she's German. Germans beat us up. Now we will beat them." I asked them to stop, and when they ignored me I got hold of them and pushed them away. I threw them into a ditch.

'In Leitmeritz, former camp inmates were running, grabbing whatever they could get hold of. Some, the older ones especially, were looking for jewellery and other valuables. I looked for food. I was fifteen years old. I was naïve. In a shop I saw rice and sugar. People were just raiding everything. Some people ran into banks and were grabbing money, but the money was no longer valid currency. I took some rice and sugar in a sack, about twenty kilogrammes, as much as I could carry. The three weeks in Theresienstadt, not being driven to work, and having sufficient sleep, restored my strength enough to enable me to carry this weight for more than a kilometre.

'When I got back to Theresienstadt I heard people crying out, "Kill him, kill him." There was a big circle. In the middle was an SS man. Anyone who could get into the circle was kicking him and hitting him. He got up. They kicked him and pushed him down. I stood there. I felt sick. The man was literally beaten to death, and yet people were still beating him up. I was very upset. I had a burning sense of justice, because of the many injustices I had experienced against myself, against my family, against the Jews of my town. Although I knew that SS man was guilty I felt that was not the way to deal with him.'[1]

Among those who also recalled the arrival of the Russian forces at Theresienstadt was Halina Reingold, who remembered 'Red Army tanks and Red Army soldiers in tattered uniforms, some without shoes. Some of them wept. The narrow streets of Theresienstadt were crowded. The huge tanks could hardly move. One officer shouted: "The war is over, you are free, you will get bread, you will never be hungry again." Today it may sound like a soap opera, but at that time those were the sweetest words imaginable. We were free, and people seemed to have formed three groups. Those who cried for joy and embraced. Those who ran to food depots. And those who started rounding up Germans and beating them. Thinking of my sick mother, wondering about the whereabouts of

[1] Ben Helfgott, in conversation with the author, 2 September 1994.

my father, a great sadness came over me. I did not weep for joy.

Now, as I write these lines almost fifty years later, I cry. My tears are the tears I did not shed then. I cry for all those who did not live to experience THE LAST DAY OF THE WAR.'[1]

---

[1] Ilana Turner (formerly Halina Reingold), letter to the author, 29 August 1994.

XXI

Trouble Brewing

The tensions that were so strong on VE-Day in central Europe were no less ominous in the Middle East. In 1939, the British Government, under pressure from Egypt, Saudi Arabia and Iraq, had agreed to restrict Jewish immigration to Palestine in such a way as to ensure that the Arabs would always be in the majority. The considerable contribution of Palestinian Jews to the war effort created an expectation however, among the Jewish rank and file, that Britain would reward their patriotism by enabling a Jewish State to come into being, even if its geographical area was restricted to a relatively small part of Palestine. The Zionist leaders were less sure that such an outcome was possible. They were being confronted at the moment of victory by the great reluctance of the British authorities to allow the survivors of the concentration camps into Palestine.

In Tel Aviv, 50,000 people marched on May 8 in celebration, but, as the *Palestine Post* reported, 'the enthusiasm over victory was mingled with sadness for the millions of Jews destroyed by the enemy, and at the centre of the mass celebrations 'a black pilaster was erected where a torch was lit in memory of the Nazi victims'. Similar pilasters were set up in Dizengoff Circus where coloured lights playing on the fountain 'were lit for the first time since 1940, and the reflection of their gay hues contrasted with the sombreness of the columns'.[1]

In Jerusalem, the celebrations of VE-Day turned into two conflicting demonstrations on May 9. At the Jewish Agency building, to which a large crowd marched that afternoon, 'the Zionist colours were draped and bordered in black in mourning for Jews murdered in Europe'. Many in the crowd were discharged soldiers of the war that had just ended. Others were veterans of the First World War. Their slogans, 'which drew prolonged cheers from the watching crowds', demanded an end to the immigration restrictions of the 1939 British Government White Paper and free immigration to Palestine 'of the Jews of Europe'. Late that night an Arab demonstration formed up at the city's Jaffa Gate

---

[1] 'Monster Parades', *Palestine Post*, 10 May 1945, p. 3, col. 3.

and the marchers, 'shouting nationalist slogans', marched through the commercial centre of the city.[1]

There were no clashes in Jerusalem that day, merely separate assertions of priorities. Both needs were quickly to be frustrated: the British refused repeated requests to allow 100,000 survivors of the concentration camps into Palestine, and interned in Cyprus tens of thousands of survivors who made their way 'illegally' to the Palestine coast. Arab national demands for immediate Arab majority rule were likewise unfulfilled.

In Amman, where Arab nationalists had successfully acquired sovereignty under British patrimony, a celebratory lunch was held on May 9, with the Emir and the British Resident present 'under the eucalyptus trees of the Roman water wells.'[2] That night bonfires and torchlight processions lit up the city, and salutes were fired from guns that were normally used only during the month of Ramadan. In the Palestinian Arab city of Nablus, the minarets of the mosques were illuminated for the second night running, having been in darkness since the outbreak of war. Off the coast at Gaza, a British leave ship, christened HMS *'Urry Up*, raised a great banner, visible from the shore, inscribed with the words: 'Burma – or Blighty!'[3]

In the Pacific, the war knew no abatement or relaxation. On Okinawa, on May 9, sixty Japanese soldiers who broke into the American lines were killed in hand-to-hand fighting. Hundreds of Americans also died that day in battles to capture Japanese strongpoints; hundreds more were the victims of battle fatigue and could fight no longer. On Luzon, more than a thousand Japanese soldiers barricaded themselves in caves. Attacked by flame throwers and explosives when they refused to surrender, all of them were killed after a few days. In Indo-China, it was the Japanese who still had the upper hand. At Lang Son, sixty French soldiers and Foreign Legionnaires, who had managed to hold out since the Japanese occupation, were killed when their fort was overrun; the few survivors, put up against a wall, were machine-gunned as they defiantly began to sing the 'Marseillaise'. Afterwards, the Japanese bayoneted any who showed signs of life. Even so, a few amazingly survived the massacre. One of them, a Greek legionnaire by the name of Tsakiropoulos, was caught three days later, and decapitated, together with two Frenchmen; the Political Resident at Lang Son, and the local commander, General Lemonnier.

[1] 'Mass V-Day Rallies', *Palestine Post*, 10 May 1945, p. 1, cols. 2 and 3.
[2] 'Bonfires in Trans-Jordan', *Palestine Post*, 10 May 1945, p. 3, col. 3.
[3] 'Gaza,' *Palestine Post*, 10 May 1945, p. 3, col. 3. 'Blighty' was soldiers' slang for 'home'.

In the British newspapers on May 9 it was reported that the only pilot to have won the Victoria Cross in the Battle of Britain, Wing-Commander James Brindley Nicolson, who was in charge of training at South-East Asia Air Force Headquarters, was reported missing. Had he lived another few weeks he would have returned to Britain as a prospective candidate at the General Election. On a thousand-mile bomber mission from a base near Calcutta to Japanese positions near Rangoon, his bomber crashed into the sea. Nine of the eleven crew were killed, including Nicolson.

The newspapers also announced on May 9 that the first Victoria Cross to be won since the end of the war in Europe had been awarded post-humously to Lance-Naik Sher Shah, of the 16th Punjab Regiment, killed in the fighting in Burma. His was the 139th award of the Victoria Cross during the war, and the twenty-third to be won by a soldier of the Indian Army.[1] In an attempt to forestall a Japanese attack on the forward section of his platoon, he had, in the words of the official citation, 'by himself stalked the enemy from the rear and broke up their attack by firing into their midst', killing seven Japanese before crawling back to his post. When the Japanese attacked again, he again went forward to infiltrate their positions. On his way back, he was hit by a mortar bomb, losing his right leg, but continued firing to help break up a third Japanese attack. He was subsequently shot through the head and died during the night. When his body was recovered, 'twenty-three dead and four wounded Japs, including an officer, were found in daylight immediately in front of the position.'[2]

During May 9 two conflicting elements in British policy in Burma came to a head. The nationalist leader Aung San, whose Burma Independence Army had earlier co-operated with the Japanese against the British, was reported to be on his way through the jungle to offer his services to Britain. Several senior British officers advised that day, in the strongest terms, that because of Aung San's pro-Japanese military record he should be treated as a war criminal and, on reaching the British lines, should be 'placed under arrest pending trial'. They were overruled. 'On no account will Aung San be placed under arrest,' Lord Mountbatten telegraphed to General Slim that same day. 'Aung San is to be informed that his assistance is appreciated,' and that while his past offences would not be forgotten and that 'he may be required to stand his trial in due course', any

---

[1] 'Posthumous VC For Punjabi', *The Times*, 9 May 1945, p. 7, col. 3. The episode had taken place on the night of 19–20 January 1945. Lance-Naik is the equivalent rank to Lance-Corporal in the British Army.

[2] 'VC lost leg, went on killing Japs', *News Chronicle*, 9 May 1945, p. 3, col. 1.

service that he rendered to the Allied cause 'both in the past and in the immediate future, will be taken into account.'[1] Aung San's offer to change sides was accepted. As one of his followers told General Slim: 'If the British sucked our blood, the Japanese ground our bones!'[2]

In the Pacific, two British aircraft carriers, *Victorious* and *Formidable*, were the base for continuous British air strikes against the Japanese air-sea force. On May 4, fourteen Japanese aircraft had been destroyed, but on May 9 both carriers were hit by *kamikazes*, and many of their aircraft destroyed by fire. Only the armoured flight decks, a recent innovation, saved the carriers from serious damage. Another technical development, the 'proximity' or Variable Time (VT) fuse, was making the heavy anti-aircraft guns much more effective.

In Berlin that night, shortly after midnight, Marshal Zhukov gave a banquet for a large array of Russian, American, British and French officers. The most senior was the Supreme Allied Commander, General Eisenhower, whom Zhukov described as 'one of the greatest generals of all time, and one of America's outstanding sons'. The banquet was held in the room which, the day before, had witnessed the German army's final surrender. Zhukov's toast to Eisenhower was the second of twenty-four. The first was to Stalin. Charles F. Kiley, the only American reporter to have been at both the Reims and Berlin surrenders, described how 'after the 13th or 14th toast – with vodka, champagne, cognac and red wine – few except the hardy Russians could keep an accurate count of the toasts.'[3]

As night fell in London on Wednesday, May 9, Churchill felt the urge to go into the streets and join the still-celebrating crowds. His detective recalled: 'At 8.30 p.m. Winston decided to go out again. He looked down his nose at the saloon I called up, and queried: "Where is the open car?" I replied with some trepidation: "It has gone, sir." Angrily Mr Churchill retorted: "All right then, I shall just walk." "Impossible, sir," I objected. "The crowd is too dense." I might as well not have spoken. Off he started

[1] 'War Diary, Wednesday 9th May 1945': War Office papers, 172/1762. Public Record Office, Kew.

[2] In January 1947 Aung San travelled to London, where he successfully negotiated Burma's independence. He was assassinated that July by a political rival. Burma became independent in January 1948. Aung San's daughter, Suu Kyi, who for five years has been under house arrest in Rangoon, is the leader of the opposition in Burma today. In 1990 her party, the National League for Democracy, won the elections but was not permitted to take power. In 1991 she was awarded the Nobel Peace Prize.

[3] Charles F. Kiley, 'Zhukov Praises Eisenhower At Victory Banquet in Berlin,' *Stars and Stripes*, 10 May 1945, p. 8, cols. 3 and 4.

and with him I had to go. Two saloons followed on my signal. When we reached Whitehall, he realized that he could not get through and announced: "I shall walk between the two cars."'

Thompson begged Churchill to wait for the mounted police, as the crowd was closing in, but he refused. 'He was taking no notice of anything I said that evening. He was still peeved because I had sent the open car away. Suddenly he decided to climb on the top of the car, which I felt he might have done earlier with advantage. He sat on the roof with his feet dangling over the windscreen. He looked very funny, and his irritation left him immediately.'[1]

The crowd in Whitehall was as large as it had been on VE-night. To its resounding cheers Churchill declared: 'London – like a great rhinoceros, a great hippopotamus, saying, "Let them do their worst, London can take it." – London could take anything.' He wished to thank the Londoners, he said, 'for never having failed in the long, monstrous days and in the long nights black as hell.'[2]

'He spoke seriously for a time,' Churchill's detective later recalled, 'and then with sudden inspiration he said, "I'm going to recite a verse of Rule Britannia. Then you must sing it." As he concluded his verse, he raised his arm and started the first note of the song. The crowd took it up with gusto, and with the sound of the voices ringing in his ears, he went inside.'[3]

Returning to the Annexe at Storey's Gate, Churchill worked until the early hours of the morning. Among the telegrams he had dictated during May 9 was one to Truman about the need for a meeting of the Big Three. 'In the meantime,' Churchill noted, 'it is my present intention to adhere to our interpretation of the Yalta Agreements and to stand firmly on our present announced attitude towards all questions at issue.'

One of the questions at issue was the control of the Italian province of Venezia Giulia. Marshal Tito's Yugoslav partisan forces had already taken up positions in parts of the province, but over most of it Allied troops under Field Marshal Alexander were in control. Tito's forces had also entered the southern part of the Austrian province of Carinthia.

'Trouble brewing with Yugoslavia,' the First Sea Lord, Admiral Sir

---

[1] W.H. Thompson, *Sixty Minutes with Winston Churchill*, Christopher Johnson, London 1953, p. 90.
[2] Speech of 9 May 1945, in Charles Eade (editor), *Victory, War Speeches by the Right Hon. Winston S. Churchill, OM, CH, MP, 1945*, Cassell, London, 1946, pp. 129–30.
[3] W.H. Thompson, *Sixty Minutes with Winston Churchill*, Christopher Johnson, London 1953, p. 91.

Andrew Cunningham, wrote in his diary on May 9, 'Tito refusing to give way and occupying up to the Isonzo River and beyond. Also crossing the borders of Austria.'[1] In a telegram that day to Tito, Churchill warned the partisan leader about Alexander: 'It would be a great mistake I am sure for you to make an attack upon him. In such circumstances he has already the fullest authority to reply.' This 'trial of strength', Churchill suggested to Tito, should be 'reserved for the Peace Table.'[2]

These disputes, being conducted in strict secrecy, could not dampen the enthusiasm of London's revellers, who were determined to party through a third day and night. Aumie Shapiro sent an account of his activities on VE+1 to his friend overseas: 'The turnings off the Roman Road, specially Armagh Road, were ablaze with bonfires. As many as four were to be found in a small turning. Street parties were being held everywhere and it was obvious that the East Enders, who had for so long suffered under the cruel blows of total warfare, were going to have a real good "do"! At one o'clock in the morning of Thursday, Sid and I were sitting on the kerb-stones of Rhondda Grove, Bow, where we lived, wearily watching the colourful flames of the street's own bonfire. Our neighbours had done a good job.'[3]

The *New York Journal-American* had a two-column exhortation on May 9: 'V-J Day Next!'. One of its advertisers, the Liggett Rexall Drug Store, offered a prayer while at the same time reminding readers of its advertisement to buy war bonds. Under the heading 'Say a Prayer and Buy a Bond and Carry On!' the company printed the prayer: 'Not now is the time to sit back and say "well done". The battle still rages on our other side. Let us give thanks to Almighty God on bended knee, humbly grateful that He has found us worthy of glad tidings from the West.

'And, strengthened and renewed by the encouragement of this day, let us turn to the terrible task in the East with such an outpouring of increased effort, that it will be swiftly accomplished. Say a prayer. Buy a bond. And "Carry On" to Victory Complete!'[4]

---

[1] Admiral Cunningham, diary, 10 May 1945. National Maritime Museum, Greenwich.
[2] Prime Minister's Personal Telegram, number 867 of 1945. Premier papers III. Public Record Office, Kew.
[3] Aumie Shapiro, letter to a friend, London, 13 May 1945. Private archive.
[4] *New York Journal-American*, 9 May 1945, p. 3, cols. 1–5.

XXII

Terrible Times

The Aftermath of VE-Day

Reaching the German North Sea port of Cuxhaven soon after VE-Day, the 32nd Guards Brigade found a German minesweeper flotilla waiting to surrender. 'The Royal Navy had not yet arrived,' Captain Vivian Herzog later recalled, 'and our Brigadier, in the time honoured tradition of the British Army, instructed an Intelligence Officer to take control of the Navy. That was me. I called the Commander of the German flotilla, Lieutenant Bisterfeld, and gave him instructions. At a certain point, he astonished me by being the first, and if I am not mistaken, the only German of the many I had spoken to, who said that he was proud to be a Nazi. He did not believe what he called the propaganda about the concentration camps. I asked him, if I proved to him that this had in fact occurred, what would he do? He said he would convene all the officers in the flotilla, and from the bridge announce to them that he was ashamed to be a German officer. "More", he said to me, "you cannot expect of me."

'I detailed an officer to take him to Sandbostel, on the road to Hamburg. One half of the facility was a prisoner-of-war camp and one half was a concentration camp. There in the prisoner-of-war camp he met the German Wehrmacht officer commanding that camp, who described to him in detail what had happened in the adjacent concentration camp. He visited the entire camp. He drove back with the escorting officer and was as white as a sheet. Without saying a word, he went up to the bridge of his ship, convened all the officers of the flotilla, and informed them that he now was ashamed to be a German officer.'[1]

For the five officers and forty-five crewmen of the German submarine *U–249* the war ended on May 10 when they sailed into Plymouth harbour flying the British ensign and escorted by two Royal Navy sloops. Theirs

[1] Chaim (formerly Vivian) Herzog, letter to the author, 26 October 1994.

355

was the first U-boat to give herself up in a British port. Six others had been sighted by the Royal Air Force, proceeding as ordered on the surface, flying a black flag or black pennant. But the dramatic post-war scuttling of the fleet in 1918 had been paralleled in 1945 with the scuttling, just before the war ended, of most of the surviving submarine fleet. More than 150 U-boats were scuttled in the first week of May, including fifty-six in Flensburg, thirty-one in Travemünde, twenty-six in Kiel, fifteen in Wilhelmshaven and ten in Hamburg. Of those surrendering, more than a hundred were taken out into the Atlantic to the west of Ireland and sunk in deep water: this was one of the last British operations of the war, Operation Deadlight.

The last German submarine to be scuttled was the *U–1277*, on 3 June 1945, west of Oporto. The last to surrender was *U–977*, on 17 August 1945, in the River Plate, a straggler from battles long gone. In the U-boat war, 39,000 German sailors had put to sea, of whom 28,000 had been lost. One historian comments: 'It was the highest mortality rate for the men of any service in any country.'[1] One might add that on the day the war ended there were, in Germany, tens of thousands of grieving parents, wives and children, of the U-boat crews alone. The same was true in Allied lands: for on the Allied side 30,000 merchant seamen lost their lives at sea.

On May 10, British soldiers were flown across the North Sea, to Oslo, to assist in the disarming of the German occupation forces in Norway. By the end of the month 272,000 German soldiers had reached their 'reservation areas' and a further 32,900 'were due to arrive'.[2] In one aeroplane taking British troops across the North Sea, which crashed near Oslo on May 10, all twenty-four soldiers and airmen on board were killed: the second such crash in two days.

Among those who reached his home in Britain on May 10 was Major Elliott Viney. From the train taking him to London, he wrote in his diary, 'we passed a cricket match'. He found London less badly bombed than he had expected 'having seen the ravaged German cities', and then said goodbye to those who had been with him since their departure from Eichstatt less than a month earlier. 'At the station everyone scattered and I suppose I shall never see most of them again – queer thought.' After meeting his father, he left London for his home in the country. That night, reunited with his mother and

---

[1] Edwin P. Hoyt, *The Death of the U-Boats*, McGraw-Hill, New York, 1988, p. 251.
[2] 'General Notes on Operations', May 1945, War Office, London: War Office papers, 193/394. Public Record Office, Kew.

brother, 'I had a *hot bath*, my first for five years, and went rather dazed to bed.'[1]

The euphoria and domesticity of returning home was in stark contrast to the situation for those whose empire had smashed into ruins. The first days of Germany's defeat saw the suicide of many of those who feared being brought to trial for war crimes should they be captured, or recognised after capture. On May 10, Konrad Henlein, who had been Governor of Bohemia and Moravia since May 1939, committed suicide in an Allied internment camp. That same day, in a naval hospital at Flensburg, SS General Richard Gluecks was found dead; it is not known whether he committed suicide, or was killed by some group, possibly Jews, who sought to avenge the concentration camp savageries over which he had presided for more than five years.

Details of the fate of the Jews under Nazi rule was emerging daily. The figure of six million dead was too enormous to grasp, but the stories of what had happened to individual communities, however painful, was easier to grasp. On May 10, Norman Lourie, a war correspondent with the Jewish Brigade, was in Trieste, where he met some of the two hundred Jewish survivors of a pre-war community of five thousand. They told him of their community's fate. 'At first the Germans took the wealthier members of the community and ultimately the poorer Corfu Jews. "No one knows where they went. They have vanished. Many died in the trains on to which they were loaded like beasts," I was told. Small children and even very old women from the Home for the Aged were despatched to their death. After extracting from the Secretary of the Community, Dr Carlo Morpurgo, all possible information, the Germans deported him too. Even Swiss Jews with Swiss protections were despatched, as was the case with Signor Gino Frederico Parin, a famous seventy-year-old Triestino painter, who died in a German concentration camp. The Swiss Consulate did everything possible to assist our people. A British Jewess, Alice Nathan, aged seventy-five, was deported too.'[2]

On May 10, Benjamin Ferencz, who less than two weeks earlier had been one of the first Americans to enter Flossenbürg concentration camp, reached Mauthausen. Five days later he wrote to his fiancée in New York: 'The little jeep churned up the narrow and steep road. Again hundreds

---

[1] Elliott Viney, diary, 10 May 1945. Private archive. After his return to Britain, Major Viney was decorated with the DSO for his part in the action in which he had commanded a battalion during the retreat to Dunkirk (when he was captured) and the MBE for his work while a prisoner-of-war (camp librarian, Education Officer, editor of a broadsheet).

[2] Norman Lourie, 'Jews of Trieste Wiped Out', *Palestine Post*, 11 May 1945, p. 3, cols. 1–2.

of people lined the way. But many of these were not walking. They were lying in the dust, their hollow eyes staring out of their bony faces. At the top of the long ascent was a massive wall of huge stone blocks. Turrets interrupted the wall at regular intervals, and behind this monumental stone fortress were 25,000 dying and dead souls. The other camps I had seen seemed to be built just for a short while. They had been made of wood with wire fencing. But this one was built to last for ever, a permanent place for the destruction of "enemies of the Reich".'

Driving slowly through the camp gate, Ferencz and his two companions 'were greeted by throngs of unclad people milling around the court. Many of them wore absolutely nothing. Most of them wore rags, and some still had on the blue and white striped trousers which had marked them as "prisoners". A small dark-skinned boy ran forward. He was thin as a rail and was barefooted. He held out one long and bony hand as he pleaded "Cigarette, Cigarette, Casablanca, Casablanca". He had obviously been taken prisoner at Casablanca and had been observing German *Kultur* since then. The hundreds of others next to him eyed him and us curiously to see the results of his begging. I did not dare to give him a cigarette for fear that I would be immediately mobbed. I shook my head sadly and walked on.'

The camp at Mauthausen was dominated by a huge stone quarry from which the camp prison itself had been cut. 'Several of the former inmates pointed to the great walls and solemnly told me "every stone has cost a life". One of the Nazi sports was to order their prisoners to jump off the high cliff. Those who were reluctant were thrown. The smashed bones are still mingled with the smashed rock. The stock holders in the quarry are the SS and the leaders of the Nazi party. The blood of the slaves is their dividend, and the fat grow rich on human misery.'

Walking through the barracks, Ferencz spoke to several Hungarian women 'who were delighted to find some one who could speak (or at least understand) their language. There were little girls and little boys too. One fourteen-year-old girl had been torn away from her parents a few years ago and had finally ended on the death block where the arrival of the Americans saved her. Her only crime, as well as that of the dozens and dozens of other children, was that she was Jewish. She started to cry when I asked her where her parents were, and I did not go into it. I asked myself when I saw the shrivelled skeleton of one old woman, "What is there that keeps that woman alive." She was nothing but bones. Her arms were thin sticks and her long gray hair seemed to be wrapped around her eyes. The next day I had the answer to my question. I saw her tiny body being carried toward the crematorium. Now she will be put in a wooden box and buried outside the prison walls.'

As he walked through Mauthausen, Ferencz saw 'little infants, only two and three weeks old, who were wrapped in rags, living in dirt, without food, and with nothing but their wails. The mothers with little hope keep asking "when will we be allowed to leave?" And I could not answer, for there are so many camps and so many thousands of similar unfortunates that it takes time, and every day is an eternity for them. There were a million other things I saw and did, but I can't describe them now, dear. It's horrible and pathetic. I don't even want to think of what the sight of all these things is doing to me. How can I ever have the tenderness to worry about your scratched finger, or the other little things which will now seem so insignificant to me?'

From Mauthausen, Sergeant Ferencz drove on into the mountains to another camp, at Ebensee. 'The camp was unique in many ways,' he told his fiancée. 'Here there were no torture devices, no gas chambers, no hangings, and few persons beaten to death. Yet to all the prisoners it was a terror. Practically their sole method of elimination was starvation.' There was a huge quarry at the camp. 'Here the prisoners were forced to labour long hours, and the diet provided meant that within six months the victim would be dead. They died by the thousands and the camp crematorium always had plenty of customers. When we took over the army immediately set up a field hospital inside the camp. I walked through "the wards" and viewed the patients. They were dying all around. Many were still alive and the Americans were trying to preserve the little life that was left.'

In front of one of the barracks was a large pail of water, in which some of the prisoners were bathing some of those who were sick. 'It was a fantastic sight. The patients nothing but skin and bones were carried out to the tub. They were carried like babies, and none of them could have weighed more than eighty pounds. They were placed standing in the tub and water was run over their bodies. Like lifeless marionettes these former humans fell over the arms of their bather. Their heads flapped loosely and their arms hung limp. Yet these skeletons being held up in a tub were live human beings, men who may have been prominent and influential at one time. Now they were but helpless animal-like puppets who might not die. No one who has not seen it can visualize the scene. It is all a wild nightmare.'[1]

*   *   *

---

[1] Benjamin Ferencz, letter to his fiancée, Austria, 15 May 1945. Private archive.

On May 12, Frank Richardson, a senior medical officer with the 15th (Scottish) Division, was stationed in northern Germany. 'On the Sunday after VE-Day,' he later wrote, 'passers by would have heard a mighty male voice chorus swelling from the church of Ahrensburg, as we sang "Now thank we all our God". If this purloining of the Germans' own great hymn of thanksgiving *"Nun danket Alle Gott"* rubbed salt into the wounds it was, I am sure, unintentional. If any passing German thought wistfully of the days when Frederick's Prussians made their victorious battlefields ring with that wonderful sound, German soldiers singing, I doubt if many inside the church spared a thought for the days when our soldiers must have heard it sung by their German allies, as at Minden and Waterloo.[1]

'Such thoughts were banished from our minds, temporarily at least, by the pathetic indeed almost awe-inspiring, spectacle of that great army in total defeat, streaming westward, leaving every field in which they had slept littered with straw and hay, of which the farmers would bitterly resent the loss in the coming months. The stern anti-fraternisation edict stifled any expression of sympathy; and indeed any stirring of comradeship towards the beaten enemy (such as would have been possible in our old western desert days with the soldierly men of the Afrika Korps) had died under the impact of Belsen and similar atrocities. I consider myself lucky not to have had to enter Belsen in those early days; the experiences of those who did so make horrific reading. The Germans had begun an attempt to conceal the magnitude of this crime, and a train load of the victims had been dumped in a hutted camp near Celle when the train taking them deeper into Germany was bombed. A Gunner colonel was close to tears when he told me about the situation demanding my attention.

'The impact of that spectacle enables me to justify to myself the harshness with which I treated the inhabitants of Celle and the two senior German army doctors, whom we compelled to do what was necessary under our supervision. The citizens had to fill the lorries, which I sent round, with their best clothing and bedding, and food for the robuster ex-captives (the most serious cases needed special diets). The German officers (of equivalent ranks to brigadier and lieutenant colonel) themselves carried out the corpses for burial. When I had to depart and hurry after our advancing division the senior medical officer begged me with tears in his eyes, "as a doctor", to believe that he had known nothing of

[1] Minden (1759), when the French defeated a British–Hanoverian–Prussian combination, and Waterloo (1815), when the British and the Prussians defeated the French.

this dreadful camp. He had, after all, thousands of German soldiers as patients in the hospitals under his control. I told him that I did believe him, and asked him, as a doctor, to do all he could for the survivors of his compatriots' brutality and neglect.'[1]

In the Brünnlitz area of Czechoslovakia, the last region in central Europe to have been under German control when the war ended, civilians and former slave labourers were still awaiting the arrival of the Russians. As one of the Jewish prisoners, Moshe Bejski, recalled, even on May 10 'the inmates were advised not to stray outside the fence. Although Russian soldiers could be seen on the road and in the distance (on horses and flatbed wagons, of all things), Germans or Vlasov's troops might still be in the field. Again the advice to take no chances was not heeded, and people approached the road. As it came time for the Polish-language news bulletin from the BBC in London, the office workers and the engineers gathered around the radio. When the broadcast began with the Polish national anthem, tears welled in the eyes of several inmates, including men, for it was clear that the anthem signified liberation this time.'

It was not until the following day, May 11, that a Russian officer 'pulled up to the camp gate on horseback. He was alone, indicating that there were no more Germans in the vicinity. The officer knew that he had reached a prison camp, but it was hard to converse with him, despite the similarity between his Russian and our Polish. He asked us to gather all the inmates at the roll call yard, and when we did so, he climbed onto a table in the yard and launched into a speech reeking of pathos. We were able to understand, or hypothesize, what he was saying: it was the Red Army that had liberated us, and we were entitled to go wherever we wished. Whenever he mentioned the Red Army, the "leader Stalin", and the Supreme Soviet, we applauded.

'At the end of his speech, he clambered down from the table. A group of prisoners tried to hug him, but the language gap made dialogue difficult. Suddenly, to everyone's astonishment, the Lieutenant began to speak in Yiddish. A Jew in the Red Army! He was immediately bombarded with questions: where are you from, have you crossed Poland, have you been in Cracow and other cities and towns, are there any Jews there? The Jewish Lieutenant replied: "I crossed Poland from east to west, I entered many cities and towns including Cracow, and I found no Jews anywhere. There are no Jews in Poland."

---

[1] Frank Richardson, 'Scenes of action', in *As You Were, VE-Day: a medical retrospect*, British Medical Association, London, 1984, pp. 133–4.

'Finally, several prisoners escorted the Lieutenant to the gate, where he had tethered his horse. Here I asked him: "You said there are no Jews in Poland. Most of us are from Cracow and the vicinity, so – where should we go now?" The Lieutenant answered in Yiddish: "Don't head east; they don't like us there. But don't head west either, because they don't like us anywhere." And he left.'

It was this statement by the 'Jewish-Russian Lieutenant', Bejski later recalled, 'who had liberated us from the Nazi confinement camp and declared us free to leave, that apprised us, the former prisoners, of the terrible reality, the horrific tragedy that we faced. There were no Jews in Poland. To wit: the hope of finding alive any member of any family that had been separated years back and sent to Belzec, Treblinka, Auschwitz, and other accursed camps, was dashed. And were it not enough that only one individual per family, and two individuals per town, remained alive, it transpired that the survivors had nowhere to go, because Jews were not liked anywhere. This was the message that the liberating Russian officer brought, and it was with this burden that the former prisoners left the camp and sought a place to drive their stakes. They faced the morrow and the future with the melancholy of this realization, not with the joy of liberation. This was the bitter reality of liberation day.'[1]

On the day of the arrival of this Russian Lieutenant at Brünnlitz, Oskar Schindler and his wife were several hundred miles to the west, near Linz, in what had become the American zone of Austria. Later he was given money and a letter of recommendation in which former prisoners stated in his defence that theirs was 'the only camp in Nazi-occupied territories where a Jew was never killed, or even beaten, but was always treated as a human being.'[2] Schindler made his way to Argentina. Ironically, Eichmann, the persecutor of those whom Schindler had helped, was to find sanctuary in Argentina as well.

In the Soviet Union, May 10 was a second day of celebration. But work had to go on, as Jakob Murkes noted in his diary five days later: 'The next day we had to come back to earth, after our flight to the stars. It was a working day, but everyone was hungover. Impossible to get down to earth! In the afternoon I happened to read the little local paper, *The Orsk Workman*, from the previous day. On the front page there was a bulletin, signed Kalinin, saying that the day of the 9th of May must be

---

[1] Judge Moshe Bejski, letter to the author, 23 October 1994.
[2] Thomas Keneally, *Schindler's Ark*, Hodder and Stoughton, London, 1982, p. 425. Schindler died in 1974 and was buried, at his request, in the Catholic cemetery in Jerusalem.

47. 'Successful?', a cartoon published in the *New York Journal American* on 9 May 1945. The surgeons have removed 'totalitarian malignancy' from Europe. One of the surgeons comments: 'I only hope, gentlemen, that we got it all!'

48. German civilians enter a British army cinema.

49. The film is about to begin: 'Belsen and Buchenwald: Atrocities – The Evidence'.

50. After the film, a German woman weeps.

51. Two girls who laughed during the showing of the film are sent back to watch it again.

52. Theresienstadt after liberation. Beyond the steps, the wall where prisoners were executed.

53. Searching for messages from lost relatives, Poland.

54. Burning the last hut at Belsen, 21 May 1945. *See page 386.*

55. German refugees walk westward along one of Hitler's pre-war motor roads.

56. German refugees, trudging westward, pass a Soviet poster, July 1945.

57. Dutch SS troops interned after Holland's surrender.

58. A Soviet victory banquet for the American General William H. Simpson, 12 May 1945. *See page 378.*

59. Sergeant F.G. Tucker returns home to Oreston, South Devon, from his air base in Lincolnshire, 15 May 1945. *See page 373.*

60. Cossack troops surrender their arms to the British Eighth Army near Klagenfurt, southern Austria, before being forcibly repatriated to the Soviet Union. *See pages 366–70.*

61. British ATS (Army Transport Service) girls visit the ruins of Hitler's Chancellery, Berlin, 20 July 1945.

"—And now let's learn to live together!"

62. An American, a British and a Soviet soldier: 'The Trustees of Humanity: "And now let's learn to live together".' A cartoon by Philip Zec, *Daily Mirror*, after the defeat of Japan, 15 August 1945.

considered a celebration of victory. The German surrender itself, took place on the 8th of May. So Mr Park was right. In this same paper my attention was drawn to a big article. It's title was:

HORRIBLE CRIMES OF THE GERMAN GOVERNMENT AT AUSCHWITZ

'This article was no doubt reprinted from *Pravda* which gave it its official character. In it there was a detailed description of the Extraordinary State Commission for the seeking out of Nazi crimes pertaining to the Auschwitz extermination camp. I was struck by a detail in this very detailed account. It was obvious that the Soviet censors were trying to take advantage of these horrors (but I couldn't conceive how), a profit for some very suspect political objectives. It was specifically pointed out in this article that the victims of these crimes were firstly Russian prisoners-of-war and secondly, people of various origins coming from all European countries. Not a word about the fact that an overwhelming majority of these victims were Jews intended for extermination, followed by incomparably smaller proportions of Poles and other various nationalities. This Soviet interpretation seemed very suspect to me, and I had the distinct impression that it boded ill. It was this news which made me feel anxious amidst yesterday's joy and euphoria.'

On the following day, May 11, those working at Orsk were told 'that the following day off, Sunday 13th of May (not because it was a Sunday) would be made into a working day by an *ukaz* of the great boss, Bachilov. The explanation was as simple as, I'd even say, horrible, and typical as the country's mentality: as the 9th of May, a working day, had become (by an act of God) a celebration of victory day, this loss must be made up for by making a day off into a working day. This *ukaz* was a real slap in the face, a disgrace for the millions of fighters who had given their lives to make the celebration of victory possible.'

Waking up on this extra workday, May 13, Murkes could not believe his eyes: 'one would have thought winter had returned. A stubborn rain mixed with big snow flakes veiled the world. Paths which had been quite dry the day before had become real marshes. The workers and foremen who had come to work were protesting, a rare phenomenon, almost unheard of. Work outdoors was impossible. Fiodor Jakovlevitch himself went off to the central office to find out the big bosses' decision. He returned, apparently very irritated, and announced uncomfortably: "Comrades, it's not raining on the site!" This was the same concentration camp saying that I'd heard several times in forced-labour camps, and which was used as a pretext to justify work in any conditions . . . The

363

weather worsened considerably and it became clear to everyone that work was quite impossible. In the afternoon all the workers and employers obtained the authorization to go back home. This Sunday is also the same day as the day of Thanksgiving designated by President Truman for the United States.'[1]

Not thanksgiving, but dire warnings, reached Truman on May 13, in a telegram from Churchill setting out the British Prime Minister's anxieties about Soviet policy, and the future of Europe. The telegram, sent to Washington on May 12, began: 'I am profoundly concerned about the European situation. I learn that half the American Air Force in Europe has already begun to move to the Pacific theatre. The newspapers are full of the great movements of the American armies out of Europe. Our armies also are, under previous arrangements, likely to undergo a marked reduction. The Canadian Army will certainly leave. The French are weak and difficult to deal with. Anyone can see that in a very short space of time our armed power on the Continent will have vanished, except for moderate forces to hold down Germany.

'Meanwhile what is to happen about Russia? I have always worked for friendship with Russia, but, like you, I feel deep anxiety because of their misinterpretation of the Yalta decisions, their attitude towards Poland, their overwhelming influence in the Balkans, excepting Greece, the difficulties they make about Vienna, the combination of Russian power and the territories under their control or occupied, coupled with the Communist technique in so many other countries, and above all their power to maintain very large armies in the field for a long time. What will be the position in a year or two, when the British and American Armies have melted and the French has not yet been formed on any major scale, when we may have a handful of divisions, mostly French, and when Russia may choose to keep two or three hundred on active service?'

Churchill's telegram continued, using a phrase that was later to symbolize the whole era of Cold War: 'An iron curtain is drawn down upon their front. We do not know what is going on behind. There seems little doubt that the whole of the region east of the line Lübeck-Trieste-Corfu will soon be completely in their hands. To this must be added the further enormous area conquered by the American armies between Eisenach and the Elbe, which will, I suppose, in a few weeks be occupied, when the Americans retreat, by the Russian power. All kinds of arrangements will have to be made by General Eisenhower to prevent another immense

[1] Jakob Murkes, diary, 15 May 1945. Private archive.

flight of the German population westward as this enormous Muscovite advance into the centre of Europe takes place. And then the curtain will descend again to a very large extent, if not entirely. Thus a broad band of many hundreds of miles of Russian-occupied territory will isolate us from Poland. Meanwhile the attention of our people will be occupied in inflicting severities upon Germany, which is ruined and prostrate, and it would be open to the Russians in a very short time to advance if they chose to the waters of the North Sea and the Atlantic.'

Churchill ended his 'iron curtain' telegram by suggesting to Truman: 'Surely it is vital now to come to an understanding with Russia, or see where we are with her, before we weaken our armies mortally or retire to the zones of occupation. This can only be done by a personal meeting. I should be most grateful for your opinion and advice. Of course we may take the view that Russia will behave impeccably, and no doubt that offers the most convenient solution. To sum up, this issue of a settlement with Russia before our strength has gone seems to me to dwarf all others.'[1]

Truman was adopting a tough stance towards communist pretensions. 'I have come to the conclusion,' he wrote to Churchill with regard to Tito's desire to annex Venezia Giulia, 'that we must decide now whether we should uphold the fundamental principles of territorial settlement by orderly process against force, intimidation or blackmail.' The problem, Truman believed, 'is essentially one of deciding whether our two countries are going to permit our Allies to engage in uncontrolled land grabbing or tactics which are all too reminiscent of those of Hitler and Japan.' It was therefore Truman's wish that Field Marshal Alexander should obtain 'complete and exclusive control' of the ports of Trieste and Pola, as well as the line of communication through Gorizia and Monfalcone, and an area 'sufficiently to the east of this line to permit proper administrative control'. Truman also suggested that Stalin be informed of the Anglo-American view. 'If we stand firm on this issue,' Truman told Churchill, 'as we are doing on Poland, we can hope to avoid a host of other similar encroachments.'[2]

Poland was high on the Anglo-American list of 'other similar encroachments'. In a telegram to Eden that day Churchill stressed the need to keep the Polish situation before Stalin, including the plight of the sixteen arrested emissaries. This should be done, Churchill explained, 'by a

---

[1] Prime Minister to President, telegram number 44, 'Personal and Top Secret': Cabinet papers 120/186, Public Record Office, Kew.
[2] President to Prime Minister, telegram number 34, 'Personal and Top Secret', 12 May 1945. Premier papers III. Public Record Office, Kew.

vigorous press campaign and by the outspokenness which will no doubt be in any case necessary in Parliament'.[1]

Poland, which had suffered so terribly from the cruelties of occupation since 1939, was not to escape a new tyranny and a new burden in 1945. With liberation from German Nazism came subjugation to Soviet Communism. In Warsaw, Pilsudski Square, which had been renamed Hitler Square during the war, was renamed again in 1945: Stalin Square. Poles who were twenty years old when the German army had entered their capital in 1939 were to be over sixty when national freedom finally returned, and Hitler-Stalin Square was renamed Victory Square.[2]

The fate of the sixteen Polish prisoners aroused considerable anger in the West. Far less known, and almost unnoticed in the newspapers, was the fate of the 'repatriates': thousands of anti-communist Yugoslavs who had found refuge with the British forces in Austria, and tens of thousands of former Soviet citizens, and pre-war refugees from Soviet communism. From all the area under British and American control they were being sent back to the Soviet Union in accordance with the terms of the Yalta Agreement. Allied soldiers who had to participate in this repatriation, often using force and at times deception, were distressed by what they had to do. The public in Britain and the United States was not given the full story of the scale or nature of the handing back of those for whom deprivation, imprisonment and, for some, execution, was in store.

On May 18, Captain Tony Crosland, who was serving with the 6th Armoured Division in southern Austria, wrote in his diary: 'The problem of the anti-Tito Croats and Slovenes is almost causing a civil war within the British Army. We have on our hands at the moment some 50,000 of them. When we accepted their surrender, they certainly assumed that they would not be returned by us to Yugoslavia. It was then decided as a matter of higher policy that they were to be handed back to Tito. The armed lot south of the Drava were dealt with thus: our troops all withdrew north of the river, and behind them took out the centre section of the bridge; after we had gone, firing broke out, a number of Croats swam back across the river, and more tried to repair the broken bridge: so we put up wire and other obstacles to stop them getting back to safety.

'The unarmed lot were shepherded into trains and told they were going to Italy: they crowded on in the best of spirits, and were driven off under a British guard to the entrance of a tunnel at the frontier: there

---

[1] Prime Minister's Personal telegram, number 905 of 1945 (Foreign Office telegram number 647 to San Francisco), 12 May 1945. Premier papers III. Public Record Office, Kew.
[2] It has now returned to Pilsudski Square.

the guard left them, and the train drove off into the tunnel. Among officers here, there is great revolt and resentment against the deception and dishonesty involved.' A few days later Crosland wrote to a friend that it was 'the most nauseating and cold-blooded act of war I have ever taken part in. Like you I am too mentally weak and spiritually weather-beaten for anything more.'[1]

The repatriation of anti-communist Yugoslavs went in tandem with the repatriation of Russians who had fought alongside the German armies. Even Russians who had reached the United States were liable to be sent back. On Ellis Island in New York harbour, at Fort Dix, New Jersey, and at Camp Ruston, Louisiana, as well as on the West Coast, many Russians due to be repatriated committed suicide. Others jumped overboard after leaving American soil.

From the day the war ended, the Soviet authorities had treated with harsh contempt not only those Russian prisoners-of-war who had been enlisted in the German army, but even those who had been put to forced labour by the Germans. A Russian officer, Lieutenant Dlynnich, recalled his fate after he had been captured by the Germans towards the end of the war. Put to work in a factory near Berlin, he was wounded by an exploding mine, and was in hospital when Soviet forces liberated the region. 'After my recovery I was sent to a screening camp and thence to a construction battalion. In the screening camp all the Russians who had been in Germany had to appear before a commission of the NKVD. A detailed interrogation takes place. How, why, and when did you get to Germany? Why didn't you join the Partisan movement? Where and with whom did you work in Germany, and so forth. Beatings are frequent. All those suspected of collaboration with the Germans (be it only on the basis of denunciations and hearsay) are sent to separate camps and then appear before the Revolutionary Tribunal in Frankfurt-on-the-Oder where after a brief trial they are sentenced to various terms of forced labour in concentration camps – usually more than five years.'

Those whose records were 'clean' had a notation made in their records: 'SO' (socially dangerous). The younger men and some of the women 'are sent to construction battalions and work details with the army, while the older men, some of the women, and the children are sent home. There the adults must report to the local offices of the NKVD, are entitled to remain home only one month, and then must serve two years in special labour camps. The terms of those remaining in Germany, with the army

---

[1] Captain Anthony Crosland, diary, 18 May 1945: Susan Crosland, *Tony Crosland*, Jonathan Cape, London, 1982, pp. 38–9.

and work details, are not known. Former Vlasovites were at first shot without much ado, but now they are usually sentenced to fifteen to twenty-five years.' Dlynnich added: 'The repatriates are depressed, especially those who had been in the American and British zones. They are forbidden to attend higher schools or occupy responsible positions for a long time. In general they are treated as "second-class" citizens.'[1]

Those among the 'repatriates' who had come from the American and British zones had been forcibly repatriated, following the letter of the Yalta Agreement. The scenes at the time of repatriation were painful in the extreme, causing considerable unease among many of the Allied soldiers who had to carry out the physical task of forcing men into trains and trucks at bayonet point. The Soviets were unyielding on the need for these men to be returned, even though some of them had fled the Soviet Union at the time of its formation more than three decades earlier.

Captain Crosland, who eleven days earlier had seen the forcible repatriation of anti-communist Yugoslavs to Yugoslavia, also saw at first hand the Russian repatriation, writing in his diary on May 29: 'I witness today the handing over to the Soviet Army of large numbers of Russian nationals who had been fighting in the ranks of the Wehrmacht. There are thousands and thousands of these men all told, mainly Cossacks, Ukrainians and White Russians. What prompted them to join the Germans I do not know: mainly, probably, the prospect of food and release from German prison camps. When we first came in to Austria, they all made strenuous and ultimately successful efforts to surrender to us rather than to the Russians or Tito. But now the Russians have demanded them back, and this was apparently agreed at Yalta: we hand them over disarmed to the Russians.

'The secret of their fate somehow leaked out a few days ago; some have already committed suicide, others tried to escape and were shot. This morning a deputation arrived, asking if they could be shot on the spot instead of being handed over. Eventually, however, the great majority are got away somehow or other.

'The scene of this particular hand-over was the bridge at Judenburg which is the frontier between our zone and the Russians. The road down to the bridge was lined for half a mile with armed British soldiers, and the armoured cars sat at vantage points in the town, to guard against any last-minute breakaway. Across the bridge was the Russian committee of welcome. At length the convoy rolled up under heavy guard. One knew that these Cossacks had committed some of the worst atrocities of the

---

[1] Lieutenant G. Dlynnich, quoted in David J. Dallin and Boris I. Nicolaevsky, *Forced Labour in Soviet Russia*, Yale University Press, New Haven, 1947, p. 284.

war: one knew they thoroughly deserved a traitor's fate: yet as they craned their heads out of the trucks to try and see what lay in front of them, one forgot all that, and felt nothing but pity. All one saw was a lot of simple uncomprehending men being shepherded off under guard to a black and hopeless future: in the case of the officers, going to certain death.

'However, it all went off with only a single hitch – one man leapt out of his truck and hurled himself over the parapet. One by one the trucks crossed the bridge: the prisoners off-loaded, and were marched off by the Russians. The bridge itself was like a paperchase: when they knew beyond a doubt that it was true, they frantically tore up and threw away all letters and photographs which might have incriminated fresh victims. For a few moments, as I looked at the youngsters particularly, I could hardly stand the whole scene, and nearly broke down.'[1]

On May 31 more than 3,000 Caucasian men, women and children were put into three trains and sent, on that day and the next, to Judenburg, in the Soviet Zone, where the NKVD awaited them. The 30,000 Cossacks were assembled for their repatriation on June 1, at several camps. They too were forced into cattle trucks, which were then bolted, after which the trains moved eastward under British armed guard. Others were forced into trucks. In the struggles at one camp, five Cossacks were killed, in another four. Others committed suicide rather than be taken back. Some British soldiers had no sympathy, citing the atrocities committed by Cossack units against the local population while they were in Yugoslavia. Other British soldiers were distressed at having to carry out their orders. 'The ordinary soldiers of "Y" Company of the 8th Argylls,' writes Nikolai Tolstoy, 'were seen by many to be weeping as they conducted their incomprehensible and much disliked job.'[2] Cossacks who managed to flee into the hills were rounded up and sent on later trains to Judenburg. When a British soldier at Judenburg station asked the Russian interpreter what would happen to the repatriates he was told that all the officers would be shot and the rest would be sent to Siberia. As the Cossacks left the trains, which then returned empty to the British Zone for another journey, all their belongings were taken from them. When the last train had disgorged its last prisoners, for that is what they had become, the massive mound of belongings was set on fire by the Soviet guards.

Repatriation continued from the British and American Zones of

[1] Tony Crosland, diary entry, 29 May 1945: in Susan Crosland, *Tony Crosland*, Jonathan Cape, London, 1982, pp. 39–40.
[2] Nikolai Tolstoy, *Victims of Yalta*, Hodder and Stoughton, London, 1977, p. 215.

Germany throughout the summer and autumn. Angered by this process, on 4 October 1945 General Eisenhower tried to abrogate the repatriation article of the Yalta Agreement and ordered the discontinuance of forcible repatriation of Russian nationals. At that time there were still 26,400 Soviet citizens in American custody. The spokesman for the Supreme Allied Commander explained that 'we are not going to risk the lives of American soldiers to make them go'. The State Department overruled Eisenhower's instructions, however, and ordered the completion of the repatriation programme. In what had been Dachau concentration camp, ten former Russian prisoners-of war committed suicide rather than go back.

Like Britain and the United States, France also adhered to the Yalta repatriation agreement, interpreting it widely. In order to accelerate the repatriation of more than 300,000 French prisoners-of-war whose camps in the east of Germany had been liberated by Soviet forces, and who were held after VE-Day in the Soviet zone, the French Government went so far as to allow Russian NKVD commissions to travel through France in search of 'non-returners'. At Beauregard, near Paris, uniformed NKVD men controlled the camp set up for those who had been rounded up. The first trains left for Russia in July 1945. Still the NKVD men continued their searches. It was not until May 1946 that the French Minister of Internal Affairs told the Soviet Ambassador that all Soviet secret police activity in France must cease. Even Sweden came under Soviet pressure to return 157 Soviet citizens, originally from the Baltic States, who had escaped from Germany to Sweden. Two historians of repatriation, David Dallin and Boris Nicolaevsky, wrote: 'Living in constant fear and under pressure from the Soviet Government, Sweden finally yielded and returned the unfortunate doomed refugees.'[1]

At Russia's insistence, British and American forces were withdrawn from a broad swathe of territory through central Germany and western Czechoslovakia that had been occupied during the final weeks of the fighting. East of Lübeck, Corporal Daniel Krauskopf was with a British military unit ordered to pull back. 'A few days after May 8th we were travelling west,' he later wrote. 'The Russians wanted their assigned territory. As we loaded on six-by-six trucks, we had to beat off with our rifle butts old, or what seemed old, women, who were trying to escape with us from the Russians.'[2]

---

[1] David J. Dallin and Boris I. Nicolaevsky, *Forced Labour in Soviet Russia*, Yale University Press, New Haven, 1947, p. 296.
[2] Daniel M. Krauskopf, letter to the author, 26 October 1994.

'When we reached Schwerin,' Lieutenant Frank Green recalled, 'we thought we would be forming part of the army of occupation in that part of Prussia, and it came as something of a surprise to be ordered out some days later. I remember the entreaties of the local inhabitants not to leave them to the Russians.' Even as the British troops pulled back 'the local householders were actually obeying the first Russian directive which was:

TO REMOVE ALL THE GLASS FROM THEIR WINDOWS AND LEAVE IT STACKED CAREFULLY OUTSIDE THEIR HOUSES.'[1]

The glass was needed for windows in Russia.

As agreed by the Allied leaders at Yalta, the demarcation of the occupation zones of Germany had come into place.

In preparing to withdraw from Czechoslovakia, the Americans refused to take with them the ten thousand soldiers of General Vlasov's First Division; Russians who had fought for a year on the German side, and then, on May 6, had participated in the Prague uprising against the Germans. Having reached the temporary haven of Schlüsselburg, in the American-occupied area of Czechoslovakia, on May 9, they were told by the Americans on May 12 that they were to be handed over to the Soviets. Their commanders then gave the order 'for the men to dismiss and fend for themselves'. Half of them fell into Soviet army hands almost at once, or were captured by Czech partisans and handed over to the Soviets. About half managed to reach the American zone of Germany but were then held in camps before being repatriated to the Soviet Union by the Americans. Vlasov and his senior commanders, including General Bunyachenko who had commanded the troops in Prague, left Schlüsselburg in a column of vehicles, hoping to reach the American zone. They were met on the road by a Soviet column, where Vlasov was identified and taken prisoner. 'He was not heard of again,' writes the historian Catherine Andreyev, 'until 2 August 1946 when *Izvestiya* announced that Vlasov and eleven others had been tried for treason by the Military Tribunal of the Supreme Court of the USSR. They had been found guilty of being agents of German Intelligence, and had carried out active espionage and terrorist activity against the USSR. They had been hanged.'[2]

On May 14 the Soviet Union announced that between May 9 and 13 the Red Army had captured 1,060,000 German officers and men,

---

[1] Frank Green, letter to the author, 27 October 1994.

[2] Catherine Andreyev, *Vlasov and the Russian Liberation Movement*, Cambridge University Press, Cambridge, 1987, p. 77.

'including ninety-one generals.'[1] That day the first Soviet medical unit arrived at the concentration camp of Theresienstadt, which had been liberated six days earlier. Seeking to save lives, they found themselves in the presence of a spotted fever epidemic in which several hundred prisoners had already died since liberation. A strict quarantine was at once imposed. The former prisoners were once again behind locked gates. Two weeks later those gates opened for good, and by September the last prisoners had gone. Between the wars, Theresienstadt (Terezin) had been a small Czech provincial town. In 1946 it was given back 'its town statute' and became a town again.[2]

The survivors who had witnessed the final days of Theresienstadt's existence as a concentration camp sought their new lives on all five continents. They live today in London and New York, in Toronto and Sydney, in Tel Aviv and Buenos Aires. Those who went back to Czechoslovakia did so unaware that more than forty years of communism were to follow. Margit Schönfeld recalled the journey back from Belsen to Prague about two weeks after VE-Day. 'I was brought with many others to Celle, where a train was prepared and waiting for us. It was partly filled with former prisoners from other camps. There were again cattle vans, this time with open doors and straw on the bottom. We had nice blankets and food that the British Army gave us. The weather was gorgeous and we enjoyed the ride. Some men climbed to the roof and sat there. There was a tunnel, not much higher than the train and this was the end of the boys above. Poor boys, after having survived the camp, they lost their life in such a way. There was also a guard in our van, maybe to protect us, a young soldier from Alabama, who was very friendly and chatted with us. He accompanied us to Pilsen, where the American Zone ended. From then on we were on our own.

'We arrived in Prague in the morning and at the main station there were those who told us where to go to get food, some money and food tickets (food was rationed). After the long journey in a cattle van I decided I needed a bath or a shower and so my first steps led to the shower at the main station. When I stepped out of the shower, I had a shock. A Russian civilian came to the door, patted my behind and called me a "*charasheja djevetchka*" ("a nice girl"), prepared to start a flirtation or even worse. At the first moment I was flabbergasted, then I got very angry and ran away not without abusing him. It was the first time I met a Russian and I was rather furious about the welcome to Prague.'

[1] 'General Notes on Operations', May 1945, War Office, London: War Office papers, 193/394.
[2] Ludmila Chladkova, *The Terezin Ghetto*, Nase Vojsko, Prague, 1991, p. 47.

At the age of twenty-four, Margit Schönfeld felt that it was 'too late for a new start'. Despite the offer of a ticket to Ecuador from an aunt who had emigrated to Quito before the war, she remained in Czechoslovakia. As her second husband, she married a man who had also been in a concentration camp, and whose family owned a small factory. 'When the communists took over in 1948 we were despised "capitalists". The harassing went on.' So too did the pain of the past. 'My parents were deported to Riga and probably shot there. My first husband, Willy Schönfeld, was deported to Birkenau with me and killed in the gas chambers of Auschwitz. My grandfather was deported from Theresienstadt to an unknown place in the East.'[1]

The last camp commandant of Theresienstadt, Karl Rahm, did not long survive the system he had served: he was arrested in Austria, condemned to death by a People's Court in Leitmeritz, and hanged.

There was still some fighting in central Europe on May 11, when Soviet troops overran several pockets of German resistance east of the Czech city of Pilsen. Further south, German troops in Slovenia, near Maribor, continued to fight against Tito's forces. Maribor itself was reached on May 11 by Bulgarian troops under Russian command, and the city handed over to Tito. In East Prussia and northern Latvia, several hundred thousand Germans were still refusing to surrender. But it was now no longer military defeat, but possible future retribution, which loomed; in Oslo, on May 11, the former German ruler of Norway, Josef Terboven, committed suicide by blowing himself up with a stick of dynamite.

In Europe, the war had been transformed into a chaos of refugees, deprivation, punishment, vengeance and the search for a new life. Throughout Europe 'displaced persons' were putting their names on registers for new lands and new lives. Former prisoners-of-war were returning home after long and painful absences. Soldiers, sailors and airmen of the Western Allies could look forward to being with their families again, freed from the worry that each visit might be their last. Newspapers and photographers caught the thrill of many such homecomings. On May 15 the caption of one published photograph was 'a hero comes to town'. It was Sergeant Frank Tucker, pictured with his wife and young child walking home through the village of Oreston, in South Devon, under a canopy of flags.[2] Sergeant Tucker was a gunner in a Lancaster

---

[1] Margit Herrmannova (née Schönfeld), letter to the author, 21 October 1994.
[2] The jacket photograph of this book: Hulton Deutsch Collection, M135280, Box 960.

bomber, based in Lincolnshire. 'I did nine raids altogether,' he recalled.[1]

An estimated nine and a half million people were on the roads of Europe in the week following VE-Day, seeking their pre-war homes. These 'displaced persons', or DPs, were seen by soldiers and journalists alike as they left Germany and moved in all directions through Europe. 'Some are civilians, newly liberated labour slaves of the Nazis,' wrote *Life* magazine, 'some political prisoners, some prisoners-of-war. Trudging on foot, hitching rides on bicycles, motorcycles, looted German cars, trucks and hay wagons, this stumbling mass of humanity moves steadily on, urged by one fixed idea: to get home.' Most DPs were 'like cogs and springs suddenly disassembled from the vast machine that kept the Nazi war effort rolling'. They had worked in industrial enterprises and farms throughout the Reich. Some were prisoners-of-war who had accepted the status of 'free workers' and been sent to private homes, factories and shops. Some were volunteers, 'attracted to Germany by promises of better conditions and a place in Hitler's "new order"'. Most were civilian conscripts, deported to Germany from the conquered nations of Europe, 'who did their stint of forced labour at bayonet point.'[2]

If the Western Allies had hoped to arrange for a phased and orderly return of these people to their homelands they were to be disappointed. Even before the war ended the DPs were on the move, and with VE-Day that movement became an immense and uncontrollable flood. At certain cities, trains were provided: goods wagons and carriages open to the elements. Some French DPs left Germany in American transport planes which had been delivering supplies and fuel to the occupation forces. But for the mass of DPs, home had to be reached on foot.

Among those leaving the rubble-strewn cities of Germany in the immediate aftermath of the war were more than eight and a half million people: 2,400,000 Russians, 2,100,000 Frenchmen, 1,500,000 Poles, 600,000 Lithuanians, 570,000 Belgians, 560,000 Latvians, 420,000 Italians and 400,000 Dutchmen. Tens of thousands of Danes, Yugoslavs, Greeks, Estonians, Bulgarians, Roumanians, Hungarians and Czechs were also on their way home. Fleeing in a counter-direction were nine and a half million German civilians. Half a million of these were from Roumania, Hungary and Yugoslavia: Germans who had been living outside Germany for several centuries. Two million were German citizens expelled from East Prussia, a province which, after several hundred years

---

[1] Francis Sidney John Tucker, in conversation with the author, 3 November 1994.
[2] 'Displaced Persons, The Millions Of People The Nazis Uprooted Start Their Great Trek', *Life*, Overseas Service Edition, 4 May 1945, p. 37.

as part of Germany, was being divided between Russia and Poland. Three million of the German citizens fleeing westward were from areas which Poland had annexed: Danzig, the Polish Corridor, Pomerania and Silesia.

Three and a half million of the Germans driven from their homes were former Czechoslovak citizens (and before 1918, Austro-Hungarian subjects) fleeing from the Sudetenland region of Czechoslovakia. The restored Czech Government wanted this German minority out of its jurisdiction, and out of the homes they had lived in for generations. From the first day of the liberation of Czechoslovkia from German rule, the Sudeten Germans were driven on to the roads and out of the country, most of them with only the bundles they could carry on their shoulders or push on handcarts.

The Allies had no means of grappling with a problem on such a scale. It was to be more than a decade before the United Nations Relief and Rehabilitation Agency (UNRRA) was to find homes for all those who were registered as DPs and living in DP camps. On May 10 the Supreme Headquarters Allied Expeditionary Force had tried to quantify the scale of the DP problem. Its report, on 'displaced persons on hand in Germany', lists 1,166,527 DPs in camps and 862,600 elsewhere in the American zone. The number of recently liberated prisoners-of-war in the American zone that day was given as almost half a million.[1] Together with the DPs, this gave a total of two and a half million people on the move, or in camps, in the American zone alone. To try to bring some order into the chaos, more than a hundred UNRRA teams were already 'in the field', assisted by 697 Allied Liaison Officers.[2]

The statistics of the displaced can be set against the impact that they made on those who saw them. In a letter to his family in the United States, written on May 15, Benjamin Ferencz described some of those whom he had encountered on the road that day: 'We stopped to rest on a shady knoll. A group of about three old women, two young mothers, and about five small children approached us. The old women were limping and the children were all crying. The heat alone was terribly exhausting. "Please, please" said one of the grandmothers, "can't you give us a lift? We have been walking since early morning and we still have twenty kilometres to go. Only for the children, they were tired and crying and can go no more." "*Sind sie Deutsch?*" I asked her. "*Oesterreicher*", she said

---

[1] The precise figure given in the report was 499,413, of whom 119,117 were listed as Russians, 98,363 as French, 33,819 as Poles, 16,167 as Yugoslavs, 10,465 as Italians and 9,189 as Belgians.
[2] Colonel A.H. Moffitt Jr, 'Daily Situation Report No. 8', 10 May 1945: War Office papers, 202/621. Public Record Office, Kew.

sort of apologetically. The non-fraternization policy applies to Austrians as well, and there was no room in the jeep for them all. I explained that we couldn't carry civilians, and that the Austrians could only thank Hitler for their troubles; there were other more worthy cases who would come first. It hurt me to see the children crying and I was very sorry for the old ladies but I had to refuse.'

In his area of Austria there were '50,000 people on the roads' who wanted a lift, Ferencz commented. 'In every direction they walked or moved as best they could. All of them were going to a place they might call home. Men in every uniform were everywhere. Even some German soldiers had been released when the war ended and they too marched along in formation. There were French and Italian soldiers too, as well as Hungarians, Roumanians, and Russians. Civilians who had been bombed out, or who had fled, or who had been political prisoners were also there. All of them moving somewhere. Very many of them just walking to try out their new found freedom.'[1]

The survivors of the concentration camps were also on the roads, making their way out of the hated perimeters of their torment, away from the walls and barbed wire of the camps in which they had been incarcerated, tortured, starved and where they had toiled. 'After four or five days I left Theresienstadt and went by train to Prague,' Ben Helfgott recalled. 'It was like being in heaven. I had a pass. I could travel free. Prague was the first civilized city I had been to for six years. There were lots of soup kitchens there, where they were giving food to former camp inmates. The city was teaming with survivors who were coming from all parts of liberated Europe. I met two other survivors who took me with them to where they were staying: a deserted apartment.'

Every morning at ten o'clock, Ben Helfgott hired a boat and went rowing until twelve. 'It gave me an opportunity to build myself up. Then, every day, I went from kitchen to kitchen until four o'clock to eat to my heart's delight. And then, each evening, I went to the cinema. I still had some of my sugar and rice, which I was either bartering or selling. I remember enjoying the beer, the lovely beer... One of the films I saw was a love story about two young Russians. He was a soldier and she was a nurse. When the war came they promised that they would meet on a bridge in Moscow at twelve o'clock when the war ended. And despite all that each of them had gone through, they did.'[2]

*   *   *

[1] Benjamin Ferencz, letter of 15 May 1945. Private archive.
[2] Ben Helfgott, in conversation with the author, 2 September 1994.

The instinct of tens of thousands of Jewish survivors was to try to reach Palestine. The obstacles in their path were considerable: even to get to an Italian port, and from there to run the gauntlet of the British naval blockade of Palestine established to keep them out, these refugees in search of a homeland had to cross almost every border in Europe. To do so, they resorted to many devices. Leib Reizer, from the pre-war Polish city of Grodno, which had just been annexed by Russia, recalled one such stratagem, as, with his wife and eight-year-old daughter, he made his way with a group of Jews who had gathered together in Grodno for the journey. 'At the time, the border between the USSR and Poland was Lososna. One young officer checking documents tried to dissuade us. "Why are you leaving?" he asked. "Are we not giving you all the privileges?" Go explain it to him! When the freight train reached the Malkinia Station near Treblinka, the Jewish passengers broke down crying. And when the train arrived in Warsaw, which lay in ruins, it was the Poles who began to cry. We helped them with a sigh. In Sosnowiec we stopped only for a few hours. We had to remain close together, because soon we would transform ourselves into – Greeks! A collective document signed by the military Commandant of Lublin was issued to us, certifying that we were all Greeks from a concentration camp, *en route* to Greece. Why Greeks? Very simple. Which Polish policeman speaks Greek – which would have been one way to expose us?'[1]

Leib Reizer made his way through Czechoslovakia to Austria, from where, after three years in various DP camps, he went to New Zealand. 'Could it be that he wanted to get as far away as possible from Europe,' his daughter has asked.[2] Some survivors were trying to rebuild their lives in the countries they had lived in before the war. In the Polish city of Lodz, a city from which tens of thousands of Jews had been deported to their deaths, several hundred Jews, from different Polish towns, gathered to study and to plan for their future. 'For one year we made every effort to pick up the broken shards of our lives out of the ashes,' Tess Wise recalled, 'but it was a futile effort, because every day brought new proof that we were not welcome. Anti-semitic attacks and pogroms were the order of the day'. The seven surviving members of her family, of which there had been eighty members before the war, made a decision to travel to the American Zone of Germany. In Munich, the establishment of a United Nations Relief and Rehabilitation Agency university became a

[1] Leib Reizer, 'We Become Greeks, Post-War Memories', published in *Di Grodner Opklangen*, Argentina, 1950 (in Yiddish).
[2] Betty Broit, letter to the author, 26 September 1994.

magnet and an opportunity for those Displaced Persons who were determined to educate themselves. 'The period in Munich was balm to my heart. There were hundreds of refugee students forming one big sad family, all rooting for one another – planning a future our parents had dreamed about for us before and during the war. To be doctors, engineers, dentists and scientists.'[1]

It was not until May 12 that the British liberation force reached St Peter Port, on the Channel Island of Guernsey. Called upon to surrender his sword, Admiral Hüffmeier could not do so: he had destroyed it, he said, 'in accordance with orders'. He was then taken on board HMS *Faulkner* as a prisoner-of-war, while the British troops marched 'through streets bedecked with flags and lined with a wildly cheering throng of people'. Champagne, hidden since the summer of 1940, was brought out in celebration.

Also on May 12, as part of the Allied mood of amity and rejoicing, the Soviet forces on the Elbe gave a banquet for Lieutenant-General William H. Simpson, commander of the American Ninth Army, followed by entertainment; a moment of relaxation and laughter caught by the camera.[2]

In mid-Atlantic, a German submarine, the *U–234*, which had left Norway nearly a month earlier to sail to Japan with General Kessler, the newly appointed German Air Attaché to Tokyo, on board, surrendered to the Americans. In the North Sea, German motor torpedo boats were making their way from Rotterdam to Felixstowe, also to surrender. Peter Scott, the son of the polar explorer Robert Falcon Scott, was one of the British naval officers who went aboard to escort the German craft to the shore. 'With some difficulty,' he recalled, 'we persuaded the Germans to fall their crew in on deck as they entered harbour, where a great crowd of spectators were assembled on all the piers and jetties. All at once the armed guards filed on board and the Germans were hustled off the boats. It was the end!'[3]

---

[1] Tess Wise, letter to the author, 30 September 1994. Tess Wise later made her way to the United States.

[2] See photograph 58.

[3] Sir Peter Scott, quoted in Winston G. Ramsey (editor), *After The Battle*, issue number 12, 1976.

XXIII

From VE- to VJ-Day

Throughout Europe victory parades were held to welcome the returning soldiers. Liberators were also fêted. On May 12, members of the Polish Armoured Corps took part in a victory parade in the small Czechoslovak town of Melnik, fifteen miles from Prague. 'It was a great privilege to me to participate at the head of my battalion', Benjamin Meirtchak later recalled. 'And the Czech girls were so pretty, with flowers welcoming the liberators "*Na Zdraw*" ("Your health").'

From Melnik, Meirtchak travelled to the Polish city of Lodz, where he hoped to find his sister Hannah. 'After tragic five years of war I met her, the only survivor or our whole family. Our parents had been killed in Majdanek camp. Nothing is known about our brother Marek. We laughed and we cried, we spoke days and nights. Hanna told me the tragic story of their life in Warsaw ghetto, about the deportation to Majdanek. She was separated from our mother in the selection. Father passed the selection, but a few days later he was killed by the Germans. I told Hanna my story. We discussed our future. We decided – no more Poland, no other countries. We shall build our new life in the land of Israel. I went back to my unit. It took us another three years to fulfil our plans. Meantime I married Fela, Hanna married Pesach, and in 1948 we came to the State of Israel.'[1]

In the Soviet Zone of Germany the apparatus of communist power was slowly being imposed. Returning to her husband's estate at Kerzendorf, fifteen miles from the centre of Berlin, Lali Horstmann, whose diplomat husband had served in Britain between the wars, later wrote: 'The mayor was a white-haired old man who bore us no ill-will, although he had declared himself a communist a fortnight before. He said he wished to co-operate with my husband in keeping order, but he had been powerless to carry out the general's instructions. During the night stray soldiers and villagers had climbed into the cellar through the smashed window-frames, and had broken open and looted cases of silver and trunks

---

[1] Benjamin Meirtchak, letter to the author, 22 September 1994.

of clothes, both our own and the belongings of friends who had entrusted them to us for safe-keeping during the bombing.

'It was as if a gale had swept through the rooms. Pictures had been slashed from top to bottom, cut-out faces of portraits still hung to the canvases by a thread, the floor was littered with my grandmother's wedding-gown, an old court-train in light blue and silver brocade, fancy dresses and pink hunting coats that we had left forgotten in the attic for years past. I enjoyed their discovery and their faded charm on that day; their possession was a great if short-lived pleasure, for soon they vanished for ever, stolen or taken by God knows whom.

'Our secret hiding-place had not been discovered, much was still safe, but it seemed impossible ever to restore the house to what it had once been. Even the stove would not work. When we tried to cook a meal the pipe was found to be blocked and soon the smoke grew so thick we could hardly open our eyes. Masses of soldiers still swarmed ceaselessly in and out of the house like pigeons in a pigeonloft, looked about in surprised curiosity, picked up what they fancied and either carried it away or threw it out of the window.'[1]

On May 14, six days after Germany's formal surrender to the Allies, 150,000 German troops surrendered to the Red Army in East Prussia, and a further 180,000 in northern Latvia. Only one German force, some 150,000 men, the remnants of the German forces in Yugoslavia, was still under arms; on the following day it surrendered to the Russians and Yugoslavs at Slovenski Gradec. For the Yugoslav partisans, May 15 was Victory Day. In the previous two months' fighting in Yugoslavia 99,907 German soldiers had been killed in action. The Yugoslavs had lost 30,000 men killed during these same final months, a small proportion of the 1,700,000 Yugoslavs who had died since April 1941 in battle, in concentration camps, or in captivity in Germany.

One of the Yugoslav partisan leaders, Milovan Djilas, who had been sent to Montenegro and the Dalmatian Coast, later wrote: 'Before the walls of Kotor only local officials and a column of skinny, shabbily dressed schoolchildren greeted us. The officials made excuses – the telephone system had broken down, as usual – and persuaded us to wait until the people had gathered: party members and Communist Youth had been sent out to round them up. As we exchanged impressions and reminisced about the war, some three or four hundred citizens showed up in their finest dress. The people of the Bay of Kotor are cultivated like the Italians, and traditionally look upon Montenegrins as savages given to plundering

---

[1] Lali Horstmann, *Nothing for Tears*, Weidenfeld and Nicolson, London, 1953, pp. 125–6.

and feuding. Perhaps that is a little how they looked upon us as well, with our uniforms and weapons. When the people had gathered, the secretary of the district committee or the district president decided that the time was now ripe to make a welcoming address, climbed up on a counter in the outdoor market place, and delivered it. After him, I climbed up too – as the main attraction. I began approximately as follows: "In the course of the National Liberation Struggle . . ."

'I was interrupted by the shrill shouting of a raw-boned girl: "Long live the National Liberation Struggle!"

The people, with a trained unanimity, shouted, "Long live!"

> I: ". . . under the leadership of the heroic Communist party . . ."
> THE GIRL: "Long live the heroic Communist party!"
> THE PEOPLE: "Long live!"
> I: ". . . and the leader and teacher of our peoples, Comrade Tito . . ."
> THE GIRL: "Long live the leader and teacher of our peoples, Comrade Tito!"
> THE PEOPLE: "Long live!"
> The girl and the people repeated this, too.

'Unsettled already, because all of this was but one single sentence, I continued: ". . . allies, primarily the Soviet Union . . ." I never finished that sentence. It was clear to me by this time that nobody was paying the least attention to the meaning; they were merely echoing hallowed clichés, repeating ritually the word symbols that it was the girl's job to signal to them. This, then, I thought to myself, is how my agitation and propaganda look out there. This is the extent to which the spontaneity of the people has been organized – it's grotesque! Even though my speech is unimportant, a matter of protocol, because of all this organization I won't even be able to deliver it. As if in jest, I blurted out, "Listen here, girl! Let me unload the heavy burden I assumed on my way down to Kotor, and I give you my word of honour that I'll mention all those slogans at the end!" The people of Kotor laughed uneasily and the officials sourly, while the girl withdrew, abashed.'[1]

In every country that had suffered German occupation, the victors sought to punish those who had collaborated with the enemy. In France, the killing of collaborators had begun from the first hours of liberation the

---

[1] Milovan Djilas, *Wartime*, Secker and Warburg, London, 1977, pp. 443–5.

previous autumn. In the concentration camps, guards whose behaviour had been particularly repellent had been cornered and killed. The quislings in every land, including Norway's eponymous Quisling and Holland's Mussert, were caught and punished, mostly by execution. Even in the tiny island of Guernsey, a stern voice could be heard. 'Those who sought to line their pockets at the expense of others less fortunate, and those who did not scruple to betray their friends – let them, until a later date, deal with their own consciences.' They could be contrasted with other Guernsey men and women who, 'risking the penalty of prison in Germany, where several who were unfortunate were sent and where one, at least, died in one of those notorious Nazi hells – retained their wireless sets through good and bad times and enabled the whole Island, in diverse ways, to hear the news. To these also: "Well done, and thank you!" '[1]

On May 14 *Life* magazine published an article by Sidney Olson on his travels through defeated Germany. To one question which many were asking, he wrote: 'The mystery of where the SS has gone is being cleared up steadily. They have gone into civilian clothes and are seeping back into the little German towns. Yesterday eight of them were caught in Dillingen, a pleasant little town on the Danube, when some blue-turbaned Hindu ex-prisoners recognized the men who used to hit them with rifle butts in their prison camp.

'The screening of all German civilians by the Military Government is necessarily very slow as it is an enormous job for a small outfit and Germany is a big place in which to hide. Meanwhile it's a very odd feeling to walk through streets in which are many husky, tanned brutal-looking Germans in civilian clothes who stand about rather stiffly or bicycle past you with averted faces.

'The conflict now seething within American soldiers, between their hatred of Germans and Germany and Nazism, and their natural Christian upbringing and kindness and susceptibility to beautiful children and attractive women and poor old ladies, is one of the great stories of today. The same doughboys who went through Dachau's incredible horrors were the very next day being kissed and wreathed in flowers by the German women of Munich. Some doughboys say they hate all the Germans, and they obviously do; and yet others who have been through just as much bitter fighting and obvious trickery will tell you that they hate only the Nazis and they like many Germans. I heard one say, "I even want to shoot all the pregnant women because I know that what's

---

[1] 'Guernsey's 5 Years Under Nazi Rule', *Guernsey Weekly Press*, 15 May 1945, p. 1, col. 6.

in their bellies will someday be shooting at my children." His buddy was giving candy to a little German girl while he was speaking.'

Olson had harsh words about the German people, thoughts which were widely felt at the time, especially by those who had fought on German soil. Few Germans, he wrote, 'can yet realize the place of Germany at the bottom of the list of civilized nations. They learn with shock and shame of the American non-fraternization policy. Many of them simply cannot understand it. They thought they were fighting in an honourable war. When parents realize that they lost all their sons in a cause unspeakably dirty they are filled with a despair that will mark the rest of their lives. Of course they should have realized it years ago when they were "Heiling" the Führer. But they lived two lives, they say, one of exaltation at his great political promises of the wonderful new Germany to come, and one of terror that the Gestapo might knock on their door that night. And yet it is clear that Josef Paul Goebbels did the job he set out to do all too diabolically well. But the over-all, inescapable fact is that the German people are so solidly, thoroughly indoctrinated with so much of the Nazi ideology that the facts merely bounce off their numbed skull. It will take years, perhaps generations, to undo the work that Adolf Hitler and his henchmen did.'[1]

The transformation of Germany was indeed to take time, more so under communist rule in the east than in the west. Fifty years after the end of the war, neo-Nazi gangs, mostly in what had been East Germany, and several violent manifestations of anti-foreigner feeling levelled against Turkish and other 'guest workers', were denounced by the society at large, and combated with vigour by the authorities: a far cry from the active connivance of the German State apparatus under Dr Goebbels.

In India, the defeat of Germany, and the realization that the British would soon return to Party politics, had stimulated nationalist sentiment. In a despatch from the Director of Military Intelligence in Delhi, the War Office was told that the main nationalist reaction to the end of the war in Europe was 'that as India was not consulted at the beginning of war she could not be expected to celebrate victory which has no significance *vis-à-vis* her political demands.' Pro-Russian sentiment was 'conspicuous'. As far as Britain's forthcoming General Election was concerned, the nationalists were 'only less sceptical of Labour than of Conservative programmes for India'.[2]

---

[1] Sidney Olson, 'Defeated land', *Life*, Overseas Service Edition, 14 May 1945, p. 51.
[2] Telegram of 30 May 1945: War Office papers 208/7614. Public Record Office, Kew.

The Indian nationalist movement had taken a great risk in 1942 by launching the Quit India movement, turning its back on Britain at the very moment when Japanese forces, claiming to be the champions of an independent India, were on the eastern border, and even in places across it. Gandhi, who in 1914 had encouraged Indians to fight for Britain, had been imprisoned in 1942 for his anti-British stance. On VE-Day, in his honeymoon hotel in Bath, Maurice Zinkin, the Deputy Financial Adviser to the Government of India, later recalled: 'The war had trained hundreds of thousands of Indians, and the classes on which we had depended, notably our own officials, had decided – as they had not in the 1930s – that they wanted to govern themselves. One still hoped that there would be some agreement between the predominantly Hindu Congress and the Muslim League, and that there would still be a place for British officials like myself who were dedicated to their Indian jobs. But it was painfully obvious that the risks of failure were high, though in 1945 I did not anticipate the massacres of 1947. It was even more obvious to me that an independent India might not want foreigners at the top of its Finance Ministry, so I decided that I must cover my rear and make some connections in the UK during our honeymoon.'[1]

Political speculation was premature, however, while the war in the Far East continued. In Chungking, Lieutenant-General Wedemeyer, commanding the United States forces fighting alongside Chiang Kai-shek in China, had high hopes that the end of the war in Europe would be to the military advantage of his own area of operations. On May 14 he wrote to the Chief of the Strategy and Policy section at the Pentagon: 'Now that the Germans are liquidated, I feel justified in asking you and your cohorts to focus your attention and support on the China Theatre. We have experienced so many frustrations here, yet we are all of good heart and will not let you down.'[2] Wedemeyer's main frustration could not be assuaged by Washington, and was a precursor of things to come: the continuing strife between Chiang Kai-shek's Nationalist forces and the Chinese Communists led by Mao Tse-tung.

'A civil war in China,' Wedemeyer warned the American Chief of Staff, General Marshall, 'would reduce the advantages gained by victory over Japan and destroy economic and political equilibrium in the Far East, the important objective for which we are fighting.' Wedemeyer had

---

[1] Maurice Zinkin, letter to the author, 12 October 1994. After Indian Independence, Maurice Zinkin embarked upon a career with Unilever, serving with them for several years in India, and becoming in due course chief of staff to the Chairman.

[2] Letter of 14 May 1945: Keith E. Eiler (editor), *Wedemeyer on War and Peace*, Hoover Press, Stanford, California, 1987, pp. 116–19.

made contact with Mao and offered him military support, but his own resources were such that the only part American forces could play was that of 'active defence'. As to the future, he wrote, whether victory over Japan came early or after an extended period of war, 'it is reasonable to expect widespread confusion and disorder. The Chinese have no plan for rehabilitation, prevention of epidemics, restoration of utilities, establishment of balanced economy, and redisposition of millions of refugees.'[1]

The ferocity of the war against Japan did not abate. On May 11, nearly four hundred American sailors had been killed on the aircraft carrier *Bunker Hill*. This was three times the American death toll in the battle of 1775 which the carrier's name commemorated. On Okinawa, the following day saw a renewed American attack against the fortified Shuri line across the southern part of the island. Hundreds died on both sides. Conical Hill fell to the Americans on May 13, nor could the Japanese drive them off again. A report on the casualties on Okinawa up to May 13 gave the figures of 6,634 American dead, 137,557 Japanese dead, and 1,800 Japanese taken prisoner. The Japanese were fighting, literally, to the death. 'Jap suicide crash dives continue to harass our fleet units', the casualty report added, 'and although some damage has been inflicted, the mounting cost in Jap planes shot down is one the enemy can ill afford.' That day, May 13, six British bombers successfully mined the Yangtze River. In an attack on a Japanese-controlled strategic railway, eight British planes 'scored seven hits on the tracks, and killed two hundred Japs who were caught standing in formation along the railroad'.[2]

On May 14, American atomic scientists and bombing experts examined possible targets for the atomic bomb. One report discussed by a special top-secret Target committee meeting at Los Alamos that day noted that the hills around Hiroshima, one of the most favoured targets, were 'likely to produce a focusing effect which would considerably increase the blast damage'. According to the report, the one drawback was Hiroshima's rivers, which made the city 'not a good incendiary target'. Another target under consideration on May 14 was Hirohito's palace in Tokyo, but this was not one of the four targets which were chosen that day for further study; they were Kyoto – the Japanese holy city – Hiroshima, Yokohama and the Kokura arsenal.[3]

---

[1] Letter of 1 August 1945: Keith E. Eiler (editor), *Wedemeyer on War and Peace*, Hoover Press, Stanford, California, 1987, pp. 124–32.
[2] 'The War Against Japan (to include 15 May 1945)', 'Secret': War Office papers, 203/5346. Public Record Office, Kew.
[3] Notes of the meeting of 14 May 1945: Richard Rhodes, *The Making of the Atomic Bomb*, Simon and Schuster, New York, 1986, pp. 631–2.

The war against Japan held many terrors for the Allies, not least that of a prolonged war, lasting well into 1946 and perhaps beyond, dominated by the need to land on the Japanese mainland islands, and to fight their way to Tokyo. On Okinawa the fighting reached a climax on May 15 with the opening of the battle for the 'Sugar Loaf', a battle which was to last for ten days, and in which nearly three thousand Marines were killed or wounded. In Burma, on May 17, a Canadian member of the British Special Operations Executive, Jean-Paul Archambault, was killed behind Japanese lines when he accidentally detonated one of his explosive charges. Only a year earlier he had been carrying out similar clandestine duties behind the lines in German-occupied France.

On May 19, as Europe entered its second week since the day the war ended, the Japanese launched a suicide attack on American positions on Okinawa. More than five hundred Japanese were killed. On Mindanao in the Philippines, as well as on Okinawa, the third week of May saw bloody battles, in which even the massive use of flame throwers could not dislodge the Japanese defenders, but could only destroy them yard by yard and cave by cave. Off Okinawa, on May 24, Japanese suicide pilots sank a fast troop transport and damaged six warships, while ten Japanese pilots, in a daring landing on Yontan airfield, destroyed seven American aircraft and damaged twenty-six more, as well as igniting 70,000 gallons of aircraft fuel, before being killed. Theirs had also been a suicide mission.

In Germany, on May 21, the last of the hundreds of wooden barracks of Belsen were burned down by flame throwers. 'The swastika and a picture of Hitler were displayed on that last barrack', Anita Lasker, a survivor of Auschwitz, wrote, 'and there was a little ceremony. We all stood there and watched as this last trace of the camp was devoured by the flames.'[1]

The Allied powers were committed, by several wartime declarations, to find and to bring to trial those responsible for war crimes. Trials were to go ahead, at Nuremberg, and in several of the camps themselves, including Belsen, where former commandants and guards were sentenced to death and hanged.

On May 22, Hitler's most senior surviving Military Intelligence officer, Reinhard Gehlen, gave himself up to the Americans at Oberursel, north of Darmstadt. He was to return to Intelligence work, under American

---

[1] Anita Lasker, typescript, 'Inherit the Truth'. Born in Breslau, Anita Lasker was a member of the prisoners' orchestra in Auschwitz. 'I was the only cellist in that orchestra – that is why I am able to talk to you now.' (Anita Lasker, conversation with author, 11 December 1994).

auspices, working against the Russians in post-war West Germany. Also on May 22 an American major, William Bromley, who had earlier been sent to Nordhausen for the express purpose of aiding future rocket research in the United States, began to despatch four hundred tons of German rocket equipment to Antwerp, for shipment across the Atlantic to White Sands, in New Mexico. Requisitioning railway wagons from as far west as Cherbourg, Bromley completed his task before June 1, when, according to the wartime agreement establishing the precise borders of the British, American, French and Russian zones of occupation, the Russians entered Nordhausen.

At Flensburg, Grand Admiral Dönitz had continued to act as if he were the head of the German Government. Every morning since VE-Day, wearing his Admiral's uniform, he had been driven in the armoured Mercedes, which Hitler had given him, from his living quarters to the nearby naval school in which his Government was housed. Each day he had held a meeting of his Cabinet. On May 21, as this masquerade continued, a British naval mission reached Flensburg by air. This mission was accommodated on board the Hamburg-Amerika liner *Caribia* in Flensburg harbour. Berthed on the opposite side of the pier was the liner *Patria*, in which was accommodated the Allied Control Commission, established by Eisenhower, under the command of an American, General Rooks. A Russian military mission was also present, with Eisenhower's authority to interrogate members of the German Government.

'As might be expected,' the head of the British Naval Mission, Commodore G.R.G. Allen, wrote in his official report, 'the political atmosphere was somewhat confused; on the one hand the German naval authorities were ready to co-operate under the terms of the capitulation, and to discuss matters of naval policy and technical matters quite freely. The German armed forces, both naval and military, apppeared to be in good shape with good morale and well-disciplined. The naval ratings were smart and well turned out, and there was no visible sign of demoralization. The civil population were evidently well-fed and appeared reasonably contented, self-confident and relatively indifferent to events happening around them. On the other hand, General Rooks told me that Admiral Dönitz himself had recently stated that the conditions were likely to deteriorate sharply in the near future if the Western Allies insisted upon maintaining their present policy of non-co-operation with the Germans in the occupied areas.'

Dönitz pointed out to the American general 'that the propaganda now being issued from London on the one hand, and that from Moscow on the other, were diametrically opposed. From London it was being continually stated that the German people must be treated harshly – that the German leaders were criminals and must be removed. From Moscow the Russians were telling the Germans that they intended to treat them well, and a policy of fraternization was to be the rule in Russian-occupied Germany. If the present conditions persisted there would soon be a movement of Germans from the west into the Russian zone; there were already some thirty million Germans in the Russian areas, many of whom were known to have communistic tendencies, and in Dönitz's opinion, if the Western Allies wish to drive Germany into communism they could not adopt a better plan than that now being enforced.'[1]

On the afternoon of May 22, Dönitz's adjutant received a telephone call summoning Grand Admiral Dönitz, General Jodl and Admiral von Friedeburg to meet the head of the Allied Control Commission, General Rooks, on board the liner *Patria* at 9.45 the next morning. When he was told this, Dönitz said curtly, 'Pack the bags.'[2]

Commodore Allen was on board the *Patria* on the morning of May 23 when the arrest of Dönitz and his Government took place. 'General Rooks had confined all officers to the ships during this event to prevent any untoward incident,' Allen reported to London, 'and a British brigade with tanks was deployed in the town to maintain order. Admiral Dönitz conducted himself with much dignity; the other two appeared nervous.'[3] Rooks told them: 'Gentlemen, I am in receipt of instructions from Supreme Headquarters, European Theatre of Operations, from the Supreme Commander, General Eisenhower, to call you before me this morning to tell you that he has decided, in concert with the Soviet High Command, that today the acting German Government and the German High Command, with the several of its members, shall be taken into custody as prisoners-of-war. Thereby the acting German Government is dissolved.'

After General Rooks had announced what was in effect the final end of the Third Reich, Dönitz commented that 'words at this moment would be superfluous'. All German naval officers at Flensburg were confined to their quarters. A detachment of British troops surrounded the police buildings in Mürwik where Dönitz and the members of his administration were brought under guard, each of them permitted one suitcase of personal belongings. Following a body search for poison phials they were

---

[1] Commodore G.R.G. Allen, Commodore for Chief of Combined Operations, Report of the Admiralty Mission to Flensburg, May 21–24: Admiralty papers 1/18222, Public Record Office, Kew.

[2] Peter Padfield, *Dönitz, The Last Führer*, Victor Gollancz, London, 1984, p. 475.

[3] Commodore Allen's report.

taken into a courtyard to face press and newsreel photographers. They and their baggage were then put on trucks and driven in an armoured convoy to the airfield. The only man not to go with them was Admiral von Friedeburg, who had appended his signature to three of the German surrenders in the first week of May. 'It is probable the past had much to do with his agitation,' the historian Peter Padfield has written, 'and that he was a victim of the all-powerful legend of the "stab-in-the-back" by the Novemberlings who had signed the armistice after the First War; on this occasion he had signed and was answerable to posterity. At all events, arriving back at his quarters to collect his belongings, he had asked the British officer escorting him for permission to write to his wife.

'After writing the letter, Admiral von Friedeburg went to the bedroom where his twenty-two-year-old son was packing his things; he was followed by the British officer, who thought he was acting "somewhat peculiarly" and walking unsteadily. He then requested to use the bathroom and I agreed provided he left the door open. I followed him to the bathroom and he entered rather slowly, then suddenly closed the door and turned the key. I called the escort and we immediately forced the door, which took approximately fifteen seconds. On my entering he was heaving by the washbasins; he half-turned round and fell into the bath backwards, striking his head on the bottom of the bath.'[1]

A doctor was called, but von Friedeburg was dead by the time he arrived. He had committed suicide by poison. Before killing himself, he had gone to the German Admiralty at Glücksburg, called his officers together, announced to them that he had been placed under arrest, and told them that from that moment the German Admiralty would cease to exist. He then drafted two farewell signals to be sent to all German naval units. These signals were seized, however, by the British Naval Control Office, and were not transmitted. Meanwhile, von Friedeburg had retired to his private flat where he committed suicide. The senior British Naval Officer with General Rooks, Captain Maund, at once sent for the senior German Admiral, Admiral Backenkohler. Friedeburg's last two signals would not be sent, said Maund. Backenkohler was to assume the function of Naval Commander-in-Chief 'temporarily'. The German Admiralty was to carry on its functions until further orders. Maund also informed Backenkohler that a military funeral for von Friedeburg would not be permitted but that proposals for a private funeral should be submitted. 'There was no disturbance,' Commodore Allen reported, 'and the

[1] Peter Padfield, *Dönitz, The Last Führer*, Victor Gollancz, London, 1984, pp. 476–9.

Admiralty continued to function as usual.'[1] The German Government had been dissolved, but the German Admiralty, twice triumphant at the outset of two world wars, and twice defeated, still had a commander-in-chief.

Late on the afternoon of May 23, Dönitz and his ministers were flown across northern Germany to Luxembourg, and then driven to a hotel at Bad Mondorf. Awaiting them there were Goering and other members of Hitler's Government, some of whom they had last seen in the bunker in Berlin. They were under arrest. Dönitz, those with him, and those whom they found at the hotel, were all to be brought to trial. For many of them, though not for Dönitz, the journey from Bad Mondorf to Nuremberg was to be their last.[2]

That day, at lunchtime, at a British interrogation centre in the village of Barfelde, an episode occurred that was bizarre even according to the standards of those days. As the Sergeant Major entered the room in which the officers were working he announced, as Vivian Herzog recalled, 'that a German with two others with him demanded to see the officer commanding the camp. When he entered the room, which was an empty barrack room with temporary arrangements, the German stood at attention and announced in German, *"Ich bin der Reichsführer SS"*("I am the Commander of the SS"),[3] in other words, Heinrich Himmler. He wore a black patch on one eye, was without a moustache, which had been shaved off, and wore the uniform of a sergeant in the field security of the German Army.[4] The officer commanding asked him who the two accompanying him were, and he introduced them as his Adjutant and his bodyguard. Both were in the uniform of private soldiers in the GFP.

'We had, like all Allied units, a book of signatures of all the Nazi leadership. We asked him to sign, and it was obviously Himmler. He was then stripped and searched, and cyanide was found in one pocket. He was covered in a blanket. The fact of his falling into our hands was telephoned immediately to Second Army Headquarters in Lüneburg, and instructions came from the Army Intelligence Officer not to talk to him, not to touch him, and to wait until they would fetch him. We did talk

---

[1] Commodore G.R.G. Allen, Commodore for Chief of Combined Operations, Report of the Admiralty Mission to Flensburg, May 21–24: Admiralty papers 1/18222, Public Record Office, Kew.

[2] Dönitz received a ten-year prison sentence. He died in 1981, in his ninetieth year. Ten leading Nazis were executed at Nuremberg. In subsequent trials the Polish authorities executed 631 German war criminals, the United States 278, the British 240, the Hungarians 149, and the French 104.

[3] *Reichsführer* was the equivalent SS rank to Field Marshal.

[4] Geheime Feld Polizei or GFP.

to him, and asked what he wanted. Why had he surrendered? He said that he wanted to meet with Churchill or Montgomery in order to offer them the forces of the SS as support in the imminent struggle against the Russians. We asked him about the concentration camps. Like all Germans, he knew that there were prison camps but denied knowing their true nature, and he had no knowledge whatsoever of what went on there. All the leading picture magazines of that period such as *Picture Post* and *Life* magazine depicting in gruesome detail all the horrors and atrocities, were produced. He was obviously flustered and uneasy, but denied having been associated with such cruelty.

'Soon the Intelligence Officer of the Second Army arrived. He was brusque and abrupt, left no doubt in Himmler's mind what his fate would be, and made most of the mistakes one should avoid if one wants to use a prisoner and extract whatever information possible. He brusquely took him out and unceremoniously pushed him into a car and drove with him to Lüneburg. Here, we were told, Himmler was examined by a doctor. When the doctor reached his mouth, Himmler pushed back his head and swallowed cyanide which had been hidden in a cavity in a tooth. He lingered between life and death for fifteen minutes, and despite all the efforts to pump him and save him, he died.'[1]

It was four hours after Himmler had been identified at Barfelde. 'The bastard's beat us!' was one British sergeant's comment when the deed was done.[2] On the following day, May 24, Field Marshal von Greim, whom Hitler had made head of the German Air Force in the last days of April, committed suicide in prison in Salzburg.

In Germany, and beyond, self-styled 'Jewish avengers' had already begun to track down and to kill a number of those who had carried out the policy of mass murder. But vengeance was the path of a minority. 'Sometimes', Israel Gutman, a survivor of Majdanek, Auschwitz and Gunskirchen has written, the 'desire and expectation of revenge' were the 'hope' that kept camp inmates alive 'during the final and most arduous stages of camp life', but once the war was over, 'we find only a few cases of revenge, or organized vengeful activity on the part of the survivors.'[3] As Dr Zalman Grinberg, a survivor of the Kovno ghetto and the death marches, told those survivors who were still living in huts in Dachau on May 27, nearly a month after liberation, but a day nevertheless on which thirty-five Jews had died as a result of continuing illness and weakness:

[1] Chaim (formerly Vivian) Herzog, letter to the author, 26 October 1994.
[2] Winston G. Ramsey, 'The Death of Himmler', *After the Battle*, issue 14, 1976.
[3] Discussion among conference participants, published in *The Nazi Concentration Camps*, Yad Vashem, Jerusalem, 1984, p. 521.

'Hitler has lost every battle on every front except the battle against defenceless and unarmed men, women and children. He won the war against the Jews of Europe. He carried out this war with the help of the German nation. However, we do not want revenge. If we took this vengeance it would mean we would fall to the depths and ethics and morals the German nation has been in these past ten years. We are not able to slaughter women and children! We are not able to burn millions of people! We are not able to starve hundreds of thousands!'[1]

In the eastern Mediterranean there was fighting on May 27, as French Moroccan troops who had been landed at Beirut ten days earlier entered the Syrian inland towns of Homs, Hama and Aleppo. So fierce was the fighting in Aleppo that the French were forced to evacuate the town. There was further fighting in Damascus two days later. Within three weeks of the end of the war in Europe, a pre-war colonial struggle had been renewed. There was an ominous note in a British Intelligence survey of the situation. 'The other Arab States are taking great interest,' it reported, 'particularly Iraq, which has hinted at sending arms to the Syrian Government.'[2]

On May 20, Henry Slamovich, one of the Jews from Plaszow who had been saved by the German industrialist Oskar Schindler, returned with about twenty-five other young Jews, all of them survivors, to his home town of Dzialoszyce. 'We thought to ourselves,' he later recalled, 'we had survived. We are alive, we are going to enjoy freedom.' Even though his own home was now lived in by non-Jews, Slamovich was determined somehow to rebuild his life in his own town. But within a week, four of the twenty-five Jews who had returned were murdered by Polish anti-Semites. The rest of the young Jews realised they would have to leave. 'It was sad, very sad,' Slamovich recalled thirty-five years later.[3]

Elsewhere in central and eastern Europe, liberation and safety had also proved inconstant partners. At the former German slave labour camp at Neustadt-Glewe, where Russian troops had taken over from the Americans within a few days of liberation, the Jewish women understood just how much Russian blood had been shed in nearly four years of fighting. 'They had paid dearly for their victory,' Lena Berg recalled, 'and they celebrated with all the forthrightness and lack of restraint characteristic

---

[1] 'Address Delivered by Dr Zalman Grinberg on the Occasion of a Liberation Celebration', Dachau, 27 May 1945.

[2] 'General Notes on Operations,' May 1945, War Office, London: War Office papers, 193/394. Public Record Office, Kew.

[3] Henry Slamovich, in conversation with the author, 5 November 1985.

of Slavs.' Those whom the Russians had liberated were recovering their health, their hair, even their looks.

Lena Berg's account continued: 'The camp teemed with amorous couples, but the majority of the liberated women, despite their sympathy for their liberators and admiration for the Red Army's heroism, were reluctant to express their gratitude with their bodies. The Russians were unable to understand that and the situation led to sharp, and occasionally tragic conflicts. "Aren't you our girls?" the Russians would say, surprised by the reluctance. "We shed our blood for you. We liberated you, and you refuse us a mere trifle?"

'Intoxicated by victory and often literally drunk, they felt they were entitled to anything and everything. Several times they took women by brute force, and I shall never forget the heart-rending screams and tears of a fifteen-year-old girl raped by a Soviet private in the barracks in front of hundreds of women. "No! No! I don't want to!" the girl raved. We heard these words for a long time afterwards.'[1]

Throughout the summer and autumn of 1945, and through the winter into 1946, thousands of concentration camp survivors still waited for the chance to leave Europe. 'Thousands and thousands of newly-freed survivors started travelling from one camp to another throughout Germany, France, Poland, looking for family,' Mania Tenenbaum, who had been liberated in Belsen in April with a dangerous infection, later recalled. 'I could not travel yet, after the illness, but put my name on every available list. The Red Cross did a superb job in putting people in touch with one another. So many happy, anxious faces! So many tears! I checked so many lists and waited and waited but found no Tenenbaum. I had no family left. I could not, because of my illness, return to Poland to the Kubicka family which was our pre-arranged meeting place that my parents decided upon so long ago. But people had been arriving in our camp from Poland too, but there was no one I knew.'

Mania Tenenbaum's sister Rella, from whom she had been separated in Auschwitz, had survived. Liberated from a camp in the East by the Russians, she eventually reached Belsen, where the two girls were re-united. Their mother Shaindla ('my wonderful, warm, delightful, loving mom') and their younger brother Jacob had been deported from Radom to Treblinka in 1943 and murdered there. Their father Tobias (always called Tovy) had survived various camps until January 1945, when he had been killed in Mauthausen.

---

[1] Lena Berg, recollections, in Alexander Donat, *The Holocaust Kingdom, a memoir*, Secker and Warburg, London, 1965, p. 317.

At Belsen in those post-war days, Mania Tenenbaum also recalled another reunion. 'One of the survivors that stopped one day in our camp was no other than my old boyfriend Moniek Horowicz. The girls wanted to surprise him and brought him to me wanting to witness the surprise embrace of old friends and lovers. He looked and looked at me and I will never forget the few words that startled me. "You look familiar" he said. I did look like a shadow weighing probably no more than eighty pounds. He stayed on in camp and simply did not know what to do for me. He looked and felt surprisingly good. He brought me additional food, like fresh milk and eggs from the farm, extra clothing, cared for me with such fatherly love and affection. He found out weeks later that his mother and wife had survived. (He had married during the war.) He left the camp to join them.

'I started gaining weight and strength. My arm partially healed, although it was badly scarred. I was so anxious to return to more normal living conditions, so tired of standing in line for food, so tired of the group life. It was then that two boys I knew from Radom stopped in our camp and told us of an enchanting little town they just passed, one of the very few not even touched by bombing, a town settled in the mountains near Frankfurt on Main, occupied by the Americans, a town called Bad Nauheim. They urged us to go there. All of us survivors received free passes for travel by train anywhere. The offer and the prospect seemed tempting. I was told that I needed more care, more nourishing food for my arm to heal completely. With the tens of thousands of survivors, our English liberators simply didn't have the medical facilities or proper food to take care of all the damage the Nazis had done to so many human beings. We were also told that the Americans had an abundance of food, facilities and medicine. I talked two of my girl friends into venturing a trip to this promising little town of Bad Nauheim which gave me a new life, the love of my life, and my future.'[1]

With that new life, Mania Tenenbaum put Poland behind her. 'Almost immediately after arriving in Bad Nauheim, I met my future husband, a Jewish soldier stationed there after the occupation. He knew me only two weeks before he proposed. We married in December 1945. I found peace, security, warmth and love which lasted thirty-seven years of marriage (he died in 1983). I arrived in the United States as a war bride in May 1946, and have been residing in a Detroit suburb since. Thirteen years ago, I returned to Poland and to my home town for a short visit.

[1] Mania Salinger, manuscript memoirs, United States Holocaust Memorial Museum, Washington DC.

It was very emotional, a sentimental visit. I insisted on going alone, without my husband. After all, he was not part of my childhood. I went home to reminisce, to find a picture, to re-live the happy years, but also to close a chapter, to say "Goodbye".'[1]

On their return home, as many as a million former Soviet prisoners-of-war, Soviet citizens who had fought the Germans in battle and been captured, were arrested and sent to labour camps. Stalin, whose own son had been taken prisoner, regarded those who had surrendered and been held in German camps with paranoid suspicion.[2] In the three Baltic Republics, Lithuania, Latvia and Estonia, and in the Ukraine, the impact of these purges was particularly harsh. Stalin knew that among the inhabitants of these non-Russian lands were those who had welcomed the Germans, collaborated with them, and in some cases even participated in mass murder. The fact that millions of soldiers, particularly from the Ukraine and other non-Russian republics of the Soviet Union, had fought the Germans as bravely as any, did not assuage his fears.

On May 24, Stalin held a reception at the Kremlin, at which he spoke to a great assemblage of senior officers, Communist Party officials and foreign diplomats. His remarks were published in *Pravda* the next day. Translating them for the British Military Mission, Hugh Lunghi later recalled: 'We were struck by the way Stalin, true Georgian in looks, more so in accent, had singled out the *Russian* people, "the leading nation of the Soviet Union, remarkable for its clear mind, its patience and its firm character". We wondered what the many non-Russian senior officers at the reception made of that. Another surprise was his acknowledgement of "the many mistakes the Soviet Government had made", but that "even in the darkest times of 1941 and 1942 the Russian people had not told the Government to go". On our part there was much hollow laughter at the very idea.'[3]

Stalin's praise for the Russians among the many nationalities of the Soviet Union, his own included, was an omen of things to come. The primacy of Russia over the other republics and regions was to prevail for

---

[1] Mania Salinger (née Tenenbaum), letter to the author, 26 September 1994.

[2] Yakov (Yasha) Dzhugashvili, Stalin's only son by his first wife, was a Lieutenant of Artillery and had been captured near Smolensk in the opening weeks of the war. While a prisoner-of-war he had been taken to see Goering, whom he is said to have astonished by predicting that Russia would become the mightiest political, scientific and economic power in the world. He died on 24 April 1943 after throwing himself on the perimeter fence of his camp, and being shot by one of the guards, apparently at his own request. H. Montgomery Hyde, *Stalin, The History of a Dictator*, Rupert Hart Davis, London, 1971, pp. 442, 484.

[3] Hugh Lunghi, lettter to the author, 22 September 1994.

four decades, until in 1991 the unified structure broke up and Russia became only one State among a dozen in a Commonwealth of Independent States. By then communism itself had collapsed, Stalin's war leadership was being subjected to the fiercest of internal criticisms, and his tyrannical rule deplored by those in whose name he had once ruled unchallenged.

Within a month of VE–Day, the Soviet control of East Berlin, and East Germany, was complete. On June 5, at Wendenschloss, just outside Berlin, the signature of a Four-Power Declaration on the defeat of Germany was the occasion for a short but unhappy celebration. Marshal Zhukov was the host. Eisenhower, Montgomery and Lattre de Tassigny represented the United States, Britain and France, the three other powers with zones of occupation in Germany. It was agreed that Berlin, which was then still under Russia's sole occupation, would be divided into four zones, one for each Ally. But the Americans also agreed to withdraw from the most easterly areas of Germany that had been conquered by their forces, transferring to Russian control a considerable area of land, including the city of Leipzig. The Americans were already in the process of withdrawing from those areas of western Czechoslovakia which American troops had liberated a month earlier.

The excesses of the Russian soldiers, especially in Berlin, had been the subject of considerable Western criticism. After the Wendenschloss ceremony one of the British war correspondents present, Alexander Werth, mentioned this to Marshal Sokolovsky, whom he had met in 1941. 'Of course a lot of nasty things happened,' the Marshal replied. 'But what do you expect? *You* know what the Germans did to their Russian prisoners-of-war, how they devastated our country, how they murdered and raped and looted. Have you seen Majdanek or Auschwitz? Every one of our soldiers lost dozens of his comrades. Every one of them had some personal scores to settle with the Germans, and in the first flush of victory our fellows no doubt derived a certain satisfaction for making it hot for those Herrenvolk women. However, that stage is now over.'

One new stage that had begun in the Soviet occupation zone was Operation Booty. Throughout the eastern occupied areas, German factories were being dismantled and their movable installations sent by train and truck to Russia. The Siemens plant near Berlin was completely emptied of machinery 'during the very first days'.[1] Inside Russia, war con-

---

[1] Alexander Werth, *Russia at War, 1941–45*, Barrie and Rockliff, London, 1964, pp. 986–8.

ditions continued for the civilian population, and in some cases worsened. In the last two years of the war American Lend-Lease programmes had supplied considerable amounts of food to the Red Army, sufficient for ten million people. That Lend-Lease now ended, leading to a sharp fall in the amount of food reaching Russia. As Alexander Werth reported in his despatches, food supplies available through the United Nations Relief and Rehabilitaion Agency (UNRRA), while accepted by the Federal Republics of White Russia and the Ukraine, were declined by the Soviet Government for the Russian Federation, 'apparently as a matter of prestige.'[1]

VE-Day was followed in the summer of 1945 by more formal parades and celebrations. The day chosen for the VE-Day parade in Paris was June 18. This was the same day that had been chosen for the victory parade in 1919, at the end of the First World War. Two invasions had been avenged. The bloodletting of Verdun and the humiliation of occupation were both as far in the past as they could be, at least for that day. General de Gaulle, who had been taken prisoner-of-war by the Germans at Verdun, took the salute. Whatever his grievances against the British and Americans for not allowing him unfettered wartime freedom in the Second World War, this was his moment of triumph.

Facing the podium on which de Gaulle took the salute was a stand specially set up for wounded soldiers. As the procession proceeded, twelve ambulances drove by. The wounded men gave a great cheer. This was the hospital unit which had been the salvation of many of them during the fighting in the Western Desert and Syria. Because the unit had been organized by Mary Borden, the energetic novelist wife of a British general, Edward Louis Spears, it flew the British as well as the French flag on its victorious drive. De Gaulle, who had been brought to Britain by Spears in 1940 but later quarrelled with him, was so angry at the cheers for the Union Jack that he gave orders for the unit to be disbanded and its British members sent home. Commented Lady Spears: 'A pitiful business when a great man suddenly becomes small.'[2]

On June 24 the Soviet Union held its victory parade. Hugh Lunghi was witness to that day of celebration and commemoration. 'It was raining,' he recalled. 'Standing in our uniforms behind the barriers at the foot of the Kremlin Wall we were soaked. It did not detract from the drama: Marshal Zhukov on horseback reviewed the troops, then the dashing

[1] Alexander Werth, *Russia at War, 1941–45*, Barrie and Rockliff, London, 1964, p. 1006.
[2] Mary Borden (Lady Spears), *Journey down a Blind Alley*, Hutchinson, London, 1946, p. 295.

Marshal Rokossovski, one-time victim of Stalin's purges, also on horse-back, led the parade. A huge military band played as the twenty-abreast columns marched through Red Square interspersed with *katyusha* rocket launchers, large calibre guns, tanks and armoured vehicles.

'A sudden silence, then a mighty roll of drums accompanied by a heavy downpour: a column of goose-stepping soldiers, two hundred strong we later learned, halted at Lenin's tomb, turned briskly right and flung onto the steps of the mausoleum two hundred German regimental and naval banners and standards, red, black and white, highlighted by the huge black swastikas on white background. It was a strikingly dramatic gesture we had seen once before on a much smaller scale when bedraggled col-umns of German prisoners had been led through the streets of Moscow.

'Much later in the day, when we returned after the parade, crowds stood round gazing at the banners. There was no triumphant gloating, let alone anything like stamping on the banners: it was, we felt, not so much the presence of the mausoleum sentries, standing stiffly with bay-onets fixed, that restrained the crowd: the mood seemed rather one of grief for remembered sacrifices. This time the limp, rain-sodden banners really seemed to mark the end of all that. An elderly woman said to me: "What we need is a new beginning".

'Two days after the Victory parade it was announced that Stalin had been awarded a second Order of Victory and, for the umpteenth time, the title of Hero of the Soviet Union. The following day the Ministry of Defence officially informed us that Marshal Stalin was now "*Generalis-simo*". News of this elevation, accompanied by large photo-portraits of Stalin in his new uniform, covered the front page of every newspaper.'[1] On the next day, June 28, in accordance with a secret accord made at the Yalta Conference, the *Generalissimo* gave orders to his chiefs of staff to prepare for offensive action against Japan.

The movement of Russian troops to the east was another step in the preparations for victory against Japan. The nine-year-old Felicija Herszkowicz, living then in a Ural settlement near Kamiensk–Uralsk, later recalled 'trains going every day through the town to the east. We children used to go to watch the trains. It was like an everyday event, soldiers were going through the station. We would run to the station, in the hope of getting some sweets. My own uncle, who was serving with the Red Army in Czechoslovakia at the end of the war in Europe was sent to Japan.'[2]

<hr>

[1] Hugh Lunghi, letter to the author, 22 September 1994.
[2] Felicija Dobroszycki (née Herszkowicz), in conversation with the author, 1 November 1994.

It was with his new rank and uniform of *Generalissimo* that Stalin reached Potsdam on July 17, for the final inter-Allied conference of the war. Churchill and Truman were his fellow-negotiators there until Churchill returned to London to learn of the defeat of his party at the polls: the election had been held on July 5 and the results announced on July 26. He was replaced as Prime Minister, and also at the conference table in Potsdam, by Clement Attlee. The outcome of the negotiations at Potsdam was to confirm what had been clear on the day the war ended: that the Soviet Union would dominate Eastern Europe, would maintain its position in eastern Germany, and would have an effective stranglehold over Berlin. It was also at Potsdam that Truman revealed to Churchill and Stalin the successful detonation of the atomic bomb at a test site in the United States. Inside a one mile circle the devastation had been complete.

The war against Japan had gained in momentum as the war in Europe receded. On May 24 more than four hundred American bombers had dropped 3,646 tons of bombs on central Tokyo, and on the industrial areas in the south of the city. More than a thousand Japanese were killed. Also killed in the raid were sixty-two Allied airmen who were being held in Tokyo as prisoners-of-war; it was later alleged that they had been deliberately locked into a wooden cell block for the duration of the raid, while all 464 Japanese prisoners and their jailers were taken to a safe shelter. On the day after this Tokyo raid, the United States Joint Chiefs of Staff confirmed November 1 as the date for the start of Operation Olympic, the invasion of the most southerly Japanese island of Kyushu.

On mainland China, the nationalist Chinese troops who had been in battle for even longer than the European combatants, were advancing against the Japanese with a renewed vigour. On May 26, the Japanese were forced to evacuate Nanning, losing their overland link with Indo-China. Two days later, off Okinawa, the Japanese mounted their last major air offensive against American warships, losing a hundred planes without sinking a single ship.

In Tokyo, at a Government conference held in the presence of Hirohito on June 8, the Japanese Cabinet resolved to prosecute the war to the bitter end. For two more months that resolve was carried out. For the Americans who had to plan the invasion of the Japanese home islands, the understanding of this resolve, which could be recognized from the tenacity of the Japanese defenders on every distant island, was terrifying. Henry Muller, then in the Philippines, recalled: 'It was in late

June or July while working on the plans for invading Japan that I was shocked to read an estimate by our medical staff that we could expect 900,000 American and three million Japanese casualties! I recall trying to frame in my mind a concept of 900,000 killed or wounded U.S. soldiers – like ten times the population of our state of Nevada or nine times the full capacity of the huge Los Angeles Coliseum. It was awful to contemplate.'[1]

The war against Japan continued for three months after the end of the war in Europe. On July 26 the American cruiser *Indianapolis* reached Tinian Island in the Pacific, carrying on board an atomic bomb. Tinian was within bombing range of the Japanese mainland. That same day the Japanese Prime Minister, Admiral Kantaro Suzuki, rejected an Allied appeal for unconditional surrender. On July 30 a top secret committee in Washington confirmed Hiroshima as the atom bomb's target. In the early hours of August 6 the bomb was dropped, with a death toll, within two weeks, of 92,000. On August 8 the Soviet Union, honouring its promise at Yalta, declared war on Japan. The Americans planned to drop a second atomic bomb on August 11, if Japan had not surrendered by then, but a forecast of bad weather led this date to be brought forward by two days. No response having come from Tokyo by then, a second bomb was dropped on Nagasaki on August 9. Within a few minutes of the explosion, 40,000 people were killed. Late that night, after an anguished debate, the Japanese military leaders accepted the Emperor's plea that the war should be brought to an end. On the following morning the Japanese Government agreed to unconditional surrender. As the final negotiations proceeded on a formula devised to accept Hirohito's request to remain ruler of Japan, Truman gave the order that no more atomic bombs were to be dropped. At midday on August 15 the Emperor broadcast to his people that the war was over.

News of the dropping of the two bombs brought exhilaration to the Allied soldiers, sailors and air force personnel for whom the continuance of war against Japan meant further intense fighting, heavy loss of life, or permanent injury. A British doctor, Sholto Forman, was in Bombay on his way to war when the bombs were dropped. He had returned to India after celebrating VE-Day in London. 'I gathered up the reins as resident medical officer, No 5 Commando near Poona,' he later wrote, 'and the sound of machine guns on exercise fired the most chilling reflex associations down my spine I can remember. But fears were liars again. The

[1] Brigadier-General Henry J. Muller Jr, letter to the author, 11 October 1994.

bombs on Hiroshima and Nagasaki were dropped as we were packing an exhausted looking tramp steamer in Bombay harbour for the invasion of Penang Island. None of us wept for the victims. Perhaps we were wrong, but on the night the war ended I don't think any of us gave a damn. Reprieve is sweet. I was home six months later.'[1]

A nuclear scientist then in Moscow later recalled his reaction to the dropping of the atomic bomb. 'On my way to the bakery on the morning of August 7,' Andrei Sakharov, later a leading human rights activist, recalled, 'I stopped to glance at a newspaper and discovered President Truman's announcement that at eight a.m. the previous day an atom bomb of enormous destructive power had been dropped on Hiroshima. I was so stunned that my legs practically gave way. Something new and awesome had entered our lives, a product of the greatest of the sciences, of the discipline I revered.'[2]

When VJ-Day came on 15 August 1945 it saw a second upsurge of joy and celebrations. Yet it too had clouds: the plight and savage memories of the returning prisoners-of-war, the gaps in homes where sons and fathers had been killed, and the concerns, even amid the euphoria of total victory, that the decisive weapon might become an evil feature of the second half of the century. Asked about the dropping of the two atomic bombs, a British housewife commented: 'I was happier when I lay listening to bombs and daring myself to tremble; when I got romantic letters from abroad; when I cried over Dunkirk; when people showed their best sides and we still believed we were fighting to gain something.'[3]

'It was predicted the war with Japan would last until 1950,' an English schoolboy, Norman Hurst, recalled, 'because it was said that her troops would indulge in a suicidal defence of her territory, island by island. It was with little emotion therefore that one heard of the detonation of the first atomic bomb and the huge casualties it caused. When the second bomb went off we were staying at a pub, on the outskirts of Monmouth, run by friends. In the orchard at the back we built the customary bonfire around which customers drank while the beer lasted. Like VE-night it was a jolly, convivial occasion notable for the self restraint of those participating. Life generally at the pub was easier, the landlord kept pigs and chickens so there was plenty of home-cured bacon, fresh

[1] Sholto Forman, 'Family celebration', in *As You Were, VE-Day: a medical retrospect*, British Medical Association, London, 1984, p. 72.

[2] Andrei Sakharov, *Memoirs*, Hutchinson, London, 1990, p. 93.

[3] Mass Observation, *Peace and the Public*, quoted in Angus Calder, *The People's War, Britain 1939–45*, Jonathan Cape, London, 1969, p. 586.

eggs and wild mushrooms. Happy that we youngsters were not going to get caught up in a fighting war, it was only later when reading John Hersey's *Hiroshima* that the full impact of nuclear war was brought home.'[1]

Victory over Japan revived the scenes and emotions of Victory in Europe. For the millions of soldiers fighting in the Pacific and Far East, VJ-Day was the moment of release from the heavy burdens and uncertainties of combat. In Britain, political change was part of the search for a better life for those who had come through the exertions and privations of almost exactly six years of war. Following the General Election the Labour Party had came to power, voted in by nearly twelve million people, 50.4 per cent of the electorate. Across the Atlantic Ocean, Ansel Harris, a Royal Air Force cadet then finishing his training at Winnipeg later recalled how the 'muted celebrations' of VE-Day in that distant Canadian city in May had been 'replaced by dancing in some of the streets' in August.[2] Even as British newspapers were reporting MacArthur's orders to the Japanese to send an emissary to Manila in a white plane to receive instructions for carrying out the surrender terms, George VI was announcing in Parliament the programme of the new Labour Government, dominated by the extension of public ownership 'that our industries and services shall make their maximum contribution to the national well-being'.[3]

As with the ending of the war in Europe, different ceremonies and moments marked the ending of war with Japan. On August 17, in one of the Japanese prisoner-of-war camps in Thailand, the men were summoned by the commandant and told that the war was over. 'So many had suffered and died,' commented one of them, Edward Dunlop, 'even now some would never see home; but the momentous day had come.'[4] On August 23 Soviet forces, who had entered the war fifteen days earlier, captured Port Arthur, from which they had been driven by the Japanese forty years earlier. On September 2 General MacArthur took the Japanese surrender on board the battleship *Missouri* in Tokyo Bay. On September 12, in Singapore, Admiral Mountbatten accepted the unconditional surrender of all Japanese forces in South East Asia. Looking at the Japanese officers during the ceremony, General Slim, the victor of the Burma campaign, later wrote: 'Their plight moved me not at all. For them, I

---

[1] Norman Hurst, letter to the author, 28 August 1994.
[2] Ansel Harris, letter to the author, 12 October 1994.
[3] *Hansard*, 15 August 1945.
[4] E.E. Dunlop, *The War Diaries of Weary Dunlop, Java and the Burma-Thailand Railway, 1942–1945*, Lennard Publishing, Hertfordshire, 1987, p. 381.

had none of the sympathy of soldier for soldier that I had felt for Germans, Turks, Italians or Frenchmen that by the fortune of war I had seen surrender. I knew too well what these men and those under their orders had done to their prisoners. They sat there apart from the rest of humanity.' Slim added: 'If I had no feeling for them, they, it seemed, had no feeling of any sort, until Itagaki, who had replaced Field Marshal Terauchi, laid low by a stroke, leant forward to fix his seal to the surrender document. As he pressed heavily on the paper, a spasm of rage and despair twisted his face. Then it was gone and his mask was as expressionless as the rest. Outside, the same Union Jack that had been hauled down in surrender in 1942 flew again at the masthead. The war was over.'[1]

General Itagaki was later charged with war crimes relating to the death and maltreatment of Allied prisoners-of-war. He was tried by the International Military Tribunal, Far East, found guilty, and hanged at Sugamo Prison in Tokyo on 23 December 1948. He was one of seven senior Japanese military leaders to be executed for war crimes.[2] A further 124 Japanese camp commandants and guards who were brought to trial as war criminals were also hanged.

A few Japanese soldiers remained in hiding in various remote regions of the former empire until long after the war, unaware, or refusing to believe, that Japan could actually have surrendered. In 1945, when the Japanese withdrew from Lubang Island, in the Philippines, Second Lieutenant Onoda Hiroo had been ordered to fight a guerrilla action until the Japanese forces returned to the island. He remained in the jungle for almost three decades. When told that the war was over, he refused to give himself up; his former commanding officer had to be flown from Japan to order him to surrender.[3] He obeyed. The year was 1974. One man's war, the last of a war of tens of millions of fighting men, had come to an end.

---

[1] Field Marshal Sir William Slim, *Defeat into Victory*, Cassell, London, 1956, p. 534.

[2] Twelve German leaders were sentenced to death at Nuremberg. Ten were hanged. One of those sentenced, Martin Bormann, was never found. Another, Hermann Goering, cheated the hangman by commiting suicide in his prison cell.

[3] Richard Fuller, *Shokan, Hirohito's Samurai*, Arms and Armour Press, London, 1991, page 13. Lieutenant Hiroo published his memoirs, *No Surrender – My Thirty-Year War*, in 1975 (Andre Deutsch, London).

EPILOGUE

On VE-Day 1945 millions of men, women and children were caught up in the celebrations: singing, dancing and carousing into the night. As on Armistice Day 1918 the immediate impact of the end to the fighting was one of relief and rejoicing. Yet many, including those who vividly recall the unbridled celebrations, also remember the doubts and problems remaining; the uncertainties which did not necessarily end with the ending of the war against Japan. I myself remember the long wait for the return of my cousin Simmy Gordon, who had been captured by the Japanese at Singapore and had been held a prisoner-of-war for more than three and a half years. On his return we glimpsed, as tens of thousands of families glimpsed, a hint of the ordeal through which those held captive by the Japanese had passed. In common with so many former prisoners-of-war, Simmy never fully recovered from his experiences, which were the subject of innumerable nightmares. In one sense, his war never ended: for him the day the war ended was more of a date in the history books than a part of real life.

The immediate aftermath of the war saw an attempt to deal with some of its detritus. Dyne Steel, who had been working in the Displaced Persons camps for more than a year, later wrote of a brief moment of particular satisfaction when, on 15 April 1946, 'members of Military Government, the UNRRA team and the other Relief units took their places in the tiny cemetery in Bergen to commemorate the handful of British soldiers who had died when the Germans surrendered the camp. A freshly painted white cross had been placed at the head of each grave with the man's name and regiment. Draped over the arms of the cross was a broad ribbon in the Polish colours of red and white with the inscription: "From grateful Poles whose lives you saved".

'A big wreath of scarlet and white flowers was placed on each grave and a bugler sounded the Last Post. Then we joined the long procession of some two thousand ex-inmates of Belsen, some waving the Polish flag, some the Star of David, as slowly they made their way to the site of their former sufferings. After the singing on the way up, there was a great silence, broken only by the sound of weeping as many of them fell on their knees beside the mass graves remembering those who had died.

There were many such graves, but of course no names, only the number of those buried in each: three thousand or more. It was a simple but fitting ceremony to commemorate the first anniversary of the liberation of Belsen.'[1]

The injustices of the war bedevilled the post-war years. Many in Britain felt uneasy at the inability of their country to maintain an independent Poland. 'Tomorrow we celebrate our victory,' Harold Macmillan wrote to General Anders on 7 June 1946, more than a year after VE-Day and nearly ten months after the defeat of Japan. 'With my colleagues in Mr Churchill's Government, I shall be at the saluting stand to watch the parade. I tell you this frankly; with all the legitimate joy and pride in every British heart will be mingled much sorrow and even shame.'[2] The personal sorrows and sadnesses of the war could likewise not be totally dissipated even by time.

At the Victory Parade in London on 8 June 1946, Marion Salter was watching the parade from an office in Whitehall. 'My thoughts were mixed,' she later wrote. 'I recalled serving with the Royal Marines at Eastney Barracks at Portsmouth, my first posting. I met Alec Aldis there, he was a regular Royal Marine with great ambitions. We were both commissioned in 1943, I served as the Assistant Secretary to the Commodore at HMS *Collingwood*. Alec having gained a Military Medal in the Battle of Crete had returned to Egypt, then home for his commission. He was then appointed Signals Officer of 41 Royal Marine Commando. We met once before D-Day, became engaged, with plans for the following Christmas, but he was killed on D-Day 6th June '44 (also my 23rd birthday). Later I met Stuart, just returned from serving five years in Burma attached to the West African Frontier Force, and I was newly engaged to Stuart as I stood by that window and anxiously scanned the masses of troops below waiting for the WAFF to march past and to try to pick out Stuart. So here I had great hope and happiness to look forward to, but the sadness of losing Alec, that brave and wonderful Royal Marine Commando, still persisted.'[3]

It was only after the end of the war that many children saw their fathers for the first time, nor was the homecoming always a happy one. Of the Australian servicemen who returned after the war, among them her own father, Germaine Greer has written: 'Thousands of them came

---

[1] Dyne Steel, *A 'One and Only' Looks Back*, Pentland Press, Edinburgh, 1992, pp. 92–3.
[2] Harold Macmillan, letter of 7 June 1946: Tadeusz Modelski, *The Polish Contribution to the Ultimate Allied Victory in the Second World War*, Worthing, Sussex, 1986, p. 272.
[3] Marion Loveland (née Salter), letter to the author, 31 October 1994. Stuart Loveland and Marion Salter were married in January 1947.

home to live out their lives as walking wounded, carrying out their mascu-
line duties in a sort of dream, trying not to hear the children who asked,
"Mummy, why does that man have to sleep in your bed?"[1] For some
children the moment of father's return was the true celebration of victory.
Cameron Hazlehurst, who was not yet four when the war ended, later
wrote: 'I'm afraid VE-Day was not a big day for me. Much more important was the day I met my father on Lime Street Station in September
or October 1946. He had been in India for four years, having left when
I was five months old. I can still see him walking down the platform to
me in his army khaki great coat, carrying a parcel under his arm which
turned out to be a present for me!'[2]

The death toll in the Second World War was higher than in any war of
recorded history. On the day the war ended, the parents, widows, children, families and friends of the dead were those for whom the ending
was sad and bitter. These, Paul Fussell has written, were 'the survivors,
those whose lives are ruined by their sons', husbands', fathers' sacrifices
for ideologies. The men don't feel anything: they're out of it. It's the
living who are the casualties.'[3]

The living sought different forms of solace. Forgetfulness was one,
made more difficult in our day as the passage of time brings back past
memories in sharp relief. Reconciliation was another, hard for those
whose lives were uprooted and crippled by suffering and loss. Retribution
was a third, pursued through the courts at the Nuremberg Trials and in
dozens of other trials in all the countries that were occupied, and in
Germany itself. Several thousand camp commandants, guards, torturers
and collaborators were executed, some after trials, some after drum-head
courts, some without any trial. Many thousands more were brought to
trial and imprisoned, albeit often for short terms. More than forty years
after the end of the war, Britain, Canada and Australia put laws on their
statute books (the British law in 1991) which give the jurisdiction to local
courts to try crimes committed during the war years by individuals who
emigrated after the war.

There was no single day on which the Second World War ended,
not even on the battlefield. Individual stories of liberation, and areas of
continued fighting, cover a wide range of moments in time. Circumstances and moods, as much as calendars and geography, also determined

---

[1] Germaine Greer, *Daddy, we hardly knew you*, Hamish Hamilton, London, 1989, p. 14.
[2] Cameron Hazlehurst, letter to the author, 23 September 1994.
[3] Paul Fussell, letter to the author, 23 October 1994.

the day on which an individual felt his or her moment of individual relief. Roger Peacock, for whom more than four years as a prisoner-of-war had made the celebrating of VE-Day so difficult, wrote: 'Governments must of necessity draw a line across the calendar and ordain a VE-Day, or two, and a VJ-Day, ditto. But for many participants such lines were of limited personal significance. It will be recalled that a quarter of a century after 1945, a solitary Japanese soldier was still hiding out in some Pacific jungle, inflexibly convinced that talk of peace was hostile propaganda. He put down his weaponry, reluctantly, only after a relative had been flown out from Japan, equipped with a few relevant newspapers, and had convinced him. We Europeans, on the other hand, needed no such convincing: all over the world Allies and Germans alike accepted gladly the cessation of hostilities.'[1]

Even the defeat of Japan did not mark the end of fighting. Despite the Japanese surrender the British decided, because of considerable uncertainty that outlying Japanese troops might disobey the surrender orders from Tokyo, to continue with the planned invasion of Malaya. On September 12 a landing was made at Port Dickson, after which the troops began to fan out in Malaya. Hardly had this movement begun than the 23rd Indian Division, one of the two assault divisions involved, was ordered to embark for Java. Alfred Doulton, who had fought against the Japanese in Burma with the 23rd Indian Division, later recalled: 'Not even VJ-Day was the end of WWII for us, as the Division was sent to Java where it fell to our lot to try and keep apart the Dutch, who thought they were returning to reclaim their Empire, and the Indonesians, who had, through the machinations of the Japanese, recently declared their independence. In the process we suffered quite heavy casualties, and I never ceased to admire the loyalty of our Indian troops involved in this fag end of the war when hostilities were over everywhere else in the world and their own country was on the verge of achieving its own independence.'[2]

The Indonesians had declared their independence from the Dutch on August 17. By the time the 23rd Division landed, a full-scale guerrilla war had broken out. When the 49th Indian Infantry Brigade landed on October 25 at Soerabaia their brigadier was murdered and, Alfred Doulton recalled, 'there were horrific scenes (and some outstandingly gallant actions) and our losses were heavy'.[3] The 5th Indian Division, supported

[1] Roger Peacock, letter to the author, 26 August 1994.
[2] Alfred Doulton, letter to the author, 2 October 1994.
[3] Alfred Doulton, letter to the author, 9 October 1994.

by the guns of the Royal Navy, had to be brought in to restore order. The troops who had borne the brunt of the fighting, the 23rd Indian Division, left Java on 28 November 1946, more than six years after the start of the war in Europe. Their casualties on the island had been 407 killed, 162 missing and 808 wounded: these were the last Allied casualties in what had become the longest war since Napoleon's defeat at Waterloo 131 years earlier.

Echoes of that war persist after half a century. On 23 September 1994 *The Times* reported that the bodies of more than two hundred Italian prisoners-of-war who had died in Magdeburg, in eastern Germany, after Italy had left the Axis, 'are being repatriated after lying buried under army training grounds for fifty years.'[1]

For the Allies, the day the war ended in Europe was the day on which good triumphed over evil. This exhilaration inevitably found an immediate echo in the art, literature, films and the history books of their respective nations. As the decades advanced, cynicism, disillusion and doubt were to tarnish the image of the 'good' war. For those who had been defeated, it was harder than for the victorious powers to confront the reality of so much destruction and so much loss, which could not easily be presented in a heroic light.

Ten years after the German surrender, the first Chancellor of the Federal Republic of Germany, Konrad Adenauer, reflected on the meaning of May 8. It had, he said, represented the defeat of the evil forces of Nazism. When Mayor of Cologne, he had been an opponent of Nazism, was dismissed from office in 1933, and twice imprisoned. 'But,' he added, 'May 8, 1945, will also be recorded by history as the day when the division of Germany began. This division has created a source of disquietude in the heart of Europe. The obliteration of the unnatural boundary between West and Central Germany will be the primary concern of every German Government. Reunification can only be achieved by peaceful means. Until it is accomplished the German people will have no domestic peace and no means of livelihood, nor will the population of the Soviet occupation zone attain freedom from want and liberty of thought.'[2]

The Central Germany to which Adenauer referred was what had become in 1945 East Germany, and the reunification to which he looked forward did eventually take place. But the 'East Germany' of his characterisation had come under Polish and Russian rule in 1945. He made no

---

[1] 'Final honour', *The Times*, 23 September 1994.
[2] Konrad Adenauer, 1955, quoted in Dennis L. Bark and David R. Gress, *A History of West Germany: From Shadow to Substance, 1945–1963*, Blackwell, Oxford, 1989, p. 91.

claim to those lands, which had been a part of the nineteenth and early twentieth-century German patrimony. The completeness of the Russian victory over Germany in 1945, the expulsion of millions of Germans from those eastern lands, and their re-population by Poles and Russians, created demographic facts that are unlikely to be reversed. For a decade after the Allied victory they were often challenged. Some of the first published historical documents to which I subscribed were volumes of testimonies and statistics from the West Germany Ministry of Refugees and Expellees. But, however much the Russian and Polish ideologies move towards the western European pattern, the lands they took in 1945 are no longer a part of the negotiable frontier changes envisaged by rulers and politicians. Breslau, the city that held out under siege almost to the last day, one of the great German cities, is unlikely to become German again. As Wroclaw, it has become as Polish a city as Warsaw or Cracow, its guide books reflecting recent Polish history, its German days of glory erased. Only the readers of Karl Baedeker's pre-war and pre-1914 guide books can catch the flavour of regions such as Silesia and East Prussia that are no longer German, and may never be again.

In *The Times* on VE-Day there had been three attempts, given prominence in readers' letters, to look forward to a renewal of German life on a basis of hope. One letter was from Robert Birley, a distinguished headmaster, who wrote of the 'unavoidable duty' of re-educating the German people. Re-education for responsibility could lead to a Germany that was 'capable of producing a stable democratic government'. The Germans must also learn to respect the Slavs. The victory of Russia over Germany, Birley believed, was probably the most valuable 'as it was the hardest' lesson the Germans had learned in the war. 'Perhaps the acid test of German re-education will be their readiness to accept the Czechs and Poles as peoples with cultures and traditions of their own.'[1]

The Western Allies were determined to restore German democracy. Germans imprisoned by the Nazis or fleeing from the Third Reich were to emerge as leaders. De-nazification and re-education were instituted as crucial elements in the creation of a new German ethic. Far from becoming a pariah nation, West Germany was to take a lead in the creation of a European community and, after reunification, in the political deliberations, economic prosperity and peace-pursuing ideology of the European Union. Of all the transformations that fifty years have wrought in Europe, the transformation of Germany from the terror of the continent to an

---

[1] 'Re-educating Germany', *The Times*, 8 May 1945, p. 7, col. 4. Birley was headmaster of Charterhouse (1935–47) and later of Eton College (1949–63).

integral, democratic and peace-loving partner was probably the greatest, and certainly the most welcome to those who had suffered most, whether as nations or individuals.

German totalitarianism had been destroyed, but national aspirations and global ideologies made the period after the war a time of continuing violence and loss of life, starting when the war ended and continuing in some lands for many years. For many individuals, the postwar period was one in which recovery from their experiences was extremely difficult. Fifty years after the end of the war, Roger Peacock reflected on the fact that his war had not ended when he was taken prisoner in June 1940, nor with his release from captivity in April 1945, nor on VE-Day, nor on VJ-Day. As he later recalled: 'After my return to Britain on VE-Day, I was in need of daily medical attention, which I received at a local hospital, and assumed that once the condition was cured – I had no doubt that it would be – I should retrain on more modern aircraft and be sent to inflict mayhem on Japan. Knowing how that enemy had treated our prisoners, I had no objection to being posted for flying duties to the Far East, but VJ came along and I noted only that I should not be needed out there.

'And still all emotion was paralyzed. This I did not query: it seemed most natural and would continue indefinitely, perhaps for ever?

'Then one afternoon I entered a Forces canteen and climbed up to the tiny chapel in the attic. There I sat alone, still dazed – my normal state over the preceding months. I picked up a Prayer Book and opened it at random, at the Epistle for the Ninth Sunday after Trinity, as it chanced. Chanced? I came to the words: "Now all these things happened to them for ensamples, and they are written for our admonition, upon whom the ends of the world are come. Wherefore, let him that thinketh he standeth, take heed lest he fall."

'My eyes read no further. A huge wave of relieving grief rose within me, would not be controlled, broke into total weeping. All the grief of 1940, of seeing friends die day by day. All the privations and separations of POW life; all the frustrations of the joyless return; all sought expression. I don't know how long I knelt there, crying. Nobody else came in and at length I dried my eyes, pulled myself together and left. From that moment, though still slowly, life returned: my war was over.'[1]

There were many in all armies for whom the pain of combat or captivity was to result in a lifetime of nightmares. With the wide newspaper

---

[1] Roger Peacock, letter to the author, 26 August 1994.

coverage in June 1994 of the fiftieth anniversary of D-Day, this mental anguish was intensified. Major Colin Crawford, the director of a British charity which cares for mental health of veterans said, as both VE-Day and VJ-Day celebrations loomed on the horizon, 'many patients suffer from nightmares every night. They are reminded all their waking lives about events they can never forget. The more they recall the events that caused them stress, the more they are distressed. Next year, when we remember VJ-Day we can expect another surge in patient numbers because of the great suffering endured by many who fought in the Far East campaigns. Many old soldiers – about four per cent are women – suffer from post-traumatic stress syndrome. Newsreel film of fifty-year-old battles can trigger feelings of guilt: they ask why they survived when comrades died.'[1]

Major Crawford reflected that as the veteran soldiers get older, 'they find it less easy to cope with their memories. Many have now retired and have no more help from their colleagues at work. They have more time to brood. Some are now widowed, and have no one to care for them.' With the growing publicity of wartime anniversaries, which will culminate on the VJ-Day anniversary in August 1995, a growing number of veterans are seeking help. 'The growing press coverage is not able to help them.'[2]

All those who remembered VE-Day, or whose letters and diaries survive, looked to the future with mixed feelings of hope and foreboding, and with aspiration they were determined to see fulfilled, whether of housing and jobs, education, or an end to wars. This latter hope had been strong in 1918. Those who held it in 1945 held it no less strongly. The 'war to end war' of 1914–18 had failed utterly to live up to that particular designation. Those born nine months after the exuberances of Armistice Day 1918 were just twenty years old when war broke out again in 1939. A cartoon by Will Dyson published on 17 May 1919 had shown Clemenceau coming away from the Paris Peace Conference at Versailles and remarking: 'Curious! I seem to hear a child weeping.' The child is a baby whom Dyson has identified as '1940 class': those boys who would be called into the army in the year 1940, when they reached the age of twenty-one.

The new war, which many saw as a continuation of the quarrels and unfinished business of the old one, was limited at first to fighting between

[1] Major Colin Crawford, quoted in David Ward, 'War anniversaries trigger stress among veterans', *Guardian*, 31 October 1994. The charity is Combat Stress, formerly the Ex-Services Mental Welfare Society, established after the First World War to help the victims of shell-shock.
[2] Major Colin Crawford, in conversation with the author, 12 December 1994.

Germany, Poland, Britain and France. There were many who thought, or hoped, that it need not spread to them. Belgium, Holland, Denmark and Norway were neutral in 1939 as in 1914. The United States was giving a lead in neutrality to the neutral world. The Soviet Union had signed a non-aggression pact with Germany a week before the outbreak of war. Italy took no military action in 1939. But within two years Germany had attacked Belgium, Holland, Denmark, Norway, Greece and the Soviet Union. Within days of the Japanese attack on Pearl Harbour, Germany had declared war on the United States.

The European war that ended on 8 May 1945 had been total war on land, in the air and at sea, fought by the armies, navies and air forces of more than twenty States, and waged mercilessly on civilians. Unlike the ending of war in 1918, the Germany of 1945 had been occupied by its enemies, and its eastern territories stripped away, including two whole provinces, East Prussia and Silesia. Unlike 1918, the victorious powers had no intention of allowing a revived Germany to threaten them militarily. The Soviet Union sought to attain this by strict political control over what was now East Germany, the Western Allies by encouraging a democratic and demilitarized regime in West Germany, later the Federal Republic. Another safeguard was the division of Germany into two halves: a division that came, ironically, to symbolize not the end of Nazi Germany but the deep gulf of belief and practice between the former Allies.

German reunification came forty-five years after VE-Day. Throughout that period it had been unthinkable: the Soviet Union had represented it as the ultimate danger to the stability of the continent. Suddenly, as the Soviet Union itself began to lose the iron bonds of communist discipline and belief, the two Germanies came together, in a spontaneous outpouring of national unity totally lacking the nationalist extremism that characterized the Third Reich. Although economically as strong as at any time in her history, the new Germany no longer represented a force to be feared on the battlefield.

Within fifty years of VE-Day, the United States and the Soviet Union, the two Great Powers which had built up their rival strengths in Europe and had filled Europe with their arsenals from the day the war ended, came to an agreement that they would no longer confront each other in Europe's territory. The whole apparatus of confrontation established and maintained at such high material and psychological cost, was dismantled. At the beginning of 1994, just over two years after the collapse of the Soviet Union, NATO, the main instrument of Western defence, established Partnership for Peace: this envisaged an individual partnership agreement between NATO and any country on the Eurasian land mass that wished to join. Each agreement offered the newly participating country a wide range of joint military activities. Among the objectives which each country agreed to pursue was the democratic control of defence forces.

More than twenty former communist countries, including Poland, Hungary and, most recently, the former Soviet republic of Armenia, had signed partnership agreements by the end of 1994, and more are planned. Britain and Russia intend to hold joint military, naval and air exercises by 1996. These shared manoeuvres are considered, for those countries that want it, and that meet the necessary criteria, a preparatory step for their eventual NATO membership, something in which the United States is particularly interested. The East–West divisions of the Cold War, and the confrontation that was so intense as the Second World War ended, dissolved almost overnight. Fifty years after the end of the war in Europe, the militarization of the continent was being replaced by economic co-operation. The political debates of the European Union, which itself hopes to draw in the former communist countries of Eastern Europe, is a far cry from the military confrontations that twice plunged the whole continent into war in the twentieth century.

On 1 September 1994 the last Russian troops (they were no longer Soviet troops, for the Soviet Union was no more) left Berlin, the city they had reached as conquerors nearly half a century earlier, and in which they had since 1945 been the dominant military presence. They left the city by train from the suburb of Karlshorst, the very place in which the final act of unconditional surrender had been signed on 8 May 1945.

On 25 January 1995 President Yeltsin of Russia issued a decree formally rehabilitating all Russian civilians and former prisoners-of-war, several million people in all, who, following Beria's proposal to Stalin on 9 May 1945, the Soviet VE-Day, had been imprisoned in the gulag immediately on their return to the Soviet Union. 'The Government has been instructed to make compensation payments to the former Soviet prisoners-of-war on a par with the citizens who were victims of Nazi reprisals,' the official announcement stated.[1] Former soldiers would receive some monetary compensation and special cards reinstating them as war veterans. The unfinished business of The Day the War Ended never ends.

---

[1] Reuter News Agency report, Moscow, 25 January 1995.

Maps

1. Europe

418

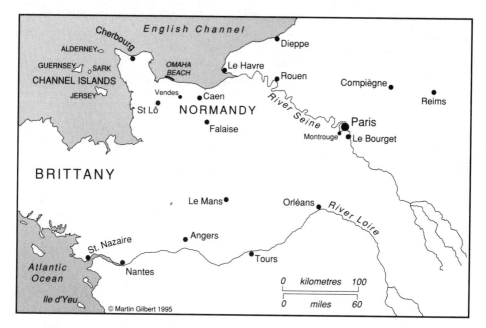

2. North–West France

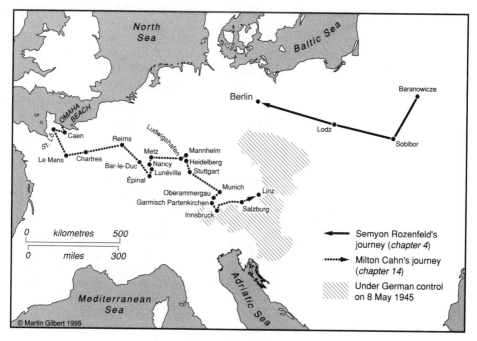

3. Two soldiers' journeys

North
Sea

Baltic Sea

Flensburg

Schleswig Kiel
SCHLESWIG
HOLSTEIN

Rostock

Wilhelmshaven

Cuxhaven

Lübeck Wismar

FRISIAN ISLANDS

Jever
Emden

Hamburg

Ravensbrück

Bad Zwischenahn

Lüneberg

Westerbork

Oldenburg
Bremen

River Elbe

HOLLAND

Bergen
Belsen Celle
Hanover

Potsdam

Amsterdam
Haarlem
Leyden Hilversum
The   Amersfoort
Hague Utrecht Arnhem
Rotterdam   Wageningen

Osnabrück

Hildesheim
Barfeld

Braunschweig
Magdeburg

Brandenburg

Lippstadt Bad Lippspringe
Paderborn

Oud Stoof

Nordhausen
Berga

Leipzig

Antwerp

BELGIUM
Brussels

Cologne

Bad Wildungen

Buchenwald
Eisenach Erfurt
Merkers Ohrdruf

Hohenstein-
Ernsthal

River Meuse

River Rhine

Waterloo

River Meuse

GERMANY

Nivelles

Bad Nauheim

Oberursel
Wittlich   Frankfurt
on Main Hammelburg
Darmstadt

Luxembourg
Bad Mondorf

Flossenbürg

Mannheim

Verdun

Metz

Nuremberg

River Neckar

River Danube

FRANCE

Karlsruhe

Eichstätt
Ingolstadt Straubing
Dillingen   Neuburg
Ulm   Moosburg Landshut
Dachau
Munich

Stuttgart

Strasbourg

Épinal

River Isar

Colmar

Lake
Constance

Salzburg

Bavarian Alps

Berchtesgaden

Oberammergau
ALLGÄU

0   kilometres   100

Basle

Girenbad

Wörgl Itter
Castle

Saalfelden

0   miles   60

Innsbruck
TYROL

Zell am See

© Martin Gilbert 1995

SWITZERLAND

VORARLBERG

ITALY

4. Western Germany

5. Schleswig–Holstein

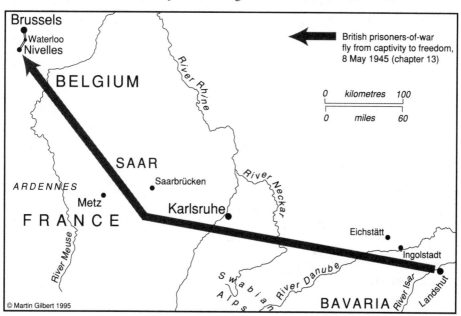

British prisoners-of-war
fly from captivity to freedom,
8 May 1945 (chapter 13)

6. A journey from captivity

Baltic Sea

POMERANIA

EAST PRUSSIA

Rostock
Peenemünde
Greifswald
Malchow
Stettin
Ravensbrück

Lauenburg
Danzig
Stutthof

Bydgoszcz
River Vistula
Malkinia

Berlin
Potsdam
Frankfurt-on-Oder
Fürstenberg
River Elbe
Spremberg
River Neisse
Bunzlau
SILESIA
Dresden
Bad Schandau
Görlitz
Gross Rosen
Breslau
River Oder

Wloclawek
Budzyn
Praga
Warsaw
Lodz
Radom
Piotrkow
Kalisz
Löwen
Birnbaumel
Dzialoszyce
Sosnowiec
Buna
Plaszow
Birkenau
Auschwitz
Cracow

SUDETENLAND
Bodenbach
Leitmeritz
Theresienstadt
Melnik
Eger
Prague
Kolin
Konstantinovy Lazne
Pilsen
Schlüsselburg
Velke Mezirici
Boskovice
Olomouc
Sternbeck
Březova-nad-Bradlom
Brünnlitz
Brno

Danube
Aigen-Schegel
Landshut
River Inn
Mauthausen
Hörsching
Linz
Piešťany
Bratislava
Vienna
River Danube

Salzburg
Fuschl
Ebensee
Altausee
Berchtesgaden
Saalfelden
River Enns
STYRIA
Zell-am-See
Judenburg
Graz
Griffen
Klagenfurt
Maribor
CARINTHIA
Slovenski Gradec
Budapest

0 kilometres 100
0   miles   60

© Martin Gilbert 1995

7. Eastern Germany and Austria

422

8. Berlin and the Elbe

423

9. Europe and the Mediterranean

10. Northern Italy

424

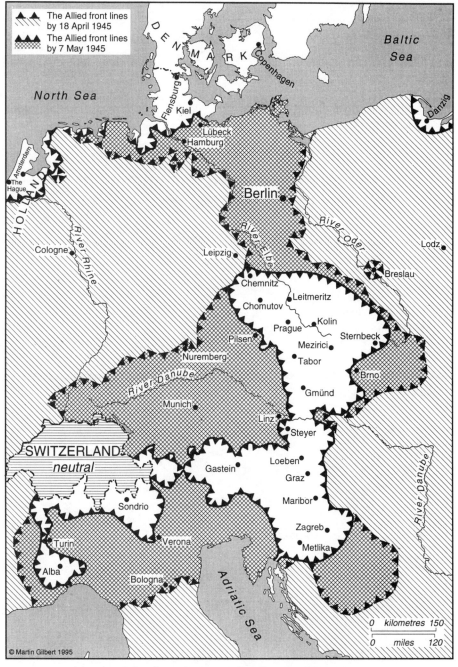

11. The front lines, 18 April and 7 May 1945

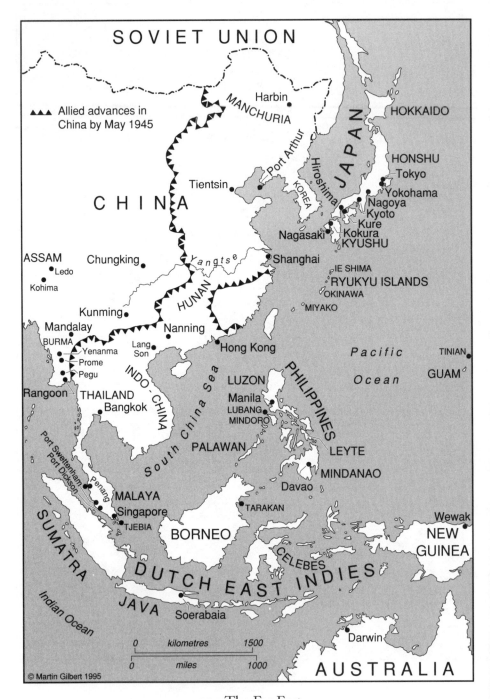

12. The Far East

13. The United States

427

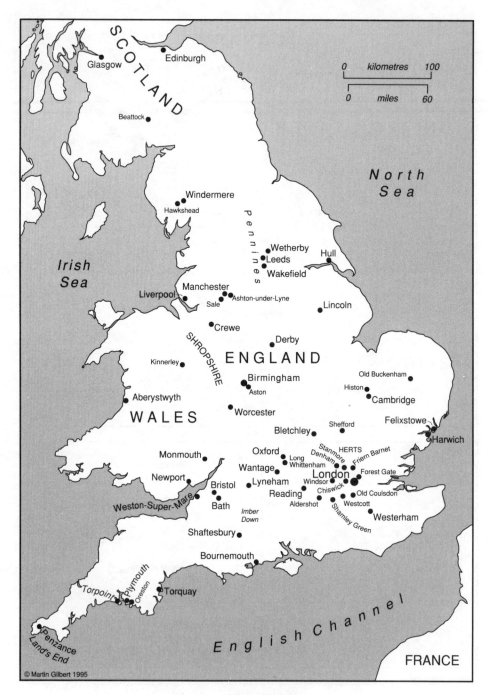

14. Great Britain

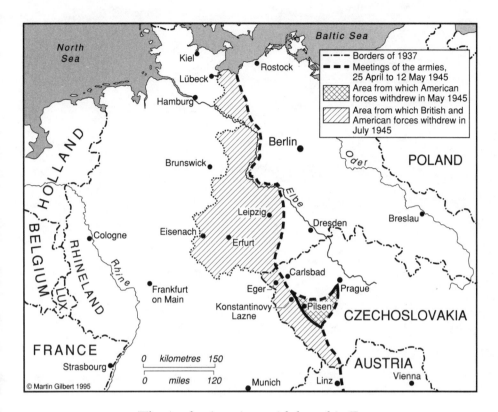

15. The Anglo–American withdrawal in Europe

BIBLIOGRAPHY OF BOOKS CITED

Ruth Andreas-Friedrich, *Shauplatz Berlin, Tagebuchaufzeichungen, 1945 bis 1948*, Suhrkamp, Frankfurt-am-Main, 1984.

Catherine Andreyev, *Vlasov and the Russian Liberation Movement*, Cambridge University Press, Cambridge, 1987.

Drago Arsenijevic, *Voluntary Hostages of the SS*, France Empire, Paris, 1978.

C.R. Attlee, *As It Happened*, William Heinemann, London, 1954.

Dennis L. Bark and David R. Gress, *A History of West Germany: From Shadow to Substance, 1945–1963*, Blackwell, Oxford, 1989.

Michael Bar-Zohar, *Ben Gurion, A Biography*, Wiedenfeld and Nicolson, London, 1978.

Antony Beevor and Artemis Cooper, *Paris after the Liberation, 1944–1949*, Hamish Hamilton, London, 1994.

Valentin M. Berezhkov, *At Stalin's Side*, Birch Lane Press, New York, 1994.

Mary Borden, *Journey down a Blind Alley*, Hutchinson, London, 1946.

Lord Boothby, *Recollections of a Rebel*, Hutchinson, London, 1978.

Robert Boothby, *I Fight to Live*, Victor Gollancz, London, 1947.

Tom Bower, *The Paperclip Conspiracy, The Battle for the Spoils and Secrets of Nazi Germany*, Michael Joseph, London, 1987.

British Medical Association, *As You Were, VE-Day: a medical retrospect*, BMA, London, 1984.

Arthur Bryant (editor), *Triumph in the West*, Collins, London, 1959.

Angus Calder, *The People's War, Britain 1939–45*, Jonathan Cape, London, 1969.

Ludmila Chladkova, *The Terezin Ghetto*, Nase Vojsko, Prague, 1991.

Clementine Spencer Churchill, *My Visit to Russia*, London, 1945.

Peter Collister, *Then a Soldier*, Churchman Publishing, Worthing, 1985.

Martin Conway, *Collaboration in Belgium, Léon Degrelle and the Rexist Movement*, Yale University Press, New Haven and London, 1993.

Susan Crosland, *Tony Crosland*, Jonathan Cape, London, 1982.

Charles Cruickshank, *The German Occupation of the Channel Islands*, Oxford University Press, London, 1975.

David J. Dallin and Boris I. Nicolaevsky, *Forced Labour in Soviet Russia*, Yale University Press, New Haven, 1947.

Geoffrey Dennis (editor), *The War of 1939*, Caxton, London, 1946.

Milovan Djilas, *Wartime*, Secker and Warburg, London, 1977.

Alexander Donat, *The Holocaust Kingdom, a memoir*, Secker and Warburg, London, 1965.

Georgii Drozdov and Evgenii Rybako, *Russia at War, 1941–1945*, Stanley Paul, London, 1978.

Alan Dulles, *The Secret Surrender*, Harper and Row, New York, 1966.

E.E. Dunlop, *The War Diaries of Weary Dunlop, Java and the Burma-Thailand Railway, 1942–1945*, Lennard Publishing, Hertfordshire, 1987.

Charles Eade (editor), *Victory, War Speeches*, by the Right Hon. Winston S. Churchill, OM, CH, MP, 1945, Cassell, London, 1946.

Keith E. Eiler (editor), *Wedemeyer on War and Peace*, Hoover Press, Stanford, California, 1987.

Dwight D. Eisenhower, *Crusade in Europe*, William Heinemann, London, 1948.

John Erickson, *Stalin's War with Germany, The Road to Berlin*, Weidenfeld and Nicolson, London, 1983.

Michael Etkind ' "Youth" Remembered', *Journal of the '45 Aid Society*, number 12, London, March 1985.

Tony Foster, *Meeting of Generals*, Methuen, London, 1986.

Richard Fuller, *Shokan, Hirohito's Samurai, Leaders of the Japanese Armed Forces, 1926–1945*, Arms and Armour Press, London, 1992.

Saul Friedländer, *When Memory Comes*, Farrar, Straus and Giroux, New York, 1979.

Ben Giladi (editor), *A Tale of One City*, Shengold, New York, 1976.

Germaine Greer, *Daddy, we hardly knew you*, Hamish Hamilton, London, 1989.

Dr Zalman Grinberg, *Address Delivered by Dr Zalman Grinberg on the Occasion of a Liberation Celebration*, Dachau, 1945.

Nigel Hamilton, *Monty, The Field-Marshal, 1944–1976*, Hamish Hamilton, London, 1986.

Alfons Heck, *A Child of Hitler: Germany in the Days when God wore a Swastika*, Renaissance House, Frederick, Colorado, 1985.

Alistair Horne (with David Montgomery), *Monty 1944–1945*, Macmillan, London, 1994.

Lali Horstmann, *Nothing for Tears*, Weidenfeld and Nicolson, London, 1953.

Edwin P. Hoyt, *The Death of the U-Boats*, McGraw-Hill, New York, 1988.

Alfred Kantor, *The Book of Alfred Kantor*, New York, 1971.

Robert Kee, *The Impossible Shore*, McGraw-Hill, New York, 1950.

Thomas Keneally, *Schindler's Ark*, Hodder and Stoughton, London, 1982.

Colonel Nathanial Kutcher, *Mauthausen Remembered*, privately printed, Miami Beach, 1994.

Leopold Labetz (editor), *Solzhenitsyn, A Documentary Record*, Allen Lane, London, 1970.

Fleet Admiral William D. Leahy, *I Was There*, Whittlesey House, New York, 1950.

J.W.J. Levien (editor), *Atlas at War*, Atlas Assurance Company, London, 1946.

Ernest W. Michel, *Promises to Keep*, Barricade Books, New York, 1993.

Samuel W. Mitcham Jr., *Hitler's Field Marshals and their Battles*, Leo Cooper, London, 1988.

Tadeusz Modelski, *The Polish Contribution to the Ultimate Allied Victory in the Second World War*, Worthing, Sussex, 1986.

H. Montgomery Hyde, *Stalin, The History of a Dictator*, Rupert Hart Davis, London, 1971.

Lynn H. Nicholas, *The Rape of Europa, The Fate of Europe's Treasures in the Third Reich and the Second World War*, Macmillan, London, 1994.

Nigel Nicolson (editor), *Harold Nicolson, Diaries and Letters, 1939–45*, Collins, London, 1967.

Chaim Nussbaum, *Chaplain on the River Kwai, The Story of a Prisoner of War*, Shapolsky, New York, 1988.

Dr Miklos Nyiszli, *Auschwitz, A Doctor's Eye-Witness Account*, Panther, London, 1962.

Peter Padfield, *Dönitz, The Last Führer*, Victor Gollancz, London, 1984.

Alan Palmer, *The East End, Four Centuries of London Life*, John Murray, London, 1989.

Graham Payn and Sheridan Morley, *The Noel Coward Diaries*, Weidenfeld and Nicolson, London, 1982.

Ben Pimlott (editor), *The Second World War Diary of Hugh Dalton, 1940–45*, Jonathan Cape, London, 1986.

Cathy Porter and Mark Jones, *Moscow in World War II*, Chatto and Windus, London, 1987.

Peter Quennell, *The Wanton Chase, An Autobiography from 1939*, Collins, London, 1980.

Anthony Read and David Fisher, *Berlin, The Biography of a City*, Pimlico, London 1994.

P.R. Reid, *The Latter Days of Colditz*, Hodder and Stoughton, London, 1982.

Leib Reizer, *We Become Greeks, Post-War Memories*, Di Grodner Opklangen, Argentina, 1950.

Richard Rhodes, *The Making of the Atomic Bomb*, Simon and Schuster, New York, 1986.

David Rolf, *Prisoners of the Reich, Germany's Captives, 1939–1945*, Leo Cooper, London, 1988.

Andrei Sakharov, *Memoirs*, Hutchinson, London, 1990.

Christopher Seton-Watson, *Dunkirk-Alamein-Bologna, Letters and Diaries of an Artilleryman 1939–1945*, Buckland, London, 1993.

Field Marshal Sir William Slim, *Defeat into Victory*, Cassell, London, 1956.

Dyne Steel, *A 'One and Only' Looks Back*, Pentland Press, Edinburgh, 1992.

Johannes Steinhoff, Peter Pechel and Dennis Showalter (editors), *Voices from the Third Reich, an Oral History*, Regnery Gateway, Washington DC, 1989.

Robert I. Straus, *In My Anecdotage*, privately printed, Santa Barbara, California, 1989.

Major Mercer W. Sweeney (editor), *Wingfoot, Rhineland and Central Europe Campaigns, 101st Cavalry Group (Mechanized)*, Weinheim, Germany, 1945.

David A. Thomas, *The Atlantic Star 1939–45*, W.H. Allen, London, 1990.

W.H. Thompson, *I Was Churchill's Shadow*, Christopher Johnson, London, 1951.

W.H. Thompson, *Sixty Minutes with Winston Churchill*, Christopher Johnson, London, 1953.

Nikolai Tolstoy, *Victims of Yalta*, Hodder and Stoughton, London, 1977.

Hugh Trevor-Roper, *The Last Days of Hitler*, Macmillan, London, 1947.

Dmitri Volkogonov, *Stalin, Triumph and Tragedy*, Weidenfeld and Nicolson, London, 1991.

John W. Wheeler-Bennett, *King George VI*, Macmillan, London, 1958.

Alexander Werth, *Russia at War, 1941–45*, Barrie and Rockliff, London, 1964.

William Whitelaw, *The Whitelaw Memoirs*, Aurum Press, London, 1989.

Charles Williams, *The Last Great Frenchman, A Life of General de Gaulle*, Little Brown and Company, London, 1993.

Ruth Winstone (editor), *Tony Benn, Years of Hope, Diaries, Letters and Papers 1940–1962*, Hutchinson, London, 1994.

Robert Wistrich, *Who's Who in Nazi Germany*, Weidenfeld and Nicolson, London, 1982.

Yad Vashem (proceedings of a conference), *The Nazi Concentration Camps*, Yad Vashem, Jerusalem, 1984.

Kenneth Young (editor), *The Diaries of Sir Robert Bruce Lockhart, Volume Two, 1939–1965*, Macmillan, London, 1980.

Marshal of the Soviet Union G. Zhukov, *Reminiscences and Reflections*, Progress Publishers, Moscow, 1985.

INDEX

compiled by the author

447